American Sociology Series

Wilbur B. Brookover
A Sociology of Education

Ernest W. Burgess and Harvey J. Locke
The Family: From Institution to Companionship,
Second Edition

L. L. Bernard and Abel L. Bernard
Morale: Adjustment of ...

Paul H. Landis and Paul K. Hatt
Population Problems: A Cultural Interpretation,
Second Edition

Andrew... Munger and Clyde V. Moore
Sociology of ... Second Edition

Lowry Nelson
Rural Sociology, Second Edition

James A. Quinn
Urban Sociology

Herbert H. Stroup
Social Work, An Introduction to the Field,
Second Edition

Carl C. Taylor
The Farmers' Movement, 1620-1920

R. Clyde White
Administration of Public Welfare, Second Edition

Kimball Young and Raymond W. Mack
Principles of Sociology, A Reader in Theory
and Research, Second Edition
Sociology and Social Life, Second Edition
Systematic Sociology, Parsons and Mahony

American Sociology Series

Charles F.
Marden
Rutgers
The State University

Gladys
Meyer
Barnard College

MINORITIES

IN

AMERICAN SOCIETY

SECOND EDITION

AMERICAN BOOK COMPANY   NEW YORK

Foreword

Throughout its history, American society has included in its membership many groups who have been considered as somehow alien, not quite belonging to the normative society: immigrants; colored people; and non-Christians. The study of these groups and their relation to the larger society about them has occupied the attention of social scientists throughout the twentieth century. They were often studied particularistically, each group by itself or sometimes as classes of groups variously described as ethnics, races, or sects. Such study began to show that the position which each of the groups occupied in American society was in conceptual terms so similar that each could be denoted by the term "minority." Social science began to generalize about the characteristics of a minority and to describe typical processes involved in the relation of the minority to the higher status host group. Thus this aspect of intergroup relations became a recognized special field of sociology.

The first edition of this book had certain features which are retained in this revision. The central unit of investigation is not minorities as such but the relation of the minority to the dominant group. At the outset such a focus required the conceptualization of the term "dominant" as the reciprocal of "minority." This term seems more appropriate than the term "majority" because the latter is commonly used as a political term, and does not carry with it the connotations of superordination and superior power which are better conveyed by the term "dominant."

v

In general this revision retains the plan of organization of the first edition. Part I is a preliminary overview of dominant-minority relations in the United States and an introductory definition of the concepts and problems involved. Part II presents each of the numerous minority situations in this country. Part III sums up the findings and relates them to social theory and to social policy.

The revision differs from the first edition in a number of ways. First of all, the past ten years have brought much change in the relations between the various minorities and the dominant group. One aim therefore has been to update the factual story. Where necessary, as with the rapid developments in Negro-white relations in the South following the 1954 school desegregation decision, we have expanded our treatment.

Secondly, this same period has brought changes in the way social science views the subject of dominant-minority relations. Older concepts have been challenged; new theoretical insights and an ever-increasing body of research findings have thrown new light on our subject. In this revision, we take cognizance of these developments, and specifically add an entirely new chapter concerned with social theory and minorities.

Among the changes in thinking about minorities are those related to the place of race or color visibility in the determination of minority status; and the earlier assumption that assimilation is the inevitable goal of the dominant-minority process. As to the former, we have found the term "social race" a useful concept. And as to latter, we are now inclined to include further possible ways in which various minorities will ultimately achieve a stabilized adjustment to American society with equal status. The conception of American society itself has been changing, and the possibility of far more cultural pluralism in the private spheres of life, together with a basic agreement on the instrumental values of equality, democracy, and freedom, appears greater now than it did in the thinking of a decade ago.

Finally, this revision differs in a most important but quite different dimension. It is the product of two sociologists in place of one, as in the first edition, with Dr. Gladys Meyer of Barnard College joining Dr. Marden as co-author in this edition.

NOTE ON NOMENCLATURE

One problem besetting us in writing about dominant and minority peoples in the United States at this time is how we should designate certain groups, and whether or not to capitalize or italicize the words adopted. We depart somewhat from previous usage for reasons here set forth (1) Often the most precisely descriptive term is awkward: for example, "Americans of North

European ancestry." Thus we welcome the fact that the short word "haole" (meaning in native Hawaiian "stranger") is widely used in Hawaii in referring to the dominant-status persons of North European ancestry. (2) Changing circumstances render earlier words inadequate. For example, the presence of a substantial number of Puerto Ricans as a mainland minority makes the use of "Spanish-speaking" or "Latin-American" imprecise for referring to the Southwestern minority of Mexican origin. Thus we employ the term "mexicano." (3) Capitalization presents another problem. The word "Anglo"—the Spanish word for "English"—is a case in point. In describing intergroup relations in the Southwest, we want a convenient generic term to describe the dominant component as a whole. Today this includes the Olsens and the Schmidts as well as the Smiths. But since the traditional term "Anglo" is the most used, we retain it with this broader meaning and its capitalization. (4) Finally, when words are first borrowed from another language, it is common usage to italicize them. But as time goes on and these borrowed words become more current in the adopted language, the tendency is to drop the italics. Thus we do not italicize "mexicano" and "nisei."

These editorial departures are in a sense symbolic of a major conclusion of the text: the increasing trend is toward thinking of all these peoples as Americans with different heritages of no status significance.

C. F. M.
G. M.

Acknowledgments

The authors wish to express their appreciation to the following persons who have given, in various ways, generous assistance in the preparation of this revision: George I. Sanchez, of the University of Texas; Rose Hum Lee, of Roosevelt University; Lyle Saunders, of the School of Medicine, University of Colorado; Douglas S. Yamamura and Clarence E. Glick, of the University of Hawaii; Norman V. Painter, United States Office of Information; Joel V. Berreman, of the University of Oregon; Ira D. Reid, of Haverford College; Paul W. Massing and Nathan H. Gould, of Rutgers, the State University; Joan Gordon, of Vassar College; and Eleanor Russell Cate, of Barnard College. The above-mentioned have not in all cases read the final draft as it appears in publication and are not, in any event, responsible for any error which may appear, nor for any failure of the authors to properly interpret their numerous and valuable suggestions.

Table of Contents

Part III

List of Tables and Figures

TABLES

FIGURES

Part I

Introduction

In later parts of this volume the main minority situations in the United States are delineated in detail. In the first part, some pertinent general considerations are introduced. In Chapter 1, we point out the significance to American society of the presence of minorities, with special emphasis on its meaning in relation to the present situation of the United States in world affairs. Chapter 2 provides a general introduction to the sociology of dominant-minority relations, portraying their essential character and defining the terms used in this book to describe and analyze this form of intergroup relations. Because "race consciousness" is a factor involved in many dominant-minority patterns and because "race" is a term about which much confusion still prevails, it seems appropriate to provide a general orientation (Chapter 3) to the meaning of race as social science now views it in contrast to the myths which large segments of the public still believe.

1

The Significance of Minorities in American Society

WEST COAST JAPANESE INDEMNIFIED FOR EVACUA-TION LOSSES—MEXICAN AMERICANS MORE ACTIVE IN POLITICS—SUPREME COURT OUTLAWS SCHOOL SEGREGA-TION—INDIAN EDUCATION IMPROVING—FIRST NEGRO COUNCILMAN ELECTED—SIT-INNERS WIN LUNCH COUNTER PROTEST—HAWAII SENDS ORIENTALS TO CONGRESS.

WHITE COUNCILS OPPOSE SCHOOL DESEGREGATION—SOUTHERN JURY FAILS TO INDICT WHITES IN JAILBREAK MURDER OF NEGRO—AFRICAN DIPLOMAT REFUSED RES-TAURANT SERVICE—INDIANS PROTEST TRIBAL BREAK-UP —SYNAGOGUE BOMBED—CHANGE IN NATIONAL ORIGINS' IMMIGRATION LAW AGAIN BLOCKED IN CONGRESS—REPORT SHOWS MEXICAN NATIONALS DEPRESS WAGE RATES IN SOUTHWEST.

In 1954 the Supreme Court of the United States handed down its decision outlawing segregation in public schools. This decision gave an official answer to a crucial question: "What is to be the ultimate national goal?" The goal is now set—and probably irrevocably: the elimination of all discrimination on the basis of ethnic and racial background in civic and public life.

3

In the first edition of this book (1952) we characterized the period follow-ing World War II as one in which emerging national self-consciousness con-cerning dominant-minority relations was the prevailing theme. During those years the recurrent concern with related subjects in newspapers and maga-zines, and frequently novels, and stage and screen presentations reflected an enormously accelerated public interest in the condition of minorities. At long last, ethnic discrimination was being recognized as a leading national problem.

This new focus on "race relations" led to increased activity on the part of liberal elements aimed at reducing if not eliminating discrimination. Since up to 1954 the trend toward increasing acceptance of minorities was gradual and sporadic, the opposing elements were on the whole publicly dormant. The Supreme Court decision had the effect of arousing those who are op-posed to such a national goal. Thus in the years since 1954 we have seen increased tension and strife in Negro-white relations. In other areas, too, tension persists. We have read many headlines like the ones above, which reflect the opposing forces in the relations between dominant and minority groups throughout the nation.

Certainly in the South, race relations have been in crisis since 1954. The crisis in white-Japanese-American relations during World War II has been followed by the phenomenally rapid acceptance of the nisei as Americans. The mexicanos somewhat belatedly are now learning to use the institutions of political democracy to improve their welfare and status. And one school of thought, represented by Will Herberg,[1] expresses the opinion that Juda-ism is being viewed by Americans as an *American* religion, that its adherents are now regarded simply as Americans who have another religion. In short, it seems appropriate to state that in the field of ethnic relations a revolution is under way in the United States.

We would expect to find also a vastly increased amount of research by social scientists in the field of minorities. In this connection it is pertinent to note that this greater focus on minorities comes at a time when social science is approaching a new level of maturity, fortunately so because the phe-nomena of dominant-minority relations are highly complicated and in peculiar ways resistant to research procedures which have yielded valid results in other fields of investigation. In opinion polling, for example, signifi-cant differences are found in the answers to the same questions by Negro respondents when Negro interviewers are used rather than white.

Science is in theory objective and consequently neutral as to values and social policy. In view of the current situation, however, it is not surprising that the focus of current research is toward obtaining further knowledge for implementing the national goal as now established. Thus much research is

[1] Will Herberg, *Protestant–Catholic–Jew* (Garden City, N.Y.: Doubleday & Co., Inc., 1956).

directed at the causes of prejudice and (by no means the same question) at the causes of discrimination by dominant people; at the behavior of minorities in response to the new situation; and at exploring what specific ways a progressive lessening of discrimination may be effected with the least possible social cost. Policy-makers increasingly turn to the social scientists for guidance. To quote from Chief Justice Warren on the Supreme Court decision reached in the school cases: "Whatever may have been the extent of psychological knowledge at the time of Plessy vs. Ferguson, this finding [that segregation in the public schools has a detrimental effect on colored children] is amply supported by modern authority."[2] The citations given refer to various social science studies. (See below, p. 288.)

The purpose of this book is to present a comprehensive description of the most important minority problems in the United States; to analyze and interpret the relations of the dominant group to minority groups within a sociological framework; to state the general principles which emerge from such a study; and, finally, to indicate how our present knowledge may be brought to bear on social policy. The central focus of the book is the interaction which takes place between the dominant and minority, the discrimination imposed and maintained by the former, and the reactions of the latter.

In this opening chapter a preview of the range and scope of our inquiry will be indicated by (1) a brief historical summary of dominant-minority relations in the modern era; (2) a preliminary summary of minority situations in United States history; and (3) a preliminary statement of some of the principal ways these intergroup relations have affected our national life, and the nature of the problems they create.

THE EMERGENCE OF DOMINANT–MINORITY RELATIONS IN MODERN HISTORY

The dominance of some human beings over others is as old as man. In modern times, however, there has emerged a distinctive form of dominant-minority relations, characterized by "race consciousness." During the past four hundred years, Europeans in general and western Europeans in particular have penetrated other continents and in various ways established hegemony over many of their peoples. The United States came into being through just such a process, and the people who founded it, mostly of British origin, were among the leaders in this European expansionism. While what happened in the United States is explainable in large measure by forces present in its own history, full explanation requires viewing America's minority situations as a part of the larger historical process. To set the record of events in the United States in its proper perspective, we need a brief account of the

[2] 347 U.S. 483.

relations of Europeans to other peoples during the course of this great expansion.

Four major patterns of dominant-minority relations have arisen in modern history: the political annexation pattern; the colonial pattern; the slave pattern; and the immigration pattern.

The Annexation Pattern

The first of these is the political problem of minorities. Through wars, European nations have annexed portions of their neighbors' lands and have imposed special discriminations on the newly acquired subjects designed to force the assimilation of the minorities to the dominant culture pattern. Alsace-Lorraine, alternately French and German; Poland, attempting to resist Russification under the Tsars; Magyar dominance over various Slavic folks in Hungary—all are illustrations in which minorities arise by means of political annexation.

The Colonial Pattern

The colonial pattern developed along several lines, all best illustrated by Great Britain. The development of a great trading economy, subsequently strengthened by the Industrial Revolution and the rapid growth of population, enabled the British to establish political control over various parts of the world and to dominate the economic life of these vast areas primarily in the interest of Great Britain. Where these areas were densely populated by native peoples, control was maintained by placating the upper-class rulers, as in India, and applying military force when needed. According to Raymond Kennedy, the outstanding characteristics of this system have been the political and economic subordination of the native population; poor development of social services, especially education, for natives; and the color line, with its rigid social barriers between the white ruling class and the subject people.[3] Of these, the most important feature for the study of minorities is the last—the color line. Concerning this, Kennedy writes:

The colonial code that dictates complete social segregation of the races is rationalized either by the commonplace assertion that natives are ignorant or unclean or uninteresting; or by the claim that they do not desire whites to become familiar with them; or by the argument that informality, camaraderie and, most of all, intermarriage would weaken the prestige of the ruling class in the estimation of their subjects. . . .

The British colonial code draws the most rigid color line of all. Paradoxically, the greatest colonizers in the world are the most provincial in their attitudes towards strange groups and cultures. The British have been in contact for a longer time with more dark peoples than any other western nation, yet they hold aloof from their subjects to an unequalled degree. They refuse to associate freely or

[3] Raymond Kennedy, "The Colonial Crisis and the Future," *The Science of Man in the World Crisis*, ed. Ralph Linton (New York: Columbia University Press, 1945), p. 311.

make friends with other races, and this exclusiveness has engendered a reciprocal feeling toward them on the part of their colonial peoples. The attitude of the latter varies from indifference to active dislike, but, except in isolated instances, it never approaches friendliness. Natives often express a grudging admiration for the moral rectitude, financial incorruptibility, and legalistic fairness of Britishers, especially government officials, in the colonies; but bonds of mutual friendship and affection are lacking. . . .

The British demonstrate by their attitudes and behavior that they do not wish the natives to develop any sense of belonging to British society, and the entire social ritual of the colonies symbolizes the separateness of rulers and ruled. Nowhere in the colonial world are the lines of caste drawn more rigidly: in clubs, residential areas, places of public accommodation, and informal cliques. Nowhere is the taboo on intermarriage stronger, and the penalty for infraction more drastic.[4]

Where the areas of British expansion were thinly populated, the British themselves often settled, pushing back and partly annihilating the native population to take over the area, as in North America, Australia, and New Zealand. The remaining remnants of these native populations eventually became wards of the British commonwealths.

The dominant-minority pattern of South Africa represents a mixture of the two foregoing types of development. Here the British settled, defeated their Boer rivals, and then joined them to establish a nation based on a pattern of interracial segregation with 20 per cent white dominant and 80 per cent black (and some Indian) subordinate. The racial hierarchy of the Republic now comprises the European-descended whites at the top, the native African Negroes at the bottom, with Indians and mixed bloods, called "coloured" to distinguish them from the natives, in between.

The pattern of European dominance and native subordination developed in South Africa has been made more explicit and more rigid by the policy of *Apartheid* pursued by the Nationalist governments continuously in power since 1948.[5] *Apartheid* has two main features: (1) the improvement of the economy and welfare of the natives in their own "reserves," presumably with eventual greater political autonomy in their own areas; and (2) the maximum possible segregation of natives and Europeans in areas of mixed residence, with complete domination, political and otherwise, by the Europeans. Since this approach to the race problem is directly opposite to the broad trend found elsewhere in the non-Communist world, it has evoked increasing resistance from the natives within the Republic and increasing criticism from abroad, frequently expressed through the United Nations. Race relations in South Africa are at a highly critical point. The Union withdrew from

[4] *Ibid.*, pp. 318, 320. By permission of the publishers, Columbia University Press.
[5] The Nationalist government is dominated by the Afrikaners (Dutch descended), found more in the rural areas, while the opposition, the United Party, is dominated by those of British descent, more concentrated in the urban areas and more moderate on the race issue.

the British Commonwealth in March, 1961, because the other member nations insisted on a declaration disapproving its racial policy.

The French, the Dutch, and the Belgians were also involved in colonial policies from which has developed deep-seated antagonism toward the white man in Asia and in Africa. Roughly in the order presented above, these European nations have been giving up their colonies after training the natives in self-government. Much of the Congo crisis precipitated in 1960 relates to the failure of the Belgians to pursue such a policy earlier. Because of the traditional ties of the United States with these powers, we have been identified with the colonial powers in the minds of the nonwhite peoples, and our own domestic practice of discrimination against colored peoples has reinforced their antagonistic attitude.

Colonization on the part of Latin nations went through the same phases, but much less efficiently and very much less successfully. Spain and Portugal both quickly lost most of their colonial empires. In their relations with the native populations, the Mediterraneans have never drawn the color line very rigidly. They have exploited native populations, but in their personal relations they have never been strongly influenced by the idea of racial superiority. Intermarriage has been frequent. Latin America has had a more rigid class system than Anglo-Saxon America, but it has never been so preoccupied with race as a determiner of superiority or inferiority. This difference is further reflected in the contrasting treatment of slavery.

The Involuntary Migrant Slave Pattern

The enslavement of African peoples and their forced immigration to newly established colonies is the third pattern—or perhaps an auxiliary pattern—of dominant-minority relations in the modern era. The British ultimately restricted their slave trade to the Negro but pursued it with characteristic efficiency, leaving Americans a legacy that was reinforced by the invention of the cotton gin, destined to generate a social problem of the utmost gravity. The Latins made slaves of Indians and whites as well as Negroes. But from the start their slave policy differed from that of the British and Americans. The Latins accorded slaves status as human beings, established rules to limit the rights of masters, set up procedures by which freedom might be obtained, and, once the slaves were freed, accepted them as free men.[6]

The Voluntary Immigrant Pattern

The fourth pattern of dominant-minority relations arose out of the voluntary immigration of peoples from nations other than those of the original colonists. The main destination of these peoples was the United States;

[6] Frank Tannenbaum, *Slave and Citizen* (New York: Alfred A. Knopf, Inc., 1947).

Canada, Australia, New Zealand, and South Africa restricted immigration largely to British peoples, thus preserving a large measure of cultural homogeneity at the expense of more rapid population growth and industrial expansion.

Immigration to Latin America Immigration to Latin America in the nineteenth and twentieth centuries has amounted to probably not more than 11 or 12 million, and practically all of this has been to two countries, Brazil and Argentina.[7] Of all South American countries, Argentina has the highest proportion of white, or Caucasian, population. It also has had the largest amount of European immigration, most of which occurred between 1857 and 1930. The greatest numbers came from Italy and Spain. The government of Argentina adopted a policy of positive encouragement of immigration and, in general, it can be said that the newcomers did not suffer discrimination. On the contrary, as Davie writes, "The foreign-born are in a better position than citizens, since they have all the advantages that the latter enjoy and are exempt from certain obligations, like military service, that weigh upon the citizens."[8]

Immigration to Brazil has not been so great. Between 1820 and 1930, official figures report a total of about 4.5 million. An important contrast in the Brazilian situation is that its native population included large admixtures of Negro strains and some Indian strains. The Brazilian census of 1940 classified the population 63.5 per cent white; 14.6 per cent black, 0.6 per cent yellow; and 21.2 per cent brown (mixed Negro and Indian).[9] Like Argentina, Brazil officially encouraged European immigration, in which Italians and Portuguese participated in about equal numbers, with Spaniards third, and a scattering of other nationalities. From 1908 on several hundred thousand Japanese immigrants entered Brazil, the largest number coming after 1930.

In summary, immigration expanded the culturally pluralistic character of these two Latin-American nations without introducing new dominant-minority situations. As we shall see, this stands in contrast to the situation in the United States.

Chinese in Southeast Asia The emigration southward of substantial numbers of Chinese to other nations in southeast Asia—notably to Thailand, Malaya, Singapore, Indonesia, and the former Indochina area (now Vietnam, Cambodia, and Laos)—has been another main immigration trend. The Chinese in these areas have generally adjusted successfully. While they are not all middle class, enough of them are that they are identified as such by the native peasant class. Despite economic adjustment and considerable

---

[7] Maurice R. Davie, *World Immigration* (New York: The Macmillan Co., 1947), p. 446.
[8] *Ibid.*, p. 448.
[9] See T. Lynn Smith and Alexander Merchant, *Brazil: Portrait of Half a Continent* (New York: The Dryden Press, Inc., 1951), p. 150 *passim* for further discussion.

intermarriage, the Chinese remain a group apart. This failure to assimilate has been due in part to the political-legal discrimination imposed on them by the host countries or their colonial rulers, but it is due as much to their own retention of Chinese culture. Comparison with Western minority situations has often led Western writers to refer to the Chinese immigrants in Southeast Asia as "the Jews of the East."[10]

MINORITIES IN THE UNITED STATES

Indians

From the earliest settlements in the colonial period until 1871, white people increasingly encroached on the land possessed by American Indians. Till 1871 the relations of the whites to the Indians were considered formally, if somewhat fictionally, as contractual relations between sovereign political entities. In 1871 Indians became official wards of the United States Government and thus formally, as well as actually, a minority. During the wardship period neither the welfare nor the status of the Indians improved much until 1934, when the broad policy established under the "new deal" began helping the Indians improve their economic welfare with maximum possible retention of their tribal identities and cultures. Controversy now exists between those white Americans who retain this "new deal" approach and those who want to see the tribes liquidated and Indians as individuals put on their own like other Americans.

Negroes

Importation of Negro slaves to the English colonies began in 1619. Thus the new nation, born in 1776, inherited a slave minority brutally forced into subservience. In spite of their long residence in this country and considerable improvement in their welfare, Negroes still occupy the lowest status of all the American minorities. Particularly in the South, relations are still at a point of critical disequilibrium and there is continuous pressure to abolish segregation in the broader national interest. Viewing minority situations as problems, those of Negro-white relations are the most serious.

European Immigrants

Even before American Negroes moved from slavery to the status of a minority caste, there began a migration which was destined to change the character of the United States profoundly. This was the influx from Europe. First came the Irish, Scandinavians, and Germans, later the southern and eastern Europeans. The customs of the large concentrated aggregates which came from various nations differed markedly from those of the "natives"

[10] Maurice Freedman, "The Chinese in Southeast Asia," in *Race Relations in World Perspective*, ed. Andrew Lind (Honolulu: University of Hawaii Press, 1955), Ch. 17.

among whom they settled. The relation of these various peoples to the older residents followed a similar pattern, beginning with indifference, antagonism, and conflict and ending with assimilation and acceptance.

Once the restriction of European immigration went into effect with the Immigration Act of 1924, an important era in United States history came to an end. While there remain some immigrants who will live out their days never fully assimilated to American life, their children and certainly their grandchildren have been, or are being, assimilated. This chapter in the history of our minority group relations, as we shall point out later, draws to a close as the result of indirect social forces rather than any direct and purposeful planning. Compared with the situation involving other minorities, it is no longer a problem. A study of America's immigration era would have historical significance only, except for two considerations. First, from an analysis of the era we can learn much that may be applied to the analysis of other minority situations. Second, as a consequence of World War II, the problem of displaced persons required a reconsideration of our present immigration policy, and the lessons learned from the great immigration period have a bearing on our current situation.

As a foretaste of this new world problem, our country received a group of immigrants fleeing from the Nazis in the late 1930's, who came to be known as "refugees." Although their numbers were not large, their tendency to concentrate in the metropolitan areas of the Middle Atlantic coast created a minor stir of nativistic reaction. However, since they were absorbed quickly into the economy of a nation with increasing employment and into the social structure of the various nationality groups which they represented, this particular "refugee" problem did not become serious.

More important than the prewar refugee immigration problem has been the postwar problem of the vast number of people in Europe displaced as a result of World War II. The resettlement of these people became an international responsibility ultimately assumed by a special agency of the United Nations. The United States, as the most prosperous and among the less crowded nations, had a major share of the responsibility. A bill authorizing the admission of 228,514 displaced persons was passed in 1948 and supplemented in 1950 by another authorizing the admission of an additional 172,230. Following the abortive revolution of 1956 in Hungary, the United States, by special legislation, accepted a substantial portion of Hungarian refugees. The refugee problem has continued as a result of subsequent outflows of political refugees from behind the Iron Curtain.

The manner in which the United States has handled the refugee immigration reflects the crosscurrents of nativism and internationalism in public thought. The specific qualifications of the Displaced Persons Act (1948) were regarded by some people as reflecting anti-Semitic and anti-Catholic attitudes. Yet the actual processing of displaced persons for immigration has been conducted with elaborate planning by government and private agencies, with the result that problems characteristic of immigrant adjustment have been largely nonexistent.

Oriental Immigrants

Overlapping chronologically with European immigration was that of the Chinese and the Japanese, who concentrated in West Coast communities. At first they were tolerated with condescension as exploitable labor. But as these people, particularly the Japanese, began to succeed in competition with native whites, further immigration was curtailed by the government. Those who remained here were fixed in a pattern of segregated minority status little altered until the drastic relocation of the Japanese during World War II. This latter unique epoch in the history of American minorities, from any long-range view an unfortunate episode, revealed a certain ineptitude and immaturity in the handling of minority group problems. Since the War the economic status of both the Chinese and the Japanese has improved, and discrimination against them has markedly declined. While evacuation dispersed the Japanese somewhat, many of the evacuees returned to the West Coast and are becoming rapidly assimilated. The Chinese, partly by their own choice, are still considerably insulated in Chinatowns.

Mexicans

Following the cessation of unrestricted immigration of Europeans there began a large influx of Mexicans into the Southwest. The usual pattern of native-immigrant interaction proceeded slowly in the case of mexicanos, but acculturation has been greatly accelerated in the past few years. Mexicans in the United States have encountered more severe discrimination than any other immigrant group except the Orientals. Numbering well over 2 million, they constitute one of the larger minority groups. In the Southwest there dwell also the hispanos, descended from the people who inhabited the region before its invasion by anglos and its subsequent annexation by the United States. Hispanos make up a substantial part of the population of New Mexico. While they have never been formally discriminated against, their economic and health conditions ranked among the lowest in the nation up to World War II. Recently their welfare has been greatly improving.

New Minorities: Filipinos, Hawaiians, Puerto Ricans

For still another phase of our minority group history, one must go back to the turn of the century, when the United States became a world power and added overseas territories to its domain. In the process of this expansion, the United States acquired new peoples: the Filipinos and the Puerto Ricans. The political and economic emissaries from the dominant homeland treated their new national compatriots as a minority group, although the upper classes of these areas were given special consideration. When Filipinos migrated to the States, being easily recognized as Orientals, they encountered in major degree the differential treatment usually accorded minorities.

Hawaii presents a distinctive picture of dominant-minority relations. The general impression prevails that this small, although in population amazingly heterogeneous, island archipelago is a paradise of harmonious interracial relations. This impression needs some qualification in the light of the relations between Caucasian and non-Caucasian groups. But the admission of Hawaii to statehood in 1959 reflects the weakening influence of mainland racist ideology, a factor which had been previously an important obstacle to the territory's admission.

The most recent new minority situation arises out of the influx of a substantial number of Puerto Ricans to the mainland. While this phenomenon was at first largely localized in New York City, Puerto Ricans are now spreading out into adjacent areas. In the communities receiving them they have encountered the usual problems of an immigrant group adjusting to a strange cultural environment. As a people with linguistic and racial visibility, they have encountered discrimination and exploitation.

Religious Minorities: Catholics and Jews

Since the United States has been primarily a Protestant nation, residents with non-Protestant backgrounds have generally had some degree of minority status. Discrimination against Roman Catholics and Jews has been a constant phenomenon, although its more overt manifestations have been intermittent. Both Catholics and Jews have also been viewed by the Anglo-Protestant dominants as immigrants. Strong antipathy toward the Irish, for example, has been directed as much toward them for being Catholic as for being Irish, partly because of the aggressive leadership of the Irish in American Catholicism. The later immigrant groups of predominantly Catholic background—Italians, Poles, Mexicans, and Puerto Ricans—were viewed more as "foreigners" than as Catholics.

In the case of Americans of Jewish ancestry, it is clearly their identification with the Jewish religion and their long struggle to maintain it that has given them a persistent distinguishable group identity. The Jews are not a race, nor do they fit the common definitions of a nationality. While to some extent their relations with natives followed the characteristic immigrant pattern, distinctive aspects arose out of the unique character of Jews as a dispersed people. Broadly speaking, Jews accommodated to American life more quickly than any other immigrant group except some of those of north European origin. Yet their complete assimilation in the United States is blocked by the persistence of strongly entrenched gentile attitudes and, to a degree, by their own cohesiveness and by their heavy concentration in metropolitan centers.

THE SIZE OF THE MINORITY GROUPS

Table 1 presents the best available counts or estimates of the number of each of the ethnic groups now occupying minority status in the United States.

TABLE 1
Estimated Numbers of the Minorities in the United States

Negroes (1960)	18,871,831*
Japanese (1960)	464,332*
Chinese (1960)	237,292*
American Indians (1960)	523,591*
Filipinos (1960)	176,310*
Mexicanos (1953)	3,000,000**
Puerto Ricans (Mainland) (1960)	903,000†
Jews (1960)	5,531,500††

* United States Census, 1960, Advanced Reports, Annual Population Characteristics, PC (A2)–1, Table 1, p. 4.
** Lyle Saunders, *Cultural Differences and Medical Care* (New York: Russell Sage Foundation, 1954), p. 288. (Estimated Spanish-speaking population of the Southwest.)
† Bureau of Applied Research, Columbia University, New York City.
†† *American Jewish Yearbook* (New York: The American Jewish Committee, Philadelphia: The Jewish Publication Society of America, 1961), p. 63.

PRELIMINARY CONSIDERATION OF THE SOCIAL PROBLEMS CREATED BY DOMINANT – MINORITY RELATIONS

Recent approaches to the subject of social problems have taken the position that whether certain verifiable social facts constitute a problem or not depends on the value system of the viewer of the facts. For example, to many Americans the segregation of Negroes is simply in the natural order of things, while to many others any group discrimination is a moral problem. Furthermore, the definition of the problem varies with personal value systems. To a traditional white Southerner the rising militancy of Negroes creates the problem of "how to keep them in their place," while to the liberal the problem is "how best to co-operate with these minority efforts to advance toward complete equality." The value system we shall adopt in this text derives from two beliefs: (1) that democracy is the most desirable form of social organization; and (2) that the welfare of the society as a whole, either the nation or the community, properly takes precedence over the welfare of any special groups within this whole. In this preliminary consideration, attention focuses on the main ways in which discrimination against minorities creates problems conceived of according to these values. Further relevant data to verify or qualify what we have considered will be found in subsequent chapters.

Effective Use of Abilities

All minorities are discriminated against to some extent in the choice of their employment; some are discriminated against in training for specific occupations. Since there is a wide range of mental capacities in all minorities, occupational discrimination results in ineffective use of potential. This waste of manpower was brought to public attention during World War II when, for example, the restriction against trained Negro nurses in white hospitals greatly aggravated severe personnel shortages. In an intensive study of the Negro occupational potential Ginsberg observes, "It is never sensible or right for a nation to waste valuable human resources through a failure to develop or utilize them."[11]

Effect on National Income

It has been argued that minority discrimination retards the growth of national income. While the disparity of incomes between Negroes and whites, for example, has been declining, the gap is still wide. In 1939 the median income of nonwhite males was 41.4 per cent of the median income of white males; by 1958 the median nonwhite male income had risen to 58 per cent of that of white males.[12] Still further rise in the relative purchasing power of minorities would stimulate the demand for consumer goods. As we know, many factors conspire to make the Deep South the poorest economic region of the nation, but the poverty of their large Negro population is clearly one of the most important reasons. And discrimination is an important factor contributing to the poverty of the Negro.

Deviant Behavior

The belief has been widely held by people with dominant status that people with minority status furnish more than their share of sociopathic deviant behavior, such as juvenile delinquency, adult crime, mental disease, or other "pathologies." Research sometimes indicates that a particular minority does in fact show a disproportionate amount of some of these phenomena; sometimes the facts show the minority group to manifest less than their proportion. We shall examine the facts in more detail as we proceed in our study of particular minorities. Social science finds that three broad factors are provocative of disorganization: (1) the inevitable strain which a people of different culture faces in adjusting to a new situation; (2) the influence of the environmental conditions associated with the spatial and economic position of the minority, such as living in slum areas; and (3) frustrations and resentments growing out of discrimination itself. It is this last class of causes which is least generally recognized and which most

[11] Eli Ginsberg, *The Negro Potential* (New York: Columbia University Press, 1956), p. 116.
[12] United States Department of Labor, Bulletin S–3, October, 1960, p. 15.

directly pertains to our interest. A Negro boy may steal because he is poor, but he may also steal as a way of "getting even" with white people. In the latter instance, the direct influence of minority status as a causal factor in delinquency is evident. Whatever the incidence of disorganization among minorities, part of it may be properly attributed to the impact of minority status on personality.

Group Tension and Violence

Dominant-minority group situations, especially in modern, rapidly changing societies, inevitably create intergroup tensions which periodically produce violent conflict with attendant bloodshed and economic waste. In the North, race riots have occurred sporadically. More recently, white violence toward Negroes has taken the form of damaging the homes of Negro families who have moved into hitherto white areas. Lynching of individual Negroes by white mobs once was frequent in the South but has rapidly declined in the past two decades. However, other forms of violence—from vociferous jeering to rioting—persist.

Inconsistency in Values

The status of minority groups in American society constitutes a basic ideological conflict, which is viewed by many people as a moral or ethical problem. Gunnar Myrdal, the Swedish social scientist, who has made a most incisive interpretation of Negro-white relations in the United States, considers the violation of the American Creed in our treatment of the Negroes a basic point:

From the point of view of the American Creed the status accorded the Negro in America represents nothing more and nothing less than a century-long lag of public morals. In principle the Negro problem was settled long ago; in practice the solution is not effectuated. The Negro in America has not been given the elemental civil and political rights of formal democracy, including a fair opportunity to earn his living, upon which a general accord was already won when the American Creed was first taking form. And this anachronism constitutes the contemporary "problem" both to the Negroes and to whites.[13]

Effect on American Position in World Affairs

The moral dilemma which Myrdal highlighted has had an incalculably adverse effect on the position of the United States in world affairs. One writer put it thus:

Of the impact of U.S. racism abroad, we all know that every outbreak of race conflict in this country is carried large on the world's news circuits. Little Rock was certainly the most heavily reported U.S. story abroad in 1957, and it began when the echoes of the Till murder trial, Clinton, the Autherine Lucy case, and the Montgomery bus boycott had barely died away. Such events also get heavy

[13] Gunnar Myrdal, *An American Dilemma* (New York: Harper & Brothers, 1944), p. 24. By permission.

coverage in the American press, but some news of American race affairs is even more fully reported abroad. One of my recent informants said: "Why I have even sent my wife clippings from Hongkong papers about things she had never even seen in the papers here in Washington. . . ."

We know that the Communists use the issue as a handy stick with which to beat the American beasts—the demonstrators who tore at the Nixons in Caracas came shouting "Little Rock! Little Rock!"—but this is mostly effect not cause. The stick is there for them to use, so is a fair sized herd of real American beasts, and so are the emotions ready to be exploited. They come spontaneously into play quite without Communist help in many places and often among people well beyond the reach of Communist manipulation.[14]

Whatever the past costs in international relations of American discrimination, the present and future costs should be calculated in the light of the handicap which discrimination imposes on America's position in the United Nations and on its efforts to contain the sphere of influence of Soviet Russia. It will be both interesting and pertinent to review the past record and present trends of Soviet policy and practice in relation to minorities.

SOVIET RUSSIA AND MINORITIES

Soviet Russia in the early years of its existence acquired a reputation for being free from prejudice toward and discrimination against ethnic and racial groups. This reputation has been a powerful ideological weapon in Russia's efforts to persuade the colored peoples of the world of the superiority of Communism. The power of this reputation is enhanced by the contrasting reputation acquired by the colonial western European nations and the United States. Let us examine how Soviet prestige in its treatment of minorities has been acquired and give consideration to its validity and significance.

When the Soviets came into power in 1917, there were four main aspects of the Russian situation relating to its minorities. First, the population of Russia was highly heterogeneous in its ethnic and racial composition. About half the population was composed of the "Great Russians," and another fifth was made up of the closely related Ukranians.[15] These two groups and the so-called "White Russians," who composed about 3 per cent of the population, were considered Slavic peoples. The rest of the population, roughly one-fifth, included nearly 200 groups sufficiently distinctive by ethnic designation to have a special identity. In racial appearance these groups varied widely over most of the range of Caucasoid peoples. There were also several Mongoloid groups and some Mongoloid admixture among the predominantly

[14] Harold R. Isaacs, "World Affairs and U. S. Race Relations: A Note on Little Rock," *The Public Opinion Quarterly*, Fall, 1958, 22: 364. By permission.
[15] William H. Chamberlin, *Soviet Russia* (Boston: Little Brown & Co., 1930), p. 211, Ch. 9, "The Babel Tower of Nationalities," summarizes the situation of minorities in Soviet Russia to about 1930.

Caucasoid peoples. Most Russians were Orthodox Christians, but among the non-Slavic groups were some Mohammedans, and scattered in the predominantly Slavic areas lived about 3 million Jews.

The second aspect of the situation as the Communist Party took over was the presence among many regional groups of strong nationalist sentiments, which had grown even stronger as a result of the policy of forced assimilation by the previous Tsarist regime. This process of Russification had discouraged or sometimes forbidden the use of non-Russian languages and had given preference to Russians in state service.

A third significant element was a strong anti-Semitic feeling in Russia, which had been fostered by the Tsarist governments, particularly those of Alexander III and Nicholas II. Places where Jews might settle were limited, and Jews were not permitted to buy land. They were generally excluded from public employment, and the number allowed to pursue higher education was restricted. Sporadically, pogroms were carried out with little or no government interference.

Finally, it is pertinent to note the absence in Russia of that kind of racial antagonism based on the consciousness of color which has been highly developed among the British and American peoples. Thus the Soviets faced primarily two problems concerning minorities: regional resentment of "Great Russian" dominance and anti-Semitism.

In the formal organization of their new society, the Soviets aimed to remove all manifestations of ethnic and racial discrimination. This official policy of ethnic equality was made ultimately explicit in the Soviet Constitution of 1936.

> The equality of the right of citizens of the U.S.S.R., irrespective of their nationality or race, in all spheres of economic, state, cultural, social, and political life, is an immutable law.
>
> Any direct or indirect restriction of these rights, or, conversely, any establishment of direct or indirect privileges for citizens on account of their race, or nationality, as well as any propagation of any racial or national exclusiveness or hatred and contempt, is punishable by law.

Nevertheless, in practice since Stalin's time the trend has been toward the standardization of culture within the Soviet Union along lines serving the purpose of the monolithic regime—a modern-day Russification. Neither local cultures nor local nationality sentiment has been permitted to stand in the way of this process. "Three autonomous republics [Crimean Tartars, Kalmucks, and Chechens-Ingushi] were disbanded because of alleged disloyalty. . . . in time of war. . . . The peoples concerned were just thrown into the vast Soviet Russian melting pot and disappeared. . . . No statistics or other official information can be obtained about them."[16]

[16] Walter J. Kolarz, "Race Relations in the Soviet Union," in *Race Relations in World Perspective,* p. 192.

Soviet Russia and Asiatics

The Russians sent to Asia as administrators and technicians to modernize the area are an elite class who expect deference as superiors. In order to reconcile the Soviet theory of racial equality with the stern requirements of the situation, the concept of the Elder Brother was devised. The Elder Brother Russian is to be looked up to, idolized, and obeyed by his younger brother Asiatic. A dominant-minority pattern likewise arises in the reverse situation, where Asiatic workers are attracted or dispatched to European industrial centers. Of this Kolarz writes with sharpness: "The Asiatic laborers. . . . are not much more than a necessary evil and constitute the very bottom of the Soviet industrial proletariat. Many of them live in a state of neglect and squalor as has been often admitted by the Soviet Press itself. They usually remain on the low level of untrained laborers and only a few ever acquire skilled jobs.[17]

Soviet Russia and the Jews

Also in contrast to the Tsarist policy, the Soviet government imposed no legal discrimination against Jews and attempted to suppress the expression of latent anti-Semitic attitudes. However, even early in the Soviet regime this policy was not wholly successful. Chamberlin found evidences in the twenties of unofficial anti-Semitism, which he attributed to the carry-over of the traditional prejudice.[18] In a scholarly study of the Jews throughout the Soviet regime to 1950, Schwarz verifies this point.[19] He finds a rise of anti-Semitism in the twenties, a decline in the thirties, and a resurgence in the forties (which has continued to the present time). He found as indications of discrimination against Jews the failure of the Soviet authorities to publicize the Nazi massacres of Jews and the striking decline in the number of Jews in high official position in contrast to the larger number so placed in previous years. This latter point relates to a campaign against "Cosmopolitanism." Of this Schwarz writes:

The elimination of Jews from departments entrusted with the conduct of the Soviet Union's relations with the outside world is not principally inspired by anti-semitism but rather reflects a rise in Russian nationalist feeling, which is accompanied by a distrust of everything non-Russian in the narrowest sense of the word. It also indicates that the government, eager to frustrate the previous influence of "internationalism," is inclined to take for granted the fact that Jews are "internationalists." The upshot is anti-Jewish discrimination. And the authorities practicing this discrimination inevitably succumb themselves to the stealthy and discreet anti-Jewishness which for years has been penetrating many spheres of Soviet society.[20]

[17] Ibid., p. 207.
[18] Chamberlin, Soviet Russia, Ch. 9.
[19] Solomon M. Schwarz, The Jews in the Soviet Union (New York: the American Jewish Committee, 1951, published by the Syracuse University Press).
[20] Ibid., pp. 363–364. By permission.

The continuance of this Soviet policy toward Jews has been indicated by studies made in the past decade. This description, based on an article by an anonymous writer, sums up the present situation: (1) Jews are the only "nationality" not permitted to organize facilities to continue their distinctive culture. (2) Following through with the conception of Jews as cosmopolitans and Jewish group loyalty as involving attachment to a foreign state—Israel— all Jews are considered security risks, and therefore barred from many occupations. (3) Whereas earlier it did appear that persons of Jewish ancestry could be treated without discrimination if they gave up Judaism, it now appears that they cannot. No matter what they do, they are suspect. This latest development falls particularly hard on those younger Jews who have considerable faith in the Soviet regime and are not so Jewish in the religio-cultural sense. Under such circumstances it should come as no surprise that instances of occasional violence against Jews should again be found.[21]

In summary it may be said that (1) the Soviet regime adopted an official policy of treating all nationalities and races without discrimination; (2) the regime used this official policy in its propaganda with some apparent success abroad—particularly among peoples not yet under Communist control— and, conversely, propagandized every unfavorable aspect of the minorities situation in the United States; and (3) in practice, the Soviet regime has imposed Soviet Russification on all local nationalities brought into the Union and has carried on a policy of anti-Semitism persistently since about 1940.

THE UNITED NATIONS AND MINORITIES

In December, 1948, after long deliberation, the United Nations accepted the Universal Declaration of Human Rights. Among the thirty articles of this document are these statements: "Everyone is entitled to all the rights and freedoms set forth in this Declaration, without distinction of any kind such as race, color, sex, language, religion, political or other opinion, national or social origin, property, birth, or other status." "All are equal before the law and are entitled without any discrimination to equal protection of the law." "Everyone, without any discrimination, has the right to equal pay for equal work."

The prominent role of the United States in the United Nations and the location of U.N. headquarters in New York City has placed the nation's treatment of its own minorities in a new perspective. The pattern of discrimination against nonwhite people in the United States causes numerous embarrassing circumstances in relation to nonwhite representatives to the United Nations, such as refusals of service in public places outside New York and subtle rejections of housing accommodations even in the New York

[21] "The Answer to Anti-Semitism," *Commentary*, Sept., 1960, 30: 194–200. Copyright American Jewish Committee. The author writes under the pseudonym "Mark Richards."

metropolitan area. Thus the task of implementing the Declaration our nation has subscribed to is a considerable one.

TOPICS FOR PROJECTS AND DISCUSSION

1. Collect from the files of any leading metropolitan newspapers all items, articles, and editorials, over a short period, pertaining to minorities. Analyze the contents in order to answer the question "How do contemporary American publics view the minorities question?"
2. In the family or neighborhood in which you were reared, what were the attitudes expressed toward peoples of different racial, religious, or nationality backgrounds?
3. If you have traveled abroad, cite any instances of the behavior of Americans in foreign lands indicative of their attitudes toward other peoples.
4. Prepare a 10-minute talk designed to convince a dominant-status audience that discrimination is costly to them.
5. Cite any current events concerned with minorities having implications that affect America's position in international affairs.
6. If you were an American representative in the United Nations, what would you say in reply to an attack by a Communist representative on the treatment of minorities in the United States?

SUGGESTED READING

Cohen, Elliot E., ed. *The New Red Anti-Semitism.* Boston: The Beacon Press, 1953. A Beacon-Commentary Study.
> *A number of articles on the subject of anti-Semitism in Soviet Russia and Soviet-dominated areas; previously published in* Commentary *and here assembled in one booklet.*

Dvorin, Eugene P. *Racial Separation in South Africa: An Analysis of Apartheid Theory.* Chicago: the University of Chicago Press, 1952.
> *A scholarly analysis of the subject.*

Lind, Andrew J., ed. *Race Relations in World Perspective.* Honolulu: University of Hawaii Press, 1955.
> *Papers read at the Conference on Race Relations in the World Perspective held in Honolulu in 1954.*

MacIver, R. M., ed. *Discrimination and National Welfare.* Harper & Brothers, 1949.
> *A number of authorities write of the many different ways in which discrimination affects the national welfare of the United States.*

McWilliams, Carey. *Brothers Under the Skin,* rev. ed. Boston: Little, Brown & Co., 1951.
> *A popularly written account of the "racial" minority peoples in the United States.*

Pierson, Donald. *Negroes in Brazil.* Chicago: University of Chicago Press, 1942.
> *A study of the status of Negroes and mixed Negro-white persons in the city of Bahia.*

Record, Wilson. *The Negro and the Communist Party.* Chapel Hill: University of North Carolina Press, 1951.

A systematic study of the efforts of Communists in the United States to win American Negroes to their cause and an appraisal of the results, showing in general Negro resistance to these efforts.

Taft, Donald R., and Robbins, Richard. *International Migrations: The Immigrant in the Modern World.* New York: The Ronald Press Company, 1955.

Part II, "Processes in the International Arena," describes immigration processes in other areas than the United States.

2

Introduction to the Sociology
of Minorities

All dominant-minority relations occur within a given society and its particular social system. A book specifically about minorities cannot undertake an analysis of the total social structure; nor can it even present the full conceptual range within which sociologists would approach such an analysis. Nevertheless, some general concepts are basic to our discussion. They will be elaborated at appropriate points to throw light on dominant-minority relations. In this chapter we will introduce them into the vocabulary as a preliminary step toward understanding the positions and problems of minorities in the United States today.

SOME BASIC TERMS OF SOCIAL ANALYSIS

Values are the beliefs governing approved actions in a society. A "good" man is one who represents these values in his appearance and behavior, in his orientation to the life of society and its goals, and in the means he employs to attain approved goals.

A *norm* is "expected behavior"—that is, the group, according to its values, defines what actions are approved or "good" or "taken for granted."

Roles are explicitly or implicitly defined ways of carrying out functions in the society in accordance with the norms. We are particularly interested in institutional roles within the family, the job, the public life of the community, and the religious organizations. It is these roles which must be correctly perceived and carried out if success in the dominant society is to be achieved. Minorities may find that they define these roles differently, either because of subcultural values or because their position as minorities has not allowed them to perceive and learn correct role behavior.

Status defines the relative position of a person or a group with regard to another person or group in the hierarchy of prestige. The general problems of status are usually discussed as they relate to social classes (or castes). We are interested primarily in the relationship between dominants and minorities with regard to their relative status. Though this is intertwined with questions of social class, it can be considered a separate matter. While some actions unite dominants and minorities on the basis of class interests, more common, in the past, and to a large measure in the present, is the alliance of dominants across class lines to keep minorities in subordinate status.

The Dominant Group: A Definition

The dominant group in a society is one whose appearance and ways of behaving are considered the "normal ones" of the society. Members of the dominant group share a common value system, a common language, and a common history. Dominant norms are historically derived, and their pre-eminence is established by custom and by law. The survival of the society is believed to depend on these norms to such an extent that subgroups which do not fully share them are restricted, formally or informally, to a greater or lesser degree, from full and equal participation in the life of the society. As Schermerhorn points out, these norms of appearance and behavior in time attain the position of cultural presuppositions.[1]

Before the rise of national states, dominant-minority relations existed between kinship groups (tribes, clans, "peoples") or religious groups, where varying patterns of subordination or "tolerance" of outgroups were to be found. In the modern world, the secular state has the military and legal prerogative to determine the protection and participation of the people within its geographic borders and, in many instances, within its extended political hegemony. The state is distinguished from the other great institutions, such as the family and the church, by its "exclusive investment with the final power of coercion."[2] Therefore, the state is the territorial unit

---

[1] Robert S. Schermerhorn, *These Our People* (Boston: D. C. Heath & Company, 1949), p. 6.
[2] Robert M. MacIver and Charles H. Page, *Society* (New York: Rinehart & Company, Inc., 1937), p. 456.

within which one must consider any contemporary analysis of dominant-minority relations. We shall consider a dominant group, then, *as one within a national state whose distinctive culture and/or physiognomy is established as superior in the society and which treats differentially and unequally other groups in the society with other cultures or physiognomy.*

Minority: A Definition

The anthropologists Charles Wagley and Marvin Harris, in presenting case studies in the Western Hemisphere from materials which, in part, were prepared for UNESCO by social scientists of five countries, have arrived at the following definition of a minority, which we have adopted as the fullest and most appropriate:

(1) Minorities are subordinate segments of complex state societies; (2) minorities have special physical or cultural traits which are held in low esteem by the dominant segments of the society; (3) minorities are self-conscious units bound together by the special traits which their members share and by the special disabilities which these bring; (4) membership in a minority is transmitted by a rule of descent which is capable of affiliating succeeding generations even in the absence of readily apparent physical or cultural traits; (5) minority peoples, by choice or necessity, tend to marry within the group.[3]

This statement gives us five criteria which can be applied to the designation of a group as a minority in a contemporary society. First, to be a member of a minority is not only to be part of a social group vis-à-vis another social group, but to be so within a political unit. Thus the political power groups, as well as the legal structure, will profoundly affect the situation of minorities. Second, attitudes of dominant members toward minorities are bound up with a system of values which devalues certain physical and cultural traits. Third, minorities are conscious of themselves as groups. In some cases members of a minority group deliberately adhere to values which vary from those of the dominant group and which they wish to preserve; sometimes they share disabilities arising from historical attitudes and discrimination. Fourth, one is a member of a minority without choice. One is born to this and may dissociate himself only by conscious decision and appropriate action, if such action is possible. Fifth, minority groups resist intermarriage, just as it is resisted by the dominant group. The minority group's resistance may be due to regard for cultural heritage, or fear that out-marriages will result in unhappiness, or to variations of these reasons.

In the application of such a general theory it is important to remember that the central problems vary in the relations of the dominant group and any particular minority. Some groups, such as American Indians, are set off

[3] Charles Wagley and Marvin Harris, *Minorities in the New World: Six Case Studies* (New York: Columbia University Press, 1958), p. 10.

by race, language, and culture; some share all these attributes with the dominant group, but differ primarily in religion, as with many Jews. Some are set off predominantly by language: German-Americans of the Middle West in the nineteenth century were such a self-conscious linguistic minority. The linguistic minorities, which our great waves of immigration produced, have largely disappeared in the United States. The leading examples of persistence are where religion and language and tradition have been interwoven to maintain a separatist attitude, as with the Pennsylvania Dutch or the French Canadians.

Relations of the dominant group to any particular minority must always be understood in a historical dimension. Present attitudes and actions derive from past patterns of interaction, even where there are now changed relations between the dominant group and the minority.

Ethnic

Ethnic is an increasingly popular term in the writing about minorities and in the vocabulary of those engaged in action in behalf of minorities. Often it is used popularly as equivalent to the term *minority*. This is, of course, inaccurate. *Ethnic* is a term which emphasizes the cultural ethos (values, expectations, and behavior) of a group and formerly, quite properly, was limited in reference to groups whose cultural characteristics are their prime distinguishing factor. Dominants as well as minorities are ethnic groups. An ethnic group, unlike a nationality group, is a population which has preserved visible elements of a tradition without primary reference to former loyalties to a nation-state. The French emigrés who came to New Orleans after the French Revolution were a nationality group. The present French-Canadians are an ethnic group. Minority status may strengthen ethnicity, just as ethnicity may contribute to minority status. Dominant status may lead to the overlooking of the cultural dimension of intergroup contacts.

Another way in which the designation *ethnic* is sometimes used is to indicate groups whose values and behavior are variants of the dominant pattern and have become stabilized in persistent accommodation to minority status. Thus it is possible to speak of the culture of the American Southern Negro as contrasted with the culture of the Jamaican Negro. These also are ethnic groups, though each has developed and established a different variant of Anglo-Saxon culture.

Ethnicity as a dimension of minority status diminishes with increasing acculturation, if the threshold of discrimination is low. National identification then takes precedence over the older cultural identification. Eventually, if assimilation takes place, cultural identification with the dominant culture may be so complete that the third or fourth generation has no knowledge of the older cultural heritage and reflects it perhaps only in idiosyncratic mannerisms or religious institutions.

DIFFERENTIAL IDENTIFIABILITY: "VISIBILITY"

The existence of a dominant-minority situation requires that two groups possess one or more differences, which are reciprocally perceptible and by which the members of each respectively may be identified. The traits which are perceived may be physiognomic ("racial"), or cultural, or both. The term *visibility* has been frequently used for this phenomenon, and we shall use this term as less awkward than "identifiability." Let us examine the two categories of visibility, biological and cultural.

Biological Visibility

Physical Type   The traits which are highly valued in American culture are the Caucasoid features. Any variation from the ideal type is held in less esteem in the popular culture. Where differences from the Caucasoid type are perceived, as illustrated by those physical features of the Japanese or the Chinese which distinguish them from the white, we speak of biological visibility.

Lineage   Lineage is invisible visibility. We consider it an aspect of biological visibility because it imputes minority status on the basis of biological descent. In cases of severe devaluation of minorities, even a small proportion of minority ancestry is enough to designate membership in a minority. "Negroes" who are so completely Caucasoid in their physical features that they cannot be identified by sight are identifiable as Negroes by the general knowledge of their Negro lineage. In periods when dominant elements strongly desire to exclude minorities from privileges and participation and when the latter's visibility is becoming too attenuated for the purpose, rules of descent have been made official, as in the case of the Jews in Nazi Germany.

Cultural Visibility

Language and Non-Verbal Communication   The presence of an accent or imperfect grammar in speaking the dominant language, or simply the practice of speaking another language in the family or among close associates, may serve as a mode of identification in both a derogatory sense for the dominant group, or in a sense of cultural pride for the minority. Many anti-minority jokes employ stereotypes of linguistic characteristics.

Much communication between people with the same cultural experience and expectations is nonverbal. The language of gesture, facial expression, posture, emotional tone, all express cultural learning and vary from culture to culture, as most actors know.[4] Different societies allow different ways of expressing emotional reactions to joy or pain or trouble, and these reactive

---

[4] Jurgen Ruesch and Weldon Kees, *Non Verbal Communication* (Berkeley and Los Angeles: the University of California Press, 1956).

patterns also are used to identify minorities in a derogatory way. For example, one study has shown that doctors and nurses with Anglo-Saxon norms of reserve in emotional expression often fail to understand and are impatient with the reactions to their illness of patients from non-Anglo-Saxon societies.[5]

Dress Although there are only a few highly coherent minorities which maintain traditional modes of dress—for instance the Amish, Hassidic Jews, and Navahoes (on the reservation)—dress has in the past been a major symbol of cultural identity. Nationality societies whose members have long since adopted the dominant modes of dress for everyday living, often still wear the traditional "costume" to celebrate patriotic or religious festivals. Modes of hair style and ornamentation may also indicate a particular cultural heritage. Sometimes an insecure group will adopt a mode of dress as part of a struggle for identification, as for example, the Zoot suits that were affected by young Mexican-Americans in the early 1940's. Sometimes wearing cultural or religious emblems is urged or obligatory, coming from the minority group itself; sometimes it is forced on minorities by dominant groups.

Institutional Behavior Different ways of behaving in family, economic, political, and religious life often make members of minorities conspicuous. For example, filial obligations and parental authority may make a young person different in his group participation from his schoolfellows. A minority member with difference of religious practice in a highly coherent Protestant community may in this sense be visible to his neighbors. Minority experiences in economic and political activity may establish identifiable sub-cultural patterns of behavior—for example, Greeks may be associated with the restaurant business, Chinese with laundries, Irish with city politics, and so forth.

Associations An aspect of visibility frequently ignored in the discussion of minorities is what we shall call *associational visibility*. An individual may have no visible traits that would designate him a member of a minority, but he identifies himself by the group with which he generally associates, particularly in his most intimate contacts. While as a means of identification associational visibility is derivative from other bases, it acquires significance through long practice.

Overlap of Traits A minority is sometimes identified only by physiognomic traits, but usually there is an overlap of physiognomic and cultural traits. Sometimes there are only cultural traits which may occur in any of

[5] Mark Zborowski, "Cultural Components in Responses to Pain," *Social Perspectives on Behavior*, eds. Herman D. Stein and Richard A. Cloward (Glencoe, Ill.: The Free Press, 1958).

several combinations. The Japanese immigrants, for example, differed in their ethnic culture generally, had a distinctive physiognomy, and were preponderantly non-Christian. Perhaps only two minority groups can easily be fitted into a simple visibility scheme: the immigrants from the north of Europe who differ in ethnic culture without basic religious difference; and contemporary American Negroes, who are distinguished almost solely by their physiognomic features.

A useful clue to arranging minorities in a classification based on visibility may be found by considering the ways in which the dominant-status group has reacted to the visibilities involved. Proceeding in this manner, it can be observed that the dominant groups in the United States have conceived of minority groups in three ways: as "foreigners," as "colored," and as nonbelievers in the faith of the dominant group. While in most specific situations the dominants look on the minority in some combination of these three ways, in each case it seems possible to accord priority to one. For example, although the great majority of Italians are known to be Catholics, it is that entire configuration of cultural elements which compose the Italian "ethos" which identifies them most prominently. Again, while the Japanese are often thought of as foreigners, it is their physiognomic visibility which comes first to the mind of the person of dominant status when the word "Japanese" is mentioned. The leading element in the consciousness of the dominant in his conception of the Japanese is appearance. In spite of the fact that "color" is one of the less accurate traits to employ in "racial" classifications of mankind, it is consciousness of color which has loomed largest in the white man's concept of the other peoples of the earth. Wherever color difference is associated with other differences in the United States, it has always taken precedence over other factors in retarding assimilation.

Numbers and Concentration as Related to Visibility

A few dispersed individuals or families, whatever their physical or cultural traits, are less likely to be subject to all of the disabilities of minority position. They may be viewed with curiosity, tolerated, or ignored. When there are large numbers of a particular minority in a community, however, there is more likely to be a consensus of differential treatment. This is all the more so if they are forced to cluster in a given area of the community, or if they do so from choice. They are then not only visible as individuals, but visible as a segment of the community.

HOW DOMINANCE IS MAINTAINED

Force, Law, and Custom as Agents

Superior numbers, or superior technology and/or organization, or entrenched positions of power may enable one group initially to establish its mode of behavior as dominant. This position is subsequently maintained by custom and law and applied to other visible groups which may be added to the population. Force remains the ultimate sanction for maintaining dominance. It may be legitimately used (law enforcement) to ensure the preservation of established relationships, or, in periods of tension, it may be used in defiance of law.

In stable periods the law has pre-eminence, with *authority* to enforce. Thus political control of the state by adherents to dominant norms will ensure laws upholding these norms. In the creation of policy toward minorities, the state may, for example, grant or deny citizenship, as in America for a long time it excluded Orientals and defined limited citizenship for the conquered American Indians. Furthermore, the state plays its role in the subjugation of minorities not only through law and policy, but through its system of education. It presents historical models of esteemed behavior: the founding fathers and other "great men." Conversely, only too often, idealized subordinate roles are also presented in the official education: Pocahontas and Uncle Tom become the faithful protectors and upholders of Anglo-Saxon dominance. Public rituals and symbols constantly stimulate or reinvoke sentiments of loyalty, affection, and commitment to dominant values.

Custom governs the whole web of traditionally appropriate behavior. When dominance is maintained in a relatively unchanging society, custom ensures the continuance of previously defined appropriate ways of interacting. These may even be elaborated into a rigid etiquette which amplifies the fact of dominance in all spheres of life. Probably the extreme example of this is the pattern of relations between whites and Negroes in the more traditional sections of the South. The common understanding of what is expected and allowable between the two groups governs almost every phase of contact.

In the American legal system, resting as it does on English common law, there can never be too wide a gap between enforceable laws and accepted customs. The problem emerges most clearly in the tension between local or regional customs and the local and state laws which are coherent with them, and federal laws, which have responded to a broader legislative representation that includes many who do not share the regional or local patterns.

MODES OF DOMINANCE

Segregation

Segregation is a pattern of settlement, or of spatial separation in the use of common facilities, designed to indicate categorically inferior status. Formal and informal restrictions may operate to limit areas of residence for minorities. Local law and custom may require a minority member to enter a public building by a separate entrance, to work in industry on a separate floor, to use separate waiting rooms and railroad cars, to attend separate schools. Segregation may be viewed as either ecological or institutional in character. It may be formally established, or formally demanded, but it is usually informally enforced. The fact that it is informally enforced makes it difficult to eliminate.

Segregated communities almost always represent a poorer average level of living with respect to quality of housing, public services, health, and education. Thus, in the long run, segregation is a cost to the total community. Where formal and informal residential restriction has kept in inferior conditions of life those people who wished to move out, the situation is analogous to the medieval ghetto and is indeed often referred to as such in sociological writing and popular discussion of minorities. The original use of the term "ghettoizing" in relation to the American subcommunity occurred in Louis Wirth's book, *The Ghetto*.[6] At the time Wirth wrote, the situations he described obtained for many nationality subcommunities in America's cities. Although these have declined in number and size, the problem of segregation is still very real for several of the minority groups.

Categorical Discrimination

Discrimination—differential and unequal treatment by the dominant of the minority—is an essential feature of the dominant-minority relationship. Discrimination is categorical when it is applied to all members of the minority. For example, Irish immigrants arriving in Boston in pre-Civil War days found signs at places of employment saying "No Irish need apply."

Discrimination may operate in hotels, jobs, social organizations, admissions to schools, colleges, and universities, and so forth, wherever there is categorical exclusion or categorical limitation of numbers. Discrimination may also operate to create unequal rewards for work that is done, in wage differentials, or in access to promotion. It may operate in the sphere of political rights, thus limiting access to the ultimate channel of power or redress. Provisions like the poll tax effectively deprive many people from their share in the political decision-making process.

Prejudice

Whereas segregation and discrimination are *actions,* prejudice is an *attitude* unfavorable to or disparaging of a whole group and all the individual members of it.

Prejudice as False Perception   Sometimes prejudice is the result of a false perception of a minority as learned from the various socializing agents to which children and youth are exposed. It is probable that most dominant-

---

[6] Chicago: University of Chicago Press, 1928.

status persons who consciously or unconsciously take the advantage over minorities accruing from their dominant status do so simply as a result of behaving in a customary way, without any individual animus and often with limited experience of contact with the minority.

False perceptions are enhanced by *stereotypes*. A stereotype is an oversimplified generalization which emphasizes only selected traits of another group. It tends to evoke a generalized reaction to any member of that group. To some extent stereotypes arise out of the tendency to save time and effort. As one author points out, "It is much easier to have a definite opinion as to the type of creatures women are, and behave accordingly, than to analyze and study each woman anew."[7] What is significant in a stereotype of a minority group is that the selected traits tend to be those that emphasize difference from the dominant norm, and they tend to make up the whole image of an entire group, thus serving as an excuse for differential treatment. The assumption is that these traits are innate and hereditary and therefore that no change in the treatment of the stereotyped minority is warranted. Since newspapers and magazines and other forms of mass communication depend on popular approval for their sales, they often serve as reinforcing agents in the maintenance and continuance of such generalized popular stereotypes.[8] They often help create a stereotype of the dominant group as well. Minorities often have stereotypes regarding dominants, especially if they have a strong cultural tradition with different values from those of the dominants.[9]

Prejudice as Personality Structure   Anthropology and psychiatry have called our attention to the fact that some personalities need to feel superior in order to have a secure self-image. In general, as far as we know from research, one can identify this need for dominance with an insecure person who has been brought up by very dominating adults. No community problems may occur if there are other outlets for his need to be superior—if, for example, the person may with cultural approval in turn dominate his children, or his servants, and if no major threat to his way of life occurs. When external circumstances challenge his way of functioning, his livelihood, his personal security, he may need to lay the blame for this at the door of members of the society whom he believes are of lesser worth—"aliens," "troublemakers," "competitors." This is the person whose prejudices grow out of his *personality needs*. His prejudices develop with regard to any given important social stereotype which impinges on his environment. It may be a

[7] Gerhart Saenger, *The Social Psychology of Prejudice* (New York: Harper & Brothers, 1953), p. 68.
[8] See, for example, Bernard Berelson and Patricia J. Salter, "Majority and Minority Americans: An Analysis of Magazine Fiction," *Race Prejudice and Discrimination*, ed. Arnold M. Rose (New York: Alfred A. Knopf, Inc., 1951), p. 522 ff.
[9] See Chapter 7 for the Puerto Rican stereotype of the "Real American."

"native" in colonial Indonesia, an African in Afrikander South Africa, a Japanese on the West Coast, a Jew in Nazi Germany. Some societies seem to produce fewer of this type of personality, while in other societies this type of personality seems to be more nearly the norm. No culture is composed *entirely* of one type of person or another.

It is these personalities that form the hard core of prejudiced citizens who resist change in the position of minorities and who refuse to surrender their stereotypes of minority groups. Persons who do not have such a personality structure may also have stereotypes which they acquired through learning in their environment, but they can relinquish them when given an opportunity for relearning. The personality type which needs prejudice to support its precarious self-esteem usually cannot modify through learning.

Prejudice as Panic Reaction A third type of prejudice may be brought into play in situations of generalized anxiety where persons are played upon by propaganda or mob psychology to share attitudes against a minority which they would not have imagined for themselves in a time free of stress and of which they are often ashamed later. The existence of dominant-minority patterns provides an outlet for frustrations which can under some circumstances be mobilized into temporary aggression against a minority.

The "Vicious Circle"

Once established, the dynamics of dominant-minority relations set in motion a continuous series of reciprocal stimuli and responses which has been frequently called the "vicious circle." Discriminatory practices operate to keep a minority in disadvantaged circumstances which may lead to low standards of living, health, education, and morals. These poor conditions then give support to the dominant group's rationale for discrimination. The discrimination and the low standards mutually "cause" each other. Myrdal points out that,

If things remain about as they are, or have been, this means that the two forces happen to balance each other. . . . If either of the factors changes, this will cause a change in the other factor, too, and start a process of interaction where the change in one factor will be continuously supported by the reaction of the other factor. . . .
If, for example, we assume that for some reason white prejudice could be decreased and discrimination mitigated, this is likely to cause a rise in Negro standards, which may decrease white prejudice still a little more, which would again allow Negro standards to rise, and so on through mutual interaction. If, instead, discrimination should become intensified, we should see the vicious circle spiraling downward.[10]

[10] Gunnar Myrdal, *An American Dilemma* (New York: Harper & Brothers, 1944), pp. 75–76.

MINORITY ADAPTATIONS TO MODES OF DOMINANCE

Separatism

In the period of colonial expansion, from the seventeenth to the nineteenth centuries, there were many groups who sought to set up enclaves in the New World which were geographically separate and in which they could maintain their particular way of life. A number of such German-speaking groups came to the colonies in the eighteenth century, of which the Amish still persist. So too, those dissenting "minorities" from England who were discriminated against in the sphere of political power—Puritans, Quakers, Catholics—saw in the establishment of new settlements an opportunity not only to survive, but to control and develop their communities according to their own values. Thus William Penn wrote to his son in 1700:

Remember these points, that it was the Government which engaged me and those that adventured with me. . . . The Government was our greatest inducement, and upon that public faith we have buried our blood and bones, as well as estates, to make it what it is: for being Dissenters, we therefore came that we might enjoy that so far of which would not be allowed us any share at home.[11]

Separatism is not the same as the clustering of a group in one area from the need to be with the familiar. It usually does not persist more than a generation. Separatism represents the decision to eschew the structure of the dominant society in order to retain values which have led to discrimination in the society from which the group has separated. Throughout the nineteenth century there were separatist settlements in the United States with religious or nationality identities which they wished to preserve. With the closing of the frontier, separatism became a less common solution. Although it persists, occasionally even in the midst of an urban community, as with Hassidic Jews, it is no longer an easy solution.

Accommodation

If the individuals in a minority remain within the framework of the dominant society and must of necessity accept conditions they cannot control, they must to a degree conform to the subordinate position and to implicit or explicit rules of behavior vis-à-vis the dominant group. When this situation persists over several generations, a pattern of accommodation develops in which both superior and subordinate positions are taken for granted. Both dominant and minority members may accept the same rationalizations for the existing pattern. Both may equally defend it. A high degree of personal sympathy and understanding may in some instances develop under

---

[11] "Papers Relating to Provincial Affairs," in *Pennsylvania Archives of History and Biography*, Second Series, Vol. VII, p. 11.

these circumstances between dominant and minority individuals, as both groups are interdependent parts of an established social system.[12]

The costs to the individual of minority status who accepts the accommodative pattern are often high, both in his perception of reality and in his difficulty in handling suppressed hostility and inevitable resentment. A variety of devices may help him ease this burden: clowning, intra-group aggression, fantasy, and psychological distortion of lesser or greater severity.

Among minorities where the barriers against the whole group are not severe enough to force a general accommodative pattern, individuals may still choose this adaptation, according to their temperament, skills, or previous social experience.

Acculturation

Acculturation is a term widely used to describe the process by which individuals whose primary learning has been in one culture take over traits from another; or sometimes the way in which whole groups incorporate traits from other cultures with which they have had contact. The sense in which we use it here is specific to dominant-minority relations. Our use of the term does not describe a process, *but an alternative mode of adaptation.* As we have seen, some minorities choose separatism. Others have accommodation forced upon them, with the result that, although some external traits are adopted, there is resistance, as with American Indians.

Acculturation has often been described in the older literature as an interim stage preceding assimilation. We wish to emphasize that this sequence by no means always takes place. Differential evaluations of one's self and of one's subculture will determine eventual assimilation.

Acculturation involves two levels of adaptation. The first is behavioral, in which the material culture, language, and secular behavior of the dominant group is acquired, but the key attitudes and the participation in private spheres of life remain subcultural. Such is true of the Norwegians of "Jonesville," described in Chapter 4.

The second level is one where (usually, though not always, in addition to behavior) the cultural *attitudes* of the dominant culture have been acquired. If there is close congruence in attitudes between the dominant culture and the subculture, what we have called the second stage may precede the first, as with the Japanese. On the whole, however, the other sequence is more common. Dominant norms become internalized and are the assumptions from which behavior emanates spontaneously. The primary *identification,* however, is still with the subgroup. Persons may choose acculturation as a mode of adaptation because they value tradition, because group identity

[12] E. Franklin Frazier, *Race and Culture Contacts in the Modern World* (New York: Alfred A. Knopf, Inc., 1957). Chapter 13 describes this in a discussion of the plantation as a social institution.

gives security, because ideologically they seek a culturally pluralistic ideal society, or because the barriers they perceive will, in their opinion, never permit assimilation.

Assimilation

Assimilation of a minority person occurs when the cultural values of the dominant culture have become the cultural assumptions of such a person. In the strictest sense, it might be argued that complete assimilation is impossible for a person born and reared in a minority subgroup and culture. If one takes the prevailing viewpoint in sociopsychological thinking that socialization in childhood is never completely changed, it would follow that a minority individual conditioned to a minority culture could never completely internalize the dominant culture. There are, however, other considerations which enter here. (1) The level of acculturation as a mode of adaptation in minority groups is typically generational—that is to say, the child of the immigrant becomes himself more acculturated than his immigrant father and thus as a parent himself socializes his children to more of the dominant culture and less of the immigrant culture. Thus in subsequent generations, those of immigrant subcultural background become increasingly conditioned to the dominant culture. By the third or subsequent generations, internalization of the dominant cultural values becomes possible. (2) In a highly dynamic society such as that of twentieth-century United States, the dominant culture itself undergoes change. For example, one might state that at the turn of the century in the United States a belief in Christianity and a belief that every individual should save enough money to care for his old age were assumptions of the dominant culture. Today one could find much support for the propositions that a belief in God (however specifically defined) and support of a "respectable" religious organization; and the belief that a person should be willing to work steadily to accumulate enough social security benefits for his old age make for a *real*, that is, acceptable, American. (3) A large-scale, industrial, urban society is *sui generis* a society with subcultures.

Taking all these factors into consideration, in defining assimilation one must either adhere to the strict position postulated above and in that case assume that assimilation is found only in a folk society or a regimented state, and that it is not possible in our kind of a society, or one must take the position that assimilation is a proper term to define the following situation: A person is assimilated when he has identified himself with the dominant culture and is accepted without discrimination by people of dominant status in both public and private roles. The ultimate test of assimilation is the absence of the rule of endogamy. Therefore an assimilated person of minority-group background must entertain the possibility of out-marriage with confidence that the rule of endogamy will not be invoked against him by persons of dominant status. For operational purposes, however, we shall consider that assimilation has occurred when a person of previous minority status, having internalized the major cultural values of the *present*, is generally accepted on a basis of equality as a neighbor, a clique member, or a personal friend. When this situation is applicable to substantially all the persons of a given ethnic or racial or religious background, the group hitherto considered a minority may be considered assimilated, and ceases to be a minority *group*.

Amalgamation

Amalgamation is the biological merging of previously distinct racial or subracial stocks. Amalgamation always takes place to some degree with or without formal approval when members of one group live in constant interaction with members of another. With members of both groups having a similar degree of acculturation and a similar position in the over-all status system, cross marriages begin to take place even in the face of group disapproval. The stress of the American family system on the nuclear family and the geographic mobility of Americans have facilitated this process. Similarly there have frequently been cross marriages at upper status levels where the frame of reference is international rather than national, as with some intellectual and social elites. And, finally, when there is a pattern of severe exploitation and subjugation of the minority by the dominant group, sexual exploitation will be one facet of the configuration.

These modes of adaptation have sometimes been treated as sequential stages in a process through which all minorities passed. This point of view grew out of observation of the fact that numbers of European immigrants "disappeared" into the dominant group, creating that blend of physical types and cultural admixture that is "American." But such sequence is not upheld by the experience of all minorities. Choices of modes are still exercised by individual minority members and by groups. Sometimes possibilities are limited by dominant-group action. In other cases, separatism persists among groups when the barriers against them are not high. Thus acculturation is not inevitably followed by assimilation, as is clear with American Negroes and a large proportion of American Jews.

To see any direction of movement one must relate the mode of adaptation to *possibilities*, and to *goals*. Louis Wirth has posited four possible goals for minority groups: secession, pluralism, assimilation, and achievement of dominance.[13] As Wagley and Harris point out, at the present time only two of these alternatives have any significant place in minority aspirations in the Western Hemisphere: pluralism and assimilation.[14] The problems and ad-

---

[13] Louis Wirth, "The Problem of Minority Groups," in *The Science of Man in the World Crisis*, ed. Ralph Linton (New York: Columbia University Press, 1945), pp. 354–364.
[14] Wagley and Harris, *Minorities in the New World*, p. 286.

vantages of each of these directions will be examined in another chapter of this book. Here it is merely necessary to note the relation of minority goals to modes of adaptation.

THE FOCI OF DOMINANT – MINORITY INTERACTION

The aspects of the social structure in which dominant-minority relations come into focus are the value system, the institutional role behavior, and the status hierarchies.

Value Systems

Any culture maintains its existing system of social organization through *the dominance of one configuration of values.* These values may not be consistent, as Myrdal has pointed out in his discussion of *The American Creed,*[15] but even in their lack of consistency on the level of formulated beliefs they show some central assumptions. For example, contemporary Western culture has been described as having the following ways of viewing the fundamental questions of the relation of man to nature: that nature is to be *overcome* and controlled (the basis for scientific and technological thinking); that the *future* should have more emphasis than the present or the past; that the normal mode of relations between men is individualistic and competitive. These orientations are the basis for the derivative expectations of behavior. The individual acquires these values in hierarchical relationship to persons in authority: parents, teachers, employers, and civic models. They are reinforced by myths and hero figures. They are acquired by indoctrination and emulation.

It is the nature of values that they seem to the group that holds them to be "the best," "the right." It is part and parcel of a value system that, except in the thinking of a few intellectual sophisticates, other value systems are held in lesser regard. Values are acquired so early in the socialization process—in the family, in the school, in the community—that for most people they are largely unconscious assumptions, governing action much more deeply than it is governed by professed creeds.

Variant Values

Variant values is a term for subcultural values. For example, among rural Spanish-Americans of the southwestern United States, the individual is socialized and becomes integrated into a traditional culture different from the "Anglo" culture of the dominant group. He will therefore act out his roles with reference to the subculture in a way that may be inappropriate to

[15] Myrdal, *An American Dilemma,* p. 24.

the expectations of the dominant culture.[16] He has merely incorporated the values of another culture than the dominant. This may place him at a competitive disadvantage, because he does not know how to assume expected roles in the dominant pattern. It may also make him appear less "valuable"—even ridiculous—to naive dominants who use his ineptness in their patterns as rationalization for restricting his privileges.

Official and Unofficial Values

Both dominant and variant value systems are sets of *official values* designed to maintain cultural continuity and give a frame for expectations, and they are acquired hierarchically. *Unofficial values,*[17] on the other hand, are concerned with present interest and are acquired and supported by present experiences, which lack an hierarchical character. These are sometimes called *deviant values.* They contain some elements which are in conflict with the official values, though there may be areas in which the two overlap. Unofficial values may be of many kinds. In our country they may be the values of a group of people in the creative arts who are opposed to the "official" American value of economic success. They may be the values held by an economic or a political protest group. They can be those of a religious cult. They can be, in a period in which official values are changing, a reactionary pattern defending the interests of a group affected by the change. Members of minority groups are often attracted to groups which adhere to unofficial values, because it may seem harmonious with their present interest to protest or deny official values, especially as these appear discriminatory, and, too, it may be a way of relieving their minority status by forming associations with a different group of people. Upholders of the official value system in conflict with groups expressing "unofficial" values have sometimes linked unofficial values with "foreign" and used anti-minority sentiment against them in their struggle with protest groups. Thus in the nineteenth century, miners' unions were described as "drunken, fighting Irish."[18]

Conflicts of dominant and variant values are most overt when separatism occurs. They arise in many modes of dominant-minority relations, however—as, for instance, in issues of separation of church and state; of Sabbath ob-

[16] Florence Rockwood Kluckhohn, "Dominant and Variant Value Orientations," *Personality in Nature, Society and Culture*, rev. ed., ed. Clyde Kluckhohn and Henry A. Murray, with the collaboration of David M. Schneider (New York: Alfred A. Knopf, Inc., 1953), pp. 342 ff.

[17] Milton L. Barron, *The Juvenile in Delinquent Society* (New York: Alfred A. Knopf, Inc., 1954), p. 203.

[18] A fair fist fight (between men of equal strength) and a drinking bout at the local tavern on Saturday night were legitimate outlets within Irish peasant culture. See Conrad Arensberg and Solon Kimball, *Family and Community in Ireland* (Cambridge, Mass.: Harvard University Press, 1940). These modes of behavior were "foreign" and devalued by Puritan America and later used to arouse sentiment against the early struggles of predominantly Irish groups of coal miners.

servance; of acceptance of technology or medical care. Official versus unofficial values emerges as the focus of conflict in periods of stress.

Institutional Roles

The failure to carry out institutional roles in the manner defined by the dominant culture is a major justification offered by dominants for discrimination against or devaluation of minorities: "They don't *do* right."

In some Near Eastern societies the pattern of commercial enterprise has been highly competitive, with the emphasis on competitors' outwitting one another. The spirit of the inviolability of contract which dominates Western European (and by heritage dominant American) commercial relations is only partially understood and adhered to in these other societies. Where the merchant with the Near Eastern role definition operates among dominant Americans, he is described as "sharp," "slick," "untrustworthy." Yankee traders in Reconstruction days were also described this way by Southern planters, who were used to a feudal pattern of economic obligations and had different expectations of the role of merchant.[19]

Occupational roles are key factors in the acculturation process. Improved occupational positions with the accompanying roles are much sought by minorities and are the point of interaction where much pressure and counterpressure is exerted. Conflict usually can be resolved only by minority members' learning new role behavior.

Although occupational roles are perhaps the most significant, other institutional roles are important also as focal points in dominant-minority relations. When the Irish entered politics the role of the political leader was defined by them in the light of their political heritage of protest and insurgence, the present necessity of vote-getting, and lack of access to the prerequisites of political leadership available to John Adams conservatives. The immigrant group created a new structure of urban politics and new roles, in the ward boss and the local party boss, which brought bitter but not always successful opposition.

Family roles as defined by one group may be alien to the other. For example, a Southern Negro mother, especially from a rural area, may take it for granted that she leaves her children for her mother to bring up. This is a carry-over from an ante-bellum pattern when older slaves took care of children and working-age women worked.[20] A social worker from the dominant culture may note this as "maternal rejection," which it may not be at all. A Puerto Rican mother may quit her job and apply for public assistance because her daughter has reached puberty and in the cultural framework it is now the mother's duty to stay home and chaperone her daughter. A

[19] Seymour Martin Lipset, "Changing Social Status and Prejudice: The Race Theories of a Pioneering American Sociologist," *Commentary*, May 1950, pp. 475–479.

[20] E. Franklin Frazier, *The Negro Family in America* (New York: The Dryden Press, Inc., 1948).

father, in many European societies, who sees his paternal role as providing for a good marriage for his daughter may be bewildered when a college scholarship committee tells him she is not eligible for scholarship aid as long as her dowry is in the bank. Religious roles have often been focal points of dominant-minority issues, especially with regard to education.

The institutional patterns of a culture are its guarantees of continuance. Honored positions in the society go to those who best fulfill significant dominant institutional roles. People who have had prolonged subordination often have no opportunity to perceive or learn these roles, or feel they must reject them because they are impossible. Others cling to roles defined by variant value systems. Yet increasingly there is the rising aspiration for the benefits to be derived from improved positions, which leads to role relearning, role conflict, or role modification. This is where the real personal crises of dominant-minority relations occur.

Social Class and Minorities

Individual improvement in economic circumstances and in social status is a dominant norm in American tradition. Benjamin Franklin says in *Poor Richard's Almanac,* " 'Tis a laudable ambition that seeks to be better than its neighbors." In a society of free enterprise, to compete successfully and to achieve wealth and respect is to fulfill a social ideal. This is usually associated with upward mobility. Discrimination places a limitation on such upward mobility for minority members. They may succeed in shifting their position within the minority group, but the new position will not be similar to a shift in the scale of the dominant group. Furthermore, the holding of minorities in less valued jobs often creates more opportunity in the higher positions for members of the dominant group who might not be able to compete successfully if there were really free competition. This problem of equality of opportunity is the problem of *status* and *class.* We have even had in the United States such rigid barriers to movement from one position to another that we could speak of a "caste-like" situation. In *caste* there are legal or religious prohibitions against moving from one's hereditary position in the social hierarchy. When legal restrictions have created this caste barrier, as under slavery, impetus has been given to the growth of parallel social hierarchies, one for the dominant, one for the minority. This also occurs without such severe barriers as caste, when there is historical discrimination enforced by association or custom even without the authority of law.

In a study made a generation ago of a middle-sized American industrial community with an ethnically heterogeneous population, it was possible to see the relation between the dominant status structure and that of the minorities.

In "Yankee City," a research team delineated a social class structure composed of three classes, or six when subdivided:[21] upper upper, lower upper; upper middle, lower middle; upper lower, lower lower. In a figure, horizontal lines can be used to indicate the hierarchical gradations. Where do the various ethnic and racial groups fit into this scheme?[22] Taking ethnic as distinct from racial minorities, it was found that in 1933 in "Yankee City" they distributed over several segments of the six-fold class structure. For example, some Italians were found as high as the lower middle class. They were thought of, however, as Italians and reacted to accordingly. Within each class level to which they rose, the ethnics were thought of as somehow not quite the same as the native members of the same class—that is, until as individuals they become assimilated. If one examines the status of ethnic minorities in the United States, the conclusion seems inescapable that it represents a combination of the horizontal and vertical principles of social differentiation. The test of the existence of a minority is to verify dominant behavior toward it within the same class. The way to express this distinction between class and minority in a figure is to take first the pyramid of the class structure of the dominants, superimpose the pyramid of the class structure of the minorities first exactly, and then to drop the latter less than a full horizontal segment to express the inferior position of each minority class segment to others within the class. The result is seen in Figure 1.

Figure 1. The Relation Between the Dominant-Minority Structure and the Class Structure

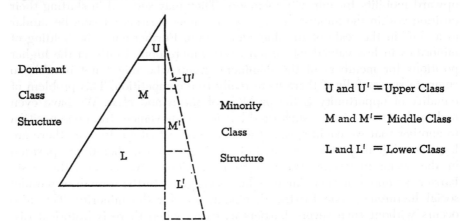

U and U' = Upper Class

M and M' = Middle Class

L and L' = Lower Class

[21] See W. Lloyd Warner and Paul S. Lunt, *The Social Life of a Modern Community* (New Haven: Yale University Press, 1941), Ch. 5, "How The Several Classes Were Discovered," and p. 225, Table 7, "Class and Ethnic Groups."
[22] Although it is now recognized, as theory of stratification has developed, that the "Yankee City" studies are classifications of "status" (prestige) rather than "class" (access to economic positions), we have retained the original terminology.

A further complication arises in the fact that the determiners for class are sometimes different for the dominant and the minority. For example, a neighborhood grocer with a family-operated store may be close to the top of the class structure of an ethnic minority, but a similarly occupied dominant might border between upper lower and lower middle in dominant class structure. To sum up, the main distinction between class and minority can be expressed by stating that in the former, people look up and down at each other, and in the latter, they look up and across, and down and across.

Minority and Caste

For our purposes it may be sufficient to point out that the term *caste* involves a situation in which the lines barring certain degrees of association between the groups are rigidly drawn. The prohibition of marriage across the caste lines is the most adamant barrier of all, and if in spite of it intermarriage does take place, the family thus formed is characteristically assigned the status of the lower caste. We shall see that the status of American minorities with marked racial visibility has often approximated caste.

Marginality—An Individual Response to Group Adaptation

Individuals caught between emulation of the dominant group and ties to the minority group we call *marginal*. In the older theory of minorities, which assumed that minority groups moved in a sequential series of steps to ultimate assimilation, specific groups were sometimes said to be in a marginal stage. This referred to the fact that the direction of the leadership and membership was toward the incorporation of dominant values and goals, emulating, even if imperfectly, dominant institutional roles, although "visible characteristics" of the minority persisted. The group then took on a double identity: "I am an Italian-American."

In searching for a more general approach to marginality which might apply in all dominant-minority situations, including pluralistic goals, we would take the position that in American society marginality is an *individual* adaptation to minority status. Where it seems to be a group phenomenon, it is because a visible number of individuals are caught in similar conflicts. The social structure of America does not define and provide for a special set of positions and a special set of roles for an intermediary stratum between the dominant and the minority culture, as with the mestizos of Mexico;[23] and as it might be argued was characteristic of the mulatto craftsmen of the ante-bellum cities in the South.

From the point of view of this analysis, then, a marginal person is one whose *reference group* is different from his membership group. That is to say, he emulates and strives to be accepted by a group of which he is not

[23] Wagley and Harris, *Minorities in the New World*, pp. 50–51.

yet, or is only peripherally, a member. Viewing marginality this way, it can be said to occur whenever an individual is abandoning the mode of adaptation that has prevailed in the group of which he is a member. This usually makes him, to a greater or lesser degree, an "outsider" to both groups.

Internally the marginal person may suffer from conflict of values and conflict of loyalties. This may operate to make him anxious and to lower his efficiency in fulfilling the roles he is seeking to carry out. His anxiety may even keep him from perceiving the subtler aspects of role behavior in the group toward which he is striving. If he is able to rationalize his striving to the point where he suppresses or disciplines any conflicts in abandoning one group for the other, he risks being regarded as a renegade by the group he strives to leave and as an "operator" by the group he is moving toward.

His problem is often easier if he does not have to carry a double burden of class marginality along with race or culture marginality. Too often, however, there is this double burden as the minority member comes to accept the dominant American norm of class mobility. There is also greater possibility of handling marginality in the multi-group society of the urban metropolis, where it is possible to segment participation in several groups without their overlapping or being visible to one another.

DOMINANT – MINORITY RELATIONS AS PROCESS

The interaction between different groups and members of minority groups is not only maintained within a structure but is part of a continuous process of change. Sociologists have identified three aspects of this process: the historical process of changing mutual relations; the contemporary processes of stable interaction; and the characteristic processes of interaction in time of stress.

In his book, *Race and Culture Contacts in the Modern World,*[24] Frazier has developed a scheme for the analysis of the historical processes of relationship. He points out that the nature of initial contact is usually one of mutual curiosity, provided the two peoples have no preconceived image of each other. This was historically true of the first contacts of Europeans with the Indians of the New World. "The fascination which natives have exhibited in their first encounter with Europeans is similar to the attitude of young children and even adults, who have not been influenced by stereotypes, when they first meet individuals of a different race. They appear to be fascinated rather than truly friendly or hostile or fearful."[25]

Frazier defines a second stage as one of silent trade and barter. Conflicts arise out of the trading when peoples are not bound by the same set of con-

[24] New York: Alfred A. Knopf, Inc., 1957.
[25] *Ibid.,* p. 41.

cepts and codes. These conflicts lead to biological struggles, forays, wars, and conquests, since there is no common cultural mechanism for the adjudication of differences. Inevitably those with superior technology establish supremacy. Frazier then describes how relationships may pass through subsequent stages of ecological, economic, and political organization, in which new modes of dominance are substituted for old.

The stable interrelations between dominants and minorities are usually defined within the traditional categories of co-operation, competition, and conflict; but these modes of interaction may have specific configurations in dominant-minority relations.

Conflict Since the interests of minority groups and their share in the benefits of the larger society are disadvantaged, there is *always* potential conflict in dominant-minority relations. Sometimes conflict is repressed, or turned against members of another minority, or aggression is directed toward members of one's own group because its expression toward the dominant would be too dangerous. Sometimes conflict is handled through established channels of negotiation. Sometimes it is held in temporary abeyance by the priority of urgent common interests.

Competition Competition may occur between dominants and minorities in the economic and the political spheres. It may occur between several different minority groups. The threat of competition from a minority may be used by members of the dominant group to create support of their own interests. For example, at one period industrialists attempted to ensure a docile white labor force by the threat of replacement with Negroes.

Co-operation Co-operation between dominants and minorities has most often been in a pattern in which each played clearly defined superordinate and subordinate roles in a unified system of social relations. When minorities as a group have had enough power (economic or political), co-operation has been in the form of an implied contractual relationship between one group as a group and the other group as a group. In associations designed for civic welfare and particularly for the welfare of minorities, there has been an increasing pattern of co-operation between dominant members and minority members, as individuals, on a basis of equality. When this type of individual co-operation on the basis of equality is not within a single delimited group directed toward a special goal, we have the phenomenon of integration. Integration thus occurs in the association of individuals when the minority still identifies itself as a minority. In this way it differs from assimilation.

In time of relative stability and general economic improvement, dominant-minority relations tend to remain more amicable within an established pattern, or within a pattern of gradual improvement of minority position. Theorists of group behavior have pointed out that frequency of interaction between individuals tends to strengthen positive attitudes toward one another. Any lessening of discrimination has the effect of bringing people of heterogeneous background into increasing contact with one another. Thus, if there is no segregation, urbanization may be looked on as a trend effecting improvement for minorities.[26]

Interaction in Times of Stress

In times of stress occasioned by war or rapid social change, or conflict between minorities and the dominant group, other processes come to the fore which tend to intensify the disabilities of minorities. The very existence of a minority provides a target on which to discharge diffuse anxiety resulting from general stress. Not only do derogating attitudes toward minorities increase in the dominant group at such times, but attitudes of one minority toward another may follow the same pattern. Sometimes such social upheaval leads to physical outbreaks against minorities, as in race riots, or to increasing restrictive measures against minorities, or simply to a reinforcement of stereotypes and scapegoating.

GENERAL FACTORS OF CHANGE AFFECTING MINORITIES

Industrialization

As Warner and Low[27] point out with regard to "Yankee City," in the early days of industrialization industrial workers had the status which had obtained for free white wage earners under the handicraft system. There was an opportunity for able individuals to rise to supervisory or management positions or eventually to become entrepreneurs, much as the journeyman had once been able to become a master craftsman, setting the standards for his workmen, marketing his product, and being a small merchant capitalist. As industrialization grew and the factory system became the dominant pattern of production, the competition to cut labor costs brought a lower wage standard and a decline not only in the style of life of the industrial worker but in the prestige of his occupational group. Since immigrants contributed largely to this growing labor force, they shared and increased the lowered position of the American industrial workers. As more and more immigrants came, there was a tendency to identify all industrial labor as "foreign," all the more so when tensions grew up around the struggle to form labor unions. A study in the 1940's of a small industry in a midwest community showed that the industrial workers were referred to as "Poles,". though in fact 50 per cent of this group were of native American stock.[28]

---

[26] See Chapter 19 for elaboration.
[27] W. Lloyd Warner and J. O. Low, *The Social System of the Modern Factory* (New Haven: Yale University Press, 1941).
[28] August B. Hollingshead, *Elmtown's Youth* (New York: John Wiley & Sons, Inc., 1941).

In the late nineteenth and early twentieth century, then, the depressed position of the industrial worker operated to lower the position of the minorities employed in industry, and the presence of the minorities offered a rationalization for rejecting efforts toward the improvement of the working and living conditions of labor. The success of the trade union movement provided new channels for minority members to improve their position individually and to achieve leadership roles; it also improved the standard of living of American organized labor to the extent that many industrial workers have been able to place their children in middle-class positions.

In recent years the more open policy in employment, the membership policy of the AFL-CIO, both perhaps given impetus by the temporary wartime legislation against discrimination in employment, have opened jobs to Negroes from which they had previously been disbarred, and are paving the way for the same improvement of position which affected the older immigrant groups.

Urbanization

The growth of our urban, multi-group society has had a significant effect on minority participation. Folk cultures, with their kinship patterns, language, and folk beliefs, have been brought in contact with other cultures, and subjected to the secularizing influence of dominant economic, educational, and legal systems. The institutional balance of folk cultures, where family and religion take precedence, is borne upon by the multi-group urban community, where the dominant institutions are economic and political.

Two urban phenomena helped mitigate the transition from folk to urban roles in the past. One was the civil services, which increased in scope with the growth of cities and which by law in federal employment or in northern states were nondiscriminatory. Local custom and local politics may have operated to enforce informal discrimination in some places, but one sees throughout the country the role of public employment in opening new positions in the social structure to minority members.

The urban political machine also became an instrument for minorities to obtain local power. For several decades it operated, through its patronage system, as a welfare agent for minorities who supported it. Changes in the welfare structure of the nation have made this function (though not always this practice) obsolete. The machine also opened career channels in politics to minority members. It became an arena for intergroup integration between various national minorities, and subsequently during and after the Depression of the 1930's, a channel for integration of minorities and dominants, eventually including racial minorities. The character of the machine has changed as its functions have changed and as urban politics has had more influence in the national political structure.

Another aspect of urbanization has been that the size, density, and heterogeneity of cities have made possible segmentation of roles, so that public and private roles need not necessarily overlap. This has aided the acculturation process.

It is significant that half the population of the United States now lives in metropolitan areas—that is, in a big city or its suburbs. Although suburban patterns of dominant-minority relations vary from the patterns of the central city, the economic dependence of suburbs on the city, as well as other ideological influences emanating from the metropolitan core, has an impact which is being felt more and more.

The Garrison State[29]

The experience of World War II and the subsequent maintaining of an elaborate system of defense has made the nation more conscious of the need of developing and using its manpower resources. Whereas war itself often brings outbreaks against minorities because of the over-all tensions, each war in which the United States has engaged has also temporarily (and permanently for some) improved opportunities for minorities through wartime employment and military participation. In World War II the Federal Fair Employment Practices Act, making discrimination in employment illegal (a temporary wartime measure), set a precedent which has now been followed by eighteen states. The post World War II integration of the armed services brings many new roles to minority members and many new opportunities for intergroup associations.

International Pressures

One large force which has affected dominant-minority relations in the United States is this country's new role in world affairs. With the rising strength of Asian and African nations, the virtual end of colonialism, and the desire to hold the prestige and influence of a social system of private enterprise and political democracy, it has been necessary for our nation to see that it is not vulnerable in its relations to those of its own population who are of other than Nordic origin.

Minorities and Public Policy

The choice between improving the welfare of minorities or improving their status is the basic policy problem. Any policy involves the definition of goals, both short-term and long-term, for dominants and minorities alike. By and large, for most sections of the country and for cultural minorities where race is not the major means of designation, dominants adhere to the long-term goal of *individual* change of status through assimilation. The

[29] Harold D. Lasswell, *National Security and Individual Freedom* (New York: McGraw-Hill Book Co., 1950), pp. 23 ff.

short-run policy may work toward this goal by opening as many channels of participation as possible to "able" minority members; or it may operate in a discriminatory way, with the rationalization that until a depressed minority has had better living conditions and education it is not "ready" for change in status.

Minorities as groups may seek change in status toward an assimilative goal, or toward a pluralistic goal, or toward a goal that concerns welfare primarily rather than status. This last choice may be because suffering so much discrimination makes these people see any other goals as unrealistic, as with some Negroes; or because they wish to preserve a cultural value system which does not include participation in the dominant culture's status evaluation, as with hispanos or certain American Indian groups.

CLASSIFICATION OF THE AREAS OF DISCRIMINATION

Discrimination to persist must be maintained by some part of the institutional structure of the society. Those institutions most closely related to the general public good, political and economic, will be the first to feel the pressure for modification of discriminatory norms. Those institutions which uphold and perpetuate private spheres of activity in family and religion will be the last to yield.

Political Discrimination

American political institutions exhibit the many variations which occur through the different balances of statutory democracy and the right to private property. Because our Constitution guarantees civil equality to all regardless of race, creed, or national origin, political institutions have become the major focus for efforts to reduce discrimination. On the whole, great strides have been made, and political discrimination persists only in localities and regions where state and local laws obtain. The several problems of political discrimination that remain are generally subsumed under the term "civil rights." Segregation in public education, rights for Indians, access to tax-supported facilities, such as recreation areas, and so forth, are also within the sphere of political discrimination.

Economic Discrimination

The problem of economic discrimination is more complex, since attempts at regulation by law can in many instances be interpreted as unwarranted interference with the rights of private property. Types of economic discrimination include discrimination in employment, either by announced policy or by private agreement, and also the subtler problem of the promotions and privileges available in certain occupational channels. Another type of economic discrimination is residential discrimination, where informal agreements of property owners exclude some minorities from some residential sections.

The economic sphere has been increasingly invaded by state regulation in the twentieth century, and legislation has barred certain types of economic discrimination in some places. Economic pressure through threat of boycott or unfavorable publicity has lessened discrimination in those sectors of business most vulnerable to such mechanisms: transportation, hotels, and retail stores, for example. Discrimination in trade unions is another type of economic discrimination.

Social Discrimination

Discrimination in the private areas of life is not subject to control by law and will be the last to disappear. Most amenable to change, even in defiance of local sentiment on occasion, have been the religious institutions, though this is not occurring without struggle. Country clubs, fraternities, private schools, and other voluntary organizations may set their own rules and will maintain varying degrees of discrimination depending on how strong the in-group feeling of their membership is. The final area through which discrimination can continue to operate longer is in the family and its attitudes, from social invitations through the spectrum of private life to intermarriage. All practices, formal and informal, which limit admission to groups, or situations that are primarily sociable or prestige-defining, are what we shall in conformity with common practice refer to as *social discrimination* without particular reference to their institutional base.

THE POINT OF VIEW OF THIS BOOK

Recent approaches to the study of minorities have selected various emphases. One is the method of comparative case studies to demonstrate cross-cultural patterns of dominant-minority relations. Another has been to stress cultural values and the contrasts between dominant and minority institutional patterns, especially those of family life. Still another has emphasized the psychological mechanisms affecting and stemming from intergroup relations.

Our approach assumes, as Arnold and Caroline Rose do in *America Divided*,[30] and Myrdal does in his study of the Negro in the United States,[31] that the minority problem is primarily a problem for the dominant culture. The assumption here is twofold: that the costs to the society as a whole outweigh any benefits to dominant individuals inherent in the patterns of disadvantage to which the minorities are subjected; and that it is at present, at

[30] Arnold Rose and Caroline Rose. *America Divided* (New York: Alfred A. Knopf, Inc., 1948).
[31] Myrdal, *An American Dilemma*, Chs. 1–3.

least primarily, in the hands of the dominant group to make or change policy affecting minorities.

We have chosen *differential visibility* as the classification of minorities which governs the arrangement of our material. We have emphasized, though not exclusively, *discrimination* as the significant mechanism by which minorities are disadvantaged. Our substantive material has drawn most heavily on *community studies,* since we feel that the problems of discrimination are not solved merely through public policy but ultimately in community adaptation and innovation. Although we share the position that minority problems are problems of the dominant segment of society, we wish to stress throughout that the process of interaction in whatever mode is a *reciprocal* one. Changes in either dominant or minority behavior will bring about reactive behavior, favorable or unfavorable, in the other group and thus affect the pattern of relationship.

TOPICS FOR PROJECTS AND DISCUSSION

1. How would you define "dominant American values"? Are the elements which you have included consistent?
2. What attitudes have you encountered on the part of employers, the police, or some other group in public life that reveal a pattern of discrimination? Is this local, regional, or national?
3. Can you describe the feelings of a minority member who cherishes some ideal of behavior or some social obligation that would not be congruent with the behavior of the dominant group? Have you felt or observed such an instance in school, college, or your community?
4. Does your state have laws against discrimination in employment? Were they easily enacted?
5. Are there people in your community who would never be invited to visit other people informally? Are these "class" attitudes or "dominant-minority" attitudes?
6. Considering the threefold classification of minorities given in this chapter under the heading of "visibility," where would you place people living in America from the following backgrounds: Turkish, Armenian, Hindu, Mexican, Puerto Rican?

SUGGESTED READING

Barron, Milton L., ed. *American Minorities.* New York: Alfred A. Knopf, Inc., 1957.
    Some more recent articles on intergroup relations.
Frazier, E. Franklin. *Race and Culture Contacts in the Modern World.* New York: Alfred A. Knopf, Inc., 1957.
    A discussion of patterns of contact, with illustrations from many countries.

Locke, Alain, and Stern, Bernhard J. *When Peoples Meet,* rev. ed. New York: American Educational Fellowship, 1946.
> *Selected excerpts from a wide variety of sources. Part III, "The Ways of Dominant Peoples," and Part IV, "The Ways of Submerged Peoples," are especially pertinent to this chapter.*

Rose, Arnold, ed. *Race Prejudice and Discrimination.* New York: Alfred A. Knopf, Inc., 1951.
> *A collection of readings in intergroup relations, many of which are drawn from sources not usually available.*

Wagley, Charles, and Harris, Marvin. *Minorities in the New World: Six Case Studies.* New York: Columbia University Press, 1958.
> *Presentations of minority situations in the Western Hemisphere, based on studies by five UNESCO social scientists.*

3

Race: Myth and Science

In dominant-minority relations "race" is a basic category and provides the most obvious cue to visibility or identification. The term is placed here in quotation marks because its meaning and significance in the popular thinking and behavior of dominants are vastly at variance with current scientific thinking. One contemporary anthropologist has suggested that, in general usage at least, the term be discarded altogether.[1] That the beliefs about race which have become established in popular sentiment may well constitute, as Montagu's title suggests, "man's most dangerous myth" was anticipated in the 1880's by a French pro-Aryan writer, Vacher de Lapouge, when he wrote, "I am convinced that in the next century millions of men will cut each other's throats because of one or two degrees more or less of cephalic index."[2]

While the wars that have ensued since de Lapouge made this prophecy have not been based primarily on race antagonism, the idea of race was employed in the propaganda—for example, in the stereotype of "the Hun" in World War I, and in that of "the Jap" in World War II. Because

[1] M. F. Ashley Montagu, *Man's Most Dangerous Myth: The Fallacy of Race* (New York: Columbia University Press, 1945), p. 12.
[2] Vacher de Lapouge, cited by Ruth Benedict, in *Race: Science and Politics*, rev. ed. (New York: The Viking Press, Inc., 1945), p. 3.

these beliefs about race are so powerful a stimulus to social conflict, it is of the utmost importance that the student of social relations learn what race really is and how significant—or, actually, how insignificant—it really is. To the student of dominant-minority relations in particular, understanding the myth and the reality of race is indispensable. For over two centuries racialist thinking in international relations has fostered the dominance of white Europeans over colored peoples. As we shall see, the beliefs about race arose after the white subordination of colored peoples began. They gave to the dominants plausible intellectual and moral justification for a pattern of relations highly disadvantageous to the minorities.

Before the scientific developments of the present century, the term *race* was often used to designate a nationality or a culture group, or some other broad class of human beings. Webster's definition illustrates how widely it has been used and how various are the nuances it may suggest:

The decendants of a common ancestor; a family, tribe, people, or nation, believed or presumed to belong to the same stock; a lineage; a breed; also more broadly, a class or a kind of individuals with common characteristics, interests, appearance, habits, or the like, as if derived from a common ancestor; as the *race* of doctors, the *race* of birds. "The whole race of mankind"—Shakespeare. "Whence the long race of Alban fathers came."—Dryden.[3]

The research of the last fifty years, in physical anthropology primarily but also in related fields, has given an entirely new perspective on the physiological groupings of man. There is now consensus in anthropology, biology, psychology, and sociology as to what races are and are not. In 1950, UNESCO published a series of research monographs which represent international scientific agreement on what is known about races.

WHAT "RACE" IS

Origin of "Races"

To begin with, mankind apparently started out as one race. Since *Homo sapiens* evolved thousands of years before written history, it is not possible to know the racial features of prehistoric man with any exactitude. However, contemporary anthropology generally accepts on the basis of fossil evidence and the logic of evolutionary and genetic principles a monogenetic rather than a polygenetic theory of man's origin. Montagu has put it thus:

Concerning the origin of the living varieties of man we can say little more than that there is every reason to believe that a single stock gave rise to all of them. All varieties of man belong to the same species and have the same remote ancestry. This is a conclusion to which all the relevant evidence of comparative anatomy, palaeontology, serology, and genetics points. On genetic grounds alone,

[3] Quoted in Harry L. Shapiro. *Race Mixture* (Paris: UNESCO, 1953), p. 8.

it is virtually impossible to conceive of the varieties of man as having originated separately as distinct lines from different anthropoid ancestors.[4]

Differentiation of "Races"

Long before written history, the major differentiation of mankind into the main varieties occurred as a result of migration, of natural selection affecting the survival of certain variations, and of the limitations of variation through the relative isolation of the major varieties in their chosen continental habitats. Subsequently limiting their further migration largely to their own continental domain, each of the main varieties "perfected," so to speak, its basic type. The older categories of "races" and "subraces" are thus descriptions of people who, through geographic isolation and barriers of social organization, have intermarried for thousands of years, bringing into prominence certain dominant biological traits. These are sometimes referred to as "Mendelian populations," a term derived from the geneticist Mendel, who demonstrated the existence of dominant strains and recessive strains in inbreeding and crossbreeding. From this point of view, the tall Watusi of Uganda, the pockets of blonde Andalusians, and the Sherpas of Nepal are "Mendelian" populations.

Such physical traits as the color of the eyes or hair and the pigmentation of the skin do pass through the genes from parents to children. The carriers have been identified and described. We know now that a group of individuals with common characteristics will procreate offspring with the same characteristics. Mankind is composed of a variety of populations which differ among themselves in the frequency of many genes. These Mendelian populations will reproduce themselves across time.[5]

As Ruth Benedict aptly writes:

No one doubts that the groups called Caucasoid, Mongoloid, and Negroid each represents a long history of anatomical specialization in different areas of the world; but the greater numbers of individuals cannot be assigned to one or another of these races on the basis even of several . . . [physical] criteria. . . . There are Whites who are darker than some Negroids; dark hair and eyes are common among all races; the same cephalic index is found in groups of the most diverse races; similar hair form is found among ethnic groups as distinct as native Australians and Western Europeans.[6]

Instability of Racial Type

Throughout history great migrations alternating with long periods of endogamous mating created and recreated visible subtypes. The American

[4] Montagu, *Man's Most Dangerous Myth*, p. 46. By permission.
[5] Oscar Handlin, *Race and Nationality in American Life* (Garden City, N.Y.: Doubleday Anchor Books, Doubleday & Co., Inc., 1957), p. 151. (Reprinted by arrangement with Little, Brown & Co., Boston, Mass.)
[6] Ruth Benedict, *Race: Science and Politics*, rev. ed. (New York: The Viking Press, Inc., 1945), pp. 45 ff.

Indian illustrates the process of subtype development. The ancestors of the Indians came from Asia and possessed general Mongoloid features. Natural selection and thousands of years of isolation, limiting the range of variability to that present in the original migrating groups, perfected a distinctive Indian type.

While throughout all history mixing has occurred across main divisions, in the past few centuries the wandering and mixing of peoples has created many new subtypes, involving combinations of traits from the main racial divisions. We may cite the Pitcairn Islanders, of *Mutiny on the Bounty* fame, and the American Negro. The present Hawaiian situation, where the various ethnic groups are intermarrying with increasing freedom, is a most interesting example of racial change going on today.

From the foregoing it can be seen that race is a highly unstable phenomenon. The racial variability of *Homo sapiens* has undergone more or less continuous modification. This changing nature of race makes the idea of a "pure" race meaningless. The greatest homogeneity in "racial" traits is found among small groups of people long isolated from the main currents of human travel and exchange.

Race and Physiology

Comparative studies of the physiology of samples of racial groups have in some cases shown significant differences and in other cases no differences at all. Differences in immunity to disease would be important to the survival of races, especially when the members of a group are transplanted to some place other than their accustomed environment. It is said that the peoples of north Europe are more susceptible to whooping cough and more resistant to goiter and cretinism, whereas the peoples of southern Europe succumb more often to the last two ailments but resist pulmonary diseases. While the rates for various specific diseases vary among racial groups, the environmental influences vary so widely that whether racial genetics has anything to do with the differences is not established. Admitting that these problems require much more explanation, Krogman concludes that science does not know "any genetico-racial biological differences in the organs which will conduce to, or inhibit, organic breakdowns under the onslaught of disease."[7] Finding some physiological differences between racial groups by no means establishes a genetic cause for them. General group differences in such matters as diet, modes of life, and other environmental factors are involved in interpreting these differences. In summary, Klineberg writes:

There are interesting and significant group differences in physiological activity, but there is no adequate proof that these are determined by heredity. The studies

---

[7] Wilton Krogman, "What We Do Not Know about Race," *The Scientific Monthly*, August, 1943, 57:103.

of blood pressure in particular show the extent to which these organic functions may be affected by cultural and environmental factors, and they throw considerable doubt upon a racial interpretation.[8]

In short, what science now knows about race differences suggests that the stocks of mankind vary more in their visible physical characteristics than in their invisible physical traits. As a final illustration we refer to "blood," about which so much superstition has developed. The four types of human blood, designated by the labels O, A, B, and AB, are inherited. But whites, Negroes, and Mongols have all these blood types.[9] Blood plasma derived from various racial groups was utilized for the wounded in World War II irrespective of their race, with no effect on the personality or physiology of the recipients.

Race Crossing

Random observation of people in large metropolitan areas of the United States will readily reveal persons of hybrid characteristics of the main races of mankind whose external features are well proportioned and handsome. An occasional unpleasing-looking hybrid may be noted, but the same can be found among persons who are not hybrids. What science has to say about the effects of race crossing may be approached by first considering some conclusions drawn from specific studies of particular interracial crossings.[10]

Polynesian-White Crossing The hybrid descendants of English mutineers and Tahitian women are taller than the average Englishman or Tahitian, and are more vigorous and healthy. They are perfectly alert. The physical type of the descendants is in every way harmonious, with white characteristics predominating.

Australian-White Crossing All unprejudiced observers agree that the offspring of aboriginal-white crossings in Australia are of an excellent physical type and that both the aborigines and the hybrids possess considerable mental ability.

In Hawaii Here are hundreds of varieties of mixed types, involving native Hawaiians (Polynesians), Japanese, Filipinos, Koreans, Chinese, and whites of many nationalities. The descendants of mixed Hawaiian unions have a much higher fertility rate than other ethnic groups and in height, weight, and other physical characteristics tend to be intermediate between their Hawaiian and non-Hawaiian forebears.

Indian-White Mixtures Boas showed that the "half-blood" Indian was taller and more fertile than the parental Indian and white stocks. Krogman concludes that Seminole Indians of Oklahoma, who are the descendants of a

---

[8] Otto Klineberg, *Race Differences* (New York: Harper & Brothers, 1935), p. 131. By permission.
[9] Ruth Benedict and Gene Weltfish, "The Races of Mankind" in Benedict, *Race: Science and Politics*, pp. 174–175.
[10] The examples given are taken from Montagu, *Man's Most Dangerous Myth*, Ch. 8.

mixture of runaway Creek Indians, Negro slaves, and whites, are on the whole good physical types, and often beautiful. There is not the slightest evidence of degeneration or disharmony in development.

The verdict of biological and anthropological science is clear and unequivocal: race crossing per se has no deleterious biological consequences. On the contrary, and most disconcerting to the exponents of racism, the preponderance of evidence points to at least an initial biological superiority of the progeny of the first hybrid generation over that of the respective racial parental generation. The phenomenon of "hybrid vigor" well known in plant and animal biology is indicated in many human interracial crossings. Of this the biologist Jennings writes:

In view of the immense number of genes carried by individuals of each race, and their separate history up to the time of the cross, the relatively few defects that have arisen are almost certain to affect genes of different pairs in the two. Hence when the races cross, the individuals produced will receive a normal gene from one parent or the other in most of their gene pairs; and since the normal gene usually manifests its effect, the offspring of the cross will have fewer gene defects than either of the parents.[11] Thus the offspring of diverse races may be expected to be superior in vigor, and presumably in other characteristics. . . . Data on this point are not abundant, but it is probable that hybrid vigor is an important and advantageous feature of race crosses in man.[12]

The merits of race crossing may be argued at the social level, but those who argue against it will find no support from biological science.

WHAT RACE IS NOT

Race and Culture

Frequently one hears people speak of the Latin race, or the French race, or the Mohammedan race. Such expressions imply that race and culture are correlated and that one is bound to manifest his raciality in corresponding forms of culture. The problem of the relation of race to culture is one aspect of the larger problem of the relation of heredity to environment, a subject which has provoked an enormous amount of controversy and volumes of research.[13] The racialist writers are one special group of biological determinists. In essence they hold that what determines differences in the cultures of ethnic groups is the distinctive genetic racial heredity of each. One such

[11] H. S. Jennings, *The Biological Basis of Human Nature* (New York: W. W. Norton & Company, Inc., 1930), p. 280. By permission.
[12] H. S. Jennings, "The Laws of Heredity and Our Present Knowledge of Human Genetics on the Material Side," in *Scientific Aspects of the Race Problem*, H. S. Jennings et al. (New York: Longmans, Green & Co., Inc., 1941), p. 71.
[13] All introductory sociology textbooks discuss the subject of heredity and environment. One of the clearest brief expositions of the topic may be found in R. M. MacIver and C. H. Page, *Society: An Introductory Analysis* (New York: Rinehart & Company, Inc., 1949), pp. 80–97.

group of writers was the "Aryan" school. From philological research which revealed similarities in the languages of the Persians and Indians and those of the western Indo-Europeans, the Greeks, Romans, Teutons, Celts, and Slavs, they concluded that all languages derived from a common source, and they posited a primitive Aryan tribe from which all the later Aryans descended. Considering these languages superior and assuming without question that language and race are related, this school expounded the theory of the "superior Aryan race." It would take us too far afield to summarize the criticisms of the Aryan theories. In brief, the wide variation in both racial characteristics, as determined by anthropologists, and the cultures among the alleged Aryan peoples indicate that these theories have little scientific foundation.

Race and Nationality

The tendency to identify race and nation is perhaps the most widely held of all beliefs relating race to culture. Here again there are instances in which a high degree of racial homogeneity parallels a fairly distinctive culture, as, for example, in modern Japan. Ironically enough, however, it is in Europe, the very region where racialist theories were most earnestly expounded, that the lack of correlation between race and national culture is most clearly illustrated. This is notably true of Germany, France, and England, where Nordic, Alpine, and Mediterranean traits have been shown to be harmoniously blended in the citizenry of each nation. Dominian writes, "Northern France is perhaps more Teutonic than southern Germany, while eastern Germany is, in many places, more Slavic than Russia.[14] Hankins points out that within Germany, "a relative purity of Germanic elements along the Baltic and North Seas (but mixed even there with Slavic Poles and Wends) gradually gives way to the southward to an increasing complexity in which Alpine and Mediterranean elements increase."[15]

Since the English were racially mongrelized within the broad Caucasian limits, it follows that the old American stock was correspondingly a mongrel mixture of European varieties. In a study of Americans descended from this English stock, Hrdlicka showed that they ranged widely in skin color, hair color, and eye color, with intermediates predominating over either the alleged Nordic type with fair skin, blue eyes, and blond hair, or the swarthy-complexioned, brunet, Mediterranean type. Altogether, the measurements indicate extensive hybridization in the old American stock.[16]

Beyond all this, the exhaustive study of the nature of culture and its processes which has gone on for the past few decades indicates that it is the

[14] Leon Dominian, *Frontiers of Language and Nationality* (New York: Henry Holt & Co., Inc., 1917), pp. 3–4.
[15] F. H. Hankins, *The Racial Basis of Civilization* (New York: Alfred A. Knopf, Inc., 1926), p. 286.
[16] Alec Hrdlicka, *Old Americans* (Baltimore: The Williams & Wilkins Co., 1925), Ch. 3.

common experience of living together that develops cultural similarities, irrespective of race. Thus American Negroes, whose lineal continuity with the American scene is almost as old as that of the English, were more Americanized in the cultural sense at the turn of the century than any of the recent white immigrant groups. An American Negro school child would have just as much difficulty acculturating himself to a central African tribe as any white child, except, of course, where differential reactions of the Africans to whiteness might place greater obstacles in the way of the acculturation of the white child.

Social Race

From the foregoing discussion it is apparent that the term "race" as traditionally used has neither descriptive accuracy nor categorical validity. Nevertheless, this traditional concept persists in cultures as a mode, among others, of ranking people socially. This is what Wagley calls "social race."

"Social race" (i.e., the way in which the members of society classify each other by physical characteristics) is but one of a series of values which give individuals rank and determine their social relations.[17]

Wagley, in analyzing populations in rural Brazil, found he had to resort to the term "race" for the concept of "social race" because this was the common term not only in the popular vocabulary but also in the collection of census statistics.

Throughout this report, when the term "race" is used, the authors hold no brief for its validity as a physical or genetic classification. In one sense or another, the term is always used in this volume in a social and cultural sense. It is well known that colour or race data in population statistics reflect the social categories of the census takers, and it is interesting to reflect upon the variety of social definitions of "race" which would inevitably be involved in any census of Brazil. . . . Even our own observations as to the probable "racial" affiliation of an individual or group of people are by necessity "naked eye" judgements certainly coloured by our own social and cultural experience. Throughout this report, then, we are interested in the social definitions of "race" . . . and in their effects upon the life of the people of the communities studied, while exact physical classification is of little interest for our purposes.[18]

In keeping with Wagley's position, we too shall have to discuss race with the understanding that we are referring only to popular social categories which affect the way in which groups behave toward one another.

Ethnic

In much contemporary writing on intergroup relations, the term *race* has been abandoned and the word *ethnic* substituted. In this book when the term ethnic is used in connection with groups which are distinguishable by

[17] Charles Wagley, ed. *Race and Class in Rural Brazil* (Paris: UNESCO, 1952), p. 14.
[18] *Ibid.*, p. 14. By permission.

physiognomic as well as cultural traits, we will be emphasizing the cultural ethos of the group. When the group is referred to as a race we will be emphasizing the barriers that are erected against them within the dominant pattern of race attitudes.

Equality and Inequality

Such myths as the belief that any races other than the European were less evolved species are now so long exploded that they do not need to be recapitulated and refuted. The growth of cultural anthropology has given a new perspective on cultures and their ability, whether simple or complex, to solve the problems of their natural environment, so that we are no longer prone to use the terms "savage" or "backward," which imply a set of criteria in which the highest development of Western European cultures is the standard of measurement. There is by no means the assurance of former times that the technologically developed world is morally superior to peoples whose modes of living still feature human labor and simple agricultural practices. With the widespread increase in education and communication, most of the literate world now knows that European civilization is not the only great civilization of history, that many technical processes were known on the continent of Africa while Europe was still tribal, and that the Oriental civilizations were in many respects far in advance of Western Europe in the Middle Ages and the beginnings of the modern period of our history.

The issues of equality of ability between the races fall again, as all the other previous arguments we have discussed, into the patterns of social relations between peoples. An issue which has been of major concern in dominant-minority relations in the United States has been the question of whether on the various mental tests the minority populations are as "bright" as native American groups.

When the tests were first applied to representatives of different ethnic groups, it was usually in the belief that the method was capable of measuring native ability, and that the results could be so interpreted. . . . The history of the mental testing of ethnic or "racial" groups may almost be described as a progressive disillusionment with tests as a measure of native ability, and a gradually increasing realization of the many complex environmental factors which enter into the result.[19]

Many illustrations of the effect of environmental handicaps on performance in mental testing can be cited. Striking examples were the army tests in World War I, in which Negro recruits of Ohio, Illinois, and New York obtained higher scores than did whites of Mississippi, Kentucky, and Arkansas.[20] In most tests, American Indians generally obtain low test scores, but in a study of American Indian foster children living in white homes,

[19] Otto Klineberg, *Social Psychology*, rev. ed. (New York: Henry Holt and Co., Inc., 1954), p. 305.
[20] *Ibid.*, p. 307.

Garth found an average I.Q. more than 20 points higher than the general Indian average.[21]

Klineberg refers to a statement by the southern sociologist Odum that among the "errors of sociology" is "the assumption that races are inherently different rather than group products of differentials due to the cumulative power of folk-regional and cultural environment."[22]

THE SOCIAL SIGNIFICANCE OF THE RACIALIST DOCTRINE

If, as it appears, there is almost no objective evidence to support any of the tenets of the doctrine of racism, how do we account for its development and persistance? First let us recall the fact that we have not had the scientific evidence which has destroyed the doctrine in the scientific world for very many years. Thus the persistence of the doctrine is in part related to the lag in discovery and to the still remaining lag in the dissemination of the twentieth-century findings.

Much light on why the racist myth arose and diffused among white men in general and north Europeans in particular can be obtained by examining the history of the doctrine and in considering some societal circumstances connected with its history.

Racialism: A Corrollary of European Expansion

A number of recent writers insist that the racialist myth, or doctrine, arose no earlier than the eighteenth century.

In the long history of the world men have given many reasons for killing each other in war: envy of another people's good bottom land or of their herds, ambition of chiefs and kings, different religious beliefs, high spirits, revenge. But in all these wars the skulls of the victims on both sides were generally too similar to be distinguished. Nor had the war leaders incited their followers by referring to the shapes of their heads. They might call them the heathen, the barbarians, the heretics, the slayers of women and children, but never our enemy Cephalic Index 82.

It was left for high European civilization to advance such a reason for war and persecution and to invoke it in practice. In other words, racism[23] is a creation of our own time.[24]

Prior to the sixteenth century the world was not race conscious and there was no incentive for it to become so.[25]

[21] *Ibid.*, p. 310.
[22] *Ibid.*, p. 311.
[23] The use of the word "racism" in place of "racialism" is becoming increasingly common. It might serve a useful purpose to retain the more traditional term to refer to the literary apologia for the phenomena concerned and to use the newer term for the behavior manifesting this point of view. We shall, however, use the two terms synonymously. [Authors' note.]
[24] Benedict, *Race, Science and Politics*, pp. 3–4. By permission.
[25] Ralph Linton, *The Study of Man* (New York: Appleton-Century-Crofts, Inc., 1936), p. 46.

When we examine the scientific literature of the seventeenth century with a view to discovering what beliefs were held concerning the variety of man, we find that it was universally believed that mankind was comprised of a single species and that it represented a unitary whole. . . . Physical differences were, of course, known to exist between groups of mankind, but what was unfamiliar was the notion that the differences exhibited by such peoples represented anything fundamental.[26]

In all modes of dynamic social conflict arising in the seventeenth century, "racism" became involved. It was invoked by the nobles of France to justify their position as superior to the masses and later by European aristocrats, generally to maintain their position as the "hereditary," and therefore all-time, superiors of the proletariat.[27]

Racialism becomes a support of nationalistic rivalries by adding to the cult of nationalism the idea that "our nation is a superior race." "Race as a factor in history . . . came into being as a concomitant of the nationalism upon which the political, economic, and cultural structure of modern civilization rests," Snyder writes.[28] But, most pertinent to our interest, racism became a strong support of slavery and imperialism. In the process of establishing their economic hegemony over most of the world and in developing less settled areas under this domination to their own greatest advantage, white Europeans, particularly the English—who passed on this tradition to the Americans—developed a caste-like relation to the "natives" of their colonies and, under an even more indisputably inferior status, to the forcefully imported slaves. In fact, it seems clear that in actual time sequence, the white men first exploited native labor and brought in slaves and then expounded a theory of the inferiority of the "colored" peoples to support their *de facto* status.[29] Montagu develops this position. "Their different physical appearance provided a convenient peg upon which to hang the argument that this represented the external sign of more profound ineradicable mental and moral inferiorities."[30] Benedict puts the same idea in these summary sentences.

Racism did not get its currency in modern thought until it was applied to conflicts within Europe—first to class conflicts and then to national. But it is possible to wonder whether the doctrine would have been proposed at all as explaining these latter conflicts—where, as we have seen, the dogma is so inept—if the basis for it had not been laid in the violent experience of racial prejudice on the frontier.[31]

In summary, the doctrine of racism appears to have developed in relation to the colored races as an ideological and moral justification for a system

[26] Montagu, *Man's Most Dangerous Myth,* p. 16. By permission.
[27] Benedict, *Race, Science and Politics,* p. 112.
[28] L. L. Snyder, *Race: a History of Modern Ethnic Theories* (Chicago: Alliance Book Corporation, 1939), p. 48.
[29] See Chapter 11 for a discussion of the development of philosophical justification of slavery in the United States long after the first slaves were imported.
[30] Montagu, *Man's Most Dangerous Myth,* p. 19.
[31] Benedict, *Race: Science and Politics,* p. 111. By permission.

already established and highly useful to white dominants. It has been continued for the same reason. The fact that at the time of contact the native races were sufficiently colored to be identified and also were at a level of civilization actually inferior (by the standards of white civilization) offered plausible demonstration of the white man's allegation of their inferiority. Once systems of dominant-minority relations became established, with the doctrine of white supremacy to reinforce them, two vicious circles were set in motion: the perpetual conditioning of subsequent generations of white children to accept the racist doctrine, and the impact of the system on the minority which served to keep them in large measure inferior by impeding the development of their capacities.

Racialism: An Adjunct of Nationalistic Movements

The potential power of racism in stimulating group conflict can be further illustrated by its application to two twentieth-century phenomena: the Japanese pan-Asiatic movement and the rise of the Hitler Reich. While it would be oversimplification to explain the aggressive policy pursued by Japan in the twentieth century wholly on the basis of their notion of race superiority, that this notion was prevalent and served a useful purpose in developing morale for aggressive political policies should not be overlooked. According to the Japanese scholar Hirata, "from the fact of the divine descent of the Japanese people proceeds their unmeasurable superiority to the natives of other countries in courage and intelligence."[32] While, like all tribes and nations, the Japanese were always ethnocentric, the development of distinct "racial pride" as part of the cultural paraphernalia essential to whip up national enthusiasm for military, imperialistic expansion was a part of the great borrowing of Western ideas and knowledge which characterized modern Japan.

In the Nazi ideology, racialism was a dominant theme. The Nazi philosophers expounded the notion that the development of a pan-Nordic (German) state was the only bulwark against chaos. First of all the German nation itself must be further purified particularly from the deteriorating effect of the Jewish "race." Goebbels once observed, "Many intellectuals are trying to help the Jews with the ancient phrase, 'the Jew is also a man.' Yes, he is a man, but what sort of a man? The flea is also an animal."[33] In practice, the Nazis subjected Jews to persecution and extermination. Once the German Nordic "race" itself was thus purified, the rest of the "race" was to be incorporated into a pan-German state, and Germans in other parts of the world, notably the United States, were to be encouraged to retain their racial purity and to foster Nazi ideas.[34]

[32] Willard Price, "Japan's Divine Mission," *The New Republic*, Nov. 17, 1937.
[33] *Time*, July 8, 1935.
[34] See Snyder, *Race*, for a discussion of racialism in the Third Reich.

Racialism in the United States

The doctrine of racialism is widely prevalent in the thinking of large segments of the population of the United States. How these racialist beliefs and attitudes serve to support dominant discrimination against minorities will be indicated repeatedly as we consider the stories of each minority group separately. At this point we shall limit our treatment of racialism in the United States to its literary expression. Writings of a racialist character directed specifically at showing the inferiority of the Negro and thus attempting to give moral justification to slavery appeared in the South in the decades before the Civil War. It was in the second and third decades of the twentieth century, however, that the racialist thesis found its greatest literary expression by the apostles of the Nordic movement, beginning with the publication by Madison Grant of *The Passing of the Great Race*.[35] Borrowing heavily from the European Nordic protagonists, Grant examined the United States. He considered the "melting pot" thesis anathema and warned the "native" Americans—that is, Nordics—to protect their heritage from being destroyed by new, non-Nordic elements. The same general thesis gained more academic respectability through the writings of Henry Fairfield Osborn, a professional paleontologist. Osborn belonged to the school of scientists who considered heredity far more determinative of human events than environment. He further believed that the Nordic racial group was superior to the Alpine and Mediterranean elements, and thus saw the gradual dying out of Nordic hereditary traits as the greatest single danger to the future of the country. Lothrop Stoddard, like Grant a lawyer, expanded the Nordic theme to encompass the doctrine of white supremacy over colored peoples. The title of one of his best known works, *The Rising Tide of Color Against White World Supremacy*, clearly indicates his basic theme.[36]

It is significant that this period in which the Nordic movement was receiving its greatest literary development coincides with the enactment of restrictive legislation against European immigration, beginning in 1921. While it is impossible to determine what effect these writings may have had on legislation, it is clear that the high quotas accorded the allegedly "Nordic" countries and the low quotas allotted the "non-Nordic" nations harmonized with the beliefs of these pro-Nordic writers.

The popularity of these pseudoscientific Nordic proponents stimulated vigorous research and writing which was ultimately to demolish, in intellectual circles, not only Nordic doctrine but all other expressions of racialism. From this exploration has emerged the scientific view of race presented earlier in the chapter. Racialism at the present time has no standing in American academic circles. Furthermore, the current antiracialist viewpoint is

[35] Madison Grant, *The Passing of the Great Race* (New York: Charles Scribner's Sons, 1916.)
[36] See Snyder, *Race*, Ch. 14, "Racialism Invades the United States."

being widely diffused throughout the population, particularly through the formal educational program. If the elimination of minority discrimination depended solely on "debunking" the racialist doctrine, such discrimination would disappear in a generation. But as the history of racialism suggests, belief in its doctrine does not rest solely on inadequate knowledge of its objective error but partly in the desire of the dominant to believe it.[37]

TOPICS FOR PROJECTS AND DISCUSSION

1. Find out how many of your fellow students have heard of the UNESCO series of pamphlets entitled *The Race Question*. What kind of reactions do you get to this inquiry that shows you something about attitudes toward other "races"? Toward UNESCO? Are these publications in your college library? In any library in your community?
2. Suggest as many reasons as you can why the comparative scores of two racial groups on mental tests may not reflect their relative mental abilities.
3. Read Hitler's *Mein Kampf*, Chapter 11, "Nation and Race," and write a critical review from the contemporary scientific view of race.
4. Find illustrations of the concept of "social race" in examples of differential treatment of several "racial" minorities. Explain the historical and other social factors that are relevant to these differences of acceptance.
5. The term "race" is frequently incorrectly used in written and oral speech. Collect as many such uses as possible. Classify your material and make an interpretative summary of your findings.

SUGGESTED READING

Handlin, Oscar. *Race and Nationality in American Life.* Boston: Little, Brown & Co., 1950. Also reprinted 1957 by *Doubleday Anchor Books.*
    A discussion of American minorities today with special emphasis on the role of concepts of race.
Klineberg, Otto. "Racial Psychology," in *The Science of Man in the World Crisis,* ed. Ralph Linton. New York: Columbia University Press, 1945, pp. 63–77.
    A critical examination of the belief that races have innate psychological differences.
Montagu, M. F. Ashley. *Statement on Race.* New York: Henry Schuman, Inc., 1951.
    An expanded and annotated account of the statement on race issues by United Nations Educational, Scientific and Cultural Organization, (UNESCO).
Thompson, Edgar T., and Hughes, Everett C., eds. *Race: Individual and Collective Behavior.* Glencoe, Ill.: The Free Press, 1958.
    An extensive selection of readings ranging widely over the field of race relations.
Wagley, Charles. *Race and Class in Rural Brazil.* UNESCO, 1952.
    A discussion of the social relations of persons of the three racial stocks and their mixtures which constitute the population of Brazil. An example of how ideology and the social system effect attitudes toward and opportunities for persons of different racial strains.

[37] See Gerhart Saenger "The Effectiveness of the UNESCO Pamphlet Series on Race," *International Social Science Bulletin,* Vol. VI, No. 3. Dr. Saenger found many resistances to using the UNESCO material in schools and colleges.

Part II

Minority Situations in the United States

In this main portion of the book we describe and analyze the numerous specific minority situations which have developed in the United States. In each case we trace the interaction between the minority and the dominant status group from the time of original contact to the present. The order of presentation broadly follows distinctions in visibility: the European immigrants with their cultural difference; the mexicanos and Puerto Ricans, where partial physiogonomic as well as cultural difference enters in; and the distinctively non-white groups—Chinese, Japanese, Negroes, and American Indians. While it still appears broadly true that non-white visibility is a stronger barrier to final acceptance on equal terms with all others, the matter now appears more flexible. For this reason we make no formal division of the section as we move from less to more racially different groups. We place the story of Hawaiian ethnic relations near the end so that the student may have the advantage of more of the other material as a background for viewing the interesting contrast found in our island state. Finally, since there are special aspects of intergroup relations where it is religion specifically which differentiates a group, we treat Catholic-Protestant and Jewish-Gentile relations each in separate chapters.

4

The Immigrant Pattern: European Nationalities

Immigration, as the United States of America has known it, has been a peculiarly American institution. One British author has described it as "the greatest folk migration in human history," and "the most persistent and pervasive influence" on the development of the United States.[1] The Great Atlantic Migration opened a continent, built an industrial nation, and was a demonstration of political democracy's capacity to survive religious, national, and racial heterogeneity. The survival of the political institutions on which identification as an American is so strongly based today did not occur without pressures and counter pressures in meeting the challenge of unity born of heterogeneity.

The European migration has traditionally been broken into three periods before the restrictive legislation of 1924: the colonial, the "old," and the "new" immigration. Although this classification has had an effect on public opinion and on policy, there is no valid reason for it. The reasons for which immigrants came at all periods were similar; the skills they brought, and their ability to adapt to the American environment show great consistency,

[1] Maldwyn Allen Jones, *American Immigration* (Chicago, Ill.: The University of Chicago Press, 1960), p. 1.

however much groups differed culturally. Some came earlier, some later. The *impact* of immigration, however, varied; and the attitudes toward immigrants varied at different periods of the nation's development.[2]

Except for slaves and transported convicts, migration involved in most instances a *decision* and a risk, which to an extent may have strengthened self-reliance, adaptability, and enterprise. Despite lingering loyalties to distant lands, the experience of migration inevitably worked against traditional values. The absence of an hereditary ruling class, the existence of representative government, and the separation of church and state which had been necessary for the co-existence of multiple sects, were significant factors in making possible national unity in the face of difference.

Immigration before 1820

Public issues related to immigration in the American colonies before the Revolution dealt with any immigrants lacking visible means of support, those convicted of crimes abroad, and Catholics. The criteria for acceptance were economic, religious, and "moral standing"; there was no nationality criterion, though from time to time the Scotch-Irish, the French, and the Germans briefly encountered hostile attitudes. The attitude toward immigrants could be summed up as "welcome tinged with misgiving."[3]

The power struggle of the Revolutionary and post-Revolutionary period assured the pre-eminence of English political institutions and the English language. The success of the War of Independence united diverse elements behind a leadership stemming from the predominance of Englishmen in the first two generations of settlement. Although only New England and the tidewater areas of other colonies had a predominance of population of English descent, these were the entrenched and the powerful.

The newcomers, of whatever origin, so far removed from Europe by the three-months voyage, were nevertheless sufficiently identified with the new world to be able to take individual positions—loyalist or revolutionary—without needing to form nationality blocs.[4]

The immediate post-Revolutionary period saw growing concern for the political influence of new migrants: political conservatives feared the growth-by-immigration of the anti-federalists; the popular democratic front was suspicious of the acceptance of emigrés from toppling European aristocracies. The Alien and Sedition Acts of 1798 had "anti-foreign" implications and were accompanied by "anti-foreign" outbreaks. The attempt was made to lengthen the period of residence before enfranchisement from two, to five, to fourteen years, but the longer periods, though enacted, were evaded by states. The tension of establishing a new nation made itself felt.

[2] *Ibid.*, pp. 4–5.
[3] *Ibid.*, p. 40.
[4] *Ibid.*, pp. 53 ff.

Throughout the late eighteenth and early nineteenth centuries there was lively public discussion of the pros and cons of migration in both the European and the American press. On the one hand, European governments felt the inroads on their artisan classes; on the other, movements to limit the participation of the foreign-born in public affairs recurred in the United States. Both the American Revolution and the Civil War acted to improve the integration and the status of the immigrant groups. But the periods of tension preceding and during wars and accompanying economic depressions occasioned outbreaks against "foreigners."

During the period from 1790 to 1812, because of restrictions in Europe on emigration of artisans, regulation of the number of passengers a ship might carry, and the conditions of embargo and war, the volume of migration temporarily diminished. Those who came were assimilated rather rapidly. But the beginning of the revolution in technology, which was to change transportation and create the factory system, brought evasion and eventual abandonment of restrictions on both sides of the Atlantic for the next half century.

THE GREAT ATLANTIC MIGRATION

The young nation of the United States in 1820 had a substantially common culture woven around three main elements: political democracy, private economic enterprise, and Protestantism with a strong Puritan tinge. Scattered in its population were other North European people in insufficient numbers to disturb the general homogeneity. Perhaps only in Louisiana, where people of French descent were concentrated, did the culture have a distinctly variant ethnic flavor. This young America was made up largely of small towns and rural communities, in which the close solidarity of primary groups prevailed. Class distinctions were not pronounced except in the few large cities and in the South, where the plantation system was built on slave labor. A vast frontier of enormous resources lay open for exploitation and settlement. The one large group of extremely different people were the Negro slaves (and some free Negroes), who in 1820 constituted approximately 18 per cent of the population. This was the social setting in which the great drama of immigration was to begin and continue for a hundred years, influencing in many ways the subsequent development of the new nation.

"America Fever"

Although an accurate census of immigration was not available till 1820, when shipmasters were first required to submit passenger lists to customs, it is a fact that the five million immigrants who came to the United States between 1820 and 1860 were a greater number than the entire estimated population in 1790. By the outbreak of World War I in 1917 immigration had reached 30 million; but the war interrupted the flow and after 1924 immigration was severely limited. Most of the attention to migration in both the domestic and the European press (pro and con) throughout the nineteenth century was due to its being recognized as unique. Contemporaries spoke of emigration as a "fever."

Figure 2. Total Immigration to the United States by Decades*

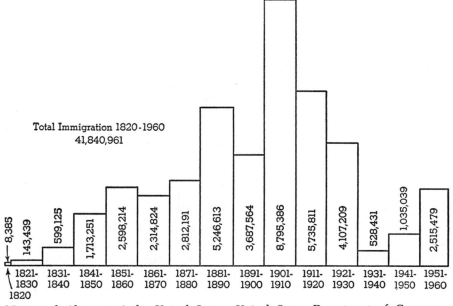

Total Immigration 1820-1960
41,840,961

| 8,385 | 143,439 | 599,125 | 1,713,251 | 2,598,214 | 2,314,824 | 2,812,191 | 5,246,613 | 3,687,564 | 8,795,386 | 5,735,811 | 4,107,209 | 528,431 | 1,035,039 | 2,515,479 |

1821-1830 1831-1840 1841-1850 1851-1860 1861-1870 1871-1880 1881-1890 1891-1900 1901-1910 1911-1920 1921-1930 1931-1940 1941-1950 1951-1960
1820

*Statistical Abstract of the United States, United States Department of Commerce, Bureau of the Census, 1961, p. 92, Table 111.

Many modes of communication stimulated immigration: books, pamphlets, letters from relatives, agents recruiting labor, transportation agents. The motives were mixed; economic improvement was paramount, but at no period was the economic motive exclusive. Jones believes that most of those who came for other than religious or political reasons or for adventure were not impoverished, but were in danger of loss of status as industrial and agricultural changes in Europe displaced old ways of life.[5]

Immigrants in the colonial period had been welcomed as buffers along the frontier. In the nineteenth-century immigration only a small proportion became frontiersmen. Those who settled in agriculture followed and took

[5] *Ibid.,* p. 107.

over (and improved) land which had already been opened. Skilled workers (Welsh miners, Staffordshire potters, British and Scottish textile workers) tended to congregate in the American centers of their craft, creating ethnic enclaves. Climate, lack of artisan employment, and the presence of slave labor made for proportionately little immigration to the Southern states. Other regions took on distinctive ethnic flavors. At midcentury, two-thirds of the Irish were in the Northeast, one half the Germans in the upper Mississippi and Ohio valleys, and one half the Norwegians in Wisconsin.

Reception of the Immigrants

The acculturation and assimilation of the nineteenth-century migration depended on a number of factors. There was at the time a public policy against grants of land to ethnic groups, although several efforts were made to have such nationality enclaves established in the West. Dispersion, as we shall see, greatly affected the rapidity of acculturation.[6] The Germans, for example, preserved the language and loyalties to the home country and culture for several generations.

Such voluntary concentration on the part of the immigrants slowed their merging with the dominant Anglo-Saxon culture; but repeated nativistic movements also affected attitudes toward these new people. It is important to distinguish between a passive dislike of foreigners based on ethnocentrism and the more violent mass zenophobia, which is cyclical in character, marked by irrational hysteria, and usually inspired by specific political interests. This latter pattern was resurgent in times of internal stress.

Early nativism (pre-Civil War) had as its most prominent theme anti-Catholicism. Economic competition was not at this time a *manifest* issue. The Know-Nothing Party, which had its heydey in the two decades before the Civil War, revived the old Federalist efforts to limit office-holding to the native-born, to extend the period for naturalization, and to exclude criminals and paupers. It was at this period that the myth of the ethnic vote emerged. Recent investigation shows that, with the possible exception of the Irish, this occurred only in some localities.

Nativism re-emerged after the unifying interim of the Civil War, particularly on the West Coast. The restrictive acts of 1882–1885 were not an integrated attempt to deal with immigration, but rather a series of unconnected measures favoring special interests. The role of organized labor in "anti-foreign" efforts began to be felt, in California and in the Midwest, in mines, and in heavy industries, where new immigrants from Europe were used as strike breakers or where other groups (such as Orientals) were willing to work for low wages. After the Haymarket bombing of 1886, the tendency to link the terms "foreign" and "radical" gained new impetus.

With growing urbanization, the crowded, substandard conditions of living

[6] *Ibid.*, p. 123.

in many cities receiving new immigrant populations aroused the concern of welfare agencies and their wealthy supporters.

The growing influence of the Irish in politics and the increase in Roman Catholic parochial education allowed for a continual revival of anti-Catholic sentiment.

At the end of the nineteenth century, and in the twentieth until the outbreak of World War I, a configuration of factors affected the reception of immigrants. The major migrations were now from southern and eastern Europe—from nonindustrialized countries, on the whole, which could supply a basic unskilled labor force to replace other groups moving up in the occupational scale as a result of earlier settlement and the nation's expansion. With the 1890 census the frontier was declared closed, and soon thereafter the myth of the frontier as the basic American experience began to take shape. Since most post-Civil War immigrants had little relation to the settling of the frontier, the myth helped devalue latecomers.

The Dillingham Commission In 1907, when the nation was experiencing the greatest volume of immigration of all time, the Dillingham Commission was created to study the question of immigration and report to Congress. It was this Commission which coined the concept "old" and "new" immigration. The theme runs through the entire forty-one volumes of the report that the "old" immigration was of a different kind, had dispersed and entered all phases of American life, whereas the "new" immigration had congregated together in such a way that assimilation was impeded. The implication was that these late arrivals constituted pockets of people without American standards, values, or loyalties. In comparing "old" and "new," the Dillingham Commission's report took no account of the longer period of settlement of the "old" immigrant group. Furthermore, it lumped all old and all new into two simple categories without taking into account the vast differences in skill, motivation, and social organization within each category.[7]

The Report came during a period of economic depression and gave support to a growing sentiment for immigration restriction. Indeed it provided the rationalizations on which the quota system subsequently was enacted. The anxieties of World War I, the increasing status of organized labor (won during the war), the fear of "radical" movements which appeared to be sweeping Europe at the close of the war, the psychological tests for the army which had showed low ratings for southern Europeans from peasant cultures, all increased the pressure for restriction. In Chapter 5 we discuss the restrictive policy adopted by Congress, beginning in 1921 and made permanent by the Johnson-Reed Act of 1924. The purpose of this act was avowedly to create a quota system to maintain "the racial preponderance [of] the basic strain of our people." Thus the Great Atlantic Migration came to an end.

[7] *Ibid.*, p. 181.

NATIVE – IMMIGRANT RELATIONS

To what extent did the relations between these diverse European peoples and the natives assume an identifiable dominant-minority pattern, and to what extent are any of these peoples minorities still? In the rest of this chapter and in the next we will seek to answer these questions.

The Northern Europeans

Although linguistically different, the Germans, Scandinavians, Swiss, and French Huguenots never suffered the categorical discriminations that most subsequent groups encountered. The more rapid acculturation and social acceptance of these Northern Europeans was facilitated by many favorable circumstances. For one thing, they were less visibly different. Their cultures had more affinity to the dominant Anglo-Saxon culture. They were largely Protestant. They were more experienced in democratic political practices. And they possessed a heritage of independent agricultural occupation. The relatively small proportions that settled initially in cities were mainly skilled craftsmen or professionals. Most of the people settled beyond the heavily populated areas. While this semi-isolation enabled them to retain much of their Old World culture, it also provided opportunity for them to make their own adjustment to American life with a minimum of friction with the native population. That they were "looked down on" and "poked fun at" is illustrated by the following jingle quoted by Smith, directed at members of an immigrant group in Minnesota:

> Swedie, Swedie, stuck in the straw,
> Can't say nuthin' but "Yaw, yaw, yaw."[8]

But with the acquisition of the English language, without an accent in their children's cases, most north Europeans became accepted Americans.

When north Europeans failed to join the mainstream of American life, one of the reasons was religious sectarianism. A number of Swiss and German separatist groups segregated themselves in distinctive colonies. The best known of these, which persists today, are the Amish, who are discussed in Chapter 17. The central facts about the Amish are that their religion and their whole culture are one and inseparable and that, a dissident sect with former experience of being persecuted, they in fact desire only a limited acculturation.

Another type of sectarian adjustment was made by a group of Norwegians in "Jonesville," a community of about 10,000 in the North Prairie Region.[9] Here sectarian emphasis on the old rural Protestant ethic of work

---

[8] W. C. Smith, *Americans in the Making* (New York: Appleton-Century-Crofts, Inc., 1939), p. 149, n. 28.
[9] W. Lloyd Warner, *et al.*, *Democracy in Jonesville* (New York: Harper & Brothers, 1949), Ch. 11.

led this group to avoid the usual channels of mobility. Although some individuals have left the group and become easily absorbed in the over-all social structure, the group has persisted for several generations content with low occupational status and strong in-group values. This group, however, is not typical of the Norse-descended people of the surrounding region.

A factor which kept north Europeans "nations within nations" was rural isolation and concentration. The Germans especially have shown amazing persistence in the preservation of language, and have maintained a foreign-language press, both religious and secular. One writer points out that as late as 1940 counties with populations primarily of German descent voted for the presidential candidate of German descent (Wendell Willkie) and that the German language press strongly supported him as a "German" candidate.[10]

Some of the persistence of sentiment for the home country, even if two or three generations removed, was consolidated for the Germans by the shock of having Germany the enemy in two major wars. Especially in World War I there was considerable hysterical action against the German-born and Americans of German descent. During World War II the antagonism toward German people was limited and only such German people who were, or who were thought to be, Nazi sympathizers received differential treatment. All such action against a nationality group tends to strengthen its identification with the "homeland," even though such homelands are "ghost nations," as one writer has called them, and no longer experienced as real.[11]

The Irish

The considerable number of Irish people who came to the colonies in the eighteenth century appear not to have been thought of as a people apart from the rest, except for a period when they arrived in large numbers. In the nineteenth century they were the first of the great ethnic migrations. They settled primarily in cities and stayed heavily concentrated in the North Atlantic states, except for those employed in mining and the construction of railways and canals. In the three decades before the Civil War they encountered much resistance and discrimination from the "native" population. For one thing, they were Catholic and anti-British. They were rural people who had settled largely in cities and towns. They entered the lower occupational ranks of unskilled work, thus starting with lower class status at a time when class distinction was becoming more important.

[10] Nathan Glazer, "Ethnic Groups in America: From National Culture to Ideology," in *Freedom and Control in Modern Society*, eds. Morrow Berger, Theodore Abel, and Charles H. Page (New York: D. Van Nostrand Company, Inc., 1954), p. 165.
[11] *Ibid.*, p. 173.

The native Americans looked down on the Irish for their whiskey drinking and fighting. "But when these were combined, as they frequently were after 1830, with religious disputes, the Irish Catholics discovered themselves in a new and unhappy situation. . . . They had become outcasts in a Protestant country, objects of positive antipathy among large groups of American working men and of cold suspicion on the part of their masters."[12]

Like many other foreigners, the Irish suffered revilement not only because of different behavior but because they came at a time when internal problems were besetting American life. The factory system was replacing the handcraftsman, and native American labor was experiencing the threatened or real decline in status concurrent with this change. The unskilled Irishman provided the urgently needed cheap labor supply for American industrial development. This was perceived by a senator from Massachusetts in 1852 when he opposed proposals to limit Irish immigration:

> That inefficiency of the pure Celtic race furnishes the answer to the question: How much use are the Irish to us in America: The Native American answer is, "none at all." And the Native American policy is to keep them away.
>
> A profound mistake, I believe . . . We are here, well organized and well trained, masters of the soil, the very race before which they have yielded everywhere besides. It must be, that when they come in among us, they come to lift us up. As sure as water and oil each finds its level they will find theirs. So far as they are mere hand-workers, they must sustain the head-workers, or those who have any element of intellectual ability. Their inferiority as a race compels them to go to the bottom; and the consequence is that we are, all of us, the higher lifted because they are here . . .[13]

The minority status of the Irish as a group was due to a number of factors: they were the largest ethnic group to come in the pre-Civil War period; a great number of them settled on the Eastern seaboard in cities where they were "culturally visible"; they were constantly renewed as a group by a steady flow of immigration well into the twentieth century; they were early and persistently engaged in politics; they became significant elements in the early attempts at labor organization; they played a special role for a long time in dominating the development of American Catholicism.

Most of those Americans descended from the earlier immigrant groups have by now become so far assimilated that their ethnic origin has little affect on their status in American society. It is interesting to note that, despite a very substantial and continuous immigration from England from 1851 to 1930, one finds little reference to English immigrant colonies. This

---

[12] William F. Adams, *Ireland and Irish Emigration to the New World* (New Haven: Yale University Press, 1932), p. 339. By permission.
[13] Edward Everett, "Letters on Irish Emigration," in *Historical Aspects of the Immigration Problem, Select Documents,* ed. Edith Abbott (Chicago: Ill.: The University of Chicago Press, 1926), pp. 462–463.

indicates that English immigrants as individuals or families were always easily absorbed into the native groups and accorded dominant status. For the Scandinavians and the Germans, the process of assimilation took somewhat longer but, except for isolated instances, has now been completed. The fact that the Irish were on the whole viewed as a minority group longer than other North Europeans is undoubtedly bound up with their role in urban politics, their Catholicism, and the constant renewal of their numbers by fresh immigration. In Midwest and Western cities, where their numbers were smaller, they seem to have disappeared as a separate group more rapidly.

THE LATER IMMIGRATION: SOUTHERN AND EASTERN EUROPEANS

As we have pointed out, by the time the heavy waves of Italians, Poles, Russians, Hungarians, Greeks, Eastern European Jews, and others came to the United States, the country had become "settled" from coast to coast, cities had grown, there was an increasing free Negro labor supply, and conditions of living and working were not so felicitous as in the early nineteenth century. The pattern of ethnic subcommunities became intensified.

The absorption of older immigrants had considerably broadened what could now be considered "native," but there is little evidence that this worked to lessen discriminatory attitudes toward the new groups; quite possibly the opposite was true; although in the "Age of Reform" which preceded World War I, a great deal of public attention was given to the plight of the immigrant. Despite humanitarian concerns, however, ethnic solidarity persisted almost to World War II in areas of residence, in work groups, and in politics, both because of and as a defense against attitudes which were devaluing. These ecological and occupational enclaves became the subject of sociological descriptive studies, and from them the earlier theories of minorities in American life derived. In the following pages we present abstracts from some of these studies.

Burlington, Vermont[14]

Burlington, the metropolis of the state, is a small city of about 25,000 people, situated on the eastern shore of Lake Champlain. It has a number of small factories and mills and otherwise is a small commercial and political center. Anderson decided to take the foreign-born themselves and their children as her criterion of membership in an ethnic group. Thus in 1930, 40 per cent of Burlington's population were "foreigners," or as the writer refers to them most frequently "new comers." Of these, the French-Canadian totaled nearly 5,000, more than all the rest put together; English-speaking Canadians slightly exceeded the 1,200 mark;

[14] Reprinted by permission of the publishers from Elin Anderson, *We Americans* (Cambridge, Mass.: Harvard University Press, 1937). The account given here is an adaptation by Charles F. Marden of various portions of Anderson's book.

and the Irish fell slightly short of it. Next were about 750 Russians and Poles, most of whom were Jewish. The 457 English, 392 Italians, and 309 Germans were numerous enough to be thought of as ethnic elements. A scattering membership from 29 other nationalities was to be found.

Anderson describes the city as dominated by the Yankees, though they were being challenged in leadership by the Irish. The Irish tended to champion the cause of all the immigrant groups. The latter tended to accept Irish leadership, although they frequently resented Irish officiousness. The French-Canadians were unaggressive, docile, and slow to rise in economic and social status. While cherishing their distinctive culture, they failed to stick together on civic issues. The Jews of Burlington presented the same picture as elsewhere when found in sufficient numbers. They were successful in economic life but lived in their separate social structure. The Germans still retained a fair degree of distinctiveness, notwithstanding their more favorable assimilability. The Italians of Burlington, being few in number, showed less ethnic coherence than is found among Italians in other American cities.

The community life of Burlington in 1934 was greatly affected by a consciousness of ethnic difference and the corresponding cleavages in its social life associated with this sense of difference. In spatial distribution, three of the six wards, those less desirable to live in, were largely inhabited by newcomers; two were identifiable as largely Yankee wards. More than half the French-Canadians, the Germans, and the Irish lived in the "foreign" wards, with the latter showing the greatest dispersion. The class and occupational structure divided largely, though not precisely, along ethnic lines, with the French-Canadians in the lower class, predominantly employed in factory and mill work; the Irish having moved up in social class and found increasingly employed in clerical and professional positions; and the Yankees with higher social prestige and the higher ranking occupations.

The social life of most people in Burlington tended to revolve around those of similar ethnic origin. In formal associational life, for example, about 70 per cent of the Jewish, French-Canadian, and Italian men belonged only to organizations with membership exclusively from their own ethnic background. With the women in each group, the proportion of ethnic exclusiveness was well over 80 per cent. The attitudes of the ethnics toward their own and toward other groups in the city were revealed in the preferences expressed for neighbors. As further choices, the newcomers rated Old Americans first, Irish second, and Negroes and Chinese (of which there were a few) last. Consistently, the Old Americans gave English-Canadians as their second preference. Somewhat inconsistently, however, two-thirds of all the people interviewed indicated that "the preservation of nationality neighborhoods was of no interest to them." Only among the Old Americans and the French-Canadians was there an emphatic minority expressing a desire to live apart from others. Granting that various circumstances conspire to make it natural, sociologically speaking, for this social distinctiveness in the earlier years, Anderson was impressed with "the persistence of a formal pattern of separation after the reasons for its existence . . . [had] disappeared." She discovered that the members of each group were conscious of a strong pressure to remain in their group, manifested by criticism of those who sought friendships among other ethnic groups. The second and third generations among all groups were more strongly affirmative than the foreign-born to the statement "One is criticized if one mixes freely with people of other nationalities in the community."

The movement outward from ethnic affiliation was influenced by religion. After their numbers became greater, French-Canadian Catholic parishes were organized distinct from those of the Irish. In the second and third generations, increasing numbers of the French-Canadians affiliated with the traditionally Irish parishes. Anderson came to the conclusion that with the decline in the strength of distinctive ethnic cleavage through the great fusion of the separate Catholic elements, the line of cleavage in community life between Catholics and Protestants as a whole became more pronounced, expressing itself in contrasting approaches to many community problems.

"Yankee City"

In 1941 the first of a series of several detailed studies of "Yankee City" was published.[15] The basic interest of the research was to test the validity of the class system as the main integrating factor in American community life. Included in the material accumulated was probably the most definitive set of data on ethnic groups yet to have been gathered for any one city.

"Yankee City"—so labeled because it has "a living tradition inherited from generations of Yankee forebears"—is situated on a harbor at the mouth of a large river within the area of metropolitan Boston. Its population at the time of the study in the early 1930's was about 17,000. About one-fourth of its working population were employed in the shoe industry. Other small factories, commerce, and the clamming industry completed its economic activities.

In basic ethnic composition, the population of "Yankee City" was 54 per cent "native" and 46 per cent "ethnic." By ethnic is meant any person who (a) either considers himself or is considered by others a member of an ethnic group, or (b) who participates in the activities of the group. Since the research team was able to appraise the status of nearly every individual in the city, we have here a more accurate count than is usually available. This procedure eliminates the counting of a few individuals of minority group origin who came before the mass influx of their compatriots and were therefore considered natives. And it counts as ethnics persons of various origins irrespective of generation who remain definable as ethnics in the terms adopted. The relations between these diverse ethnics in "Yankee City" are summarized as follows:[16]

The "natives" of Yankee City" number 9,030, or 54 per cent of the population. They comprise mainly the descendants of colonial British stock. Included as natives, however, are a few descendants from French Huguenot stock and German Jews who settled in the city early in its history. Also included are more recent immigrants from the British sources. "Predominant in number, this native group dominates the economic, political, and social structures of the community."

Of the remaining 7,646 individuals in "Yankee City" about half are Irish, the first large group of immigrants to enter, beginning around 1840. Though, like the Yankees, they spoke English, they differed in being Catholic and having a rural

[15] William Lloyd Warner and P. S. Lunt, *The Social Life of a Modern Community* (New Haven: Yale University Press, 1941).
[16] Condensed adaptation by Charles F. Marden of Warner and Lunt, pp. 213–217. By permission.

and agricultural background in a city whose economic life was geared to ship-building and maritime commerce.

The French-Canadians came next, around the 1880 period. They became more distinctive, a group apart, with high internal solidarity centering around their Catholicism, the French language, and a strong solidarity of family life. Next in order was the influx of Polish Jews beginning around 1903, which, added to a few German Jews who had come in earlier, formed a Jewish aggregate of 397 persons. The Jews differed from the rest in language, religion, and family and cultural tradition. Being, however, from urban occupational backgrounds, the Jews maintained their original occupational pattern, while the others did not. An Italian influx into "Yankee City" came about the same time as that of the Jews. Since their numbers were few—284 in 1933—they were not organized in separate parishes from the Irish. They were, however, split into antagonistic north and south Italian subgroups. The Armenian group at the time of the study was only slightly less than the Italian: 246. They had come into the city around 1900 and were more than other ethnic groups employed in one industry, shoe manufacture. This Armenian subcommunity lacked integration because it was split along religious lines between Congregational Protestants and eastern Orthodox communicants.

While the greatest movement of Greeks into "Yankee City" occurred in the 1920's, their number increased steadily, and in 1933 they were the fourth largest ethnic group, totaling 412. About two-thirds were employed in factory work; others were confectioners, restaurant owners, barbers. Their cultural accommodation centered around their separate Greek Orthodox Church and its parochial culture, their patriarchal type family, and their coffee houses. Still more recent arrivals were the Poles and Russians. The Poles had come to number 677, thus being the third largest ethnic group. First they worked in the textile factories, but following the decline of the textile industry found employment in other factories. Interestingly enough in view of the antagonism between Poles and Russians in Europe, the "Yankee City" researchers found "close and amicable relations existing between them in Yankee City." This arose from the knowledge of each other's language, from frequent and informal meetings in their local provision stores, and from the smallness of the Russian group.

The Metropolis

No such over-all community studies of the interaction between native and ethnic peoples in America's great metropolises are available. In some eastern cities the proportion of people who would qualify as ethnics under our definition comprised a substantial majority of the population. Illustrative of the principle of ecological segregation, the great city had many distinctive ethnic and racial areas, each comprising a little world of its own: Little Sicily, Yorkville, Spanish Harlem, Chinatown, and so on. One systematic study of Greenwich Village, one section of New York City, describes the different ethnic communities in some detail, their interrelationship with each other, and with at least the native population nearest to them.[17]

Greenwich Village

The Village is located on the lower west side of Manhattan, roughly bounded on the south by Houston Street, on the east by Sixth Avenue, on the north by

[17] Caroline F. Ware, *Greenwich Village* (Boston: Houghton Mifflin Co., 1935).

11th Street and again 14th Street, and on the west by the Hudson river. In 1930, three years before this study was made, the population was about 38,000. In ethnic terms these people divide into "Villagers" and "local" people. The former refers to persons of more native American origin with a bohemian way of life—artists, writers, and other people who wished to live, at least during their early adult years, in an "emancipated" atmosphere. These people and their doings, and the night clubs and foreign restaurants which they and sightseers patronize, made up what is known to the outside world as Greenwich Village. But these Villagers comprised in 1933 only a small part of the population. At least four-fifths were people of more recent immigrant origin, called in the study "local" people. Of these the largest element was Italian, next the Irish, a scattering of Jews, a small colony of Spanish, and a noticeable number of Germans.

The Villagers and the local people lived in two distinct social worlds. Very little personal contact took place between the two groups. Their respective values and the corresponding behavior patterns and forms of social organization presented a striking contrast and resulted in lack of understanding, mutual mistrust, and occasional antagonism. The Villagers were careless about money; the local people were frugal and hard bargaining in money matters. The "experimental" approach to love relations and the equality accorded women by the Villagers were in sharp contrast to the patriarchal, Catholic conception of family life held by the local people.

The social life of the local people was divided very largely on ethnic lines. The Irish, by virtue of longer residence in the area, possessed higher social status but were being pressed by the ever-larger Italian group. The tendency for the Irish to send their children to parochial schools and of the Italians to public schools further separated them. Any earlier intermingling of children was frequently arrested at the adolescence ages. While a sufficient amount of intermarriage had taken place between Irish and Italians to be a source of comment among the local people, the two groups remained substantially apart. As for the Spanish, Ware writes:

> The Irish considered the Spanish dirty as well as dangerous, regarding them, even more than the Italians, as foreigners and lumping together all Spanish-speaking peoples of various complexions—Cubans, Filipinos, Mexicans —as "niggers". . . .
> The Italians had practically no contact with the Spanish . . . [but] were much more ready to say a good word for them than were the Irish. . . . Although most [Spanish] had been in this country for more than ten years, few of those interviewed could speak English.
> The only two groups in the locality which had really shown social amalgamation had been the Irish and the Germans.[18]

Immigrants in Rural America

As the earlier European immigration was, except for the Irish, primarily a movement to rural America, so the later immigration was primarily an urban phenomenon. Reflecting the assimilation of these earlier rural immigrants is the absence in general texts on contemporary rural American society of much treatment of European ethnic groups. One of the most com-

[18] Charles F. Marden's adaptation of material in Greenwich Village, drawn from Chs. 4, 5. The quotation is from p. 141. By permission.

prehensive studies of this topic was that of Brunner, published in 1929.[19] This study, which attempted to ascertain the degree of assimilation of immigrant farmers and their children, was based on a survey of seventy rural communities. The main conclusion was that in more than two-thirds of the communities the immigrant groups "were progressing more or less surely along a well chartered course leading toward complete assimilation into the life of rural America."[20] In the one-third of the communities where assimilation had been slow, Brunner found three main circumstances which retarded the process: (1) situations where the immigrant group was especially remote from its native neighbors; (2) situations "where the issue of the [first] World War and of the right of self-determination for formerly subject peoples" had been permitted to disturb neighborly relations; (3) a few situations in which "settlements of north Europeans, especially Germans, remained aloof and unassimilated, from choice."[21]

Another significant finding in this survey was that where the foreign settlement was mixed, or polyglot, adjustment to the life of the American rural community was more rapid than in a one-nationality settlement. In these mixed situations, less native opposition was encountered, and the lack of a common cultural background and language forced on the immigrants a more rapid process of "self-Americanization."[22]

Among the later immigrant groups, the Czechs and the Poles were the two groups with the largest number of rural settlements. About half of all Czech immigrants engaged in farming on farms owned by Czechs. While the rural setting encouraged their carrying on for a longer period many of the traditional aspects of their homeland culture, it also gave a greater stability than is found among the city groups. The Polish farmers more often entered agriculture beginning as farm laborers. Many subsequently bought abandoned or run-down farms and by arduous effort made them self-sustaining. As with the Czechs, the rural milieu provided for greater stability in Polish group life, though the assimilation of Polish farmers did not proceed as far as with other immigrant groups.[23]

PATTERNS OF NATIVE – IMMIGRANT INTERACTION

A good deal of the classical description of the initial problems of immigrants stems from the tradition of the crusading journalists of the first decade of this century. At this period of heaviest immigration, particularly

---

[19] Edmund deS. Brunner, *Immigrant Farmers and Their Children* (Garden City, N.Y.: Doubleday & Co., Inc., 1929).
[20] *Ibid.*, p. 115.
[21] *Ibid.*, p. 115.
[22] *Ibid.*, p. 106.
[23] See R. A. Schermerhorn, *These Our People* (Boston: D. C. Heath & Company, 1949), for the general facts and bibliographical sources on Poles in American agriculture, pp. 281–283; and for Czechs in rural areas, pp. 300–303.

in the port city of New York, conditions were deplorable. We do not have data to estimate accurately the conditions which obtained for new migrants throughout the great century of migration from 1820 to 1920, but it is likely that they were similar. We know that it was a common pattern for immigrants to send for relatives and help establish them, as best they could, often house them, and induct them into some kind of community living. We know that until contract labor was made illegal in 1882 many came with committments to jobs, however low paid. Until the closing of immigration, agents of major industries waited at Ellis Island to meet the boats and to select skills or brawn as needed for America's industrial expansion. Skilled industrial workers were at a premium. There was also continually a small group of professionals or small businessmen with some capital who established themselves rather easily.

For most of the immigrants the voyage was hard, even with attempts to regulate the number of passengers and conditions of passage. Even when they were met by relatives, many experienced what is now termed "culture shock." Immigration officials were often harsh, and the Ellis Island interim, with its great bare sheds, was a depressing end to an overcrowded voyage.[24] In the later immigration many a self-respecting peasant felt a marked loss of status in a low-paid job (and in a home with no land). The added problem of imperfect communication for those who did not speak English compounded the distress of the newcomer. As we have said earlier, at various times, depending on many internal factors, the immigrant might be greeted with open hostility on the part of the natives. At other times he was largely ignored. Sometimes he was avidly seized upon: to serve in the Union Army; to be quickly naturalized in an election year; to become a strike breaker for the Pinkerton agency.

The Ethnic Subcommunity

Wherever immigrants settled in considerable numbers they at first clustered with people from home. Sometimes they even had little sub-sub communities, where they had discovered neighbors and friends not only from the home country but from the home district, and they brought their district or regional rivalries with them. Then, as now with the Puerto Ricans, they settled in the sections of the city which were least desirable residentially, since this was what was available to them. Then as now, landlords discovered that exorbitant rents could be extracted for little space and poor quality of housing. Families were forced to crowd into single rooms or "old law" tenements, some of whose rooms had no windows. In the evenings the people spilled out on the street, weather permitting, and gossiped, quar-

[24] Robert E. Park and Herbert A. Miller, *Old World Traits Transplanted* (New York: Harper & Brothers, 1921). Chapters 3 and 4 give documentary material on the demoralization of some immigrants in their early days in America.

reled, exchanged news from home, shopped from the pushcarts, and insofar as possible recreated the life of the home village. The Irish had their taverns, the Greeks a little restaurant that served as a coffee house for the men, the Germans their sport clubs. They read the foreign language press: *The Irish Echo*, the *Staatszeitung*, *Il Populo*, the *Jewish Daily Forward*, and so on. These subcommunities flourished through the first quarter of the century, renewed by a continued influx from the old country. They persisted in most of our large industrial cities until World War II, but now are gradually thinning out as a result of improved circumstances for the younger generation, efforts at urban renewal, and the dying out of the old generation.

This ecological separation of nationality groups let them build up as an integrated subsociety which had little interaction with the dominant group except through economic, political, welfare, and occasionally religious contacts. Caroline Ware, in her study of Greenwich Village, describes such an Italian subcommunity.

The culture which the Italian peasant brought with him to America was closely rooted in the soil, and centered in the family which was patriarchal in form and integral with the land. It rested on oral tradition rather than literacy. It accorded a place of dignity to manual skill and fine craftsmanship. It took for granted Catholic faith, but accepted religious indifference as well as piety. It contained a body of superstitions revolving around the "evil eye" and the use of occult powers. It contained no element of community participation or social organization beyond the family group. Although this pattern had been substantially modified before emigration among some emigrants, especially those who had lived in cities in Italy and some of those from the north who were more literate, most of those who came to America brought with them this pattern intact.[25]

The formal social organization of the Italian community was composed mainly of the family, the church, and numerous associations combining mutual aid and sociability formed on the basis of the part of Italy from which the people had come. The family was highly patriarchal, with women extremely subordinate and seclusive. Women stayed home, had children, took care of the house and family, and did little else. Children were expected to obey their parents and to work to support them. Daughters were peculiarly guarded. Any interest shown in them by males was interpreted as warranting marriage promptly. The formal allegiance of Italians to the Catholic church was unquestionable, although in the particular area under study the Church faced handicaps. The most important disadvantage was the higher prestige enjoyed by the Irish Catholics. According to Ware,

In its effort to make and hold a place for itself in the changing community, the Italian church pursued three principal courses. It abandoned those characteristic Italian religious practices which marked it in the eyes of the younger generation as "foreign," while at the same time it retained enough of the atmosphere of a characteristically Italian church to make the older generation feel that it belonged

[25] Ware, *Greenwich Village*, p. 173. By permission.

to them; it sought to attain prestige and to give evidence of being able to meet an American situation in American terms by the construction of an imposing church building conspicuously "up-to-date" in its fittings; and it adopted the institutional programs which the Irish churches scorned, in an effort to bring members within the fold and to compete with the social agencies and the Protestant missions of the locality.[26]

Immediate consciousness of minority status was borne in upon the Italians more by their subordinate position to the majority Irish than in regard to any natives. "The Italians questioned found it much easier to state what they disliked about the Irish than to name anything which they liked."[27] The vehemence of this Italian attitude may be interpreted as evidence of the actually higher social position of the Irish. It was the sense of being looked upon as inferior which made for the solidarity of the Italian community. "Consciousness of being Italian was a defense reaction against . . . being treated as a 'Wop'—rather than a positive manifestation of group solidarity."[28]

Acculturative Institutions

Initiated by Ethnics In the new environment, nationality groups developed formal associations for their own protection and improvement. Mutual benefit societies, limited to the members of a specific common nationality, replaced village informal patterns of mutual aid. Nationality societies— "Polish-American," "Hungarian-American"—preserved some of the old tradition, celebrated national holidays, but more importantly were a structure through which group interest could be expressed to the larger community in political and civic affairs. Participating in such formal organizations was in itself a training for established roles in American life, and thus contributed to the adjustment of the immigrant.[29]

For almost every large immigrant group in America there arose newspapers printed in their own language, some with national and others with local circulation. Such papers printed news of activities in the old country and therefore have been considered as retarding assimilation. Yet, for those many immigrants who could not read English the newspapers brought a wider knowledge of American public affairs and the native cultural values.

Initiated by Native Americans The concern about immigrant welfare led to the development of organized efforts in their behalf on the part of various groups of native Americans. Most of these efforts were at first religiously motivated. The Methodists, for example, in the middle of the nineteenth century organized a German-speaking section of their denomination specific-

---

[26] *Ibid.*, pp. 311–312.
[27] *Ibid.*, p. 131.
[28] *Ibid.*, p. 169.
[29] Mary B. Treudley, "Formal Organization and the Americanization Process, with Special Reference to the Greeks of Boston," *American Sociological Review*, Feb. 1949, 14:44–53.

ally to serve the German immigrants; later they extended their efforts to other immigrant nationalities and their publishing house for a time supported a religious press in several languages. Another example of religious effort is that of the Roman Catholic religious order, the Maryknoll Fathers and Sisters. Founded in the early twentieth century, this order is devoted to the service and education of Orientals abroad and in the United States.

The initial motivation for the settlement movement was religious also, although settlement houses have largely lost their religious orientation and have become secular. The settlement house was an institution developed at the end of the nineteenth century to aid the slum-dweller, which in the United States at that time meant the immigrant. Such centers as Hull House in Chicago and the Henry Street Settlement in New York became neighborhood centers providing educational, recreational, and cultural activities in immigrant communities. Though it cannot be claimed that the settlement movement reached the mass of immigrants, it did contribute significantly to all contemporary thinking about immigration and welfare. From the Henry Street Settlement the first visiting nurses went into homes to care for the ill, thereby creating the pattern of modern public health nursing. In New York and Chicago, settlement houses were active in promoting legislation concerning working conditions in factories, child labor, and housing and health. The first expressions of the value of cultural pluralism came from the settlements. As a direct service, settlement houses often tended to reach the more ambitious individuals anxious to move out of the immigrant world into the mainstream of American life. On the debit side, one study, made in Boston in 1940, has pointed out that settlement workers have often been unable to bridge the gap between their own middle-class American attitudes and the real needs and indigenous leadership of the immigrant group whose ways were alien.[30]

Interaction in the American Institutional Structure

The urban political party, the lower ranks of the civil service, and the trade union were each major modes of involving the immigrant in American life.

The involvement of the immigrant in politics is as old as the nation and the early struggles between the propertied and the popular parties. The immigrant vote was marshaled for every election, often with the individual voter understanding the issues only very vaguely at best. The heavy concentration of the Irish in the port cities of the East let them very early play an active role in organizing local politics. As urban centers grew throughout the nineteenth century, "machine" politics developed, seeking local control and party influence in the state and national elections. In the East, and to

[30] William Foote Whyte, *Street Corner Society* (Chicago, Ill.: The University of Chicago Press, 1943).

some extent in other industrial areas, the machine was Democratic and the leadership initially was Irish. The political machine operated on a basis of patronage and personal favors, which aroused the criticism of the "good government" organizations. However, the machine was able to make politics more personal for the immigrant, and therefore more meaningful, than could forces whose approach to civil life was impersonalized and abstract.[31]

Handlin describes machine politics as more characteristic of the second generation than of the immigrants themselves. Since the group that migrated often was too involved in other pressures, did not command the language, and had no history of political participation, it therefore remained apathetic.[32]

During the nineteenth century, the lower civil service jobs in the cities became a channel for the establishment of immigrants and their children. The police force, the fire department, and the post office had their lower ranks filled from the new groups. The link between political patronage and the police allowed for a considerable amount of corruption, but it also kept the police of America free of the authoritarian and severe disciplinary attitude found in some of the immigrants' home countries.

The labor movement, too, involved the immigrant in an organizational structure which helped him adapt to the conditions of the new country. Throughout the nineteenth century, factories tended to deploy their labor force in a way which maintained ethnic solidarity, each department or shop having a particular ethnic character. Union locals therefore similarly were largely or exclusively composed of one ethnic group. But in the experience of a strike or in the conduct of union affairs above the shop level, native Americans, British, Irish, German, Welsh, Polish, Russian Jewish, Italian, and many others worked together. The major involvement of immigrant workers in unions came in the early twentieth century, but immigrants were prominent in the Workingmen's Party, a labor party, before the Civil War, in the Knights of Labor, and in the formation of the American Federation of Labor.

While the school was a more important factor in the assimilation of the native-born children of the immigrants, it deserves mention in relation to the immigrant generation as well. Many cities set up night-school programs for the instruction of adult immigrants, with the curricula stressing the English and civics necessary for naturalization. The main influence of the school on the adult immigrant, however, has been largely indirectly mediated, through their children. For example, as Galitzi says of the Rouman-

---

[31] After the restriction of immigration, leadership passed from the Irish to other national groups, and by the 1948 national election the political pattern had changed so that the "ethnic vote" was no longer a meaningful category. Samuel Lubell, *The Future of American Politics*, 2nd ed., rev. (New York: Doubleday Anchor Books, 1956). See the index for analyses of nationality votes from 1929 to 1948.

[32] Oscar Handlin, *The Uprooted* (Boston: Little, Brown & Co., 1952), Ch. 8.

ians, "The children hearing the English language become the carriers of the new language and new ideas into the Roumanian home. They interpret to their parents the American standards of health, economic efficiency, civic duties, and fair play."[33]

But even with these bridges of contact with the dominant natives, the typical immigrant became only partially acculturated to American life. The pattern of subcommunal segregation described above retarded the process; yet, given the situation as it was, such a response was logical and necessary. Mass immigration was encouraged and tolerated because the rapidly growing industrial society greatly needed cheap labor. Yet, for the most part, the immigrant was not desired as a neighbor, a friend, or a competitor by the dominant natives. Segregation suited perfectly the natives' attitudes and arose in part in response to them. And temporarily it met a need of the immigrant for a sense of self-respect, for expressing his accustomed mode of life, and for social security—the sense of belonging.

The Dilemma of the Second Generation

The concentration of immigrants in subcommunities, however, intensified the problems of the second generation. What gave security to their elders created conflict for the children of the immigrant growing up in America. Like all other parents, immigrant parents conditioned their children to their accustomed social heritage. The children, as a result of their school experience and the other outside stimuli which their growing knowledge of the English language opened to them, desired to become Americanized. The children began to perceive that the culture of their parents was not American as defined by the outside dominant native world. Furthermore, the immigrant children learned that the ways of their parents were defined as inferior and that they, too, were socially rejected because of their background. Handlin discusses the fact that a great deal of the generational problem was compounded by the insecurity of the immigrant parents in their own roles. In the new environment a confusion came as to the old established rights and duties between husband and wife and parents and children. Without the protective cover of well-defined roles, father, mother, son, and daughter faced each other as individuals under the most trying conditions.[34]

An example from a case study of one second-generation girl illustrates both the external and internal conflict:

You see, we young people live in two worlds, and learn the ways of both worlds—the ways of our parents and the ways of the big world. Sometimes we get mixed up and we fight, we fight our parents and we fight the big world. Some-

[33] Christine A. Galitzi, A Study of Assimilation Among the Roumanians in the United States (New York: Columbia University Press, 1929), p. 228.
[34] Handlin, The Uprooted, p. 239.

times I feel I am not much of an American. I was raised by the Russians, I understand Russians, I like Russians. At other times, I think that I am not much of a Russian; except to my parents, I never speak Russian, and all my friends are Americans. Well, I am American, we live in America—why shouldn't we take their ways? When my parents object to my American friends, I say: "I work with them, I do everything with them; why shouldn't I go out with them?" Then they come back at me and say: "Why don't you sleep with them?" They think they would disgust me with Americans, but I get mad and say; "Well, I will!" and they have nothing more to say.

I almost always have a good comeback. I say, "This isn't Russia. When you go to Russia, you can be Russians; but you can't be Russians in America." I have learned American ways. I can't go against my freinds and do the Russian way. . . .

Many times I get mad, and then I leave the house. You see, I don't want to hurt my parents and still I want to live like I see is right—that is, right according to American ways. They can't see it my way, and I can't see it their way.[35]

While in the long run it was to be free education that assimilated the descendants of immigrants, in the short run too often the school fell far short of solving the emotional problems of these culturally marginal young people. Smith's appraisal of the school's impact epitomizes the dominant attitude toward the immigrant minorities:

On the basis of the available data, we are forced to the conclusion that the American school, although well intentioned, has not dealt wisely with the children of immigrants. Unknowingly it has been actually ruthless in ignoring and belittling the cultural heritages of the diverse elements in our population while glorifying the dominant civilization, thereby bringing about permanent and often tragic estrangements. The school should have paid some attention to counteracting the various influences in the community which tend to produce conflicts between the two generations.[36]

The school not only tended to depreciate or ignore the cultural heritage of the children of immigrants, but the very models they presented of Americans and American life were alien to these children and contributed to their feeling of inferiority. Handlin points out that the elementary-school textbooks which were offered to immigrant children were based on the vocabulary and images of rural America, which were unreal and meaningless to the children of urban slums. "Falsity runs through all the books, which were written to be used by other pupils in other schools; even the arithmetic sets its problems in terms of the rural countryside . . ."[37]

In the face of these two worlds of home and school, the children as they grew older developed perforce a life of their own, an intermediary world, whose locale was the street. Here they formed their own social groups and established their own code of behavior. Sometimes these groups were hostile

---

[35] Pauline V. Young, *The Pilgrims of Russian Town* (Chicago: The University of Chicago Press, 1932), pp. 114–115. By permission. The entire case from which these excerpts are taken is to be found on pp. 114–118.
[36] W. C. Smith, *Americans in the Making*, p. 303. By permission.
[37] Handlin, *The Uprooted*, p. 246.

and destructive. Sometimes they were merely friendship groups. Whyte has described one such group in detail in his study *Street Corner Society*. "Doc" and his gang, the "Corner Boys," rejected the dominant values as represented by school and settlement house, since they had been rejected by teachers and social workers. Theirs was a friendship group which "hung around together." Their chief norm was loyalty to and sharing with one another. Some of the difficulties for these Italian American boys are summed up by Whyte.

Some ask, "Why can't those people stop being Italians and become Americans like the rest of us?" The answer is that they are blocked in two ways: by their own organized society and by the outside world. Cornerville people want to be good American citizens. I have never heard such moving expressions of love for this country as I have heard in Cornerville. Nevertheless, an organized way of life cannot be changed overnight. As the study of the corner gang shows, people become dependent upon certain routines of action. If they broke away abruptly from these routines, they would feel themselves disloyal and would be left helpless, without support. And, if a man wants to forget that he is an Italian, the society around him does not let him forget it. He is marked as an inferior person—like all other Italians. To bolster his own self-respect he must tell himself and tell others that the Italians are a great people, that their culture is second to none, and that their great men are unsurpassed.[38]

The second generation did become Americans in their incorporation of the American goal of achievement and success. The traditionally sanctioned means to business success was frequently closed to them, however, because of ethnic discrimination and low socioeconomic status. For many, achievement or monetary success could be found in politics or the rackets and, as Daniel Bell has pointed out, both politics and crime in the large urban areas have experienced successive invasions by ethnic groups.[39]

Whyte indicates the forces at work in the dominant community and the immigrant community that determine the alternatives for the ambitious second-generation Italian.

To get ahead, the Cornerville man must move either in the world of business and Republican politics or in the world of Democratic politics and the rackets. He cannot move in both worlds at once; they are so far apart that there is hardly any connection between them. If he advances in the first world, he is recognized by society at large as a successful man, but he is recognized in Cornerville only as an alien to the district. If he advances in the second world, he achieves recognition in Cornerville but becomes a social outcast to respectable people elsewhere. The entire course of the corner boy's training in the social life of his district prepares him for a career in the rackets or in Democratic politics. If he moves in the other direction, he must take pains to break away from most of the ties that hold him to Cornerville. In effect, the society at large puts a premium on disloyalty to Cornerville and penalizes those who are best adjusted to the life of the district. At the same time the society holds out attractive rewards in terms of money and

[38] Whyte, *Street Corner Society*, p. 274. By permission.
[39] Daniel Bell, "Crime as an American Way of Life," *Antioch Review*, Summer, 1953. Also in Bell, *The End of Ideology* (Glencoe, Ill.: The Free Press, 1960).

material possessions to the "successful" man. For most Cornerville people these rewards are available only through advancement in the world of rackets and politics.[40]

Marginality Some individuals in the second generation were caught between their association with the immigrant community and their desire to be identified with the wider community or the dominant group. Such individuals were marginal because they took the dominant group as their reference group, incorporating their values as their own, and yet were not treated as equals by the dominant group. As Whyte has said, even if the individual wanted to forget his ethnic background, the larger society would not let him. In his description of Chick Morelli, Whyte has presented a portrait of a marginal man. In contrast to the "corner boys," Chick modeled his values after the wider community. He identified with the schools and his teachers, thought money should be saved, was generally concerned with his own advancement, and came to believe that Italians themselves were to blame for the discrimination they experienced.[41] The most important associations for Chick were with people outside of Cornerville, but he was frequently made to feel inferior.

Assimilation

Like the earlier immigrants, most of the southern and eastern European immigrant peoples have become or are in the process of becoming completely assimilated—that is to say, acculturated and accepted socially without reference to their ethnic origin. As a typical example of how assimilation takes place, the case of Paul Stanley is pertinent.

Stanley becomes a native. Paul Stanley through the aid of his athletic prowess had graduated from college and gone to law school while supporting himself working in the law office of a local lawyer of upper middle-class (native) status.

Paul's father and mother had come from Poland when they were children. They had both worked in the shoe factory and had gone to an "Americanization school" to improve their English. They were proud of their home, which they owned outright, kept well painted, and landscaped with cast-off tires, a border of half-buried beer cans, and a well-tended garden and lawn. They looked down on their less ambitious neighbors and also the Riverbrookers (lower-lower class people) with "native" status.

Mr. Stanley was very fond and proud of his son, for whom education had opened the door to greater social heights. Their first serious rift came when Paul became interested in Annie Tylor, a Riverbrooker girl; Paul wanted to marry her and eventually did, much to the disappointment of his parents. Annie's family were a typical ne'er-do-well low-class family known to the truant officer. Annie herself was the most ambitious and respectable of the lot and had in school managed to be accepted in "better-class" cliques of girls. Because of all the in-law complications, Annie and Paul ran away to get married, causing a split in Annie's family, who said she had married a "damn foreigner" and a Catholic fellow. Following their marriage, the new Stanleys drew away from both sets of parents, who

[40] Whyte, *Street Corner Society*, pp. 273–274. By permission.
[41] *Ibid.*, pp. 52–56.

were not after all the kinds of parents they wanted their new friends to meet. Their new home was in a nonethnic neighborhood.

After graduating from law school Paul had been invited to join the Caribous, made up mostly of Yankees, with only a few Poles. Within a year after his marriage, Paul became a member of the Antlers (higher social rating than the Caribous) and played bridge there several nights a week. He began to neglect his Caribou contacts. The Stanleys were now in a social clique made up of Yankee lower-middle class folks but were not, of course, ever invited to dinner at the home of the still higher-class Antlers whom Paul knew at the club, or ever called on by the nice ladies of Hill Street—upper class. "And anyway," they said, "we're going to see to it that our children have every advantage."[42]

It will be seen that Paul Stanley's assimilation involved a repudiation of his parent's ways of life; marriage into the native group, even though in this particular instance to a girl of lower-lower-class status; admission into associations with "native" membership; and an increasing number of intimate friendships with others than those of Polish backgrounds. In short, Paul Stanley in becoming an American moves both outward from his own ethnic affiliations and upward in class status.

Various explanations have been advanced to account for the differences in the rate of assimilation of immigrant groups into the dominant group. Those that have been the most widely held at various times in our history are probably the least tenable, for in general they have assumed that the only factor determining the rate of assimilation had to do with the characteristics of the immigrant group itself. Some of these explanations are of interest and import because they were factors in the assimilation process in that they represent the attitudes and beliefs of the dominant group. The general belief that the "old immigration" assimilated easily and that the "new immigration" did not is one such popular belief that we have already discussed.

Another widely held generalization is that groups are not assimilated because they are not acculturated. They are not treated as equals and admitted into close association because they are different. This too may tell more about the state of mind of the dominant group than it does of the degree to which the immigrants have taken on American ways. The same behavior that is lauded in the dominant group may be condemned when it is found in the minority group.

A sociological theory of assimilation must take into account the characteristics and goals of the immigrant group, the characteristics and goals of the dominant group, and the type of social structure at the time of migration. Thus immigrant groups have varied in their cultural characteristics and in their goals, the former ranging, for example, from the cultural complex of the peasant which is in marked contrast to the culture of the immigrant who came from urban environment. The goals too have ranged from those of

[42] Warner and Lunt, *The Social Life of a Modern Community*, adapted by Charles F. Marden. Pp. 188–193. By permission.

separatism to assimilation. The bulk of the immigrants to the United States were peasants and they arrived at a time in American social development when free land was no longer available. The only opportunities were in the urban industrial world, where their skills, habits, and customs were not only useless but often a disadvantage. Interestingly enough, however, those immigrants with agrarian skills who arrived when the United States was still largely an agrarian society were not rapidly assimilated into American life. On the contrary, they represent, even today, ethnic enclaves in some of the rural areas of the Middle West. This appears to be due to either their relative isolation, to separatist goals, or to both. The major immigrant group that brought urban skills to an urban-industrial society with the goal of assimilation was the German Jews. Generally speaking, however, they have not been entirely assimilated because the dominant group has chosen to exclude them.

The major systematic attempt to delineate the variables in assimilation has been made by Warner and Srole.[43] Their criteria of assimilation are the amount and kind of participation permitted the ethnic group by the dominant group as measured by residential mobility, occupational mobility, social class mobility, and membership in formal associations. On the basis of their research they suggest certain variables as determining the rate of assimilation. In each case the variable mentioned should be read as if preceded with the phrase "other things being equal."

The Recency Factor   The more recently the ethnic group has come into the community, the slower the degree of assimilation.

The Cultural Similarity Factor   The more divergent the culture of the ethnic group from the normative culture of the dominant status group, the slower the degree of assimilation.

The Concentration Factor   The larger the numerical proportion of the ethnic group in relation to the total population of the area, the slower the degree of assimilation.

The Physiognomic Factor   The "darker" the general physical appearance of the group, the slower the degree of assimilation.

The Permanency Factor   The more temporary the ethnic group conceives its residency in the host society, the slower the degree of assimilation.[44] These variables lend themselves to the following proposition regarding the assimilation of ethnic groups.

The greater the difference between the host and the immigrant cultures, the greater will be the subordination, the greater the strength of the ethnic social systems, and the longer the period necessary for the assimilation of the ethnic group.[45]

[43] Warner and Srole, *The Social Systems of American Ethnic Groups* (New Haven: Yale University Press, 1945), pp. 102, 283–296.
[44] Compare with the list given by Warner and Srole, p. 102.
[45] *Ibid.,* p. 285.

Though the work of Warner and Srole is a major step forward in the development of theory in the field of majority-minority relations, it should be noted that the propositions they have developed tend to treat the attitudes and behavior of the dominant groups as a dependent variable. The behavior of the dominant group may be in some situations the independent variable determining the rate of assimilation of ethnic groups. For example, the dominant group may be considered as having certain privileges and advantages which it wishes to monopolize. The unwillingness to admit the minority group to equal status thus becomes the crucial factor in assimilation. The need to exclude others from these privileges may be most pronounced among those who have themselves been only recently assimilated into the dominant group. The history of the official and unofficial attitudes and acts of the dominant group discussed earlier in this chapter indicates a rich source for tentative hypotheses about attitudes and behavior of the dominant group as these determine the amount and type of participation they are willing to share with ethnic minorities.[46]

SUMMARY

The immigrants who came to America developed this continent. At different periods in the history of the United States different opportunities and differing problems of adjustment confronted them. Attitudes toward immigrants fluctuated with political interests, the closing of the frontier, the growth of industry, and the growing size of cities.

The questions arising from the limitation of immigration and from the present position of immigrants from Europe and their descendants are discussed at the conclusion of the following chapter, after we have considered the twentieth-century European migration to America.

TOPICS FOR PROJECTS AND DISCUSSION

1. How would you account for the fact that there has been little immigration to the United States from South America?
2. Recalling your high school education, what did you learn about the cultural heritages of the immigrant groups to be found in the American population?
3. Ask a number of people who migrated to the United States from continental Europe to talk about their first year or two in this country. Try to direct the conversations to the difficulties they experienced, particularly how they got along with the natives. Write an account of these conversations.
4. Make a chart of your own family history since migration to this country. Show the ethnic identity, occupation, and place of residence of each generation.

[46] Early formulation of such hypotheses may be found in Richard Hofstadter, "The Pseudo-Conservative Revolt" and in Seymour Lipset, "The Sources of the 'Radical Right,'" both in *The New American Right*, ed. Daniel Bell (New York: Criterion Books, 1955).

Summarize what this shows you about migration to and opportunity in the United States.

5. If you have had experience with a family which has foreign-born parents and American-born children, try to discover the chief areas of dispute between parents and children. To what extent are these similar or different in content and emphasis from the usual disagreements between American parents and children as discussed in popular magazines?

6. Select one group from the European migration and see what you can discover that their culture had contributed to American life: to language, (words, expressions), foods, customs, enterprises, public service, scientific or artistic achievement, and so on.

7. John F. Kennedy is a third-generation American. What attributes, other than his office, define him as assimilated?

SUGGESTED READING

Abbott, Edith, ed. *Historical Aspects of the Immigration Problem, Selected Documents.* Chicago, Ill.: The University of Chicago Press, 1926.
    A fascinating array of documentary materials from records and publications on many facets of immigrant problems and attitudes toward immigration.
Brunner, Edmund de Schweinitz. *Immigrant Farmers and Their Children.* Garden City, N.Y.: Doubleday & Co., Inc., 1929.
    The most complete single-volume study of European immigrant minorities in rural areas.
Handlin, Oscar. *The Uprooted.* Boston: Little, Brown & Co., 1951.
    A lively account of the voyage and settlement of American immigrants.
Jones, Maldwyn Allen. *American Immigration.* Chicago, Ill.: University of Chicago Press, 1960.
    A brilliant re-appraisal by an Englishman of the great migrations to America.
Park, Robert E. and Miller, H. A. *Old World Traits Transplanted.* New York: Harper & Brothers, 1921.
    One of the earliest sociological studies of the process of immigrant adjustment with much interesting case material.
Warner, W. Lloyd, and Srole, Leo. *The Social Systems of American Ethnic Groups.* New Haven: Yale University Press, 1945.
    A classic study of the ethnic patterns in a small New England manufacturing city.
Whyte, William Foote. *Street Corner Society.* Chicago, Ill.: University of Chicago Press, 1943.
    Problems of adjustment to American life in an Italian slum neighborhood.

5

The Effect of the Later Immigration
on the United States

At the beginning of the twentieth century, public opinion in the United States began to regard European immigration as a serious problem. While, as we have seen, there had been difficulties arising from the adjustment of the older immigrant groups and strong feeling against the Irish, somewhat localized, in the nineteenth century, it was not until after the frontier had closed and the newer immigrant groups became highly visible that native Americans began to be seriously disturbed about immigration. In the main, two broad questions were raised: (1) Should immigration be restricted? (2) What should be done to bring about a more satisfactory adjustment of immigrants to American life? The final answer to the first question was the adoption of a policy of drastic numerical restriction of European immigration on a nationality quota basis. With reference to the second question, various schools of thought arose, ranging from the advocacy of programs of rapid assimilation to promotion of the idea of "cultural pluralism," in which the various nationality cultures would remain in high degree distinctive and the ethnic groups involved would be considered equal to the native ethnic group. The development of American thought and action concerning these two questions will constitute the first portion of this chapter.

The adoption of restrictive immigration brought to an end a colorful and highly significant phase of American history. Since, as we have seen, by the third generation at least, the ethnic group tends to be assimilated, America would soon cease being a land of foreigners. Long before this, Asiatic immigration had become negligible. Thus only the other nations of the Americas were left as sources of large-scale immigration. In fact, since 1924, Canada and Mexico have been the main sources of extensive immigration. French Canadian immigration, which had reached a peak earlier, continued to keep alive the typical pattern of native-immigrant interaction. Mexican immigration, commencing on a large scale after 1910, reached its peak in the later 1920's. This latter immigration became in a sense the new immigrant "problem," although highly localized in the Southwest. In fact, it reached such dimensions that we shall give it separate treatment in Chapter 6.

While restriction became the national policy toward European immigration, there has continued an articulate public which considers this policy unsatisfactory. In general, it was felt that the total quota was too small, and even more strongly opposed was the manner by which the allocation of quotas discriminated for or against the nationalities of the later immigration. Ever since the restrictive policy has been in practice, numerous native status groups have called for its revision in these respects. To furnish a background against which to weigh the arguments for and against revision of our present immigration policy we shall consider in another section the effects of the later immigration on the developing American culture. Whatever may have been the merits or flaws of the restrictive policy at the time it was adopted, subsequent events abroad, perhaps more than those at home, have exerted pressure for some change. First arose the problem of the political refugees created by the rise of Naziism in central Europe before World War II; second came the problem of the persons displaced by the war; and third there developed the problem of the political refugees from the areas of Communist expansion in eastern Europe. And beyond all these specific problems lies the fact that with the establishment of the United Nations it became both appropriate and inevitable that immigration and emigration be considered in an international as well as a national perspective. The present chapter, therefore, concludes with a consideration of these current international aspects as they relate to the immigration policy of the United States.

THE RESTRICTION OF EUROPEAN IMMIGRATION

Until 1882 immigration into the United States was practically unrestricted. A few states had passed laws which established some selective, but not exclusive, standards, but their effect was negligible. There was ample room for a growing population and plenty of work for all to do. Under these conditions it is not surprising that the first general federal legislation, the

Act of 1882 (not to be confused with the Chinese Exclusion Act passed the same year), should do no more than bar obviously undesirable immigrants. This act prohibited the entry of convicts (political offenders excepted), lunatics, idiots, and other persons likely to become paupers, but it placed little restraint on the total volume of immigration, which continued to rise until 1914.

The movement to restrict immigration gained backing from three public groups. The first, and probably most influential, was organized labor.[1] Labor's position was based primarily on the practical consideration that immigrant labor accepted low wages and was generally more tractable, thus retarding union efforts to improve the workers' economic position. A second public favoring restriction was composed of those various individuals scattered throughout the country who attributed many of the nation's ills to the presence of "too many ignorant foreigners." These were the "racist"-minded people to whom the racialist writers mentioned in Chapter 3 appealed. In examining the newspapers and magazines from 1900 to 1930, Woofter found that from 1907 to 1914 there occurred a marked change in public sentiment toward immigration. "The undesirability of certain racial elements" was becoming more persuasive than economic argument against restriction.[2] Finally, there was a growing feeling among the more thoughtful and scientific circles that the nation could not go on indefinitely trying to assimilate such large masses of people of different cultures. This point of view is reflected in the report of the United States Immigration Commission in 1911, which recommended restriction on economic, moral, and social grounds. The first congressional act to give expression to these pressures was the measure to bar as immigrants any aliens who were illiterate (a measure passed in 1917 over President Wilson's veto).[3] This kind of test was aimed at curtailing southern and eastern European immigration. Actually, it failed to reduce materially the volume of immigration, and Congress turned to a system of numerical limitation.

The Quota System

Congress first passed the Immigration Act of 1921, the most important aspect of which was that it restricted immigration on a basis primarily numerical—the first time this principle had been applied. The act provided that the number of aliens of any nationality admissible to the United States in any one year be limited to 3 per cent of the number of foreign-born persons of such nationality who were residents of the United States in 1910.

[1] See Mary Beard, A Short History of the American Labor Movement (New York: The Macmillan Co., 1927), p. 72.
[2] T. J. Woofter, Jr., Races and Ethnic Groups in American Life (New York: McGraw-Hill Book Co., 1933), p. 31.
[3] Literacy test bills were passed by Congress in 1896 and again in 1909, but were vetoed by Presidents Cleveland and Taft.

The Act did not apply to the Western Hemisphere or to countries otherwise regulated, such as China and Japan. The total yearly quota admissible under this Act was 357,803. The effect, although not the wording, of this law was discriminatory against southern and eastern European nationalities. The quotas set up permitted about 200,000 from the northern and western countries and 155,000 from the others. Since from 1910 to 1914 the average annual immigration from the northern European countries had been less than the quotas allowed, in practice the law did not greatly limit emigration from these areas. But it did greatly restrict southern and eastern European immigration, which had averaged 738,000 annually during the 1910–1914 period.

The Immigration Act of 1921 at its expiration was supplanted by the Immigration Act of 1924. Two different systems of quota apportionment were now set up, one temporary, in order to give the Immigration Commission time to work out proper quotas for the other, the permanent quota allotment. The temporary quota, which was to operate for three years, provided that "the annual quota of any nationality shall be 2 per cent of the number of foreign-born individuals of such nationality resident in continental United States as determined by the United States Census of 1890, but the minimum quota of any nationality shall be 100." The effect of this Act was to reduce the number of yearly immigrants still further to 164,667 and to discriminate even more strongly against the "newer" immigrant countries. Northern and western Europe now was allotted 80 per cent, whereas the southern and eastern nationalities had only 20 per cent of the quota. The permanent provisions of the Act of 1924, which was to take effect in 1927, reduced the annual quota to 153,774.[4] The law called for the apportionment of the total quota among the countries to which the Act applied according to their relative contribution to the American population as enumerated in 1920. Correctly apportioning the quotas was a difficult task, which involved retracing the entire immigration figures almost since the beginning of the nation, for which many of the essential statistics were lacking. No records of immigration by nationality were kept before 1820, as we know; and the recording of the country of origin of persons born here of foreign-born parents was not started until 1890.

Table 2 indicates the European nationality quotas allotted under the 1924 immigrant act and the number of immigrants admitted from European nations under this system in 1959. We have separated the northern and western nations from the southern and eastern in order to show (1) the extent to which the quotas favor the former; and (2) the failure of the former to use up their quotas, and the full use by the latter of their quotas. Great Britain used only one-third of its allotment, and Eire well under one-half.

[4] The revised quota system under the Act of 1924 actually did not go into effect until July 1, 1929.

On the other hand, nearly all the southern and eastern nations used up or exceeded their 1959 allotment, which suggests that many more applicants were not able to enter. The net result for 1959 was that against a permissible quota of 149,667 European immigrants, 89,145 were actually admitted. An additional 68,878 European immigrants were admitted, some under regular

TABLE 2
European Annual Quotas and Quota Immigrants Admitted During Year Ending June 30, 1959[5]

SOUTHERN AND EASTERN EUROPE			NORTHERN AND WESTERN EUROPE		
		QUOTA			QUOTA
NATIONALITY OR COUNTRY OF ORIGIN	ANNUAL QUOTA	IMMIGRANTS ADMITTED	NATIONALITY OR COUNTRY OF ORIGIN	ANNUAL QUOTA	IMMIGRANTS ADMITTED
Poland	6,448	6,382	Gr. Britain and		
Italy	5,645	5,746	No. Ireland	65,361	22,650
Czechoslovakia	2,859	2,005	Germany	25,814	24,757
U.S.S.R.	2,697	2,863	Eire	17,756	7,251
Austria	1,405	1,428	Sweden	3,295	2,081
Yugoslavia	933	1,016	Netherlands	3,136	3,096
Hungary	865	949	France	3,069	2,979
Finland	566	541	Norway	2,364	2,267
Portugal	438	453	Switzerland	1,698	1,604
Lithuania	384	426	Belgium	1,297	1,137
Rumania	289	343	Denmark	1,175	1,128
Greece	308	392	Other European		
Spain	250	292	Countries	200	175
Latvia	235	262			
Turkey	225	263			
Estonia	115	138			
Other European Countries	800	529			

non-quota provisions of the basic law,[6] but the largest number, 25,395, entered under the special act passed by Congress in July, 1958, to admit refugees from the Hungarian revolution of 1956.

Immigration from Europe since 1924

The adoption of the policy of restriction of immigration by the quota method had the effect of drastically curtailing the flow of immigrants to the United States. Table 3 presents the immigration flow from Europe by five-

[5] Adapted from *Annual Report of the Immigration and Naturalization Services* (Washington, D.C., 1959, p. 21, Table 7).
[6] Immigration law provides for the admission of spouses, children of American citizens, and ministers and their families, these not to be counted in the specified quota.

TABLE 3
European Immigration to United States
by Five-Year Intervals, 1925–1959[7]

1925–29	872,800
1930–34	309,163
1935–39	213,523
1940–44	132,355
1945–49	417,349
1950–54	778,012
1955–59	784,496
Total	3,507,698

year intervals following the Act of 1924. An examination of the table reveals marked fluctuations in the volume of immigration for the period.

Immigration Adjusts to the Quota Limits: 1925–1930 During this period practically all European nations utilized their quotas to the full. The fact that the total immigration exceeded the quotas is accounted for by the admission of nonquota immigrants as permitted by the Act of 1924, the largest group of which were the wives, husbands, or minor children of resident immigrants.

Immigration Far Below the Permissible Limits: 1931–1935 The drastic decline in European immigration beginning with 1930 clearly reflects the economic depression of these years, which made coming to America less attractive to Europeans. In addition, the federal government instructed its consulates abroad to apply rigidly the clause in the immigration legislation denying entry to persons likely to become public charges.

Refugees Increase the Totals: 1936–1940 While the rise in European immigration beginning in 1936 may have reflected in part the improved economic conditions in the United States, it was substantially advanced by the arrival of thousands of Europeans who sought asylum from persecution in the expanding Nazi Reich.

World War II Virtually Cuts off All Immigration: 1941–1946 Interestingly enough, because of the manpower shortage during the war, the United States imported on temporary visas from Mexico, Canada, and the West Indies some 350,000 laborers.

Displaced Persons Increase Immigration After 1946 Further discussion of the immigration of refugees and displaced persons will be pursued below.

The McCarran-Walter Act, 1952
No basic change in the national origins quota legislation has been made since its inception in 1924. The issue over nationality discrimination in

[7] Adapted from the *Annual Reports of the Immigration and Naturalization Service*, United States Department of Justice, 1949 and 1959.

quotas has been debated ever since. It was debated in Congress from 1946 to 1952, when the McCarran-Walter Immigration Act was passed, the advocates of increasing the annual quota and of altering quotas to provide more places for the southern and eastern European nations losing on both counts. The McCarran-Walter Act did not change the policy but involved setting up preferences within the same system. Immigration officials were ordered to give first preference to persons with skills currently in short supply and second preference to relatives of persons already in this country.[8]

The failure to "liberalize" the original quota system in the bill reflected primarily the long-nourished "nativist" preference for northern and western nationalities and a greater than ever fear of possible "subversive" infiltration. According to Divine, the economic factor received least emphasis in the passage of the McCarran Bill.[9] Both President Truman and President Eisenhower recommended changes to remove the discriminatory features, but no bill has gone beyond committee since 1952, except the special refugee acts.

THE EFFECTS OF THE LATER IMMIGRATION ON THE DEVELOPMENT OF THE UNITED STATES

Among the main social trends in the United States in 1880, the following appear most significant as a background against which to evaluate the effect of the later immigration: (1) The population was growing at a rapid rate, although signs of a decreasing rate of natural growth were already discernible. (2) The economy of the nation was rapidly shifting from a primarily agricultural to an industrial basis under the stimulus of the private enterprise system, which it was generally believed should have minimum regulation by government. (3) Correspondingly, community life was shifting from a primarily rural to a primarily urban basis. (4) The preoccupation with pecuniary values was retarding interest in the arts, efficient government, and social welfare. (5) The secular approach to problems of life, derivative from Protestant tradition, was stimulating scientific discovery and invention and its application to social problems. It was into a society undergoing these processes of change that the southern and eastern Europeans came. While the ethnic groups varied, for the purposes at hand the people of the later immigration may be characterized broadly in the following terms: they were rural, peasant folks used to working on the land or possessing skills in the handcrafts; they were accustomed to a simple social life based on kin relations, the church—for the most part Greek or Roman Catholic—and communal festivals; they were strongly familistic—that is, patriarchal—with high

[8] Other provisions of the McCarran-Walter Act included codifying the entire series of immigration bills and allotting quotas for the first time to Asiatic nations, in most instances 100 per annum (185 for Japan).
[9] Robert A. Divine, *American Immigration Policy, 1924–1952* (New Haven: Yale University Press, 1957), p. 186.

family integration and stability; and, finally, they were essentially super-naturalistic rather than scientific.

Effect on Population Growth

Reuter has calculated the relative contributions of net immigration as against natural growth for the United States since 1820. For each of the decades ending 1880 to 1920, he has shown that growth by immigration accounted for between 25 and 35 per cent of the total growth.[10] Reuter included not only net immigration but also the natural increase of immigrants arriving during the period. Their rate of natural increase was assumed to be the same as that of the total population. Such a procedure underestimates the contribution of immigrants to population growth because the immigrants were for the most part young adults at the most reproductive ages. Furthermore, they derived from peasant, Catholic cultures, whose mores encouraged large families. While most studies show that the longer these immigrants were here and the more they rose in social status, the smaller their families became, it seems reasonable to suppose that during the lag attendant on their assimilation to the small-family mores of America they contributed a more than proportionate share to the birth rate.

Controversy arose concerning whether the gain in population coming from the later immigration was a real net addition to the population. Walker, noting the decline of the native birth rate, contended that this was due to the unwillingness of the native status population to compete with the lower economic standards of the immigrants. In essence he argued that the population would have grown as fast or faster without immigration because then the original stock would have had larger families.[11] Such an argument overlooks the many other factors which influenced the declining birth rate, more marked among the native Protestant groups, such as urbanization, the desire for a constantly higher standard of living, and the changing status of women. Indirectly it is possible that the differential family size of the old stock and the new may have been affected by the greater upward social mobility made possible for the native stock by the constant replenishing of the low-class levels by newcomers. The relatively low birth rates, however, of Australia, Canada, and other pioneer nations of Anglo-Saxon stock suggest that the fertility of this stock in the United States would have declined if there had been no further immigration. The idea has been advanced that immigration indirectly hastened the approach to a stationary population by accelerating the process of urbanization and industrialization. Whether or not in the long run the population of the United States would have been

[10] E. B. Reuter, *Population Problems* (Philadelphia: J. B. Lippincott Co., 1937), pp. 59–60.
[11] Francis A. Walker, *Discussion in Economics and Statistics,* ed. Davis R. Dewey (New York: Henry Holt and Co., Inc., 1899), pp. 417–454.

any different in size with or without immigration, there is no doubt that during the period in which it took place immigration contributed to the rapidity of national growth by providing a larger base upon which natural reproduction operated. Without immigration the development of the United States to the size of a leading world power would not have occurred so soon.

Economic Effects

Mass immigration greatly stimulated the rapid industrial growth of the United States by furnishing both the needed supply of labor and, through population growth, an ever-increasing domestic market for goods. The role which immigration played in furnishing the brawn is indicated by a number of characteristics in the situation.[12] (1) Immigration was a fluid method of matching labor demand and supply through its tendency to increase or decrease in relation to the business cycle. (2) Immigrants came at an age when they were ready to work. (3) Immigrants tended to flow to those places and industries where the demand was greatest. (4) Because they needed work right away and lacked skills suitable for employment at other levels, they were willing to do the most menial and unskilled jobs, which native workers tended to shun. Thus immigration was in a sense almost "made to order" as a device for meeting the needs of expanding industrial growth under the private enterprise system. On the other hand, it is argued by some writers that the very cheapness and availability of immigrant labor may have retarded the technological advances in labor-saving devices which were later to characterize so markedly the American industrial system.[13]

The argument formerly advanced that immigration aggravated unemployment is scarcely ever voiced today. Unemployment is now understood to be related to a wide set of factors connected with the cyclical nature of the free enterprise system and to many conditions involved in world trade on which neither immigration nor emigration have any marked influence. Furthermore, as already indicated, immigration has a tendency to decrease in periods of depression, regardless of legal regulations. The complaint that immigration had the effect of lowering the wage scale and therefore the standard of living of the nation has validity only in a temporary sense. Immigrants did work cheaper than native labor at first. But as they became more adjusted to life in America and as they became unionized they pressed for higher wages and adopted higher standards of living. In the meantime their labor contribution had helped create the greater national wealth essential to a higher standard for all classes.

In a somewhat similar manner, the immediate effect of mass immigration

---

[12] See *The Immigrant Problem in the United States,* Research Report, No. 58, National Industrial Conference Board, New York, 1923, pp. 29–36.
[13] *Ibid.,* p. 32.

may be said to have retarded the growth of unions. On the one hand, industrialists took advantage of the weak bargaining position of the immigrants. "That employers make capital out of racial rivalries, playing off 'Wop' against 'Hunkie,' for example, and so preventing a united labor front, is well enough established."[14] On the other hand, the unions made it difficult for the new immigrant to obtain membership. "Foreign born craftsmen have been driven to unskilled labor, for the conditions imposed on them . . . were utterly beyond their reach."[15] Eventually the later immigrant groups became a substantial portion of union membership, but the barriers to their admittance imposed by the unions themselves retarded the development of a united labor movement.

Political Effects

In Chapter 4 we noted how the involvement of immigrants in politics contributed to their adjustment. Here we consider how this involvement affected American political development. Unfamiliar with American politics, immigrants were successfully courted by city political machines, whose political practices were not always savory. Edward J. Flynn, long-time political boss of the Bronx in New York City, writes of the time around World War I, "The immigrants, . . . being human, wanted friends, jobs, and the chance to become citizens. Tammany was smart enough to offer them all three in return for lifetime and often second, third, and fourth generation fealty to the party."[16] As the political strength of the various immigrant peoples increased, political parties tended to consider issues involving their homelands with the view to avoid alienating any ethnic group. This was well illustrated in the debate on the national origins act itself, as Divine brings out: "The opposition to national origins was founded on a strange alliance between restrictionists from the Midwest who favored German, Irish, and Scandinavian immigration and anti-restrictionists who wanted larger quotas for Southeastern Europe. The latter group hoped to discredit the principle of restriction by encouraging the battle between the Nordics."[17]

Part of the opposition to the later immigrant groups was based on the fear that they were more loyal to their homelands than to their adopted country, and that they were radical or subversive. The political behavior of these immigrant groups shows such fears to be groundless. Various "progressive" movements had their greatest strength in the Midwest, where, insofar as the ethnic element may have been an influence, it was the northern European rather than the southern and eastern European cultural influences which

[14] Robert F. Foerster, *The Italian Emigration of Our Times* (Cambridge: Harvard University Press, 1919), p. 402.
[15] Peter Roberts, *The New Immigration* (New York: The Macmillan Co., 1912), p. 73.
[16] Edward J. Flynn, *You're the Boss* (New York: The Viking Press, Inc., 1947), p. 11.
[17] Divine, *American Immigration Policy, 1924–1952*, p. 47.

predominated. In particular, the co-operative movement had its greatest strength in this area. The various socialist movements and parties have indeed arisen in the industrial-metropolitan areas where the heaviest concentrations of recent immigration are to be found; but both the small size of the organizations and the insignificant vote which they have generally drawn for candidates for political office indicate that only a small minority of the population of recent immigrant lineage has been attracted to their causes. As Hansen put it, "Probably more immigrant Socialists were lost to the cause in the United States than were won from the ranks of the newcomers. Those who did not join the Republican party as the protector of the industries that employed them, found a home in the more liberal atmosphere of the Democratic party. Neither group, of course, questioned the fundamentals of capitalism."[18]

Personal Disorganization

Writers about immigrant problems have struggled with the question "To what extent did immigration affect the volume of various sorts of personal maladjustment in the United States?" Comparisons of the rates of criminality, delinquency, mental disease, and pauperism of three groups—the foreign-born, the native-born of foreign parentage, and the native population—are difficult to set up, particularly because of wide differences in age compositions and in socioeconomic levels. For example, Davie cites these figures on mental disease for 1923: "The rate per 100,000 . . . was 159.8 for native whites of native parentage, 207.0 for native whites of foreign parentage, and 513.9 for foreign born whites."[19] But the foreign-born population contains relatively few children, and mental disease appears more frequently in adult groups. Furthermore, the foreign-born population in this country is highly concentrated in urban areas, and the rate of admission to mental hospitals, on which the statistical comparisons are based, is twice as great in urban as in rural areas. Finally, the foreign-born population is predominantly male, and the rate of admissions of males exceeds that of females by about 4 to 3.

Let us try to interpret the real meaning of some facts about juvenile delinquency. A 1910 census report indicated that the ratio per 100,000 population was 99.8 for native-born whites of native parentage and 153.3 for native-born whites of foreign parentage. A number of factors other than those related to minority status per se are needed to explain these comparative figures. In spite of the difficulties involved in the statistical approach, substantially every writer who has described the life of ethnic groups in American cities emphasizes such factors as cultural conflict and marginal status in

---

[18] Reprinted by permission of the publishers from Marcus Lee Hanson, *The Immigrant in American History* (Cambridge, Mass.: Harvard University Press, 1940).
[19] Davie, *World Immigration*, p. 279.

accounting for personal disorganization in these groups.[20] Thus it is difficult to avoid the conclusion that, over all, mass immigration did add to the total volume of personal disorganization, not because of the nature of the immigrants or their cultures, but because of the problem of adjustment to a new situation.

Effects on American Culture

We use the word "culture" here to denote the arts, sciences, religion, and recreation, in contrast with government, economics, and other instrumental phases of civilization.[21] The Anglo-American culture placed little value on the arts, and its people were markedly inconspicuous in aesthetic expression. In contrast, the folk cultures of the continental nations, and those of the later immigration in particular, were far more elaborated in music, the dance, colorful folk festivals, and the arts in general.[22] Thus the later immigration enriched the aesthetic quality of American life not only through the contributions of their great artists but also by diffusing a greater sensitivity and heightened evaluation of the arts. The Puritan influence which inhibited the development of the arts among the Anglo-Americans had carried over into their whole concept of enjoying life. The pursuit of pleasure for its own sake was in a sense a "sin." Such an attitude was in marked contrast to the continental cultures, which placed high value on spontaneous gaiety, less inhibited expressions of passion, and enjoying life each day as it came. So the later immigration contributed to the decline of the Puritan outlook on pleasure.

The Anglo-American culture became increasingly secular in its approach to human problems, not only in economics but also in such fields as health and welfare. In contrast, the folk cultures of the later immigrant nationalities were more supernaturalistically oriented. In the earlier periods of adjustment to their new environment, many difficulties were encountered in such matters as enforcing regulations pertaining to sanitation and public health and in rationalizing the approaches to problems of human conduct, particularly in family relations. The later immigration had the effect of retarding the trend toward the application of a secular as distinct from a supernaturalistic approach in human relations.

Finally, the later immigration, since it was predominantly Catholic, greatly altered the religious composition of the nation. Since their Catholicism is the one differentiating aspect of the later ethnic groups which has

[20] See, for example, Mabel A. Elliot and Francis E. Merrill, *Social Disorganization*, 3rd ed. (New York: Harper & Brothers, 1950), Ch. 28.
[21] See R. M. MacIver and Charles H. Page, *Society* (New York: Rinehart & Company, Inc., 1949), for this distinction, especially pp. 486–487.
[22] See William C. Smith, *Americans in the Making* (New York: Appleton-Century-Crofts, Inc., 1939), pp. 423–431. The continental Europeans of the earlier immigration also had a creative influence on the development of the arts in the United States.

been most completely retained, this change may be considered one of the most profoundly important permanent effects of the later immigration. Indeed, we consider it so significant that we shall devote Chapter 17 to its implications.

Immigrant Contributions Limited by Minority Status

No brief discussion can, of course, exhaust the list of contributions of the later immigrants to the development of American culture. Among the many millions of immigrants were many highly creative minds, whose artistic creations and scientific discoveries added enormously not only to American but to world civilization.[23] Innumerable items, such as foods, words, and clothing styles, have been incorporated into the general mode of American life. Nevertheless, as we recall the processes by which immigrant adjustment took place and as we look at the cultural product now prevailing, it is obvious that the contribution of the immigrant groups was limited by their minority status. Native Americans who considered these foreigners as inferior people were not disposed to borrow elements from their Old World cultures. Even more important was the impact of minority status on the native-born of the later immigration. Since rise in status and acceptance by the dominant group was contingent on the loss of ethnic visibility, those of immigrant lineage themselves looked down on their heritage and failed to perpetuate even those elements consistent with modern American living.

The European ethnic groups became Americanized, if not quite into the Protestant, then into the Anglo-Saxon mould. The melting pot boiled, but the emergent product was indigenously American rather than a mere amalgam of variegated European cultures. The result was more a creation of the reciprocal responses of many groups to the rapidly changing circumstances of the twentieth century in an environment fortuitiously rich in natural resources than a static reintegration of elements from times past. The cultural product is now essentially American, not foreign. The extent to which European ethnic groups may continue to be differentiated is considered at the conclusion of this chapter.

Summary

The foregoing discussion suggests the following propositions as a summary of the effects of the later mass immigration on American society:

1. It accelerated the population growth of the United States during the period in which it took place and thus further advanced the position of the United States among the world powers.

2. It expedited industrial expansion and urbanization.

3. It temporarily retarded the growth of unionism.

[23] See Francis J. Brown and Joseph S. Roucek, *One America* (New York: Prentice-Hall, Inc., 1949), Part II, for the most exhaustive listing in one volume of the significant contributions to American life of each of the 39 different ethnic groupings described.

4. It facilitated the perpetuation of the "Tammany Hall" type of urban politics until such time as increasing assimilation of the native-born descendents and their class differentiation broke up any marked tendency toward ethnic political blocks.[24]

5. In its total impact, it increased the volume of personal maladjustment with particular reference to ethnic persons in marginal status positions.

6. It elaborated the artistic and esthetic elements of the general culture, and facilitated the trend away from the Puritan outlook on pleasure and personal morality.

7. It retarded the trend from a supernaturalistic toward a secular approach to problems of human welfare, particularly the application of newer social science approaches in human relations.

8. While innumerable specific items in the various ethnic cultures became incorporated into the general national or regional cultures, the minority status of ethnics limited the extent of this influence.

FUTURE IMMIGRATION POLICY OF THE UNITED STATES

Whether or not the present immigration policy of the United States should be revised, and in what ways, is related to questions of population, economics, international relations, and harmonious community life, which interrelate in so many ways that it is difficult to discuss each separately. Whatever may have been the motivation behind the Immigration Act of 1924, it seems indisputable that some limitation of immigration is a necessity for the United States, as well as for any other modern state. The problem thus centers on how many should be admitted and what qualifications should be required.

Population Considerations

The perspective on population problems affecting the United States and certain other Western nations, such as England, France, and Canada, has greatly change since World War II. Earlier in the century, the declining rate of population growth in these nations pointed to a stationary population by the latter part of the twentieth century. To some sutdents of social problems this possibility was viewed with forboding in the face of the higher rates of population growth in the less developed nations. What has actually happened, however, has been a substantial rise in the rate of population growth in the United States in the postwar period, reflected in an 18 per cent increase in population in the decade 1950–1960. During the same time, the rates of population growth in the less developed regions of Asia and

---

[24] For example, the only hope for better government in New York during the 30's was to elect a mayor with minority background on the "fusion" ticket. This happened with the election of Fiorello La Guardia in 1934.

South America reached such staggering proportions that the central problem came to be potential overpopulation in the world as a whole.[25]

The substantial rate of population growth of the United States, together with the increasing significance of technological superiority over sheer human numbers, particularly when the latter involves continuing impoverishment, has largely allayed concern over any inadequacy in the size of this nation's future population. Since immigration to the United States has been so limited since 1928, obviously the recent upswing in the rate of population growth has been little influenced by further immigration. Thus public debate over immigration policy centers on other considerations than population —particularly on domestic economics and international relations.

Economic Considerations

It seems reasonably clear that a steady increase in population aids economic expansion and helps raise the standard of living of a nation situated like the United States. Since, as we have seen, growth will take place without increase in immigration, attention focuses on other ways in which immigration can affect the economy of the nation. The economic system is cyclical, which means that there is fluctuation in employment. It is important, therefore, that at periods of high unemployment immigration not aggravate the situation. The present quota restrictions are severe enough to preclude this happening.[26] This point, however, is a valid argument for continuing the policy of numerical control of immigration, without necessarily supporting the particular quota number now in effect. A second aspect of the economy related to immigration is fluctuation in the need for workers in particular occupations. Selective immigration is one way to facilitate adjustment of supply to demand in specific occupational categories. A current illustration is the shortage of physicians for hospital service, which is being met in part by foreign doctors, and the difficulty of obtaining hospital service workers (a relatively low-paid field), which is being met in part in New York City by the employment of recent immigrants from Puerto Rico. Similarly, immigration from Mexico has filled the need for agricultural workers which would apparently not have been filled by native labor.[27]

International Considerations

Justification of the differential quotas favoring the nations of the older immigration as against those of the newer, is a difficult matter. Neither our past experience with immigrants nor our present social science furnishes

[25] Philip M. Hauser, *Population Perspectives* (New Brunswick, N.J.: Rutgers University Press, 1961).

[26] The less restricted immigration from Mexico and Puerto Rico has generally shown tendencies to respond automatically to increased or decreased employment opportunity in the United States. See pp. 124–125 for further discussion.

[27] Other aspects of the agricultural migrant worker problem are discussed on p. 135, below.

objective bases for assuming that ethnic lineage affects the relative capacity of any foreigner to adjust successfully to American life. The case is therefore strong for the adjustment of national quotas so that all nations are considered equal. As a temporary procedure in this direction, it has been frequently recommended that quotas unused under the present system be placed in a general pool which in the immediate subsequent period could be used by countries whose quotas have been exhausted or be made available for special groups in distress.[28]

Finally, the question of political affiliation must be considered. When a nation is engaged in a struggle against another nation, it is inevitable that it will want to bar as immigrants people whose loyalty is on the other side, as is the case with many European Communists today. A real danger to democracy in the application of political tests for admission to the United States is the danger of confusing beliefs—as, for example, Communism—with mere belief in social change.

Summary

It may be suggested in summary that the present immigration policy of the United States calls for revision in the following directions:

1. It is obvious that some numerical limitation be maintained. The present figure of 150,000 a year is easily within the capacity of the nation to absorb without economic or social disturbance, and should not be lowered. Whether it should be raised depends on the position taken on the controversial question "Is it desirable to stimulate the present rate of population growth in the nation?"

2. Two considerations suggest flexibility in the number to be admitted in any given year: (a) fluctuations in the business cycle; and (b) the varying need to provide refuge for groups in distress.

3. While nationality quotas are essential to give opportunity to all foreigners to compete for admission, their allocation on a somewhat more equitable basis than now prevails seems called for. At the minimum, a provision that the unused quotas of nations might be pooled for the use by other nations would seem to balance in part the present disparity.

4. Since the migration of the peoples of the world will come increasingly under the purview and administration of the United Nations, the United States should stand ready to supplement or revise its basic policy in relation to any future international programs.

The significance of this last consideration has been illustrated already in situations arising since the present policy was adopted: (1) that of the refugees from Naziism, (2) that of the displaced persons of World War II, and (3) that of the Hungarian refugees following the revolution of 1956.

[28] William S. Bernard, ed., *American Immigration Policy* (New York: Harper & Brothers, 1950), p. 275.

THE REFUGEES

Throughout our entire history American society has been added to periodically by immigrants who left their native lands primarily to escape persecution for political or religious opinions. The term "refugees" was applied to individuals who fled from the Nazi persecution beginning in Germany in 1933 and carried on further in the Nazi-occupied areas after 1938. To quote Davie and Koenig,

The recent refugee movement has also been marked by (1) the extremely cruel treatment of the victims of political, religious, and "racial" persecution; (2) by the difficulty which these victims encountered in escaping and in finding a secure refuge as Naziism spread to ever larger areas; (3) by the reluctance of the countries not immediately affected to admit them because of the deep economic depression then existing; and (4) by the breaking up of families on a scale previously unknown. Such has been the refugee movement which began with the rise of Hitler to power in 1933.[29]

Davie and Koenig estimate the total number of immigrants in the United States who can be called "refugees" at 243,862. The period from 1938 to 1941 marked the peak of this particular immigrant movement. America was not, as many natives put it, "swamped" with refugees, since the total amount of all immigration to our shores from Europe from 1933 to 1944 totaled only 365,955, only 16.8 per cent of the total permissible from Europe under the quota laws. Over half the people came from Germany or Austria, with Poles, Czechoslovakians, Russians, French, Italians, and Hungarians following in this order. Of the entire group about two-thirds were Jewish, a fact explained by the Nazi persecution of Jews which was most systematic and categorical. These refugees eventually were distributed throughout the country, although they settled largely in cities.

This particular group differed from the earlier mass immigration in having a far larger proportion of highly educated, professionally trained, and commercially experienced persons. For example, 5,000 were physicians; 25,000 merchants; 1,800 manufacturers; and 3,500 college and school teachers. The proportion of skilled and unskilled laborers was far below that of the earlier immigration. This unusual distribution of occupational backgrounds is explained by the difficulties of escaping and the need of some wealth to get away. Relatively more of the refugees were wealthy, although many of the well-to-do who did not come early were unable to bring their wealth with them.

Davie and Koenig sum up their answer to the question "What do Americans think of the refugees?" as follows:

The general reaction of Americans toward the refugees may be summed up as one of compassion for the victims of persecution seeking a haven here. The

---

[29] Maurice R. Davie and Samuel Koenig, *The Refugees Are Now Americans*, Public Affairs Pamphlet, No. 111, 1945, p. 4. By permission.

refugees report that, on the whole, Americans have shown an attitude of friendliness and helpfulness. As the number of refugees increased, however, a certain amount of antagonism developed. Refugees began to be looked upon as serious competitors, especially by certain professional and wage-earning groups and in certain communities. These fears were allayed with the increased demand for labor brought about by the war.

Nevertheless, a certain degree of resentment has persisted in certain quarters and against certain groups of refugees.[30]

Within a short time these refugees became well adapted, if not assimilated, to American life. On the one hand, their relatively few numbers offered little serious competition to Americans except in an occasional locality; on the other hand, they had a beneficial influence out of proportion to their numbers. Some started new business enterprises and introduced new manufacturing processes; others were highly skilled workers in trades where a dearth of native trained workers existed. If in any sense the presence of the refugees constituted a "problem," it has long since ceased to be one.

DISPLACED PERSONS

In the years since World War II the United States has been receiving a new category of immigrants who have become technically designated displaced persons. These people are Europeans who were rendered homeless through the destruction of the last war or who for various reasons could not with safety resume residence in their prewar community. By the end of 1950 the heart-rending task of resettling these people had been substantially accomplished. It would therefore perhaps be adequate for us to confine our discussion of the topic to indicating how many came to this country, who they were, and how they fared among us. But the role which the United States played in this co-operative world problem is a good barometer for evaluating the present climate of American sentiment toward certain minorities, and a good test of the attitude of the American people toward international co-operation. We shall therefore treat the topic of the displaced persons in detail.

The Circumstances Creating Displacement

During the period of the German conquest up to 1943, millions of persons were evacuated by the German army or fled before it. At the same time prisoners of war and slave labor from non-German nationals were taken to Germany. More than two million Poles, French-speaking Alsace-Lorrainers, and Slovenes were expelled from border areas incorporated into the Reich in order to make room for foreign nationals of German stock who were thus repatriated nearer the homeland. As the tide of the war reversed, a series

[30] *Ibid.*, p. 28. By permission.

of other population movements took place. Inhabitants of German cities, perhaps as many as six million, were evacuated to other places within the Reich. As Russian victories occurred, Reich Germans from eastern and southeastern Europe, together with some non-Germans who feared the Communists, fled back to the fatherland. At the conclusion of the war, the Allied armies liberated from the notorious Nazi concentration camps the surviving Jews and non-Jewish political opponents of the Nazi regime. And later on, as the Iron Curtain began to surround their countries, thousands fled from their homes to seek asylum in lands controlled by the Allied governments.

Characteristics of the Displaced Persons

Surveys made in Europe of the displaced persons indicated a fairly even sex distribution, a heavy concentration in the age groups 18 through 44, and a high birth rate in the camps of 35.5 per thousand.[31] One survey estimated 70 per cent Roman Catholic and 20 per cent Jewish.[32] The percentage of skilled laborers was high. Most of the displaced persons were Poles, Ukranians, Yugoslavs, and Balts.

The Role of the United States

The response of the United States to this problem was slow and cautious. During the early period, when the emphasis was on repatriation, the United States admitted 20,000 displaced persons, each of which was required to have a sponsor in this country who would guarantee that he would not become a public charge. The United Nations organized the International Refugee Organization in 1947, and in the first year about 200,000 displaced persons were resettled, of whom the United States admitted 16,836, a rather small number. One reason for this was that most of the displaced persons were ineligible for admission under our quota system. The Administration urged Congress immediately upon IRO's call to pass special legislation making it possible for a substantial number of displaced persons to be admitted on a nonquota basis. Congress did not act until the closing hours of its 1948 session, on June 2. The bill then passed had the following main provisions.

1. Permitted the admission of 205,000 displaced persons over a two-year period.
2. Charged the displaced persons entering up to 50 per cent against future annual quotas of the countries of birth.
3. Restricted eligibility to those entering Germany, Austria, and Italy before December 22, 1945.

[31] E. D. Kulischer, "Displaced Persons in the Modern World," *The Annals of The American Academy of Political and Social Science*, March, 1949, 262: 172–173.
[32] William S. Bernard, "Homeless, Tempest Tossed," *Survey Graphic*, April, 1948, 37: 189.

4. Required that at least 40 per cent of the total admitted must be persons coming from areas annexed by foreign powers.

While the number allowed under this act was more commensurate with the size and position of the United States, the specifications made it difficult to find 205,000 displaced persons who could qualify. The cutoff date excluded the large number of Jews who fled from eastern Europe after December, 1945. The areas which had been annexed by foreign powers, from which 40 per cent must be drawn, included the Baltic States, whose population contained substantial numbers of Protestants. Since, as indicated above, 90 per cent of the displaced persons were either Roman Catholic or Jewish, it is not surprising that the bill was considered by many as highly discriminatory against peoples of non-Protestant faith. Sharing this sentiment, President Truman, in a statement released when he signed the bill, put it in these words: "In its present form, the bill is flagrantly discriminatory. . . . It is a close question whether this bill is better than no bill at all. . . . [It] discriminates in callous fashion against displaced persons of the Jewish faith. . . . [It] also excludes many persons of the Catholic faith who deserve admission."[33]

As admissions began to lag, the Administration pressed for revision of the 1948 Act, and on June 16, 1950, a new bill was signed by the President. This revised act permitted the entry of 228,514 displaced persons in addition to the 172,239 admissions already granted. It removed the qualifications as to occupation and nationality in the previous bill and the prior "cutoff date" for time of displacement, thus making eligible Poles, Rumanians, and Catholics in general who had fled in 1946 and 1947 from Communist-controlled countries. By the end of 1952, when the displaced persons legislation ended, the United States had admitted about 400,000.

SUMMARY

The response of the American government and public to the various refugee problems reflects the ambivalence characteristic of its response to earlier immigration, but with certain changes. Opposed to acceptance of these refugees have been the various nativist publics, to whom "foreigners" are *ipso facto* undesirable, and the anti-Semitic public. As before, liberal elements have favored a generous policy in accordance with democratic principles. Unlike the early period, there has been a shift in the position of organized labor, which at least officially supported the admission of displaced persons. The growing recognition of the international responsibility of the United States and the "cold war" implications of the refugee problems made acceptance of a substantial share of these people imperative.

The admittance to the United States of these various refugee groups cre-

[33] See the *New York Times*, June 26, 1948, p. 7.

ated no serious problems at all. They were dispersed widely enough that there was no marked visibility or noticeable economic competition with natives. The ethnic backgrounds were all from nationalities which already had furnished assimilated elements in the American population.

An outstanding new feature of refugee immigration is the addition of new procedures. The screening of applicants and their preparatory orientation abroad, the pre-planning of first home and job in this country before arrival, and the co-operative assistance of voluntary agencies with governmental officials in facilitating the adjustment of the new arrivals marks a new approach to the handling of immigration. This new approach was utilized in connection with the admittance of some 25,000 Hungarian refugees from political persecution following the abortive Hungarian revolution of 1956, again by special legislation outside the quota system.

THE PRESENT POSITION OF IMMIGRANT GROUPS IN AMERICAN SOCIETY

The history of the great migration of European ethnic groups to the United States contains nearly all the problems and patterns of dominant-minority relations in this country, except slavery and its effect on Negroes and whites. Groups of both the earlier and later migrations have experienced discrimination, been subject to prejudice, shared the life of a nationality subcommunity, and seen many of their members abandon the traditional ethnic culture and merge with the dominant group. It is clear also that the type and degree of discrimination against any one or any several groups has varied according to other pressures than that of immigration.

To assess the present position of ethnic groups in America, it is relevant to ask "How far do people of a particular nationality background remain identifiable and identify themselves as ethnic groups, and to what extent are they discriminated against."

Nationality Groups are American in Language, Secular Behavior, and Loyalty

The European nationality groups, since the limitation of immigration, now contain a preponderance of American-born children and later descendants of the immigrating generation. The foreign-born are an older population and, with the exception of the displaced persons, they migrated more than forty years ago. America is their home. Almost all of them speak English—if not at home, outside the home. Since the pattern of later migration was on the whole to urban areas, the influences of the dominant culture have surrounded them more closely, through politics, mass communication, and changing urban residence patterns which have led to the disintegration of many distinctive nationality neighborhoods.

The second generation has attended American schools, associated with children of other ethnic background, and developed common ways of behaving on the job or in leisure pursuits. Their models are what they know of America, not what they know of the "old country." They share the patterns of daily living of most urban Americans at whatever level they have been able to achieve them. It is our hypothesis that in a systematic study of the entire range of activities pursued day by day in the lives of families entirely composed of native-born people of the later immigration, a wide preponderance of activities listed would give no clue at all to their ethnic heritage. On the basis of their range of activities and without reference to their names or their associates, identification of ethnic origin, if correctly made at all, would be made on the basis of a very small percentage of activity items.

The effect of this growth in secular participation of immigrants and their children in American life has been to achieve a merger of the dominant and the parallel ethnic status structures. There has grown up a national pattern of social status in which a significant factor is period of migration, and in which class attitudes increasingly replace anti-ethnic attitudes. This, however, is subject to regional variation.

The fact that even ethnic groups which have preserved a strong sentiment for the home country are first and foremost American in loyalty was demonstrated by the German-Americans in World War I, when they disappointed the Imperial German government, which had expected their support.

Discrimination Against Ethnic Groups
The degree to which there is economic discrimination against nationality groups is difficult to determine. From such materials as *Cornerville* we may assume that it is the access to training and jobs conveying greater prestige that is the focal point of economic discrimination. The "good" law school, the grade-A medical school, the managerial-level job may in some regions be open to only a few exceptional representatives of the eastern or southern European groups.

Social discrimination persists, also, often rationalized on class or religious grounds. Many ambitious members of ethnic groups find themselves discriminated against, in the sense that ambition and mobility in a person of "old American" background, say from a Midwestern small town, is regarded favorably and welcomed as a sign of individual enterprise, whereas it is felt to be inappropriate in the "ethnic."

The Persistence of Ethnic Identity
Ethnic identity, in the sense of persistence of cultural values and sentiments of attachment, continues most markedly among groups who have been kept, or have kept themselves, to a greater or lesser degree separate from the larger society. Thus rural settlements where there has been little

population change may see a long persistence of ethnic subculture. Lubell describes one such German rural community in Minnesota, where the language of the family, the church, and the daily community life was still German and the children complained of school because "English is so hard."[34]

When a national religion strengthens other nationality ties, the group identity may persist longer, as with Greeks. After-school classes maintained by the Greek Orthodox Church help hold children to the religion and culture of their forefathers, even when English is spoken at home. When the religious identity is confined to one nationality or the nationality to one religion, there is more pressure toward maintaining marriage within the group. As outmarriage begins to occur, it is likely to be most frequent among members of the same religion.

The proportion of the European migration that consciously and distinctly holds to values different from the dominant is now very small and, as we have said, is more likely to be rural. The values longest preserved without modification will be religious and familial, though, as with some sects, attitudes toward occupations occasionally vary from dominant attitudes. Some ethnic identity is kept alive through the pressures of discrimination. The members of a nationality group are thrown back on association with one another in the absence of access to other associations. Thus to some extent patterns of ethnic association persist in certain occupations and industries. We must conclude, however, that even under these circumstances the attachment to the country and culture of their forefathers is largely symbolic. What the meaning to the individual is of these symbolic attachments we know very little, or how it may affect critical decisions with which he is faced. Sociologists have raised the point that the significance may be deeper than we have tended to believe.[35]

One effect of the closer examination of what is happening to the European groups and their descendants is to change our way of looking at assimilation and cultural pluralism. Assimilation is not so complete and inevitable as the writers of the early 1900's thought; nor is cultural pluralism—a United States composed of different but equal ethnic groups—currently seen in such simple terms as was true in the 1930's and '40's. We shall devote attention to this question later, but it is relevant here to point out that increasing conformity in secular life may sharpen the need for subcultural identities that preserve continuity, bind sentiment, and enrich and personalize the fabric of life.

---

[34] Samuel Lubell, *The Future of American Politics*, 2nd ed., revised (New York: Doubleday Anchor Books, 1956), p. 158.
[35] See Nathan Glazer, "Ethnic Groups in America: From National Culture to Ideology," in *Freedom and Control in American Society*, Morroe Berger, Theodore Abel, and Charles H. Page, eds. (New York: D. Van Nostrand Co., Inc., 1954).

TOPICS FOR PROJECTS AND DISCUSSION

1. From a number of general histories of the United States covering the period since the Civil War compile the views expressed concerning the effects of the later immigration on the development of American social life. To what extent do these views agree or disagree with the hypotheses advanced in the summary on pages 108–109?
2. Do you think the present international situation is more likely or less likely to bring about a revision of our present immigration laws? Why?
3. Analyze all the possible effects which mass immigration had on the composition and size of the population of the United States.
4. Discuss the effects of immigration on the economy of the receiving nation. Do these effects vary at different stages in a nation's development?
5. Consult the files of periodicals dealing with current affairs for the first half of 1948 for material concerning the Congressional debate on the first Displaced Persons Act. Summarize the leading views expressed.

SUGGESTED READING

Bernard, William S. ed. *American Immigration Policy: A Reappraisal.* New York: Harper & Brothers, 1950.
> *A brief, comprehensive account of the effects of immigration and an appraisal of national policy from a liberal viewpoint.*

Bowers, David, ed. *Foreign Influences in American Life.* Princeton: Princeton University Press, 1944.
> *Essays on the influence of European immigrants on the politics, economic ideas, and cultural life of the United States.*

Davie, Maurice R. *Refugees in America.* New York: Harper & Brothers, 1947.
> *The most comprehensive account of the pre-World War II refugee immigration.*

Divine, Robert A. *American Immigration Policy, 1924–1952.* New Haven: Yale University Press, 1957.
> *Includes treatment of post-World War II immigration acts through the McCarran Act.*

Gross, Feliks. "Political Emigration from Iron Curtain Countries," *The Annals of the American Academy of Political and Social Science,* September, 1950, pp. 175–184.
> *Discusses the political emigration from eastern Europe since World War II and analyses its implications for Western democracy.*

"Reappraising Our Immigration Policy," *The Annals of the American Academy of Political and Social Science,* Vol. 26, March, 1949.
> *The issue is devoted to the background of the immigration policy of the United States and a reappraisal based on world conditions following World War II.*

Taft, Donald R., and Robbins, Richard. *International Migrations.* New York: The Ronald Press Company, 1955.
> *A comprehensive study of immigration in the modern world. Part III deals with the United States.*

White, Lyman Cromwell. *300,000 New Americans.* New York: Harper & Brothers, 1957.
> *A study of the procedures of an immigrant aid service.*

6

Mexicanos

The Southwest of the United States is characterized by a pattern of dominant-minority relations with a background different from that of the later European immigration. Large-scale migration from Mexico into the Southwest began about 1910. In describing the intergroup situation that followed, the problem of nomenclature arises. The literature on this subject designates the minority variously as "Latin-Americans," "Spanish-speaking Americans," "Mexican-Americans," "mexicanos," and "hispanos." Since all these terms are more or less interchangeable, let us choose the term "mexicano" for all Mexican-descended people, except, of course, in quoting from writers who use one of the other terms. For the dominant group we will employ the term "Anglos."

The distinguishing feature of Anglo-mexicano relations is the fact that, long before the period of large-scale immigration from Mexico, the Southwest bore a cultural imprint of Spanish-Mexican origin, as symbolized by the many "Los" and "Santa" community names in the region. In the area were many hispanos, especially in New Mexico, whose families traced their lineage locally to long before the intruding Anglos entered. Thus the migrating Mexicans moved into an area in one sense less alien than that into which the European immigrants came. By this time, however, the Anglo cultural imprint had clearly established dominance over the Spanish-Mexican, and any adoption of hispano culture by the Anglos was largely superficial.

Although not as far from their homeland as the European immigrants had been, the mexicanos did not possess a cultural heritage which would make rapid acculturation likely. They started off at the bottom of the occupational scale, in particular as agricultural workers. And they were discriminated against by the Anglos. The process of acculturation has gone on, as we shall see, but it has been relatively slow.

ANGLOS AND THE SPANISH PEOPLES OF THE SOUTHWEST[1]

Spanish-speaking people have been in the Southwest for over 350 years. Some of the villages north of Santa Fe, New Mexico, were founded in 1598. A century later Spanish settlements were made in Texas, and almost two centuries later, in California. In each of these three areas, distinctive Spanish cultures developed. Another influence was the relations of the Spanish to the many different Indian groups with which they came in contact. "Until about the middle of the 19th century, the *californios*, the *nuevo mexicanos*, and the *texanos* went their separate cultural ways, held together only slightly by, at first, the slender ties to Spain, and later, briefly, by the uncertain and flimsy bonds of independent Mexico."[2]

The Southwest today bears the indelible marks of these influences. Many of the methods and processes of sheep-raising, cattle-raising, mining, and irrigation farming were borrowed from the Mexican-Indian culture of the area. Now blended with new techniques which developed after annexation, these contributions are not adequately accredited to the people who were responsible for them. Some Mexican influence is reflected also in state laws governing land use and property rights between husband and wife. More visibly recognized as "Spanish influence" are architectural forms, clothing, and language. American vocabulary in the region includes many Spanish words. The whole nomenclature of the rancho and vaquero (cowboy) culture is largely Spanish.[3]

From the turn of the eighteenth century to the Mexican-American war, intergroup relations ranged from individual friendships to competition, antagonism, and, in many instances, violent conflict rising out of ethnic and racial distinctions. The Mexican society was sharply divided between upper-class property owners and peons. The invader-immigrant Anglos as individuals often competed and sometimes came in conflict with the upper-class Mexicans for economic gain; however, there were many who co-operated with the ruling Mexican elements and through intermarriage became part

---

[1] We are indebted to Prof. George I. Sanchez, of the University of Texas, for supplying "Spanish-speaking People in the Southwest—A Brief Historical Review" (mimeographed), which has been drawn upon in this section.
[2] *Ibid.*, p. 2.
[3] See Carey McWilliams, *North From Mexico* (Philadelphia: J. B. Lippincott Co., 1949), Ch. 8.

of Mexican society. Both upper-class Mexicans and Americans considered the peons an inferior, servile class. With the increasing infiltration of Americans, however, relations between Mexican and American became more antagonistic. In Texas, where by 1836 Americans far outnumbered Mexicans, this antagonism expressed itself in a successful revolution resulting in the formation of the Republic of Texas.

By the treaty of Guadalupe-Hidalgo, terminating the Mexican-American War, all the Mexican territory north of the Rio Grande became part of the United States. From this point on, American influence became dominant over Spanish-Mexican; upper-class Mexicans attempted to join American society; and the poorer and illiterate Mexicans became a distinct ethnic minority, notwithstanding the fact that they were now citizens of the United States. The antagonistic character of Anglo-Mexican relations is reflected in the terms "gringo" and "greaser," which each group came to apply to the members of the other, with contemptuous implications. In popular usage before the conquest, "gringo" referred to any foreigner who spoke Spanish with an accent. The term "greaser" referred to a native Mexican or a native Spanish-American, and was originally applied disdainfully by the Americans of the southwestern United States to Mexicans.

Given this situation against the setting of the "trigger-fingered" frontier, it was not surprising that violence should frequently arise. Paul S. Taylor in his study of a border community testified to many instances of violence from both groups. He cites the comment of a local official: "Undoubtedly robberies and murders by Mexicans have continually been perpetrated in Texas, but in retaliation Americans have committed terrible outrages upon citizens of Mexican origin."[4] McWilliams notes that "the first person to be lynched in California was a Mexican," and Leonardo Cordoba, Clement Lopez, and Jesus Saguaripa were lynched in Tucson . . . (1873), with a coroner's jury defending the lynching."[5]

Race Consciousness in Anglo-Mexican Relations

In Anglo-mexicano relations, the element of "race consciousness" on the part of the Anglos has been more pronounced than when European immigrants have been involved. From an objective basis, the Mexican immigrant group does possess greater racial variance. The racial composition of the population of Mexico has been in this century approximately 10 per cent white, 60 per cent mestizo (mixed Indian-white), and 30 per cent Indian.[6] Since the immigrants to the United States have been drawn largely from the latter two elements, especially the mestizo, it is not surprising that the re-

[4] Paul S. Taylor, *An American-Mexican Frontier* (Chapel Hill: University of North Carolina Press, 1934), p. 65.
[5] McWilliams, *North From Mexico*, pp. 127-128.
[6] See Maurice R. Davie, *World Immigration* (New York: The Macmillan Co., 1936), p. 215. Also, *Encyclopedia Americana*, 1960, p. 472.

sults of the United States Census of 1930, enumerating the Mexican stock by racial designation as "white" and "colored" for the first and only time, showed less than 5 per cent as "white," 65,968 out of 1,422,533 total Mexican stock listed.[7] This considerable admixture of Indian traits does not have any significance in relation to behavior capacities or traits, since there is no evidence that Indians are inferior in innate capacity. The mestizo cultures are more Latin-American than Indian. The Indian strain does, however, give the Mexican-American group a darker appearance. In the earlier days, this color visibility affected Anglo attitudes toward Mexicans. Writing about race consciousness in 1930, Gamio stated,

The darkest-skinned Mexican experiences almost the same restrictions as the Negro, while a person of medium-dark skin can enter a second-class lunchroom frequented also by Americans of the poorer class, but will not be admitted to a high-class restaurant. A Mexican of light-brown skin as a rule will not be admitted to a high-class hotel, while a white cultured Mexican will be freely admitted to the same hotel, especially if he speaks English fluently.[8]

SIZE AND DISTRIBUTION OF THE MEXICAN – AMERICAN POPULATION

Accurate figures for the number of people of Mexican descent living in the United States are not available. This is due in part to the difficulty of deciding on a single criterion by which Mexicans can be distinguished. Concerning the efforts made by the Bureau of the Census to count this population, Lyle Saunders wrote,

The Bureau of the Census in 1930 attempted to enumerate them under the heading "Mexican," defining them in their instructions to enumerators as "all persons born in Mexico or having parents born in Mexico, who were not definitely white, Negro, Indian, Chinese, or Japanese." The principal difficulty with this definition, aside from the confusion of racial and cultural concepts it contained, was that it excluded persons whose grandparents, great-grandparents, or even more remote ancestors had come to the Southwest by way of Mexico. In New Mexico, for example, where the Spanish-speaking people have lived for more than three centuries, only 61,960 "Mexicans" were enumerated although it was a matter of common knowledge that the Spanish-speaking group made up about half the population of the state, or something over 200,000 persons.

In 1940 the Bureau of the Census dropped the classification "Mexican," except for foreign-born persons actually natives of Mexico, and attempted to determine the size of the Spanish-speaking and other foreign language groups by asking of a five per cent sample of those enumerated the question: what was the principal language, other than English, spoken in your home during your childhood? From the answers to this question an estimate was made of the number of Spanish-

---

[7] United States Census, 1930, *Population*, Vol. 2, pp. 27, 34.
[8] Manuel Gamio, *Mexican Immigration to the United States* (Chicago: University of Chicago Press, 1930), p. 53. By permission.

speaking people in states and large cities, but the sample was not large enough to permit estimates for counties, small cities, or rural areas.[9]

The above consideration led Saunders to conclude that the census enumerations have always been an undercount. In 1953 he estimated the mexicano population in the five southwestern states of California, Arizona, New Mexico, Colorado, and Texas at two and a half to three million. Since there are some in other states, the total aggregate probably well exceeds three million. Between 1940 and 1950 the population counted as Mexican in the five states increased 45.8 per cent, as against a general increase in the region of 36 per cent. Saunders feels that some of this increase reflects only a greater accuracy in the 1950 census count.[10] In any event, Mexican-Americans constitute one of the largest ethnic elements in the United States who remain in considerable degree differentiated from the Anglo population and, with high birth rates, they are a rapidly growing minority.

The population of Spanish-Mexican origin is largely composed of persons of twentieth-century Mexican immigrant background. The relatively small portion of this population which is descended from Spanish-speaking families who lived in the area annexed by the United States is concentrated in New Mexico and southern Colorado. They may be differentiated by the term hispanos. The non-hispano portion of the mexicano population is largely concentrated in three states and was estimated in 1950 to be in Texas about a million; in California about 750,000, and in Arizona, 130,000.

As we shall see, trends in Mexican immigration have been largely affected by the "pull" of employment opportunities in the Southwest, particularly in agriculture, and the "push" of adverse economic conditions in Mexico.[11] Immigration in substantial numbers began in the first decade of this century and increased sharply in the next two decades. As with other groups during the depression, the immigration of mexicanos declined sharply in the decade of the thirties.[12] The great demands for manpower during World War II precipitated a trend of immigration from Mexico which reached a peak around 1953. Much of this involved transient harvest hands who had entered the country illegally, popularly designated as "Wetbacks," because many had swum the Rio Grande. The "Wetback" migration reached startlingly high proportions in the post-World War II period. In 1953 the Border

[9] Lyle Saunders, "The Spanish-Speaking Population of Texas," *Inter-American Education Occasional Papers*, V (Austin: University of Texas Press, 1949), p. 8. By permission.
[10] Lyle Saunders, *Cultural Difference and Medical Care: The Case of the Spanish Speaking People of the Southwest* (New York: Russell Sage Foundation, 1954), pp. 285–288.
[11] See "Migratory Labor in American Agriculture," *Report of the President's Commission on Migratory Labor* (Washington, D.C.: Government Printing Office, 1951).
[12] In 1929 the United States established a Border Patrol and required Mexican nationals entering the United States to register. This enabled the immigration authorities to control the volume of immigration, but it turned out to be somewhat unnecessary in the depression decade that followed.

Patrol apprehended 750,000. These were returned to Mexico, and others went back of their own accord, but a sizeable proportion escaped detection and remained in this country. The general decline in immigration after the early 50's means that the Mexican "immigrant" group is now increasingly native-born. A special 1950 census reported 83 per cent of the Spanish-surname people in the Southwest as native born. The percentage for those born in Mexico was for Arizona 17; for California 19; and for Texas 18. In the "hispano" states of New Mexico and Colorado, the Mexican-born were less than 4 per cent.[13]

INITIAL PERIOD OF IMMIGRATION—
ANGLO – MEXICANO RELATIONS TO WORLD WAR II

In broad outline, the process of adjustment of the Mexican immigrant group follows the pattern delineated for European immigrant groups. For the initial period, the studies of Paul Taylor in four different areas of the Southwest are the most extensive.[14]

In the Southwest, 1927

Mexican immigrants in the Southwest found employment in unskilled occupations, chiefly as agricultural laborers. Their wages, in common with agricultural labor generally, were low—usually lower than that paid any Anglos employed in the same kind of work. Employers often maintained that this differential was justified because Anglo laborers were more productive than Mexicans. These Mexican laborers were slow to become unionized. Earlier efforts at organization, opposed strongly by the agricultural employers, were generally unsuccessful. While by the late 20's an increasing number of the Mexicans were buying or building homes of their own, they did not buy farm land for themselves, and they showed little interest in sharecropping. Few opportunities existed for Mexicans in higher ranking occupations, both because they were not equipped to fill them and because of the discrimination against their employment in occupations involving Anglo fellow workers or serving Anglo trade. Some Mexican clerks were employed in low-priced stores for the purpose of encouraging Mexican trade.

The housing of the more settled Mexicans was of the lowest standard;

[13] Saunders, *Cultural Difference and Medical Care*, pp. 300–307.
[14] Paul S. Taylor, *Mexican Labor in the United States* (Berkeley: University of California Press, Publication in Economics, Vol. 6, 1928). In this volume are included three monographs: No. 1 on Imperial Valley, California; No. 2 on the Valley of South Platte, Colorado; and No. 5 on Dimmit County, South Texas. Taylor also wrote *An American-Mexican Frontier* (Chapel Hill: University of North Carolina Press, 1934). While Taylor, an economist, was primarily interested in the labor situations of the Mexicans, his field of inquiry embraced the general pattern of social relations between the Anglos and Mexicans.

and that of Mexicans employed in agriculture of a nondescript variety, sometimes haymows or improvised shelters in the woods. In spite of these poor economic conditions, Mexicans were not often on relief rolls, partly because of their tradition of mutual aid. Nor did Taylor find their criminal arrests more than proportionate.

The pattern of group relations distinctly separated the Mexican from the Anglo group in each community. The Mexicans lived apart. Although their low economic status and their desire to be with fellow compatriots in part account for this, the studies clearly indicate that in the case of those few more successful Mexicans who aspired to rent or buy in Anglo areas, where restrictive covenants were not specific, social pressure in the Anglo group kept them out. Keenly sensitive to their not being wanted as neighbors, few Mexicans made the effort to live outside their colony. The social line drawn between the two groups was as sharp as that in housing. Taylor cites the comment of a soda clerk in the Texas border area: "We serve Mexicans at the fountain but not at the tables. We have got to make some distinction between them and the white [sic] people. The Negroes we serve only cones."[15]

In short, the picture Taylor draws shows that Mexican labor was welcome in the Southwest because it filled a labor need not likely to be met by workers of Anglo status at the wages and under the working conditions which the farmers of the Southwest were prepared to provide. The warmth of their welcome was in proportion to their willingness to continue to fill this need without becoming ambitious for something different, and to their willingness to keep their place in social matters. To what extent the situation had changed in the next fifteen years can be seen in Tuck's study of "Descanso," a Southwestern community in the early 40's.[16]

Descanso: The *Colonia*

Descanso is a small Southwestern city set in fertile valley, half cupped by mountains. It is a railroad junction, surrounded by large-scale farm operations. "Railroads and ranching . . . set the tempo" of its economy. While it lacks the clear-cut ecological pattern of Eastern cities, the tendency is for the east and north sections toward the mountains to be the preferred native residential section. The south section is the dilapidated area of shacks and cheap bungalows now inhabited about equally by Mexican-Americans, poor native Americans, and Negroes. It is in the western section, the Monticello district, that the Mexican colony lives. To quote Dr. Tuck:

On both sides of Monticello Avenue, a small Mexican business district has grown up—cafés, grocery stores, *cantinas*, a barber shop, a bakery, a drugstore, and a couple of *tortillerias*. The hiring and provisioning agency for the Santa Fe

[15] Taylor, *An American-Mexican Frontier,* p. 250.
[16] Ruth D. Tuck, *Not With The Fist* (New York: Harcourt, Brace & Co., 1946).

is also here. Much of the life of the Mexican-American colony centers on this street, and the colony itself is larger, more homogeneous, and more progressive than the smaller group in Spring Valley. The district has one or two Italian families, a few Filipinos, and recently the area has experienced a considerable invasion of Negro families from its east end, close to the railroad tracks. Practically no Anglo-Americans live in the heart of the district, although, toward the north, Mexican-Americans of higher economic status are beginning to occupy houses on streets with Anglo-Americans.[17]

The social life of the *colonia* is rooted primarily in the family system, secondarily in the church. The family system follows the usual Latin patriarchal form, resembling the Italian pattern we saw in Chapter 5: subordination of women, although much reverence for mothers; subordination of children, with differential training of the sexes in line with patriarchal ideals; permanency in family relations; strict parental protection of girls, together with a double standard of sex morality. While most Mexicans in Descanso were and are today Catholics, Tuck feels that the local church does not constitute as important a focus in the life of the Mexican-Americans as it does in Mexico. In practice, the males scarcely ever go to church. "The most admired and influential man in the colony is non-Catholic. . . . Another outstanding and respected man is a frank, effective critic of the Church."[18] The Church makes no effort to adapt itself to the situation. It makes few attempts to offer recreational facilities to youth or cultural stimulation for the adults.

"Most of the social life of the *colonia* is essentially informal in nature."[19] The proliferation of societies, clubs, and associations which distinguishes American life has not yet intruded on the *colonia*. The number of kin of each family is extensive enough to provide a wide circle of friends. There is one large men's organization, the Confederation of Mexican Societies, a council of four mutual insurance groups, whose chief activity is to celebrate two Mexican national holidays. It rather vaguely acts for the "economic, moral, and cultural improvement of the Mexican people."[20] Its constitution specifically restricts any civic activity which is political in nature. From time to time, other organizations had arisen which were more definitely political; however, "most of them have had brief, fitful lives."

Descanso's *colonia* falls into a two-class division: the "big people" and their satellites; and the commoner folk. "The top group contains some persons whose origins in Mexico were 'folk,' many quasi immigrants whose parents had such origins, and an increasing number of second generation persons who have risen within the structure of the *colonia*."[21] The criteria of

---

[17] *Ibid.*, p. 5. By permission of the publisher.
[18] *Ibid.*, p. 153.
[19] *Ibid.*, p. 157.
[20] *Ibid.*, p. 160.
[21] *Ibid.*, p. 133.

class mobility are much the same as with other people, with one exception. Higher education, higher status occupations, money, and service to the group raise one's status. The exception seems to be pride in being a Mexican.

This self-respecting pride in one's background and origins strikes a rather new note in American immigrant histories. The man who changed his name, denied his background, and was ashamed of the old folks with the accented English and foreign ways is a commonplace type among other immigrant groups. He is a distinct rarity among Mexican-Americans, except for some badly confused adolescents; and his actions, rather than being admired as a hallmark of success are described as "his misfortune," as though he had a strange affliction. "Assimilation! I am tired of that word," said one of the *colonia's* leaders. "Fusion is what we want—the best of both ways." A young American of Mexican descent, speaking at a club luncheon, was told by a gentleman of Swedish ancestry: "We Scandinavians get ahead because we dropped our old-country ways." "Perhaps that was your misfortune," was the reply.[22]

How does the native community react to these Mexicans? Broadly speaking, it exhibits all the characteristic dominant-group attitudes and discriminations, applied "not with the fist" but in all other possible ways. Here are some examples:

"I'm for giving everybody a fair chance, but will you tell me what good it does to educate the average Mexican? They just don't take to it." (A native businessman)

"Of course, I pride myself on my tolerance, but I simply won't have my daughters attending a youth center where there are Mexicans." (A clubwoman)

"Sure, I'm hiring skilled Mexicans now. I've got a war contract and I have to . . . . But I'm not going to have them after the war. A Mexican's a darned good worker, but you don't want to have too many of them around in top positions." (An employer)

"This town will never stand for Mexicans in the same pool with white kids. Okies? But Okies are white." (A public official.)[23]

While there are Mexican-Americans who can honestly say that they have never encountered any of the cruder forms of discrimination and others who experience them only infrequently, still "it is safe to say that the entire population . . . is aware of barriers against it."[24]

A young college graduate said—"Discrimination? Of course, all of my life, since I was a little boy. I make my way, I enjoy myself, I have good Anglo-American friends, in spite of it, but I never forget."

[22] *Ibid.*, p. 134. By permission of the publishers.
[23] *Ibid.*, p. 53. By permission of the publishers.
[24] *Ibid.*, p. 52.

An extremely successful man [Mexican] by colony standards, said: "I don't know why it is, but I've had to fight ever since I first crossed the threshold of a public school. Even now, I seldom sit down in a restaurant without expecting the waiter to come up and say, 'Sorry, we can't serve you.' I'm careful to go where I know such things won't happen, but I still half expect them."[25]

Welfare

Like most immigrant minorities, mexicanos had low indices of welfare in their earlier years in this country. They did not improve as rapidly as many other groups. A Texas survey found their housing substandard, their sanitary facilities and services inadequate; their diet insufficient, causing much malnutrition; and their health generally poor. High incidences of the communicable diseases—especially tuberculosis—were reported, in some cities higher than the rates for Negroes. Child mortality and maternal mortality rates far exceeded the Anglo rates.[26]

Underlying the low welfare of the mexicanos up to this time had been low income due to occupational distribution in the poorest paid jobs. From the outset the extremely low economic status was related to the large numbers employed as agricultural workers, an occupation always the poorest paid in American occupational hierarchy. Even in 1950 about one-fifth of Spanish surname workers were still farm laborers and another third were in occupations below the skilled level.[27]

Anglo Attitudes Toward the Mexicanos

As is characteristic of dominant groups, Southwestern Anglos tended to play down the extent of their discrimination and to rationalize what could not be denied by invoking an unfavorable stereotype of the mexicano. Tuck put it thus:

There is nothing Descanso will deny more stoutly than any intention of keeping its Mexican-Americans disadvantaged in order to derive an economic gain from their position. That is why it resents the words caste or semicaste being applied to its practices. Descanso argues, rather, that the bulk of its Mexican-Americans are so low in type that they could not profit by advantage. It seems rather odd to prove this point by making sure that they have continued inferior advantage, but Descanso sees no hint of a vicious circle in this procedure. The "low type" of Mexican, says Descanso, is getting about what he deserves. If he encounters segregated schooling, segregation in use of public facilities, unequal employment opportunities, unequal pay for equal work, or prejudiced law enforcement and justice—what of it? Descanso does not see that, in making these and a thousand other decisions, it is casting a vote that amends, not only the rights and liberties of a certain group, but the very nature of its democratic procedure. Descanso

[25] *Ibid.*, pp. 52–53. By permission of the publishers.
[26] Pauline R. Kibbe, *Latin-Americans in Texas* (Albuquerque: University of New Mexico Press, 1946).
[27] Robert H. Talbert, *Spanish-Name People in the Southwest and West* (Fort Worth, Texas: Leo Potishman Foundation, 1955), p. 72.

would not think of revising a certain historic document so that it guaranteed life, liberty, and the pursuit of happiness somewhat more to "high types" than to "low types." No, says Descanso, we are just making a few social distinctions, several million of which cannot possibly affect a democracy. You have to recognize, argues Descanso, that some people are just born inferior, generation after generation. As the leader of a church study group put it, "there are always hewers of wood and drawers of water."[28]

In a study of a south Texas community, Simmons found that the Anglo stereotype of the mexicano emphasized his inferiority, which seemed to the Anglos self-evident.[29] He is identified with menial labor, but as a worker is considered improvident, undependable, childlike, and indolent. Other features of the stereotype are uncleanliness, drunkenness, criminality, and spitefulness toward Anglos. Viewing the mexicano in this unfavorable light, Anglos feel justified in their practices of exclusion. Even the favorable features of the stereotype reinforce the Anglo notion that mexicanos belong in subordinate status.

Among those [traits] usually meant to be complimentary are the beliefs that all Mexicans are musical and always ready for a fiesta, that they are very "romantic" rather than "realistic" (which may have unfavorable overtones as well), and that they love flowers and plants and can grow them under the most adverse conditions. Although each of these beliefs may have a modicum of truth, it may be noted that they can reinforce Anglo-American images of Mexicans as childlike and irresponsible since they support the notion that Mexicans are capable only of subordinate status.[30]

Minority Status of Mexicanos

Two factors perhaps distinguish mexicanos from other Latin immigrants from Europe: their peasant, nonliterate cultural background; and their conspicuous lack of political adaptability, this preventing them from exercising the potential political power which their numbers warrant to improve their conditions. A number of other factors and circumstances differentiate them from other minorities in the United States: the recency of their immigration in large numbers; their entrance into the Southwest, with its long history of Anglo-assumed superiority over the Mexican and of Anglo violence and exploitation in dealing with Mexicans; their high admixture of Indian blood; their original occupational concentration as agricultural laborers, very frequently migratory; and their nearness to the homeland, which has made frequent visits back and forth feasible, with a retarding effect on acculturation. On the Anglo side we note the crystallization of the "inferior-immoral-childlike" stereotype, associated patterns of discriminatory behavior, and the

[28] Tuck, *Not With The Fist*, pp. 53–54. By permission of the publishers.
[29] Ossie G. Simmons, "The Mutual Images and Expectations of Anglo-Americans and Mexican-Americans," *Daedulus: Journal of American Academy of Arts and Sciences*, Spring, 1961, 90: 286–299.
[30] *Ibid.*, p. 292. Reprinted by permission of the Editors of *Daedalus*.

persistent exploitation of cheap labor of Mexican descent by special employing interests, notably in agriculture.

The status of Anglo-mexicano relations in the Southwest as the United States entered World War II approximated semicaste. While there were few if any legal restrictions against them, in subtle ways, Mexicans were "kept in their place." The pattern of discrimination is summed up in an extensive survey in Texas, conducted during the war years.

Economic Discrimination. (1) Unfair employment practices forcing low economic status upon the majority of Latin Americans. (2) Discrimination exercised by both management and Labor unions in the admission and upgrading of Latin Americans. (3) Exploitation in agriculture. (4) Demand of growers for cheap labor carried to the extreme of favoring illegal seasonal influx workers, thereby denying employment opportunities to resident workers.

Inequitable Educational Opportunities. (1) Arbitrary segregation in public schools. (2) Inability of working children to attend schools. (3) Lack of interest of school administrators in enrolling Latin American children and encouraging attendance. (4) Improperly trained teachers and inferior buildings and equipment.

Social and Civic Inequalities. (1) Refusal of service in some public places of business and amusement. (2) Denial of the right to vote in some counties. (3) Denial of the right to rent or own real estate in many cities. (4) Denial of the right to serve on juries in some counties. (5) Terrorism on the part of law-enforcement officers and others.[31]

THE EFFECT OF WORLD WAR II

World War II affected the minority status of mexicanos in the same way it affected most other minorities—improvement of welfare and lessening of discrimination—but the changes were not as great for the mexicanos as for some others. The war opened up new avenues of employment and increasing unionization. Higher wages and more regular employment improved welfare. The experiences of Mexican veterans broadened them and left them less willing then before to accept minority status in civilian life. The following is not only illustrative, but, as we shall see later, prophetic:

A discharged private in the infantry said: "I'm glad I'm going to have one of those little buttons to wear in my coat. And a flock of foliage to put on my uniform for Armistice Day parades. I'm going into politics. There's seven or eight of us, all from Southern California, who've talked it over. Things are going to happen in these colonies, and we're going to see that they do."[32]

The agencies of the federal government brought pressures to bear on local areas during the war to improve the position of minorities. Through the Office of the Coordinator of Inter-American Affairs, intercultural committees were formed throughout the Southwest to improve the relations between

[31] Kibbe, *Latin-Americans in Texas*, pp. 271–272.
[32] Tuck, *Not With The Fist*, p. 221. Reproduced by permission of the publishers.

Anglos and mexicanos. With the war's end, a let-down in this ameliorative trend was noticeable. But there was a net gain in status for many mexicanos, and, of course, increasing acculturation.

Increasing acculturation without complete acceptance, however, inevitably results in some disorganization, particularly among persons in a marginal position. A manifestation of the growing pains accruing to marginal status were the "zoot suit" riots in Los Angeles in 1942, much over-publicized and exaggerated as they were. The evidence is clear that in some of the most serious clashes between "zoot suit" Mexican youth and Anglos, it was the Anglos who precipitated the riots by attacking the Mexicans. Because of the minority status of the Mexicans, however, the reaction of the community at large was to presume the Mexicans guilty; to exaggerate the prevalence of delinquent behavior among all Mexican youth; and to apply abnormally drastic penalties to the Mexican participants and light or no punishment to the Anglos. Bogardus in his analysis of gangs of Mexican youth in Los Angeles puts their significance in proper perspective by indicating that perhaps 1,000 out of about 35,000 Mexican youth in the city between 6 to 17 were members of juvenile gangs, and a small portion of these were members of *Pachuco* gangs, as the older groups and those more inclined to delinquency were called.

The causes for the formation of these gangs and their behavior follows the same pattern found in every American urban slum. There is nothing peculiarly Mexican about it. The underlying factors are the physical sordidness of the environment, the growing inability of parents to control their children, lack of interest in school because of handicaps, the special obstacles in getting work, and lack of adequate wholesome recreational outlets.[33] The following quotation from a nineteen-year-old mexicano youth illustrates much of the above:

A lot of the trouble the Mexican boys get into is just because they are rebelling against their parents. Mexican parents can't accept American customs and don't approve of their kid's ways. But then the Americans don't ever really accept Mexican kids either—so the boys have to stick together. That's why the gangs are so important. Some guys really get bitter about this and they carry things so far that they are out to "get even" with everybody.[34]

POST – WORLD WAR II TRENDS
IN ANGLO – MEXICANO RELATIONS

Since World War II the relations between Anglos and mexicanos have followed broadly the same course as that in all minority situations (the

[33] Emory S. Bogardus, "Gangs of Mexican Youth," *Sociology and Social Research,* September, 1945, 28: 55–56.
[34] Margaret Clark, *Health in the Mexican-American Culture* (Berkeley and Los Angeles: University of California Press, 1959), p. 142. By permission.

Southern scene excepted). Mexicanos have been becoming increasingly acculturated; their welfare has improved; and discrimination against them has decreased. Yet progress in all three of these ameliorative trends has been slow—slower, for example, than with the Japanese. A study of the *colonia* in San Jose, California, more than ten years after the Descanso study sums up as follows:

The Spanish-speaking people of San Jose refer to themselves as the "colonia." The people differ in many ways, and find themselves divided by socioeconomic class differences, national loyalties, religious affiliation, provenience, and age differences. However, a sense of group loyalty within the colony is fostered by such factors as common language, common channels of communication, kinship, formal organizations, special events of common interest to Spanish-speaking people, Mexican-American business establishments, and a sense of separation from the Anglo population of San Jose.[35]

Language is a sensitive index of acculturation. In San Jose, Clark found that "certainly knowledge of English is not universal in the colonia, but neither is it limited to a 'few of the educated.'" Even in the most insulated and underprivileged area of the *colonia*, "there is a growing use of English in the home." and most parents want their children to speak both English and Spanish well.[36] In health, likewise, there is much holding on to the traditional as well as taking on Anglo ways. For example, as Saunders writes, "a number of Spanish-Americans interviewed in the San Luis Valley of Colorado in 1952 indicated that in general they utilized the services of both folk and Anglo scientific practitioners and that their knowledge of remedies for various conditions included items drawn from both cultures."[37]

Political Participation

One of the most recent areas in which the mexicanos have been adopting the Anglo American way of life is their participation in politics. Of this Sanchez[38] writes:

Probably most symbolic of the changes that have taken place among Americans of Mexican descent in recent years, and undoubtedly fundamentally causal in those changes, are those in the area of politics. While the hispanos of New Mexico have been very vocal politically, and politically effective since World War I, their fellow mexicanos in the other states have had a political awakening during the past ten years that verges on a revolution.

Nowhere is this as spectacularly illustrated as in Texas. There, in the face of great odds—the poll tax, poverty, prejudice, ignorance, and the like—the Latin

[35] *Ibid.*, p. 33.
[36] *Ibid.*, pp. 53, 55.
[37] Saunders, *Cultural Differences and Medical Care*, p. 193.
[38] George I. Sanchez, Professor of the History of Philosophy and Education at the University of Texas and long-time student of Anglo-mexicano relations, at the request of the authors wrote an otherwise unpublished note on recent trends in the Southwest, from which we gratefully quote.

American (so-called) has taken very large political strides indeed. Whereas a few years ago only the border counties elected Latin-American officials, and then nearly always on a token basis and for minor local positions only, today Latin Americans are found in all sorts of elective positions throughout south central and south Texas—as school board members, as county commissioners, as city councilmen, as mayors, in the state legislature, and so on. A most encouraging feature in this development is the increasing independence of the mexicano vote. Where a few years ago that vote was listless and frequently controlled by bosses and machines, it has demonstrated in recent years a vigor and an independence which already make it a power to be reckoned with in elections. For example, had this vote followed the old pattern in the recent presidential election and split badly on its choice of candidates, Texas would have gone handily into the Republican column. As it was, the Latin Americans of Texas, for the first time in a national election, voted solidly for one candidate, Senator John F. Kennedy, giving him several times the number of votes that were his margin of victory in the state. Of particular significance is that, in the estimation of this observer, the vote would have been the same if Senator Kennedy had not been a Catholic.

These political developments in Texas are duplicated in some parts of California. New Mexico continues its close two-party operation, with the Hispanos choosing and picking between the two to come up with mixed slates in the final elections. Colorado and Arizona follow the New Mexico pattern closely. In all of the states, the mexicano vote is, by contrast with what it was a decade or two ago, a remarkably sophisticated one, and one which soon should make itself felt in bringing about long-needed major reforms at the local, state, and national levels.

Further indication of the rising political influence of mexicanos was seen in 1961 in the appointment of Raymond Telles, first mayor of Mexican descent of El Paso, Texas, as Ambassador to Costa Rica by President Kennedy and in the election of Henry Gonzales to Congress from a Texas district.

Decline in Discrimination

While there has been a decline in discrimination against mexicanos in the Southwest, the traditional stereotype which the Anglos have held of the mexicano and the associated patterns of discrimination still show much vitality. Both the decline and persistence of discrimination are illustrated in the field of housing. It is often difficult to determine how far spatial concentration of a minority is due to their own inclination and their relative poverty and how far dominant discrimination is the cause. In a study of Latin-American housing in San Antonio, Dodson found "no rigid line of segregation, even though the vast majority of the Latin-American population is concentrated in one area."[39] And still further, "before the war, there were no Latins in North San Antonio, but now Latins are scattered through the area." On the other hand, Dodson found that "real estate agents while deny-

[39] Jack E. Dodson, "Housing in Two Texas Cities," in *Studies in Housing and Minority Groups,* eds. Nathan Glazer and Davis McEntire (Berkeley and Los Angeles: University of California Press, 1960), p. 93.

ing discrimination admit 'too many Mexicans can ruin a neighborhood.' and 'people can never tell about Mexican neighbors.' "[40] The same study finds a tendency for Latin-Americans to withdraw from situations where housing discrimination is sensed. The Negro minority in San Antonio was found to be more aggressive in seeking to enter new housing areas than were the mexicanos.

Union Participation

In the area of union participation there is ambivalence in regard to discrimination. In urban areas workers of Mexican lineage are being increasingly unionized but at the same time discriminated against as union members. A study of labor union practice in Los Angeles County clearly documents widespread discrimination in the upgrading of Mexicans, as well as Negroes, in the unions studied. The main thesis emerging was that improvement of the position of ethnics depends on the extent to which the power structure of the union permits ethnic pressure in its own behalf. In other words, Anglo members tend to discriminate against mexicano members so far as they can within the prevailing structure of their organization.[41]

Unionization of agricultural farm workers, still a major occupation for mexicanos, has been slow. The mexicanos have been apathetic, and there has been strong opposition from the grower interests and increasing mechanization. The earnings and working conditions of migrant workers, long known to students of social affairs to be exceptionally inadequate, were more broadly publicized in a television documentary[42] in 1960. Improvement in agricultural wages is believed by many people to have been retarded by the practice since 1951 of importing Mexican nationals on temporary visas under contract between the Mexican and American governments. Despite safeguards in the legislation designed to protect the wage level and the employment of available domestic farm workers, in effect this procedure has held down wages and militated against better working conditions in this occupation. In 1960 Congress shifted position by refusing to extend the expiring legislation beyond six months, as against the two year renewal which the grower interests had requested.[43]

Civil Liberties

Perhaps the most spectacular developments in the decline of discrimination have been in the area of civil liberties. Of this Sanchez writes for us:

---

[40] *Ibid.*, p. 97.
[41] Scott Greer, *Last Man In* (Glencoe, Ill.: The Free Press, 1959).
[42] "Harvest of Shame," Columbia Broadcasting System, November 25, 1960.
[43] The contract labor bill—Public Law 78—was passed by Congress in 1951 with a time limit which has been re-extended at each date of expiration up to 1961.

Even ten years ago, gross violations were common—in school segregation, in denial of service by businesses catering to the public, in segregation or denial of service in public parks and swimming pools, in police brutality, in exclusion from jury service, and in many related areas where discriminatory treatment takes more subtle forms and is just as real but more difficult to pin-point. And such violations of social justice were not restricted to any one state—for, in one form or another, they were to be found in California, Arizona, New Mexico, Colorado, and Texas.

Of what is probably the greatest significance, overt segregation of "Mexican" children in the public schools has been eliminated to all intents and purposes. The federal court cases in California, Arizona, and Texas—both those that came to trial and those which did not—have made it abundantly clear that American children of Mexican descent cannot be segregated in the public schools. Even where school authorities have sought to use pseudo-pedagogical reasons for separating "Anglos" from "Latins" the courts have either condemned the practices or have made it patent that the proof of the pudding would be in the eating, thus discouraging the use of subterfuges to cover up "racial" segregation. This break-through in school cases has served as precedent for the attack on segregation in other public services, with wide-spread success. In all areas there still remain many fronts on which the civil liberties battle will have to be fought. Recalcitrant communities (rather, recalcitrant governing boards) will seek "legal" ways to perpetuate segregation—in education the devices will include "neighborhood schools," "free choice" in the selection of a school, "ability grouping," "special" provision for migrant children, and the like. Most of these subterfuges will be the subject not of court action but of political action, as has been demonstrated already in a number of communities.

In the area of civil liberties, the *Pete Hernández Case* (Supreme Court of the United States, No. 406, October Term, 1953) has not drawn the attention is deserves, for it is significant not only for Spanish-Mexicans in the United States but for all groups that are treated as a class apart. This case, about a "Mexican" who was tried and sentenced by a jury in a county where "Mexicans" had never served on juries, was carried on up to the Supreme Court of the United States by lawyers of Mexican descent who were financed entirely by funds raised by people of Mexican descent. The unanimous judgment of the Court, written by the Chief Justice, finding for the plaintiff, included the following:

Throughout our history differences in race and color have defined easily identifiable groups which have at times required the aid of the courts in securing equal treatment under the laws. But community prejudices are not static, and from time to time other differences from the community norm may define other groups which need the same protection. Whether such a group exists within a community is a question of fact. When the existence of a distinct class is demonstrated, and it is further shown that the laws, as written or as applied, single out that class for different treatment not based on some reasonable classification, the guarantees of the Constitution have been violated. The Fourteenth Amendment is not directed solely against discrimination due to a "two-class theory"—that is, based upon differences between "white" and Negro.

This far-reaching decision, handed down two weeks before the *Brown v. Board of Education* (segregation of Negroes) case, laid down a principle on which the Americans of Mexican descent (as well as others) can rely for protection against discrimination and the mistreatment of their class in every area of official public endeavor. The Hernandez case served another cause of equal importance: it gave heart to the "Mexican" leadership, a leadership whose sights had been raised with their victory in the previous Mendez and Delgado (school segregation) cases.

Welfare

Change in the welfare picture with respect to mexicanos shows much the same situation as with acculturation and discrimination. Their welfare has improved, but the process is slow. The housing of Latin-Americans in San Antonio was found to be worse than that of the city's Negroes.[44] In a section which has long been a slum, "even some areas of newer housing have been ramshackle slums from the day they were constructed."[45] Specific area studies indicate that the health of the Spanish-speaking population is lower than among the general population of the Southwest. These tend to show undernourishment, a high infant mortality rate, and a greater prevalence of some infectious diseases, notably tuberculosis and dysentery.[46] As Sanchez puts it:

For all the progress that has been made, the mexicano of the Southwest is still the forgotten man. In terms of health, wealth, education, and welfare he is, with the possible exception of some of the Indians, the most disadvantaged—and, unlike the Indian, he has been left to pull himself up by his own bootstraps. His progress in recent years, his increase in stature, his dearly won growth, still has before it the challenge of his persistent nemesis: poverty.

HISPANOS

As we have noted, included in the population of the Southwest are those Spanish-speaking people who are descended from Spanish-Mexican lineage indigenous to the area at the time of the annexation, some of whose ancestry goes back to the sixteenth century. In view of the general statistical confusion concerning Americans of Latin ancestry, their numbers and proportion are difficult to establish. It is clear, however, that in New Mexico and southern Colorado a large proportion of the Spanish-speaking people derive from this hispano lineage as distinct from migrant Mexican lineage; in Texas and Southern California the situation is roughly reversed.

Hispanos in New Mexico

Hispanos comprise about half the population of the state. There are several counties where they number more than 80 per cent of the population. Both Spanish and English are official languages in the state. Compared with the obvious minority status of immigrant Mexicans in other southwestern states, hispanos do not appear at first to be a minority at all. They are all citizens, and no efforts are made by Anglos to deny them civic privileges. All over New Mexico there are hispanos who participate actively in politics, and in counties where they predominate heavily they frequently run the government. Free and equal access to all public places is accorded all ethnic and racial elements—the Indians and the relatively few immigrant Mexicans,

[44] Dodson, in *Studies in Minorities and Housing*, pp. 92–93.
[45] *Ibid.*
[46] Saunders, *Cultural Differences and Medical Care*, p. 76.

as well as the hispanos. In the entire Southwest region, New Mexico exhibits the least "racial" intolerance. The reason for New Mexico's distinctiveness in this connection appears to lie in the fact that through a long part of the state's history as United States territory, Anglos were a distinct numerical minority, and that, therefore, a pattern of racial tolerance was developed at the outset of Anglo-Hispano contact which has been strengthened by tradition. Anglo-hispano relations in New Mexico show an interesting similarity to haole (white) relations with the "colored" races in Hawaii (see Chapter 16). But beneath the surface of this substantial intergroup harmony lie subtle discriminations against the Spanish-speaking people of middle-class status and until recently the pitifully low welfare status of the lower-class, largely rural, hispanos.

Rural Hispanos: "Forgotten People"

In rural New Mexico live an hispano folk whom Sanchez calls "forgotten people."[47] Relatively isolated for generations, these rural hispanos developed a "folk" community life based on a subsistence, noncommercial agricultural economy organized along semicommunal lines. Over the years since annexation, the encroachment of Anglo "big business" agriculture whittled down their domain, so that their economic resources, coupled with their outmoded techniques, brought them to a pitifully low economic level. Their culture did not so much change in its traditional character; rather it deteriorated as a result of their unequal struggle to survive in a modern civilization. Their low welfare status was reflected in New Mexico's statistics on health and literacy. In 1930 the state had a death rate of 13.8, almost 3 more deaths per 1,000 population than the nation at large. Its percentage of illiteracy in 1930 was 13.3, placing it third from the lowest among the states.[48]

The native, rural hispano New Mexicans were not so much discriminated against, in the usual dominant-minority sense, as neglected. They were exploited in the impersonal ways characteristic of the free enterprise system where groups are unequally able to compete, but the Anglos did not assail their culture.

In the past ten years the welfare of hispanos has somewhat improved. Hispanos in New Mexican cities are becoming assimilated. According to Saunders:

Increasing numbers of young hispanos have migrated into the cities of New Mexico and Colorado, where they have married, found jobs, and moved in the direction of becoming indistinguishable in their life-ways from the Anglo population among whom they live. Their full assimilation is slowed somewhat by a continuing tendency to live in separate, largely hispano sections of the cities and for a preference toward endogamy. But even though thus slowed, assimilation is pro-

[47] George I. Sanchez, *Forgotten People* (Albuquerque: University of New Mexico Press, 1940).
[48] *Ibid.*, pp. 29–33.

ceeding rapidly and the cultural differences that have distinguished hispano and Anglo are diminishing.

Rural hispanos, while helped considerably by job opportunities opened through federal spending for defense projects (especially in central New Mexico—up and down the Rio Grande Valley), and by the rising level of prosperity of the nation in recent years, remain a somewhat disadvantaged population in terms of welfare status. Their incomes are lower, their health status less good, their education less complete than those of their urban counterparts. Selective migration has resulted in high proportions of the very young and the very old in some rural areas with the consequent need for institutionalized Anglo-type educational, health, and welfare services. The old hispano culture has proved remarkably resistant—Spanish is still the preferred language in the homes of many rural families—but it is gradually being eroded by the intrusions of Anglo technologies and Anglo institutions. The discovery of uranium and other new and valuable minerals and the increased exploitation of oil and gas resources have brought boom conditions and urban-type employment to some rural areas; but in the core area of hispano culture, the upper Rio Grande Valley, the rate of change, though steady, is slow, and there is much in the life of the area now that would be familiar to one who knew the area a quarter of a century ago.[49]

CLASS DIFFERENTIATION: SPANISH – AMERICANS

Our discussion of mexicanos thus far has dealt with them largely as a lower-class people in the general American system of class differentiation where, measured by objective criteria of income, occupation, and education, the large bulk of mexicanos would be located. The middle- and some upper-class persons of this ethnic background derive from two sources: those who come from families that have been in higher class status (largely hispanos), and those of recent immigrant background who have risen to higher class position, especially those in professional occupations. There is a tendency for people within these strata to identify themselves as "Spanish-Americans," to differentiate themselves from "Mexicans." In some instances "pure" Spanish descent (unmixed with Indian) is a real or alleged basis of distinction. The old-line families, although highly acculturated, take pride in retaining aspects of upper-class Spanish culture, being, for example, completely fluent in both English and Spanish. The more recent middle-class mexicanos tend more to seek complete Americanization. When these higher-status people live in communities with large immigrant Mexican populations, the relations of the Spanish-Americans with the latter are ambivalent. On the one hand, their attempt to be "Spanish," and therefore superior to Mexicans creates hostility between the two Latin elements; on the other hand, Anglo discrimination against both groups creates a bond of common interest. Thus the middle-class, Spanish-speaking person appears to occupy a status of marginality in some degree comparable to that of middle-class Jews in Northern cities.

[49] Lyle Saunders made these observations for the authors.

ASSIMILATION OR CULTURAL PLURALISM?

We shall observe that some minorities desire assimilation involving the loss of ethnic identity. As we have seen, the European immigrant peoples have substantially reached this position. In the case of the people of Mexican descent, several factors suggest the possibility of their adjustment to American society on a basis of distinctive ethnic identity, with co-ordinate rather than minority status: (1) The mexicanos are not yet so far along the assimilative process as to preclude this outcome. (2) There is the example of co-ordinate ethnic pluralism in New Mexico. (3) There is a current tendency for the various Spanish-Mexican subgroups to co-operate in recognition of their common identification in *la raza* (see below). (4) These people are located close to (and in the case of the hispano still in) the homeland of their ancestors. The further questions remaining are, Will Anglos accept mexicanos on this basis? And will subsequent descendants of mexicanos want to remain mexicanos? Observing that students and writers frequently distinguish between the hispano, the Spanish-American, and the Mexican-Americans, Sanchez writes,

In the last analysis, these are all Indo-Hispanic peoples, Spanish-Mexican peoples, with all that that implies in terms of their bio-social make-up. Furthermore, these peoples, in New Spain and then in Mexico and in the United States, have been consistently disadvantaged peoples, much in the same boat as to socioeconomic circumstances. These common antecedents have given a fundamental sameness to their culture and, as a consequence, to their behavior. Therefore, while the hispano of Santa Fe is a mexicano with a tradition somewhat different from that of the mexicano of Laredo or of Fort Collins or of Fresno or of Tucson, and each has backgrounds that are different from that of each of the others, they are all mexicanos—they all belong to *la raza,* that vague but very real community that has nothing to do with nationality or patriotism or race.

The recent past has been eloquently illustrative of this little-appreciated fact. One cannot view developments throughout the Southwest (and in the Mexican-American communities in such places as Chicago) without marveling at the similarity and, in the last analysis, the cohesiveness of these peoples. Probably the most dynamic and popular leaders of the Mexican-Americans in California are a New Mexican and a Coloradoan. In New Mexico, a Texas-Mexican has done wonders in rallying the hispanos for much-needed reforms in government. In Texas, a New Mexican has been in the middle of the state Latin-American leadership. The American G.I. Forum of the United States, composed almost entirely of veterans of Mexican descent, a powerful force for good in about twenty states, is the creature of a tremendously energetic and a selfless Texas-Mexican medical doctor. These men and their work attest to the commonalty of the people of Mexican descent in the United States.

One of the most persistent problems arises out of the peculiar status of these Spanish-Mexican peoples in the United States. They are really not immigrants in the same sense that the Italians, Irish, and others like them in the United States are immigrants. In the Southwest, certainly, the Spanish-Mexican is in his traditional home. His Indian antecedents, of course, give him a status very different from that of the European immigrant. Bolstering this is the fact that his Spanish ancestors were here since the sixteenth century and that this vast region, the Southwest, was a part of New Spain until a little over a hundred years ago. The Mexico-United States boundary meant little until some thirty-five years ago, and the freedom of movement across that boundary has become virtually a traditional and much-exercised right—one, unfortunately, exploited by the employers of cheap labor.

This peculiar status of these Spanish-speaking peoples has made them unusually resistant to the superficial features of Americanization. Under no compulsion to repudiate the "old country" and to become 150 per cent American, they have clung tenaciously to their language and to other manifestations of their sense of identity. This in spite of widespread blind, misguided pressures by schools, employers, news media, and the like. In some public schools, children are still punished if they speak Spanish on the school grounds; and it is the exception, rather than the rule that by all reason should prevail, when a school system seeks to capitalize on the Spanish vernacular of its children. The pressures have been so great that, on occasion, a Spanish-Mexican leader has sought to champion the obliteration of this basic cultural heritage of his people. Fortunately, these instances have been rare and, in most cases, the proponent has recanted. One of the most encouraging of recent developments has been a conscious and vocal resistance to these pressures. This is in part the result of the action of the leaders, of whom there are many more with good education; in part this results from the increased maturity and sophistication of the entire society, which daily appreciates more the value of foreign languages; and in part the slowly spreading realization among educators that, instead of being a disastrous handicap, the Spanish mother-tongue of these Americans of Mexican descent can be transformed into a decided asset.

The progress noted in the language field, slow though it still is, may be seen reflected when other features of Spanish-Mexican culture are considered. Southwestern history, as now presented to the student and the public, is much less chauvinistic than it was a few years ago—though, for instance, in Texas, Cabeza de Vaca still doesn't rank with Jim Bowie and, in New Mexico, Kit Carson far overshadows Father José Antonio Martínez. The "anti-Mexican" climate has been much reduced in the past ten years.

Whether the mexicanos will retain cultural identity or become merged into the Anglo population depends largely, according to Simmons, on how the Anglos continue to react to the mexicanos. "Mexicans want to be accepted as full members of the larger society, but do not want to achieve this at the cost of giving up completely their cultural heritage." If full acceptance of Mexicans by Anglo-Americans is contingent on the complete disappearance of cultural differences, it will not be accorded in the foreseeable future.[50]

TOPICS FOR PROJECTS AND DISCUSSION

1. Do you think the story of the adjustment of Mexican immigrants to the United States would have been any different if the immigrants had migrated to the

[50] Simmons, "The Mutual Images and Expectations of Anglo-Americans and Mexican-Americans," p. 298.

great industrial regions of the Midwest and Northeast during the twenties? Develop your answer.
2. Often Spanish-speaking Americans prefer to live in communities where there is no Mexican immigrant group. What reasons would you give for this preference?
3. Do you think the Southwest as a region would be more prosperous or less prosperous if there had been no Mexican immigration during this century?
4. What reasons would you suggest for the fact that some employers prefer Mexican nationals to Mexican-Americans better adjusted to life in the States?
5. How significant are the relations of Anglos to persons of Mexican origin in the United States for Pan-American solidarity in international affairs? Discuss.

SUGGESTED READING

Clark, Margaret. *Health in the Mexican-American Culture: A Community Study.* Berkeley and Los Angeles: University of California Press, 1959.
>   *The first part of this field study provides a general picture of a Mexican-American community in northern California; a concluding part deals specifically with health.*

Gamio, Manuel. *The Mexican Immigrant: His Life Story.* Chicago: University of Chicago Press, 1931.
>   *Analysis of the adjustment of Mexican immigrants to the United States in the decade 1920–1930; personal life stories.*

Hadley, Eleanor M. "A Central Analysis of the Wetback Problem," *Law and Contemporary Problems,* 1956, 21: 334–357.
>   *Analyzes the problem of Mexican agricultural workers in relation to the national immigration problem.*

McWilliams, Carey. *North from Mexico.* Philadelphia: J. B. Lippincott Co., 1949. Peoples of America Series.
>   *Covers the history of the relations between Anglos and people of Mexican descent living in the United States; a short, popularly written book.*

Sanchez, George I. "Pachucos in the Making," *Common Ground,* Vol. 4, Autumn, 1943, 4: 13–20.
>   *The writer finds "Pachucos" the product of Anglo discrimination and documents extensively the practice of discrimination against Spanish-speaking Americans.*

Saunders, Lyle. *Cultural Differences and Medical Care: The Case of the Spanish Speaking People of the Southwest.* New York: Russell Sage Foundation, 1954.
>   *A comprehensive analysis of the culture, social organization, and welfare of the Southwest's Spanish-speaking population. Contains also a useful appendix on the demographic characteristics of this population.*

Simmons, Ossie G. "The Mutual Images and Expectations of Anglo-Americans and Mexican-Americans," *Daedalus: Journal of American Academy of Arts and Sciences,* Spring, 1961, 90: 286–299.
>   *Analysis of the stereotypes held by the Anglo-Americans and Mexican-Americans of each other, based on a community study of a south Texas city.*

Taylor, Paul S. *An American-Mexican Frontier.* Chapel Hill: University of North Carolina Press, 1932.
>   *A study of Anglo-Mexican relations in a Texas border county. The most sociologically oriented of Taylor's specific community studies.*

7

The Puerto Ricans on the Mainland

Since the annexation of Puerto Rico after the Spanish-American War, there has been a stream of migration to the continental United States, rising and falling according to circumstances in both areas. At the close of World War II there was a sharp upswing in the volume of immigration, which has varied from less than 30,000 to over 50,000 a year since then, responding to fluctuations in economic conditions and employment opportunities.[1] On December 31, 1959, there were an estimated 903,000 Puerto Ricans living in the United States, two thirds Puerto Rican born and one-third born here of Puerto Rican parents. Three-quarters of the entire number were living in New York City. There are colonies of some 40,000 each in the Chicago metropolitan area, the Philadelphia metropolitan area, and northern New Jersey; up to 10,000 in upper New York State, Hawaii, California, and Connecticut; and smaller numbers throughout industrial centers of New England, Pennsylvania, Ohio, Michigan, Wisconsin, and Miami, Florida.[2]

PUERTO RICO AND THE UNITED STATES

Before 1932 the federal government assumed a laissez-faire attitude to-

[1] Clarence Senior, *Strangers—Then Neighbors: From Pilgrims to Puerto Ricans* (New York: Freedom Books, 1961), p. 22.
[2] *Ibid.*, pp. 60–61.

ward the island's economy, with the result that American investment in the development of Puerto Rico came from mainland private capital. The extent of absentee interest in the Puerto Rican economy was summarized in 1930 as follows:

. . . Sugar is 60 per cent absentee-controlled; fruit is 31 per cent, or more; tobacco is 85 per cent; banks are 60 per cent; railroads 60 per cent, or more; public utilities, 50 per cent; and steamship lines, approximately 100 per cent. There is no important source of wealth that is not partially in the hands of outsiders, and in some instances, such as steamships, outsiders control the entire business. Any estimate of Porto Rico dependence on absentees which places the total at less than 60 per cent of the island's wealth is certainly too low. Not all of the industries belong to absentees, but those which do not are so indebted to continental banks as to be virtually in their possession. Not all of the good land is in the hands of outsiders, but a large portion of it is, and much of the remainder is heavily mortgaged. And finally, there is that type of dependence on absentees which Porto Rico suffers, because of her long dependence on a monopolizing mother country, the necessity of importing vast quantities of food, clothing, machinery, chemicals and drugs. The control of the absentee is all but complete and with the aid of the Coastwise Shipping Act and the American Tariff bids fair to absorb all of the profitable enterprise.[3]

Under Franklin D. Roosevelt's early administrations, governmental effort at reorienting the Puerto Rican economy with more regard for the welfare of the islanders themselves was undertaken. The Puerto Rico Relief Administration was succeeded by the Puerto Rico Reconstruction Administration, which undertook irrigation projects, new highways, new schools, new houses and other development efforts. In 1942 Pattee said "There is little doubt that the present administration . . . postpones, at least, a collapse in Puerto Rican economy."[4]

"The Puerto Rico Reconstruction Administration . . . made definite progress but did not achieve that complete reform that was so desperately needed."[5] An indigenous reform program developed from the emergence of a new political party on the island, the Partido Popular Democrato. By somewhat faltering steps, democratic political institutions have been established, with increasing degrees of self-government permitted. On November 2, 1948, Puerto Rico elected its own governor for the first time. Except for the Presidential appointment of the auditor and supreme court justices, and for the power of the United States Congress to annul any law passed by the Insular Legislature (something which has not yet been done), Puerto Rico has attained complete self-government.

[3] W. Bailey Diffie and Justine Whitfield Diffie, *Porto Rico: A Broken Pledge* (New York: The Vanguard Press, 1931), pp. 135–136. By permission.
[4] Richard Pattee, "The Puerto Ricans," *Annals of the American Academy of Political and Social Science*, Sept. 1942, 223: 52.
[5] *Ibid.*, p. 52.

Operation Bootstrap

Under self-government Puerto Rico launched "Operation Bootstrap," a development program to raise the levels of living on the island. In twenty years these efforts of the Puerto Rican government have raised the per capita income on the island 307 per cent. The program has concentrated on two areas of economic improvement. The first has been diversification of agriculture. Many of the large sugar areas have been made available for smaller landowners under the "500 acre law," which had been on the books since 1900 but was not enforced. Many new crops have been introduced, and cattle-raising and dairying have become important sources of income. The second effort has been to encourage industry. By February, 1960, some 600 new factories had been established, creating jobs for 45,000 people. The government aided in the training of personnel by building factories for rent at reasonable rates, and by other measures. In 1956 the income from manufacturing surpassed the income from agriculture for the first time. Puerto Rico has surpassed every Latin-American country in increase in per capita income. The social aspects of Operation Bootstrap have included a major public health effort and marked achievements in education. Although Spanish is the primary language, English is a required subject from the first grade on. Now almost the only illiterates are older people. The number of school rooms, teachers, and pupils has more than doubled; higher education has tripled; extension services in education have been developed; and the Division of Community Education has become a focus of interest and training for workers from many countries engaged in development programs.

Despite these advances, in 1958–59 unemployment on the island averaged 90,000: 14 per cent of the labor force. A large proportion of this has been and is being drained off into the labor market of the continental United States.[6]

The Islanders

While from the practical point of view of distinguishing islanders from mainlanders, Puerto Ricans often refer to themselves as Puerto Ricans and to mainlanders as Americans, they nevertheless go on to indicate that they consider themselves members of the American nation. They are American citizens, and as such have unrestricted migration.

As a sociocultural group, the Puerto Ricans at the time of annexation by the United States, had adopted and adapted Spanish institutions and Spanish culture to form their own variant of Latin-American civilization. Into the composition of the population had gone white, Negro, and Indian strains. The social structure was that of a plantation economy in which a small upper class, chiefly of landed proprietors, was distinguished from a peasantry, some of it on plantations, some in mountain villages.

Since the abolition of slavery in the island there has been no civic and

[6] Data on Operation Bootstrap from Senior, *Strangers—Then Neighbors*, pp. 55–59.

public discrimination in Puerto Rico because of race. None of the forms of inter-racial conflict or violence which have been found on the mainland has occurred. This formal absence of discrimination is similar to other patterns in Latin cultures in the Western hemisphere. Furthermore, the population of Puerto Rico presents so wide a range of combinations of physiognomic features that a pattern of dominant-minority relations based on "race" would be difficult to maintain.

Although Puerto Rico is often cited for its absence of prejudice based on "color" visibility, and intermarriage between people of different racial heritages has long been recognized, there is some consciousness of differences. Taken together with the factors of wealth and education color may affect status. "Whites"—very light-skinned people—are at the top if they also have wealth and education. Very dark-skinned people are at the bottom unless they have wealth and education. They are then sometimes designated as "trigueño" (brunet) as a circumvention for the term "Negro," or they borrow the French usage, "a man of color." "Indios" are an intermediary group; "grifo" designates the light-skinned, kinky-haired individual.

Students of Puerto Rican society indicate that in its more subtle and less explicit aspects prejudice and discrimination based on color visibility are widespread. Maxine Gordon writes, "We maintain . . . that no Puerto Rican is unaware of his position in Puerto Rican society as determined by the color of his skin."[7] In support of this position the writer cites the terminology by which the varying degrees of Negroid-appearing people are designated in informal conversation; folklore which makes much of whether or not one has a Negro ancestor; first-hand knowledge of social discrimination based on color at the university; and evidence that while intermarriage is outwardly tolerated social discrimination nevertheless follows for certain kinds of mixed marriages. Armstrong expresses a somewhat similar view, although disclaiming systematic study of the subject.[8] President Truman's Civil Rights Committee reported discrimination in the employment of Negroes on the island. The perception of Negro ancestry has a different meaning, however, to a Puerto Rican than to the average mainland American.

The milder form of color prejudice and discrimination on the island has been influenced by three factors. (1) It is in part a reflection of class prejudice, since Negroes in general occupy lower economic positions. (2) It is in part derivative from Spanish colonial influence and slavery. (3) Race consciousness as a determiner of status has increased as a result of the affiliation of Puerto Rico with the United States. Mainland white tourists tend to project their mainland attitudes toward Negroes on Puerto Ricans. During

---

[7] Maxine W. Gordon, "Cultural Aspects of Puerto Rico's Race Problem," *American Sociological Review*, June, 1950, 15: 382.

[8] Robert G. Armstrong, "Intergroup Relations in Puerto Rico," *Phylon*, Sept., 1949, 10: 220–224.

World War II, Army camps on the island segregated Puerto Rican troops, and the Navy would not take Puerto Ricans.[9]

Knowledge of the mainland reaction towards migrants to the United States also affects the island viewpoint. Although the mainland influence which has increased race consciousness is resented by the islander, it produces ambivalent reactions. It promotes, on the one hand, a tendency for those Puerto Ricans who appear "white" to draw apart from those who do not, both on the island and on the mainland. On the other hand, the dark Puerto Rican migrant to the mainland may choose to make his adjustment in the Negro community, especially among Negroes from the Caribbean region.

The Puerto Rican Journey

The Puerto Rican migration has been the heaviest foreign language migration to the Atlantic states since before World War I. Up to 1947 and 1948, a large proportion of the Puerto Ricans who came to the continent were contracted for agricultural and domestic labor. There was much unethical traffic in human beings until the island legislature enacted legislation to control and correct the situation. Offices of the Commonwealth of Puerto Rico, set up to assist migrants, were established in New York and Chicago. At present the Migration Division of the Department of Labor of the Commonwealth of Puerto Rico maintains offices in San Juan and in twelve mainland cities. The division's personnel work in approximately one hundred mainland towns and cities each year.[10] Co-operation has also been established between the Puerto Rico Employment Service and the United States Employment Service. Since Puerto Ricans are citizens, job orders from American industry pass through the United States Employment Service to the Puerto Rico Employment Service when qualified local workers are not available. Employers may recruit labor in Puerto Rico directly only with the approval of the Puerto Rican government, and only when a legitimate order is cleared through regular United States Employment Service channels.[11]

In 1948 the Columbia University study[12] of Puerto Ricans in New York City found that 85 per cent of the immigrants had quit jobs in Puerto Rico to come to the United States. What they sought was not so much any job but a *better* job. The data on age of immigrants also suggest that the principal motive for migration has been economic. In 1958 a total of 73 per cent of the Puerto Ricans migrating were between 15 and 44 years of age. Only 8 per cent were over forty-five, and 19 per cent were under 14.[13]

[9] Gordon, "Cultural Aspects," p. 387.
[10] Senior, *Strangers—Then Neighbors*, p. 60.
[11] *Ibid.*, p. 61.
[12] C. Wright Mills, Clarence Senior, and Rose Kohn Goldsen, *The Puerto Rican Journey* (New York: Harper & Brothers, 1950).
[13] Petroamerica Pagande Colon, *Migration Trends* (New York: Commonwealth of Puerto Rico, Migration Division of the Department of Labor), May, 1959, pp. 7–8.

Other benefits, too, are sought. Education is thought by many to be better on the mainland, and the ultimate opportunity for improved status is encouraging. There are some for whom life in the home village has become unsatisfactory because of social situations. On the mainland, health and security benefits are easily available. Then there is the glamor of New York. And there are kinship ties to those who have already migrated.

One aspect of the Puerto Rican migration is the ease and frequency with which the migrants may return to Puerto Rico. Although it was also a feature of some of the older migrations to have a proportion of migrants who viewed their sojourn in the United States as a way to improve their economic circumstances, after which they would return home, for Puerto Ricans, because of the nearness to the island and their citizenship status, there is more turnover in population. There is also a considerable amount of seasonal labor, principally for agricultural work. Those who do establish permanent residence and intend to become part of mainland life still keep ties in the island and take frequent vacations "at home" when they can afford it.

Of the current migration, Senior reports that 40 to 45 per cent of the new arrivals speak English, but many are timid about speaking it with strangers. In 1957, a survey found that 63 per cent of the Puerto Rican families living in New York City speak English at home. Those who come from rural areas experience more difficulty in the cities than those who have had urban experience. Those who come from mountainous areas tend to be individualistic, while those from cane plantations are more accustomed to co-operative group actions.[14]

Puerto Rican labor is vital to the economic future of some American industries. The Harvard University study of the New York metropolitan region points out:

> The rate of Puerto Rican migration to New York is one of the factors that determine how long and how successfully the New York metropolitan region will retain industries which are under competitive pressure from other areas.
> To the extent that some of these industries have hung on in the area they have depended upon recently arrived Puerto Rican workers, who have entered the job market of the New York area at the rate of about 13,000 each year. But the New York area is beginning to lose its unique position. . . . [T]his stream of migration is now spreading to other mainland areas as well, and the spread promises to accelerate.[15]

The character of the migration has been changing. In 1948, 82 per cent of the migrants were from urban areas. With the industrialization and development of white-collar occupations on the island the proportion of urban Puerto Ricans coming to the mainland has declined. By 1958, 75 per cent of

[14] Senior, *Strangers—Then Neighbors,* pp. 63–64.
[15] *Ibid.,* p. 65.

the migrants came from rural background. This has brought a large un-skilled labor force to American cities. As of 1957 more than 50 per cent of the employed male heads of families of the Puerto Ricans in New York were in unskilled and semi-skilled occupations, another 22 per cent were service workers, 16 per cent were enther skilled craftsmen or foremen, 6 per cent were clerical and sales workers, and 3 per cent were professional, mana-gerial, and technical.[16]

THE PUERTO RICANS IN NEW YORK CITY

Migrating Puerto Ricans initially concentrated in a section of Manhattan just south and east of Harlem. This district is referred to by Puerto Ricans as "El Barrio Latino," and by the New York press as Spanish Harlem. With the heavy influx since World War II, Puerto Ricans have spread all over the city creating different patterns of neighborhood relationships in different situations. Thus on Manhattan's West Side the avenues have large middle-class and upper middle-class apartment houses occupied by "continental whites," while the side streets are filled with Puerto Rican families crowded into converted former private residences that have been abandoned as single-family dwellings in the changing pattern of city and suburban living. Here social class as well as cultural barriers create social distance, and often tension, between mainlanders and migrants.

In New York's Lower East Side, housing conditions are often not as bad for the migrants because of extensive urban renewal in this district. Further-more because of its historic role as an immigrant neighborhood, the Lower East Side is one of the best serviced and most intercultural subcommunities in New York City.

Many of the longer established Puerto Rican families are, like other New Yorkers, going to the suburbs, and to the less crowded boroughs of the city. In the deteriorating sections of the city the newcomers have found places in the slums with other slum dwellers.[17]

Although the Puerto Ricans are not concentrated in a single ecological subcommunity, they are nevertheless, to a large extent a community in identity. Puerto Ricans are pridefully conscious of their Spanish cultural heritage. They usually refer to themselves as Hispanos or Latinos, linking themselves with other New World Spanish cultural groups.

The Hispano group includes Puerto Ricans, their descendants who may or may not be Spanish-speaking individuals, and also Spanish-speaking persons from Latin America and Spain. . . . Sources of solidarity and bonds of understandings

[16] *A Summary of Facts and Figures* (New York: Commonwealth of Puerto Rico, Migra-tion Division of the Department of Labor, January, 1959), p. 17.
[17] For a vivid description of the ecological distribution of Puerto Ricans in New York City, see Christopher Rand, *The Puerto Ricans* (New York: Oxford University Press, 1958), Ch. 1.

among Hispanos are partly derived from the historic common general cultural traditions of the peoples who are considered Hispanos. But, partly, too, they are a reaction to the position of the group as a minority in New York.[18]

Puerto Ricans gain on several counts from this sense of identity. It clearly differentiates them from American Negroes and is seen as protection from the threat of the racial attitudes of mainlanders. Among other Spanish-speaking people, Puerto Ricans gain status by being American citizens. According to Padilla, members of other groups of Spanish cultural origin often claim to be Puerto Rican when they are not.[19] Identity born of language and culture is consciously reinforced by symbolic and ceremonial efforts. Rand describes a Columbus Day celebration in which wreaths were laid at the statue of "the Spanish Columbus" in Central Park (as distinguished from the other statue of the presumably Italian Columbus in Columbus Circle). One placard at this demonstration read

WE DO NOT KNOW WHERE

HE WAS BORN BUT WE DO KNOW

HIM AS A CITIZEN OF SPAIN

AND AS THE ADMIRAL

OF THE SPANISH EXPEDITION

IN WHICH THE NEW WORLD

WAS FOUNDED[20]

There are losses also from this sense of identity, for it is not strong enough to solve all the problems confronting Puerto Ricans in New York. The young person of Puerto Rican descent is subjected not only to conflicts of values and behavior patterns that persist in modified and transformed modes between hispano and mainland culture, but he must seek status and approval both within and outside the hispano group. Furthermore, the dominant culture presents no uniform set of standards in the variety of status and ethnic traditions in metropolitan New York.[21]

Visibility

Most Puerto Ricans, especially the poorer ones, are biologically or culturally visible. Padilla has made a chart which shows the differences in the way in which biological visibility is perceived by mainlanders, by other Puerto Ricans, and by individuals with regard to themselves.[22]

[18] Elena Padilla, *Up From Puerto Rico* (New York: Columbia University Press, 1958), pp. 47–48.
[19] *Ibid.*, p. 11.
[20] Rand, *The Puerto Ricans*, p. 158.
[21] Padilla, *Up From Puerto Rico*, pp. 89 ff.
[22] Padilla, *Up From Puerto Rico*, p. 76. By permission.

REFERENCES OF OUTGROUP (MAINLANDERS)	REFERENCES OF INGROUP (HISPANOS)	REFERENCES OF INDIVIDUALS DESCRIBING SELF
White	White	White
	Trigueno Hispano	Hispano
	Grifo	Trigueno
	INTERMEDIATES*	
Puerto Rican	Negro	De Color (of color)
or	Trigueno	Trigueno
Mixed	Indio	Hispano
	Grifo	Indio
	Hispano	
Negro	Negro	De Color
	Trigueno	Trigueno
	Indio	Hispano
	Grifo	Indio
	Hispano	

* A category to include the numerous racial terms used by Puerto Ricans, used by C. Wright Mills, Clarence Senior, and Rose Kohn Goldsen, in *The Puerto Rican Journey* (New York: Harper, 1950).

This table shows us that no individual in the group of migrants studied designates himself a Negro. Neither will he call himself Grifo. The Hispano group, however, may call him either of these, with implied derogation. When appearance is predominantly "white," the outgroup, mainlanders, may accept the individual as white where both Hispano individuals and the Hispano group will make some differentiation.

Cultural visibility is especially marked among new migrants. Even without hearing the rapid Spanish chatter which goes on in the streets of New York, lower-class Puerto Ricans can usually be identified by their dress, especially the women. Styles favor full Spanish skirts in bright colors. Movement is free, swinging, and graceful. In old-fashioned Puerto Rican families little girls' ears are pierced in babyhood and toddlers will wear earrings. Young men often affect bright jackets and shirts.

Acculturation

The value system of Puerto Ricans shares much with other Spanish cultures. The importance of *dignitad* (self-possession, pride) is paramount in the conception of the ideal person. The culture and social system are male dominated, with strong emphasis on proving masculinity. A man must be, ideally, stable and strong, sexually virile, honest and reliable in work, aggressive in combat, and sensitive to honor. He is logical and can reason. Women, on the other hand, are frail, illogical, and easily deluded. Therefore women must be guarded and accompanied by the responsible males of the family.[23]

The human condition is such, in the value scheme, that man is buffeted by many forces. Fatalism underlies much of the thinking, operating sometimes to lower individual aspirations, or quite usually to explain failure and disappointment. Time is infinite. Hurry robs one of dignity; thus commitments within time have wide latitude. Gaiety is valued, singing and dancing enjoyed by all. Emotional expressiveness in word and gesture are the norm. Puerto Ricans sometimes refer to dominants on the mainland as "the cold people."[24]

These values are carried out in the institutional patterns. Within the island social structure the family and the extended kinship form the dominant institutional configuration. Obligations of kinship are strong, as are those of village ties, which for rural families have been the *locus* of the extended family. Male virility is honored by the evidence of many children. Girls are watched over by their mothers before marriage and women by their husbands and mothers-in-law after marriage. The marriage age is early in rural Puerto Rico, often soon after the onset of puberty. "Consensual marriage," like the common-law marriage of our own rural colonial heritage, is acceptable whether or not it is ever formally sanctioned by church or state.

Economically, the segment of Puerto Rican society which migrates largely represents labor or small enterprise (shopkeepers). Women have a tradition of fine needlework, and Puerto Ricans as a whole seem to have manual dexterity. To the degree that they fulfill the expectations of their own traditional culture they are workmanlike and reliable in their jobs, as is testified by some mainland employers.[25] Many Puerto Ricans have shown business and entrepreneurial skill.

Politically, Puerto Ricans are only beginning to participate in modern democratic ways. Old respect for authority and position invest the bureaucrat or the teacher with honor.

Most Puerto Ricans are Roman Catholic. For many this is a nominal identification with only a tenuous discipline exercised by the affiliation. In New York City, a minority of Puerto Ricans, perhaps 20 per cent, have been attracted to Protestant Evangelical groups. Store-front churches have sprung up, and the Penticostal Holiness sect and Jehovah's Witnesses have been successful proselitizers. Some of the poorest stratum have embraced various Asiatic and Caribbean cults.[26]

Puerto Ricans come from a society which until recently had very marked stratification, with little chance for mobility. In migration the old criteria of

[23] J. Mayone Stycos, *Family and Fertility in Puerto Rico: A Study of the Low Income Group* (New York: Columbia University Press, 1955), pp. 28–34.
[24] Rand, *The Puerto Ricans*, p. 97.
[25] *Ibid.*, p. 146.
[26] *Ibid.*, pp. 20, 117.

status are weakened, though not destroyed. However, a new precedence is given to the united, stable family ("familia unida"). A family of this sort usually consists of several biologically related nuclear families which recognize mutual obligations toward each other. In the new environment it is the symbol of stability and respectability.[27] Income, occupation, and level of education affect a person's status, as do occupational position and familial connections in Puerto Rico before migration.[28] A small percentage of Puerto Ricans have established themselves as members of middle-class dominant society, or as members of the world of celebrities in the arts and sports.[29]

Status in the hispano group in New York is otherwise largely related to "old residents," the "born and/or brought up in New York," and "new migrants." Old residents, unless they are middle-class and educated, may not speak much English, having considered themselves too old to learn—"that's for the children"—but they have adapted in other ways, survived, acquired know-how, offered advice and help to those who came later. They consider new migrants "very old-fashioned people," since the newcomers are often closer to the older folk beliefs and cultural ways of the island. Many old migrants are members of a united family, whereas newcomers may be single men, nuclear families, unmarried young women ("daughters of family"—that is, virgins) "women" (mujeres)—single women about whom there has been some scandal in the village and who it is hoped can start over again in the new environment, or disorganized persons.[30]

Those brought up in New York do not regard Puerto Rico as home. They are oriented to mainland life as they understand it and speak English among themselves. Women value men of this group—"he is a good man, he was brought up here," which often means he will help around the house. The women brought up here are viewed more dubiously, since it is often felt that they have departed too much from the traditional confinement to the household and submissive domesticity.

Obstacles to Acculturation

There are a number of areas which become focal points of attention in adjustments between traditional acceptable ways of the island and the dominant norms of the mainland. Adjustment has been eased to some extent by the fact that the people of the older urban migration were familiar with public education, wage systems, large hospitals, mass communication, and the electoral process. New migrants have increasingly had experience with these forms as a result of the development of the island. Rand mentions an informant in Chicago who felt that the Puerto Ricans had an advantage

[27] Padilla, *Up From Puerto Rico*, p. 115.
[28] *Ibid.*, Ch. 2.
[29] Senior, *Strangers—Then Neighbors*, p. 59.
[30] Padilla, *Up From Puerto Rico*, p. 58.

over the Mexicans in that city because of the longer exposure, in the island, to certain key structures of mainland society, as well as to entrepreneurial values.[31]

The most obvious problem of acculturation is language. Employers complain of a labor force with which they can communicate only through one or two bilingual members, and they are not sure whether or not directions are being communicated accurately. The Employment Service finds trouble placing workers with little English.[32] The problem for the schools is acute, since hundreds of children enter the public school system with little or no English. The language problem cannot be divorced, however, from the central cultural value of *dignitad*. Many Peurto Ricans understand more English than mainlanders realize, but their pride prevents them from speaking English if they do not speak it well.

The problem of punctuality is acute for the migrants from rural background, who have not had the experience of industrial society, and for women who have been confined to a limited sphere of activity.

Since the family is the dominant institution in the island culture, it is in family patterns and roles that many adjustments are required. Consensual marriage is not recognized in New York State, which outlawed, by statute, common-law marriage nearly half a century ago. Thus the mother of children born in a consensual marriage is ineligible for welfare benefits which might accrue to her on the disability, death, or desertion of a husband in a registered marriage. The custom of early marriage comes in conflict with the New York State age of consent, which is sixteen with parents' permission and eighteen without. The role of women in traditional hispano culture is often at variance with the expectations for women in institutional structures. Independent participation in church and school activities may be denied a Puerto Rican woman by a conservative husband or by the extended kinship group. One finds the phenomenon of a husband having to take a leave of absence from his work to take his wife and children to the clinic, "since she could not go alone." Yet, because New York City is the center for the needle trades, and needlework has been a traditional skill among the women, many Puerto Ricans have found employment in the factories of the garment district and in the sewing rooms of custom dress shops. Often a woman in the garment industry can earn more money than the men of her family, a fact which creates conflict of roles within the family.

The American ideal of the nuclear family, if adhered to, often can neither provide security nor assure authority. Roles of parents and children become confused without the support of kinship and hispano community approval. Nevertheless, Puerto Ricans are criticized by mainlanders for kinship obligations that take precedence over work or school commitments.

Economically, Puerto Rican acculturation is retarded by the low skill level

[31] Rand, *The Puerto Ricans,* p. 144.
[32] *Ibid.,* pp. 142 ff.

characteristic of many migrants. According to Rand, there has been some evidence that some Puerto Ricans have not accepted the possibility of moving on to more highly skilled jobs, and are content to remain at the level they have learned.[33]

In politics Puerto Ricans have been handicapped by the requirement for voters to pass literacy tests in English. Since most Puerto Ricans in New York read the Spanish daily papers, many people feel that literacy tests should be given in Spanish if, as it is claimed, the issue is literacy and not literacy-in-English. The participation of Puerto Ricans in city politics has been relatively slight, although it has increased in the last decade. Since the political machine has not the coherent power it had in the beginning of the century when the immigrant vote was wooed, there have only been sporadic efforts to reach the Puerto Ricans, and this usually by a factional group of one or another political party. On the whole, Pureto Ricans have not benefited in New York politics.

The role of the church, functioning primarily as it does in the sphere of personal belief and loyalty, and in welfare, is a point of conflict for the migrant in two areas. In education, parochial schools in New York City have not had the space or staff to accept the non-English-speaking child. Many middle-class Puerto Ricans, or those who are conservative, prefer parochial education, especially for the upper grades. They feel that discipline is better, that respect for the teacher is maintained, and they approve of the segregation of the sexes. It is the feeling of organizations concerned with public education in New York that Puerto Rican children with language or disciplinary problems are "dumped" on the public schools, that the best group is syphoned off to the parochial schools, thereby helping to maintain a derogatory image of Puerto Ricans and driving more middle-class families among the mainlanders to use private schools or to move to the suburbs. The second area of conflict within the institutional pattern of religion is that of family planning. Because the marriage age is low and because there are cultural values related to fertility, many young families find themselves with numerous children before they are thirty. The government of Puerto Rico has had a public policy of fostering family limitation, but this is contrary to the established doctrine of the Roman Catholic Church. On the mainland, health and welfare agencies, reform groups, and often the hispano mothers themselves are interested in smaller-sized families, especially in the situations of low income and poor housing.[34]

Discrimination

New York State has statutory prohibition of discrimination in employment. New York City has a law prohibiting discrimination in housing. No other place in the United States, probably, gives as much lip service to the ideal

---

[33] Rand, *The Puerto Ricans*, p. 145.
[34] *Ibid.*, p. 83.

of non-discrimination against religious, ethnic or racial minorities. Nevertheless, there is much discrimination through evasion of laws and in the areas of daily living not covered by special codes against it.

Since Puerto Ricans form such a large part of New York's unskilled labor force, they have found employment readily in the lowest paying jobs. Discrimination at the lower levels of the occupational structure seems to be linked with the factors of the language handicap, union policies, and traditional "corners" on certain types of employment that have been held by some other ethnic group. The old-line unions in the building trades and on the waterfront have succeeded fairly well in keeping out Puerto Ricans. However, other unions—in the garment trade, the hotel workers and the retail and department store union—have had anti-discrimination policies. Union control of a shop's choice of workers through hiring halls has sometimes been used to break the hold of a particular ethnic group on a shop by forcing mixed crews on the employers.[35] In the white-collar field, public employment is, for Puerto Ricans as for earlier immigrant groups, the chief channel of access.

One important issue is that of whether or not to license professionals trained in Puerto Rico. The Board of Education will take graduates of the University of Puerto Rico as Substitute Auxiliary teachers, a non-classroom position designed especially to aid Spanish-speaking parents and children. The Department of Welfare has followed this precedent for special personnel. The acceptance of nurses whose examinations were not taken in English has been resisted, despite the urgent need for Spanish-speaking nurses for ward and clinic service in hospitals throughout the city.

Discrimination in housing continues in many parts of the city. The housing law is new, and the enforcement agency is part of a larger section of city government with many other responsibilities. It is too soon to evaluate the adequacy of the law and the feasibility of enforcement. Eagle, in a recent study of the housing of Puerto Ricans in New York City, was surprised to find so few Puerto Ricans feeling themselves discriminated against. To the question, "Do you think you can live anywhere in the city if you have the money to pay the rent, 87 per cent answered "Yes," and only 5 per cent stated that they felt they had actually experienced discrimination in seeking housing. A partial clue to this apparent unawareness of discrimination lies in the fact that the great majority of Puerto Ricans can afford to seek housing only in the less desirable dwellings. The same study found that while only 3 per cent of those who had lived in the city three years or less complained of discrimination, 10 per cent of those who had lived in New York longer voiced such a complaint.[36]

---

[35] *Ibid.*, pp. 143–144.
[36] Morris Eagle, "The Puerto Ricans in New York City," in Studies in Housing and Minority Groups, eds. Nathan Glazer and Davis McEntire (Berkeley and Los Angeles: The University of California Press, 1959), pp. 166–167.

Political discrimination is primarily linked with the question of English language literacy. Some Puerto Ricans feel there is discrimination in the courts, since the procedure of American courts deprives them of a chance to plead their cause with emotion, gesture, and Latin eloquence.

The situation of the Puerto Ricans is an example of the limitations and advantages of formal controls on discrimination. Since the Puerto Ricans are the newest minority, visible and present in large numbers, there is considerable derogation of the group as a whole. Individual middle-class Puerto Ricans have been well accepted in middle-class city and suburban neighborhoods. The group, however, is largely at the bottom of the economic scale and is looked down on by both white and Negro New Yorkers. Hostility between Negroes and Puerto Ricans is apt to be high. The efforts to eliminate discrimination have challenged New Yorkers to live by the creed of equality of opportunity. These efforts have brought abuses to public attention, and have made possible for many Puerto Ricans a more rapid establishment and improvement than was possible to immigrants in the earlier part of the century.

THE PUERTO RICANS OF "EASTVILLE"

A large proportion of the Puerto Ricans in New York find themselves the new slum-dwellers of the city. Elena Padilla has made a study of one such neighborhood, "Eastville," which makes an interesting comparison with Tuck's study of the Mexican community, Descanso, which we presented in Chapter 6. "Eastville" is not "El Barrio Latino." It is an interethnic slum, not a homogeneous nationality subcommunity.

Regardless of how long they have been melting in the pot, the people of Eastville are seldom identified as just plain Americans. They are designated "Hungarians," "Puerto Ricans," "American Negroes," "American Indians," "East Indians," "Russians," "Italians," "Chinese"—and all of these group labels are conceived as indicating something about the personal, social and biological traits of various group members. It makes little difference in this categorizing whether the individuals were born or have lived all their lives in this country if they still possesss characteristics—real or assumed—in physical appearance, in styles of wearing apparel, in knowledge of another language than English, and in their names, that allow them to be distinguished from "real Americans." The term "American" is used, as a rule, with reference to outsiders who do not live in the neighborhood and who, although they may themselves be members of ethnic groups, do not meet the criteria that suggest to Eastvillers membership in any particular group with which they are familiar.[37]

In "Eastville" there are ties of neighborhood that cut across ethnic lines and other identifications that are ethnic.

Among Eastvillers there are levels on which feelings of neighborhood solidarity bind members of all ethnic groups together. By the process of discrimination and

[37] Padilla, *Up From Puerto Rico*, pp. 1–2. By permission.

dislike people get involved in relationships of conflict, and by common under-standings and participation in common activities sentiments of solidarity develop. Both the positive feelings and the negative ones work together to shape the social body that is the neighborhood. The idea that the neighborhood is a bad place in which to live is a shared one among Eastvillers. So, too, is their attitude toward discrimination by outsiders against them. . . .

On the other hand, it is difficult to organize programs of social action in East-ville when ethnic group barriers are ignored or when the sources of loyalty within an ethnic group are not recognized. Beneath the intergroup tensions and conflicts among ethnic groups are working interpersonal relationships among individuals, which override ethnic affiliation.[38]

Although there is neighborliness and often mutual helpfulness, the urban slum neighborhood lacks the homogeneity and long residence of the village.

First and last names are seldom known or recognized in Eastville. People are identified according to whatever characteristic they are best known by in the neighborhood—the man from Italy, the lady who owns the candy store, the woman from Ponce . . .[39]

Housing is a problem in "Eastville," although the overcrowding is not comparable to that in some districts where there are whole families in one room. The 1950 census reported an average of three persons per room for "Eastville." Apartments are self-contained units which include a bathroom (sometimes with the tub in the kitchen). Some are "old law" (pre-1911) tenements with windows only in the front and back rooms and airshafts for the intervening rooms. Rents in the middle 1950's, at the time of Padilla's study, ranged from $14 to $80 a month, with "under the table" fees from $800 to $1,500 "for the key." Utilities are extra. The entire area is rat-infested; repairs in electric installations, plumbing, and plaster must usually be undertaken by tenants themselves, as complaints are consistently ignored by the absentee landlords. City garbage collection is less frequent in these slum areas: twice a week as contrasted with daily pick up in middle-class neighborhoods. When weather permits, much of the life of the neighbor-hood goes on on the street.

Strewn with garbage though they are, the streets and alleys are notable for the number of people of every conceivable ethnic group who spend a considerable part of their time there to get away from their apartments. Day and night the juke boxes in the candy stores deluge the streets with the tunes of the latest records of the season, and it is not strange to see youngsters or young adults dancing by themselves inside the stores or on the sidewalks to rock 'n' roll rhythms by the Velvets or to Xavier Cugat's mambos and meringues. Others watch and then try the ones they like under the tutelage of those who know the steps and proper motions for the dances. Noise of music and of words in Yiddish, Spanish, Italian and English, barking dogs, movement of people, cars' horns, are inter-woven in a polyphonic soundtrack which records the pace of the neighborhood.

[38] *Ibid.*, pp. 11–12. By permission.
[39] *Ibid.*, p. 12.

Only very cold weather or news echoed through the grapevine that gang fights are scheduled, keep people off the streets. Otherwise the streets, the sidewalks, the stores, and the bars are filled with people meeting, chatting, and relaxing.[40]

Living in the midst of people who have conscious ties to ethnic groups, hispanos have continued the pattern of vesting individuals with ethnic identity. The principal ethnic groups recognized by hispanos in "Eastville" are Cubans, Americans, American Negroes, Italians, and Jews. Of these, Americans and Italians are the most highly rated. Jews, Cubans, and American Negroes are, as a rule, less favored, especially the two latter groups.[41]

An undisputed American, or someone who is American and nothing else, is conceived as having a name that cannot be identified with or traced to a foreign origin; as being reddish and white in complexion, tall, blond and blue eyed; as doing professional work; and as not knowing Spanish or having an accent when speaking it. He does not understand the Hispano people. Americans are nice, honest, beautiful and funny. Should one or more of these traits be missing, the individual is suspected of not being a "real American," but something else instead.[42]

THE PUERTO RICAN "PROBLEM"

New Yorkers are apt to see the influx of Puerto Ricans as a problem for the city. To what extent is this true? The Puerto Rican influx has occurred at a time when housing patterns in New York have changed from single residences to suburban and apartment house dwelling. The deteriorating side streets in "good neighborhoods" have brought the problems of a low-paid working class literally to the doorsteps of the secure. The "problem" might not be so much discussed if it were enclaved in a distinct subcommunity. As it is, this geographically, culturally, and often biologically visible group must carry the onus for the living conditions and behavior of any exploited, underprivileged, poorly educated, urban slum population with some special cultural variations. As Oscar Handlin points out,

By habit and tradition New Yorkers have been unwilling to acknowledge that they have allowed themselves unjustly to discriminate against some of the residents of their city or that certain disorders are inherent in the situations or urban life. They are particularly reluctant to do so now when a large percentage of them are the children and grandchildren of immigrants who themselves suffered from the debilitating effects of settlements in slums.[43]

One of the most acute problems has already been mentioned—the schools. The public education system has not only the challenge of absorbing a large

[40] *Ibid.,* p. 9. By permission.
[41] *Ibid.,* p. 89.
[42] *Ibid.,* p. 90. By permission.
[43] Oscar Handlin, *The Newcomers* (Cambridge, Mass.: Harvard University Press, 1959), p. 96.

foreign-language child population, which will probably increase in view of the age group of the migrating Puerto Ricans, but there are many problems besides language for the child of the newer migrants. Many schools find that they must run clothing pools, as the newcomers are unprepared for the winter climate in New York and are without resources to buy adequate clothing. In a recently migrated family, absence from school is regarded as natural if the child is needed at home. Teachers complain of having so many peripheral welfare problems that there is no time for teaching.

As with other immigrant groups, the adolescents and young adults have difficulty finding their identity between "American" models and Spanish expectations and under slum conditions. Many Puerto Rican adolescent gangs have developed, as well as interethnic gangs which include Puerto Ricans. Young Puerto Ricans have been particularly preyed upon by the dope trade. "Crimes of passion" take place, but there has been no development of adult criminal gangs among Puerto Ricans.

Family disorganization is always high in the poorest segment of an urban population. As might be expected, the case loads of welfare agencies in the city include a large proportion of Puerto Ricans. Health problems too are widespread.

Puerto Rican Welfare

More intelligent effort has been made to meet the problems of the Puerto Rican migration than was possible with the older European migrations. The structures of labor and welfare in the United States have changed. The development of the social sciences has made more knowledge available to influence planning. The position of Puerto Rico as a United States dependency facilitates co-ordination between the island and the mainland.

The Migration Division of the Office of the Commonwealth of Puerto Rico works both on the island and in its offices in the United States to aid the adjustment process. Each week twenty-nine radio stations throughout the island carry a program, "Guide to the Traveler," based on the experience of previous migrants. In 1960 there were thirty-five committees on migrant orientation in cities and towns in Puerto Rico. Television, radio, newspapers and printed leaflets are urging knowledge of English, giving information about climate and clothing, the documents needed for schools, the need for driver's licenses, and warning about installment buying and many other topics.[44]

In New York the Migration Division has organized a campaign to urge the newcomer to go to night school. The Spanish-language press and Spanish-language radio carry these appeals, and there are thousands of

[44] Senior, *Strangers—Then Neighbors*, p. 62.

leaflets distributed by clergy, social workers, health stations, settlements, and banks.[45]

Some progress is being made on the housing problem through efforts at urban renewal. New York City has a program of low-cost, subsidized housing in areas where there have been particularly bad slum dwellings. Renewal of the side streets between middle-class housing is beginning, and clergy, social agencies, and political clubs have aided in bringing negligent landlords to court.

The school system, where it is practicable, has attempted to draw zone lines so that the ethnic balance of a school's population will not exceed one-third Puerto Rican. The problem is aggravated, however, by the principle of homogeneous grouping, which syphons off the better students into separate classes. Since the number of Puerto Ricans who have qualified for these classes is still not large, the other classes have disproportionately more Puerto Ricans. The Board Education has been experimenting with ""culture-free" intelligence tests and with special programs for the gifted of less privileged background. There are about a hundred Spanish-speaking Substitute Auxiliary teachers assigned to schools in the city. The efforts of Negro parents and Negro organizations for improved schools and for revised testing have benefited Puerto Ricans also.

The public welfare agencies, the private nonsectarian welfare agencies, various Protestant denominations, and Catholic parishes and religious orders have given thought and effort to meeting the needs of the new migrant group.[46] The Riverside Church, an interdenominational, interracial Protestant Church built by John D. Rockefeller, Jr., and located adjacent to Columbia University, has a Spanish-speaking minister on its staff and services in Spanish every Sunday. The settlement houses, some with the aid of state and federal funds, have undertaken imaginative programs in districts where there are large Puerto Rican populations.

Padilla gives an account of one "welfare" family in "Eastville":

Mr. Rios was injured in an industrial accident in 1953. This later involved orthopedic surgery. Workmen's Compensation was paid for a short period and for the subsequent surgery, but after the discontinuance Mr. Rios continued to suffer pain, and with his injured arm could not find a job. A visiting nurse suggested the family should seek help from the Department of Public Welfare—"go on welfare," and she herself made the contact for the family. The case with the Compensation Board was reopened and Mr. Rios now receives $18 a week from this agency. Mrs. Rios and the three children have supplemental aid from the Department of Welfare. Mr. Rios has been attending night school, has finished grammer school and is now in junior high school. He still has pain and receives treatment from both public and private clinics. He still consults lawyers in the hope of getting indemnification for his injury. In the last seven years the rent has been doubled.

[45] *Ibid.*
[46] Rand, *The Puerto Ricans*, pp. 118–124.

The Rios family have been in New York for twenty years. They belong to a store front church, and the children have been to the church camp summers, although when the daughter reached puberty, her parents no longer allowed her to go to camp. The children are not allowed to play on the streets, though the boys are often "given permission" to go to the park. The children are doing well in school. Mrs. Rios earns a little money by caring for the children of working mothers in her home. Mr. Rios hopes when he "has completed his education" to be able to get a job so they can get off welfare. He is 45 years old.[47]

Adaptive Institutions

There are three Spanish-language newspapers in New York. One, a conservative paper in sober format, is primarily oriented to the whole Spanish-speaking colony, including businessmen and diplomats. It contains much news of Spain and Latin America. Another, the New York edition of a San Juan paper, contains chiefly news of Puerto Rico. The most popular paper among New York's Puerto Rican population is a tabloid daily slanted expressly toward Puerto Rican migrants. In addition to carrying the usual type of copy it offers itself as the champion of the Puerto Rican against the police and other agents of authority, as well as giving information about night classes, P.T.A.'s and so forth. It plays a considerable role in creating minority identity.[48] By its format and the character of its news emphasis it also makes a bridge to the popular English-language press and the mass attitudes appealed to by this segment of the press.

A number of indigenous organizations have developed. The Spanish Merchants Association has 200 Puerto Rican members. The Puerto Rican Civil Service Employees Association is thirty-five years old, owns its own building, and has established a successful credit union. The Spanish Club of the New York City Police Department has 250 members, mostly Puerto Rican. The Association of Puerto Rican Social Workers has more than 1,000 members. There are organizations of lawyers, ministers, teachers, nurses, electricians, barbers, bar owners, taxi owners and drivers, and baseball umpires.[49] The Council of Puerto Rican and Spanish-American Organizations of Greater New York now includes fifty-four civic, social, cultural, religious and fraternal organizations. The Federation of Puerto Rican Organizations of New Jersey has thirty member groups.

Although political parties and political clubs have not yet become a major mode of adaptation, the Puerto Rican vote in New York City rose from 35,000 in 1954 to 230,000 in 1960. There are three Puerto Rican members of the New York State Legislature. Rand believes the major Spanish-language daily paper has hopes of welding the Puerto Ricans into a political force.[50]

Labor unions, some with locals that are almost 100 per cent Puerto Rican

[47] Padilla, Up From Puerto Rico, pp. 134–141, adapted by the authors.
[48] Rand, The Puerto Ricans, pp. 24–25.
[49] Senior, Strangers—Then Neighbors, pp. 70–71.
[50] Rand, The Puerto Ricans, p. 25.

serve also as adaptive institutions. A 1959 survey found that 63 per cent of New York's Spanish-speaking households had one or more union members.[51]

TRENDS AND PROSPECTS

The future of the Puerto Rican minority is bound up with many factors: the development of the island, the dispersion of Puerto Ricans on the mainland, the opportunity for advancement, the consciousness of themselves as a cultural minority, and the future position of racially visible people in the continental United States.

The amazing development of the island economy, if it continues at the present rapid rate, may change the pattern of migration. We have already noted a shift from the urban to the rural migrant. The development of the island may reduce the available cheap labor force by a considerable amount, especially if the Puerto Rican efforts toward population control begin to show effects. The preparation of migrants can be expected to improve also. Nevertheless, for some time to come, opportunities in the continental United States will outstrip those in Puerto Rico, and the remoter rural areas may still be a source of supply for the mainland labor force, and these rural people are the ones who will have the severest problems of adaptation to mainland urban life.

The future of the island politically is also a factor influencing both the increase or decrease in migration, as well as the feelings within the Puerto Rican group already settled in the United States. Various groups on the island have at one time or another favored either independence or statehood. Independence would at the very least create new problems, and perhaps new emphases, in the development of the island. Statehood would also slow development efforts, since Puerto Rico would then be subject to federal taxation, from which it is now exempt. The present Governor, Muñez Marin, sees great cultural as well as economic benefits in the present relationship, which allows self-government within "a commonwealth of the American political system." He foresees a future in which Puerto Rico will carry its share of the federal financial burden, and he poses the question of whether eventually a new relationship may not be defined which is neither statehood nor independence.[52] The political future of Puerto Rico, however, is also bound up with other developments in Latin America and the Caribbean, as well as with American policy.

The dispersion of the Puerto Ricans on the mainland, urged by the Columbia University Study in 1948,[53] is already taking place and will prob-

---

[51] Senior, *Strangers—Then Neighbors,* p. 68.
[52] Luis Muñez Marin, *Puerto Rico Does Not Want to Become a State* (The *New York Times Magazine,* August 16, 1959).
[53] Mills, Senior, and Golden, *The Puerto Rican Journey,* Appendix, pp. 84–102.

ably increase. Opportunity for advancement seems to be promising for Puerto Ricans as compared with most early twentieth-century immigrant groups. According to David W. Barry, Executive Secretary of the New York City Mission Society,

No previous immigrant group so quickly numbered among its members so many policemen, welfare workers, teachers and social workers, office workers and independent business men, and even doctors and lawyers—after barely a dozen years in New York. And the signs of the future are in the substantial enrollment of young Puerto Ricans in the city's colleges and universities.[54]

Puerto Ricans are beginning to move into home-owning areas in the suburbs. One Cleveland, Ohio, realtor is quoted as saying, "they are becoming a credit to the community, although many old timers protested when they moved in."[55]

Whether the Puerto Ricans will assimilate or whether their identity as a cultural minority will be strengthened will be influenced by larger trends in America, and in United States-Latin American relations. Even the efforts to achieve nondiscriminatory legislation in a city like New York heightens the awareness of descent as a criterion of identification. In the face of this there is an inevitable strengthening of cultural bonds, which may be reinforced if there is unabating migration.

For the dark-complexioned Puerto Ricans the future is bound up with the future of race attitudes. Many continue to segregate themselves from American Negroes and are a powerful factor in maintaining the Spanish cultural subgroup. But in the end their opportunity is associated with the ultimate opportunity of other dark-skinned Americans.

TOPICS FOR PROJECTS AND DISCUSSION

1. Compare the Puerto Rican and the Italian migrations to the United States. How are they alike and how do they differ?
2. What are the gains and losses to an immigrant in a geographic nationality subcommunity as compared with a mixed neighborhood?
3. Why are Negroes and Puerto Ricans sometimes treated as if they were a single "problem" group? Is this justified or not? Explain.
4. How do you account for the lack of organized crime among adult Puerto Ricans? How do you explain, then, the high rate of juvenile delinquency?
5. One of America's leading musicians, Leonard Bernstein, has made young Puerto Ricans in New York the central figures in *West Side Story*. Listen to the songs from this musical. Compare it with Padilla's account of "Eastville." Do they agree or disagree in their presentation of young people in a city slum?

[54] Quoted in Senior, *Strangers—Then Neighbors*, p. 67.
[55] *Ibid.*, p. 70.

SUGGESTED READING

Eagle, Morris. "The Puerto Ricans in New York City," in *Studies in Housing and Minority Groups*, eds. Nathan Glazer and Davis McEntire. Berkeley and Los Angeles: University of California Press, 1959.
> *Studies the housing of New York's Puerto Ricans and how they themselves view the situation.*

Handlin, Oscar. *The Newcomers: Negroes and Puerto Ricans in a Changing Metropolis*. Cambridge, Mass.: Harvard University Press, 1959.
> *A part of the New York Metropolitan Region Study. The new migrants' problems appraised in the light of the history of the New York City labor force.*

Padilla, Elena. *Up From Puerto Rico*. New York: Columbia University Press, 1958.
> *A social anthropologist describes and analyzes the daily living of Puerto Ricans in one New York neighborhood.*

Senior, Clarence. *Strangers—Then Neighbors: From Pilgrims to Puerto Ricans*. New York: Freedom Books, 1961.
> *An up-to-date summary of facts about Puerto Ricans on the mainland, with an excellent bibliography.*

Stycos, J. Mayone. *Family and Fertility in Puerto Rico*. New York: Columbia University Press, 1955.
> *An analysis of the values governing family life among working-class Puerto Ricans in Puerto Rico.*

Wakefield, Dan. *Island in the City: The World of Spanish Harlem*. Boston: Houghton Mifflin Co., 1959.
> *A vivid description of life in "El Barrio Latino," the Spanish subcommunity of New York.*

8

The Chinese in the United States

In the mainland population of the United States there were in 1960 some 600,000 people of Asian lineage. There were 206,877 Japanese, 199,095 Chinese, and 107,240 Filipinos.[1] While altogether these people make up only a small percentage of the total mainland population, their relations with the dominant population have been significant, for their treatment by white Americans has had serious repercussions in the relations between the United States and Asian governments.

In broad outline, the interaction of these Oriental immigrants parallels that of all native-immigrant interaction. The discrimination displayed against them was, however, on the whole, much stronger. While, as we have seen, most of the subsequent generations of European lineage became assimilated, the Asian immigrants, up to World War II at least, remained only partially acculturated to American society. In part, of course, this may be explained by the fact that their cultures were in some aspects more alien to the United States than that of the European immigrants. The ranking of Asian immigrant groups below that of European immigrant groups on social

---

[1] The Asian population of Hawaii is given in Table 15, p. 353. These figures were obtained by subtracting the data for Hawaii from the United States total as given in the Advance Reports of the 1960 Census. Data for Asian Indians, Koreans, and Polynesians are not given, but all other Asians living in mainland United States are few in number.

distance scales indicates that the fact that they are Mongoloid in appearance and therefore viewed as another "race" by Caucasian Americans has imposed an additional obstacle to their acceptance.

In this chapter on the Chinese and the following one on the Japanese we shall be describing the mainland situation. Hawaii, where Orientals play so prominent a role, will be treated in Chapter 16.

The picture in the mind of the average American of the Chinese in this country is probably more compounded of myth and legend than is true of any other minority. The word "Chinatown" is associated with things exotic, mysterious, curious, and alien to American life. The popular stereotype is derived more from the movies and mystery novels than from actual contact with the Chinese themselves. The lack of real knowledge of the Chinese is explained by their small numbers and their concentration in a few large cities. But it also arises from the fact that even in the communities where they do live, the Chinese have been until recently the most socially isolated of all minorities, a point which takes on added significance when we remember that the Chinese immigration antedated the period of later European immigration.

THE CHINESE POPULATION IN THE UNITED STATES

Chinese immigration to the United States, as Table 4 shows, beginning in large numbers in the 1850's rose to a peak in the decade of the 1870's and declined sharply after the First Exclusion Act (1882). Beginning with the depression through World War II, there was little immigration at all. Since the war, immigration has increased sharply again. How are we to account for the fact that, while during 140 years more than 400,000 Chinese have migrated to the mainland of this country there are apparently not half that number living in the country in the 1960's?

CHINESE IMMIGRATION TO THE UNITED STATES

First, the Chinese Exclusion Act drastically curtailed, though it did not completely eliminate, further immigration after 1882. Second, during several decades the number of Chinese returning to China exceeded the number of arrivals. "From 1908, when records of departures began, to 1930, while 48,482 Chinese immigrant aliens were admitted, 72,796 departed, thus showing a net loss."[2] Third, normal natural increase was prevented by the disproportion of the sexes. In 1910 there were 1430.1 males to every 100 Chinese females; in 1920, 695.5; and in 1940, 258.3. Finally, because of exclusion there had been an undue proportion of elderly Chinese in the population, which accounted for a relatively high death rate for the group. Thus the

[2] Maurice R. Davie, *World Immigration* (New York: The Macmillan Co., 1936), pp. 315–316. By permission.

TABLE 4

**Chinese Immigration to the United States and Population of Chinese Ancestry
as Recorded by Census**

YEAR	TOTAL ADMITTED*	TOTAL RECORDED**	PER CENT INCREASE OR DECREASE
1820 to 1830	3	-----	---
1831 to 1940	8	-----	---
1841 to 1850	35	758	---
1851 to 1860	41,397	34,933	---
1861 to 1870	64,301	63,199	80.9
1871 to 1880	123,201	105,465	66.9
1881 to 1890	61,711	107,488	1.9
1891 to 1900	14,799	88,869	−16.4
1901 to 1910	20,605	71,531	−20.4
1911 to 1920	21,278	61,639	−13.8
1921 to 1930	29,907	74,594	21.6
1931 to 1940	4,928	77,504	3.4
1941 to 1950	16,709	117,140† (150,005††)	51.8
1951 to 1960	9,657	190,095† (237,292††)	62.3 (58.2††)
TOTAL	408,539		

* *Annual Report of Immigration and Naturalization Service,* Washington, 1960, Table 13, p. 41.
** *United States Census* for each decade.
† Includes mainland United States without Hawaii.
†† Includes Hawaii.

Chinese population declined from a peak of 107,488 in 1890 to a low of 61,639 in 1920. From 1921 to 1940 the Chinese in America increased but slightly, to a 77,504 total in 1940.

The 1940–1950 decade showed an increase of 51.8 per cent in the Chinese population. Part of this may reflect a more accurate census count gained through the use of Chinese recorders for the first time. But it is a question if even this measure succeeded in getting all the resident aliens counted, since many avoid official contacts because of illegalities in their status— fraudulent claims to derivative citizenship, "jumping ship" by seamen, cross- ing borders without detection, and "smuggling." Much of the increase actu- ally occurred in the postwar years, when an unprecedented number of female immigrants admitted under the War Brides Act helped bring the sex ratio of this population to 1.89. (In 1890 there had been 27 Chinese males to every 1 Chinese female.)

The above considerations likewise explain why there was such a high per- centage increase in the Chinese population on the American mainland from

1950 to 1960 (62.3 per cent). In addition to more accurate counting, some Chinese students stranded in the country by the Chinese revolution who were given permanent entry, the large number of relatives of Chinese American nationals, and refugees from the mainland of China—mostly merchants and scholars—all swelled the total. For example, of the 5,722 immigrant aliens from China admitted for the 1959 period, 1,348 were wives of American citizens.[3]

The American Chinese population is highly urbanized. By 1950, as many as 94 per cent were officially counted in cities of various sizes, and according to Lee only 1 per cent could be said to have really rural residence.[4] The trend has been toward concentration in a few large cities. In addition to San Francisco, with the largest Chinatown in the nation, enough Chinese to form a local "colony" are found in Chicago, Detroit, Los Angeles, Brooklyn, New York, and Philadelphia. The most interesting recent change in the geographical distribution of the American Chinese population has been the southward movement. In 1950 there were 10,432 in the South. While this was still a small percentage of the then 117,629 national total, it represented an increase over 1940 of 112.5 per cent. Of this Lee writes:

> The southern movement gathered momentum during the depression, when the South surpassed all other regions in attracting families who owned and operated general merchandise, food, and service establishments. The Chinese function as middlemen in a multi-racial society where the social relations between the whites and Negroes are strained and hostile. They also play this role in the Southwest, where Mexicans and American Indians are numerous and the Chinese cater to all groups. This is similar to the position the Chinese occupy in South-East Asia, the Caribbean, and elsewhere.[5]

It is of interest to find that in 1940, a hundred years after the Chinese immigration started, for the first time, the American-born Chinese exceeded the foreign-born Chinese population. The exceptional tendency for Chinese immigrants to return to their homeland and the long period in which the group had had an excessively high male preponderance account for the delay.

THE EARLY PERIOD

The discovery of gold in California was the magnet which first attracted mass immigration of Chinese to California. Perhaps much of the peculiarly violent and rough treatment accorded these first Chinese immigrants can

---

[3] *Annual Report of the Immigration and Naturalization Service*, Washington, D.C., 1959, p. 17, Table 6.
[4] Rose Hum Lee, *The Chinese in the United States* (Hong Kong: Hong Kong University Press, 1960), p. 38. Distributed in the United States by the Oxford University Press.
[5] *Ibid.*, p. 39.

be understood when it is remembered that Chinese-native white interaction first took place in the especially lawless setting of the frontier. Opposition arose to the Chinese as gold miners because they were industrious and persevering, often taking on mining locations that whites considered worthless and making them pay. Thus began the cry that the Chinese depressed the wages and the living standard of the whites, an allegation which was to dog the Chinese as they subsequently became laborers in all the menial occupations available—in railroad construction, on the farms, and in domestic service. Antagonism toward the Chinese expressed itself in lawless violence, in discriminatory city ordinances and state legislation, and finally in successful persuasion of the federal government to exclude further Chinese immigrants.

Acts discriminating against the Chinese, imposing special taxes on them and prohibiting them from entering the state, were passed by the California legislature in the 1850's and 1880's. Opposition to the Chinese was manifested also in city ordinances which attempted to reach the Chinese indirectly. For example, "San Francisco had a laundry ordinance imposing a license fee as follows: on laundries using a one-horse vehicle, $2 per quarter; two horses, $4 per quarter; no vehicle, $15 per quarter. The Chinese laundries commonly used no vehicle. It was made a misdemeanor for any person on the sidewalks to carry baskets suspended on a pole across the shoulders—a typical Chinese practice."[6]

Frequently the Chinese were exposed to violence, especially in periods of hard times. As a result of the panic of 1873, riots occurred during which the Chinese were robbed, beaten, and murdered by hoodlums who made the Chinese the scapegoats for the ills of the times. Eye-witness accounts report that "it was a common sight in San Francisco and other cities to see the Chinese pelted with stones or mud, beaten or kicked, having vegetables or laundry stolen from their baskets, and even having their queues cut." It was also reported that their washhouses were set afire, and when they tried to escape from burning houses they were beaten and sometimes compelled to die in the flames. The police afforded little protection against these outrageous attacks and the victims did not retaliate. The Chinese government, however, demanded an indemnity, which was paid by the United States government.

All of the California city ordinances and state laws specifically discriminating against the Chinese were eventually declared unconstitutional by either the state Supreme Court or the United States Supreme Court.[7] Fur-

---

[6] Davie, *World Immigration*, pp. 311–312.
[7] Below we refer to the Alien Land Holding Laws passed in the three Pacific Coast States for the purpose of barring foreign-born Japanese from owning land. They constituted a legal discrimination against the Chinese as well, but since the Chinese were less inclined toward land ownership, this discrimination had less practical importance in their case.

thermore, the violence against Chinese persons was protested by the Chinese government, prompting the federal government to investigate the situation. Eventually Congress passed the first Chinese Exclusion Act in 1882, suspending all Chinese immigration for ten years. This was repeated for another ten years in 1892; and in 1902 suspension of Chinese immigration was extended indefinitely, to remain thus until 1943 when, under the spur of the war situation, China was added to the quota immigrant nations and allotted 105 annual entries. Included in each of these measures were various other humiliating provisions, such as the denial of the privilege of becoming citizens to foreign-born Chinese.

The exclusion of the Chinese by federal legislation is a clear illustration of Congress yielding to the specific will of one of its individual states in the absence of any general national demand. McWilliams has noted the following factors in the situation which help explain it: (1) All but one of some eight anti-Chinese measures passed by Congress were passed on the eve of national elections and for avowed political purposes; (2) the interrelationship of the Southern attitude toward the Negro and the California attitude toward the Oriental prompted Southern representatives to side with California on a *quid pro quo* basis; (3) there was no real knowledge of the Chinese on the part of white Americans throughout the nation, and they failed to recognize the issue as related to national interest.[8]

URBAN ADJUSTMENT

In time sequence, the above discussion of the legislation limiting Chinese immigration has trespassed briefly upon the second phase of native-Chinese relations in the United States. Numerically few, and destined by the exclusion acts to remain so, and culturally conditioned by their Chinese heritage to be meek and pacific rather than aggressive and militant, the Chinese reacted to this vehement Caucasian opposition in the most inoffensively accommodative ways. They dispersed to a few of the largest cities in the nation, thus removing the concentration factor. In these large cities they segregated themselves in very compact areas and have confined their lives within them. They have entered the least competitive occupations, particularly domestic and personal service. The small professional and clerical group had been limited to serving their own people, but since World War II, more American-born Chinese residing outside California co-work with Caucasians in servicing the general public. Since "Chinatowns" are a point of interest to tourists, some people make their livelihood through curio

---

[8] See Carey McWilliams, *Brothers Under the Skin* (Boston: Little, Brown & Co., 1943), pp. 87–96, for an extensive account and interpretation of the legislation against the Chinese.

shops and restaurants serving the tourist trade.[9] Two distinctive types of business have developed—entirely unrelated to their own cultural background—the Chinese laundry and the Chinese restaurant, both designed to provide low-price service not conspicuously competitive with white businesses in the same field. Many came in the early period only as contract labor and returned at the end of the contract.

Like other immigrant minorities in the initial stage, the Chinese developed a segregated community within the large city. But because of the racial barrier to their gradual assimilation, Chinatowns have become more compact and more permanent. No other ethnic folk remained so long so completely isolated from the rest of the community.

While the insulation of the Chinese in the United States and the prolonged delay in their movement through the characteristic course followed by other immigrants have been affected by the prejudice and discrimination of dominant-status Americans, apparently more than with other immigrants the Chinese themselves have contributed to the process. This will be better understood by examining certain broad categories of Chinese in this country and the social organization of the Chinese community.

Sojourners

This term applies to the Chinese who have lived in this country with the idea of making enough money to return to the homeland to live at a higher-status level. Siu describes this category thus: "The Chinese sojourners maintain a psychological and social separateness from the larger society and insulate themselves against the full impact of the dominant societies' values, norms, attitudes, and behavior patterns."[10] With this attitude, the sojourner lives a dual existence "which contributes to his sense of non-belongingness in both societies, a fact that is seldom admitted by the sojourner."[11] It is this psychological orientation which marks a Chinese as a sojourner whether foreign or native-born, irrespective of his class position, or whether the time ever comes that he feels affluent enough to return to his homeland.

Students and Intellectuals

From 1847, when an American missionary brought three Chinese boys to study at an American academy, to 1954, some 18,000 Chinese nationals have studied in the United States. Most American institutions of higher learning have trained some Chinese nationals. The peak of Chinese student enrollment came in 1949, at 3,916. Since most of this student group have come from the upper strata of Chinese society, their relations with dominant

---

[9] Today this is largely true of the San Francisco Chinatown, and possibly that of Los Angeles. Most Chinatowns are now being razed for slum clearance. The trend since World War II has been to surround Chinatowns with other ethnic groups or commercial buildings, as in New York.

[10] Paul C. Siu, "The Sojourner," *American Journal of Sociology*, July, 1952, 58: 34–44.

[11] *Ibid.*

people have been different from those of other Chinese. Confining themselves largely to the academic community, they have been well received and often welcomed into social relations with their fellow American students. Thus they have little identification with the American Chinese, and less with sojourners, whom they think of as "peasants."

American Chinese

Statistically this designation may be applied to persons of Chinese origin who were born in the United States and who are therefore American citizens. Sociologically the term is best applied to the Chinese who are in fact predominantly American in their culture and behavior and who think of themselves as Americans more than as Chinese. This group desires assimilation, but for the most part its members experience varying degrees of non-acceptance by dominant Americans.

THE SOCIAL STRUCTURE OF THE CHINESE COMMUNITY IN THE UNITED STATES

We have seen that it is characteristic for an immigrant group in the United States to develop adaptive institutions to facilitate adjustment to the larger society. The Chinese in this country established an elaborate associational network which still dominates the life of those Chinese who live in Chinatowns or whose businesses or social life bring them in contact with the leaders of these associations. The best example of this social structure is in the San Francisco-Oakland-Berkeley Bay area. There are four main groups: Family Associations; District Associations; the Chinese Consolidated Benevolent Association; and Tongs.

The family, or clan, associations are composed of all Chinese in the nation bearing the same surname. Since surnames are limited, there are many Chinese bearing each of them, and the associations are of considerable size. The professed activities of the family associations are to promote the welfare of the particular clan, especially the newly arrived members; their latent function is to perpetuate old betrothal and festive marriage customs. The district associations recruit members on the basis of the part of China from which the immigrant generation came. Smaller district associations have been consolidated into larger ones, and in recent years they appear to operate largely in San Francisco. The functions of these district associations seem to overlap those of the family associations, being concerned with the welfare of persons of a given district. By far the most inclusive is the Chinese Consolidated Benevolent Association. The name is, according to Lee, for the benefit of the outside community.[12] It is known to Chinese as the All Chinese United Association.

---

[12] *The Chinese in the United States*, p. 148.

There are several local organizations, but that of San Francisco, known popularly as "The Six Companies" (from a previous consolidation), is best known. While its professed functions are charitable, the Six Companies actually operates as the main agency of social control of the unacculturated Chinese, performing functions ordinarily performed by legally constituted American authority, such as settling disputes between individuals or groups. The more American-oriented Chinese resent the influence of the Six Companies, as well as other local Chinese Benevolent Associations, but are often not in a secure enough position to challenge it.

Tongs have been the type of Chinese association most publicized in the dominant community. In the earlier days, tongs functioned as a special underworld, controlling the operation of illegitimate enterprises within the Chinese communities. Since such enterprise involves more or less constant conflict between tongs, "wars" between them frequently ended in violence. While there was a tendency for the general community authority to let the tongs alone so long as open violence was limited to the Chinese area, it finally became necessary to curb their activities. In self-protection, the tongs "went respectable," claiming to be henceforth only "merchants associations" promoting the interests of legitimate Chinese-operated business. There are indications, however, that they still play a part in whatever remaining illicit activities operate in Chinatowns or involve Chinese living outside Chinatowns. But in any case, in deference to possible outside interference, their methods of control are more circumspect.

Chinatown, San Francisco

Nearly half the Chinese in the United States live in the San Francisco Bay area, and the Chinatown of the city itself is the main center of this minority group.[13] The following provides a recent picture.

Immigration officials estimate that there are 80,000 Chinese in San Francisco, one-tenth of the city's total population. Of these, roughly 50,000 are estimated to live in the now thirty blocks which comprises Chinatown around Grant Avenue, the "alley like" main thoroughfare. Another 30,000 Chinese live outside this area but have many ties with Chinatown proper. The area is marked by "antiquated structures with pagoda like upper stories," amber pagoda lights and strings of oriental lanterns . . . old smells of rotten fish, exotic shops with Chinese lettering that still use the ancient abacus to click off the prices of miniature trees, incense, elephants on blackwood stands, silk, images, jade rings, and baskets of tea . . . Chinese restaurants . . . with pidgin English speaking waiters.

Many of our Chinese denizens still cannot speak the English language and a large number do not vote. . . . Barred off in their tiny, ofttimes squalid quarters in Chinatown's ghetto, more than half do business only among Chinese, maintain only Chinese friends, belong only to Chinese organizations, and even pray at Chinese churches. While a growing minority have moved into white neighborhoods, and send their children to predominantly white schools, thousands more

[13] The 1960 Census recorded 95,600 Chinese in California.

send their children to school in and around Chinatown, where they learn and play only with other Chinese. Thus the social barrier is perpetuated.[14]

Concerning membership in the four major associations, the reporter found:

Not all Chinese in San Francisco are members of all four; some are not members of any. Almost all are members of the family and district associations, no one knows how many belong to tongs because so few will admit it, and every one is supposed to be represented in the Six Companies. Membership in one or more of these associations is felt by some Chinese, generally those not yet assimilated, as necessary to have status, to avoid economic or social boycott, despite the inevitable griping at the dues and very frequent further requests for money. These organizations are the chief agencies of social control (aside from the strong control of each family over its immediate members). The unassimilated Chinese does not think of the larger city government as his, and feels his relations with the larger community must be mediated through the Chinese organizations. These interlocking associations are controlled by leaders chosen by more or less self-perpetuating cliques with no semblance at all of democratic processes.[15]

The student of urban sociology will not be surprised to learn that in a group so situated some illegal activities will be found. Cited in this special survey are the problems of narcotic peddling and gambling. More disturbing is the discovery of the relatively new problem—supposedly new among the Chinese—of juvenile delinquency. In view of the belief long held by outsiders that the strong family system of the Chinese has prevented juvenile delinquency in this group, it is interesting that this recent investigation still finds that the children of the American-born Chinese seldom get into trouble with the law.[16] It is the teen-agers born in China and arrived in the United States within the past five years whose names are found on the police blotter. Lacking well-established family ties, such youths are frequently taken under the tutelage of the tongs that play a part in the illicit activities.

The "Slot Racket"

Unique to the Chinese in the United States has been the so-called slot racket. A section of the 1870 citizenship law passed by Congress recognized the right to confer citizenship on Americans born abroad. Chinese residents in this country have made much use of this law to secure entry of others, especially relations with the same surnames. As we have seen, many male Chinese immigrants returned to China from time to time for protracted visits to their families abroad and conceived children there. In countless instances, "sons never born" were reported, thus creating a "slot" on the family tree. Those "slots" enabled people to claim derivative citizenship and enter

---

[14] "Chinatown, U.S.A." *The Californian*, San Francisco, California, February, 1960. Adapted by permission of the Editor of *The Californian*, a monthly newspaper.
[15] *Ibid.*
[16] However, in Lee, *The Chinese in the United States*, pp. 334–341, material is cited which suggests that even the children of the native-born show more juvenile delinquency than the outside community has understood.

the United States. Persons claiming derivative citizenship, if born before 1934, were eligible for admission to this country if they could prove that their fathers or grandfathers resided in the United States at one time. The "racket" aspect has been in the selling of these "slots" by legitimate claimants. Arrangements are made to sell the "slots" through Hong Kong brokers for prices ranging from $2,500 to $6,000.[17]

The slot racket has had seriously disorganizing consequences in the American Chinese community: (1) It adds an illegal activity. In addition to "paper" families, many Chinese men had wives in China whom they could not or would not bring to this country. In time these men remarried here, thus victimizing native-born girls and their offspring. (2) It increases the tendency for the Chinese to fail to co-operate with American authorities. Even innocent resident Chinese who might want to expose the perpetrators are likely to fear to do so. (3) The "slotted" residents lead a dual life, fearful of exposure which might lead to deportation. (4) It helps perpetuate the tongs, because many slotted individuals rely on them to protect their false status or that of their "illegal" families in the United States.

THE CURRENT SITUATION

We can now consider the present situation and possible future of the Chinese as an immigrant minority accorded minority status.

Welfare

Economic   Whatever may have been their earlier situation, the Chinese in the United States are now by no means a poor people. Their residence in dilapidated ghetto areas and their frugality, engendered by their sojourner orientation have obscured their actual economic progress. For the Chinese fourteen years of age and over in 1949, the median income was $1,799; among the nonwhite groups, only the Japanese had a higher income during the same year.[18] Upward occupational mobility is indicated in the 1940–1950 decade, when there was an increase in the number of American Chinese in professional, technical, sales, and clerical occupations, a decline in the number of operatives, and a marked decline in the number of males engaged in domestic service occupations.[19]

Health   The Chinese have had lower then national average longevity, and much higher rates of tuberculosis and infant mortality, although in this connection their situation is improving.

Education   In 1950 the median school year completed by a Chinese male was 8.4. This figure seems quite low when one considers how long the

[17] *Time*, January 20, 1958, p. 17.
[18] Lee, *The Chinese in the United States*, p. 50.
[19] *Ibid.*, p. 48.

Chinese have been in this country and that traditional China placed a high value on education. Somewhat curiously, the median schooling for the Chinese female in 1950 was nearly two years greater, 10.3.[20]

Acculturation

Outside San Francisco, where, as we have seen, the largest Chinatown with a distinctive old-world orientation still prevails, the Chinese in the United States appear at long last to be becoming essentially American rather then Chinese. A close-up view of the extent of acculturation may be seen in a study of Chinese families in Chicago.[21] In 1950 roughly half of the 164 families in the study lived in Chicago's small Chinatown. Those employed or owning Chinese stores were less Americanized than those working in establishments catering to the general public. About half celebrated both Chinese and American holidays. Most prepared food in both American and Chinese style. About one-third of the families were entirely English-speaking. Parents were finding it more difficult to get their children to conform to Chinese ways. In one-third of the families the wives appeared to have equal status with the husbands; and the dominance of and perference for sons as against daughters was giving way, partly because the girls were more often able to find work outside the ghetto. In one-fourth of the marriages, the partners had selected their own mates without parental assistance.

Trends Toward Assimilation

There are influences from both the minority and the dominant sides which retard assimilation. Lee has summarized the attitudes of the Chinese themselves as follows:

> The alien born retain their sojourner status and mentality throughout their years abroad and hope for eventual resettlement in China. The second generation—or first generation born in the United States—favor the retention of the old world heritage as a device for achieving social solidarity within the minority group itself. They do not feel a deep sense of belonging to the host society. The third and succeeding generations of American-born, however, desire to effect integration; their policy emerges victorious and the other two wither away.[22]

A strong obstacle to assimilation from the Chinese side is found in the vested interests of the present leadership in retaining Chinese group distinctiveness in order to maintain their own status position. We noted above how particularly strong this type of leadership is in San Francisco's Chinatown. These San Francisco Chinatown leaders have influence on the Chinese nationally. Assimilation will be more rapid as the present leadership is supplanted by assimilation-oriented leaders and as Chinatowns disappear.

[20] *Ibid.*, p. 49.
[21] Liang Yuan, "The Chinese Family in Chicago," Unpublished Master's Thesis, University of Chicago Libraries, 1950.
[22] Lee, *The Chinese in the United States*, pp. 408–409.

Initial steps in the assimilation of immigrant groups have frequently been made through participation in the American political system, through membership in labor unions, and through education, particularly higher education. The Chinese still show minimal participation in all these areas. While there are labor unions in the larger Chinatowns, these are not usually affiliated with the larger American organizations and thus are less likely either to improve the economic welfare of the Chinese or to bring them into contact with the dominants. Underlying this union situation one finds an often repeated inconsistency. On the one hand, American labor unions have effectively barred the Chinese from many occupations, thus engendering hostility to unions on the part of Chinese; on the other hand, it is claimed that "concerted attempts to organize Chinese workers have met with little success."[23] Lee finds that even the native-born Chinese and those with derivative citizenship are not active in American politics.[24] San Francisco excepted, and of course in Hawaii, the number of Chinese in any one community is too small to be actively wooed by dominant politicians. The still deeply engrained attitude that government is an instrument of oppression rather than a protector of the public welfare continues to hold back the Chinese from active participation in the larger political process. This belief is bolstered by those of their leaders who use whatever political powers they may have for their own political advantage.

Finally, assimilation of the American Chinese continues to be retarded by the infrequency of outgroup marriages. Twenty-nine states have had laws which make marriage between Caucasians and Mongoloids illegal. When contested, these miscegenation laws have been declared nonenforceable (in California, for example), but despite the removal of legal disabilities, strong pressure continues to be exerted within the Chinese group itself against mixed marriages, especially if their social life is localized within the Chinese community.

Dominant Reaction to the Chinese

The earlier period of open and sometimes violent discrimination and anti-Chinese agitation subsided with passage of the Exclusion Act, which guaranteed that the numbers of Chinese would not pose any threat. Since then, the attitude of dominant Americans toward the Chinese has been aloof and patronizing. Because of the aloofness, aided by Chinese passiveness, Americans actually know little about their Chinese residents. Patronage is manifested by dominants who find them useful employees and by Chambers of Commerce who find the presence of an exotic Chinatown a splendid tourist attraction. Moreover, many white leaders like to believe they are helping the Chinese by "letting them take care of their own."

[23] *Ibid.*, p. 180.
[24] *Ibid.*, pp. 178–179.

On social distance tests, designed to indicate varying degrees of social acceptance, dominant respondents have usually put the Chinese near the bottom of the list of ethnic groups, although above Negroes.[25] The stereotyped image of the Chinese held by dominant Americans has not been shown to be very clear, although "sly," "superstitious," "law-abiding," "take care of their own" are commonly heard attributes. As with most national stereotypes of minorities, the image of the Chinese is not based on contact or observation but spread by diffusion through mass media among the dominant groups.

The major test now looming as to the present disposition of the dominants to accept American Chinese without reference to racial origin is in housing. Despite the removal of all legal disabilities affecting free choice of residence, American Chinese frequently face obstacles similar to those facing other minorities, particularly Negroes (see pp. 311–315). The following case is illustrative.

The Southwood Case. A China-born student who served in the Chinese army, advancing to the rank of captain in World War II, came to this country in 1943 and graduated from an American College intending to go in the consular service of his country. Following the Communist revolution, he decided to remain in this country, having in the meantime married an American-born Chinese girl. They settled in an apartment in a South San Francisco suburb and the husband worked as an airplane mechanic. This couple answered an "ad" of a house for sale, bought it successfully, and were preparing to move in when the "news" of their coming leaked out and spread through the neighborhood. Late that afternoon, a neighbor paraded up and down in front of the house, shouting with raised fist, "The Chinese are coming." The white sellers received irate letters and were later threatened with economic reprisals. The Chinese couple received threatening phone calls and letters. Not easily dissuaded, the young couple called for a public meeting in the area to discuss the situation. This was followed by informal voting on the matter. The tally was 174 I object; 28 no objection; and 14 no opinion. The couple gave up the house.[26]

The above case is not cited to suggest that the entrance of a Chinese family to all Caucasian neighborhoods is always opposed in this fashion. Lee indicates that many Chinese families have settled in the surburban neighborhoods of San Mateo and Burlingame. And even in Southwood this couple had some white supporters and received many expressions of regret from various dominant status people.

AMERICAN CHINESE AND THE TWO CHINAS

The accession to power of the Communists on the Chinese mainland and the Korean War raised problems for the Chinese in the United States. The

[25] See Lee, *The Chinese in the United States of America*, pp. 355–357, for a summary of the rank of the Chinese on various social distance tests.
[26] Adapted from Lee, *The Chinese in the United States*, pp. 315–319. By permission.

impact of this crisis fell differentially on various subgroups. Many Chinese, especially the China-oriented group, feared the possibility of a general anti-Chinese sentiment similar to that developing against the Japanese in World War II. There were a few outbreaks of violence in isolated spots such as the following:

In Woodland, California, a family lost their son recently in the battlefield in Korea. When the Defense Department notified them, parents, wife and brother were deeply grieved. Filled with a desire for revenge, they gathered their friends and relatives and headed toward a Chinese restaurant in that town. They broke into the establishment and destroyed everything within. Dishes, glasses, furniture, etc. were all ruined. The damages were estimated to be very great.[27]

On the whole, however, there were no concentrated strong outbursts of anti-Chinese feelings. This is due in part to the fact that official Sino-American relations during most of this half-century have been generally friendly. Furthermore, it has been widely believed that any Chinese who still has orientation to the mother country is pro-Nationalist.

For the sojourners already living here before the influx of immigrants after World War II, the Communist Revolution ended all dreams of returning to the home village and living at a higher status with their accumulated savings. All they had invested painstakingly over the decades through periodic remittances was confiscated by the new regime. The newer immigrants from Communist China, however, though likewise sojourners, are more frequently in favor of the political change. They were transplanted here by their husbands, brothers, or close relatives; depending upon where they reside and how many are grouped together, the climate favoring the "homeland regime" is manifested. Since most are non-English speaking and interact within the in-group, few dominants know about their activities in various organizations whose leadership is actually on the mainland. Were this not so, the various apprehensions since 1956 associated with the smuggling of aliens, narcotics, art objects, and other merchandise from the mainland, through "rings" extending from Hong Kong to Canada, to Mexico, to Cuba, and to Europe, and thence to the United States, would not have occurred.[28]

When the Communist Regime forced the Nationalists to flee to Taiwan, the most immediate problems were faced by the students, trainees, and other Chinese nationals here on temporary visas. Their funds were cut off, and they had to face the question of what their status would be if they re-

[27] The excerpt is from an editorial in the *Chinese Journal*, New York, December 1, 1950. The editorial warned the Chinese in America that they face close scrutiny from the F.B.I. under the present circumstances, particularly those who would be classified as enemy aliens in the case of formal declaration of war.
[28] See Kirk Durig, *Social Change in San Francisco Chinatown*, Ch. 4, a master's thesis at San Francisco State College, August, 1961.

turned to mainland China or to Formosa. The United States government furnished some funds to enable stranded students to complete their courses and to seek employment for the time being. Some students wanted to return to the mainland; others wanted to remain in this country; few would resettle in Taiwan. The American government did not want to harbor Communist-sympathizing students, nor did it want to return to Red China skilled professionals and technicians who had been trained here. The immigration service did permit the return to Communist China of a small number of the stranded students who desired to return; and many of the rest still here are being given permanent visas to remain.

SUMMARY

In summary, the following factors characterize the Chinese in the United States as a minority:

1. Their small numbers in mainland United States.
2. Their small numbers in any one community, the San Francisco-Oakland Bay area excepted.
3. The relatively few urban communities in which the Chinese are numerous enough to be perceived as an ethnic element in the population.
4. Their tendency to react to dominant discrimination in markedly non-aggressive ways. Their occupational adaptation has been exceptionally noncompetitive.
5. Their marked tendency, until recently, to insulate themselves from the larger American community by perpetuating their own distinctive social organizations; and to have their unavoidable instrumental relationships with the larger community mediated indirectly through their own social organization.
6. From the above, the tendency for the Chinese to take care of themselves, as reflected in low public relief applications and low known juvenile delinquency.
7. The various illegal activities within their own community, sometimes getting sufficiently out of hand to require the interference of the authority of the larger community.
8. As a consequence of this combination of factors, the fact that the American people in general know little about the Chinese and do not perceive them as a threat or a problem. Dominant reactions are indifferent, curious, supercilious, amused, or patronizing, rather than overtly hostile. Studied avoidance is one method of showing social distance; agitations against living near or with Chinese is another.
9. Integration of Chinese is progressing, and they are often local leaders and buffers as other "racial" minorities achieve greater integration.

PROSPECTS FOR THE CHINESE IN THE UNITED STATES

With the now greater preponderance of native-born over foreign-born and their high degree of acculturation, the later generations of Chinese are now oriented more toward the larger community. While dominant discrimination has not disappeared in housing, employment, club memberships, and intermarriage, it would seem, in the present climate of increasing acceptance of all minorities, that white Americans will not interpose permanent barriers to the assimilation of the Chinese. Much depends too on the individual Chinese and the type of mental, social, educational, and class orientation he possesses. As is true of other ethnic groups, the degree of acculturation is uneven. Length of residence is not the crucial criterion as much as life style, socioeconomic attainment, mode of livelihood, and membership in civic and other formal organizations of the larger society.

TOPICS FOR PROJECTS AND DISCUSSION

1. Suggest as many reasons as you can for the fact that the number of Chinese in this country is now much less than the number who ever came here.
2. What reasons would you suggest for the fact that the Chinese tend to live in or near large metropolitan areas?
3. Design a questionnaire aiming to find out the attitudes of white Americans toward the Chinese living in this country and to find out the source of their attitudes. Try out your research plan.
4. Discuss the implications of the changed international situation for Chinese living in the United States.

SUGGESTED READING

Huang, Lucy. "Dating and Courtship Innovations of Chinese Students in America," *Marriage and Family Living,* Vol. 18, February, 1956, pp. 25–30.
> *Based on interviews with Chinese students of both sexes.*

Konvitz, M. R. *The Alien and the Asiatic in American Law.* Ithaca, N. Y.: Cornell University Press, 1946.
> *Deals with the various civic discriminations imposed by law on aliens and Asiatic peoples resident in the United States.*

Lee, Rose Hum. "The Stranded Chinese in the United States," *Phylon,* Second Quarter, 1958, pp. 180–194.
> *Analysis of problems faced by Chinese students stranded in the United States as a result of the collapse of the Nationalist Government of China.*

Lee, Rose Hum. *The Chinese in the United States of America.* Hong Kong: Hong Kong University Press, 1960. Distributed in the United States by Oxford University Press, New York.
> *The most comprehensive and informative single volume on the Chinese in the United States.*

Siu, Paul C. F. "The Sojourner," *American Journal of Sociology,* July, 1952, 58: 34–44.
> *Analysis, based partly on interviews.*

9

The Japanese in the United States

Like the Chinese, the Japanese settled on the West Coast, but in a more stable period in that region's history. While eventually they may have incurred more antagonism from the natives than the Chinese did, they were spared the physical violence suffered by the Chinese in the lawless frontier days. Japanese culture was Asiatic, like that of the Chinese, but Japan had already entered a period of technological development so that their literacy was greater and their skills better suited to rapid economic adjustment. It is perhaps because of this superiority from the standpoint of making a living that their subsequent relations with the natives followed a different course than those of the Chinese.

Although most of the Chinese remained on the West Coast, a considerable number scattered in cities throughout the northern part of the country. But up to the time of their relocation the Japanese remained highly concentrated in the Pacific coast states. While the Chinese reacted to native opposition with extreme passivity, as has been shown, the Japanese were less tractable. They held their ground, refusing to disperse like the Chinese, and made ingenious adaptations to the various economic discriminations inflicted on them, such as devising a plan whereby an alien father bought land in the name of his native-born son. Consequently, while the native population

183

came to think of the Chinese in stereotype A—the inferior, humble, and ignorant, who could be condescendingly tolerated—the Japanese came to be treated according to stereotype B—the aggressive, cunning, and conspiratorial, requiring more active and outright dominance to keep them "in their place."

Like the Chinese, the Japanese retained a greater interest in their homeland than the European immigrants, as manifested in the large number constantly returning to Japan. Yet the Japanese population in the United States shows an almost steady rise, while up to 1930, as we have seen, that of the Chinese showed some years of decline. Finally, both groups suffered from the humiliation of severe legislative discrimination, culminating in drastic federal laws. The manner, however, of handling the federal restriction of immigration was noticeably more diplomatic in the case of the Japanese, a contrast attributable to the greater power of the Japanese government, a government able to protest more effectively against the discriminatory treatment of their nationals in this country.

JAPANESE POPULATION TRENDS

For over 200 years, from 1638 to 1868, Japanese citizens were forbidden to go abroad, and foreigners, with few exceptions, were forbidden to enter Japan. The first to go out from the Land of the Rising Sun were students sent to gain knowledge from the rest of the world. Soon after, a limited number of laborers were permitted to leave. But it was the agreement signed by the Japanese government and certain Hawaiian sugar plantation owners in 1885, by which Japanese contract laborers were permitted to go to Hawaii, that set emigration into momentum. From then until 1924 there was considerable Japanese migration to Asiatic Russia (302,946), to Hawaii (238,758), to the United States (196,543), and to China (105,258); and, in more limited numbers, to Canada, Brazil, the Philippines, Peru, Korea, and Australia. Considering the enormous rate of population growth in Japan during these decades and the consequent population pressure, the relatively modest amount of emigration is surprising. The failure to emigrate in larger numbers to the areas of the world settled by Europeans was due in part to the unfriendly manner with which the Japanese were received and to the legal restrictions imposed. The special circumstances leading to substantial Japanese immigration to Hawaii are discussed in Chapter 16.

With overlapping in the 1881–1890 decade, Japanese immigration to the continental United States takes on where Chinese immigration falls off. Tables 5 and 6, respectively, show the number of Japanese immigrants admitted from 1861–1947 and the total Japanese population, which of course includes the native-born, at the decennial years.

TABLE 5
Japanese Immigration to the United States[1]

1861–70	186
1871–80	149
1881–90	2,270
1891–00	25,942
1901–10	129,797
1911–20	83,837
1921–30	33,462
1931–40	1,948
1941–50	1,555
1951–60	46,250

TABLE 6
Japanese Population in Mainland United States[2]

CENSUS YEAR	NUMBER	DECADE	PERCENTAGE RATE OF INCREASE
1860	0		
1870	55		
1880	148	1870–80	169.1
1890	2,039	1880–90	1,277.7
1900	24,326	1890–00	1,093.0
1910	72,157	1900–10	196.6
1920	111,010	1910–20	53.8
1930	138,834	1920–30	25.1
1940	126,947	1930–40	−13.1
1950	141,768	1940–50	11.6
1960	260,877*	1950–60	83.3**

* The 1960 Census includes Hawaii, giving a total Japanese population of 464,332.
** Based on mainland figures without Hawaii. The percentage increase of the Japanese population for the United States including Hawaii for the 1950–1960 decade was 42.3.

The increase in the Japanese population from 1880 to 1910 was due largely to immigration itself, since the great preponderance of the new-comers were male. After the agitation on the West Coast for restricting Japanese immigration, President Theodore Roosevelt negotiated directly with the Japanese government, and the so-called Gentlemen's Agreement was made in 1907. It provided that Japan would not issue passports for the continental United States to laborers unless they were coming to resume a

[1] *Annual Reports of the Immigration and Naturalization Service.*
[2] Advanced Reports, United States Census, 1940, Vol. II, Table 4, p. 19; also Advanced Reports, 1960, Annual Population Characteristics, PC(A 2) −1, Table 1, p. 4.

formerly acquired domicile, to join a parent, husband, or child, or to resume control of a farming enterprise which they had left. This agreement did not completely close the door to Japanese immigration, and the growth of the population was due partly to that continued, though greatly diminished, immigration. More significant, however, is the fact that many of the immigrants after 1907 were women, frequently "picture brides." By 1930 the sex ratio among the Japanese in this country had declined to 143.3 males for every 100 females—much more normal than that of either the Chinese or the Filipinos living here. The only decennial decline in Japanese population occurred in the 1930–1940 decade, during which the number of returning homeland emigrants exceeded 8,000, while slightly fewer than 2,000 new immigrants came in. This trend apparently continued up to the time of Pearl Harbor, since the estimated population in 1942 was only 122,000.

As Table 6 shows, the population of Americans of Japanese descent on the mainland has continued to increase, reaching 260,877 in 1960.[3] The surprising increase in the 1950–1960 decade cannot be accounted for by births or by the allocation to Japan of an annual quota of 185 for the first time under the immigration revisions of the McCarran-Walter Act in 1952. It is largely due to the admission of wives of male American citizens, Oriental or Caucasian. In 1960, of the 5,699 Japanese aliens admitted as immigrants, 3,990 were wives of citizens.[4] During the period from 1951 to 1960, there were 46,250 Japanese immigrants admitted to this country.[5]

As we have noted, the Japanese population, unlike the Chinese, remained heavily concentrated on the West Coast, particularly in California, up to the time of the attack on Pearl Harbor. In 1940, of the 127,000 Japanese, both foreign-born and native-born citizens, 111,000, or about 88 per cent, resided on the West Coast. In California alone there were 83 per cent, and most of these were in Los Angeles County. Outside of the West, the only two cities having enough Japanese to form a distinctive colony were Chicago and New York. Chicago had a larger Japanese population than any other city except Los Angeles, estimated at 15,000 to 20,000.[6] In New York a Japanese colony has existed since the late nineteenth century, reaching at one point nearly 5,000, but at the outbreak of the war numbering about 2,000.[7] The relocation of the Japanese resulting from their evacuation from the West Coast and their resettlement has considerably changed the pattern of distribution, as will be discussed below.

[3] Figure obtained by subtracting the Japanese in Hawaii in 1960 (203,445) from the total Japanese population of the United States (464,332). See note (*) in Table 6.
[4] *Annual Report of the Immigration and Naturalization Service*, 1960, Table 6A, p. 19.
[5] *Ibid.*, Table 13, p. 41.
[6] *People in Motion: The Postwar Adjustment of the Evacuated Japanese*, United States Department of Interior Publication (Washington, D.C.: Government Printing Office, n.d.), p. 168.
[7] Bradford Smith, *Americans from Japan* (Philadelphia: J. B. Lippincott Co., 1948), p. 336.

CULTURAL BACKGROUNDS OF THE JAPANESE IMMIGRANTS

The culture in which the Japanese immigrants had been reared differed more markedly from that of America than the culture of the European immigrants; yet in some aspects it prepared the Japanese for more successful adjustment to life in this country. Before the period of Japanese immigration, Japan had begun transforming itself from a semifeudal into a modern industrial nation. Thus its culture was a mixture of the traditional and the new. Basic in its traditional culture was the intricate set of mores which defined the strong obligation of the individual to the group, to the family, to those of superior class, and to the state. The strongly authoritarian character of Japanese social organization produced markedly obedient and self-effacing personality traits in the Japanese people. The strong sense of subordination of the individual to the welfare of the group was reflected in the solidarity of Japanese groups in this country. Deriving also from long tradition was the intricate pattern of etiquette and ritual which prescribed the proper way of behaving in every situation. To conform punctiliously to these elaborate social rituals was a major drive in the Japanese personality, accounting for the reputation for courtesy and good manners which the nineteenth-century Japanese acquired.

The ferment of rapid change had begun in earnest at the beginning of the Meiji Era (1868–1912). The conscious policy of the ruling elite was to transform Japan into an industrial nation with western technological methods under a centralized government. To the already great skill in farming, necessitated by population pressure and little tillable acreage, new scientific agricultural methods were added. Public education was developed to a high level. The development of scientific medicine and programs of public health were encouraged. While it is difficult to know how much all these new influences affected the mass of the Japanese people, nevertheless, in the willingness to learn and to experiment in matters technological and economic, the Japanese did surpass not only all other Asians but many European immigrant groups.

INITIAL ADJUSTMENT

The first Japanese in the United States were employed in domestic service. As their numbers increased, some became engaged in a wide variety of menial jobs and others began to operate small shops. Because at first their numbers were small and the jobs they took did not affect the employment opportunities of white American workers, little opposition was felt. Beginning about 1890, however, antagonism began to be displayed by members of labor unions. In that year Japanese cobblers were attacked by members of the shoemakers' union. In 1892, a Japanese restaurant in San Francisco was attacked by members of the local cooks' and waiters' union.[8] From then on, anti-Japanese activity grew steadily in California, rising to a climax in the famous School Board Affair in 1906, when the San Francisco Board of Education passed a resolution requiring the segregation of all Oriental children in one school. At the time there were ninety-three Japanese attending twenty-three different public schools of San Francisco. The resolution brought protest from the Japanese government and precipitated a crisis between the Imperial Government and that of the United States, which led to the signing of the Gentlemen's Agreement in 1907.

The rising antagonism toward the Japanese in the cities led them to turn to agriculture.[9] They started out as farm laborers and by the late 1890's outnumbered the Chinese laborers. By 1909 they constituted a large part of the farm labor force in the western states. It was natural for the Japanese to turn to agriculture: they brought with them knowledge of intensive cultivation of the soil superior to that of many American native farmers. It was likewise natural that more and more of them should aspire to operate farms themselves. By 1909 there were 6,000 Japanese operating farms, the greater number by far as tenants.[10] They experimented with small-scale farming, finally concentrating on fruits and vegetables. They were adaptable, thrifty, and industrious, and the number of Japanese-operated farms increased until 1920.[11]

The success of the Japanese in moving from laborer to entrepreneur, even though on a small scale and usually involving the payment of rent to white owners, led to opposition from white farmers, culminating in the passage in California of the first alien land holding act in 1913. Under this legislation, aliens ineligible for citizenship could lease agricultural land for periods not to exceed three years but could not own it. When it was discovered that the Japanese were buying stock in land-owning corporations and acquiring land in the name of their native-born children, further pressure resulted in a new act, which in substance prohibited the leasing of land by any method by Japanese foreign-born. Similar laws were passed by other Western states, and their constitutionality was upheld by the United States Supreme Court in a test case in 1923. From then on the role of the Japanese in agriculture declined, and return to the cities increased. Nevertheless, at the time of Pearl Harbor they controlled large segments of California's berry and vegetable crops.

[8] Yamato Ichihashi, *Japanese in the United States* (Stanford: Stanford University Press, 1932), pp. 229–230.

[9] Ibid., see Chs. 11, 12, 13, for an account of the progress of the Japanese in American agriculture.

[10] *Ibid.*, p. 178.

[11] *Ibid.*, p. 193.

URBAN ADJUSTMENT

As with all urban-dwelling minorities, the Japanese established a separate community within the larger community. On the West Coast, the main "Little Tokyos" were in San Francisco, Los Angeles, and Seattle. For a close-up view of life within such a colony we turn to Seattle around 1935.

The Seattle Japanese Community, 1935[12]

The Japanese began coming to Seattle around 1900, establishing a colony with a transient character that reflected the frontier nature of Seattle itself at the time. Since in a growing community there was plenty of work to do, the few Japanese were welcome. There were mostly men eager to make money and return to Japan. Many stayed, however, and, after the Gentlemen's Agreement, when more Japanese wives came to the United States, a more settled community life developed. While discrimination against the Japanese was pronounced, the opportunity to earn a living remained, furthered by the labor demand during World War I. The Immigration Act of 1924, which had prohibited further Japanese immigration, marked the beginning of what Miyamoto called the "second generation" period. "From a community geared to expect a constant flow of immigration," it became a community geared to the greater opportunity which the American-born could claim as their birthright. By 1930, of Seattle's 8,448 Japanese, 47 per cent were native-born.

The Japanese colony was located directly to the southeast of Seattle's central business district. Between 1920 and 1935, the distribution of Japanese residences showed a marked trend away from solidly Japanese areas to a scattering about the central areas. The more successful Japanese families were diffused throughout practically every section of Seattle.

While the Japanese were found in a wide range of occupations, considerable concentration is noted. Of those employed in Seattle in 1935, 31 per cent were in domestic and personal service and 45 per cent in the trades.[13] In general, the range of family incomes was not great, which meant that the absence of class difference was added to the forces uniting the members of the Japanese colony. The number of Japanese operating small mercantile enterprises of their own reflected a considerable individual initiative and participation in the private enterprise system. But few could accumulate enough capital for these ventures; most required the aid of friends and relatives for the start. Often small groups formed pools from which various members could draw in initiating new enterprises.

The social life of the Japanese colony in Seattle revealed a mixture of Old World, accommodative, and acculturative institutions. The traditional heritage was most clearly seen in the continuance of the patriarchal Japanese family, with its extreme emphasis on male authority and filial obligations. In recreation likewise, their play life tended "to revolve about activities that are essentially Japanese in character."[14] The two Japanese daily newspapers in Seattle in 1935 were heavily devoted to activities of the homeland, and few of the foreign-born Japanese read American papers.

[12] Adapted from Shotaro Frank Miyamoto, *Social Solidarity Among the Japanese in Seattle,* University of Washington Publications in the Social Sciences, Vol. 11, No. 2 (Dec., 1939), pp. 57–130.
[13] *Ibid.,* p. 71.
[14] *Ibid.,* p. 122.

Among the accommodative institutions there were, in the economic area, the *tanomoshi,* or "pools" described above, and a Japanese chamber of commerce, patterned after the American form. In addition there were the *Ken-jin* and the Seattle branch of the Japanese Association of North America. The former were organizations of Japanese who came from a particular region, or *ken,* of Japan. Their functions were primarily social and, occasionally, charitable. The Japanese Association was the nonofficial equivalent of community government. It acted as the agency of social control throughout the Japanese community and represented it in its relations with the larger community.

In addition to their rapid adjustment to American economic institutions, the Japanese subscribed to the high value placed by Americans on education. While most of the immigrants themselves lacked higher education, they encouraged their children not only to continue school but also to excel in their studies. The strong discipline of the Japanese parents over their children was employed to reinforce the authority of the school. Between 1930 and 1937 in the nine Seattle high schools fifteen Japanese students were either valedictorians or salutatorians of their classes.

Turning to the sphere of religious affiliations, it is somewhat striking to note that 1,200 Seattle Japanese belonged to Christian churches in 1936,[15] more than belonged to all the Japanese religious groups combined. Miyamoto suggests that the many practical services rendered by the mission churches encouraged Japanese membership.

The general picture one gets from examining the situation of the Japanese in Seattle, which was representative of their situation throughout the West Coast, is that the Japanese successfully adapted to American life but still lived as a group apart. Much of their continued ethnic identity can be accounted for by forces within the group itself, which have been described above. Nevertheless, without question their continued solidarity and distinctiveness were manifestations of their rejection by white Americans as full-fledged participants in the life of the larger community. Once the more strongly voiced opposition was felt, the Japanese accommodated themselves to limited opportunity on a separate and discriminatory basis, which was the pattern up to the time of Pearl Harbor.

Increasingly, however, the succeeding generations of Japanese born in this country were becoming acculturated. We turn to consider these native-born as a group and the effect of their increasing acculturation on the position of the Japanese in American society.

THE AMERICAN – BORN JAPANESE

The increasing acculturation of the nisei, as the Japanese born in America of foreign parentage are called, developed cleavages in the closely integrated and self-sufficient Japanese community life. Cultural conflict similar to that noted in the European groups produced similar strains in family life. The younger Japanese considered their parents "too Japanesy" and began to defy their attempts to discipline them according to the traditional family pattern. The children became interested in American sports, desired free-

[15] *Ibid.,* p. 99.

dom in their out-of-school life, and wanted to dress in the fashion of their white schoolmates. For the parents this Americanization brought much sorrow. They could not understand that this desire on the part of their children to act like Americans was dictated by the wish to be accepted as Americans.

The typical conflict between generations among immigrant groups was made more intense for the Japanese by the unusual age distribution of their population. The great disparity in the sex ratio of the earlier immigrant group resulted in a great preponderance of males in the older generation. The middle-age generation was proportionally small, and not until the third generation were large numbers of both sexes present. "As late as 1940, only 27,000 of the 80,000 Nisei were over twenty-one."[16] Many Japanese parents sent their children back home to be brought up in the fatherland culture. In 1942 it was estimated that at least 25,000 United States citizens of Japanese ancestry had been educated in schools in Japan. Among these kibei, as they were designated, were the Japanese considered most probably disloyal in sentiment at the time of Pearl Harbor.

As with the Chinese, the conflict of the generations, typical in immigrant patterns, had a different sequel from that of the European nationalities. Anxious as the nisei were to become Americans and forget Japan, they found that, despite their acculturation, the native community looked upon them as "Japs" because of their racial visibility. They continued to be discriminated against in three areas—employment, public places, and social contacts.

In employment the educated nisei had three choices. He could accept prejudice for what it was, and assume the inferior tasks of houseboy, dishwasher, migratory laborer, cannery hand—just what the dominant group expected him as an inferior to do. He could go to Japan and forsake America. Or, if he tried hard, he could get a job at a higher level, though far below his actual qualifications.

Many barbershops, restaurants, and hotels refused service to Orientals. Several large coastal cities had restrictive covenants which kept the Japanese out of any of the attractive neighborhoods. And there were other aspects of discrimination in the social sphere.

The fear of rebuffs, the constant horror of being humiliated in public, made the Nisei draw together in a tight circle, even at college. They formed their own clubs even though some felt that such organizations only perpetuated their difficulties. They formed noticeable groups on campus. "There's a barrier between Nisei and the other students," said one. "You can feel it. They never feel easy with each other."

Hostility in the social sphere did not as a rule become noticeable until adolescence. The fear of "miscegenation," the old superstitions about racial "hybrids," the fear that friendship might be construed as having a sexual intent introduced at

16 Bradford Smith, *Americans from Japan*, p. 245.

courting age, a stiffening of attitudes. Yet the Nisei were quite as set against inter-marriage as the Caucasians, their own fears and superstitions as deeply rooted.[17]

EVACUATION AND RELOCATION

The processes of conflict and acculturation were rudely shattered by Pearl Harbor. On February 19, 1942, the Army was given authority to establish military zones from which any persons, citizens or alien, might be evacuated and excluded. All Japanese people were ordered to leave the West Coast. This action was the most unprecedented single national action against a large group of people in our history. Analysis of its causes provides insight into the dynamics of dominant-minority relations in the United States. (We shall return to this after carrying forward an account of what happened to the Japanese after February 19.)

At first the Japanese were given time to remove themselves. A few did leave, but it was soon discovered that they were not wanted elsewhere. A report from the *Los Angeles Times*, March 24, 1942, reads, "Japanese evacuees moving inland from California in a great mass migration will be put in concentration camps if they enter Nevada, Governor E. P. Carville warned tonight."[18] Therefore, on March 27, the Japanese were ordered to stay where they were pending their mass evacuation under military supervision. A new federal agency, The War Relocation Authority, was established to plan for the supervision of the Japanese under detention. Between then and August 8, all West Coast Japanese (over 110,000) were transferred to ten hastily built centers in the Rocky Mountain states and in Arkansas.

In addition to the shocklike psychological effect and the bitterness which evacuation engendered, the Japanese faced enormous economic losses. While the government took steps to protect the material property owned by the Japanese, the guarantees appeared so uncertain that many sold their effects—under the circumstances, of course, at a loss. A business enterprise and a crop in the field could not be "frozen." They had to be disposed of for whatever they would bring at hurried sale or lease, or be abandoned.

Life in the Settlement Centers

The War Relocation Authority faced a unique problem in American history. How the personnel met these problems and how life in the centers affected the Japanese have been extensively studied by highly qualified social scientists.[19] The policy of the WRA was to organize the community

[17] *Ibid.*, p. 250. By permission.
[18] Alexander H. Leighton, *The Governing of Men* (Princeton: Princeton University Press, 1945), p. 36.
[19] *Ibid.* See also Dorothy Swaine Thomas and Richard S. Nishimoto, *The Spoilage* (Berkeley: University of California Press, 1946).

life with maximum self-control by the Japanese. All the evidence indicates that the personnel were highly sympathetic to the Japanese, an attitude criticized by the same elements of the white population which had clamored for evacuation in the first place. As was almost inevitable under such circumstances, a number of rebellious activities followed. Of these the most serious was a strike by some evacuees at Poston Center, Arizona, arising out of a feeling that two alleged attackers of a white official had been unfairly punished. In consequence of incidents of this nature, Tule Lake Center, California, became a segregation camp where active malcontents from all other centers were placed and controlled under strict discipline.

Resettlement

The other branch of the WRA's operation was engaged through regional offices throughout the nation in trying to find employment for the Japanese outside the center. The WRA also assumed responsibility for helping the resettler adjust to his new community, as well as to his job. One of its hardest tasks in this connection was to find a place for him to live. This phase of operations has not been given the systematic study which it deserves as a reflection of dominant attitudes. Its activities beginning in the spring of 1943 included the resettlement of the Japanese particularly in the Midwest and the Mountain States. Lack of extensive resettlement in the East was due to Army opposition. Most of those leaving the camps were young adult nisei who, when they became successfully resettled, often sent for relatives to join them. In the large metropolitan centers it was fairly easy to place Japanese in a wide range of menial and semitechnical jobs. It was difficult to place them in industries with war contracts or in positions calling for contact with the public. Frequent opposition from unions arose. Among the reasons often given for not hiring the Japanese were distrust of their loyalty; that other employers would resent it; that customers would resent it; and "my son is in the Pacific." While many of the resettlers left their jobs for the same reasons one might under normal circumstances, they also left because of their interest in finding work where they could acquire new skills and get ahead.[20]

Up to January 1, 1945, the date after which evacuees were permitted to return to the West Coast, the WRA had resettled 31,625 Japanese in other parts of the country. Interestingly enough, when the opportunity came, the vast majority of the evacuees returned to their former communities. Since the date for terminating the WRA had been set, their choice had to be quick and the WRA was no longer able to give them individual assistance. It is probable also that many of the Japanese who had been resettled in other areas subsequently returned to the West Coast.

[20] The authors are indebted to Gordon Berryman, a former employee of the WRA, for sharing these insights into the resettlement process.

JAPANESE EVACUATION: A CASE HISTORY
IN WHITE AMERICAN DOMINANT BEHAVIOR

As we have noted, the evacuation of all persons of Japanese ancestry from the West Coast and their subsequent internment was a governmental action without precedent in American history, involving constitutional issues of grave significance. The Supreme Court of the United States upheld the constitutionality of evacuation in wartime,[21] although strong dissents were written by a minority of the justices. However, in retrospect, the whole incident appears to have been a serious error in judgment. For this reason some analysis of the circumstances which led to the steps taken is highly pertinent to the study of dominant-minority relations. The central question engaging our attention is this: To what extent was the decision for evacuation and internment of the Japanese arrived at as a logical necessity for national security; or to what extent was the decision made in response to regional pressures unrelated to security? Since the Western Defense Command of the United States Army was responsible for the decision, it is appropriate to consider first the case which it presented in justification.[22]

Military Authority

The Final Report referred to as fact some illegal signaling from shore to sea on the West Coast, although it presented no specific proof that Japanese were involved. It cited the result of one spot raid made by the Federal Bureau of Investigation on Japanese homes in which "more than 60,000 rounds of ammunition, and many rifles, shotguns, and maps of all kinds" were found. Such articles, as well as some others, had been declared contraband for enemy aliens. To what extent they were possessed by enemy aliens or by American citizens of Japanese ancestry and to what extent the articles found were evidence of conspiracy is not stated. The report indicated that in three instances in which Japanese submarines shelled West Coast areas, the particular spots chosen were the very ones most out of range of American coastal batteries at the time. It assumed that the Japanese Navy must have had "inside" information, although no evidence was presented to connect West Coast Japanese with this knowledge. The above is in substance the entire case made regarding acts of sabotage or espionage.

Much more of the case presented by the Western Defense Command concerning the security menace of the Japanese was based on the fact that the Japanese were in a position to do much damage and on the assumption that many of them would take such opportunities. The military authorities were much impressed by the residence distribution of the Japanese, which seemed

[21] *Koramatsu v. United States*, 323 U.S. 214.
[22] "Need for Military Control and for Evacuation," *Final Report, Japanese Evacuation from the West Coast* (Washington, D.C.: Government Printing Office, 1943), pp. 7–19.

too singularly adjacent to strategic points to be fully coincidental. Surprisingly enough for a military document, the report rested much of its case on sociological phenomena. Reference was made to "ties of race" as well as strong bonds of common traditional culture which make the Japanese a tightly-knit group. Major emphasis was placed on the considerable number of Japanese associations on the West Coast whose purposes and activities reflected great interest in the ancestral homeland and in some instances involved contributions in behalf of Japan's war with China. Finally, the report stressed and statistically verified the fact that a considerable number of the American-born Japanese had been educated in Japan and subsequently returned to live in the States. The military authorities conceded that many Japanese living in the country were loyal but felt that the task of screening the loyal from the disloyal presented too great a problem and that therefore the only safe course was to evacuate everybody of Japanese ancestry.

The sociological observations just noted comprised facts about the Japanese in the United States well known to many people on the West Coast. In fact, the Japanese had been the subject of much detailed study by Pacific Coast social scientists long before Pearl Harbor. These students could have greatly assisted the military in making valid interpretations of Japanese society on the West Coast. In this connection Grodzins writes, "as later research has shown military officers did not in a single instance rely on the large mass of scientific materials that had been gathered about American Japanese by such men as Steiner, Park, Strong, Bogardus, and Bailey."[23]

Espionage and sabotage are inevitable concomitants of war. It is reasonable to suppose that some of the enemy aliens would be engaged in the task, although it is also logical to suppose that among the enemy agents would be some who were not Japanese at all. Even in the absence of much specific proof of disloyal behavior on the part of Japanese Americans, the general logic of the situation clearly called for special vigilance over this group by the agents of the Justice Department and prompt action against any particular individuals, even perhaps on reasonable suspicion. With such a policy, actually already in practice before evacuation orders, few Americans, and perhaps even few Americans of Japanese ancestry, would have quarreled. This was, indeed, the policy advocated by the Justice Department. As late as January 12, 1942, Attorney General Biddle said, "Wholesale internment, without hearing and irrespective of the merits of individual cases, is the long and costly way around, as the British discovered by painful experience; for by that method not only are guiltless aliens themselves demoralized, but the nation is deprived of a valuable source of labor supply at a time when every available man must be at work.[24]

---

[23] Morton Grodzins, *Americans Betrayed: Politics and the Japanese Evacuation* (Chicago: University of Chicago Press, 1949), p. 305.
[24] Leighton, *Governing of Men*, p. 17. By permission.

But the case submitted was highly unimpressive as a justification for such drastic action as mass evacuation. How then is the evacuation to be explained? Two possible answers appear. One is that General De Witt, Commanding General of the West Coast Area, believed it necessary on the basis of his no doubt sincere, but sociologically inaccurate, judgment of the Japanese, and his judgment was accepted by various higher officials, including President Franklin D. Roosevelt, who finally issued the order. A second possible explanation is that De Witt was influenced by the pressure of people on the West Coast who were either fearful of or imbued with strong antagonism toward the Japanese. Grodzins stresses the latter influence: "The most active proponents of mass evacuation were certain agricultural and business groups, chambers of commerce, the American Legion, the California Joint Immigration Committee, and the Native Sons and Daughters of the Golden West."[25] The list of pressure groups can be divided into those with economic motivation for getting rid of the Japanese and those with a nativist, anti-foreign orientation. The following excerpt from a resolution adopted by an Oregon American Legion Post illustrates the sort of pressure that was exerted:

[that] this is no time for namby-pamby pussyfooting. . . . that it is not the time for consideration of minute constitutional rights of those enemies but that it is time for vigorous, whole-hearted, and concerted action . . . toward the removal of all enemy aliens and citizens of enemy alien extraction from all areas along the coast and that only those be permitted to return that are able to secure special permit for that purpose . . .[26]

Ten Broeck and his associates[27] place greater responsibility on the commanding officer and his superiors, and on the people of the West Coast generally, among whom there was widespread fear and frustration engendered by the war and Japan's early military successes.

In summary, we suggest that the evacuation resulted from the interaction of a series of factors: (1) the well-established pattern of dominant-minority relations, long nurtured throughout the history of the relations between native Americans and the Japanese on the West Coast; (2) the crisis of war, engendering fear of those racially identified with an enemy nation; (3) a situation ripe for special groups antagonistic to the Japanese to exploit; (4) the failure of liberal West Coast native Americans to bring sufficient counter pressure; (5) the position of authority of a commanding officer with particularly unsophisticated sociological judgment; and (6) the fact that higher federal officials had to make a decision while beset with the enormous burdens of conducting a war.

[25] Grodzins, *Americans Betrayed*, p. 17.
[26] *Ibid.*, p. 42. By permission.
[27] Jacobus Ten Broeck, Edward N. Barnhart, and Floyd W. Matson, *Prejudice, War, and the Constitution* (Berkeley and Los Angeles: University of California Press, 1954).

The Hawaiian Contrast

It will be instructive to conclude the discussion of the evacuation episode with a brief account of a contrasting situation in Hawaii.

At the outbreak of war with Japan, persons of Japanese ancestry comprised about a third of Hawaii's population. Following Pearl Harbor, rumors arose of espionage activities on the part of some island Japanese. Both the military and the insular authorities, failing to find specific evidence, placed their official weight on the side of allaying the rumors and indicating their confidence in the loyalty of the Hawaiian Japanese as a group. Limited restrictions were imposed on the alien Japanese similar to those imposed on the West Coast, and a few Japanese whose records before the war rendered them suspicious were interned. But there were elements of the general insular population who, fearful of the possible dangers from the Japanese and other groups, called for firmer action. As Lind indicates, there was an increase in public demonstrations against Japanese persons, apparently more from the Filipinos in Hawaii than from the white or other ethnic elements.[28] Nevertheless, the authorities held firm to their policy of active vigilance over the Japanese and arrest of only those who acted in a suspicious manner. General suspicion and fear of the Japanese as a group subsided, and the relations of the Japanese to the rest of the archipelago's population resumed, in the main, their prewar character. The correctness of the official judgment that the Japanese in general constituted no serious security threat to Hawaii was borne out by future events. Subsequent hearings on the charges of subversive activity by local Japanese brought forth emphatic denials from the War Department, the Federal Bureau of Investigation, and from various insular authorities.[29] On the whole, it can be said that the Japanese were cooperative in accepting the mild restrictions, continued their economic role in Hawaiian production, and ultimately made contributions to the armed services. Lind states that "The final count of Hawaiian war casualties revealed that 80 per cent of those killed and 88 per cent of those wounded throughout the war were of Japanese ancestry."[30]

How can we account for the strikingly different policies adopted in Hawaii and on the West Coast? Contrary to what one might at first think, the much greater proportion of Japanese in the islands operated against a policy of internment. To have tried to police one-third of the population would have been a costly process. More important, however, the removal of the Japanese from the general labor force would have drastically reduced the productive capacity of Hawaii just when a maximum increase in production was essential to the war effort.

[28] Andrew Lind, *Hawaii's Japanese* (Princeton: Princeton University Press, 1948), pp. 56–61.
[29] *Ibid.*, pp. 38–47.
[30] *Ibid.*, p. 126.

Underlying the more favorable treatment of the Japanese were certain facets of the general pattern of intergroup relations in Hawaii, which are discussed in more detail in Chapter 16. At this point we shall briefly call attention to two factors which stand in sharp contrast to the West Coast situation. First, a more friendly and less discriminatory pattern of intergroup relations prevailed in Hawaii. Tradition frowned on any public or explicit color discrimination. Second, the economic position of the Japanese in Hawaii had developed few antagonisms based on competition. While by 1940 the Japanese as a group had moved far from their earlier role as plantation workers toward various city occupations, this transition had not yet brought them into much direct competition for jobs with the socially dominant white population.

The Effects of Evacuation

The short-range effects of the evacuation and temporary resettlement on the national welfare were costly indeed. Particular segments of the West Coast population, as we have seen, made substantial gains out of removal of the Japanese from competition. For these gains, the nation paid a heavy price. The removal of the Japanese retarded the war effort. While eventually many Japanese did find useful work during the war, they would have contributed more if they had remained where they were. In fact, there were so many high-paying opportunities in California created by the manpower shortage that many Mexicans and Negroes migrated there. The whole process of evacuation, the operation of the centers, and the effort of the WRA to relocate the evacuees cost time, money, and energy which could have been used to more constructive purpose.

The effect of the evacuation on the prestige of the United States in world opinion is difficult to appraise. Because of their imperialist activities in Asia, the Japanese abroad were thoroughly hated by many other Asiatic peoples. Nevertheless, the way in which the Japanese in this country were dealt with in contrast to our treatment of Germans and Italians reflected our color bias, and cannot have raised our moral stock with nonwhite people in general.

POST – EVACUATION READJUSTMENT

Following the end of the evacuation order on January 1, 1945, the Japanese were free to go where they wanted. As we have seen, many returned to the West Coast. In 1960, the number of Japanese in the states of California (157,317), Washington (16,652), and Oregon (5,016) was 178,985, accounting for 69 per cent of the mainland Japanese population. Since in 1940 as many as 88 per cent were concentrated on the West Coast, the difference reflects the dispersive effect of evacuation. The largest number located in any one community not on the West Coast is in Chicago.[31] The Los Angeles-Long Beach area, with 81,204 in 1960, occupies first place ahead of Chicago, having about one-third of all the Japanese on the mainland.

Chicago's Japanese Americans

Caudhill and Devos report on an intensive study of the Japanese in Chicago from 1947 to 1950.[32] Their main findings concern the marked acculturation of Chicago's nisei to American middle-class norms. Objective measures of this phenomenon are seen in an educational level which exceeds that of the general American average, and in the occupational distribution. The authors found that, as early as 1947, of their sample, 35 per cent were in white-collar employment, 6 per cent owned small businesses, and 9 per cent were professionals. Employed nisei women were largely in white-collar occupations. As young adults, the nisei were still moving up the occupational scale.

Since various studies had indicated that the range of mental ability of Japanese Americans conformed to the general population range, Caudhill and Devos sought the explanation of such unusual occupational success in Japanese culture. The chief hypothesis emerging was that "There seems to be a significant compatibility (but by no means identity) between the value systems found in the culture of Japan and the value systems found in American middle class culture."[33] Thematic apperception tests indicated scores in positive achievement responses more comparable to those of the researchers' middle-class white sample (in fact higher) than their sample of white lower classes. The cultural influence, as mediated through the parents, was further confirmed in the still higher positive achievement responses of the issei, as the foreign-born are called, (who were themselves less successful) than those of the nisei. The study further reports highly favorable opinions of the Japanese by employers, who attributed many middle-class virtues to the Japanese workers: efficiency, honesty, punctuality, neatness, good moral character. Significantly, the occasional negative evaluation took the form of criticizing the nisei for being too ambitious, for wanting to move on to a better job too quickly. Thus in a new setting where no community pattern of hostility is traditional, the Japanese have created a highly favorable image of themselves as a group.

In other urban areas of relocation as well, favorable results were met. Of St. Louis, for example, Smith writes "Acceptance was good from the very

[31] Various nonofficial estimates of Chicago Japanese population, ranging from 16,000 to 20,000 were apparently too high, since the 1960 census records only 13,067 Japanese for the standard metropolitan statistical area of Chicago.
[32] William Caudhill and George Devos, "Achievement, Culture and Personality: The Case of the Japanese Americans," *American Anthropologist*, 1956, 58: 1102–1126.
[33] *Ibid.*, p. 1107.

first, thanks to good planning."[34] Acceptance of the evacuees in rural areas, however, was not generally good. One exception was Bridgeton, New Jersey. Here the community reacted with considerable anxiety when Seabrook Farms, a large vegetable growing and preserving corporation, announced it was going to employ interned Japanese. But the anxiety quickly abated after the white community had a chance to judge the Japanese for themselves.

Economic Readjustment

Bloom and Riemer have estimated that the evacuated Japanese sustained an economic loss of $367,500,000, if income losses were added to all other losses incurred from forced sale of their assets, loss of business good will, and other losses attendant on their rapid removal.[35] Making a sample survey of 206 Japanese American families, these authors found the median loss per family to be $9870, counting household and personal loss, total property loss, fees and expenses, and loss of income figures at the 1941 values of the dollar.[36] Individual economic loss is illustrated in these words of a Santa Clara County issei:

Before War I had 20 acres in Berryessa. Good land, two good houses, one big. 1943 in camp everybody say sell, sell, sell. Maybe lose all. Lawyer write, he say sell. I sell $650 acre. Now the same land $1500 acre. I lose. I cannot help. All gone. Now I live in hostel. Work like when first come to this country. Pick cherries, pick pears, pick apricots, pick tomatoes. Just like when first come. Pretty soon, maybe one year, maybe two years, find place. Pretty hard now. Now spend $15,000 just for land. No good material for house. No get farm equipment.[37]

Some small part of this loss was compensated under an Act of Congress in July, 1948 (Public Law, 886, H. R. 2999), which empowered the Attorney General to reimburse any person not to exceed $2500 for "damage to or loss of real or personal property. . . . that is a reasonable and natural consequence of the evacuation." Claims had to be filed within eighteen months, and any claims for loss of anticipated profits or earnings were excluded. Evacuees filed 24,064 claims. By March 1, 1956, all but 1,936 had been adjusted and paid. The delayed settlements involved claims in excess of the original $2500 limit. In 1956, Congress amended the act to permit settlement up to $100,000. The problem in settling these claims involved the difficulty of proving the losses and the fact that few Japanese had obtained documentary proof of sales in anticipation of such indemnity.

The evacuation undermined the occupational position of the Japanese and forced readjustment upon return at lower socioeconomic levels. Few farmers

[34] Bradford Smith, *Americans from Japan*, p. 335.
[35] Leonard Bloom and Ruth Riemer, *Removal and Return* (Berkeley: University of California Press, 1949), pp. 202–204.
[36] *Ibid.*, p. 144.
[37] *People in Motion*, p. 53.

could re-establish themselves, and produce dealers were far fewer than before the war. Many went into contract gardening, which provided a measure
of the independence they formerly enjoyed. The great shortage of housing
available for the Japanese increased the number of boarding and rooming
houses where the Japanese who did have homes added to their income by
charging high prices of fellow Japanese. The housing shortage also increased
the number of returnees who went into domestic service, which often provided housing. In general, the pattern of employment for the returnees involved a shift from being either independently employed or working for
other Japanese to working for non-Japanese employers. Bloom and Riemer
estimate that before the war, not more than 20 per cent of the Japanese
labor force in Los Angeles County worked for non-Japanese, but place the
figure in 1948 at 70 per cent.[38]

Reaction of Dominant Americans

On the West Coast, knowledge that the Japanese were coming back
evoked reaction from racist-minded groups who had been instrumental in
causing their evacuation. The American Legion, Veterans of the Foreign
Wars, Native Sons of the Golden West, the California Farm Bureau, all protested. New "Ban the Jap" committees sprang up. A number of newspapers
ran scare headlines which made many Californians uneasy. "Hood River had
jumped the gun by erasing the names of its sixteen Nisei soldiers from the
honor roll" [subsequently restored].[39] In the first half of 1945 more than
thirty serious incidents occurred throughout California.

This time, however, there was a second set of reactions, which had been
missing before. Many individuals and groups demanded that the Japanese
be given fair play and became active in insisting that they get it. The Fresno
Fair Play Committee organized to file eviction suits in behalf of those Japanese unable to move back into their former homes. In Hood River a Christian pastor organized the League for Liberty and Justice, which "made a
frontal attack on the shameful practice of refusing to sell groceries and other
necessities to Nisei."[40] When machinists of the San Francisco Municipal
Railway threatened to strike in protest against the employment of a nisei,
Mayor Roger Lapham averted the strike by going to the shop in person and
explaining to the men why the nisei was entitled to the job. Churches up
and down the Coast were focal points of support for the nisei. This second
reaction finally won out.

The pressure of public opinion all over the country put California on the defensive. It came to a point where the civic pride of the several communities was challenged and race baiting lost favor. At the beginning of 1945 the West Coast

[38] Bloom and Riemer, *Removal and Return*, pp. 67–68.
[39] Bradford Smith, *Americans from Japan*, p. 346.
[40] *Ibid.*, p. 348.

papers had been four to one against the Japanese. A year later they were four to one in favor of fair and equal treatment.[41]

Court Decisions Favorable to the Japanese

A number of court decisions invalidating laws and practices which discriminated against both the Japanese and the Chinese were handed down between 1948 and 1950. In June, 1948, the United States Supreme Court (*Takahashi* vs. *Game Commission of California*) declared unconstitutional a California law prohibiting the issuance of fishing licenses to persons ineligible for citizenship. In October, 1948, the Supreme Court of California ruled that this state's law barring interracial marriages was unconstitutional.

Three significant court decisions bearing on West Coast laws prohibiting Oriental aliens from owning agricultural land were handed down in the same period. The United States Supreme Court in January, 1948, ruled in the case of *Oyama* vs. *California* that that section of the California alien land law raising presumption of fraudulent ownership and occupation of agricultural land by persons ineligible for citizenship was unconstitutional. In March, 1949, the Oregon Supreme Court held unconstitutional the state's 1923 Alien Land Law, which prohibited renting and leasing land to Japanese aliens. The District Court of Appeals, sitting at Los Angeles in April, 1950, held that California's law barring aliens ineligible for citizenship from owning land was contrary to the Constitution of the United States. In this case the Court made a further point of great significance when it stated that the law involved was contrary to the Charter of the United Nations. The citing of this international sanction in relation to a domestic issue has profound implications for the future of dominant-minority relations in the United States.

Nisei Acculturation

Under these more favorable circumstances the Japanese made rapid acculturative strides. By breaking up the continuity of the group life, the evacuation had weakened group solidarity. Leadership was gradually transferred to the nisei. The experience in relocation gave the nisei more independence, since they often earned more money by working in the vicinity of the camps than their parents. Many nisei relocated in Eastern cities; and many came to choose their own mates. A government survey reported, "The institution of arranged marriages is very nearly out of the picture as far as Nisei are concerned."[42] Community-managed Japanese schools were not reopened. The number of Japanese language newspapers was fewer than before the war, and those published had smaller circulations.[43]

[41] *Ibid.*, p. 349. By permission.
[42] *People in Motion*, p. 201.
[43] *Ibid.*, p. 203.

The nisei increasingly participated in political and civic life. Because the issei could not become citizens earlier, the American-born were not much oriented toward civic life. The Japanese American Citizens League, founded in 1930 to protect their group interests, had failed to win the united support of the Japanese. But the attitude changed after evacuation, so that by the end of 1947 this association had reached a membership of 7,000 with local chapters in fifty cities. Its activities involved not only efforts at reducing discrimination but also the formulation of a streamlined American welfare program, dealing with juvenile delinquency, recreation, and health. Although concerning itself with problems peculiar to the Japanese, the JACL invited membership from other groups.

In the process of Americanization, the Japanese are reacting to other minorities in typical American fashion, as the following conclusions reached in the Report of the United States Department of Interior indicate:

> Attitudes of Japanese Americans toward Negroes, Mexicans, and other minority peoples vary as greatly and in about the same proportion as may be found in the general population.
>
> One result of the evacuation was to place a large number of Negroes in the former Little Tokyos. As we have seen, adjustments have been made so far with no appreciable trouble. The fact that the Japanese businessmen have a considerable amount of trade with Negroes, which they did not have before the war, has already resulted in some shifts in attitude. In general, Negro attitudes towards Japanese Americans have been friendly . . . There is, however, some resentment of the favorable attention and the community assistance given Japanese Americans.
>
> Among Japanese American leadership there is some division of opinion whether their group should become involved in problems relating to discrimination against Negroes. In a number of cases the JACL has appeared as a "friend of the court" in legal actions resulting from restrictive covenants on residential property where Negroes were involved . . .
>
> Conversely, the degree of economic and social discrimination affecting Japanese Americans is so far below that placed upon Negroes, Mexicans, and most other minority groups, that there is very great hesitation among many in associating themselves with problems which do not immediately concern them. Japanese Americans living in cities which maintain a segregated social pattern may attend white schools, use white playgrounds, and be admitted to all hospitals. The fear on the part of Japanese Americans that identification with efforts to open these institutions to Negroes might result in added disabilities to themselves has undoubtedly had a deterrent effect on closer association between the two groups.[44]

In the ensuing years, the acculturation of the nisei has become substantially complete. Gladwyn Hill, reporting from the West Coast in 1956 stated, "Instead of encountering prejudice when they apply for jobs, Japanese Americans now are more often in special demand because of their reputation for keenness and diligence. . . . The stereotype of the shadowy minority

[44] *Ibid.*, pp. 224, 226.

group with sinister alien ties is gone."[45] As in Chicago, the Japanese on the West Coast are more identified with the middle class.

The remaining area of discrimination is in housing. An intensive study of the housing situation in the San Francisco Bay area in 1956 showed the Japanese more dispersed than before evacuation.[46] Their housing was found to be physically adequate, although most of the homes were old. The nisei indicated more dissatisfaction with their neighborhoods than with their homes. When asked whether they had themselves experienced discrimination in trying to find better homes, 39 per cent of those sampled replied they had; 5 per cent replied they had not looked; and 56 per cent said they had not experienced discrimination. Of this latter group, Kitano writes, "probably many had 'played it safe' by finding houses through friends or Japanese real estate agents. It is clear that there is consciousness of discrimination, and that it has affected the free choice of Nisei in housing."[47] Those who claimed to have been discriminated against were asked who had discriminated. In 22 per cent of the cases, discrimination was attributed to the owner of a desired house; an equal number cited the neighbors; and, in 57 per cent of the cases, it was the real estate agent who had discriminated.[48] Nevertheless, even housing discrimination is considerably less than before the war. It is precisely because the Japanese are upwardly mobile, however, that this housing discrimination is felt as a serious deprivation. But, Kitano concludes, "while their economic potential tends to increase the amount of discrimination Nisei will experience, their tendency to avoid trouble tends to decrease it."[49]

SUMMARY OF NATIVE – JAPANESE RELATIONS IN THE UNITED STATES

1. From the beginning, Japanese immigrants showed a capacity for successful economic adjustment. Bearing on this was a cultural background more attuned to the developing middle-class culture of the United States than was so for southern European and Mexican immigrants.
2. Their ambitiousness led the Japanese into competition with Caucasians, engendering strong antagonism from the latter. To the general pattern of discrimination against minorities were added specific legal discriminations and the restriction of further immigration.

[45] Gladwyn Hill, "Japanese in U.S. Gaining Equality," New York *Times*, August 12, 1956, p. 38.
[46] Harry H. L. Kitano, "Housing of the Japanese-Americans in the San Francisco Bay Area," in Glazer and McEntire, *Studies in Housing and Minority Groups*, p. 183.
[47] *Ibid.*, p. 193.
[48] *Ibid.*, p. 193.
[49] *Ibid.*, p. 196.

3. The issei generation accommodated to American life, retaining strong solidarity as a group not accepted by West Coast natives as real Americans.
4. The West Coast Japanese underwent a unique form of discrimination by being evacuated from the region during World War II.
5. In the postwar period, the nisei have become substantially acculturated and reached new levels of status and acceptance by other Americans. Legal disabilities have been repealed; other forms of discrimination have rapidly decreased, with housing remaining the last serious area of discrimination.
6. The attitudes of dominant native Americans toward the Japanese have changed toward a favorable stereotype. Aside from a remaining hesitation to accept Japanese as social equals, the dominant group considers them good Americans.
7. This remaining social rejection still keeps the Japanese Americans a distinctive group when their numbers in any community are sufficient for them to develop a separate group life. But present trends point toward the increasing assimilation of succeeding generations.
8. Finally, the admission of Hawaii as a state should strengthen the position of Japanese Americans on the mainland as well as on the islands. Congressional representation from Hawaii would logically be expected to speak in their behalf in any future emergency.

TOPICS FOR PROJECTS AND DISCUSSION

1. How do you account for the currently more assimilated situation of the Japanese than that of the Chinese in the United States?
2. Design a project aimed to determine the knowledge of white Americans about the wartime evacuation of the Japanese and their attitudes toward it. Try out your design on an appropriate sample.
3. Some writers on minorities have drawn parallels between Gentile-Jewish relations and West Coast white-Japanese-American relations. What parallels occur to you?
4. In view of the greater antagonism toward Orientals on the West Coast, how do you account for the fact that the great majority of the evacuated Japanese returned to this region to live after release from internment?
5. Discuss the significance of white-Oriental relations in the United States in connection with the present international situation.

SUGGESTED READING

Bloom, Leonard, and Riemer, Ruth. *Removal and Return.* Berkeley: University of California Press, 1949.
>   *A careful study of the readjustment of the Japanese to the West Coast since World War II, with particular reference to economic adjustment.*

Embree, John E. *The Japanese Nation: A Social Survey.* New York: Rinehart & Company, Inc., 1945.
> *A short but comprehensive description of the culture and social organization of modern Japan.*

Leighton, Alexander. *The Governing of Men.* Princeton: Princeton University Press, 1934.
> *A study of the administration of the Japanese evacuation centers; concerned with the contribution of the experience to social science study and theory.*

McKenzie, R. D. *Oriental Exclusion.* Institute of Pacific Relations Study. Chicago: University of Chicago Press, 1927.
> *An authoritative account of effects and implications of the acts attempting to exclude further Oriental immigration.*

Strong, Jr., E. K. *Japanese in California.* Stanford University Publications, University Series, Education-Psychology, Vol. 1, No. 2, Stanford: Stanford University Press, 1933.

————. *The Second Generation Japanese Problem.* Stanford: Stanford University Press, 1933.
> *These two volumes give a comprehensive picture of the situation of the Japanese in California up to 1930.*

Ten Broeck, Jacobus, Barnhart, Edward N., Matson, Floyd W. *Prejudice, War and Constitution.* Berkeley and Los Angeles: University of California Press, 1954.
> *A study of the Japanese evacuation directed at assessing responsibility for the episode, with special attention to the legal aspects.*

Thomas, Dorothy S., and Nishimoto, Richard S. *The Spoilage, Japanese-American Evacuation and Resettlement.* Berkeley and Los Angeles: University of California Press, 1946.
> *An intensive study of those Japanese who became bitter enough about evacuation to renounce their citizenship.*

10

Negro-White Relations:
Biology and Background

Among the manifold dominant-minority situations occurring in this country, Negro-white relations occupy first place as a social problem. While the pattern and the process of Negro-white relations resemble in some measure the generalized dominant-minority type, there are elements of uniqueness which make it necessary to treat them as distinctive.

The Negro minority constitutes about one-tenth of the total population of continental United States. It is by far the oldest minority,[1] the first slaves having been brought to Jamestown in 1619, and it is accorded the lowest rank among all the minorities. A large portion of the Negro population has the lowest standard of living, although, as we shall see, the welfare of Negroes at present is highly variable. And virtually all of their original culture has disappeared through the long years of servitude and caste conditions, with the result that racial pride can be built, for the most part, only on a heritage of slavery and minority discrimination.

Two factors which explain why Negroes have so long remained a minority in the United States are (1) that they are Negroid in their visible racial characteristics or in their known lineage; and (2) that their ancestors were slaves. In the first of these chapters devoted to Negro-white relations we

[1] Indian-white relations did not become dominant-minority relations in the true sense until the Indians became wards in 1870.

207

shall discuss the racial characteristics and population trends of the Negro and deal briefly with the period of slavery and its immediate aftermath.

CHARACTERISTICS OF THE AMERICAN NEGRO POPULATION

The minority status of Negroes in the United States has rested in large measure on the beliefs developed and sustained in the minds of the dominant white population that American Negroes are Negroid in their biological traits and that being Negroid means they are innately inferior. Scientific evidence establishes beyond question important qualifications to any such beliefs.

Racial Ancestry of the Negro Population

The "visibility" of the Negro minority is accounted for by the fact that all the members have some genetic lineage from Negro ancestry. In the United States a person is considered a Negro if he has any known Negro lineage, whether he can be identified by his appearance or not. There is no precise data indicating what distribution of the basic Negroid traits are now present in the population known as Negro. The United States Census count in 1920—the last year a distinction between mulatto and black was made—gave the figure of 15.9 per cent for mulattoes, which all students of the question consider a gross undercount. Obviously, census takers are not physical anthropologists. When a study was made by Herskovits combining genealogical and anthropometric methods, a high correspondence between the measurements and the genealogical data was found.[2] Only 22 per cent of his sample of 1,551 Negroes were unmixed Negro, the rest showing varying degrees of Caucasian and American Indian admixture. Although Herskovits' sample contained a disproportionate number of more educated Negroes, known to have a greater percentage of white ancestry, the probability that many Negroes in his sample did not know of white ancestry from several generations back may have served to counterbalance the selective bias.

Most Negroes in the United States show one or more of the basic Negroid traits—dark skin, thick lips, "woolly" hair, and prognathism; in a minor proportion, the evidences of these traits are so faint that one cannot be sure of identifying them; and in a relatively small percentage there is absolutely no somatic evidence of Negro lineage, but either the individuals themselves, or others who know them vouch for some Negro ancestry. The American Negro population of today is, biologically speaking, quite different from that of colonial days. The processes by which this change has come about will now be described. Since the matter of sexual relations is a subject generally ig-

[2] Melville Herskovits, *The American Negro: A Study in Racal Crossing* (New York: Alfred A. Knopf, Inc., 1930).

nored by scientific investigation, even more so when, as in this case, they frequently have been illicit, we shall find the details none too exact.

Selective Mating Processes and Genetic Composition

Intertribal Mating   Knowledge of the ancestry of American Negroes is not very precise. It is now considered, however, that most of the present Negro population traces the Negro part of its ancestry back to slaves who originally came from the West Coast of Africa, from Gambia down to Angola.[3] Although there is little known about their genetic traits, there can be no doubt that persons from as wide a tribal range as is indicated presented considerable variation. Since under slavery in the United States their mating was not tribally endogamous, the first step in the process was the intermixing of these original tribal variations. This would have produced a new, but African, Negro type if it had not been for the crossing of slaves very early with both Indians and white people.

Negro-Indian Crossing   In the United States before the nineteenth century there was extensive intermingling between Indians and Negroes, with the result that some of the admixtures disappeared into the Indian population. A few Indian tribes may have been lost almost completely by this process. In the sample study of Negro racial traits by Herskovits, 27 per cent of the subjects were found to have some Indian lineage.[4] Additional Indian genetic strains resulted from the increasing importation, in the later periods, of slaves from the West Indies, where "crossing" with the natives had occurred.

Negro-White Crossing   The population from which the African slaves were recruited already had some admixture of Caucasian genes, as a result of miscegenation with the Portuguese who settled on the Guinea Coast for slave trading purposes and through contact in Europe, whence some slaves were brought to the West Indies.

In the colonies themselves, indications are that the first extensive Negro-white crossing took place between indentured white servants and Negro slaves. As the indentured servant disappeared and the Negro slave system developed, mating between white and colored people continued through the access to Negro slave women which the system gave the white male owners and white men in general. Mulatto women were most frequently chosen.

The next stage came with the Civil War and its aftermath. "The Northern army left an unknown amount of Yankee genes in the Southern Negro people."[5] Under the caste system which supplanted slavery, interracial crossing resumed more or less the same pattern of white male exploitation of

[3] E. Franklin Frazier, *The Negro in the United States* (New York: The Macmillan Co., 1949), pp. 4–6.
[4] Herskovits, *The American Negro*, p. 9.
[5] Gunnar Myrdal, *An American Dilemma* (New York: Harper & Brothers, 1944), p. 127.

Negro women, although the women had somewhat more freedom than under slavery. While evidence is scarce, most writers on the Negro agree that the amount of miscegenation has declined in the twentieth century. Among the factors frequently cited to account for this tentative conclusion are, on the part of the white people, a decline in sexual congress with Negro women because of an increasing casualness in white female sexual behavior and, on the part of the Negroes, the increasing number who have adopted white middle-class attitudes toward sexual conventionality and have developed a maturing sense of racial pride. The increasing use of contraceptives has also affected the selective process, since sex relations that do occur between the two races do not generally result in offspring.

"Light" Selection in the Negro Population It is generally acknowledged even by Negro students of race relations that mate selection within the Negro population itself has been in favor of those Negroes who possessed the greater visible indices of Caucasian traits. The higher status of mulattoes has been due not only to their "lightness" but also to the fact that the dominant white population has been somewhat more favorably inclined to them. Thus in general mulattoes have had more economic and educational opportunity. This selective mating bias among Negroes has had the effect of increasing the distribution of white genetic factors in the Negro population. This effect is partially offset, however, by the further consideration that "lighter" Negroes, tending to imitate white middle-class standards, incline to have fewer children. And the development of Negro race pride, stimulated by certain elements of Negro leadership, may well reverse the effect of the process here being considered. To the extent that a trend toward the devaluation of lightness increases, the Negro population will veer toward a mulatto norm and toward greater homogeneity about that norm. The extensive use at present of the term "brown" Americans in place of "black" in the literature concerning Negroes symbolizes the effect of this most recent process.[6]

Passing By "passing" is meant the successful and permanent assumption of "white" status by a person who knows he has Negro ancestry. In studying the African ancestry of the white population in the United States, Stuckert, using the method of genetic probability tables, estimated that during the years 1941–1950 an average annual mean of 15,500 Negroes passed. There was an annual rate of 1.21 per 1,000 Negro population, and the rate was found to be increasing.[7] The effect of passing is the removal from the Negro

[6] For further discussion of this subject, see Otto Klineberg, ed., *Characteristics of the American Negro* (New York: Harper & Brothers, 1944), Pt. V, Ch. 9, "The Future of the Hybrid," by Louis Wirth and Herbert Goldhamer.
[7] Robert P. Stuckert, "African Ancestry of the White American Population," *The Ohio Journal of Science*, May, 1958, 58: 155–160. The main finding of this study was that 28 million white persons have some African ancestry, and most of these are classified as white.

population of strains which would increase the Caucasian admixture in the Negro population. The process adds some Negroid admixture to the white population, but very little, since the Negroes who pass have very few Negroid genes to add. The Negroid influence is further diluted by the tendency of "passers," when they marry, to select either white mates or equally white Negro mixtures. In this connection, it is pertinent to call attention to the fear which many white people and many "passable" Negroes have concerning the possible Negroid characteristics of children resulting from marriages of two white-appearing Negroes or of one of them to a white person. The probabilities of progeny from such unions are now known. Representative of the accepted view are these summary statements by Julian Lewis, a biologist:

Two very fair-complexioned Negroes will produce children 18 per cent of whom are pure white, 65 per cent the same color as the parents, and 17 per cent a shade darker than both parents.

When a white person mates with a very fair Negro who is sometimes able to pass for white but not of the "pure white" type, 40 per cent of the resulting children are of the same color as the white parent, less than 60 per cent are the color of the Negro parent, and less than 1 per cent is darker than the Negro parent. The possibility of this one exception frequently causes untold worry and concern in such unions.

Some of the children of matings involving fair Negroes are pure white according to accepted standards of whiteness. Such types are known to geneticists as "extracted whites." When an extracted white mates with a full white or another extracted white, none of the children will ever be darker than the parents.[8]

Summary and Future Possibilities

Through the operation of these many selective processes, and differential birth rates, to which we next turn, the Negro population of contemporary America varies widely in its biological traits. The range is fairly well known, but the frequencies at various intervals of the range are not all well known. Therefore, in the strict scientific sense of the term, it is not clear that the term "race" should be applied to the American Negro population. Future trends in the biological characteristics of American Negroes depend in large measure on social and cultural influences, some of which have already been discussed above. In general, there appear two alternative possibilities. First, the Negro population may tend toward a more homogeneous type, which may be indicated by the term "brown Americans." This development would be favored by the continued decline in miscegenation, illicit or legal, by passing, and by the continued increase in the development of Negro race consciousness and pride. The second possibility is the gradual disappearance

---

[8] Julian Lewis, "What Color Will Your Baby Be?" *Negro Digest*, Nov., 1945, 5: 6–7. By permission. For fuller treatment see Julian Lewis, *The Biology of the Negro* (Chicago: University of Chicago Press, 1942).

of the Negro population through absorption into the white population.[9] Only a steady increase in the amount of intermarriage between Negroes and whites, contrary to the present trend, could bring this about and, like all similar biological processes, it would take centuries. Therefore, as a possible "solution" of America's twentieth-century Negro problem, amalgamation into the white population may for all practical purposes be dismissed.

THE GROWTH OF THE NEGRO POPULATION

Numerical Increase but Proportional Decrease

Table 7 shows that the number of Negroes in the United States has grown

TABLE 7

Growth of the Negro Population Since 1790[10]

CENSUS YEAR	NUMBER OF NEGROES	PERCENTAGE OF TOTAL POPULATION	PERCENTAGE INCREASE OF NEGROES DURING DECADE	PERCENTAGE INCREASE OF WHITES DURING DECADE
1960	18,871,831	10.5	25.4	17.5
1950	15,044,937	9.9	17.0	14.4
1940	12,865,518	9.8	8.2	7.2
1930	11,891,143	9.7	13.6	15.7
1920	10,463,131	9.9	6.5	15.7
1910	9,827,763	10.7	11.2	21.8
1900	8,333,940	11.6	18.0	21.2
1890	7,488,676	11.9	13.8	27.0
1880	6,580,793	13.1	34.9	29.2
1870	4,880,009	12.7	9.9	24.8
1860	4,441,830	14.1	22.1	37.7
1850	3,638,808	15.7	26.6	37.7
1840	2,873,648	16.8	23.4	34.7
1830	2,328,642	18.1	31.4	33.9
1820	1,771,656	18.4	28.6	34.2
1810	1,377,808	19.0	37.5	36.1
1800	1,002,037	18.9	32.3	35.8
1790	757,208	19.3		

[9] Ralph Linton has stated this thesis in an article, "The Vanishing American Negro," *The American Mercury*, Feb., 1947, 64: 133–139, and further suggests that the Negro will thus "vanish" in about two hundred years. An effective criticism of Linton's position is to be found in the *American Sociological Review*, Aug., 1948, 13: 437–443, "Is the American Negro Becoming Lighter? An analysis of the Sociological and Biological Trends," by William M. Kephart.

[10] United States Bureau of Census, *Negroes in the United States, 1920–1932*, pp. 1–2; *Sixteenth Census of United States, Population*, Vol. II, p. 19. 1960 Census, P. C. (A2)–1, p. 4.

each decade since 1790, the time of the first census count. It also shows, with some temporary decennial rises, that the proportion of the Negroes to the total population declined until 1930. Although influenced by net reproduction rates, this decline is due primarily to the proportionally great increase in the white population brought about by immigration from Europe. Between 1930 and 1960 the proportion increased slightly. Since an analysis of the population growth in the past would serve little purpose in understanding the current scene, we will focus on the recent rise. The net reproduction rates[11] for the white and Negro population in 1930 were substantially the same—110 and 111 respectively. From 1940 the comparable rates for whites were 94 and for Negroes 107. Thus about this time the Negro population began to reproduce itself more rapidly than the white population, a reversal of the previous situation. This change is reflected in Table 7, where it is seen that the percentage increase of Negroes in both the decades ending in 1950 and in 1960 was greater than that of the white population. It is possible that the proportion of the American population that is Negro will continue to increase slightly. Improved welfare should reduce the Negro death rate; on the other hand, as with all other groups, upward class mobility would be expected to reduce the birth rate. The prospect for the rest of this century is that Negroes will compose a little more than ten per cent of the national population.[12]

Summary Prediction

The significant probabilities emerging from this analysis of the qualitative and quantitative changes in the Negro population are these: (1) that throughout this century the United States will have a Negro element sufficiently visible in somatic characteristics to be distinguished from the rest of the population; and (2) that this Negro element will remain for the country as a whole a definite numerical minority. Thus the Negro population will possess two attributes useful to the dominant white group in keeping Negroes in minority status, if the dominants so wish to utilize them.

Distribution of the Negro Population

The Negro population in the United States has always been highly concentrated in the South. In 1790 only a scattering of Negroes lived outside

[11] The net reproduction rate (NRR) is a measure of the average number of daughters that will be produced by women throughout their lifetime if subject to prevailing birth and death rates, or life-table rates on which such calculations may be based. Many nations (and the United Nations) express the NRR in terms of one woman (U. S. NRR 1946, 1.359), while the United States Bureau of the Census expresses the NRR in terms of 100 women (U. S. NRR 1946, 135.9).

[12] A new procedure adopted by the census in 1960 may have unpredictable effects on the statistical count of Negroes. Before 1960 the enumeration of persons as Negroes was left to the census taker; but in 1960 householders themselves were asked to fill out for the taker a form in which racial designation was included.

the South;[13] in 1940, there were 77 per cent of all American Negroes still living in that region. Since 1860 the two most important regional migrations have been the so-called "Great Migration" to the North, commencing in 1915, and the small, but hitherto unprecedented, westward movement, beginning about 1940.

Under slavery, Negro migration was of course governed by the owners and traders of slaves. The southern and southwestern expansion of the plantation economy from the upper South was paralleled by a corresponding expansion of the Negro population in these areas. In spite of the technical freedom for Negroes to move where they desired after the Civil War, very few migrated to the North, and almost none to the West. There was considerable shifting about in the South itself, the net result of which was to increase the proportion of the Negro population living in Southern cities. Between 1910 and 1940 the proportion of the Southern Negro population living in cities increased from 22 per cent to 37.3 per cent. Aside from this urban drift, the other most important demographic change in the South has been the decreased concentration of the Negro population in the "Black Belt," composed of counties in eastern Virginia and North Carolina, all of South Carolina, central Georgia and Alabama, and a detached tier of counties in the lower Mississippi River Valley. From 1900 to 1940, the Negro population in this area declined from 4,057,619 to 2,642,808. While in 1880 over half (57 per cent) of the total Negro population of the country was located in the Black Belt, only about one fourth (26.15 per cent) was residing in this area in 1940.[14]

The great migration of Negroes to the North began in 1915 in response to the heavy demand for labor created by World War I. Almost all the migrants moved to Northern cities, concentrating particularly in the largest urban centers. By 1940, New York City had 16.9 per cent of the Northern Negro population, and large Negro populations were located in Chicago, Philadelphia, Detroit, Cleveland, and Pittsburgh.[15] Because of the total numbers involved, the concentration of Negroes in the metropolitan North is especially noted, yet the distribution of Negroes in many smaller cities of the North reached such a proportion even before 1940 that race relations had become a significant community problem there too. There were, for example, 15 cities in New Jersey in which Negroes comprised 10 per cent or more of the population and 12 more in which the Negro population ranged from 5 to 9 per cent.[16] The northern and western migration of Negroes con-

---

[13] Throughout this book the term *South* will mean, unless otherwise stated, the following states: Alabama, Arkansas, Delaware, Florida, Georgia, Kentucky, Louisiana, Maryland, Mississippi, North Carolina, Oklahoma, South Carolina, Tennessee, Texas, Virginia, West Virginia, and the District of Columbia.

[14] Frazier, *The Negro in the United States*, pp. 187–190.

[15] Myrdal, *An American Dilemma*, p. 183.

[16] United States Census, 1940, *Population*, Vol. II, New Jersey, Tables 32, 34.

tinues, as the 1960 census shows. In 1910, of the total Negro population 81 per cent lived in the eleven states of the old Confederacy;[17] by 1960 the percentage had dropped to 52 per cent. In the decade of 1950–1960 the Negro population of New Jersey rose 63 per cent; of Illinois, 61 per cent; of New York, 54 per cent.

The most recent trend in the migration of Negroes has been to the West. Just as World War I stimulated the northward migration, the labor demands of World War II precipitated a westward movement. There were a few Negroes living in the West before 1940, but during the 1940–1950 decade the increase of Negroes was 237.4 per cent, making the Negro population (approximately 576,000) 2.5 per cent of the region's total population. California leads all the states of the Union in the percentage rise of Negro population during the 1950–1960 decade with 90 per cent, bringing the total number of Negroes in that state to 883,861.[18]

The Significance of Negro Population Movements

We shall have occasion to consider later the bearing which the size of the Negro population in any community, state, or region has on the character of race relations in a given locality. For example, in those local areas of the South where Negroes exceed whites in number, it is understandable that the thought of a breakdown in the caste system would create a fear in the minds of most whites that approaches the intensity of an obsession. In contrast, in some Northern cities where a few Negroes live in the community, from the white side at least, there may be scarcely a conscious awareness of race relations as a problem. Despite this, however, the tendency for Negroes to concentrate in certain large Northern metropolitan areas continues.

CHARACTERISTICS OF THE AMERICAN NEGRO PEOPLE

We have already pointed out that a feature of dominant-minority structure is the stereotype of the minority held by the dominant group. In a recent treatise on slavery, Elkins has delineated the stereotype of the American plantation Negro slave:

Sambo . . . was docile but irresponsible, loyal, but lazy, humble but chronically giving to lying and stealing; his behavior was full of infantile silliness. . . . His relationship with his master was one of utter dependence and childlike attachment; it was indeed this childlike quality that was the very key to his being. Although the merest hint of Sambo's manhood might fill the Southern breast with scorn, the child "in his place" could be both exasperating and lovable.[19]

---

[17] Alabama, Arkansas, Florida, Georgia, Louisiana, Mississippi, North Carolina, South Carolina, Tennessee, Texas, and Virginia. Mississippi and Arkansas, together with West Virginia and Wyoming, claimed a loss in Negro population during the decade.

[18] United States Census, 1960, Advanced Reports, PC(A2)6, p. 4.

[19] Stanley M. Elkins, Slavery: A Problem in American Institutional and Intellectual Life (Chicago: University of Chicago Press, 1959), p. 82.

The stereotype of the American Negro current in twentieth-century white thought characterizes him in about this way: The Negro is lazy, won't work unless he has to, and doesn't know what to do with money when he gets it. He is dirty, smelly, careless in appearance, yet given to flashy dressing. He is much more "sexy" than the white man, and exercises no restraint in sexual expression. He has low mental ability incapable of anything but menial labor. He is naturally religious, but his religion is mostly emotion and superstition. On the other hand, in his simple way, the Negro is a likable fellow, clever in a childlike way, and has natural abilities as a singer, dancer, and actor which surpass those of most white folks. Obviously, by this time an increasing number of white Americans no longer hold this image of the Negro, and even those who hold it in diluted form are at least rationally forced to exclude the rising number of educated and middle-class Negroes.

The contributions of social scence to the study of the distinctive features, if any, of Negro personality are quite limited. Studies of differences in personality traits are not extensive and, according to Klineberg,[20] have yielded few definite conclusions. The testing of small samples has indicated that Negroes are more extrovertive than whites; that they are more suggestible; and that Negro children are more sociable in their play habits than white children. Other studies of particular traits have failed to show significant differences in, for example, color preferences, handwriting, and the perception of emotional expression. Comparative mental testing of whites and Negroes has been more extensive. To our earlier discussion of this subject in Chapter 3 we here add Myrdal's conclusion:

The large amount of overlapping brought out the fact that both Negroes and whites belonged to the same human species and had more similarities than differences. The averages themselves tended to come nearer each other when the measurements were refined to exclude more and more the influence of differences in environment, such as education, cultural background and experience, socioeconomic class; and the social factors in the test situation itself, such as motivation and rapport with the tester.

The intensive studies of these last influences proved, in adidtion, that no psychological tests yet invented come even close to measuring innate psychic traits, absolutely undistorted by these influences. *They rather rendered it probable that average differences would practically disappear if all environmental factors could be controlled.*[21]

In support of the unfavorable stereotype of the Negro, certain comparative figures showing a larger percentage of sociopathic behavior for Negroes than whites are often cited. It is true that as a whole Negroes are less educated; found more often on police records and in penal institutions; and

[20] Klineberg, *Characteristics of the American Negro,* Part III, "Experimental Studies of Negro Personality," pp. 99–138.
[21] Myrdal, *An American Dilemma,* p. 147. Italics ours. By permission of the publishers, Harper & Brothers.

have higher incidences of homicide and illegitimacy. But the explanation can be found through analysis of the environmental conditions associated with their slave, caste, and subsequent minority status in American society. To take a hypothetical research problem in this connection, let us set ourselves the task of measuring the relative quantum of ambition found in a white and a Negro group. Since we recognize that the economic and living conditions of the two groups as a whole are quite disparate, we first seek to equalize the factors in our selection of a sample for measurement. We seek whites as well as Negroes who are poor, who have little schooling, who live in overcrowded homes. Let us assume that our results still show a significant lesser quantum of ambition in the Negro sample. Before attributing this remaining difference to racial heredity, we would have to investigate in detail what the effect of minority status, a factor which is still different in our samples, may contribute to the difference.

The Influence of African Culture

With all the minority groups thus far considered, cultural differences derived from their nationality and ethnic origins have played a major part in influencing their adjustment and final acculturation to American life. The situation of Negroes in this respect is considerably different. The sharp impact of slavery went far to destroy the many tribal cultures which the Negroes brought with them. Scholarly controversy prevails among the students of the history of the Negro in the New World concerning the extent to which African culture traits have survived, or to what extent Negro cultural adaptations in the New World were influenced by their aboriginal culture.[22] A considerable number of scattered, specific cultural traits have been found in specific Negro groups which can be directly traced to African origin. It is significant, however, that more of these have been found among Negro groups in the West Indies, and that among those found in the United States the groups involved were especially isolated. For other, more prevalent aspects of American Negro culture and behavior which present a vague, general similarity to African cultural forms, the continuity of African heritage is highly debatable. For example, is the frequency of common-law marriage in Negro rural life derivative from African customs, or can it be explained by the highly destructive impact of slavery on the stability of Negro family life? Is the predilection of American Negroes for the Baptist denomination, which features total immersion, due to the surviving influence of West African "river cults," as Herskovits speculates, or is it more simply attributable, as Frazier suggests, to the vigorous proselytizing activities of

[22] A brief introduction to this historical problem is found in Frazier, *The Negro in the United States*, Ch. I, "Significance of the African Background." For fuller discussion of the topic, see Melville J. Herskovits, *The Myth of the Negro Past* (New York: Harper & Brothers, 1942).

the Baptist denomination?[23] In any question there are few facets of Negro personality or cultural expression for which an explanation cannot be suggested by the adaptation to conditions of slavery, caste, and minority status.

Thus Elkins concludes: "No true picture. . . . of African culture seems to throw any light at all on origins of what would emerge in African plantation society as the stereotyped 'Sambo' personality. The cultural level and the social organization of the various African societies from which the slaves were obtained entitles one to argue that they must have had an institutional life at least as sophisticated as Anglo-Saxon England."[24]

Elkin's reference to the high level of civilization of African societies in earlier periods points up an important factor regarding the advancement of American Negroes. As we have mentioned, because of their long servile position in American society, American Negroes have known little of the history of African Negro societies, and therefore have had little race pride. The increasing outstanding contributions of individuals of Negro ancestry to American society in recent years is changing this attitude.

STAGES IN NEGRO – WHITE RELATIONS

The history of Negro-white relations in the United States may be divided into four stages: (1) the period of slavery, 1619 to 1863; (2) the period of reconstruction, 1864 to 1880; (3) the period of biracial accommodation, 1881 to 1940; and (4) the period of emergent assimilation, 1941 to the present. The first and second of these stages will be discussed in the rest of this chapter.

THE PERIOD OF SLAVERY

The Colonial Period

Since there was no precedent in English law regarding slaves when the first twenty slaves were bought by Virginia settlers in 1619, it sems to have been assumed that their status was similar to that of white indentured servants, with stipulated ways of being manumitted. Early in colonial history, however, differential treatment of Negroes began. For example, when three bound servants, two white and one Negro, had been brought back to Virginia from Maryland after attempting to escape from servitude, the court, having ordered thirty lashes for all three, further ordered that the white servants should serve three years extra time in bondage, but that the Negro should serve his master for the rest of his life.[25] By court actions such as these, the differential status of Negroes evolved into a clear pattern of

[23] Frazier, *The Negro in the United States*, pp. 10–18.
[24] Elkins, *Slavery*, p. 97.
[25] Frazier, *The Negro in the United States*, p. 24.

slavery, which eventually became established by more explicit law. In Virginia the slave status was fixed by a law making all non-Christians who came into the colony as servants from across the seas slaves for the rest of their lives. In 1682 this law was repealed and in its place another substituted "making slaves of all persons of non-Christian nationalities thereafter coming into the colony, whether they came by sea or land and whether or not they had been converted to Christianity after capture."[26]

Although early developing into a fixed institution, Negro slavery grew indispensable only as the plantation system of agriculture became important and more widespread. This system involved the large-scale production of a staple crop for commercial exchange and required cheap labor. At a time when land was either free or cheap, white men wanted to work as independent farmers, not as wage earners. Thus Negro slaves filled the increasing manpower demand. The colony of Georgia, founded in 1735, first prohibited the importation of Negro slaves, but by 1750, as the plantation system began to spread into the new colony, the act was repealed. The number of Negroes in Georgia increased from a reported 349 in 1750 to 15,000 by 1773.[27] The nexus between the plantation economy and slavery is further illustrated by the difference between the two Carolinas. In North Carolina the plantation economy failed to develop on a large scale and so did slavery; in South Carolina, where the plantation system developed on a large scale, "the number of Negroes had become so numerous that it was felt necessary to encourage the importation of white servants to secure the safety of the colony."[28] Finally, as is well known, in the North, where there was no plantation economy, no large-scale slavery developed. By 1790, when the first federal census was taken, the proportion of free Negroes to those in slavery ranged from the all-free Negro population (5,462) in Massachusetts to other states where from a third to a half of the resident Negroes were still slaves.[29]

The introduction of slavery into the colonies came as an extension of the institution already established in the West Indies. The slave trade to the colonies was carried on largely by the British, although subsequently colonists themselves took a hand in it, especially New England port merchants.[30] This trade was a highly hazardous and adventuresome occupation. It was not easy to get the slaves or to deliver them since, aside from the problem of holding them by force, great mortality occurred from the usually overcrowded conditions in the "Middle Passage" journeys. However, when things went well, as they obviously often did, the profits were high. Franklin

[26] *Ibid.*, p. 26.
[27] *Ibid.*, p. 32–33.
[28] *Ibid.*, p. 32.
[29] *Ibid.*, p. 34.
[30] Maurice R. Davie, *Negroes in American Society* (New York: McGraw-Hill Book Co., 1949), p. 18.

writes, 'It was not unusual for a ship carrying 250 slaves to net as much as £7,000 on one voyage. Profits of 100 per cent were not uncommon for Liverpool merchants."[31] The exact number of slaves imported to the colonies, and later to the states, is not known, but estimates range from 500,000 to 700,000. And, in spite of the fact that the importation of slaves was officially prohibited after 1808, the evidence is incontrovertible that a substantial contraband trade continued after that date. Collins estimates that about 270,000 slaves were imported into the United States between 1808 and 1860.[32]

From all accounts the total number of slaves imported from Africa to all the New World from the fifteenth to the nineteenth century must be reckoned in the millions. Williams writes, "The importation into Jamaica from 1700 to 1786 was 610,000, and it has been estimated that the total import of slaves into all the British colonies between 1680 and 1786 was over two million."[33] Bearing in mind the number who died resisting capture and the heavy mortality on shipboard, it can be seen that the slave trade constituted a great drain on the manhood of Africa, particularly in the West Coast area, and especially since the traders tried to take the youngest and healthiest men.

From the Revolutionary War to the War Between the States

In spite of the fixed position of slavery in the colonial economy during and for a short period following the Revolutionary War, there were signs that the slavery system might be abolished. Slavery was coming under increasing attack from a moral viewpoint, not only from Northerners but from enlightened slaveholders such as Washington and Jefferson. The first President desired "to see a plan adopted for the abolition of it [slavery];[34] and Jefferson wrote in his autobiography, "Nothing is more certainly written in the book of fate than that these people are to be free."[35] The attitude of the public was affected by economic interests as well as moral idealism. Frazier indicates that opposition to slavery was expressed in Delaware, Maryland, and Virginia, where a diversified agriculture was supplanting the production of tobacco, whereas in the lower South, where the production of tobacco, rice, and indigo was still important, there was strong opposition either to suspending the slave trade or to the emancipation of the Negro.[36] In the midst of these conflicting attitudes toward slavery, the Constitution of

---

[31] John Hope Franklin, *From Slavery to Freedom* (New York: Alfred A. Knopf, Inc., 1947), p. 57.
[32] Winfield H. Collins, *The Domestic Slave Trade of the Southern States* (New York: Broadway Publishing Company, 1904), p. 20.
[33] Eric Williams, *Capitalism & Slavery* (Chapel Hill: University of North Carolina Press, 1944), p. 33.
[34] Myrdal, *An American Dilemma*, p. 85.
[35] *Ibid.*
[36] Frazier, *The Negro in the United States*, p. 35.

the new republic compromised on the issue by setting 1808 as the date after which the importation of slaves was to be abolished. The abolition of slavery in many state constitutions in the North and its declining economic significance led many people to share with Jefferson the belief that slavery was on its way out.

But the hopes of those opposed to slavery were destined to be dashed by the invention of the cotton gin. With this invention Southern cotton planters were able to meet the rapidly growing demand of the English market. The expansion of cotton economy increased by leaps and bounds, especially from 1815 on. This development was accompanied by the growth of the slave system and the slave population. (See Table 8.)

TABLE 8
Growth of the Slave Population in the United States, 1790–1860[37]

Census Year	Slave Population	Decennial Increase
1790	697,624	
1800	893,602	28.1
1810	1,191,362	33.3
1820	1,538,022	29.1
1830	2,009,043	30.6
1840	2,487,355	18.8
1850	3,204,313	28.8
1860	3,953,760	23.4

From 1790 to 1808 the natural increase of the slave population was supplemented by foreign importation of over 100,000 slaves. Although, as Table 8 shows, the percentage of increase after 1810 declined, a substantial number of slaves were smuggled in to augment the natural increase. And since there was an increasing demand for slaves because of the prohibition, a domestic slave trade developed. As the plantation system spread south and west away from Maryland, Virginia, and Kentucky, many slaves were sold by their first owners to work in the new areas.

Having built not only its economy but a total society on the foundation of slavery, the South needed rationalizations which would justify it. Thus there began to emerge in the pre-Civil War period learned treatises solemnly concluding that "the Negro" was naturally meant to be a slave and that he was obviously inferior to the white. Many of these treatises invoked Biblical sanction and two of the most scholarly were written by Presbyterian ministers.[38] The growing intellectual support for the established system reached

[37] United States Bureau of the Census, *A Century of Population Growth*, p. 132.
[38] Frazier, *The Negro in the United States*, p. 42.

its climax in the words of Chief Justice Taney, who in his famous decision in the Dred Scott case declared, "A Negro has no rights which a white man need respect."[39]

Thus it appeared clear that, far from declining, the slave system during the early nineteenth century in the South grew constantly stronger. This is important to keep in mind as we turn to the reconstruction days. It does much to explain why the Emancipation Proclamation, which freed slaves in the legal sense, did not protect them from the caste barriers that were erected to supplant those of slavery.

The American Slave System: Comparison with Latin America

Among the many instances of slave systems, there is considerable variation. The degree of authority accorded to the master is affected by many factors, of which the economic role of the slaves and the character of the other institutions in the society are important. The actual exercise of the permitted authority is always influenced by the human qualities of affection, on the one hand, and of aggressiveness, on the other, qualities which are in part structured by the general culture but which always vary to some extent with individual personalities. Too, the responses of slaves to their condition vary with their cultural level and their personality variables.

In Latin America, where a slave system flourished for many years, law, religion, and the mores of the society made the status of slaves vastly different from, and on the whole superior to, that of slaves in the British-settled area of South America and in southern United States. First, in Latin America, slaves had rights protecting them against many specific abuses from their masters. The power to inflict certain physical punishments upon slaves was limited by law, and slaves could obtain legal redress if the master overstepped these bounds. Married slaves could not be separated from each other against their will. "The children followed the status of their mother, and the child of a free mother remained free even if she later became a slave."[40] By contrast, in the American system, the slave had practically no protection by law from the arbitrary exercise of authority by the master.[41]

[39] Part of the decision rendered in the Dred Scott Case (Mar. 6, 1857) as quoted in *The Columbia Encyclopedia* (New York: Columbia University Press, 1940), p. 1728. Dred Scott, a Negro slave, was taken by his master from the slave state of Missouri into free territory. Upon return, Scott sued for his freedom on the ground that residence in Illinois, a free state, and in Minnesota, a free territory, made him a free citizen. The case came up in the Missouri courts, but after Scott was purchased by a citizen of New York, suit was filed in the federal courts. Financed by Abolitionists, the case reached the Supreme Court, where Chief Justice Roger B. Taney rendered the opinion taken as that of the majority. (1) It upheld the Missouri courts in declaring that Scott, still a slave, was not a citizen. (2) It declared the Missouri Compromise unconstitutional. The Negro was branded inferior, "altogether unfit to associate with the white race."
[40] Frank Tannenbaum, *Slave and Citizen* (New York: Alfred A. Knopf, Inc., 1947), p. 49. Most of the material for this comparison is derived from Tannenbaum.
[41] Myrdal, *An American Dilemma,* pp. 530–531.

He had no property rights. Married partners could be separated from each other, and children from their parents. That they were is attested in a number of advertisements, of which the following is typical.

> NEGROES FOR SALE. A negro woman, 24 years of age, and her two children, one eight and the other three years old. Said negroes will be sold SEP-ARATELY, or together, *as desired*. The woman is a good seamstress. She will be sold low for cash, or EXCHANGED FOR GROCERIES. For terms, apply to Matthew Bliss and Co., 1 Front Levee.[42]

Second, the Latin system favored manumission, and a more-or-less steady change from slavery to freedom was going on all the time. "A hundred social devices . . . encouraged the master to release his slave, and the bonds-man to achieve freedom on his own account." For example, in Cuba "a slave worth six hundred dollars could buy himself out in twenty-four installments of twenty-five dollars each, and with each payment he acquired one twenty-fourth of his own freedom."[43] The American system operated to prevent manumission. While some slaves were freed, as the system grew in strength during the early nineteenth century the pressures against freeing slaves became greater.

A third contrast is seen in the difference in the status of former slaves once they became free. In Latin America the freed person, whatever his racial lineage, assumed a place equal to that of all others in the civic community. Authorities differ as to whether or not Negro ancestry might have been a handicap in the class status system of Latin America, but there seems little doubt that many Negroes came to occupy high public position and that white-colored intermarriage was never looked upon with the abhorrence that it is looked upon in the United States. Although the position of the Negro freed before general abolition was in some respects higher than that of those still enslaved, the fact that he was still a Negro meant that he was considered an inferior person.

Among the various social forces which Tannenbaum offers in explanation of the contrasts in these two slave systems was the presence in the Latin-American legal system of Spanish law, with its established precedents of specific definition of slave status, and the absence of any corresponding precedents in British law. Furthermore, the influence of Catholic doctrine in contrast to the position of Protestantism should be noted. Although the

---

[42] *New Orleans Bee*, quoted in Tannenbaum, *Slave and Citizen*, p. 77. By permission of the publishers, Alfred A. Knopf, Inc.
[43] *Ibid.*, pp. 53–54.

Church did not interfere with the institution when the domestic law accepted it, it had early condemned the slave trade and officially prohibited Catholics from participating in it, even though not altogether successfully. Still further, the Church considered that slave and master were equal in the sight of God, gave slaves the right to baptism, and insisted that masters bring their slaves to church. This stands in sharp contrast to the total neglect of Negroes by the Episcopal Church in the British West Indies, and to the position of the Protestant denominations in the South of the United States. After 1700 there was no systematic opposition to teaching the Christian doctrine to the Negro slave, but the churches in the South generally made no attack on the institution of slavery itself.

Slavery as a Social System

Slavery as a system of human relations cannot be maintained without the use of force. While most slave states passed statutes designed to protect the slave from unnecessary sufferings, Myrdal writes, "In general, the Negro slave had no 'rights' which his owner was bound to respect."[44] Thus the disciplining of Negroes was left largely to the master or his white overseer, who in exercise of this function was restrained only by his own conscience and such group pressure as the white mores of the community brought to bear. When it was felt to be necessary, the masters did inflict corporal punishment and even death on the slaves.

Nevertheless, the relations between the two racial groups came to be ordered by a system of etiquette and ritual which more or less explicitly defined the proper reciprocal behavior whenever members of the two races were together. The actual relations between groups never perfectly coincides with the formal status. White-Negro relations under slavery were often overlaid with a sense of mutual responsibility and reciprocal affections. This was particularly true with house servants who identified themselves with the family, and who were often biologically related to it.

Aptheker has called attention to the fact that there were some rebellious reactions. He has noted about 250 slave insurrections and rebellions involving ten or more people.[45] Better known is the fact that many slaves attempted to flee to free territory, some successfully. The odds, however, against either rebellion or escape were so overwhelming that some form of accommodation to the inevitable was the price of survival. Accommodation to slavery required taking on—at least as role playing—all the traits of servility and dependence.

[44] Myrdal, *An American Dilemma*, p. 530.
[45] Herbert Aptheker, *American Slave Revolts* (New York: Columbia University Press, 1943), p. 162.

THE RECONSTRUCTION PERIOD

The emancipation of slaves was forced upon the South against its will, of course, and the implication of freedom could be carried through only by a costly, large-scale federal program and the application of considerable pressures upon the South. The problem was twofold: how to implement and guarantee the new political status of Negroes as free men; and how to reconstruct the economy of the South in such a manner that Negroes would have a secure economic position.

The war had wrought enormous material property losses on Southern whites, as well as taking away their slaves. Many of the freed slaves who, both during the war and immediately after it, had flocked to the cities or to the vicinity of Northern army camps found no means of livelihood. In 1865 the Bureau of Refugees, Freedman, and Abandoned Lands was established to aid in, among other things, the economic rehabilitation of the freedmen, as well as the propertyless whites, and to promote an educational program for the Negroes. The general plan was to furnish land and tools with which the freedman and landless whites might become self-sustaining farmers.

However, during the seven years of its existence (1865–1872), the Bureau was unable to accomplish its economic objectives. It had woefully inadequate funds for the size of the job. The amnesty granted former Confederates restored to them the land which had already been leased to Negroes, who consequently became landless again. When efforts were made to re-settle both white and Negro tenants on public lands in the Gulf areas, inability to raise enough capital and general discouragement with the whole program spelled failure. The desire of the more influential portion of the white South to retain the traditional system of agricultural production and to keep the Negro in his servile place did nothing to help. And the half-hearted support of Northerners contributed to the failure of the government to carry through the program. The lukewarm support was due in part to the usual reluctance to appropriate the rather large funds needed for the task. Northerners, although believing in theoretical freedom for Negroes, were far from advocating that they be accorded full, equal status. The combination of proprietary interest in the South and the traditional white attitudes toward the proper status of Negroes, shared by many Northerners as well as nearly all the white South, conspired to defeat what appears in retrospect to have been a validly conceived plan for the economic rehabilitation of the South.

The same combination of interests and attitudes appeared in opposition to the fulfillment of the other objective in the Northern plan for reconstruction of the South: the civic and social integration of Negroes and the rehabilitation of Negroes as first-class citizens. Soon after the close of the war, eight

Southern states instituted the so-called Black Codes. By various statutes affecting apprenticeship, labor contracts, debts, and vagrancy, these codes went far to re-establish the servile position of Negroes. Of the examples of these codes which Frazier cites, the following is significantly illustrative. "The Florida code states that if any person of color failed to fulfill the stipulations of a contract into which he entered with a plantation owner or was impudent to the owner, he should be declared a vagrant and be subject to punishment for vagrancy."[46]

When the Republican government of the North realized that the South was in fact nullifying the Emancipation Proclamation, it set about to exert pressure to force acceptance. Through the Fourteenth Amendment to the Constitution, declared effective in 1866, abridgement of the full civic equality of all citizens was declared unlawful, and the supplementary Fifteenth Amendment, effective in 1870, specifically denied the right to abridgement of the voting privilege "on account of race, color, or previous condition of servitude." Still further, Congress passed in 1867 a series of reconstruction acts which called for the temporary governing of the South by military rule until such time as genuinely democratic elections could be held and governments so elected should get under way. In the governments which followed, many Negroes were elected to state assemblies, and twenty were sent to Congress. Some of these Negro officials demonstrated unusual ability.

In these turbulent years the majority of Southerners naturally resented the attempt of the "carpetbaggers" to reconstruct their society, aided by their own "scalawags," as the Southerners who co-operated with the Yankee officials were called. They made much of the point that complete civic equality for Negroes would give the colored population control over the South. Actually, in no state were Negroes ever the dominating factor in the government, though in several states they constituted about half the population. The Southern attitude toward the Negro was not reconstructed, as the testimony of Carl Schurz indicates:

Wherever I go . . . I hear the people talk in such a way as to indicate that they are yet unable to conceive of the Negro as possessing any rights at all. . . . The people boast that when they get freedmen's affairs in their own hands . . . "the niggers will catch hell."

The reason of all this is simple and manifest. The whites esteem the blacks their property by natural right, and however much they admit that the individual relations of masters and slaves have been destroyed by the war and by the President's emancipation proclamation, they still have an ingrained feeling that the blacks at large belong to the whites at large.[47]

The next phase of the reconstruction drama opened as the Republican

[46] Frazier, *The Negro in the United States*, p. 127.
[47] Report of Carl Schurz, Senate Executive Document, No. 2, 39th Congress, 1st Session, cited by W. E. B. DuBois, *Black Reconstruction in America* (New York: Harcourt, Brace & Co., 1936).

Congress began to weaken. In 1872, the disabilities imposed on the former Confederate leaders, which prevented their participation in political affairs, were removed. The Freedmen's Bureau was abolished, depriving many Negro laborers and tenants of much-needed economic support and moral aid. The climax came when the Civil Rights bill of 1875 was declared unconstitutional. This bill, as Myrdal puts it, "represented the culmination of the Federal reconstruction legislation, was explicit in declaring that all persons . . . should be entitled to the full and equal enjoyment of the accommodations, advantages, facilities, and privileges of inns, public conveyances on land and water, theaters, and other places of public amusement . . . applicable alike to citizens of every race and color, regardless of previous condition of servitude."[48] When the bill was declared unconstitutional, at least as far as the "social" equality phases were concerned, the North seems to have given up.

From 1875 on, the door was open for the unreconstructed white Southerners to carry out their own program of reconstruction. The result was the biracial pattern of race relations in which the dominance of white over colored was assured. This social system has remained broadly intact down to the present and will be the subject of detailed examination in the next chapter. Reconstruction on this biracial basis involved the use of both legal and illegal procedures. Since in the white Southern view Negroes had already advanced too far, it was first necessary to apply illegal force and terror to compel a return to their original status. This phase of the reconstruction was spearheaded by a number of secret societies, of which the Ku Klux Klan is the most widely known. Extralegal activities were supplemented by further Black Code legislation, which segregated Negroes and otherwise accorded them unequal privileges. While it took some years to accomplish the task, the white South succeeded in establishing a color-caste system.

Reconstruction: An Object Lesson

What happened in the reconstruction period is an excellent object lesson in social science. It illustrates the consequences of attempting swift and radical social change without adequate social planning. In hindsight, it is clear that the federal government attempted to accomplish too sweeping objectives in too short a time against too strong a set of opposing forces and with too little public support from the North itself. For example, how could it have been expected that white Southerners, long steeped in the tradition of slavery, could change their complex attitudes and habits concerning Negroes overnight? Again, how could it have been expected that slaves, held to such a low level of literacy and moulded into a servile, dependent, per-

[48] Myrdal, *An American Dilemma*, p. 579. By permission.

sonality pattern, could immediately become self-reliant and civically active? Furthermore, how could it have been expected that such a program could be carried on without a greater consensus of Northern opinion to support it? To raise such questions in hindsight and to leave the matter there is obviously unfair to the many intelligent and socially conscious white people, both North and South who set the objectives and tried to carry them out. Neither the theoretical knowledge of human nature and social processes nor the accumulated practice of social engineering had advanced to a point in 1865 to have made success possible. We cite the lesson for its value at the present time.

The United States is now in an extraordinary period of disequilibrium in white-Negro relations, precipitated by the Supreme Court's school desegregation decision. We face this period with a considerably greater body of social theory, techniques, and practices in intergroup relations. In areas of the nation where the attitudes of the dominant group are not too intransigent, some of this knowledge has been usefully applied. As we have before commented, social knowledge affected the decision of the Court itself. The nature and scope of this accumulated knowledge will be discussed in Part III.

TOPICS FOR PROJECTS AND DISCUSSION

1. Discuss the relative importance of (a) sociological factors and (b) biological factors in determining whether an American is or is not a Negro.
2. The "Negro" population of the United States could decline even with higher birth rates and lower death rates among people of Negro ancestry. Explain how this could happen.
3. Discuss the various effects on Negro-white relations which you would see following from the increasing development of race pride among American Negroes.
4. Trace carefully the role which economic and technological factors played in the development of the slavery system in the South.
5. Consult appropriate historical sources to determine the extent to which Negroes in the South following the War Between the States were or were not prepared for citizenship.

SUGGESTED READING

Aptheker, Herbert. *American Negro Slave Revolts*. New York: Columbia University Press, 1943.
    The most complete history of the subject.
Coulter, E. Merton. *The South During Reconstruction, 1865–1877*. Baton Rouge: Louisiana State University Press, 1947.
    A Southern view of the Reconstruction Period.
DuBois, W. E. B. *Black Reconstruction*. New York: Harcourt, Brace & Co., 1935.
    A Negro leader presents his view of the role of Negroes in Reconstruction.

Elkins, Stanley M. *Slavery: A Problem in American Institutional and Intellectual Life*. Chicago: The University of Chicago Press, 1959.
> *An institutional approach to the subject.*

Holmes, S. J. "The Trends of the Racial Balance of Births and Death," in *Race Relations and the Race Problem*, Edgar T. Thompson, ed. Durham: Duke University Press, 1939.
> *The analysis anticipates increasing proportional gain of Negro population in relation to the growth of the white population.*

Lewis, Julian H. *The Biology of the Negro*. Chicago: University of Chicago Press, 1942.
> *Most complete summary and analysis of the subject.*

Myrdal, Gunnar, *et al. An American Dilemma: the Negro Problem and Modern Democracy*. New York: Harper & Brothers, 1944.
> *The most comprehensive assemblage of facts about Negroes in relation to whites in American society. The Swedish writer has presented his own interpretation of the data and researches provided by scores of American scolars. Ch. 7, "Population"; Ch. 8, "Migration"; and Ch. 10, "The Tradition of Slavery" bear on this chapter.*

Stampp, Kenneth M. *The Peculiar Institution: Slavery in the AnteBellum South*. New York: Alfred A. Knopf, Inc., 1956.
> *A scholarly analysis of slavery.*

11

Negro-White Relations:
The Traditional Southern Pattern

In the preceding chapter the period of Negro-white relations in the United States from 1881 to 1940 was designated "the period of biracial accommodation." This phrase was selected as the most suitable to subsume the two markedly different patterns of racial relations which developed in the South and outside it during these years. While Negroes occupied a minority status throughout the United States, the difference in their position in the North and in the South was so great that separate treatment is mandatory. This chapter delineates the system of race relations which developed in the South following the Northern abandonment of reconstruction. The pattern was essentially crystallized by 1910. While from then on it was not completely unchanging, it was sufficiently so to permit its delineation as a substantially fixed structure of intergroup relations. Since 1940, as we shall discuss in Chapter 13, Negro-white relations have been changing rapidly. In consideration of these changes we employ the past tense generally in this chapter. But it should be remembered throughout that much of this traditional pattern still prevails, especially in the Deep South. Why there continues to be such strong resistance to change in the South is better understood if one keeps constantly in mind that today's white Southerners have been conditioned since birth to the biracial system here described.

The chapter describes the traditional system of race relations for the South as a whole, comprising the following states: Alabama, Arkansas, Delaware, Florida, Georgia, Kentucky, Louisiana, Maryland, Mississippi, North Carolina, Oklahoma, South Carolina, Tennessee, Virginia, West Virginia, and the District of Columbia. Some of the main variations in this pattern will be considered under a separate heading at the end of the chapter.

CASTE SYSTEM

In common with many other, although not all, students of minorities, we shall designate this Southern interracial pattern as a caste system. In its ideology and in the institutions which governed race relations, the categorical segregation of the two races in a large number of social relations was clear. Intermarriage was flatly prohibited. While specific identification with a particular occupation, as was characteristic of the traditional Hindu caste system, was not so marked, nevertheless the Southern pattern did not generally permit the performance together of the same tasks by members of the two races. Furthermore, the rising middle class of Negroes in the South was in the main segregated from the white middle class. It was the absence of explicit religious sanctions in support of its biracial system which mainly distinguished the Southern pattern from other caste systems.

The Southern caste system had two main features—segregation and the so-called caste etiquette. The former involved the physical separation of Negroes from whites; the latter included the rules to be followed when interaction must unavoidably take place between one or more members of each race. Both the patterns of segregation and the caste etiquette always symbolized the superordination of the white people and the subordination of the Negroes.

Housing Segregation[1]

Residentially, in rural areas, Negroes were scattered but did not live close to whites except on plantations, where the mansion was separated conspicuously, though often not far, from the Negroes' shacks. In small towns there was a clustering of Negro homes on edges of the community. In Southern cities there were varieties of Negro residential patterns: the back-alley residence plan, as seen in Charleston; the isolated community, as in Tulsa; the one large Negro area with smaller scattered clusters found in many cities. Interestingly enough, Southern whites did not appear to object to having Negro families live near them, as Northern whites did. However, in the South when homes of Negro families were spatially proximate to those of

[1] See Charles S. Johnson, *Patterns of Negro Segregation* (New York: Harper & Brothers, 1943), for the fullest single-volume discussion of segregation at the height of the development of the system.

white families, there was usually some outward manifestation of the superior-inferior status—for example, whites facing the streets and Negroes the alley, or the comparatively more run-down appearance of the Negro homes. Neighborliness prevailed, but always in conformance to the etiquette of race relations.

Education

Seventeen states had entirely separate school systems. No contact at all took place between the teachers or pupils of the two systems except the unavoidable contact of the superintendent, who was white. This separation in schooling during the early years went far to root firmly in the attitudes and habits of children of both races the practice of race segregation. Negroes were not admitted generally into public libraries in the South, and a Negro had no access to library facilities unless he could get a white friend to take out a book for him. In a few large cities Negro branch libraries were established.

Social Discrimination

Public recreational facilities were generally scarce in the South outside the large cities, and whites in the nonurban areas did not share those that existed with the Negroes. In Southern cities, Negroes were generally excluded from public parks, and in only a few cities did they have parks of their own. Except in a few instances where a special section of a public playground was set aside for them, the colored people were not permitted to utilize public playgrounds.

In hotels and restaurants the segregation was absolute and complete. Outside the larger cities, where some Negro hotels and restaurants exist, it was impossible for Negroes who were traveling to get a meal or lodging unless some Negro family gave them hospitality. In public buildings, such as post offices, tax offices, an so on, Negroes usually waited in line until every white person appearing had been served. Separate toilets for each race was the general rule in public places where both races were admitted. The best-known device of the segregation system was "Jim Crow" transportation. In local transportation, where the vehicles were often not physically partitioned, Negroes had to go to the rear and whites to the front, the dividing line being set on each trip by the proportion of each race aboard. Of this Johnson wrote: "The operator is empowered to regulate the space occupied by each race in accordance with the respective number of passengers. This system is subject to abuse since it permits the attitude of the operator to become a factor in segregation."[2]

One of the most striking examples of segregation was in hospitalization.

---

[2] *Ibid.*, p. 49.

In some places there were isolated wards for Negroes. But more often the hospitals would not admit Negroes, and there were few Negro hospitals. Instances occurred of Negroes in need of emergency operations dying because the nearest hospitals would not admit them.

Economic Discrimination

Segregation in economic life had two main aspects: in employment and in the role of the Negro as a customer. In regard to employment, the basic principle was that Negroes must not work alongside whites on equal functional terms. For instance, one restaurant might have all Negro waitresses and another across the street all white waitresses, but no restaurant would mix the two. The first would probably have a white cashier; the second would probably have Negro dishwashers; but here the functional differentiation was clear. This principle operated to limit Negro employment to those occupations which whites did not care to enter. (The one important exception was tenant farming, in which both races engaged but in which they did not work together.) As a result, occupations which were the most menial and the poorest paid were left for the Negroes. When technological improvements came along to make any particular occupation more rewarding, the whites tried to keep the Negroes out, as they did following the introduction of farm tractors and the mechanical cotton picker. (In these particular instances white farm labor has not been wholly successful in keeping a race monopoly.)

Until 1935 labor unions in the South excluded Negroes from membership, or at most permitted them to organize in separate auxiliary locals. Since the earlier days of the caste period, Negroes had become a majority in certain semiskilled or skilled trades; the development of unions had the effect of driving them from these occupations. The elimination of Negroes as engineers on railroad locomotives and the gradual decline in the number of Negro firemen and brakemen correlated with the rise of the railway workers' unions.

The color line was less rigidly drawn against the Negro as a customer in commercial establishments. Two generalizations held largely true. The cheaper the price level of the goods to be sold, the more welcome was the Negro trade. Thus the five-and-ten-cent stores and the chain food stores generally welcomed Negro trade and provided reasonably courteous service, while the more exclusive stores either refused or discouraged Negro patronage through discourtesy. The other general rule was that the more intimate the personal relationship involved in a commercial transaction, the more likely the Negro was to be excluded. In beauty parlor and mortuary services the races were strictly separated. But when the services rendered, though involving considerable interpersonal relationships, were such that the position of the vendor was clearly superior to that of the buyer, as in the case of medical or legal counsel, white professional people generally would take Negro clients.

The Code of Race Etiquette

Since Negroes were an important part of the economic life of the South, they could not be totally segregated. To allow for some interpersonal relations there developed an elaborate pattern of racial etiquette,[3] the function of which was to make clear the superordinate and subordinate caste positions. For example, a white man did not shake hands with a Negro when introduced to him. An exception would be when a white man visited a Negro college or, sometimes, a Negro home. The white person did not address the Negro person as "Mr." or "Mrs.," but rather by his first name or by his last without the courtesy title; the Negro always addressed the white person as "Mister," "Marse," or "Misses," or better still by some such title as "Colonel," which often the white man did not actually possess. Interestingly enough, professionally trained Negroes could be addressed as "Professor," "Doctor," or "Reverend." Thus most Negro male school or college teachers were "Professors," however limited their education may have been. Negro women were never referred to as "ladies," but either just "women," or, irrespective of age, as "girls." Negro men were expected to doff their hats when they spoke to white men, but the latter were not expected to reciprocate. Whenever Negroes had occasion to call at or enter white men's homes, they did so at the rear door; the white man, of course, always appeared at the front door. Whenever circumstances brought Negroes and white people together at mealtime or on recreational occasions, the races were not expected to sit together at the same table or play together. Thus when a white person visited a colored home, if the Negro hostess wished to provide food for her guest, etiquette prescribed that they not eat together. With the exception of quite young children, Negroes and whites did not ordinarily play together. A significant exception was where there was opportunity for the Negro to serve his white companion in a servile role, as in hunting or fishing.

Endogamy is the primary principle of caste. Marriage across caste lines was not recognized and was forbidden by law in Southern states. Most adamant of all the taboos was the one against any sort of casual interpersonal relations between a white woman and a Negro man. No one thing was more dangerous to a Negro male than to be in a situation that could be even remotely construed as indicating personal interest in a white female. That Negro men understood this and acted accordingly can be seen in the following instance. A white woman, the wife of a white man in charge of a migrant labor camp for Southern Negroes in the North, attempted to engage Negro men in the camp in friendly conversation and was nonplussed at their

[3] See Bertram W. Doyle, *The Etiquette of Race Relations in the South* (Chicago: University of Chicago Press), 1937, for a fuller description of the subject.

attempts to avoid the situation. Brought up to know that the rope or faggot awaits the Negro accused—falsely or otherwise—of "sexual" interest in a white woman, Negro men in the South, as a general rule, avoided white women.

The Interrelation of Class and Caste

In the South the class system was linked with the caste system in significant ways. In most Southern communities, particularly in cities, class differentiation had developed within the Negro caste as well as in the white caste. Negroes performing higher-ranking functions—for example, ministers, teachers, doctors, farm agents—had achieved a higher-class status within their racial group. The class position of such Negroes was generally recognized by the white people, and the Negroes so recognized were accorded differential treatment from that accorded the lower-class Negroes. Frequently upper-class whites came to the defense of upper-class Negroes who got into trouble with lower-class whites. Warner and Davis cite the case of a colored professional man who accidentally ran down and killed with his car a drunken lower-class white man. Local bankers offered money for the Negro's defense, and upper-class white women called at his place of business to indicate that they supported him in his difficulty.[4] This class bond which cut across caste lines prompted upper-class whites on occasion to attend special functions conducted by upper-class Negroes, and at such occasions special courtesies not generally accorded Negroes by caste etiquette might be extended by the whites, such as addressing the Negro women as "Mrs."

This class-differentiated aspect of the caste system operated more to strengthen caste, however, than to undermine it. While it accorded upper-class Negroes some differential privileges, these were limited and always fell clearly short of equality. And to receive these class privileges upper-class Negroes had to accept caste, at least outwardly. This special relation also served practical purposes in the maintenance of the biracial system. While caste relations are fundamentally antagonistic, they cannot exist without some degree of co-operation. In spite of the vastly superior power position of the whites, an orderly community under caste required co-operation from the Negro group. In their function as leaders, the middle- and upper-class Negroes were expected to exert their influence to control the Negro masses in the interest of preserving order.[5]

---

[4] W. Lloyd Warner and Allison Davis, "A Comparative Study of American Caste," in *Race Relations and the Race Problem*, ed. Edgar T. Thompson (Durham: Duke University Press, 1939), p. 243.

[5] These class-linked relations should not be confused with the intergroup relations which are in substance nonconformity to caste. There have been, of course, throughout the whole period considered, a few white people here and there, more particularly in cities, who did not believe in caste and who, with due deference to the personal costs of nonconformity, have participated in informal mixed gatherings on a plane of social equality.

METHODS OF ENFORCING CASTE

The methods employed for sustaining this caste pattern of race relations in the South may be conveniently treated under the headings of "legal methods"; "illegal force and intimidation"; and "custom." Bearing in mind that at many points these three methods of social control reinforce each other, we shall discuss each separately.

Legal Methods

Specific local and state laws required segregation of the two races in many of the categories of interaction noted above. Southern state supreme courts upheld these laws, and until recently the Supreme Court of the United States upheld Southern segregation laws in the cases reaching it. One important exception concerns housing segregation by state or municipal law. In 1915, a Louisville, Kentucky, city ordinance forbidding Negroes to reside in certain areas was declared unconstitutional by the United States Supreme Court.[6] It further ruled that the segregated public facilities and services provided Negroes should be equal to those provided for whites. As we shall presently indicate, every description of the facilities for Negroes in the South documented the fact that Negroes did not have equal public facilities, in spite of this interpretation of the Constitution. Segregation continued to be upheld by local law.

Illegal Violence and Intimidation

The whole pattern of segregation and race etiquette, however, was not upheld by law. That part of it not so covered was reinforced by intimidation and extralegal violence. The Negro who violated the customary etiquette found himself brought to order by whites by abusive language and warnings. If he persisted in violation or if the breach was considered particularly heinous from the dominant caste's viewpoint, he might be physically maltreated or even lynched. If the violations appeared to be in any sense en masse, a whole Negro street or area might be destroyed by white groups as a way of "teaching the nigger to keep his place." The authors of the book *Deep South* write:

> In fact, it is considered entirely correct for the white person to resort directly to physical attack upon the Negro. Thus, if a Negro curses a white, the white may knock the Negro down; and the failure to do so may even be considered as a failure in duty as a white. . . .
>
> It is a common belief of many whites that Negroes will respond only to violent methods. In accordance with the theory of the "animal-like" nature of the Negro, they believe that the formal punishments of fines and imprisonments fail to act as deterrents to crime.[7]

[6] See Johnson, *Patterns of Negro Segregation*, p. 175.
[7] Allison Davis, Burleigh Gardner, and Mary R. Gardner, *Deep South* (Chicago: University of Chicago Press, 1941), pp. 45–46. By permission.

The authors quote a planter who puts the traditional Southern white viewpoint in these words:

The best thing is not to take these young bucks into the court house for some small crime but to give them a paddling. That does them more good than a jail sentence. If I catch a Negro stealing a hog or some chickens, what is the use of taking him into court? He would get a fine or a jail sentence and unless I pay him out he will lie up in jail, and when he gets out he will keep on stealing.[8]

As a result of this traditional support of intimidation and violence, law itself was caste-patterned. It applied very unequally to the two races. When any altercation occurred involving a white and a Negro, the Negro was usually presumed to be wrong. The word of a white person was ordinarily taken against that of a Negro, even when many whites knew that the white person was lying. Furthermore, the law failed to protect the Negro against extra-legal violence on the part of whites. It was generally impossible to get anybody to testify that he had any knowledge about illegal acts of violence perpetrated against Negroes. As a result, lynching after lynching occurred in the South. Even those reported in the national press, where the fact of lynching was incontrovertible, seldom resulted in indictments and trials. Negroes were carefully kept off juries in the South. However, Federal Supreme Court reversals of Negro convictions where the defense argued successfully that Negroes in the communities involved were purposely not called to jury duty began to break this caste practice to a degree.[9] For a long time the only chance for some measure of justice for the Negroes was if they had a white protector who would intercede for them. Frequently a landlord or other employer would say a good word for his Negro employee and get the case dismissed or the sentence lightened.

Custom

The casual traveler in the South would not have noticed the intimidation we have mentioned. He saw for the most part an orderly pattern of segregation and race etiquette. On the surface he saw no resentment. But, although indications of intimidation were not present each day, no Negro brought up in the South was unaware of the threat of violence. Negro children were taught by their earliest experience with white people to conform to the established pattern. Negro parents had to punish the rebellious inclinations of their children who naively approached white persons as equal human beings. And the white children in the South were, of course, conditioned to assume all the appropriate attitudes and behavior patterns of the dominant caste. Any tendency to really like Negro children had to be sternly disciplined to make sure that they were not treated as equals. Thus the Southern caste pattern was supported by the conditioning and custom of

[8] *Ibid.,* p. 46.
[9] Myrdal, *An American Dilemma* (New York: Harper & Brothers, 1944), p. 549.

the Southerners of both races to assume the reciprocal social roles required to keep it intact—the white to be arrogant, exploitative, superior; the Negro to be submissive, exploited, and inferior. Most of the time this combination of implicit intimidation and habituation worked quite successfully. The Negro who occasionally threw caution to the wind and rebelled against the pattern was dealt with summarily. The white person whose conscience occasionally pricked him submerged his inclination under the pressure of public sentiment.

Caste Control Illustrated: Keeping Negroes from Voting

The mixture of law, intimidation, and custom in sustaining caste is well illustrated in the devices by which Negroes in the South were prevented from exercising the ballot. As noted in the discussion of reconstruction, Negroes after emancipation had voted and been elected to office, but between 1890 and 1910, eleven Southern states adopted special requirements for voting designed to deny Negroes the franchise. One such device was the poll tax. In order to vote, the citizen was required to pay a special tax of a dollar or two for the privilege. While this was not a large sum, by various other devices it was made to serve its purpose. Sometimes the tax was retroactive—that is to say, in order to vote in any one year, poll tax receipts for a number of years had to be shown if asked for by the election official. An arrearage of, say, $10 was effective in keeping a Negro from voting.

Negroes were barred from voting in the Democratic primary with the excuse that any political party may restrict its membership. Before 1941 the United States Supreme Court in decisions concerning these white primary regulations failed to overrule the specific laws in this connection. Other qualifications for voting left opportunity for discrimination through their administration. For example, educational tests were sometimes stipulated. By asking Negro applicants for registration questions concerning government which they could not possibly answer, officials could keep them off the list. Or such devices as giving the Negroes only a day for registration when the white officials were not available were further employed.

In addition to these state statutes of questionable constitutionality, and to administrative discrimination, white Southerners at times resorted to intimidation and violence for the purpose of preventing Negroes from voting. Davie furnishes the following example: "There are numerous instances of Negroes who attempted to register or vote being driven away, beaten up, or killed. More generally the opposition took the form of intimidation. For example, a Negro went to the registration booth in his county and asked if he could register. The white official replied: 'Oh, yes, you can register, but I want to tell you something. Some God-damn niggers are going to get killed about this voting business yet.' Intended to terrorize Negro citizens who might seek to vote in the primaries in Dennison, Texas, in the fall of 1932, handbills were scattered throughout the town reading as follows:

NIGGER!

The white people do not want you to vote Saturday.
Do not make the Ku Klux Klan take a hand.
Do you remember what happened two years ago, May 9th?
George Hughes was burned to death, the county courthouse
destroyed . . . For good reason.

Riots on election day in which both whites and Negroes were killed occurred in various sections of the South."[10]

EFFECTS OF CASTE SYSTEM

In discussing the effects of the race caste system as it operated in the South we will consider its effect on personality and behavior; on the welfare of the Negro; on social organization in Southern communities; and on the political and economic development of the region.

Negro Personality and Behavior

Students of social life know that personality is determined through the interaction of the individual with the total system of social relationships which circumscribe his life. As was shown in Chapter 3, the factor of biological racial heredity has little to do with it. The personalities of the many individuals who are brought up in the same cultural society tend to possess a certain similarity. In heterogeneous societies such as ours, group personalities or social types can be noted, such as the "Babbitt," the "club woman," the "worker," or the "bohemian." The experience of being a dominant or a minority person likewise tends to structure a certain kind of personality. What this kind of status experience did to the personalities of Negroes and whites in the Southern scene is analyzed by John Dollard through an intimate study of class and caste relations in a Southern cotton community.[11]

Dollard has analyzed the "gains" accruing to white people under the caste system which were in turn "losses" to the Negroes. First, there was the economic gain. The system enabled white people to exploit Negroes as workers and consumers. A typical year for the Negro tenant farmer ran as follows: After the cotton had been sold and the Negro had paid his debts, he was broke. The landlord advanced him "furnish" to carry him through the next harvest. The charges for this "furnish" were not regulated and, since the

[10] By permission from *Negroes in American Society*, by M. R. Davie. Copyright 1949. McGraw-Hill Book Co., Inc., p. 266.
[11] John Dollard, *Caste and Class in a Southern Town* (New Haven: Yale University Press, 1937).

Negro lacked education, the accounting was typically in the landlord's hands. Dollard does not maintain that this exploitative advantage was always completely utilized, but it was difficult for the Negro to get justice if his accounting differed from that of the landlord.

Second, Dollard mentions the "sexual gain." By this is meant that the caste system operated to give white men exploitative advantage in sexual satisfaction among Negro women, as well as among whites, while any sexual advances of Negro men toward white women were absolutely tabooed and infractions often punished by death. The caste system did not require Negro women to accept the sexual overtures of white men, but the economic and social disadvantages which Negro women suffered through the caste system often made acceptance of these advances attractive. While by no means all white men took advantage of this opportunity, it was a general part of the rationalization of the white caste ideology that Negro women are sexually promiscuous and that relations with them were hardly to be taken seriously in an ethical sense.

The third gain Dollard saw accruing to the white caste was "ego" gratification. The daily expressions of superiority toward all Negroes which the whites could indulge and the responses of submissiveness by the Negroes bolstered the self-esteem of the whites, especially those among the less privileged ranks.

In the face of these "gains" to the whites, what could Negroes do? Obviously, these advantages to the whites generated an enormous amount of additional frustration among Negroes. Dollard suggests five ways in which Negroes could react.[12] (1) They could become overtly aggressive against the white caste. This some Negroes did, though infrequently and almost always unsuccessfully. (2) They might suppress their aggression and supplant it with accommodative attitudes. This was the slavery solution, and it still existed under the caste system. Negroes sometimes got what they wanted from whites by exaggerated flattery and thus exploited the "ego inflation" of whites to their own advantage. The clever Negro might act "dumb" in order to get around the white person. Frequently Negroes lied to white people because they feared to disagree with anything whites said. (3) Negroes might turn their aggression from the white caste to individuals within their own group. While the stereotype of Negroes carrying razors is highly exaggerated, a very considerable amount of physical violence toward one another did take place. The homicide rate among Negroes was high. (4) Negroes might give up competition for white values and accept other forms of gratification than those secured by whites. This was the solution characterizing lower-class Negroes. Since in tenant farming they were completely dependent on the planter, they assumed an attitude of "let's enjoy today, since tomorrow will be no better." Again, sex gratifications could be

[12] *Ibid.*, Ch. XII.

indulged more fully since no "social climbing ambitions" would be jeopardized. Broadly speaking this caste system encouraged Negroes to give direct, emotional expression to their basic desires because restraint in the interest of "getting ahead" had no meaning. (5) Dollard suggests that some Negroes might compete for the values of white society by attempting to raise their class position within the Negro caste. This involved managing "aggression partly by expressing dominance within their own group and partly by sheer suppression of their impulse as individuals."[13] This was the solution characteristic of the Negro middle class.

Mark of Oppression

Many years ago Herbert A. Miller referred to the high prevalence among minorities of the attitudes of fear, hatred, resentment, jealousy, suspicion, and revenge—which he labeled the "oppression psychosis." One manifestation of this is the frequency of hypersensitivity to dominant behavior—interpreting remarks or acts as having derogatory implications even when they are not meant to be such. The essential point made by Miller has been substantiated by research, even though the term "psychosis" may be applicable only to those more intensely affected by discrimination. Kardiner and Ovesey, after studying twenty-five Negro males by personality tests and psychoanalytic techniques, concluded as follows:

> On the whole we must be satisfied that the conclusions derived from the three different experimental approaches—the psychodynamic analysis, the Rorschach test, and the T.A.T.—are essentially the same. The major features of the Negro personality emerge from each with remarkable consistency. These include the fear of relatedness, suspicion, mistrust, the enormous problem of the control of aggression, the denial mechanism, the tendency to dissipate the tension of a provocative situation by reducing it to something simpler, or to something entirely different. All these maneuvers are in the interest of not meeting reality head on. . . . The defects in adaptation are not of mysterious or racial origin but owe their existence entirely to the arduous emotional conditions under which the Negro in America is obliged to live.[14]

Karon studied a small but rigorously selected sample of Northern and Southern Negroes and Northern whites, employing the Tompkins-Horn Picture Arrangement Test. His findings were that caste sanctions have an effect on the personality structure of Negroes born and reared in the South in eleven characteristics, six of which are related to the problem of handling aggression. This research rejects the formerly oft-stated hypothesis that the Southern Negro, because he lives in a consistent interracial system, is not disturbed by caste sanctions, in contrast to the Northern Negro, who lives in a more ambiguous racial situation. Karon's findings show a consistent rela-

---

[13] *Ibid.*, p. 253.
[14] Abram Kardiner and Lionel Ovesey, *The Mark of Oppression* (New York: W. W. Norton & Company, Inc., 1951), p. 337–338. By permission.

tionship between the severity of the caste sanctions and the appearance of these disturbed traits. Rural Southern Negroes are "worse off" than the urban Southern Negroes; Northern Negroes born in the South are worse off than those born in the North. In fact, the latter quite closely resemble the white Northern sample, which the author attributes possibly to the inadequacy of the tests to determine small discriminants.[15]

The fact that Negroes seldom openly manifested hatred for white people should not be interpreted to indicate that they do not cherish such a feeling inwardly. Warner and Davis write that "Anyone who believes that the hostile statements uttered by Southern whites toward Negroes are extreme should be allowed to hear those uttered by Negroes, even Negro children and adolescents toward whites."[16]

White Personality

Reciprocally, the caste system had its effects on the dominant caste personality, a subject which has received little scientific attention. In the description of the effect of caste on Negro personality and behavior, as in Dollard's study, the white reciprocals are revealed. Exploitative and "bullying" behavior were stimulated by the dominant position of whites in the caste situation. There arose a disdain for certain forms of physical labor which was traditionally associated with the minority caste. Obviously, the cultivation of a genuinely democratic personality was made difficult by the kind of upbringing which white children got in a caste-stratified community.

The Negro Community

Under the caste system the organization of Southern communities was a dual structure, in which the white community and Negro community were distinct. In the latter were parallel associations and institutions, Negro churches, lodges, schools, recreational places. As the description of segregation above indicates, there was not a completely parallel set of economic institutions. For many goods and services, Negroes patronized white stores and salesmen. However, for economic services of a personal sort, such as eating places, beauty parlors, undertaking services, and so on, separate Negro enterprises existed.

In 1944 Myrdal characterized the Negro community as a "pathological" form of the average American community.[17] (The characterization holds true for the 1960's in considerable degree.) It was like the white community except that it was more deteriorated in its physical structures; its associational structure tended to exaggerate parallel aspects of the white com-

[15] Bertram P. Karon, *The Negro Personality* (New York: Springer Publishing Company, 1958), pp. 169–175.
[16] "A Comparative Study of American Caste," p. 237.
[17] Myrdal, *An American Dilemma*, p. 927.

munity, for example, in the number of lodges;[18] and many of its institutions expressed an earlier stage of the parallel white institutions—for example, in the case of the church. Since few traces of African cultural background were to be found, the social organizations within the Negro community were not the product of a distinctive cultural heritage. They were American, developed by people who were American in their culture. The pathological manifestations grew out of the discriminations attached to the lower-caste position. These general characteristics of Negro community life are revealed by looking at the basic institutions.

Negro family life was characterized by a greater maternal dominance and weaker institutional stability than white family life.[19] Both of these characteristics arose in part from the heritage of slavery and from the difficult conditions under which Negro families lived, especially in cities. The frequent enforced separation of father from mother and children under slavery; the greater frequency of monogamic unions without legal sanction; and the low economic status stimulating married Negro women to work outside the home—all contributed to increasing the independence of Negro women in the family and to making the mother-child relationship the more enduring bond. The high frequency of common-law marriage and the high rates of illegitimacy were indices of greater institutional instability. An official table for 1936 shows Negroes having eight times as much illegitimacy as native whites and sixteen times as much as foreign-born whites for the United States as a whole.[20]

The actual "social disorganization" of the Negro family was somewhat less than it appears as measured by white standards. In the rural South particularly, adaptive mores developed which greatly mitigated the disorganizing tendencies in the situation. Illegitimacy did not have attached to it the stigma found in the white community and therefore did not produce the same psychological effects. A high value was placed on children, and the larger kin groups of the rural family tended to provide group security to all children, however irregular their status. According to Myrdal, this type of family was "conducive to social health even though the practices are outside the American tradition. When these practices were brought into closer contact with white norms, as occurred when Negroes went to cities, they tended to break down partially and to cause the demoralization of some individuals."[21]

[18] In 1935 in Natchez, Mississippi, where the total Negro population was about 7,500, there were more than 200 Negro associations.
[19] See E. Franklin Frazier, *The Negro Family in the United States* (New York: The Dryden Press, Inc., 1948), for the most complete description and interpretation of the subject.
[20] United States Bureau of the Census, *Births, Stillbirths and Infant Mortality Statistics,* 1936, pp. 9–13.
[21] Myrdal, *An American Dilemma,* p. 935.

The church, particularly in the South, has always been a most fundamental institution in Negro life. In form it resembled that of lower-class white Protestant churches: small in congregation size; fundamentalist in belief; its services characterized by great emotionalism; Puritanical in its views of morals, but unable to do much to stop "sin" except preach against it. Generally speaking, its chief function was to furnish an opportunity for release of frustrations attached to caste status and to bind the members of the community together. Because of this orientation, the lower-class churches were not as important as agencies for intellectual growth or as centers for promoting constructive activity to improve the Negroes' status as were some middle-class Negro churches in Northern cities. The limited range of other avenues of cultural expression open to Negroes appears in part to explain the high rate of church membership among Negroes; the frustrations of the caste status account for its escapist character.

The Negro community also resembled the white community in class differentiation into lower, middle, and, in large cities, upper classes based on income, education and, to some extent, occupation. The segregated system itself was in considerable measure a causal factor in Negro class differentiation. The taboos on personal interracial contact created the need for various professional and semiprofessional services which had to be rendered by Negroes. The degrees of difference in income among Negroes were so much narrower than those in the white class gradient that in small communities class ranking required supplemental basis. Thus in a small Piedmont community, Lewis found a status distinction based on morality between the "respectables" and "nonrespectables":

In general, the respectable persons are defined by what they do not do; they are people who are careful of their public conduct and reputation: they don't drink whiskey in public or get drunk in public; they don't frequent the taverns; they don't get in trouble; and they are proud of their lack of contact with the law and the courts. The respectables are not clustered in any particular section of the town, nor does any of the churches have a monopoly on them. Although the category is not composed exclusively of persons with the best jobs, the most property, or the highest incomes, these features are positively associated with the status. The reason is that respectability—or conventionally-moral conduct—is an expected accompaniment of education and a good or responsible job.[22]

The Welfare of the Negroes in the South

In most indices of human welfare, the Negro population of the United States, as well as the South separately, has always ranked well below the white population in general. For the period here under review, the unfavorable situation of Negroes is seen in the following discussion.

Occupation and Income   Negroes had in 1940 a much higher proportion of male nonfarm workers employed in the lowest occupational levels and an

---

[22] Hylan Lewis, *Blackways of Kent* (Chapel Hill: The University of North Carolina Press, 1955), pp. 233–234.

extremely small percentage employed in the three highest levels as compared with whites. A 1935–1936 study of Negro families not on relief revealed that in the Southern cities of 2,500 or more the median income for
white families was $1,570 against $525 for Negroes.[23] In the same occupations there was a tendency for Negroes to get less pay than the whites. Rural
area studies showed that white tenant farmers had an average higher family
income than Negro tenant farmers. At the other end of the scale, for Negroes
throughout the nation with college education, only 3.9 per cent had incomes
of $2,500 or over, compared with 34 per cent of similarly educated whites.[24]

Housing   Negro housing was of poorer quality than that of whites. Three
per cent of all Negro farm homes had screens in good condition, in contrast
with 24 per cent of the white homes; 10 per cent of Negro homes were without toilet or privy of any kind as against 2 per cent of white homes. In
Southern villages two-thirds of the large Negro families were living in
homes with 1.5 persons per room, as against 28 per cent of the white families of similar size in the same area.[25] The comparison in Southern cities
runs along similar lines.

Education   Comparing the educational level of the Negro population in
the South in 1940 with its level at the time of emancipation indicates tremendous strides. In 1870, 81.4 per cent of Negroes were illiterate; in 1930
this figure had been reduced to 16.3 per cent.[26] Comparing the educational
facilities for Negroes with those of white persons in the South at any given
time, however, reveals gross disparities. During the year 1939–1940, the
Southern states spent $58.69 per white child in average daily attendance in
schools as against only $18.82 for each Negro child.[27] Regarding the value
of the equipment used in the two racial school systems in eleven Southern
states in 1940, a study showed that $162 was spent for every white pupil in
contrast with $34 per Negro pupil.[28] In 1940, 29 per cent of the Negro school
teachers had completed four or more years of college, as compared with
53 per cent of the white teachers.[29] At the higher educational levels the
differential opportunity of Negroes was even more striking. In 1933–1934
only 19 per cent of the Negro children of high school age were in high
schools, as compared with 55 per cent of the white children of the same
ages. In many counties of the South with substantial Negro populations
there were, before 1940, no high schools available for Negroes.[30]

Education of Negroes at the college level in the South before 1890 was

[23] United States National Resources Committee, *Consumer Incomes in the United States*
(Washington, D.C.: Government Printing Office, 1938), p. 28.
[24] E. Franklin Frazier, *The Negro in the United States*, rev. ed. (New York: The Macmillan Co., 1957), p. 607.
[25] Myrdal, *An American Dilemma*, pp. 376–377 and 1291.
[26] Davie, *Negroes in American Society*, p. 139.
[27] See Frazier, *The Negro in the United States*, p. 437.
[28] Davie, *Negroes in American Society*, p. 150.
[29] *Ibid.*, p. 153.
[30] Frazier, *The Negro in the United States*, p. 436.

exceptionally limited, and the schools available were supported largely by private contributions, chiefly from Northern religious denominational sources. In 1890 an amendment to the original Morrill Act adopted in 1862 required that federal funds be divided fairly between the white and the Negro institutions in states having the dual system. Subsequently, seventeen land-grant agricultural and mechanical colleges for Negroes were established, receiving some of their support from federal funds under this Act. But wide disparities continued to exist in both the quantity and the quality of Negro higher educational institutions in the South.

Health   Most studies of comparative Negro-white health conditions have shown widely disparate conditions unfavorable to the Negro. On a nation-wide basis some of the significant figures run as follows: in 1939 the life expectancy of Negroes at birth was ten years less than that of whites; the infant mortality rates per 1,000 live births in 1945 were 56.2 for Negroes and 35.6 for whites; the maternal mortality rates in 1940 show that of Negro mothers about two and a half times that of white mothers. In 1938 Mississippi had 0.7 hospital beds per 1,000 Negroes compared with 2.4 beds for whites.[31]

Crime and Delinquency   The rates of crime and delinquency for this period for the Negro population as a whole compared with the white population as a whole generally show the Negro rate to be significantly higher. In 1933, among the prisoners in the county and city jails, the rate per 100,000 population 15 years and older was 236.8 for Negro males as compared with 71.9 for white males, and 24.4 for Negro females as compared with 3.4 for white females.[32] Negroes accounted for 22.8 per cent of the arrests reported to the Federal Bureau of Investigation in 1940, whereas they comprised about one-tenth of the population. In other words, in the same year, there were 1078.4 Negroes arrested for every 100,000 of the Negro population, against 391.6 white arrests for every 100,000 of white population.[33]

Students of criminology constantly caution against the use of such statistical data without qualification. The reporting of crime data is far from uniform, and therefore we rarely have a full count. And there are many factors which influence the categories of criminals who are arrested and who are placed in penal institutions. We have seen that the administration of justice is caste-patterned, particularly in the South. This in itself affects the statistical figures. Where the offenses of Negroes are against the white race or disturb the white community, Negroes are more frequently arrested and more often found guilty. On the other hand, crime within the Negro community is often left unpunished or treated lightly. Bearing in mind such con-

[31] *Ibid.*, p. 586.
[32] United States Bureau of the Census, *County and City Jails, Prisoners in Jails and Other Penal Institutions under County or Municipal Jurisdiction*, 1933 (Washington, D.C.: Government Printing Office).
[33] See Myrdal, *An American Dilemma*, p. 973, Table 3.

siderations as these, we cannot really make an exact comparison of the actual amounts of criminal behavior in the two groups. What is perhaps of more practical concern has been the relatively high prevalence among Negroes of arrests for murder—largely of other Negroes—assault, and petty larceny.

In general, the positive association of crime rates and low economic position is well established, irrespective of the social characteristics of the groups involved. Further, there are certain persistent influences carrying over from the traditional servile position of Negroes. Petty thievery, for example, such as stealing food or a piece of clothing, was generally condoned by whites, much as one treats a similar act among little children. The traditional pattern of sexual exploitation of Negro females by white males persisted to aggravate the volume of prostitution among Negro women. Again, from Dollard's analysis of Southern town race relations it is clear that the frustrations engendered by discrimination provoked a large volume of aggression, which, in the case of Negroes to whom other aggressive outlets are limited, resulted in much criminal aggression against their own people and against whites.

Violent Conflict: Lynching The caste system also generated violence directed against Negroes by whites. The two characteristic modes of expression of this violence have been lynchings and riots. Lynching may be defined as the murder of a person by a group of people infused by the mob spirit. In American history lynching of native-status people and of minority persons other than Negroes has taken place. Statistics of lynchings have been provided by Tuskegee Institute for the years since 1882. (See Table 9.) In 1884, lynchings of white people still exceeded the lynchings of Negroes by a substantial margin—whites, 160; Negroes, 51. The peak year of Negro lynching was 1892, and for each year from 1891 through 1901 the number was over a hundred. From 1892 on, Negro lynchings have greatly exceeded white lynchings. With minor fluctuations, the trend has been sharply downward.[34]

TABLE 9
Lynchings, Whites and Negroes, 1882–1959 By Decades[35]

Period	White	Negro
1882–1891	751	732
1892–1901	381	1124
1902–1911	76	707
1912–1921	50	553
1922–1931	23	201
1932–1941	10	95
1942–1951	2	25
1952–1959 (8 years)	1	4

[34] After 1936 the recorded number was under ten annually. In 1952, for the first time, no lynching was reported. From 1952 through 1959 this zero record was broken by three lynchings in 1955 and one in 1959.
[35] Tuskeegee Institute, Department of Research and Records.

With the closing of the frontier, lynching became primarily a Southern phenomenon (see Table 10). As with other characteristics of the caste system, in total number of lynchings the Deep South exceeds the border states. It is also of interest to note that the four non-Southern states leading the list are those adjacent to the Southern region: Illinois, Kansas, Ohio, and Indiana.

TABLE 10

States in Which Highest Number of Negro Lynchings Occurred, 1882–1959,
by Rank Order[36]

MISSISSIPPI	538	NORTH CAROLINA	84
GEORGIA	491	VIRGINIA	83
TEXAS	352	OKLAHOMA	40
LOUISIANA	335	WEST VIRGINIA	28
ALABAMA	299	MARYLAND	27
FLORIDA	257	ILLINOIS	19
ARKANSAS	226	KANSAS	19
TENNESSEE	204	OHIO	16
SOUTH CAROLINA	156	INDIANA	14
KENTUCKY	142		

Concerning lynching the Myrdal study finds:

Lynching is a rural and small town custom and occurs most commonly in poor districts. There are some indications that lynchings go in waves and tend to recur in the same districts. The accusations against persons lynched during the period for which there are records were: in 38 per cent of the cases for homicide, 6 per cent for felonious assault, 16 per cent for rape, 7 per cent for attempted rape, 7 per cent for theft, 2 per cent for insult to white persons, and 24 per cent for miscellaneous offenses or no offense at all. In the last category are all sorts of irritations: testifying at court against a white man or bringing suit against him, refusal to pay a note, seeking employment out of place, offensive language or boastful remarks. Regarding the accusations for crime, Raper testifies: "Case studies of nearly one hundred lynchings since 1929 convince the writer that around a third of the victims were falsely accused." The meaning of these facts is that, in principle, a lynching is not merely a punishment against an individual but a disciplinary device against the Negro group. . . .

The actual participants in the lynching mobs usually belong to the frustrated lower strata of Southern whites. Occasionally, however, the people of the middle and upper class take part, and generally they condone the deed, and nearly always they find it advisable to let the incident pass without assisting in bringing the guilty before the court. Women and children are not absent from lynching mobs; indeed, women sometimes incite the mobs into action.[37]

Among the various conditions which have been suggested as related to lynching are poverty and economic fear, social fear that the Negro is "get-

[36] Tuskegee Institute, Department of Research and Records.
[37] Myrdal, An American Dilemma, by permission of the publishers, Harper & Brothers, pp. 560–562. See Arthur Raper, The Tragedy of Lynching (Chapel Hill: University of North Carolina Press, 1933), for an extensive analysis of the lynching problem.

ting out of place," the dullness and general boredom of everyday life in the rural areas and small towns of the South.

Lynching has a "psychological importance out of all proportion to its small frequency."[38] Analyzing its effects, the Myrdal study has this to say:

> The effects of lynchings are far reaching. In the locality where it has happened and in a wide region surrounding it, the relations between the two groups deteriorate. The Negroes are terror stricken and sullen. The whites are anxious and are likely to show the assertiveness and suspicion of persons with bad, but hardened, consciences. Some whites are afraid of Negro retaliation or emigration. Every visitor to such a community must notice the antagonism and mutual lack of confidence between the two groups.[39]

Lynchings in the United States unfailingly receive wide publicity abroad with adverse consequences to the nation's prestige.

It should be mentioned that, however committed they were to segregation as a basic policy for the South, many white Southerners deplored lynching. Influential in this connection was the organization in 1930 in Atlanta of the Association of Southern Women for the Prevention of Lynching. In the basic statement of the association's purpose, lynching was declared "an indefensible crime destructive of all principles of government, hateful and hostile to every ideal of religion and humanity, debasing and degrading to every person involved."[40] This association succeeded in securing the signatures of 50,000 white women of the South to its pledge, which read in part: "We solemnly pledge ourselves to create a new public opinion in the South which will not condone for any reason whatever acts of mobs or lynchers."[41]

Race riots have been more characteristic of the Northern scene and will be discussed in that connection. In the South, they tended more to be mob action by whites directed at defenseless Negro areas.[42]

Political Effects

The South as a region has had a political development which differs from that in the rest of the country. (1) The proportion of people who participate in politics has been markedly smaller than in the rest of the nation. We have already referred to the virtual disfranchisement of Negroes. Bunche estimated that in eight Southern states, the so-called Deep South, never more than 80,000 to 90,000 Negro votes had been cast in general elections up to 1940, and only a handful in the primaries, the elections which really count.[43]

---

[38] *Ibid.*, p. 564.
[39] *Ibid.*, p. 564, by permission of the publishers, Harper & Brothers.
[40] Davie, *Negroes in American Society*, p. 354.
[41] *Ibid.*, p. 355.
[42] For dramatic accounts of violence in the Southern scene, see Walter White, *A Man Called White* (New York: The Viking Press, Inc., 1948).
[43] Ralph J. Bunche, "The Negro in the Political Life in the United States," *Journal of Negro Education*, July, 1941, 10: 567–584.

The proportion of the white electorate which participated in politics was also decidedly less than in the rest of the nation. In 1940 only 28 per cent of the adult population of twelve Southern states went to the polls, in contrast with 53 per cent for the rest of the country. (2) The South for all practical purposes has had a one-party system, the Democratic party. The primary contests in this party constituted in essence the final decision. (3) From this it followed that political opposition was more confined than elsewhere to rivalries between factions and personalities in which the basic issues contested in the nation as a whole were not debated. Since the Democratic Party in the South has represented traditional and conservative influence in the national Congress, the same kind of liberal political pressures which had arisen elsewhere in the nation, representing broadly liberal and human welfare interests as opposed to conservative and propertied interests, had not manifested themselves in any marked degree in the South. Since wide exercise of the franchise, a two (or more) party system, and the vigorous debate of new ways to further the democratic ideal are signs of a healthy democracy, the democratic political process in the South may properly be regarded as having been retarded.

To what extent are these distinctive developments in Southern politics attributable to the effect of its system of race relations? Since we adhere to the general principle that the causal factors in such complex social phenomena are always multiple and interact with one another, we shall not suggest that the system of race relations is all-determinative. Nevertheless, the interrelationship between the phenomena of race relations and these political developments is highly impressive. The elaborate devices to limit the electorate arose primarily as a way of preventing Negroes from exercising active citizenship. The one-party system, with its "white" primary, developed for the same reason. Once established, these political phenomena furthered the politicoeconomic interests of the middle and upper classes of the white South in opposition to those of the lower-class whites. The failure of the latter group to generate more effective political expression of its interests is in considerable measure related to its preoccupation with "keeping the Negro in his place."

Effect on the Economy of the South

Rupert Vance, an outstanding student of the Southern region, described the South's position (1930) in the national economy in these terms: "The statistical indices of wealth, education, cultural achievement, health, law and order reduced to a per capita basis combine in every instance to give the Southern states the lowest rankings in the Union."[44] After a careful ap-

[44] Rupert B. Vance, *Human Geography of the South* (Chapel Hill: University of North Carolina Press, 1932), p. 442. By permission.

praisal of the natural resources of the region, Vance concluded that it was not lack of adequate natural resources which accounted for the South's relative poverty. He found the chief explanation in the manner in which the Southern economy had been organized.

After the Civil War, Southern economic reconstruction called for carrying on the plantation agricultural economy, with chief emphasis on cotton production and such modifications as the emancipation of the slaves required. Since this economy required cheap labor, the caste system developed in part as a means of guaranteeing the continued employment of Negroes in their accustomed role at subsistence wages. Furthermore, in order to hold its place competitively in a national economy generally more efficient than its own, the South was forced to exploit the soil to the point of diminishing returns. In this way, a cycle of reciprocal forces was established which operated to retard the economic development of the region. The relatively inefficient economy could provide only subsistence wages for the laborers involved. Their marginal income in turn retarded the regional demand for goods which would have favored the development of industrial enterprise. Furthermore, the marginal economy was unable to produce enough to furnish the capital needed for industrial development. This capital had to be furnished, therefore, from outside the region, which meant that part of the gains were drained from the region itself. In order to get this capital, the South offered the inducement primarily of cheap labor costs, which still further aggravated the low standard of living, extending it to a wider segment of its white population. While the expanding industrial economy offered some opportunity to transfer Negroes from farm work to city work, the caste system prevented their employment in other than the lowest-paying capacities.

Clearly, many factors are involved in interpreting the cycle just described. Nevertheless, the influence of the caste system is apparent at every turn. As Vance has written: "The South holds the Negro back; the Negro holds the South back; and both point in recrimination."[45]

VARIATION IN THE SOUTHERN PATTERN

The foregoing description has disregarded variations in order to indicate the general Southern pattern. Some significant rural-urban contrasts, however, should be noted. The city environment permitted some relief to Negroes from the omnipresent impact of caste through the opportunity it afforded to build a separate community structure. At least within this area, Negroes could live their own lives.[46] Compared with the smaller places,

[45] *Ibid.*, p. 43.
[46] One of the authors was told by a Negro physician in a Louisiana city that the members of his family went "down town" as seldom as possible because they so profoundly disliked the caste requirements.

there was less actual personal interaction between the members of the two races in the city. Since traditionally the caste system carried with it much direct personal dependence of individual Negroes on particular white people, through which conformity to the mandates of caste could be closely scrutinized, the greater drawing apart of the two races in the Southern cities placed the control of caste on a more impersonal basis.

The Border States

A major variation in the Southern pattern of race relations is seen by considering certain border states, including Oklahoma, Kentucky, West Virginia, Missouri, Maryland, and Delaware, and The District of Columbia. In none of these was the "white primary" to be found; among them, only Oklahoma had "Jim Crow" streetcars. In these states the code of etiquette was frequently less explicit and less binding. However, in all of them intermarriage between Negroes and whites was prohibited by law, and the segregation of Negroes in schools remained up to 1954.[47]

The pattern of race relations in Washington, D.C., is naturally of particular significance, not only because it is the capital but because it is visited by foreign officials of all other nations. On the one hand, Washington, as part of the Southern area, reflected in many ways the Southern attitude and behavior in Negro-white relations. On the other hand, the influence of the federal government imposed certain exceptions to the traditional Southern pattern. Thus Negroes were not "Jim Crowed" in District transportation; they had equal access to all institutions and services directly operated as federal government property—for example, federal cafeterias and playgrounds operated for government employees. Before World War II, the national government as an employer offered to a limited number of Negroes employment in higher-ranking occupations, qualified by the tendency to place them in special assignments dealing with Negro problems. But aside from these exceptions, Washington in the period before World War II presented substantially the same picture as other border cities. School segregation, for example, prevailed, and Negroes were denied the use of general restaurant and amusement facilities in the city.

CHANGES IN THE SOUTHERN PATTERN

Between 1880 and 1940 race relations in the South reveal changes which went rather rapidly in one direction and rather slowly in another. As we have seen, in the short period when Northerners directed the reconstruction program, Negroes achieved certain gains in status, especially in politics. When the white South regained control, its aim was to put the Negro back

---

[47] See Myrdal, *An American Dilemma*, p. 1072, Table 1, "Various definitions of the South," for a check list of the various features of the caste system for the Southern states.

into his inferior status through the establishment of the caste system. In the 1900–1910 decade this adjustment was virtually complete, and it remained broadly unchanged until World War II. The change in the opposite direction is revealed in the improvement in the welfare of Negroes as a group, even though at all times with wide discrepancies in comparison with the welfare of the whites as a group. One of the forces operating to effect this improvement was the opportunity presented by World War I for Negroes to find employment in the North, which helped somewhat to improve their bargaining position in the South. The tendency of the federal government to insist on more equitable use of federal funds for Negroes, especially during the 1930's, also improved Negro welfare. Furthermore, the beginnings of a breakdown in color discrimination in the unions began to show in the mid-1930's.

The earnest efforts of a small group of Southern white liberals in behalf of Negroes deserve recognition as an influence in keeping the Southern pattern unfrozen. The group comprised a few writers, journalists, educators, and some club women, whom Myrdal has described as "mostly a fraternity of individuals with independent minds, usually living in, and adjusting to, an uncongenial social surrounding."[48] Because for the most part they possessed high social prestige either through their lineage from Southern aristocracy or through the national pre-eminence they had acquired in professional fields, their espousal of the Negro's cause was tolerated. Their first efforts were directed at striving for equal justice, particularly against lynching, and gaining for the Negro a fairer share of public monies spent for education, health, and other aspects of welfare. They were unable to challenge the system of segregation itself. The Southern liberals were not able to influence political life to any marked extent, and their influence was largely confined to the higher social and educational levels of Southern society. The main organization through which Southern liberalism found expression was the Commission on Interracial Cooperation, founded in 1919. In Myrdal's judgment its most far-reaching effect is *"to have rendered interracial work socially respectable in the conservative South."*[49]

Finally, we consider the effect of Negro leadership and organization on the course of Southern race relations during the caste period. Under slavery the organized activities of Negroes in their own behalf consisted, as we have seen, largely of abortive slave revolts. The outstanding leader among Negroes in the nineteenth century was Frederick Douglass. Following emancipation, which he had urged upon Lincoln, he worked to secure full equality for the Negroes, but saw the fight lost during the Southern reconstruction. Organized movements among Negroes subsequently divided into "protest" or "accommodative" patterns. The former, which Douglass es-

[48] *Ibid.*, p. 467.
[49] *Ibid.*, p. 847. Italics in original.

poused, aimed to secure full equality for Negroes; the latter aimed to secure the betterment of conditions without challenging the institution of caste itself. During the twentieth century the protest type of acivity was almost exclusively confined to Negroes in the North, which we shall consider in Chapter 12. In the South the unquestioned spokesman for the Negro was Booker T. Washington, who is generally considered a leader of the accommodative type, though some of his biographers think the extent of his compromising has been overstressed, particularly in view of the circumstances which he faced. Rose summarizes the role which Washington played and the philosophy behind it:

It is wrong to characterize Washington as an all-out accommodating leader. He never relinquished the right to full equality in all respects as the ultimate goal. But for the time being he was prepared to give up social and political equality, even to soft-pedal and protest against inequalities in justice. He was also willing to flatter the Southern whites and be harsh toward the Negroes—if the Negroes were allowed to work undisturbed with their white friends for education and business. But neither in education nor in business did he assault inequalities. In both fields he accepted the white doctrine of the Negroes "place." In education he pleaded mainly for vocational training. Through thrift, skill, and industry the Negroes were gradually to improve so much that later the discussion could again be taken up concerning their rights. This was Washington's philosophy.[50]

However one views the relative merits of the protest as against the accommodative program of action, beyond question Washington had the greatest influence of any single Negro on the development of Negro welfare during his time. His influence was most concretely evidenced in the development of Tuskegee Institute, over which he presided for many years.

TOPICS FOR PROJECTS AND DISCUSSION

1. Interview two or more Northern-bred whites who have traveled in the South and two or more Southern-bred whites who have traveled in the North. Ask each to talk about his first experiences with the different etiquette in race relations and his reactions to it. Present the findings of your interviews.
2. Debate the topic—Biracial segregation in principle is consistent with equality of opportunity for both groups.
3. How would you account for the fact that some Negro women in the South accede voluntarily to the sexual overtures of some white men?
4. Discuss the topic—The effects of the Southern caste system on the personalities of Southern white people.
5. How do you account for the apparently greater overt antagonism manifested by lower-class Southern whites as compared with that shown by middle- and upper-class whites?

[50] Arnold Rose, *The Negro in America* (New York: Harper & Brothers, 1948), p. 240. By permission.

SUGGESTED READING

Cayton, Horace R. "The Psychology of the Negro Under Discrimination," in *Race Prejudice and Discrimination*, Arnold M. Rose, ed. New York: Alfred A. Knopf, Inc., 1951, pp. 276–290.
    A brief but incisive analysis of the effects of discrimination upon Negro personality

Davis, Allison, and Dollard, John. *Children of Bondage*. Washington, D.C.: American Council on Education, 1940.
    An intensive study of eight Negro adolescents in the Deep South indicating the effects of the Southern pattern on the Negro personality.

Davis, Allison, Gardner, Burleigh B., and Gardner, Mary R. *Deep South: A Social Anthropological Study of Caste and Class*. Chicago: University of Chicago Press, 1941.
    A community study of race relations around Natchez, Mississippi, distinguishing class relations from the interracial caste relations.

Johnson, Charles S. *Growing Up in the Black Belt*. Washington, D.C.: American Council on Education, 1941.
    Study of the impact of Southern system on the personality development of Southern rural Negro youth through intensive case studies.

Johnson, Guy B. "Patterns of Race Conflict," in *Race Relations and the Race Problem*, ed., Edgar Thompson. Durham: Duke University Press, 1939.
    Traces the history of race conflict, showing that the patterns had not changed much in spite of changing conditions.

Lewis, Hylan. *Blackways of Kent*. Chapel Hill: University of North Carolina Press, 1955.
    A comprehensive and intimate account of the life of Negroes in a typical biracial community of the Piedmont area.

Raper, Arthur F. *The Tragedy of Lynching*. Chapel Hill: University of North Carolina Press, 1933.
    A detailed analysis of the lynchings occurring in 1930. The study was sponsored by the Southern Commission on the Study of Lynching.

Rohrer, John H., and Edmonson, Munro S. *The Eighth Generation: Cultures and Personalities of New Orleans Negroes*. New York: Harper & Brothers, 1960.
    An intensive follow-up study of the subjects of Davis and Dollard's study of the children of bondage who as adults comprise the eighth generation of New Orleans Negroes.

Vance, Rupert P. "Racial Competition for the Land," in *Race Relations and the Race Problem*, ed., Edgar Thompson. Durham: Duke University Press, 1939.
    Shows how racial competition for land in the rural cotton South contributed to depressed conditions for both races and stimulated migration to the cities.

12

Negro-White Relations:
The Traditional Northern Pattern

While the status of Negroes outside the South up to 1940 was in some ways similar to that within that region, the differences in the North were sufficiently striking to make a separate discussion essential. In the North, Negroes were discriminated against substantially everywhere, but not in as many aspects of life nor so intensely as in the South. The welfare of the Negro in the North was the lowest of all large minorities, but the relatively higher general standard of living in the North was reflected in the higher standards of Northern Negroes as compared with those of Southern Negroes.

A basic difference between the Northern and Southern situation has been the absence in the North of any such precise institutionalization of the minority position of Negroes as the Southern caste pattern involved. In the South, caste relations were well defined in law and in the regional mores; and control mechanisms for maintaining the caste pattern had become standardized through years of practice. In the North the discrimination and segregation which did exist lacked explicit sanction in the mores; and there were also lacking established control devices for holding the Negro in minority status. For Southern white people in general the attitudes and values of the caste system were an integral part of their personalities; and for Southern Negroes brought up under this system the reciprocal attitudes and behavior patterns were deeply structured in their personalities. Caste was an intrinsic part of the Southern social structure and daily touched the lives of the people of both races. In the North the segregated position of Negroes was only a fragmentary aspect of Northern community life, and many white people, even in communities with sizeable Negro populations, were scarcely aware of its presence.

Many contrasting circumstances in the two regional situations account for this basic difference, some of which can be stated only briefly in this over-view. The North did not have the tradition of slavery, having abolished slavery decades before Emancipation. And in no Northern community did the number of Negroes approach a majority. Thus, while Negroes were highly useful to the economy of the North, their labor was never considered essential to Northern economic life, especially as long as European immigration furnished cheap labor. The concentration of Negroes in the larger cities of the North, where their residential segregation resembled that of other ethnic and racial minorities, made their position appear less sharply in contrast to the dominant white community than in the South, where Negroes were the only considerable minority.

THE PATTERN OF DISCRIMINATION

A close-up view of the general pattern of Negro-white relations in the North may be obtained from the comprehensive study of Chicago made by Drake and Cayton. While examining only one city, in essence their book, *Black Metropolis*, typifies the Northern situation. Much of the material was gathered for this volume in the 1930's, though some of it refers to the impact of World War II.[1] Since 1940 there have been enough changes in the situation in Chicago, as well as elsewhere in the North, to prompt the use of the past tense in this chapter. Much of the description which follows, however, is still applicable in the 1960's.

Residential Segregation

Negroes in Chicago were highly concentrated in residence; 337,000—90 per cent of all—lived in the Black Belt.[2] The difference between this and other ethnic colonies found in cities was that while the others tended to break up in time, the Negro area became increasingly concentrated. The particular area was on the lower South Side, long considered by Chicago planning boards a "blighted area," the most dilapidated section of the city. The extent of congestion is indicated by the fact that Negroes were living

[1] St. Clair Drake and Horace R. Cayton, *Black Metropolis* (New York: Harcourt, Brace & Co., 1945).
[2] *Ibid.*, p. 174.

90,000 to the square mile, as compared with 20,000 in neighboring white apartment house areas.[3] This high degree of spatial segregation "is primarily the result of white people's attitudes toward having Negroes as neighbors. Because some white Chicagoans do not wish colored neighbors, formal and informal controls are used to isolate the latter within congested all-Negro neighborhoods."[4]

The real force of the measures to contain the Negro area began when the mass invasions took place. "It was only after 1915, when 65,000 migrants came into the city within five years, that resistance became organized."[5] Property-owners associations began to take active steps to forestall sale and rent of property to Negroes outside the Black Belt. "A wave of violence flared up, and between July 1917 and March 1921 fifty-eight homes were bombed. . . . The victims of the bombings were Negro families that had moved into white neighborhoods, as well as Negro and white real-estate men who sold or rented property to them."[6] The major device for controlling the Negro community was the restrictive covenant—an agreement between property owners within a certain district not to rent or sell to Negroes.

Since the consequences of housing discrimination remain the key to analysis of the Northern interracial situation, we reserve fuller discussion for Chapter 14. It is pertinent here, however, to point out that attempts to upset restrictive convenants legally were for a long time unsuccessful.[7] In 1917 the Supreme Court (245 U.S. 60) ruled that a municipal zoning ordinance which segregated Negroes and whites was unconstitutional, but it was not until 1948 that the highest tribunal declared that restrictive covenants in private housing transactions could not be upheld by law (334 U.S. 1–1948).

Occupational Discrimination

Discrimination in jobs can be seen in the tendency to deny Negroes jobs when white people were out of work. Drake and Cayton state that in 1940, *"while Negroes made up only 8 per cent of the available workers, they constituted 22 per cent of the unemployed. All along the line, Negroes had been displaced in a ratio of roughly three to one. Almost half of the Negro domestic servants, a third of the semiskilled workers, and a fourth of the unskilled were unemployed in 1935."*[8] There were numerous pursuits from which Negroes were substantially barred. "The job ceiling for Negroes . . . [tended] to be drawn just above the level of semiskilled jobs, with the skilled, clerical, managerial, and supervisory positions reserved for white

---

[3] *Ibid.*, p. 204.
[4] *Ibid.*, p. 174
[5] *Ibid.*, p. 177.
[6] *Ibid.*, p. 178.
[7] See Robert C. Weaver, *The Negro Ghetto* (New York: Harcourt, Brace & Co., 1948), Ch. 13, "The Villain-Racial Covenants."
[8] *Ibid.*, p. 217. By permission. Italics in original.

workers."[9] Another index of job discrimination is seen in the fact that the Negroes had not consistently held their competitive position in certain occupational fields. For example, during the depression Negroes lost out to whites in restaurant and hotel jobs. In the occupational areas where Negroes and whites competed for jobs, it should be remembered that before World War II, whites in general were able to refuse to work with Negroes in the same level job. Thus if a restaurant wanted to employ white waitresses, there could not be any Negroes in a similar capacity.

As compensation for these inequities, Negroes had a substantial monopoly in the two occupations of Pullman porter and redcap. In both these occupations "the earnings and the prospects of advancement are dependent upon cheerful and, if necessary, ingratiating service. . . . Even very well-educated Negroes did not scorn such jobs."[10]

The low economic position of Negroes is in part explainable by their relative lack of skills and training for the higher ranking jobs, and by the tendency of Southern Negroes to flock to the North in numbers in excess of the job opportunities available to them, in search of the real but exaggerated "freedom" of the North. But in considerable measure it was due to racial discrimination: to the tendency of white workers to refuse to work alongside Negroes and of employers to assume that this was always so; to the tendency of white customers to resent being waited on by Negroes, except in the most servile services, and of employers to assume the universality of this reaction by white clients; and to the tendency to consider the Negro as somehow different, "not quite one of us," and therefore inferior.

Social Discrimination

In contrast to the South, Negroes in Chicago were not segregated in their utilization of many public facilities. Public parks, public transportation facilities, stores, and public toilets were open to them. However, the more intimate the situation, the more doubtful the acceptance of Negroes on equal terms. In theaters, restaurants, and particularly swimming places, Negroes were discouraged by every possible means from associating with whites. In the Midwest metropolis, bathing beaches and swimming pools were among the primary tension points. The Negro press reported:

POLICE OBJECT TO MIXING OF RACES ON BEACH; ARREST 18. SAY THEY ARE TRYING TO PREVENT RACE RIOT.[11]

While the color line was seldom drawn in theaters or at large public gatherings, in recreational situations that emphasized active participation as

[9] *Ibid.*, p. 262.
[10] *Ibid.*, p. 237.
[11] *Ibid.*, p. 105.

distinct from merely looking on, Negroes were barred; and in all situations where men and women participated together, there was a rigid line. Whatever may have been their ultimate hope, Negroes themselves put less stress on the desirability of achieving equality in this more intimate sphere than in others. This difference in the relative importance attached to social equality by the two races was favorable to facilitating adjustment in Negro-white relations in the North. In such borderline situations as "social affairs" held by civic or occupational clubs with biracial membership, Negro members present resented either being ignored or being dealt with as "a special problem."[12]

Civic "Equality"

In marked contrast to the South was the civic "equality" accorded Northern Negroes. However, the term "equality" is here placed in quotes because what Negroes had in Chicago and elsewhere in the North was limited by the framework of dominant-group attitudes toward minority groups. It is hard to prove that a teacher "looks down" on Negroes, or that a juror will not believe Negro testimony when it contradicts that of a white person. But one cannot study the events without being convinced that equality was qualified by prejudice.

Drake and Cayton wrote that "To Negro migrants, fresh from the South, Midwest Metropolis presents a novel experience—a substantial measure of equality before the law. Here, they can expect a reasonably fair trial in the courts, with a choice of colored or white counsel. There are no lynchings."[13] In Chicago, as elsewhere in the North, Negroes had full political rights. Even though they were thought of as a minority group, their right to vote and participate in political organization was not denied. In *Black Metropolis*, what this opportunity to be a citizen meant to Negroes is described as follows:

Politics became an important, perhaps the most important, method by which the Negro sought to change his status. It was often the only avenue open for struggle against caste tendencies. This struggle invested his political behavior, even when corrupt, with an importance and a dignity that similar behavior could not command in any other portion of the population. To paraphrase Lincoln Steffens, the Negro favored *representative* government, even if it was not always *clean* government.[14]

As a result of their political activities, Negroes made substantial gains in Chicago.

Within a decade after the Great Migration, Black Metropolis had elected two Negro aldermen, one State Senator, four State Representatives, a city judge, and

---

[12] *Ibid.*, p. 123.
[13] *Ibid.*, pp. 108–109.
[14] *Ibid.*, p. 343. By permission.

a Congressman. . . . Wielding such political power, Negro politicians have been in a position to demand appointive positions for a few hundred individuals and equitable treatment in the courts for the masses (as well as dubious "benefits" from the great Chicago enterprise of "fixing" and "rigging" everything from traffic tickets to gambling dens). They have also been able to expose and check discrimination in the administration of the civil service laws and in the enforcement of the Civil Rights Law. They have created, among influential white politicians of all parties, an awareness of the Negro's desire for equal opportunity.[15]

The minority status of Negroes was reflected, however, in politics as in all other phases of their lives. Of this Drake and Cayton write:

The color line in politics is also reflected in the types of political plums that go to Negro politicians and their henchmen. The big contracts and the heavy graft are reserved for whites. Negroes get the petty "cuts" from gambling and vice protection. In fact, a tradition has developed that Negroes will not demand big political rewards. . . . Political leaders in Midwest Metropolis, balancing the pressures of ethnic, economic, and religious blocs, are forced to grant some of the demands of Negroes, and Negro politicians shrewdly demand all that they think the traffic will bear.[16]

Education

Curiously, in view of their exhaustive coverage of Negro life in Chicago, Drake and Cayton wrote very little about education. For the North in general during this period, Myrdal, however, noted the following:

There is little school segregation required by law in the Northern and Western states: Arizona requires it in elementary schools and makes it permissive in secondary schools; Kansas, Wyoming, Indiana, and New Mexico make school segregation permissive in the elementary grades and sometimes also in the secondary grades. Some communities in the southern parts of New Jersey, Indiana, Pennsylvania, Ohio and Illinois use organized pressure contrary to law to segregate Negroes in at least the elementary grades. In practically all other areas of the North there is partial segregation on a voluntary basis, caused by residential segregation aided by the gerrymandering of school districts and the system of "permits." This segregation is fairly complete for elementary schools, except where Negroes form only a small proportion of the population, but there is much less segregation in secondary schools. In few cases—if any—is this segregation accompanied by discrimination, however, except that form of discrimination which inevitably arises out of isolation. In fact there is probably more discrimination in the mixed schools than in the segregated ones in the North: frequently Negroes in mixed schools are kept out of swimming, dancing, and other athletics, and out of social clubs. There are, however, some Negro teachers in mixed schools in many Northern cities, and Negroes sit on the boards of education in a few big Northern cities.[17]

The opportunity for Negroes to acquire higher education in the North

[15] *Ibid.*, pp. 109–110. By permission.
[16] *Ibid.*, p. 111. By permission.
[17] Myrdal, *An American Dilemma* (New York: Harper & Brothers, 1944), p. 633. By permission of the publishers.

was less than for secondary schools. Northern state universities did not prohibit Negro enrollments, but the vast majority of the private institutions either categorically did not accept Negroes, or accepted only a "token" Negro or two. Myrdal concludes that there was no serious restriction on higher education of Negroes in the North, supporting his view by pointing out that only four Negro colleges, all of these established before the Civil War, were located in the North. However, it is pertinent to note that before 1940 a large number of Northern Negroes had gone South to attend Negro colleges—3,000, for example, in 1938–1939.[18] They may have done this because these colleges were less expensive or because they received scholarships. However, it is also possible that they had the feeling that they would face a number of unpleasant discriminations in Northern colleges. Caliver writes that Negro students "seldom lived on campus and in general, they seemed not to belong in the same way that white students felt themselves a part of the university."[19] Discrimination in higher education was likewise seen in the fact that before World War II not more than five white colleges had a Negro on their faculty.

METHODS OF ENFORCING THE NORTHERN PATTERN

Generally speaking, segregation outside the South was not supported by law. A few non-Southern states banned intermarriage; and certain local communities officially segregated Negroes in schools, but such laws were usually overridden by court decisions. In some communities the police attempted to keep Negroes out of certain public areas, such as beaches, but these actions were nowhere legally supported. Subterfuges, like making the commercial recreational place a "club," were sometimes successful. In a left-handed way law-enforcing agencies frequently supported segregation by refusing to arrest whites who molested Negroes.

Segregation was upheld by common practice—practices by whites to keep Negroes within the bounds of minority status and the reciprocal practices of Negroes to accept this status. While Negroes bitterly resented this, to have some peace of mind, they put up with discrimination most of the time. The fact, however, that these practices were of doubtful legality meant that Negroes could challenge civic discrimination on occasion, and by this means kept the pattern of relationship unfrozen. Sporadic gains here and there were made. Generally, when Negroes pressed cases of discrimination involving civil rights they won them. But, of course, since legal vindication is a costly process, such cases were not numerous.

---

[18] Ambrose Caliver, *United States Office of Education, National Survey of Higher Education of Negroes,* Vol. IV (Washington, D.C.: Government Printing Office, 1942–43), p. 13.
[19] *Ibid.*

As in the South, the Northern pattern was supported by the prevalence of the "racial ideology" which looks upon Negroes in the mass as inferior. There was, however, a wider variation in racial attitudes and beliefs in the North. What in comparison appears clearest is that Northern attitudes were not crystallized into any uniform public opinion. As Drake and Cayton wrote: "In the South, every white man feels impelled to protect every white family, clique, and church from 'Negro contamination.' In Midwest Metropolis, each person is concerned only with his own."[20]

VARIATIONS IN THE NORTHERN PATTERN

In minor aspects the picture of Chicago's Negro community and its relation to the larger community is affected by its particular locale; but less extensive studies of other large cities indicate that *Black Metropolis* was a typical picture of Negro-white relations in the metropolitan areas of the North, where the far larger proportion of the Northern Negro population lived.[21] Variations in the Northern pattern were in the main related to three situational factors: (1) the recency of the migration of substantial numbers of Negroes into any particular community; (2) the smaller-city situation as against the large-city situation; and (3) the relative exposure of the community to Southern influence.

Recency of Migration

The status of Negroes in Northern cities varies with the extent to which a given city shared in the Great Migration. Generally the status of Negroes in the North as a whole declined in the years attending this migration. Furthermore, the occurrence of the depression of the 1930's, during which so large a proportion of Negroes were on relief, retarded improvement. Even in New England, which did not greatly share in the Great Migration, the traditional tolerance toward Negroes declined. Frazier writes, "The increase in the Negro population [of Boston] during and following World War I accentuated race consciousness among Negroes as well as whites."[22] Frazier further cites a study of Milton, Pennsylvania.

The [Negro] population of this town had continued inconsequential until Negro laborers were brought in during World War I. Before that time the few Negroes had found employment in personal and domestic service among the well-to-do white families. Negroes had been accepted to the extent that white and colored children went to school together and they mingled socially to some extent. The importation of Negro laborers from the South created race consciousness among

[20] *Black Metropolis,* p. 119.
[21] See for example, Robert A. Warner, *New Haven Negroes* (New Haven: Yale University Press, 1940).
[22] E. Franklin Frazier, *The Negro in the United States* (New York: The Macmillan Co., 1949), p. 254.

both Negroes and whites. Since the Negro laborers have left, race relations have tended to assume their former character.[23]

Interesting confirmation of the principle that animosity to a minority rises with the sudden influx of a new group into a particular area comes from a study of the situation in the Northwestern communities to which Negroes migrated during World War II.[24] Before 1940, Negroes comprised less than 0.5 per cent of the population covered in this study; by 1945 the Negro population had increased 300 per cent. The very small and inconspicuous group of Negroes living in the area before this recent migration "had learned gradually to adjust themselves to white patterns, and whites had in turn more or less come to accept this small Negro minority as a natural part of the population." However, "with the appearance of new faces, unfamiliar with the community's mores, tensions began to be apparent."[25] Contributing to the tension was the fact that the white "newcomers" to these localities came from areas with more discriminatory patterns, and they translated their usual attitudes into behavior in the new situation. Furthermore, the change in white attitudes was resented by the old-time Negro families, whose status deteriorated in the face of the general rise of antagonism toward Negroes, producing friction within the local Negro group. Insofar as social policy can be brought to bear on future adjustment of Negro-white relations, these Northern and Western experiences point toward discouraging a large influx of Negroes over a short period of time into any one community.

The Smaller City versus The Metropolis

Since the major portion of the Northern migration went to the large cities, little attention has been given to Negroes in the smaller cities. In Muncie, Indiana, the Lynds found in 1929 that "the sense of racial separateness appears in widely diverse groups." Negroes were not permitted in the Y.M.C.A., for example. "News of the Negroes is given separately in the papers under the title 'In Colored Circles.'"[26] In 1935, in their post-depression study of the same city, the authors found Negroes had better leadership and organization but that they "occupy a more exposed position . . . than before the depression."[27] In the Yankee City study, the position of Negroes is summarized thus: "Negroes have been present in Yankee City from the days of the New England slave trade . . . [By 1933] the Negro group had dwindled to eighty individuals, only 0.48 per cent of the population. The caste barrier,

[23] *Ibid.*, p. 253. By permission of The Macmillan Co.
[24] T. H. Kennedy, "Racial Tensions Among Negroes in the Intermountain Northwest," *Phylon*, 1946, 7: 358–364.
[25] *Ibid.*, p. 360.
[26] Robert S. and Helen M. Lynd, *Middletown* (New York: Harcourt, Brace & Co., 1929), p. 479, footnote 1.
[27] Robert S. and Helen M. Lynd, *Middletown in Transition* (New York: Harcourt, Brace & Co., 1937), p. 465.

or color line, rigid and unrelenting, has cut off this small group from the general life of the community."[28] In smaller communities, Negroes were further handicapped because their numbers were inadequate to furnish for themselves a complete, separate community life.

Influence of the Southern Pattern on the North

From what we have considered in this chapter so far, it should be clear that white Americans living in the North were not prepared to accept Negroes with full equality. In concluding the discussion of variables in the Northern scene, it is pertinent to note two influences of the Southern pattern on the North and West. First we call attention to the migration of white Southern workers to the North which, when it was recent and in substantial numbers, tended to disturb the pattern of toleration of Negroes in many Northern communities. This was notable as a factor in the tense Detroit situation of World War II. Second, in those Northern states bordering on a state with a Southern pattern, variation in race relations from south to north was noticeable. In New Jersey, for instance, before state government policies inaugurated in the 1940's, school segregation was more pronounced in the southern than in the northern portion of the state. The part of Illinois which dips down into the South shows more Southern caste influence than the northern section of that state.

IMPACT OF THE NORTHERN PATTERN
ON NORTHERN COMMUNITIES

The kind of pattern of Negro-white relations which we have described in this chapter affected the life of those Northern communities with any substantial Negro population in many ways. We shall consider the following effects: (1) Negro minority status created and more or less perpetuated a "black ghetto," which as a physically deteriorated area yielded the high rates of crime, delinquency, ill health, and other social pathologies characteristic of slums everywhere. (2) The discriminations imposed on Negroes directly engendered frustrations in their personality structure, further provoking antisocial behavior. (3) The dominant-minority character of race relations created a continuous intergroup tension in community life which sporadically broke out into violent intergroup conflict. (4) The more dynamic, less rigid character of race relations in the North, on the one hand, led to confusion, handicapping adjustment, but on the other hand afforded greater opportunity than in the South for Negroes themselves to advance their race.

[28] W. Lloyd Warner and P. S. Lunt, *The Social Life of a Modern Community* (New Haven: Yale University Press, 1941), p. 217.

The Black Ghetto: a Blighted Area

The assignment of Negroes to minority status in Northern cities resulted in separate subcommunal structures within the larger communities. While in many cities there were a few scattered Negroes living among whites, most Northern Negroes lived together either in one large area or in several scattered but compact Negro areas. And, though the area was small, there was a distinctive community composed of separate churches, clubs, recreational organizations, and civic groups. Off the job, Negroes associated almost exclusively with each other, whether in informal or formal relations. The development of separate Negro communities fitted easily into the ecological pattern of Northern city life, where various ethnic colonies were no new phenomenon. But as time went on, while the ethnic colonies tended to disappear through assimilation of subsequent generations, the Negro separate colony, as we have noted, persisted and grew, posing a problem of serious dimensions. Resistance to admitting Negroes into new areas resulted in fantastic overcrowding. Weaver writes that in 1939 in Detroit rates for overcrowding were twice as high as for the white population.[29] When finally the walls of the black ghetto burst, infiltration of Negroes into other dilapidated areas began. However, when some Negroes did get a foothold, whites began to move out and more Negroes moved in, until the new block, or section, came to be generally Negro. This process was attended by considerable animosity between both racial groups, sometimes climaxed by race rioting. Through it all Negroes had substandard housing, for which they paid abnormally high rents.

It has been demonstrated that all slum areas, regardless of who lives in them, although highly profitable to particular special interests, are an economic drain on the community at large, and unvaryingly yield a disproportionate share of the social pathologies—delinquency, crime, high disease rates. That the presence of a Negro ghetto in a Northern community is no exception has been amply demonstrated by many studies of such areas.

Pertinent illustrations are these:

[I]n Chicago the percentage of Negro boys among juvenile delinquents increased from 4.7 in 1900 to 21.7 in 1930. . . . During this same period, the proportion of Negro juvenile delinquents in Indianapolis, Gary, and Dayton was three to four times as large as their relative numbers in the population.[30]

[I]t is practically certain that Negroes have more mental disease in the North than do whites.[31]

[29] Weaver, *The Negro Ghetto,* p. 115.
[30] Frazier, *The Negro in the United States,* 1949, p. 649. By permission of The Macmillan Co.
[31] Myrdal, *An American Dilemma,* p. 980.

Tuberculosis rates in five Northern cities for 1939—41 run from three to five times as high for all Negroes as for all whites.[32]

Northern Discrimination and Negro Personality

In Chapter 11 we discussed the effects of the Southern interracial pattern on Negro personality. It is here recalled that Karon found the same effects on Northern Negroes reared in the South, though in lesser degree. Illustrations of these effects are seen in the following cases.

A young Negress in one of the Northern industrial centers who is engaged in housework is encouraged by her white teacher to take the civil service examination. She passes at the top of the list and is assigned to a public swimming pool. Negro patronage of this swimming pool has been prohibited; nor does the director wish to employ Negroes. His objections are overruled by the civil service authorities. He employs the Negro girl in a lower capacity than she merits—in cleaning work. The girl works without complaint. After a few weeks she thinks of swimming in the pool herself. Immediately a group of white boys approach her, treat her none too gently, make her stop swimming. The shock is so great that she not only quits her job but refuses to try for any other job to which she is eligible in the civil service. The white teacher from whom I got these facts told me that she came upon the Negress some time later as an elevator girl in a department store. The teacher tried to encourage her to apply once more for a civil service position, but the girl seemed to have lost all faith and all interest in anything better than a subservient place.

Such a degree of breakdown made me suspect that as a child this Negress had had particularly friendly relations with white children on an equal footing. An inquiry showed that she had indeed grown up in a group of children without discrimination between whites and Negroes.[33]

While in the above case discrimination led to withdrawal and passive reaction, in the following case of Arthur Brown, the ultimate result was aggression.

"Hey, you lazy 4-F," growled the cop, "why don't you get yourself a job and stop hanging out on street corners?" His nightstick swung menacingly.

Arthur Brown choked back the anger and resentment that rose in his throat. His fist itched to take the measure of that cop, but he knew too well that in Harlem that just didn't go. Hit a cop and the whole force gangs up on you.

"Mind your business," he said sharply. "I can take care of myself."

Actually Arthur had tried during the day to get employment as an International Business Machines operator or supervisor, work for which he was well qualified. While there were such positions open in the community at the time, Arthur was turned down for reasons indicated. In his first personal

[32] Dorothy J. Liveright, *Tuberculosis Mortality Among Residents of 92 Cities of 100,000 or More Population: United States, 1939–41*, United States Public Health Reports, July 21, 1944, pp. 942–955.

[33] Kurt Lewin, *Resolving Social Conflicts* (New York: Harper & Brothers, 1948), pp. 172–173. By permission.

interview, he faced a woman employment officer in a Business Survey Systems Office. In turning down Arthur for the job, the white woman said:

"But you realize we've never had a colored supervisor. Now so far as I'm concerned, personally, I'd take you on in a minute. I haven't any prejudice at all. I have a great many Negro friends. But these girls we have here—they're young, impressionable—and some of them are very prejudiced. I just couldn't put you over any of them. They'd walk out on me—right smack out of the place."

Arthur tried his second reference, this time in the office of a shipyard building naval vessels. His conversation with the assistant general manager ran as follows:

"So they sent you down to get that I.B.M. job, huh?" he asked. "Well, son, I can't give you that."

"Nope. But I'm afraid you wouldn't fit into our office. We have five men on those machines. As it happens, they're all white."

"I'll get along with them."

"Well—" The general manager chewed speculatively on a big cigar. "Maybe you would and maybe you wouldn't. My experience says you wouldn't."

"How about letting me try?"

"Nope, couldn't do it. And I'll tell you why. About five or six years ago I took a colored fellow outa' the yard and put him on an office machine. He was no good—just couldn't do the work. The other fellers said he balled up the whole department, and I had to take him out. I learned a lesson from that—colored boys are all right for the heavy yard jobs, but they don't work out in an office."

"But he wasn't competent," Arthur Brown argued "I've had experience. Besides, you can't judge a whole race just by one guy—"

"Son—" The general manager's tone was patronizing. "When you've been in business as long as I have you learn what works and what don't work. We're too busy now with war orders to try out experiments. I'll give you a job, this minute, as a shipfitter's helper. It's a good trade for you to learn. But I'm not going to buck human nature and put you on an office job, and that's that."

Later the same evening, while walking up Lenox Avenue, Arthur spied a couple approaching in his direction.

Suddenly he ducked into the sheltering darkness of an unlighted storefront. A tall, good-looking brownskin girl brushed by without a second look at him. A merchant seaman held her arm, and they laughed together as at some great joke. Lucy!

Lucy was Arthur Brown's girl—or was she, any more? Since he'd lost his last job, since he'd no longer been able to take her out, buy her drinks, show her a good time—

Lucy was a fine girl. But after all, what more could he expect?

Arthur Brown walked along the avenue, shoulders hunched against the gathering twilight chill.

He paused before a theater, fingering the fifteen cents remaining in his pocket. He'd need the fifteen cents for breakfast in the morning.

He reached an intersection and stood there on the corner, watching traffic. He didn't see the cop until he tapped him on the shoulder.

"Hey," growled the cop, "didn't I tell you to stop hanging out around here? Why don't you get yourself a job—do some work to help the war effort?"

It was then he hit the cop. Why he did it he could never quite explain. He knew in Harlem that just didn't go. But somehow he didn't care.[34]

The above two cases suggest that minority status imposed on Northern Negroes had effects on the personality structure and behavior similar to those of the caste system in the South. The passive reaction of the young woman in Lewin's case, in contrast to the aggressive reaction of Arthur Brown, may reflect the variables in the psychological constitution of the two as individuals; but the intensity of the reactions noted can be considered as arising from discrimination.

Sporadic Violence

The presence of Negroes in minority status was a constant source of tension and a sporadic source of race rioting in Northern communities. While there had been race riots in the North before the Great Migration, such as one in Springfield, Illinois, in 1908, most of the serious riots occurred during and following the two great wars of this century. During World War I, aside from a notorious riot in Houston, Texas, involving servicemen of both races, the most important riot occurred in East St. Louis, Illinois, during which at least 39 Negroes and 8 whites were killed. In 1919, riots occurred in at least 26 American cities. After this flurry of disturbances, race riots were relatively few until the beginning of World War II.

In Detroit in 1942 one of the worst race riots in recent history occurred. Myrdal writes of it:

. . . [I]n trying to move into a government defense housing project built for them in Detroit, Negroes were set upon by white civilians and police. The project was built at the border between Negro and white neighborhoods but had been planned for Negroes. Encouraged by the vacillation of the federal government and the friendliness of the Detroit police (many of whom are Southern born) and stimulated by the backing of a United States congressman and such organizations as the Ku Klux Klan, white residents of the neighborhood and other parts of the city staged protest demonstrations against the Negro housing project, which led to the riot.[35]

It will be noted that the outbreaks just mentioned occurred under conditions of stress or crisis in the larger society. This suggests the value of special analysis of the responses of dominant and minority people under such stressful conditions, which we have assayed in Chapter 20.

A somewhat different pattern of race riot was illustrated by the Harlem Riot of 1935. This was an outbreak of sporadic violence in the

[34] Edward H. Lawson, "Arthur Brown Applies for a Job," *The Journal of Social Issues,* February, 1945, 1: 11–14. By permission.

[35] Myrdal, *An American Dilemma,* p. 568. By permission of the publishers, Harper & Brothers.

Negro area itself, an outgrowth of the inevitable high degree of social disorganization to be found in physically blighted, "burstingly" overcrowded, and socially depressed areas such as the black ghettos of the North. Ottley describes this riot in these words:

> The morning of March 20, 1935, the nation awoke to learn to its dismay that the home of happy feet, Harlem, had exploded into violence. Whipped to a frenzy by radical street speakers, upwards of ten thousand had tumbled from taverns and tenements, barber shops and basement dives, and surged through the streets grappling in hand-to-hand struggles with the police. They smashed store windows, hurled bricks and assaulted white merchants. Bands plundered and looted stores with amazing discrimination—choosing only those owned by whites. When the police finally restored order in the early morning, three Negroes had been killed, thirty-odd hospitalized for bullet wounds, and two hundred white and Negro persons treated for injuries. Two hundred shops were smashed and gutted, and two million dollars in property was destroyed. One hundred Negroes were in the lockup for inciting to violence, unlawful assembly, and looting.
>
> The police hunted the answer in poolrooms, basements, and gambling joints, places where the criminal elements gathered. But actually the outburst was a manifestation of deep social unrest and unhappiness.[36]

Ambiguity of the Northern Pattern and Negro Adjustment

It is a well-demonstrated sociological principle that the adjustment of adult migrants to a new social environment is characterized by a certain amount of disorganization. A large proportion of the Negroes living in the North, certainly before 1940, had been brought up in the South; and of the rest many were children born in the North to Southern-bred parents. In a number of instances, the Negro migration involved movement from a rural or small-town Southern setting to a Northern, urban milieu. These shifts in environment would themselves account for some of the problems arising from the adjustment of Negroes to Northern life. Adjustment was further complicated, however, by the fact that this migration likewise involved a shift from a clearly defined and firmly established pattern of caste relations to a less rigid and more ambiguous dominant-minority pattern.

The particular kind of conditioning which Negroes had had made the Northern scene peculiarly upsetting. The Southern Negro generally had adjusted himself, with whatever inner psychic costs, to a lifetime of minority status. In the North this pattern of adjustment was considerably upset. The Negro was in many ways freer to do things he could not do in the South, but was frequently at a loss to know just how much freer. He could go to this restaurant, but that one refused him service. He could play on the school team, but he could not go to the dances. And, while treating him like a minority person, the Northern practice at the same time held the Negro

[36] Roi Ottley, *Black Odyssey* (New York: Charles Scribner's Sons, 1948), p. 258. By permission.

more accountable to behave according to the general norms of the community. Petty thievery was almost expected of the Negro by the white Southerner, and was dealt with as one ordinarily deals with it in the case of children. But the Northerners put him in jail for it. "Illegitimacy" in the South (often occurring within stable monogamic unions) was laughed off by Southern whites as "natural for darkies," but in the North it frequently brought investigation by a white welfare worker.

Finally, while the South held out no prospect to the Negro of ever rising above the confines of caste (allowing only for some upward class mobility within caste), the Northern situation, ill defined and perplexing as it was, was sufficiently fluid to encourage Negro aspirations. But since Northern white attitudes were by no means ready for the full step, Negroes' hopes were frequently raised too high, only to be dashed. The relatively better education offered the Negro in the North encouraged him to prepare himself for occupations employment in which he would subsequently be denied. His desire for better housing, and often the means to pay for it, was raised only to be frustrated by restrictive covenants. He was at the same time encouraged to develop higher cultural interests and refused a seat in a theater. Thus the lack of clear definitions of expected Negro behavior and the uncertainties and fluidity characterizing their relations with whites placed considerable strain on Negro personality.

IMPACT OF NORTHERN "FREEDOM" ON NEGROES

In spite of the disorganizing effect of the none-too-well defined situation of the Negro and of the very considerable discrimination against him, compared with the South the North afforded far more real freedom and opportunity. Two advantages in the North were the opportunity for individual Negroes to reach higher levels of success, and far greater opportunity to work effectively to advance the race.

Rise of Individual Negroes

Although Negro society in the South had some class differentiation, in the North the class structure was more elaborated, reaching, as with the white class structure, its greatest complexity in the metropolis. The social class structure of "Black Metropolis" is described as follows:

The process of differentiation among Negroes in Bronzeville has given rise to a loose system of social classes which allows for mobility upward and downward. This class structure operates as a system of social controls by which the higher-status groups "protect" their way of life, but admit "strainers" and "strivers" who can make the grade. Individuals and organizations on the higher-status levels become models for imitation and also serve as an incentive toward social mobility. . . . At the top are the uppers, oriented predominantly around "Society" and Race Leadership, and with a small group of Gentlemen Racketeers who have gained some status as Race Leaders but who are not accepted socially. Below them is the middle class with four "centers of orientation"—church, social club, "racial advancement" (including *individual* advancement), and "policy." At the bottom is the lower class with a large "disorganized segment," but also with a "church-centered" group and a small group of "secular respectables" interested in "getting ahead." Underlying the whole structure is the "underworld" of the Black Ghetto.[37]

A few individual Negroes in the North had gained fame and fortune in areas competitive with white people: Joe Louis and, even earlier, Jack Johnson in prizefighting; Roland Hayes and Paul Robeson in concert singing; Paul Lawrence Dunbar, Countee Cullen, James Weldon Johnson in literature. It is to be noted also that the theme which the artists emphasized was often related to Negro life and problems.

For the larger part of the Negroes who achieved higher social and economic status, it was the very separation of the Negro community from the rest that provided much of their opportunity.[38] Negroes had been conspicuously underrepresented in business, even compared with some other racial minorities, such as the Chinese and Japanese. Rose writes, "In 1939, there were not quite 30,000 Negro retail stores, giving employment to a total of 43,000 persons. The total sales in 1939 were less than $\frac{2}{10}$ of 1 per cent of the national total.[39] Nevertheless, the pattern of segregation itself created a monopoly for Negroes in certain kinds of businesses—those involving intimate contact with the person of the Negro, such as hairdressers, restaurant and hotel service, and undertaking.

In professional service, however, where the relationship to the client is less personal and also not servile, aspiring Negroes, when they managed to hurdle the difficulty of acquiring professional training, were in competition with white professionals for the trade of the Negro population while being generally barred from competition for the white trade. In 1940 there were about 3,500 Negro physicians in the whole country, which means about forty-five times as many white doctors as Negro. Negro physicians were handicapped by the lack of hospitals for their patients, and frequently were not permitted to treat their patients in mixed hospitals. In 1940 there were 1,063 Negro lawyers in the United States. Although this was less than 1 per cent of all lawyers in the country, the North provided an opportunity here which was substantially closed in the South. Thus two-thirds of this small number of Negro lawyers were to be found outside the South, where less than one-fourth of the Negro population lived.

The ministry in Negro churches was, of course, an exclusively Negro occupation. Clergymen were the second largest group among Negro profes-

[37] Drake and Cayton, *Black Metropolis*, pp. 710–712. By permission.
[38] This is not to imply that many of these same people would not have achieved comparable status in competition with whites in a social structure in which racial distinctions did not prevail.
[39] Arnold Rose, *The Negro in America* (New York: Harper & Brothers, 1948), p. 108.

sionals. Teaching exceeded the ministry, largely because in the South only Negro teachers are allowed to teach Negro children. While the influence of ministers as leaders of the church-going Negro people was strong, in the North their leadership was shared and sometimes overshadowed by other educated Negroes.

Interestingly enough, one of the largest of all Negro businesses was insurance. Frazier writes, "For the year 1945, the 44 member companies of the National Negro Insurance Association reported nearly 4,000,000 policies in force, of which 3,860,890 were health and accident and nearly 80,000 unspecified."[40] The opportunity here arose from the reluctance of general insurance companies to underwrite Negro policies on the same actuarial basis employed for whites because of the known wide differentials in risks in health and mortality between the two races. That the reluctance to underwrite Negroes was by no means absolute, however, is indicated by Frazier's statement that "one large white insurance company has insurance in force on Negro lives amounting to more than twice the insurance in force in all the Negro insurance companies."[41]

Another occupation arose from semisegregation of Negroes in the North and the necessity of integrating them somehow into the civic life of the community, which provided an opportunity for some Negroes to become the liaison agents, or specialists, representing Negroes in community-wide civic activity. Much more in the North than in the South, although the tendency was increasing there, such liaison activity was assigned to Negroes. The very real participation of Negroes in Northern politics, as described previously for Chicago, afforded opportunity for leadership in party politics, with occasional appointment to public positions either as reward or through civil service.

Finally, it is inevitable that among a people so situated there should arise an "underworld," often abetted and patronized by whites, and affording opportunity for some Negroes to achieve financial, if not social class, reward.

Thus the Northern scene afforded Negroes qualified opportunity for getting ahead and accounted for the growing upper and middle class in the Northern Negro communities. The values and modes of life among the middle-class Negroes were similar to those in the white middle class. Drake and Cayton put it thus:

The whole atmosphere of middle-class life is one of tension, particularly at upper-middle-class level, or among people on the way up, but not yet secure in their position. The drive to get ahead, to "lay a little something by," to prepare for the education of children, and at the same time keep up "front" by wearing the right kind of clothes, having a "nice home," and belonging to the proper organizations—the pursuit of these goals brings into being definite social types

[40] Frazier, *The Negro in the United States*, p. 401.
[41] *Ibid.*

which Bronzeville calls "strivers," and "strainers." With limited incomes, the problem of striking a balance between the conspicuous consumption necessary to maintain status, and long-range goals like buying property and educating children, becomes a difficult one. During the depression years particularly, Bronzeville's middle-class families faced a continuous crisis.[42]

The very considerable extent to which the opportunity for the more educated and ambitious Negroes in the North to rise to higher status as individuals rested on the maintenance of segregation itself and presented something of a dilemma regarding their attitudes toward advancing the race. In developing this theme, Frazier has pointed out that segregation protects certain Negro professionals to some extent from competition with whites in corresponding occupations—a competition which is keener and which he feels many of the Negro professionals could not meet successfully.[43] It is clear that a rapid breakdown of the segregated pattern would create much insecurity for the Negro middle class, and it is reasonable to hypothesize that, unconsciously at least, this would temper the vigor of the participation of its members in desegregation movements.[44] On the other hand, esteem among Negroes, as well as other minorities, is bestowed on those who champion the advancement of the race.

Opportunity to Advance the Race: Negro Leadership and Organization

We have seen that throughout the long history of the Negroes in the New World there have always been some members of the group who have actively protested against their minority status. Under slavery, Negroes organized rebellions; under caste, Negro leadership took the accommodative road of trying to improve the welfare of the group and to obtain better treatment without challenging the basic principle of segregation. In the North in the twentieth century, Negro leadership and organization to advance the race has embraced a wider range of activities and programs.[45] Here we shall discuss those preceding the current efforts, which will be presented in Chapters 12 and 13.

Among the many Negro movements, brief attention may be pertinently directed to those with an escapist character directed by charismatic leadership. Of these, the "Back to Africa" movement led by Marcus Garvey comes first. Garvey, a West Indian full-blooded Negro, rejected the idea that

[42] Drake and Cayton, Black Metropolis, pp. 667–668. By permission.
[43] E. Franklin Frazier, "Human, All Too Human," Survey Graphic, January, 1947. See also E. Franklin Frazier, The Black Bourgeoisie (Glencoe, Ill.: The Free Press, 1957), for fuller treatment of the rise of the Negro middle class.
[44] Thus, many Negro teachers in the South currently view the prospect of school desegregation with anxiety. While, theoretically, integrated schools should involve integrated teaching staffs, Negro teachers cannot be sure of this, and those with higher administrative rank face the possibility of demotion.
[45] See Ira DeA. Reid, "Negro Movements and Messiahs," Phylon, 1949, 10: 362–368, for a brief treatment of the leading Negro movements of this century.

Negroes in the United States could ever become fully assimilated into the general white society. He developed an organization, The Universal Negro Improvement Association, whose broad aim was the establishment of an African republic to be led by Negroes. Garvey was imprisoned in 1925 on the charge of using the mails to defraud in connection with his financial manipulations, and the movement collapsed. During the brief period of its existence, the Garvey movement elicited great response from the Negro people. Myrdal contends that this movement was the first organized Negro activity of the protest variety which really gripped the imagination and enthusiasm of the Negro masses in this country.[46]

Likewise of an escapist variety, though in many other ways completely opposite to Garvey's movement, was the much-publicized movement by George Baker, generally known as Father Divine. Preaching a doctrine of love among all peoples, Father Divine established a cult in which those who joined one of his "heavens" turned over their possessions and lived under his protection and security. This remarkable leader was shrewd in managing the affairs of the movement and, on the whole, took care of the followers who placed their trust in him. While most of his followers were Negroes, some white people entered his "heaven."

There were a number of "glamour" personalities who functioned as leaders among Negroes, not so much through actual reform activities but because they achieved national popular fame and considerable fortune in their occupations. Such people as Duke Ellington, Jackie Robinson, and Marion Anderson were accorded extraordinary respect and still are. White people in comparable positions do not necessarily play a leadership role in community affairs. In the case of Negroes, however, a sort of "race" leadership is thrust upon them by the very novelty of their success as members of a minority group, whether they have the capacity or inclination to assume the role.

We turn now to consider those movements and organizations which have had a more enduring and a more far-reaching effect on improving the position of Negroes in American society.

The Development of Protest Activity

The first effort to organize a movement among Negroes in protest against their minority status was launched in 1905, when twenty-nine Negro intellectuals met at Niagara Falls and planned the formation of a national organization to challenge all forms of segregation and discrimination. Such a bold program was opposed by Booker T. Washington and thus in a way challenged his accommodative leadership. Although the organization itself ceased to be effective after 1910, it prepared the way for the formation of the National Association for the Advancement of Colored People (N.A.A.-

[46] *An American Dilemma*, pp. 746–749.

C.P.), presently to be considered, through which in part the spirit of the Niagara movement lived on.

Following the Great Migration and World War I, some younger Negro leaders in the 1920's, of whom A. Philip Randolph, president of the Brotherhood of Sleeping Car Porters, was to become the most influential, saw the Negro's greatest hope in alignment with the postwar Socialist movements. It is clear, however, from the relative failure of urban radical movements as far as election results were concerned that the majority of Negroes aligned themselves politically with the major parties. Generally it appears that this element merged with the New Deal element of the Democratic Party except for an occasional convert to Communism. As we shall see in our account of the trends since 1940, the protest line of activity continued to gain ascendancy over the accommodative approach.

The Negro Intelligentsia

The 1920's saw the emergence of a group of Negro intellectuals whose purpose was to enhance the self-respect of Negroes by glorifying the great accomplishments of Negroes past and present. Prominent among the leaders of this movement were W. E. B. DuBois, editor of *The Crisis;* Charles S. Johnson, editor of *Opportunity;* Alain Locke, editor of the volume *The New Negro;* and Carter G. Woodson, who had organized The Association for the Study of Negro Life and History in 1915 and begun the publication of *The Journal of Negro History.* This movement had much moral support and financial aid from liberal-minded white people.

The high position occupied by Negro college and university professors in the leadership of American Negroes during this period is worthy of note. To take the field of sociology alone, one may cite Dr. Charles S. Johnson, president of Fisk University; Dr. E. Franklin Frazier, professor of sociology at Howard University and formerly president of the American Sociological Society; and Dr. Ira DeA. Reid, chairman of the sociology department of Haverford College.

The Leading Interracial Organizations

The two organizations which have continued to be the most influential in working for the improvement of Negro welfare and status are the National Association for the Advancement of Colored People and the Urban League. These two organizations are not exclusively Negro but interracial, with substantial white membership. While they operate in the South, their origin in the North and their greater support in this region make it appropriate to discuss them in this chapter.

The N.A.A.C.P. was formed in 1909 following a severe race riot in Springfield, Illinois, the previous year. It was started on white people's initiative, but its active workers have usually been Negroes. The long-run objective of the Association has always been to win full equality for the Negro as an American citizen. Its specific activities have been in the field of civil liberties, constantly fighting legal cases of discrimination, such as anti-lynching legislation, the abolition of poll taxes, and so on. The strategy of its approach has been practical and opportunistic. The Association did not conduct an omnibus legal campaign against the Southern caste pattern but selected strategically important cases in specific fields of discrimination. It saved many Negroes from unequal court treatment; prevented the extradition of Negroes from North to South for trial; and helped establish the precedents by which the exclusion of Negroes from jury service constitutes a denial of equal protection of laws as guaranteed by the Fourteenth Amendment—to select only a few of its many legal successes.

The Urban League was founded in 1910, also as an interracial movement on white initiative. It arose primarily to help the recent Negro migrants adjust to Northern city life. It has become a general social welfare agency performing various welfare services: health work, recreational work, delinquency prevention, and acting as an informal employment agency for Negroes. In the postwar period, the Urban League has concerned itself more with advancing desegregation but, in contrast to the N.A.A.C.P., has used informal and educational methods in pursuing this goal rather than a legal approach. In 1960 there were sixty-three local branches of the League, twelve of which were located in the South.

In 1944 Myrdal wrote that one great weakness of both these organizations was their lack of support from the Negro masses.[47] This was due in part to the generally low educational and economic status of the Negro masses and the widespread prevalence among Negroes of a resigned and hopeless attitude as far as cracking the color line was concerned. The lack of mass support was also due to the fact that, as in all class structures, the interests of the Negro middle class and the Negro lower class were not identical in all respects. Since 1940, however, as we shall see, these two organizations have made substantial gains in mass support.

RACE RELATIONS: A REGIONAL ISSUE

Before turning to consider the trend since World War II, during which great changes in Negro-white relations have occurred, it is pertinent to emphasize that the very existence of regional attitudes and practices as disparate as those portrayed in the past two chapters has been a perennial source of regional conflict affecting in many ways the political and civic unity of the nation. The slavery issue threatened national unity until the close of the War Between The States. From 1880 to the First World War,

[47] *Ibid.*, pp. 835–836.

the North in general tended to leave the Negro problem, as far as it was thought of as such, to the South. The Great Migration to the North brought the problem home. The discriminatory pattern which developed appeared at first to suggest a moving of the region closer to the view of the South. However, throughout the entire period a segment of Northern opinion continued to propagandize against discrimination toward Negroes. Finally there began to emerge a new definition of the problem as one of national significance. More Northern people began to believe that the prevailing patterns of dominant-minority relations between the two races could not permanently endure in a political democracy. This emerging new definition of the race problem received great impetus from the New Deal. In the operation of large-scale relief and in other government-planned projects, the tendency was toward providing Negroes a fairer share. Here and there Negroes were placed in new situations alongside whites. The number of Northern organized groups, especially religious groups, that became interested in democratizing race relations grew. Among the minorities themselves, a trend arose toward integration of protest activities in behalf of all, in which Jewish associations took a prominent lead.

While these new trends were developing in the North, there was no perceptible indication of the South's readiness to accept this redefinition of the race problem or to basically alter its traditional biracial system. Thus the approach of World War II found a long-standing regional issue assuming new dimensions, more sharply focused by the greater influence of the North —as the predominant center of national opinion-making—in the formation of national policy.

TOPICS FOR PROJECTS AND DISCUSSION

1. If you have lived in or are well acquainted with any community outside the South which has any considerable Negro population, compare the extent of their segregation in this community with that of Chicago as depicted in this chapter. If your comparison shows any marked difference, suggest circumstances which seem to you to explain why your community so deviates.
2. It is frequently said that Negroes prefer to associate with their own kind. Do you think this is true?
3. Since the indications are that Negroes do have a considerably larger measure of opportunity in the North, how do you account for the fact that far more of them have not left the South?
4. Consider carefully all the reasons which occur to you to explain why it is that Negro youth, although accorded equal right in the North to complete their high-school education, do in fact drop out of school in larger proportions than white children.
5. Find out from the best available sources whether or not the delinquency rate is higher for Negroes than it is for non-Negroes in some delimited local area. Having established the comparative rates, study the situation and account for them.

SUGGESTED READING

Cantril, Hadley. *Psychology of Social Movements.* New York: John Wiley & Sons, Inc., 1941.
> Chapter 5, "The Kingdom of Father Divine," interprets this movement as a search for satisfaction which the "real" society denies.

Frazier, E. Franklin. *Black Bourgeosie: The Rise of the Negro Middle Class in the United States.* Glencoe, Ill.: The Free Press, 1957.
> Interpretation of the Negro middle class in American society.

Kardiner, Abram, and Ovesey, Lionel. *The Mark of Oppression:* A Psychological Study of the American Negro. New York: W. W. Norton & Company, Inc., 1951.
> Twenty-five urban Negroes were studied by psychoanalytic techniques, and the results indicate how the neurotic symptoms present had been affected by the impact of discrimination.

Lee, Alfred M., and Humphrey, Norman D. *Race Riot.* New York: The Dryden Press, Inc., 1943.
> Provides excellent analysis of the Detroit Belle Island race riot and suggests a program for prevention which has general application.

Lee, Frank F. *Negro and White in Connecticut Town.* New York: Bookman Associates, 1961.
> Study of race relations in a small town emphasizing the techniques of social control.

Locke, Alain. *The New Negro.* New York: Albert and Charles Boni, Inc., 1925.
> One of the first books surveying the literary and artistic contributions of the Negroes to American culture.

"Race Relations on the Pacific Coast," *Journal of Educational Sociology,* November 1945, Vol. 19.
> Issue contains a number of special accounts of race relations in Pacific Coast cities in 1945.

Reid, Ira DeA. *The Negro Immigrant.* New York: Columbia University Press, 1939.
> Most definitive account of the subject, treating especially the West Indian migrant.

Warner, W. Lloyd, Junker, Buford H., and Adam, Walter A. *Color and Human Nature.* Washington, D.C.: American Youth Commission, 1941.
> Studies the impact of the Chicago milieu on the personality of Negro youth.

Weaver, Robert C. *The Negro Ghetto.* New York: Harcourt, Brace & Co., 1948.
> A long-time student of the effect of housing segregation on Negroes provides a comprehensive treatment of the subject in this volume.

13

Negro-White Relations:
World War II and the Changing South

In the previous two chapters, Negro-white relations North and South have been viewed as substantially fixed structures of accommodative relations. In this chapter we shift focus and view the period since 1940 as a changing process. By all odds the most significant single event in the period has been the decision of the Supreme Court of the United States in 1954 declaring segregation in public education unconstitutional. The impact of this decision has produced such dramatic consequences that whatever took place from the onset of World War II until the decision is overshadowed. It must not be forgotten, however, that the Supreme Court acts only on cases brought before it. Situations arising in World War II made breaches in the pattern of segregation at many points and set in motion a trend toward further changes in the same direction. The social climate of the nation was much more favorable for such a momentous decision in 1954 than it would have been fifteen years earlier. Since to date the trend continues in the same direction and shows no sign of arrest, the years since the beginning of World War II may be considered as the period of movement toward assimilation in Negro-white relations.

THE EFFECT OF WORLD WAR II ON
NEGRO – WHITE RELATIONS

World War II marked a significant point in Negro-white relations primarily because a nation engaged in a great war must utilize its manpower to the utmost. It is also probable that, as in all war periods when the nationality sentiment rises to its highest intensity, the dominant people acted more democratically toward Negroes, as well as toward other minorities, except those of "enemy" background. Moreover, the appeal to democracy was utilized to persuade, cajole, or force white people—as in the instance of the Fair Employment Practices Committee—to alter their traditional attitudes enough to permit a more effective utilization of Negro manpower. For whatever reasons, the facts are clear enough that the welfare of Negroes improved greatly throughout the war years and that some changes in status occurred.

In Economic Life

The greatest gain accruing to Negroes in the World War II period was to have constant employment, at considerably higher real wages, in a wider range of occupations, than was previously tolerated.[1] This improved occupational situation led to advancement in Negro standards of living. Weaver writes:

Thus . . . colored, as all defense workers, bought more and better food, clothing, and, when available, household equipment. The crowded waiting rooms in the offices of Negro professional men and women and the high earnings they enjoyed during the war . . . attested to the fact that the residents in the Black Belt were demanding more and better medical and dental attention, spending more time and money on personal appearance, and seeking legal advice when such was needed. All of this meant that colored people, who had always accepted the American standards of living, rapidly took steps to achieve them once they had more money.[2]

With this came some improvement in status. In many of the new war jobs Negroes worked alongside whites under equal terms so far as wages and work privileges were concerned. In Chicago, for example, Drake and Cayton write, "Colored girls . . . became salespeople in a few Loop stores, and colored Western Union messengers appeared on the streets of Midwest Metropolis for the first time."[3]

What was to prove in the long run most significant in improving the status of Negroes was their increasing acceptance into labor unions. Johnson

[1] See Robert C. Weaver, *Negro Labor A National Problem* (New York: Harcourt, Brace & Co., 1946).
[2] Robert C. Weaver, *The Negro Ghetto* (New York: Harcourt, Brace & Co., 1948), p. 136. By permisssion.
[3] St. Clair Drake and Horace R. Cayton, *Black Metropolis* (New York: Harcourt, Brace & Co., 1945), p. 296. By permission of the publishers.

cites several estimates ranging from a total Negro union membership in 1943 of 400,000 to claims of the unions themselves which would put the figure at over a million at the close of the war.[4] But the unionization of Negroes was not accomplished easily. Acceptance was by no means whole-hearted on the part of white workers. The national trade unions often had to discipline local groups for their refusal to accept Negroes and for sometimes striking over the matter. Nevertheless, Embree wrote in 1945: "The greatest asset in employment is the new attitude of the unions. The Congress of Industrial Organizations is the strongest force against discrimination that has arisen in these fervid years."[5]

While, as might have been expected, in many instances separate Negro unions were formed, some unions became mixed, and as time went on, discarding the rules of caste etiquette became more frequent in these mixed unions. The practice of electing a white president and a Negro vice-president began.[6]

The Fair Employment Practices Committee   A further influence on wider employment opportunity for Negroes, as well as other minorities, was the Fair Employment Practices Committee, which came into being on June 25, 1941, when President Roosevelt issued his now famous executive order No. 8822. The order provided:

1. That all government agencies concerned with training programs should take measures designed to prevent discrimination.
2. That all government contracting agencies should include in defense contracts a provision obligating the contractor not to discriminate against any worker because of race, color, or country of national origin.
3. That there should be established a Committee on Fair Employment Practices to investigate complaints of discrimination and to take appropriate steps to redress valid grievances.

This action was taken in part as a result of a movement to organize a Negro march on Washington, led by A. Philip Randolph, head of the Brotherhood of Sleeping Car Porters, and had the immediate result of forestalling the march.[7] The Committee was strongly opposed in many communities, and violently opposed throughout the South. It had neither legislative sanction nor any real powers of enforcement. But, in spite of these handicaps, in the first eighty weeks of its existence "Negro employment increased in commercial shipyards from 6,952 to 12,820; in navy shipyards

[4] Charles S. Johnson, *Into the Main Stream* (Chapel Hill: University of North Carolina Press, 1947), pp. 114–115.
[5] Edwin R. Embree, "Balance Sheet in Race Relations," *Atlantic Monthly*, May 1945, 175: 89.
[6] See Herbert R. Northrup, *Organized Labor and The Negro* (New York: Harper & Brothers, 1944), for an account of the subject.
[7] For fuller details of this movement see Myrdal, *An American Dilemma* (New York: Harper & Brothers, 1944), pp. 851–852.

from 6,000 to 14,000; and in aircraft from 0 to 5,000."[8] The F.E.P.C. was abolished at the war's end, but similar agencies were subsequently adopted on the state level by many states.

Social Discrimination

Beyond the job situations and unions, however, the line of segregation between white and Negro remained substantially the same. Traditional discrimination against Negroes in housing generally held fast, as is documented in Weaver's study.[9] Even the National Capitol Housing Authority bowed to the prevailing community pattern in building low-rent housing units. The 2,700 housing units built by this federal agency for Negro occupancy were all located in Negro areas, thus reducing the space available for all Negroes.[10]

In the still more intimate area of social relations, substantially no change took place during the war. For example, on one occasion a federal agency planned a riverboat excursion for its employees, for which two boats were chartered and tickets were assigned for the appropriate boat on the basis of race. The recreational staff was embarrassed by the attempt of some Negro workers to insist on tickets for the white boat.

In the Armed Services

The armed services, with a few exceptions noted below, practiced a policy of segregation. In the Army, Negroes were assigned to colored units, most of which were in supply services where the tasks were largely menial labor. A few thousand Negro officers were trained and placed over Negro troops, frequently under the command of a white captain. In army posts, separate recreational rooms were maintained, and nearly all communities which any considerable number of soldiers frequented—North as well as South—restricted colored troops to the Negro areas and set up separate USO's. For the most part, Negro units were kept out of combat. According to Rose, "In Europe there were some efforts made to keep Negroes from fraternizing with the civilian population, when no such bar was set up against the white troops."[11]

The policy of segregating Negro troops reflected the wishes of the white troops. A survey of the attitudes of servicemen on the matter of race segregation made in March, 1943, revealed that about 80 per cent of the white troops preferred to have the two groups separated in PX's, service clubs,

[8] Carey McWilliams, *Brothers Under The Skin* (Boston: Little, Brown & Co., 1946), p. 314. Also see *Fair Employment Practices Committee, Final Report, June 28, 1946* (Washington, D.C.: 1947).
[9] *The Negro Ghetto*, Ch. 7.
[10] *Segregation in Washington, A report of the National Committee on Segregation in Washington* (Chicago, 1948).
[11] Rose, *Negro in America* (New York: Harper & Brothers, 1948), p. 138.

and nonmilitary units.[12] While, as would be expected, over 90 per cent of the Southern white respondents on each of the three counts listed above approved segregation, it is significant that over 70 per cent of the Northern white troops likewise indicated approval.[13] The Negro respondents showed far more opposition to being segregated, as would also be expected, but the detailed findings in this respect were highly significant as an indication of how Negroes viewed their situation generally. Of the Negro sample 37 per cent disapproved separation in military units; 36 per cent approved; 17 per cent thought it made no difference; and 10 per cent were undecided.[14] Comments, such as the following, made on the questionnaire by some of the anti-segregation Negro soldiers emphasized primarily the democratic principle involved. "Separate outfits shows that the Army continues segregation and discrimination. Is this the Democracy we are told we are fighting for?"[15] The 36 per cent of Negro soldiers who approved of segregation did so on the basis of expediency, based on their realistic appraisal of white prejudice. Among the reasons given for taking the pro-segregation viewpoint were a fear of interracial friction, illustrated by the comment, "A white soldier would call a colored soldier 'nigger' and it would be a fight"; a desire to withdraw from the situation of not being wanted, or, as one soldier put it, "so long as there are so many prejudiced white people, it would be too unpleasant"; a desire to prove that Negro groups can match the achievements of white groups; and finally, a desire to associate with those who understand each other, illustrated by the remark, "I had rather be with my own color. Then I know where I stand."[16]

Ultimately some cracks appeared in the race segregation pattern of the services, of which Dollard and Young write:

The first was a decision to abandon segregation in all officers' candidate schools except those for Air Force flying personnel. At the peak, there were about a score of such integrated camps, each producing specialists for some one branch of the service—artillery, tank corps, infantry, and so on. White and Negro slept, ate, and trained together with a minimum of friction and with no "incidents" worthy of record.

The second crack in the pattern resulted from a single experiment. On December 26, 1944, Lieutenant General John C. H. Lee issued an order permitting Negro enlisted men in service units within his command to volunteer for duty as infantrymen, with the understanding that after the necessary training, they would be committed to front line service with white companies. In spite of the fact that

[12] Samuel A. Stouffer, et al. The American Soldier, Vol. 1 (Princeton: Princeton University Press, 1949), pp. 566–580. Chapter 10 of this volume, "Negro Soldiers," contains probably the most definitive research material ever gathered on how the young adult males of both races look at one another and think about the "race" problem.
[13] Ibid., pp. 568–570.
[14] Ibid., p. 568.
[15] Ibid., p. 575.
[16] Ibid., p. 574.

all volunteers had to sacrifice any ratings they held, about twenty-five hundred took advantage of the opportunity and eventually saw combat duty. For the first time in the recent history of the army, Negroes and whites operated as members of a single company.[17]

In spite of segregation policy and practice, the total impact of experiences in the armed services had effects disturbing to the traditional pattern of caste relations. More objectively measurable was the introduction of colored servicemen to new standards of welfare—in diet, health, and sanitation; and the increased training in many new skills, some of which could be useful in peacetime. One measure of the Negro soldiers' own feeling about the vocational value of their army experience is provided by a study made by the office of Army Education and Information. Soldiers were asked to indicate whether or not they felt that their army training would help them get a better job after the war than they had ever had before, and 61 per cent of the Negro respondents replied in the affirmative as contrasted with only 39 per cent among the whites.[18]

Less tangible but perhaps in the long run more significant was the impact of service experience on the attitudes of GI's of both races. Northern-born Negro servicemen trained in the South came face to face with the stricter Southern caste system. Southern Negro GI's stationed in the North experienced some measure of unaccustomed freedom. In Europe many Negro GI's found white people wishing to accept them like any other American soldier. Equally disturbing to traditional attitudes and habits was the impact of war service on many white Southerners. This is most dramatically illustrated in Margaret Halsey's account of her experiences operating a servicemen's center in a large Northern city.[19] The policy of accepting all men in uniform on the same terms was successfully maintained, and some Southern-bred young women who were hostesses danced with Negro servicemen. Many Southern white servicemen, though first somewhat shocked to see white women dancing with colored servicemen, both in conversation and in correspondence with Miss Halsey indicated that they were doing some inner struggling with their attitudes.

The Situation at V-J Day

To take stock of the position of Negro-white relations at the close of the war as a base from which to analyze the trends since 1945, Myrdal's summary observations, though written a little before the war's end, will be employed.

[17] Charles Dollard and Donald Young, "In the Armed Forces," *Survey Graphic*, Jan. 1947, 36: 68. By permission.
[18] Stouffer, *The American Soldier*, p. 537.
[19] Margaret Halsey, *Color Blind* (New York: Simon and Schuster, Inc., 1946).

Of the North, Myrdal observes:

The social paradox in the North is exactly this, that almost everybody is against discrimination in general but, at the same time, almost everybody practices discrimination in his own personal affairs.

It is the cumulation of all these personal discriminations which creates the color bar in the North and for the Negro causes unusually severe unemployment, crowded housing conditions, crime, and vice. About this social process the ordinary white Northerner keeps sublimely ignorant and unconcerned. This aloofness is, of course, partly opportunistic but it can be fought by education. When now, in the war emergency, the Negro is increasingly given sympathetic publicity by newspapers, periodicals, and the radio, and by administrators and public personalities of all kinds, one result is that the white Northerner is gradually waking up and seeing what he is doing to the Negro and is seeing also the consequences of his democratic creed for his relations with Negroes. We have become convinced in the course of this inquiry that the North is getting prepared for a fundamental redefinition of the Negro's status in America. The North will accept it if the change is pushed by courageous leadership. And the North has much more power than the South. The white South is itself a minority and a national problem.

In contrast, Myrdal writes of the South:

The situation in the South is different. Unlike the white Northerner, who is most inclined to give the Negro equality in public relations and least inclined to do so in private relations, the white Southerner does not differentiate between public and private relations—the former as well as the latter have significance for prestige and social equality. Moreover, he is traditionally and consistently opposed to Negro equality for its own sake, which the Northerner is not. He may be privately indulgent much more than the white Northerner but he is not as willing to give the Negro equal treatment by public authority.[20]

PROLOGUE: THE POSTWAR PERIOD

The dramatic changes which have taken place in Negro-white relations in the United States since World War II can be better understood if the broad social forces operating on the interracial process are kept in mind. We develop these forces in more detail as part of our over-all interpretation of dominant-minority relations in the United States in Chapter 20. More briefly stated here, the major social forces pressing for change in a more equalitarian direction are the following: (1) the dynamics of the democratic process, particularly as embodied in the political and governmental structures; (2) the continued expansion of the national economy providing new job opportunities for Negroes and encouraging their migration cityward and out of the South; (3) the cumulative effect of each new Negro advance in encouraging more Negroes to press for still more gains; and (4) the growing awareness of white Americans of the adverse effect of American race relations on its prestige abroad. As social forces operating counteractive to the above may be noted (1) the traditional attitudes and corresponding institutions

[20] Myrdal, An American Dilemma, pp. 1010–1011. By permission of the publishers, Harper & Brothers.

and habits of white Americans which define the Negro as inferior and sanction discrimination against him; (2) special economic interests for which discrimination and segregation are still profitable; (3) the inevitable effects of long induration to minority status on Negroes, holding them back from activity in their own behalf.

THE SOUTHERN SCENE

Following World War II and before 1954, significant developments in the South were as follows: an increase in Negro voting—595,000 Negroes were on the voting rolls in 1947 and 1,008,614 in 1953;[21] some increase in Negro jury service prompted by a growing disposition of the federal courts to overturn convictions where the failure to call Negroes into service was attested; some beginnings of arresting and trying white people for crimes of violence against Negroes; the appointment of some Negro police officers to cover Negro areas. The Civil Rights program of the Truman Administration led to the formation of the States Rights party in the 1948 Presidential election, carrying the electoral vote of four southern States. No precipitate rise in violence toward Negroes was apparent, although the virtual disappearance of lynching was somewhat offset by a rise in the bombing of Negro homes. More than forty such bombings were reported for a year and a half period during 1951 and 1952.[22] While there was some reactivation of racist organizations, such as the Ku Klux Klan, white public opinion against such extremists was evidenced by the outlawing of masked gatherings in some Southern cities.

In the educational area, two significant developments in the postwar years should be noted. First, a breach in the pattern of segregation occurred in higher education at the graduate level. It was estimated that more than 200 Negroes were enrolled in hitherto exclusively white graduate schools in 1951. Second, a trend toward greater equalization of the segregated Negro school system as compared to the white system was marked. A comprehensive study of public-school education in the South in 1952 found the two systems most nearly equal in regard to teacher salaries, levels of teacher preparation, and the number of days of the school year. Some lessening of the disparity between the two systems since 1940 was found in the provision of better school plants, the number of and amounts spent for library books, and in various vocational offerings. However, the study concludes that "in spite of the rapid improvement of Negro schools . . . substantial further progress is needed before equalization can be achieved."[23]

[21] Margaret Price, *The Negro and the Ballot* (Atlanta: The Southern Regional Council, 1959), p. 9.
[22] "Blight, Bigotry, and Bombs," *The New South* (Atlanta, Ga.: Southern Regional Council, July, 1952).
[23] Truman M. Pierce, and others, *White and Negro Schools in the South* (Englewood Cliffs, N. J.: Prentice-Hall, Inc., 1955), p. 292. See pp. 291–292 for summary.

Thus on the surface, race relations in the South did not appear unduly critical, and in a sense the situation seemed ameliorative. Then came the Supreme Court decision outlawing school desegregation.

The Supreme Court Decision Outlawing School Segregation: May 17, 1954

This famous decision concerned five separate cases, which the court elected to consolidate since it considered the same legal question was involved in each of them. In each case Negro children through their legal representatives had sought admission to white public schools, had been denied this right by local courts, and eventually had appealed the unfavorable decisions to the Supreme Court of the United States. The core of the decision is found in the following excerpts:

We conclude that in the field of public education the doctrine of "separate but equal" has no place. Separate educational facilities are inherently unequal. Therefore, we hold that the plaintiffs and others similarly situated for whom the actions have been brought are, by reason of the segregation complained of, deprived of the equal protection of the laws guaranteed by the Fourteenth Amendment. This disposition makes unncessary any discussion whether such segregation also violated the Due Process clause of the Fourteenth Amendment. . . .

Segregation of white and colored children in public schools has a detrimental effect upon the colored children. The impact is greater when it has the sanction of law; for the policy of separating the races is usually interpreted as denoting the inferiority of the Negro group. A sense of inferiority affects the motivation of the child to learn. Segregation, with the sanction of the law, therefore has a tendency to retard the educational and mental development of Negro children and to deprive them of some of the benefits they would receive in a racially integrated school system. . . .

Whatever may have been the extent of psychological knowledge at the time of Plessy vs. Ferguson, this finding is amply supported by modern authority. Any language in Plessy vs. Ferguson contrary to this finding is rejected.[24]

The manner in which the court handled this case indicates awareness that strong negative reactions would be forthcoming and that enforcement would be beset with special difficulties. The fact that the decision was unanimous and read by Chief Justice Earl Warren gave the decision the sense of finality and probable irrevocability. The Court did not propose implementing decrees. It held another hearing at which attorneys general from states affected

[24] 347 U.S. 483. The number 1 case was Brown, *et al.* v. Board of Education of Topeka, Kansas. Three other cases were linked together with Brown, *et al.*: Briggs v. Elliott (South Carolina); Davis v. County School Board of Prince Edward County, Virginia; Gebhart v. Belton (Delaware). A separate decision in Bolling v. Sharpe, 347, U.S. 497, to the same effect was read following Brown, *et al.* This case concerned segregation of public schools in the District of Columbia and therefore involved the federal government directly.

Footnote 11 in the text of the decision lists the following writings: K. B. Clark, *Effect of Prejudice and Discrimination on Personality Development* (Midcentury White House Conference on Children and Youth, 1950); Witmer and Kotinsky, *Personality in the Making* (1952), c. VI; Deutscher and Chein, "The Psychological Effects of Enforced

and other interested persons presented arguments concerning implementation. On May 31, 1955, the Court ordered compliance "with all deliberate speed." This phraseology indicated that the Supreme Court did not expect the affected states to integrate completely all schools at once. It was interpreted to mean that some reasonable plan for eventual complete integration should be made and a beginning announced. The highest court left to district federal courts the task of deciding whether a particular plan presented in a particular community in its area was in fact a plan designed to accomplish complete integration in a reasonable time.

As we turn to discuss the trend of race relations in the South following the school case decision, it is essential to emphasize that the significance and impact of the decision goes far beyond the matter of schools. While the decision specifically ordered school desegregation, it seems clear that the line of reasoning presented has general application. The court said in effect that all state-imposed racial segregation is unconstitutional. By stating that it was reversing Plessy vs. Ferguson (1896), which held that segregation in public transportation was legal provided the segregated transportation facilities were equal, the court has led most professional students to derive this more general implication. Subsequent decisions by various courts within the federal system in such widely divergent fields as public transportation and public recreational facilities support this interpretation. In short, by inference the school decision appeared to undermine the entire legal basis of segregation throughout the United States.

The Extent of School Desegregation

How far school desegregation in the South and border states had proceeded by June, 1961, is indicated in Table 11 which may be summarized and interpreted as follows:[25] (1) The District of Columbia, governed by the United States Congress, integrated immediately following the 1954 decision. (2) In the border states of Delaware, Kentucky, Maryland, Oklahoma, and West Virginia, substantial integration has taken place. In Arkansas, North

---

Segregation: A Survey of Social Science Opinion," 26 *J. Psychol.* 259 (1948); Chein, "What are the Psychological Effects of Segregation Under Conditions of Equal Facilities?" 3 *Int. J. Opinion and Attitude Res.* 229 (1949); Brameld, *Educational Costs, in Discrimination and National Welfare* (MacIver, ed., 1949), 44–48; Frazier, *The Negro in the United States* (1949), 674–681. And see generally Myrdal, *An American Dilemma* (1944).

See Albert P. Blaustein and Clarence C. Ferguson, Jr., *Desegregation and the Law: The Meaning and Effect of the School Desegregation Cases* (New Brunswick, N.J.: Rutgers University Press, 1957), for an extensive account of the legal proceedings and the text of significant cases related to the desegregation decision.

[25] The factual material up to May, 1961, is taken from "Statistical Summary of School Segregation-Desegregation in the Southern and Border States," published by Southern Education Reporting Service, May, 1961. The extensive coverage of the school desegregation developments by this organization, made public in monthly issues of *Southern School News*, makes the school desegregation process probably the most thoroughly documented phenomenon of the times.

TABLE 11
Segregation-Desegregation Status, May, 1961[26]

STATE	SCHOOL DISTRICTS			ENROLLMENT		IN DESEGREGATED DISTRICTS		NEGROES IN SCHOOLS WITH WHITES	
	TOTAL	BIRACIAL	DESEG.	WHITE	NEGRO	WHITE	NEGRO	No.	%
Alabama	114	114	0	516,135**	271,134**	0	0	0	0
Arkansas	422	228	10	317,053†	105,130†	52,126	12,639	113	.107
Delaware	92	26	24	66,630	14,973	47,932	8,628	6,738	45.0
Dist. of Columbia	1	1	1	24,697	96,751	24,697	96,751	81,392	84.1
Florida	67	67	1	807,512	212,280	133,336	27,502	28	.013
Georgia	198	196	1	626,377	295,255	0	0	0	0
Kentucky	211	172	130	593,494**	41,938**	445,000*	32,000*	16,329	38.9
Louisiana	67	67	1	422,181**	271,012**	37,490	51,113	1	.0004
Maryland	24	23	23	461,206	136,882	456,410	136,882	45,943	33.6
Mississippi	151	151	0	287,781**	278,640**	0	0	0	0
Missouri	1,889	214*	200*	758,000*	84,000*	—	75,000*	35,000*	41.7
North Carolina	173	173	10	832,200	307,800	117,404	54,746	82	.026
Oklahoma	1,276	240	190	504,125	40,875	266,405	30,725	9,822	24.0
South Carolina	108	108	0	354,227	258,667	0	0	0	0
Tennessee	154	143	7	675,648*	152,352*	130,953	21,881	376	.247
Texas	1,531	720	132	1,840,987*	288,553*	800,000*	85,000*	3,500*	1.21
Virginia	130	128	11	668,500*	211,000*	177,731	52,286	208	.099
West Virginia	55	43	43	416,646	21,010	416,646	21,010	14,000*	66.6
Totals	6,663	2,813	783	10,173,399	3,088,261	3,106,130††	706,163	213,532	6.9

* Estimated.
** 1959–60.
† 1958–59.
†† Missouri not included.

[26] *Statistical Summary of School Segregation-Desegregation in the Southern and Border States.* Published by the Southern Education Reporting Service, May, 1961, p. 3.

Carolina, Tennessee, Texas, and Virginia a few school districts have started integration. However, in these areas the integration is still token, involving only a few Negroes in each instance. For example, despite federal intervention in Little Rock, Arkansas, in 1957, four years later only ten of the state's 422 school districts were integrated, and only 113 of the over 100,000 Negro children of school age were actually in schools with whites. (3) Most significant is the Deep South situation, where at the close of the school year 1960 no integration at all had taken place in Alabama, Georgia, Louisiana, Mississippi, and South Carolina. The first break in this situation came in New Orleans, where in November, 1960, under court order the Orleans Parish school board admitted three Negro girls to the elementary school, McDonough 19, and one to the William Frantz school. Strong negative reactions came from the Louisiana state government and from some segments of the New Orleans community. Another form of resistance arising even within compliance is seen in the frequent withdrawal of white students when Negroes are admitted. At McDonough 19 all the white students withdrew; and at William Frantz the former white enrollment of 570 dropped to less than twenty. Similarly, at Orchard Villa school in Dade County, Florida, the admission of a few Negroes resulted in the gradual withdrawal of white students, so that at the year's end the school was all Negro. Two Negroes were admitted, again under court order, to the University of Georgia in January, 1960.

While the developments just mentioned are significant in the long run, the very slow pace of school integration in the Deep South is seen in the reports following the opening of schools in the fall of 1961. For the region as a whole there was an increase of 114 more school districts desegregated than at the previous spring. But much of this increase is accounted for in Delaware, where a federal court ordered the school system of the entire state desegregated by September, 1961, and to a lesser extent by Texas, where sixteen more biracial districts had desegregated at this time. In the Deep South most significant was the admission of nine Negro children to eleventh and twelfth grades in hitherto white Atlanta high schools by court order and without incident. The proportion of Negro school children in the entire region attending schools with whites increased in September of 1961 only 0.4 per cent over the previous school year.[27]

The faculties of the public schools in nine states of the South remained segregated, including five that have desegregated schools. Some degree of teacher desegregation is reported in eight states, although in four states—Missouri, Oklahoma, Texas, and West Virginia—several Negro teachers lost their jobs in the change to biracial schools.[28]

[27] "Statistical Summary of School Desegregation in the Southern and Border States," November, 1961. Published by *Southern Education Reporting Service.*
[28] *Ibid.,* p. 3.

(4) Finally, it is important to stress that up to this time there had been no voluntary desegregation in five states of the Deep South. Apparently the process of school desegregation there will be slow.

Various analyses of the uneven progress of school desegregation broadly agree that the following factors favor desegregation: (1) a smaller proportion of Negroes in the total population; (2) urban as distinct from rural areas; (3) higher educational level of the white person. In detail, however, fortuitous circumstances make the relationship between various social factors and the timing of desegregation difficult to predict. For example, the personal decision of influential politicians on whether to take an adamantly opposed or a moderate position on the desegregation issue can delay or expedite the process in their particular localities.

SINCE 1954

The school case decision of 1954 precipitated a crisis for the South, especially the Deep South. Since the implications of the decision were, from the Southern point of view, revolutionary, it is not surprising that what followed has been a bitter, continuous struggle between those committed to traditional continuity and those intent on basic change in the Southern interracial system. The active agents on the side of change in this struggle were national Negro leaders, supported by a growing body of the Negro population; the federal court system; and an influential and articulate body of Northern public opinion, expressed in mass media. In sequence the roles played by these agents follow the order as just presented. Courts act when cases are brought before them. It was therefore the deliberate decision of the National Association for the Advancement of Colored People to test the constitutionality of school segregation which brought on the crisis at this particular time. On the side of traditional continuity were the institutions of race discrimination and the corresponding attitudes which found a substantial majority of Southern white people psychologically unprepared and unwilling to accept the drastic changes implied by the various court decisions against segregation. Some open support was received from racist-minded Americans outside the South—who were not, however, persons of much influence.

Following the school case decision, the interracial struggle has followed a course which we will describe in the following stages: (1) Southern whites viewed the situation as a crisis and the prevailing segment reacted accordingly with strong resistance. (2) Negroes challenged further areas of segregation with considerable success. (3) Further extra-regional pressures were brought upon the South with reference to other forms of segregation: from Congress in the form of Civil Rights legislation which led to increasing intervention by the federal government, and from voluntary groups, such as the "Freedom Riders." (4) Under the impact of all these pressures, the resistance movement began to weaken and reluctant compliance with desegregation orders increased.

THE CRISIS BEGINS

Following the school desegregation decision, race relations in the South veered sharply from the ameliorative trend which we mentioned earlier. Tension and conflict between the races rose sharply. Biracial relations in most communities were polarized between active Negro groups and reactionary white groups, pitted against each other on the desegregation issue. Moderate white leadership was unable to exert influence; liberals faced extraordinary reprisals.[29] Effective communication between the white and Negro communities broke down. The situation was no longer one where white groups could debate among themselves, consult with accommodative Negro leaders over improving Negro welfare, or criticize particular whites who had over-abused the privileges of the system by maltreating a Negro. The issue had become the abolition or survival of the segregation system itself, a system for so long an integral part of the Southern way of life that the conflict between the races was raised to the level of a crisis.

White Resistance

That the white South would react with strong resistance to the school decision, and to any other areas of desegregation, would be expected from an understanding of the Southern interracial system as described in Chapter 11. Further measure of the unreadiness of the white South to accept desegregation can be gained from public opinion polls.[30] On the school issue itself, the extent of Southern white disapproval is indicated by a Gallup Poll in 1954 which found 71 per cent of its Southern white sample disapproving the school decision, as compared with 30 per cent outside the South and 46 per cent for the nation as a whole.[31] The strength of Southern white support for the traditional system is further attested in another poll, where the respondents were requested to choose between "keeping the races apart," and "bringing them together" as the best solution to the Negro-white problem.

[29] We define a segregationist as one who believes that retention of the biracial system is the most important thing to the South; a moderate as one who believes in segregation but gives many other things priority to this issue and who is therefore willing to compromise on the race issue; a liberal is the white Southerner who believes that desegregation in varying degrees of rapidity is desirable.

[30] See Melvin M. Tumin, *Segregation and Desegregation: a Digest of Recent Research* (New York: Anti-Defamation League of B'nai B'rith, 1957), pp. 94–112.

[31] Data furnished by American Institute of Public Opinion, Princeton, New Jersey, which has conducted polls on the question of desegregation since 1954.

Nearly three-fourths of the Southern white respondents chose the former answer, as against about one-sixth who chose the latter.[32]

The Range of Southern White Attitudes

An analysis in more depth of the range of Southern white attitudes toward desegregation comes from a study made in Tallahassee, Florida, in 1956.[33] The respondents are classified as Accepters, Compliers, Delayers, and Resisters. Table 12 defines each category and shows the proportion of the Tallahassee sample in each. Killian and Haer found that, when faced with specific racial issues, the Delayers tended to side with the Resisters, and the Compliers with the Accepters. Thus, according to their data, the combination disposed to act against discrimination was about 74 per cent.

TABLE 12

Responses to Question Concerning the Supreme Court Ruling on Desegregation in the Public Schools[34]

ATTITUDE	NUMBER OF RESPONSES	PER CENT OF RESPONSES
1. It was a good decision—we should start trying to let Negro children into white public schools. (Accepters)	67	12.50
2. It was a bad decision—but it's the law and we should start trying to let them in. (Compliers)	63	11.75
3. It was a bad decision—we should do all we can legally to keep them from getting in. (Delayers)	305	56.90
4. It was a bad decision—we should never let them in even if it goes against the law. (Resisters)	92	17.16
5. Don't know	6	1.12
6. Other answers	3	.56
Total	536	99.99

Given this attitudinal climate, it is not surprising to find white Southern resistance to desegregation intensified by so sweeping a challenge as the school decision. A report of increased tension in the area from 1955 to 1958 found 530 cases of violence, reprisal, and intimidation as an aftermath of the various court decisions.[35]

[32] Poll conducted by the Ben Gaffin Associates Research Agency for *The Catholic Digest* in 1956. See Melvin M. Tumin, *Segregation and Desegregation*, p. 98.
[33] Lewis M. Killian and John Haer, "Variables Related to Attitudes Regarding School Desegregation among White Southerners," *Sociometry*, June, 1958, 21: 159–164.
[34] *Ibid.*, p. 161.
[35] "Intimidation, Reprisal and Violence in the South's Racial Crisis," published by the Southeastern Office, American Friends Service Committee, Department of Racial and Cultural Relations, National Council of Churches of Christ in the United States of America; and the Southern Regional Council, 1959.

Legal Inventions to Prevent Desegregation

The various attempts to evade the school desegregation process may be divided roughly into two main categories: (1) Proposals designed to permit the continued operation of schools on a segregated basis. Here are found changes in pupil assignment, ostensibly on the basis of health, morals, academic background, and so on, made without outwardly mentioning race but designed to permit *de facto* racial segregation. (2) Proposals designed to abolish public schools and institute state-supported private schools. Mississippi and South Carolina amended their constitutions to provide for the abolition of public schools if necessary to avoid integration. Georgia made grants of public funds available to parents and also would make school property available for rent to a private organization for educational purposes if integration actually took place.[36]

White Citizens' Councils

Of the various unofficial movements arising to oppose school desegregation, the most prominent was the White Citizens' Council movement.[37] This organization originated in Mississippi shortly after the school decision and continued to be strongest in that state. Similar councils arose in other states, and some liaison between the various councils in the South developed. Members were recruited from people of considerable status and power, which may explain the fact that, in general, control was exercised to keep its activities nonviolent. In addition to influencing state legislation, the Councils' chief method was at first to apply economic pressure against both Negroes and whites who participated openly in desegregation. As criticism of the use of economic sanction arose, the movement abandoned it officially, though it may have continued to practice it covertly. At least temporarily, the use of economic pressures was quite effective in discouraging the desegregation efforts of Negroes and sympathetic whites.

Thus it can be seen that the methods employed by the resistance movement were largely to secure new legislation and to apply economic reprisal. The former had mainly a delaying effect, since federal courts tend to overrule municipal ordinances or state laws causing segregation directly or indirectly. Illustrating the effectiveness of economic reprisal was the widely publicized eviction by white landlords of Negro tenants from their rented farms in Fayette and Haywood counties, Tennessee (1960). The reason given for this action was that because of mechanical improvements the Negroes were no longer needed. The evicted tenants included Negroes who

[36] See James M. Nabrit, Jr., "Legal Inventions and the Desegregation Process," *The Annals of the American Academy of Political and Social Science*, March, 1956, 304: 35–43, for a summary of these attempted legal circumventions.
[37] See Hodding Carter, III, *The South Strikes Back* (Garden City, N.Y.: Doubleday & Co., Inc., 1959), for an extensive treatment of White Citizens' Councils.

had been active in attempting to register to vote. A case carried to a federal district court on this matter resulted in an order to stop these evictions.

The white resistance movement met with considerable success. We have already noted the lack of speed in integration into the public schools. Further indications of effective resistance can be seen in the slowing down of the pre-1954 trend toward integration of Negroes in colleges and universities, and similarly, of the trend toward increased Negro voting.

Decline in Desegregation in Higher Education

The slowing down of integration of Negroes in Southern colleges and universities is attested in a recent report of the United States Commission on Civil Rights which found six states still effectively resisting integration at this level. Excerpts from the report follow:

> Compliance in some degree with the requirements of the equal-protection clause in 55.9 per cent of the formerly segregated public white colleges and universities of the South is progress indeed, but unfortunately, in many of these institutions compliance is not complete. In some, Negroes are admitted only to the graduate division; in others, they are admitted to the undergraduate division, but only if they wish to enroll in a course of study not offered in the college for Negroes maintained by the state. Such limitations are clearly in violation of the Fourteenth Amendment.
>
> The most serious equal-protection problem in public higher education, however, does not arise from the occasional instances of discrimination that occur, but from overt official resistance to any desegregation at all.[38]

Voting in the South

Efforts to limit the further extension of the franchise to Negroes in the South have been effective. We have already noted the considerable increase in the number of Negroes on the voting rolls of southern states, from 595,000 in 1947 to 1,008,614, in 1953. In 1958 the figure had increased to 1,313,827. In some Louisiana parishes a movement to purge Negroes from the registration rolls gained much headway.[39] A Florida study shows that while the Negro major party registration increased from 5.5 of the adult Negro population to 37.5 from 1944 to 1956, the largest increases took place between 1944 and 1950.[40] The author comments: "Increasing tension over the segregation issue is making it more difficult for officials and candidates in the South to maintain a moderate position on this [the voting] issue, or to seek Negro support on other issues."[41] We shall presently discuss the efforts of the federal government to accord Negroes in the South the privilege of voting.

[38] United States Commission on Civil Rights, *Report on Racial Discrimination in Higher Education, 1961,* as reported in the *New York Times,* January 16, 1961.
[39] Margaret Price, *The Negro and the Ballot,* pp. 15–17.
[40] H. D. Price, *The Negro and Southern Politics: A Chapter of Florida History* (New York: New York University Press, 1957), p. 33.
[41] *Ibid.,* p. 106.

The predominance of the resistance elements of the white South over moderates seems clear at least to 1960. The unseating of a moderate white southern Congressman, Brook Hayes, of Little Rock, Arkansas, in 1958 by a write-in vote sponsored by segregationists illustrates why other Southern politicians who may privately hold moderate views have not outwardly opposed the resistance movement. Further indication of the dominance and effectiveness of the segregationist influence comes from a study of the reaction of Little Rock's clergy to the school desegregation crisis in that city in 1957.[42] The main thesis of this study runs as follows:

> Those ministers who were openly or privately integrationist did not receive from any source, sufficient support to make their position viable. They were opposed not only by the community-at-large but by their own congregations, and by the ministers of the sect churches as well. Denominational executives, while often integrationists in their attitudes, were inclined to give greater or at least equal weight to what amounted to a contradictory value, namely, the maintenance of congregational harmony. The desire to keep the congregational peace also moved the ministers themselves, inducing some to keep silent, others eventually to give up the hope of being able to fight their cause through. Despite the difficulties, a small handful of ministers continued to make their views manifest out of personal conviction, only to be confronted with economic pressures, or in some cases with transfer to parishes outside the South.[43]

NEGRO REACTION IN THE DESEGREGATION STRUGGLE

To many white Americans the most surprising consequence of the school decision has been the reaction of Negroes. Their surprise arises from long-held illusions concerning the real feelings and attitudes of Negroes in regard to discrimination and segregation. While there was an awareness that educated Negroes were discontented with their status,[44] it appeared to many white people that the Negro masses had resigned themselves to minority status and had worked out a reasonably contented way of life on this basis. Thus, while it would be expected that the school case decision would greatly encourage Negroes, whites were unprepared for the great outpouring of concerted action in their own behalf which Negroes North and South have manifested.

That the real feelings of Negroes in the United States were quite different than the whites thought had been well documented in a survey conducted among soldiers in 1943. A representative sample of all Army troops was asked the question, "If you could talk to the President of the United States, what are the three most important questions you would ask him about the

---

[42] Ernest Q. Campbell and Thomas F. Pettigrew, *Christians in Racial Crisis: A Study of Little Rock's Ministry* (Washington, D.C.: Public Affairs Press, 1959).
[43] Quoted from Paul Y. Glock, who reviews Campbell and Pettigrew, *Christians in Racial Crisis* in *Public Opinion Quarterly*, 1960, 24: 378. By permission of the Editors.
[44] See Rayford W. Logan, ed. *What the Negro Wants* (Chapel Hill: University of North Carolina Press, 1944).

war and your part in it?" After analyzing the replies of the Negro troops in this study, Stouffer and his associates have this to say:

Four out of five Negroes came forward with at least one question, the same proportion as in a cross section of white soldiers queried at the same time . . . [H]alf of the Negroes who responded with questions to the President wrote explicit questions or protests about racial discrimination. Of the remaining comments, an unknown proportion were stated in terms which at least implied a racial emphasis but could not clearly be placed in this category on the basis of explicit statement. For this reason, the proportion of men reported as making racial comments is a minimum estimate of the racial response to the question. It will be noted that the question was so worded as to encourage focusing attention on the war and contained no manifest reference to race. While the results must be interpreted in the light of evidence . . . that the better educated and more critical were more likely to offer free answers, the fact that four-fifths of the Negroes volunteered at least one response means that a correction for nonrespondents would not alter the picture much. The high incidence of "racial" comments, therefore, is evidence of the Negro soldiers' concern with racial questions.[45]

Further indications of the preoccupation of Negro young adult males in general with their minority group status and of the specific aspects of discrimination which they resent can be seen in the kinds of questions raised in the Army survey, which are classified under seven headings substantially as follows:

1. Will there be less discrimination after the war?
2. Why doesn't he (the President) make people stop discriminating against us?
3. Why is there discrimination in the Army?
4. What does the Negro have to fight for?
5. If we have the duty to fight, why shouldn't we be given equal rights now and in the future?
6. What is the Negroes' part in the war?
7. Why can't Negro troops be moved out of the South?[46]

The wide discrepancy between the way the white people thought the Negro viewed the situation and the way the Negro actually viewed it arose in part from the social distance between the two groups. Whites seldom learned much of the Negroes' feelings. This was further aggravated by the tendency of Negroes when in conversation with white people to conceal their real feelings. Finally, the misinterpretation on the part of white people was in considerable measure a matter of wishful thinking. Many believed what they wanted to believe, which helped to justify the situation.

With the description of the Southern pattern delineated in Chapter 11 in mind, it is easily understandable that induration to minority status prevents many Negroes from active participation in the desegregation movement. Custom, with its associated habits and the experience of intimidation,

[45] Stouffer, et al., The American Soldier, pp. 503–504. By permission of publishers, Princeton University Press. Among the white troops asked the same question, there were no questions listed pertaining to racial discrimination.
[46] Ibid., pp. 504–506.

are still deeply rooted in the personalities of Southern-born Negroes, particularly the older generation. Not only is fighting for their rights fraught with danger, but it is often otherwise unpleasant. The experience of integration itself is often uncomfortable, which explains why many Negroes fail to exercise new rights even after they have been won. After the experience of integration in white schools, some Negro students prefer to go back to all-Negro schools. But this is not the prevailing mood in Negro response.

The Supreme Court's decision in the school cases raised the level of aspiration of American Negroes to new heights. For the first time since the Southern Reconstruction, younger Negroes have begun to feel that first-class citizenship is a possibility within their own lifetime. This is the key to understanding what has seemed to many Americans the most "unexpected consequence" deriving from a single event—the school decision—the previously unparalleled amount of united action among American Negroes themselves to press the advantage which the present favorable social climate presents. For an increasing number of American Negroes, "Uncle Tom" is now dead.[47] This prevailing mood among Negroes has been demonstrated in various protest movements, to which we now turn.

The Montgomery Bus Protest
"Jim Crow" laws as applied to public transportation have always been a major source of irritation to the colored minority. Aside from the principle involved, they have been a practical inconvenience, heightened by the fact that Negroes use public transportation more than whites. The practice promotes inefficiency and is costly. It is therefore not surprising that a Negro challenge on this point should be one of the next steps.

As is often the case in such a situation, the precise time and the particular place resulted from a fortuitous incident, in this instance in Montgomery, Alabama, in 1955. Montgomery's "Jim Crow" regulations were more than ordinarily cumbersome. Negroes were required to enter the front door of the bus, pay their fare, then disembark and go to the rear door to re-enter, and sit in a rear section.[48]

On December 1, 1955, a Negro woman refused to "move back" on a crowded bus so that a white woman could have her seat. For this the bus driver had her arrested. The Negro community of Montgomery reacted by organizing a boycott of the buses. The Negroes walked or arranged car pools. The movement was led by the Montgomery Improvement Association, formed for the purpose. The leader of the organization was the Rev-

[47] The name "Uncle Tom" has long been used among Negroes to designate those Negro leaders who have placated whites by not challenging the segregation system.
[48] See L. D. Reddick, *Crusader Without Violence: A Biography of Martin Luther King, Jr.* (New York: Harper & Brothers, 1959), Chs. 8, 9, and 10, for an account of the Montgomery bus protest movement.

erend Martin Luther King who, as a result of his role in the protest movement, emerged as a nationally recognized Negro leader. A remarkable development in this affair was the practically unanimous and well-disciplined co-
operation of the Negroes of the city. At the outset, the M.I.A. made the
modest demand for a "first come, first served" procedure in bus seating, the
Negroes to start from the rear, the whites from the front. Since this did not
challenge the Jim Crow principle directly, the National Association for the
Advancement of Colored People would not lend its assistance. However,
when this modest demand was rejected, the M.I.A. adopted the N.A.A.C.P.
viewpoint, calling for complete integration, and received the national organization's support.

The bus boycott continued for many months at great loss to the local bus
companies, while a legal case was carried finally to the United States
Supreme Court. On November 14, 1956, the Supreme Court upheld a previous district court decision declaring the transportation segregation laws of
the State of Alabama unconstitutional. On December 21, 1956, integrated
buses rolled down the streets of Montgomery for the first time, with Dr.
King and other M.I.A. leaders sitting up front.

The Tallahassee Bus Protest Movement

A somewhat similar situation arose in Tallahassee, Florida, six months
later.[49] On May 27, 1956, two coeds from a Negro college in Tallahassee
were arrested for having failed to move from the seat they had taken beside
a white woman in a crowded bus. The incident aroused the Negro community to organize a bus boycott, which elicited nearly unanimous support
of the Negro population in the community. Harassing tactics of all sorts
were employed by the white official community against the boycotters, such
as arresting drivers of "pool" cars on various pretexts. The boycott continued
into the winter of the following year. While it officially ended after a series
of law suits were filed, the Negroes generally stayed off the buses until the
outcome of the suits was announced.

The "Sit-Ins"

A new challenge to the caste system arose in 1960 in the form of so-called
"Sit-Ins." We have noted that the etiquette of the caste system prohibited
whites and Negroes from eating together seated at the same table. Increasingly, large merchandizing establishments, especially of the chain store
variety, have installed lunch counters as part of their business. No objections
have been forthcoming to Negroes shopping in such places; on the contrary,
their patronage has been welcomed. In deference to local custom, however,

[49] Charles U. Smith and Lewis M. Killian, *The Tallahassee Bus Protest* (New York:
Anti-Defamation League of B'nai B'rith, 1958).

these stores adhered to the practice of not serving Negroes at their lunch counters. Early in 1960, Negro students in Rock Hill, South Carolina, sat down at a local store lunch counter and requested service, which was refused. This began the "sit-in" movement, for the idea spread to other Southern cities. The management of the stores reacted at first by refusing service to Negroes and sometimes closed their counter service at the appearance of a Negro. Here and there "sit-inners" were arrested, and often high bails were set. Groups of white youths frequently gathered to jeer at the "sit-inners" and occasional physical abuse was used against the Negro youths. On the other hand, some white Southern students joined in the sit-ins.

The movement caught the imagination of Northern college students, both white and Negro, who indicated their support of the Southern Negro by picketing the Northern branch stores of the national chains involved. These pressures and the Negro students' persistence led to a sweeping victory. Within a year, most of the Southern branch stores were ordered by their top management to serve Negro customers on the same basis as whites. Following the first such change-overs, later ones tended to be put into effect without public announcement in order to avoid undue publicity or incidents.

Negro activity in the struggle for desegregation has been marked by spontaneity, discipline, and nonviolent techniques. While the Negro movements described above were aided by organizations once they were started, the origin of these and similar movements has often been in spontaneous acts by single individuals. Perhaps the most striking characteristic has been the orderliness maintained by Negroes in their various protest movements. News and television pictures of incidents arising in these protests usually show the whites in a most unfavorable light by comparison with the Negroes. The aid and training given the student "sit-inners" by organizations such as the Congress of Racial Equality (CORE) helps account for the discipline maintained. The widespread adoption of the techniques of passive resistance has been influenced by the leadership given by clergymen such as the Reverend Martin Luther King, and laity motivated by Christian pacifism.[50]

These activities also reflect the increasing impatience of younger and more educated Negroes with the slowness of the integration process, and with what they feel is the too-conservative leadership of the National Association for the Advancement of Colored People. This is well illustrated in the Freedom Rider Movement.

The Freedom Riders

In May, 1961, a group of Northerners of both races decided to test the extent to which certain Southern cities had complied or would comply with

[50] Reddick, *Crusader Without Violence*, pp. 133–135.

court rulings that segregation in the public facilities provided for passengers in interstate commerce was illegal. As the riders proceeded farther south they met with increasing resistance. Violence broke out in Alabama cities, culminating in a race riot in Montgomery. Finding evidence that the Montgomery officials had not attempted to protect the riders from white violence, Attorney General Robert F. Kennedy ordered federal marshals into the city, to remain until the immediate tension was abated. The freedom riders proceeded on to Mississippi, stopping in Jackson, where they were promptly arrested when they ignored police orders to leave a white waiting room. Despite the request by federal authorities to let matters "cool off," other, similar rides took place through various areas of the South, meeting with varying degrees of interference.[51]

FURTHER EXTRAREGIONAL PRESSURES: CIVIL RIGHTS LEGISLATION

The next important development in the desegregation struggle came from outside the region—from Congress and the Attorney General's Office.

Civil Rights Legislation: Federal Action on Voting

While the federal courts were continuing to issue orders of desegregation, the Congress of the United States made no supplementary moves to further the desegregation process until 1957, when the first Civil Rights Act for many years was passed.[52] Its main provisions were

(1) to authorize the establishment of a Commission of Civil Rights, whose duties were: to study the entire problem, including specifically denials of the right to vote; to collect information concerning legal developments denying equal protection of the laws; and to appraise the laws and policies of the federal government with respect to equal protection.
(2) to empower the Attorney General to seek court injunctions against interference with the voting rights of any individual.
(3) to establish a Civil Rights Division in the Department of Justice.

The Commission found that Negro registration had increased from 595,000 in 1947 to 1.2 million in 1956. This figure still represented only about 25 per cent of the nearly five million Negroes of voting age as of the 1950 census. In contrast, about 60 per cent of voting-age Southern whites were registered. Further analysis showed relatively greater Negro registration in the large Southern cities, such as Atlanta, Miami, and New Orleans, and from 5 per cent to none at all in rural counties, where Negroes constitute a large proportion of the population.

[51] See "Report on Freedom Riders" (Atlanta, Ga.: Southern Regional Council, 1961).
[52] Students of the realities of politics and government in the United States will know how the Southern congressional representation has special means at its command to block any legislation dealing with racial discrimination.

The fact that the Commission waited five months before a single complaint was forwarded to it is strong testimony to the influence of the intimidation implicit in the Southern segregation system. Complaints finally came, first from Alabama and Louisiana. In the hearings held in these states, local authorities tried to resist the purpose of the Commission by refusing to testify on the basis of state law, and adopted other obstructive procedures.[53] The hearings amply documented registration discrimination against Negroes. But the Commission found that the federal government faced difficulties in prosecuting violations.

The history of voting in the United States shows, and the experience of this Commission has confirmed, that where there is a will and opportunity to discriminate against certain potential voters, ways to discriminate will be found. The burden of litigation involved in acting against each new evasion. . . . county by county, and registrar by registrar, would be immense. Nor is there any presently available effective remedy for a situation where the registrars simply resign.

If any state were to pass forthrightly a law declaring colored citizens ineligible to vote, the Supreme Court would strike it down forthwith as in flagrant violation of the Fifteenth Amendment. The trouble, however, comes not from the discriminatory laws, but from the discriminatory application and administration of apparently nondiscriminatory laws.[54]

In order to strengthen the hand of the federal government, another Civil Rights Act was enacted in 1960 which (1) made any attempt to obstruct any court order a punishable offense; (2) required state officials to retain voting records for a period of 22 months; and (3) in the most important provision in the act, which was hotly debated in Congress, provided for the appointment of federal referees in cases where a district federal court finds persistent denial of voting rights. Such referees have the power to issue certificates enabling the defrauded citizen to vote.[55]

RELUCTANT COMPLIANCE

The dramatic character of the Southern interracial struggle has overshadowed the numerous instances of desegregation which are taking place without publicity. Illustrating this more ordinary process are instances of library desegregation.

Greenville, South Carolina, had separate branch library buildings for whites and Negroes. In the spring of 1960, some local Negro ministers and Negro high school students entered the white branch for service and were arrested. When the case was appealed, the library trustees and the city council closed the library. Subsequent decision by a federal court made it clear that the library must be

[53] "With Liberty and Justice for All," an abridgement of the *Report of the United States Commission on Civil Rights, 1959*, Chs. 4 and 5.
[54] *Ibid.*, p. 88.
[55] U.S. Public Law 86–449, May 6, 1960.

operated on a nonsegregated basis. Two weeks later the trustees decided to open on an integrated basis but with the reading tables to be segregated by sex. While Negroes continue to use the Negro branch, a moderate number of them now make use of the former white branch because of its superior holdings. The sex segregation of tables is no longer maintained.[56]

In a somewhat similar development,

a Danville, Virginia, library reopened on an "integrated basis" but removed all the tables so that the library functions only as place to borrow books for outside reading. Even browsing is not permitted. Card holders were required to fill out a four page form before getting a card.[57]

Desegregation has generally occurred in "piecemeal" fashion—that is, by a particular desegregation in a particular locality. It is significant that there have been few if any instances in the Deep South where the appropriate white authorities initiated a specific desegregation. Change in the pattern of race relations has occurred typically in this manner: (1) Negroes have challenged a specific form of segregation either by requesting that it be abolished or by deliberately violating a local law for the purpose of testing its legality. (2) White authorities then have denied the requests or arrested and found the Negroes guilty. (3) The Negroes, often with the aid of interested organizations, have carried the cases to court, preferably and eventually to a federal district court. (4) When faced with a court order to desegregate, white authority has either closed the public facility or reluctantly complied. Obviously, until the initiative to desegregate voluntarily becomes more common on the part of white authority, the process of desegregation will be slow. Nevertheless, reluctant compliance appears now to be superseding adamant resistance as the characteristic mode of Southern white response to the integration challenge.

Strengthening the trend toward compliance are certain consequences of the increased tension and conflict which affect the region adversely. (1) Unfavorable economic effects have been felt. The South loses many national conventions because the cities are unable to guarantee nondiscriminatory treatment of Negro members. Certain businesses otherwise disposed to locate in the South are waiting until the racial atmosphere is clearer. (2) The education of white as well as Negro children has been seriously disturbed. In Prince Edward County, Virginia, it was decided to close twenty-one schools rather than obey a specific court order to integrate. (3) Southern politicians with aspirations to national office have found that the segregationist label, necessary for election in the South, is often a disqualifying mark outside the region.

[56] We are indebted to Mr. Charles Busha, a library intern in Greenville at the time of this incident for this account.
[57] Gerald Tetley, "Danville Reopens," *Wilson Library Bulletin,* Nov. 1960, 35: 210.

SOUTHERN WHITE DESEGREGATION ACTIVITY

Despite the preponderant white sentiment in the South supporting the bi-racial system, we have noted that there has always been a white minority which believed in changing it, and that some of its members have actively worked toward this end. It is difficult to appraise the extent to which Southern white sentiment is changing. A Gallup poll in 1961 found substantially the same percentage of its white Southern sample—74 per cent—disapproving of school desegregation as in a similar poll in 1954, indicating no shift in attitudes.[58] Prominent among the organizations which seek to improve race relations is The Southern Regional Council. The creative function of this organization in reporting and analyzing the region's interracial situation has been seen in our frequent reference to their reports.

Labor Unions

Labor unions in the South have been a significant force pressing toward desegregation, despite the presence within many locals of the ambivalent attitudes we have noted in the discussions of other minority situations. Increasing unionization of Negro workers and the racial intermixing of local units has been a continuing, though sporadic, trend in the South since the mid 1930's.

A series of intensive studies[59] of Negro employment in selected areas of the South between 1948 and 1953 showed, in general, the following: (1) Wage differentials between Negro and white for the same level of work had largely disappeared. (2) Negroes were being increasingly unionized, and union contracts were increasingly protecting their wage and job seniority. (3) Mixed unions were increasing, but slowly; upgrading of Negroes was increasing, but no supervisory positions were open to Negroes where they would be in authority over whites. (4) Appraisal of the extent of intermixing Negroes and whites in the same work units was made difficult by the tendency to think of certain functional tasks as belonging to the Negroes and others to the whites. A later report on union race relations indicates further projection of these trends.[60]

Extra-regional pressures are involved. Since management tends to approach the problem on a purely economic basis, when these favor Negro employment and upgrading, national corporations override local custom.[61] Likewise, local unions are pressured by their national organization to implement the fair employment policy of the latter.

[58] Poll reported in the *New York Herald Tribune*, June 23, 1961.
[59] *Selected Studies of Negro Employment in the South* (Washington, D.C.: National Planning Association, 1955). Prepared for the NPA Committee of the South.
[60] Harry Fleischman, "Partial Report of Union Race Relations Progress, 1955—60" (American Jewish Committee, 1960), mimeographed.
[61] See *Selected Studies of Negro Employment in the South*, Case Study No. 1.

SOCIAL SCIENCE AND THE SOUTHERN RACIAL CONFLICT

Social science's interest in the changing Negro-white relations centers on these areas: the contributions which the events make to knowledge of social processes, especially the process of social change; and the contributions which existing social science can offer social actionists. In the concluding chapters we shall consider these topics in more detail. At this point we wish merely to draw attention to certain aspects of the Southern conflict which bear on theoretical problems.

Strain Toward Cultural Consistency

Social science has postulated that there is a strain toward consistency in each culture. The major values in the United States include freedom, equality, democracy, respect for the individual person, and a somewhat distinctive "moral" orientation.[62] The segregated interracial system of the South is grossly inconsistent with these values. Thus ultimately either the basic value system must change to conform to racial discrimination or racial discrimination must be abandoned. In Chapter 1 we noted that this moral dilemma was the basic theme of Myrdal's study, and that he expressed no doubt that race discrimination would have to give way.

Social Forces versus Direct Action

In analyzing social change, social science has found it useful to distinguish between change which is brought about by pressure of social forces and change brought about by social action—that is, by conscious, planned action. In the last analysis, the adaptive changes "forced" by social factors require social action. The central problem, then, is at what point concerted social action can be introduced to influence trends more directly or immediately. We have stressed that the balance of social forces in the postwar period was strongly in favor of the increasing integration of Negroes into American society. National Negro leadership chose to introduce direct action to accelerate this process, with, for the South, radical implications. The central query is, will this action accelerate the trend?

Law versus Other Means of Social Action

During this century social theorists have debated whether law can be an instrument for initiating social change as against other measures. During the first half of the century, influenced by William G. Sumner, theory leaned toward the viewpoint that law is powerless to change strongly held mores.[63] In the past two decades the conviction that law has power to effect

[62] Robin M. Williams, Jr., *American Society* (New York: Alfred A. Knopf, Inc., 1955), pp. 388–442.
[63] William G. Sumner, *Folkways* (Boston: Ginn & Company, 1907). The orthodox interpretation of Sumner's views on legislation is challenged in an article by Harry V. Ball, George Eaton Simpson, and Kiyoshi Ikeda, "Law and Social Change: Sumner Reconsidered," soon to be published.

change has gained more adherents. These contrasting modes of social thought have been reflected in the actual trends in social action. Before World War II social action against ethnic discrimination was directed generally at changing attitudes and persuading people of dominant status to cease discrimination, employing propaganda, education, and religio-ethical persuasion as methods. The postwar period has been marked by the use of law as the chief instrument to secure the desired ends, outside the South as well as within it.

On the basis of our materials we would suggest that the recent Southern events indicate that the value of a new law as an instrument of change is relative to the prevalence and intensity of the localized patterns of behavior and supporting institutions for or against it. Law appears to have been more immediately valuable in accelerating change in the North than in the South, and more immediately valuable in the local Southern areas where caste sanctions were less strong.

From another viewpoint, a case can be made that the pressure of outside law against the South was the only means by which a national objective could be achieved, if the national objective is considered to be racial equality within, say, fifty years. The resistance to the new legal interpretations in the South and the slow pace of compliance in even the border areas of the region suggest that the South by itself would have moved quite slowly in desegregation. One should expect to have to wait a generation or so, however, for the forced situational changes to be translated into intrapsychic acceptance; and one should expect protracted tension and conflict during this socially painful process.

The Strategy of Social Action

Social action to change social institutions always faces difficult problems of strategy—in this case, at what point in the segregation pattern to strike first. Insofar as the choice of attacking school segregation offered the best chance to obtain a reversal of the Plessy v. Ferguson decision, the result vindicates the strategy of the National Association for the Advancement of Colored People. However, an equally valid case can be made for the proposition that in a political democracy the right to vote can be a powerful lever in securing other rights and gains. For this reason we view with considerable interest the current action under the new Civil Rights legislation to secure the voting rights of Negroes.

The Interacting Effect of a Single Change on Other Points

The above considerations have to be considered in the light of what the effect is of change at a single point—in this case, the wall of caste in schools —on other points in the entire system. On the one hand, in the absence of the school case decision, white resistance to more moderate breaches might have been less vigorous at other points, as in the case of voting by Negroes. On the other hand, without the legal victory, Negroes might not have had the courage to undertake the bus and sit-in demonstrations.

The "Unexpected Consequences" of a Single Act

In planning a course of direct action to change a social situation, every effort should be made to anticipate what else will happen. Admittedly, social science has nowhere reached the point of being able to predict for social actionists exactly "what will happen if you do this." Certainly substantial resistance to school desegregation by white Southerners was to be expected, but it may be questioned whether the supporters of this line of action could have anticipated that some Southern communities—such as Prince Edward County, Virginia—would abandon all public school education rather than integrate even on a token basis. Similarly, while it was to be expected that a favorable court decision would greatly buoy the hopes of American Negroes, it may be questioned whether anyone anticipated that substantially all Montgomery Negroes would display the determined, united front seen in the bus protest movement.[64]

Passive Resistance as a Weapon for the Weak

While the protest movements carried on by Southern Negroes have been direct action, the techniques by which they have been conducted are associated with the term "passive resistance," as it has come to be known since Ghandi's time. Negro protest activities have on the whole been noncombative, as well as orderly and well disciplined. The relative success achieved in the areas where passive resistance has been demonstrated supports the view that it is an effective method for a heavily underpowered group in a struggle against the more powerful. It must not be overlooked, however, that the power of outside agencies—legal, governmental, and economic— has been arrayed on the side of the Negroes. Without this, passive resistance might have been less effective.

TOPICS FOR PROJECTS AND DISCUSSION

1. Explore the reasons why desegregation occurs more easily in Southern cities than in Southern smaller communities.
2. Explain why the trend of migration of Southern Negroes outside the region is not even more rapid. Why do so many of the migrants tend to concentrate in a few metropolitan areas rather than spreading out more widely?

---

[64] See A. Lee Coleman, "Predictions About Desegregation, 1950–55," *Social Forces*, March, 1960, 38: 258–262. The author summarizes the consensus of predictions by a number of social scientists concerning what would happen following the Supreme Court order to desegregate schools. The predictions have on the whole been verified by events.

3. Assuming that school desegregation in the South will take place in each community by some gradual plan, what sort of plan do you consider the best?
4. Design a project aimed at determining the attitudes of Northern whites toward the slow pace of school desegregation in the South thus far. Try it out and report your findings.
5. Compare the news coverage and opinions expressed in any available foreign publications with those in American publications following some outstanding "incident" in race relations.

SUGGESTED READING

Ashmore, Harry S. *An Epitaph for Dixie.* New York: W. W. Norton & Company, Inc., 1957.
> *A Southern liberal interprets the Southern interracial struggle following the school desegregation decision.*

Blaustein, Albert P., and Ferguson, Clarence Clyde, Jr. *Desegregation and The Law.* New Brunswick, N.J.: Rutgers University Press, 1957.
> *The legal developments and proceedings pertaining to the Supreme Court school desegregation decision are treated in detail.*

Carter, Hodding, III. *The South Strikes Back.* Garden City, N.Y.: Doubleday & Co., Inc., 1959.
> *An account of the White Citizens' Council Movement.*

Reddick, L. K. *Crusader Without Violence: A Biography of Martin Luther King, Jr.* New York: Harper & Brothers, 1959.
> *The biography is centered around King's role in the Montgomery Bus Protest.*

Williams, Robin M., Jr., and Ryan, Margaret W., eds. *Schools in Transition: Community Experiences in Desegregation.* Chapel Hill, N.C.: University of North Carolina Press, 1954.
> *Describes and analyzes school desegregation in areas outside the South before the 1954 school desegregation decision was made.*

14

Negro-White Relations:
The Changing North

Negro-white relations in the North since World War II have undergone significant change even though less dramatically than in the South. The war-induced trends resulted in lessened discrimination and increased integration of Negroes into Northern economic and civic life. Discrimination against Negroes in public facilities and services—restaurants, theaters, hotels, and so on—has markedly declined. In public community life, Negroes are found more actively participating in voluntary organizations and are often given recognition as representatives of their racial group and sometimes in their own right as persons. In politics, an increasing number of Negroes have been appointed and elected to public office. The armed services have been integrated.[1] Probably the greatest gains of all, and underlying all the other advances, have been the increasing vertical and horizontal mobility of Negroes in the occupational hierarchy and the increased income that has come with it, which we shall document in detail. At these more formal levels of interaction, interpersonal relations between Negroes and whites are increasing.

[1] See James C. Evans and David A. Lane, Jr., "Integration in the Armed Services," *The Annals of the American Academy of Political and Social Science*, March, 1956, 304: 78–85.

Despite these integrative trends in the North, in communities where Negroes are present in substantial numbers the Negro population still comprises a subcommunity set apart residentally and socially. The one area in which marked discrimination still prevails is in the denial of free access to housing. Since housing discrimination lies at the base of so much of the race relations problem in the North, we shall give it extensive consideration in this chapter.

The continued improvement in the status of Negroes in the North, proceeding with far less tension and conflict than in the South, stems from the earlier contrasts in Negro-white relations which we described in Chapters 11 and 12: segregation and discrimination lacked, for the most part, legal sanction; the economy of the North had no such clear pattern of occupational roles designated for Negroes as had the South; the presence of Negroes in large numbers was a more recent phenomenon; because of the presence of other minorities, focus on Negro-white relations as "the race problem" was never so marked. From the sociopsychological viewpoint, the greater prevalence of attitudes favorable to improvement in Negro status has been generally indicated in polls comparing the South and the rest of the nation. In a 1956 poll (see p. 294) 32 per cent of the Northern sample felt that it was "better to bring the races together" than "to keep them apart," as compared with 17 per cent of the Southern sample. The annual poll made by Gallup which found in 1961 only 24 per cent in the South favoring the school decision found 75 per cent in the North in favor. While the differences here are striking, the substantial numerical minority of Northern opinion still favorable to segregation and discrimination should not be overlooked.

RESIDENTIAL SEGREGATION OF NEGROES

In large cities with substantial Negro population, the residential distribution of Negro people tends to follow this pattern: (1) There is a main Negro area—Harlem, for example—not far from the central business district, where a large part of the population dwells and major businesses and recreational enterprises catering to Negroes are located. (2) There are other smaller pockets of almost exclusive Negro residents, typically sections becoming less desirable for residence. (3) There are some mixed white-Negro areas in the inner core of the metropolitan area where the white people are of lower economic level. (4) In general, no Negroes live in the suburbs or in white middle-class areas.

It follows from this kind of distribution that Negroes tend to live in substandard houses. "In 1950, nearly 70 per cent of nonwhite families lived in dwellings which were delapidated . . . nearly three times the proportion of white families living under such conditions."[2] "If the population density in

[2] An Abridgement of the Report of the United States Commission on Civil Rights (Washington, D.C.: Government Printing Office, 1959), p. 144.

some of Harlem's worst blocks obtained in the rest of New York City, the entire population of the United States could fit into three of New York's boroughs."[3] Usually somewhere on the fringe of some Negro or other area there is a Negro "middle-class" section, where higher-income Negroes have managed to keep relatively old dwellings in good condition. No significant break in the pattern of Negro residential segregation and concentration has occurred. According to the Griers, numerous local studies agree that segregation actually increased during the decade of the fifties. For example, in Syracuse, New York, in 1950, Negroes lived in one broad area, but in no particular tract were they more numerous than whites; by 1957, Negroes made up two-thirds of one tract and were rapidly approaching a majority in two more.[4] Forecasts are that by 1970 Negroes will compose one-third of Chicago's population, and that by the same year Negroes and Puerto Ricans will make up 45 per cent of Manhattan's population and one-third of the entire city.

The process by which Negro residential segregation comes about is roughly as follows. Start with a sizeable compact Negro area with population growing by births and even more by migration from the South. White resistance makes any movement directly outward or jumping to other low-rent areas difficult. However, some vacancies do occur in these other areas as upwardly-mobile non-Negro families move out. One or two Negro families thus manage to get into a new block or section. Whites, having tried first to prevent this "invasion" and failed, now react in panic and begin to move out rapidly. More Negroes move in, and the section becomes all Negro.[5]

White Reaction to Residential Concentration

Aside from other factors, a substantial amount of concentration of Negroes in the less desirable housing areas would occur because of low income and because there are no white people seeking such low rent areas. However, there is a growing number of Negro families who could afford better housing but cannot get it.

What are the main reasons—beliefs, fears, rationalizations—given by white people for rejecting Negroes as neighbors?

Deteriorating Property Values   The belief is widespread that entrance of Negroes into an area inevitably causes property value to decline. This belief does not objectively imply any personal prejudice.

Negro "Bad" Housekeeping and Disorderly Behavior   These two closely related beliefs held by whites are part of the long-held stereotype of Negroes

[3] *Ibid.,* p. 148.
[4] Eunice and George Grier, *Discrimination in Housing* (New York: Anti-Defamation League of B'nai B'rith, 1960), p. 11.
[5] See "Where Shall We Live?" *Report of the Commission on Race and Housing* (Berkeley and Los Angeles: University of California Press, 1958), Ch. 2.

as inferior people. They serve as logical reasons for not wanting Negroes as neighbors. Whites who hold these beliefs fear deterioration of the physical appearance and moral climate of their neighborhood.

Interracial Conflict   Whites express the fear that there will be interracial conflict in which their own safety will be endangered.

Fear of Inundation   It is commonly believed that once any Negro family moves into their block, others will follow and the neighborhood will become all Negro. As we shall see, it is this belief which stands as the last barrier to developing racially mixed residential areas.

Fear of Loss of Status   A revealing illustration of this feeling on the part of whites is seen in this incident:

A white woman, commenting on a Negro family's purchase of a house a few doors away, observed that it was a "fine" family, the husband was a surgeon, and she had no personal objection to them whatever. But, she added, people driving by see the little boy playing on the sidewalk. "How are they to know he is a doctor's son?"[6]

White Beliefs: Myth or Fact

The widespread belief of whites that the entrance of nonwhites into a neighborhood will automatically cause deterioration of property values has prompted extensive study of this subject. In an investigation by Laurenti,[7] price changes in property values in areas of seven American cities following the entry of nonwhites were compared with price changes in "control areas" of the same cities over the same periods of time. The main finding was that

. . . during the time period and for the cases studied, the entry of non-whites into previously all-white neighborhoods was much more often associated with price improvement or stability than with price weakening. A corollary and possibly more significant finding is that no single or uniform pattern of non-white influence on property prices could be detected. Rather, what happens to prices when non-whites enter a neighborhood seems to depend on a variety of circumstances which, on balance, may influence prices upward or downward or leave them unaffected.[8]

The major variables interacting in these local situations appear to be (1) strength of whites' desires to move out; (2) strength of nonwhites' desires to move in; (3) willingness of whites to purchase property in racially mixed neighborhoods; (4) housing choices open to nonwhites; (5) absolute and relative levels of house prices; (6) absolute and relative purchasing power of nonwhites; (7) state of general business conditions; (8) long-run trend values in areas involved; (9) time.[9] The first three of the above variables

[6] *Report of the Commission on Race and Housing*, p. 18.
[7] Luigi Laurenti, *Property Values and Race* (Berkeley and Los Angeles: University of California Press, 1960).
[8] *Ibid.*, p. 47.
[9] *Ibid.*, p. 47–48.

are not economic factors at all but sociopsychological. Thus what happens to property values when Negroes enter a new area is basically affected by how whites behave in general and the state of race relations in the community at the time.

From the extensive research of the University of California team on race and housing the following three generalizations emerge: (1) Where whites do not move in en masse, there is often little effect on property values, aside from those which might have taken place because of the changing situation of the areas as a whole. (2) It is after the area begins to reach a point of all-Negro occupancy that the less desirable consequences of overcrowding and downgrading of the area begin to set in. The first Negroes to take advantage of a vacancy in the white area tend to be similar in income, education, habits, and manners to their white neighbors. (3) Interracial conflict is generally less in the areas of mixed occupancy after the initial stages. (Interracial conflict is more frequent on the borders of Negro-white areas and at the beginning of the intrusion of Negroes in new neighborhoods.[10]

In their more detailed findings Glazer and McEntire stress the extent to which the minority develops a middle class which manifests the approved characteristics of the American middle class in general.[11] Such a development undermines the unfavorable stereotype, which is generally more easily applicable to the lower-class members of a minority. This favors the Japanese, for example, who are now largely middle class and have no new lower-class Japanese coming in. While the Negro middle class is growing, it is still disadvantaged by the continued recruitment of lower-class Negroes from the South, who serve to reinforce the northern white stereotyped image as pertaining to all Negroes. In another discussion, these authors find difficulty in isolating the role of prejudice for evaluation in the racial housing picture. On the one hand, the point that "the decisive factor in this poor housing is Negro economic weakness and white middle class fears of the deteriorating neighborhoods on Negro entry" leads them to state that "Prejudice in its pure form—that is to say as unreasoning and inflexible antipathy—rarely plays a decisive role in the determination of the housing of minority groups."[12] On the other hand, they state that "it is likely that color alone, serving as an almost unmistakable cue to behavior, plays a dynamic role in the situation. And for this reason changes in the character of the Negro group are likely to have less effect on their housing than real changes in the character of the Mexican or Puerto Rican group."[13]

[10] See Nathan Glazer and Davis McEntire, *Studies in Housing and Minority Groups*, and Davis McEntire, *Residence and Race* (Berkeley and Los Angeles: University of California Press, 1960).
[11] *Studies in Housing and Minority Groups*, p. 8.
[12] *Ibid.*, p. 4.
[13] *Ibid.*, p. 10.

Methods of Segregating Negroes in Housing

The methods used to keep Negroes from moving into white neighborhoods are numerous. Real estate boards have practiced a policy of racial discrimination, and most real estate agents will not handle transactions involving the entrance of Negroes into white residential areas. Too, home builders (with a handful of exceptions) do not build homes or developments for mixed occupancy. "It has been estimated that only about one per cent of all new private homes built in America in recent years have been available to nonwhites; and of these a large proportion were within the confines of cities."[14] In the suburbs, Negroes have apparently even lost some ground: the few suburban areas in which they have been permitted to locate are segregated developments, with sales only to Negroes. In general, mortgage-lending institutions refuse to finance the purchase of homes by nonwhites in white neighborhoods. These practices by the agencies involved in the housing business do not necessarily indicate prejudice but, rather, reflect business judgment based on their understanding of the basic prejudices against Negro neighbors of their dominant clientele. Finally, the policies, and more often actions, of government agencies and officials have supported racial housing segregation. While the Federal Housing Administration now has an open occupancy policy, in practice it does not attempt to control discrimination by private builders or lenders. The public housing program has insisted that minorities get a fair share of public housing but has generally left the matter of racial occupancy up to local authorities.

The Effects of Metropolitan Segregation

The large-scale concentration of Negro populations in the inner parts of the great metropolitan areas is a most significant development in the Northern scene. For an analysis of the implications of this phenomenon we draw upon the presentation of Morton Grodzins.[15]

The general picture for the future is thus clear enough: large non-white concentrates (in a few cases, majorities) in the principal central cities; large white majorities, with scattered Negro enclaves in their suburbs.[16]

Among the economic consequences of this phenomenon, Grodzins notes the decline of parts of the central city's business activity and associated property values. The replacement of higher quality stores and amusement places with all-night jewelry auctions and hamburger stands is characteristic notably of Chicago, Boston, and Los Angeles. While the present authors feel that there are other factors contributing to this trend, minority concentrations certainly reinforce it.

[14] Eunice and George Grier, *Discrimination in Housing*, p. 13.
[15] Morton Grodzins, *The Metropolitan Area as a Racial Problem* (Pittsburgh: University of Pittsburgh Press, 1958).
[16] *Ibid.*, p. 4.

Grodzins finds that a number of social consequences follow from metropolitan segregation. (1) The spreading of the slums. Given limited space for a growing population, relatively low incomes, and disproportionally higher rents for substandard dwellings, overcrowding will continue to be inevitable. Slum dwellers tend to be augmented by newcomers adjusting to a new environment. Thus the high rates of social pathologies characteristically associated with the above conditions may be expected to continue or increase. (2) Interracial conflict. It has been generally found that interracial conflict of the more explosive sort tends to occur along the boundary areas where the dominant race residents are trying to stem minority invasion. (3) Increased social isolation of Negroes from whites. Within the black belt, "hundreds of thousands of Negroes live, eat, shop, work, play and die in a completely Negro world with little or no contact with other people."[17] This statement appears to us to be too sharply drawn, particularly by including work with other phases of isolation. In fact, Grodzins refers to some participation of Negroes in mixed labor unions, some mixed blocks where friendly interracial neighborliness prevails, and a few newly formed interracial church congregations. Nevertheless, "the larger evidence is not that of integration nor intracommunity social gains. Rather it is in the direction of more uncompromising segregation and larger Negro slums."[18] (4) Finally, these large Negro concentrations have political consequences. Negroes are in a position to use their increasing political power to gain advantages for their group, as witness the increasing number of Negro officeholders. There is always the disturbing possibility of sharpened political conflict along race lines in the city proper as the nonwhites threaten to become a majority. Similarly, there is potential political conflict between the Negro-dominated city proper and the white-dominated suburbs, an old type of political conflict in the United States, acerbated by the consciousness of racial difference.

Concerning the above political analysis, we would suggest some qualification. The total Negro population of any community cannot be thought of as a political unity. Both major parties have their followers among Negroes. Through the respective political organizations Negroes are joined with whites against the opposing group, which is also mixed. Furthermore, with the increasing class differentiation in the Negro group, there is a tendency for political behavior to reflect class status rather than racial status. "Block" voting is seldom found among Negroes except when a particular immediate civil rights issue is involved.[19]

[17] *Ibid.*, p. 11.
[18] *Ibid.*, p. 12.
[19] Some political analysts of the 1960 national election suggested that the heavy Negro voting for the Democratic national ticket in Texas and South Carolina reflected a greater immediate concern over economic problems, especially growing unemployment, which always falls heavily on Negroes, than with the so-called racial issues.

"Segregation" in Northern Schools

The Supreme Court school decision had less impact on the North, because with some few exceptions segregated schooling for Negroes as an official policy had been abandoned wherever it had existed. Nevertheless, the decision prompted review of school districting and assignment practices. Since there remains much *de facto* school segregation arising from housing segregation, changes were made in some communities to promote more mixed enrollments. In New York City, a survey found that about ten per cent of the city's public schools were high concentration (Negro and Puerto Rican) schools. It was found also that these schools had relatively more teachers per pupil and more special services than the average. The less desirable findings were that these schools tended to be older structures and to have more substitute teachers. The survey led the New York City Board of Education to adopt a policy of more permissive school assignment, affording parents the right to apply for their children to be admitted into any city school, subject, of course, to available space. Nevertheless, it is obviously impossible actually to intermix the races in every school. In Manhattan, for example, three-fourths of the school children are Negro and Puerto Rican.[20]

In some smaller communities, tendencies to arrange pupil assignments in ways to minimize mixing the races have been alleged in cases brought to federal courts.[21]

Urban Redevelopment and Negro Housing

The housing segregation of Negroes (and in varying situations, of other minorities) is inextricably interrelated with metropolitan planning. For example, both the erection of low-cost housing developments and higher-class apartments on the fringes of the slums require the displacement of present occupants, who are frequently Negroes. In any building financed by federal funds, suitable relocation of displaced residents is supposed to be accomplished before new buildings can start, but when the present occupants are Negroes, finding a new residence is a difficult task. Thus either new developments are delayed or the displaced Negro residents face great hardship. A further development is predicted for the New York Metropolitan Region. "The major part of the further increase in Negro and Puerto Rican population in the Region is expected to occur outside the established areas of con-

[20] Nathan Glazer, "Is Integration Possible in New York Schools?" *Commentary,* September, 1960, 30: 185–193.

[21] In New Rochelle, New York, in 1961, local Negro parents brought the local school board to court on the charge of segregating Negro school children in the Lincoln School, which was over 90 per cent Negro. The Court found for the Negro parents, and an order to change the policy of assignment was upheld in appeal. In September, 1961, 267 pupils formerly registered at Lincoln were transferred to other schools in the city. See the *New York Times,* June 1, 1961 p. 1; August 3, p. 25; and September 2, p. 18, for the legal developments.

centration. That trend, plus the accelerated relinquishment of housing by middle income groups in fairly old urban areas of the Region, and the growing urban renewal effort, produces a continuing dispersion of the Region's slums."[22]

Breaks in Housing Segregation

In view of the strategic part that housing segregation plays in arresting the otherwise rapidly accelerating trend toward the integration of Negroes outside the South, special attention to the positive action taking place in this connection is pertinent. Such action has taken three forms: (1) public housing, (2) privately developed experiments in interracial housing, and (3) community organization to facilitate harmonious adjustment in areas of mixed occupancy.

Public Housing　We have noted certain problems affecting Negroes in slum clearance projects. According to McEntire, Negroes have received their appropriate share of the new housing; in fact, this has been their major source of good housing.[23] The main issue has been the matter of segregation or open occupancy, where federal authority has tended to defer to the wishes of local authority. Thus in the South public housing is entirely segregated; in the North the situation varies. McEntire finds Weaver's earlier judgment (1942) that public housing was "an instrument for the spread of segregation" was even more accurate in 1957.[24] On the other hand, where local authority supports mixed occupancy, public housing has provided successful demonstrations of integrated housing. In a special study of an integrated public housing project in Minneapolis, Deutsch and Collins found an increase in the favorability of attitudes toward their Negro neighbors and toward Negroes in general on the part of the white residents.[25]

Private Housing Developments　While observing that there has been a wide range of characteristic relations between the races in privately developed interracial experiments, the Griers note that such problems as did arise were not related to the interracial nature of the neighborhoods. "Seldom, however, was there a reported incident of hostility in which racial tension was a causative factor or in which race was mentioned by any of the participants even at the height of the acrimony. In no community studied was there any evidence of a hostile split between groups of residents organized along racial lines."[26]

Community Organization　There have been a few efforts at organizing

---

[22] Edgar M. Hoover and Raymond Vernon, *Anatomy of a Metropolis* (Cambridge, Mass.: Harvard University Press, 1959), p. 237.

[23] Davis McEntire, *Residence and Race*, p. 328.

[24] *Ibid.*, p. 321.

[25] Morton Deutsch and Mary E. Collins, *Interracial Housing: A Psychological Evaluation of a Social Experiment* (Minneapolis: University of Minnesota Press, 1951).

[26] Eunice Grier and George Grier, *Privately Developed Interracial Housing: An Analysis of Experience* (Berkeley and Los Angeles: University of California Press, 1960), pp. 199–200.

community groups in areas of mixed occupancy for the purpose of establishing a pattern of friendly relations, usually initiated and led by civic-minded people of dominant status. The following is an example.

For years a high class residential area around the University of Chicago, Hyde Park-Kenwood, began developing pockets of slums, then found itself turning from a white to a Negro neighborhood. Concerted community action, with citizens' participation on a scale perhaps unmatched in the nation, has done much to slow the drift toward blight. Moreover, the neighborhoods set out to do so on a deliberate interracial basis. In the process, their residents learned much about how the ideals of brotherhood differ from the practices. Leaders of the effort found out how to make the city government help them enforce decent living standards. But continuing Negro pressure for more housing raised doubts as to whether this unique and pioneering effort could succeed in the face of overwhelming odds.[27]

Experience in all three of these forms of racial integration in housing indicates that the obstacle to success is the fear by whites of inundation. Polls of white attitudes over twenty years show an increasing willingness of white people to live in an integrated area.[28] But by an integrated area the respondents do not mean one that is largely Negro. The crucial factor in planning mixed areas is to prevent too many Negroes from entering. While "the tipping point" cannot be defined with precision, it appears to be well below 50 per cent Negro. In a private interracial development in Concord Park, in the Philadelphia region, the builders hoped for a Negro proportion of about 20 per cent. When forty of the first fifty houses built went to Negroes, the management placed a 45 per cent limit on sales to Negroes in an effort to preserve the interracial character of the project.[29] In an integrated section of Lakeview, Long Island, Negro residents took the initiative themselves in trying to discourage further Negro purchases in the area. A nonwhite leader of the community organization involved complained that some real estate dealers of both races showed white-occupied homes up for sale to Negro prospects only and advised white owners to "sell now or it may be too late."[30]

Reflecting the problems outlined above and the kind of social action likely to increase in the future is this development reported for Teaneck, New Jersey, a residential suburb in the New York Metropolitan Area. When Negroes from the neighboring community of Englewood began to move into Teaneck in 1954 there was at first the usual reaction by white residents. This was followed, however, by community action through workshops aimed at stopping panic selling and otherwise bringing about amiable interracial relations.[31]

[27] Martin Millspaugh and Gurney Breckenfeld, *The Human Side of Urban Renewal* (Baltimore, Md.: Fight-Blight Fund, Inc., 1958), p. 91. By permission.
[28] McEntire, *Residence and Race*, p. 81.
[29] *Ibid.*, p. 214.
[30] The *New York Times*, June 20, 1961, p. 35.
[31] See "Teaneck Studies How to Integrate," the *New York Times*, March 5, 1961, p. 60.

THE ECONOMIC SITUATION OF THE NEGRO IN THE UNITED STATES

1960 survey by the Federal Department of Labor attests to the continued improvement in the economic situation of the Negroes in the United States.[32]

Occupational Distribution

Table 13 reflects the changes in the occupational distribution of Negro males for the nation as a whole from 1940 to 1960. The percentage gain of Negroes is noticeably higher than that of whites in all the nonfarm occupations above the laborers' level except at the professional and technical levels, where the percentage increase of both groups is about the same. (It will be recalled that segregated racial communities create opportunities for Negro professionals to serve a Negro clientele.) A similar table comparing the distribution of Negro women wage earners shows still heavy concentration in service work, about 59 per cent in 1960 as against 68 in 1940. Over these twenty years the percentage of Negro women engaged in household domestic service decreased and the percentage engaged in other service occupations increased. While the percentage is still small, it is significant to note the increase in the employment of Negro women in the clerical and sales

TABLE 13
Per Cent Distribution of Employed Males by Major Occupation Group, Color, and Sex, April 1940 and April 1960[33]

MAJOR OCCUPATION GROUP AND SEX	WHITE		NONWHITE	
	1940	1960	1940	1960
Total employed men	100.0	100.0	100.0	100.0
Professional, technical, and kindred workers	5.9	11.3	1.9	4.0
Managers, officials, and proprietors, except farm	10.6	14.6	1.6	2.7
Clerical and kindred workers	7.1	7.3	1.2	5.1
Sales workers	6.7	6.5	.9	1.9
Craftsmen, foremen, and kindred workers	15.5	20.0	4.4	9.0
Operatives and kindred workers	18.8	19.1	12.2	24.4
Laborers, except farm and mine	7.5	6.3	20.5	23.3
Service workers, except private household	5.8	5.7	12.4	14.6
Private household workers	.2	.1	2.9	.2
Farmers and farm managers	14.0	6.3	21.3	5.7
Farm laborers and foremen	6.8	3.0	19.9	8.9
Occupation not reported	1.0	—	.7	—

[32] United States Department of Labor, *The Economic Situation of Negroes in the United States*, October, 1960, Bulletin S–3.
[33] *Ibid.*, p. 15.

categories. In clerical and kindred occupations, the percentage of Negro women jumped from 1.0 to 8.9. In 1940 only 0.6 per cent were employed as sales workers, while in 1960 the figure was 1.5 per cent.

Income of Negroes

The Labor Department's 1960 survey summarized its findings concerning the wage and salary income of Negroes as follows:

Since earnings vary with occupation, the relative rise in Negroes' occupational levels, as well as their continuing disproportionate concentration in the less skilled jobs, is reflected in their earnings. Whites average higher earnings than Negroes, but the gap is somewhat less wide than in earlier years. In 1939, nonwhite male workers earned, on the average, 41 per cent as much as whites; by 1958, 58 per cent. The corresponding percentages for nonwhite female workers were 36 and 45.

These averages are reduced by the inclusion of many part-time or part-year workers. If figures are limited to those who worked a full year, nonwhites do relatively better. For full-year full-time work, nonwhite males in 1958 averaged $3,368, which was 65 per cent of the rate for white males.

When family rather than individual incomes are compared, the Negro-white difference is somewhat less, as a higher proportion of Negro family members are in the labor force.[34]

Unemployment

The summary picture of the unemployment situation among Negroes as compared with others is shown in the same survey.

Unemployment rates are generally higher among Negro than among white workers. One factor is the disproportionate number of Negroes who are in unskilled work, where unemployment is regularly heavier. Another is the frequently lower seniority ratings of Negro workers, because of their more recent entry into factory and office work.

In the 1958 downturn, unemployment rates rose in all groups. The rate rose about as much for nonwhite as for white men, and continued roughly twice as high. About 14 per cent of the nonwhite male workers, a large proportion of them from unskilled and semiskilled occupations, were unemployed and seeking work in 1958, compared with an average of about 6 per cent of white workers. By 1959, both rates had declined, but that of nonwhites had declined relatively less. About 11.5 per cent of nonwhite men were still unemployed, compared with 4.6 per cent of whites.[35]

Aside from the general over-all national trend favorable toward increasing integration of minorities, two important specific forces have accelerated the process in the employment of Negroes: government, at all levels, and labor organization, especially at the national level. Government has pursued, at least outside the South, a vigorous policy of nondiscrimination with regard to its own employees. In 1940, of the total employment in federal, state, and

---

[34] *Ibid.*
[35] *Ibid.*, pp. 6–7.

local government, 5.6 per cent, was nonwhite; by 1960 the percentage had increased to 10.7, roughly about the percentage of the national nonwhite population. A second significant governmental activity promoting Negro employment has been the establishment by an increasing number of states of a state agency similar to the wartime Federal Fair Employment Practices Commission abandoned by the federal government at the end of World War II. By the end of 1960, seventeen states, having half the population of the country and a fourth of its Negro population, had passed enforceable fair employment practices legislation.[36] While generally these agencies have enforcing power, in practice they have proceeded through public education and by informal efforts to persuade offenders to stop employment discrimination. Such efforts have met with much success; so far few cases have reached formal hearing or the courts.

When the new constitution of the merged AFL-CIO national union was adopted in 1955, one of the objectives listed was "To encourage all workers without regard to race, creed, color, or national origin to share equally in the full benefits of union organization."[37] The new organization also established a Civil Rights Department to further this objective. In unions organized along industrial lines, the trend has been toward the integration of Negroes in mixed unions. In the trade or craft unions, however, the fact that only a limited number of apprentices are admitted makes it especially hard for members of minority groups to enter. For example, in May, 1958, in San Francisco, there was reported only one Negro apprentice in the metal trades and none in the apprentice programs of other trades. Recent studies have shown a somewhat similar situation in a number of other cities.[38]

THE NORTHERN PROSPECT

On the assumption that the present social forces impinging upon Negro-white relations in the North are likely to continue for some time to come, the prospect ahead appears to involve a projection of the current trends. In summary, these are as follows:

1. Continued decline in discrimination against Negroes in employment, more particularly their increasing placement in higher-ranking positions. The rapidity with which Negroes will improve their occupational status depends not only on the decline in discrimination but also on the extent to which Negroes acquire the necessary training and education to qualify for

[36] Several of these agencies are also charged with enforcing nondiscrimination rules in public accommodation, housing, or education.
[37] Ibid., p. 23.
[38] New York State Commission against Discrimination, Apprentices, Skilled Craftsmen and the Negro, p. 15. This publication describes historical and national aspects of the subject.

new occupational opportunities. Employers ready to employ Negroes in new positions frequently cannot find qualified Negro applicants.

2. Continued improvement in the welfare of Negroes, which will follow from their improving occupational status.

3. Continued decline in discrimination against Negroes in all aspects of Northern community life except housing. From this will follow an increasing association of Negroes with whites on a nominal basis of equality in formal relations.

4. Growth of the Negro population outside the South at a rate noticeably higher than that of the general population, primarily because of continued migration of Negroes out of the South.

5. Dispersion of the Negro population in uneven fashion. Both population growth and urban redevelopment will force a spreading out of Negroes in two main patterns: (a) Dispersion to other deteriorating areas in either the inner core of the metropolis or satellite cities. This will mean a spreading of the slums, with their associated physical appearance and social conditions. (b) On a smaller scale, the invasion of better residential areas in the suburbs by the growing Negro middle class.

6. Each of these dispersive movements will be accompanied by a localized rise in interracial tensions, with occasional overt conflict as white residents resist Negro invasion. In most such situations the initial period of tension will be followed by some new accommodation on a relatively harmonious basis, either by the area's becoming all Negro through white withdrawal or by adjustment to mixed occupancy as long as the Negro proportion remains a minority. Thus the state of race relations in the North will be quite uneven from area to area in each of these stages. As more neighborhoods or communities experience this same situation, the development of community planning for the smoother adjustment of this repeating process may be anticipated.

7. The above trends are interactive, each reinforcing the other. As more whites associate with Negroes on the job and in the political club, the possibilities of interracial friendship emerge. As well-kept Negro suburban homes increase, white fears of the consequences of having Negro neighbors will decrease. As more whites observe the competent performance of individual Negroes in higher-prestige roles, the illusion that low mental ability is associated with Negroid genetic heritage will disappear. In short, the white American image of the Negro will fade.

8. In each Northern community with substantial Negro population a distinctive Negro subcommunity will continue to exist for a considerable time. In their informal relations and in those formal associations in which "sociable" interaction is extensive, Negroes will largely associate with other Negroes. Corollary with this will be the continuance of distinctive national Negro organizations—the press, church organizations, and national lodge as-

sociations, as well as the national organizations devoted to improving Negro status.

The persistence of a separate Negro structure is not to be considered cultural pluralism. American Negroes are not a culturally distinctive component of American society. The common heritage of slavery and the common experience of discrimination account for whatever "consciousness of kind" American Negroes possess, and dictate whatever separate social relationships remain. Racial pride manifests itself largely in elation over the contributions —increasing in number—made by Negroes to the common *national* life. Thus the continued separateness of Negroes in the United States is a function of their distinctive biological heritage and the still persistent belief of white Americans that this alone is a barrier to full acceptance.

TOPICS FOR PROJECTS AND DISCUSSION

1. Design a project aimed at discovering the attitudes of Northern whites toward having Negroes as neighbors. Try it out on a sample of Northern whites, preferably in an area where no Negroes now live. Report your findings.
2. Discuss the topic "Vested Interests among Northern Whites as an Influence Perpetuating Discrimination." Follow with a discussion of "Vested Interests among Northern Negroes Having a Similar Consequence." These are also good subjects for term papers.
3. Design a project aimed at determining the attitudes of Southern whites toward the Northern manner of dealing with Negroes. If you live in the South, try out your design on a sample of Southern whites and report your findings.
4. State and defend as many reasons as you can to account for the fact that comparatively fewer Negro young people than whites aspire to higher education.
5. Do you agree with the proposition that Negroes in the United States are not a distinctive cultural group? Discuss. Consider hypothetical circumstances under which Negroes in this country might become a more distinctive cultural group.

SUGGESTED READING

Laurenti, Luigi. *Property Values and Race.* Berkeley and Los Angeles: University of California Press, 1960.
> *An excellent research into the crucial problem of minority housing.*
Lincoln, C. Eric. *The Black Muslims.* Boston: The Beacon Press, 1960.
> *A scholarly study of a Negro sect illustrating Negro nationalism.*
McEntire, Davis. *Residence and Race.* Berkeley and Los Angeles: University of California Press, 1960.
> *The final summary of the extensive research into the housing of minority groups conducted by the author and numerous associates.*
Markham, R. H. "The Case of the Negro Wacs." *The Christian Science Monitor* (Boston, May 5, 1945).
> *The case of insubordination on the part of Negro female soldiers illustrates the changing status aspirations of Negroes.*
Reitzes, Dietrich C. *Negroes and Medicine.* Cambridge, Mass.: Harvard University Press, 1958.

An outstanding study of the situation facing Negroes who apply for admission to medical schools.

Stouffer, Samuel S. *et al.* "The Negro Soldier," Chapter 10 in *The American Soldier*. Princeton, N.J.: Princeton University Press, 1949.
Presents the results of the most definitive research conducted on Negro soldiers in the United States Army during World War II.

Vose, Clement E. *Caucasians Only: The Supreme Court, the NAACP, and the Restrictive Covenant Cases*. Berkeley and Los Angeles: University of California Press, 1959.
Describes the sociological and political events leading to decisions in restrictive covenant cases and appraises the results of the Supreme Court's rulings.

Wilson, James Q. *Negro Politics: The Search for Leadership*. Glencoe, Ill.: The Free Press, 1960.
A study of the participation of Negroes in political and civic life in Chicago in particular, and in the North in general.

15

Indians in the United States

An account of the relations between the Indians of the Americas and the white Europeans who invaded their domain reveals significant contrasts between the areas dominated by conquerors from the Latin nations and those dominated by the English. The Spaniards employed various devices to force the Indians to work for them. While this exploitation greatly decimated the Indian population, in the Latin-American nations which Gillen has described as Mestizo America, there are to be found today many Indian groups who remain distinctively Indian in their culture. The large mestizo populations of these nations indicate that, to a far greater extent than north of the Rio Grande, the descendants of the Indians of colonial times have been integrated into the general national societies, largely into the peon class. The general cultures of Mestizo America have pronounced Indian influences.

In contrast, the English settlers in North America pushed the Indians off the land to work it themselves, subsequently with the aid in the South of Negro slaves. As in Latin America, the Indian population in the United States was greatly decimated, but more as a result of unsuccessful warfare with the whites and the expropriation of their land and resources than through harsh conditions of slavery or peonage. Again as in Latin America, many Indian societies survived and retained their tribal cultures. But they survived largely on the fringes of the new North American society, isolated from it rather than a part of it.

The problems arising from these two contrasting patterns of Indian-white relations likewise differ. In Mestizo America, the groups remaining Indian in their way of life constitute substantial portions of the population; and the welfare of such groups effects in high degree the welfare of the nations involved.[1] The problems of the large mestizo group are not peculiarly Indian but are interrelated with the broad problems of class difference and the development of democratic institutions. In the United States and Canada, on the other hand, the Indian problem is in comparison more particularistic and relatively minor. The special character of the Indian problem in the United States is attested by the establishment of the Indian Service as a branch of the federal government with no counterpart in all the other minority situations. Its minor place is seen in the fact that the Service concerns itself with less than 0.5 per cent of the total national population.

THE INDIAN POPULATION

Composition of the Population

Estimates of the number of aborigines in the Western Hemisphere at the time of the white man's coming vary widely. Lorimer cites estimates ranging from 8 to 13 million.[2] Means, however, estimates the number of Indians of the Inca Consolidation alone to have been 16 million.[3]

Any estimate of the present Indian population of the Americas is exceedingly unreliable, not only because of inadequate statistical counts but also because persons of varying degrees of Indian ancestry have been so largely incorporated into the common national populations that the lines of racial division have become highly obscured. Lorimer summarizes the situation as follows: "The number of pureblood Indians in the Western Hemisphere may be greater today than at the time of Columbus; with the number of persons usually considered as Indian it is almost certainly greater; and the total Indian stock, including its fractional elements in the whole population, is far greater."[4] The same author further observes: "Mestizos, or Ladinos, who draw their genetic heritage in part from Amerindian and in part from other stocks now outnumber pureblood Indians both in Latin America and in the United States."[5]

[1] John Gillen, "Mestizo America," *Most of the World*, ed. Ralph Linton (New York: Columbia University Press, 1949), pp. 156–174. Mestizo America includes all the nations south of the Rio Grande except Argentina and Uruguay, which are practically all Caucasian in composition, and Brazil, where there is a proportionally smaller Indian population, and where Indians have not been as integrated into the total national life as in Spanish America.
[2] Frank Lorimer, "Observations on the Trends of Indian Population in the United States," *The Changing Indian*, ed. Oliver La Farge (Norman: University of Oklahoma Press, 1942), p. 11.
[3] Philip A. Means, *Ancient Civilization of the Andes* (New York: Charles Scribner's Sons, 1931).
[4] Lorimer, "Observations," p. 11. By permission.
[5] *Ibid.*, p. 12.

Estimates of the number of Indians in 1492 in the area which is now the United States range from 700,000 to 1,000,000. By the time Indians became official wards in 1871 their population had been reduced to less than half a million. It is generally agreed that under the early reservation system the population declined still further, reaching its lowest around 1900. In the official census count, these trends are reflected in the following figures:

TABLE 14
Indian Population of the United States[6]

1890	248,253
1920	244,437
1940	333,369
1950	357,499
1960	523,591

Students of Indian affairs have considered the census counts an under-estimate. Thus it may be that the 46.5 per cent increase reported in the Indian population between 1950 and 1960 reflects a more accurate count.

The difficulties in determining the actual number of Indians stem from problems of definition, particularly in regard to the classification of mixed bloods. Census enumerators are instructed "to return as Indians, not only those of full Indian blood, but also those of mixed white and Indian blood, except where the percentage of Indian blood is very small or where the individual is regarded as a white person in the community where he lives."[7] However, persons of whatever admixture of Caucasian genetic strains, or in many instances, of Negro-Indian mixture, who have remained in the tribes and therefore on the Indian Service rolls are considered Indian because they live as Indians. The future size of the Indian population depends not only on natural growth but also on the extent to which mixed bloods choose to remain "Indian" or to pass into the white world.

Distribution of the Indian Population

While there are people classified by the census as Indian in nearly every state in the Union, our interest focuses on those who live as Indians in groups. Some Indian landholdings are to be found in 32 of the 50 states. Their distribution has remained generally the same for many years.[8]

1. *The Southwest.* Primarily Arizona and western New Mexico. Major groups are the Navaho, Hopi, Papago, Pueblo, and Apache. In this area live nearly one quarter of the Indians of the United States, numbering about 110,000 in 1960.

[6] United States Census data for the specified years.
[7] H. L. Shapiro, "The Mixed-Blood Indian," in *The Changing Indian*, p. 20.
[8] See Sol Tax, "What the Indians Want" in the Chicago *Sunday Sun Times*, June 11, 1961, Secton 2, p. 1, for a map showing the numerical distribution of Indians by states. See G. E. E. Lindquist, *The Indians in American Life* (New York: Friendship Press, 1944), for a map showing the distribution of Indian Tribes by area.

2. *California and the Northwest.* An intermittent scattering of Indian tribes through California, Nevada, and Utah, including many Shoshone and Paiute. A further intermittent but less wide scattering of reservations in Washington, Oregon, Idaho, Montana, and Wyoming.

3. *The North Central.* The area of greatest concentration here is in South Dakota with its large Sioux population, followed by substantial reservations in North Dakota and Minnesota and scattered small bands in Nebraska and Iowa on the south and in Wisconsin and Michigan on the east.

4. *Oklahoma.* Next to the Southwest region, this former Indian territory has the largest concentration of Indians, totaling about 52,000 in 1960. Linked with this area are small bands in Northern Kansas.

5. *North Carolina.* While some small Indian groups are located in widely scattered places in Texas, Louisiana, Mississippi, Alabama, Florida, South Carolina, and Virginia, the Cherokee tribes of North Carolina far outnumber all other Indian groups combined in the South.

6. *New York.* Of the relatively few Indians to be found in the Northeast, most are located in the rural areas of New York state, including the Seneca, the Onondaga, and the Tonawanda. There are very small bands in Rhode Island and Maine.

Racial Characteristics

The aborigines of the American continents are generally classified as a variety of the Mongolian stock. Their distinguishing physiognomic features, according to Kroeber, are straight hair, slight facial and body hair, brown skin color. They are variable in head form, medium in nasal index, medium in prognathism, tall to medium in height, and generally broad faced. Having migrated to the Americas perhaps eighteen thousand years ago and having subsequently been hemispherically endogamous until 1492, the Indians developed a type distinguishable from the original Asiatic strains. It is interesting that Kroeber considers the Indians, along with present-day Malaysian types, to be earlier developments of the Mongoloid family than the so-called Mongoloid proper, typified by the modern Chinese. The oblique or "Mongoloid" eye, typical of the latter, which the Indians generally lack, is considered by Kroeber a later development.[9]

Intelligence

Earlier studies comparing the intelligence test scores of Indians with whites generally showed Indians averaging below whites.[10] As with many other minorities, lack of motivation affects performance; and more than with Negroes, language difficulties handicap Indians. For example, the Indian

[9] A. L. Kroeber, *Anthropology* (New York: Harcourt, Brace & Co., Inc., 1948), pp. 136–137.
[10] See Otto Klineberg, *Characteristics of the American Negro* (New York: Harper & Brothers, 1944), pp. 70–71; also see pp. 86–88 for a brief summary of comparative Indian-white mental test studies.

children who chose "dust" or "excitement" as a response to the item "crowd," may have been just as logical based on their own experience as those who chose the "right" answers: "closeness" and "numbers." Later and more comprehensive mental testing programs yielded results more favorable to the Indians, pointing to the conclusion that Indians are innately as intelligent as any other ethnic group.[11]

INDIAN SOCIETIES AND CULTURES

From the viewpoint of current minority problems, it is perhaps more important for the Americans of dominant status to understand the culture and personality of Indians than similar characteristics of immigrant groups. The latter, as we have seen, early desire to become American and are, for the most part, quickly assimilated. Indians, however, in considerable measure, do not want to become assimilated.

The future of Indian culture and welfare depends very largely on the policy adopted by the white population. And no policy will be successful which is not based on an understanding of Indian culture. Acquiring such an understanding is immeasurably complicated by the fact that Indian culture is not one but a variety of cultures developed over thousands of years before the white man's coming and greatly changed by his presence. Space permits only a brief tracing of the post-Columbian development of Indian societies and a general statement of their characteristics.

At the time of discovery by the European invader, there existed north of the Rio Grande in the area to become the United States more than 600 distinct tribal societies. Contrary to the trend in Mexico and South America toward consolidation, the North American natives had remained in small units. The process of subjugation of the North American Indians tended to keep them distinct from each other and to retard their acculturation to colonial societies. In spite of this, the general principle that cultural diffusion always takes place when different peoples meet, operated between Indian and white societies. The influence of white culture on the Indians is illustrated in Radin's comments:

The use of iron, the adoption of the horse, and the impact of Christianity and of European culture in general, often produced new expansions of native culture that were rarely felt by the Indians themselves to be anything but legitimate extensions and growths of their own civilizations. . . .

In the United States proper the three outstanding examples of such new developments and recreations are the Iroquois, the Southwestern Pueblos, and the Navajos. The three major traits we ordinarily associate with the last tribe—sheepherding, silverwork and blankets—all represent borrowings from the Spaniards. Practically all the great rituals, so distinctive of their life today, come from other

[11] See *Annual Report of the Secretary of Interior for the fiscal year ending June 30, 1948* (Washington, D.C.), p. 383, for comparative Indian-white mental test studies.

Indian tribes with whom they have come into contact indirectly through the intermediation of their white conquerors. And yet no Navajo would understand what an anthropologist or an historian meant if he pointed out that most of what he possessed today had come to him from non-Navajo sources.[12]

Among the many elements of white culture which the North American Indians borrowed to which Wissler calls special attention are the horse, the gun, and alcohol drinking.[13] Of these, the horse was clearly the most useful. On the Great Plains, where the hunting of buffalo constituted a main economic activity, the greater speed and safety which the horse provided was highly advantageous. The role of the gun was more ambivalent. Its value for hunting and for warfare with other tribes was in part offset by its very efficiency. It promoted too great a decimation of both Indian and game populations. The drinking of alcohol, which Indian tribes first learned from the white man, was altogether a disorganizing influence, the more so because with no previous experience with this beverage, the Indian cultures lacked mores to control its use.

The contributions of the Indian to the normative American culture and indeed to world culture have been more considerable than the average American realizes. In brief summary may be noted food plants introduced to the white man by the Indian—maize, potato, tomato, chocolate—to name only a few; medicinal plants, such as cascara, cocaine, and quinine; hammocks, snowshoes and toboggans; linguistic adoptions into the American English language such as "pow wow," "ambush," and whole phrases such as "bury the hatchet"; in art, geometric designs and styles in basketry and pottery, and many melodies which have been adapted in American music.[14]

General Characteristics of Indian Societies

Notwithstanding the difficulties of generalizing about such widely varying cultures, certain broad characteristics of Indian societies may be noted, with some reference to their contrast with the cultures of the white invaders. The characteristic features which we shall discuss here apply to the Indian people before the period of wardship.

1. The Indian cultures were all preliterate. Thus knowledge and mores were inculcated through the spoken word and the teaching of youth by the elders.

---

[12] From *The Story of the American Indian* by Paul Radin. Published by Liveright Publishing Corporation, New York City. Price $2.98. Copyright, 1934 and 1944, by the Liveright Publishing Corporation, pp. 374–375.

[13] Clark Wissler, *Indians of the United States* (Garden City, L. I.: Doubleday & Co., Inc., 1946), Ch. 20.

[14] See Clark Wissler, "Contributions of the American Indians," *One America*, eds. Francis J. Brown and Joseph Roucek (New York: Prentice-Hall, Inc. 1946), Ch. 32. Also, see Irving Hallowell, "The Impact of the American Indian on American Culture," *American Anthropologist*, 1957, 59: 201–211.

2. While all preliterate societies appear small in contrast with modern societies, Indian societies north of the Rio Grande tended to be small even in the perspective of primitive societies. Tribal relationships were almost entirely personal, and the Indians lacked experience with those secondary, impersonal, formalized relationships characteristic of larger-scale civilization.

3. The Indian economies were primarily hunting and gathering, with fishing in certain areas. In what is now the United States, hoe agriculture was practiced among the Eastern tribes and the Southwest, where maize growing was prevalent. When hoe agriculture was practiced, it was usual for the women to perform the gardening tasks,[15] a point to keep in mind when noting the later efforts to transform Indian men into farmers. The attitudes of nonagricultural Indians toward the land are revealed in the words of Wowoka, a Nevadan Indian who founded a new religion among the Western Indians in the nineteenth century.

You ask me to plow the ground . . . Shall I take a knife and tear my mother's bosom? Then when I die she will not take me to her bosom to rest. You ask me to cut grass and make hay and sell it, and be rich like white men but how dare I cut my mother's hair?[16]

4. While individuals sometimes owned items of personal adornment and had property rights to certain songs and crests, property with economic value usually belonged to extended kin or tribal groups. It was inconceivable that any individual member of the group should lack necessities as long as they were available to any one else.

5. Class distinctions were generally less marked than in preliterate societies in other areas, and where they did exist the material standard of living did not vary greatly from commoner to noble.[17] Too, individual power was greatly limited. Thus in comparing the position of chief among four widely contrasting North American tribes, Goldenweiser writes, "in no case is he [the chief] permitted to exercise actual control over the actions of his people —barring such drastic situations as war or other temporary exploits—and . . . in his daily life he is scarcely distinguishable from any of his subjects.[18]

Indian Personality
Despite the wide varieties of Indian cultures which structure correspondingly different personality characteristics, the Spindlers feel it is possible to generalize about North American Indian personality.

[15] Robert H. Lowie, *Primitive Society* (New York: Liveright Publishing Corporation, 1947), p. 75.
[16] Radin, *The Story of the American Indian*, p. 368. By permission of the Liveright Publishing Corporation.
[17] See Harold E. Driver, *Indians of North America* (Chicago: the University of Chicago Press, 1961), Ch. 19, "Rank and Social Classes."
[18] Alexander Goldenweiser, *Early Civilization* (New York: Alfred A. Knopf, Inc., 1922), p. 120.

. . . [W]e can tentatively describe the psychological features most widely exhibited among the North American Indians as a whole in the following way: nondemonstrative emotionality and reserve accompanied by a high degree of control over interpersonal aggression within the in-group; a pattern of generosity that varies greatly in the extent to which it is a formalized social device without emotional depth; autonomy of the individual, a trait linked with sociopolitical structures low in dominance-submission hierarchies; ability to endure pain, hardship, hunger, and frustration without external evidence of discomfort; a positive valuation of bravery and courage that varies sharply with respect to emphasis on highly aggressive daring in military exploit; a generalized fear of the world as dangerous, and particularly a fear of witchcraft; a "practical joker" strain that is nearly everywhere highly channelized institutionally, as in the common brother-in-law joking prerogative, and that appears to be a safety valve for in-group aggressions held sharply in check; attention to the concrete realities of the present—what Rorschachists would call the "large D" approach to problem solving—practicality in contrast to abstract integration in terms of long-range goals; a dependence upon supernatural power outside one's self—power that determines one's fate, which is expressed to and can be acquired by the individual through dreams, and for which the individual is not held personally accountable, at least not in the sense that one's "will" is accountable for one's acts in Western cultures.[19]

INDIANS AND THE WHITE GOVERNMENT

The ancestors of the Indians of present-day United States came in contact with four groups of white people: the Spaniards, the French, the English, and the Dutch. The Spaniards, as has been indicated, although quite ruthless at times, aimed at integrating the Indians into a new Spanish American civilization. Since the French came primarily to trade rather than to settle, they aimed, on the whole, simply to keep on friendly terms with the Indians. The French interfered little with them, and those who remained borrowed much of the Indian culture. Many married Indian women. In the struggle between the French and the English for control of the eastern portion of North America, Indian tribes became involved on opposite sides; thus sometimes Indian was pitted against Indian in a conflict in which they were to become the losers whichever European power prevailed. Since the English finally prevailed, further discussion will be devoted to their relations with the Indians.[20]

Period of Community Diplomacy: 1607–1778

During the colonial period each local English or Dutch settlement dealt with the Indians by whatever means seemed best to it. In Virginia the first

[19] George Spindler and Louise Spindler, "American Indian Personality Types and their Socio-cultural Roots," *Annals of the American Academy of Political and Social Science,* May 1957, 311: 148–149.
[20] The Dutch established the policy of buying the land from the Indians, as in the famous purchase of Manhattan Island for a purported $24. The Quakers in Pennsylvania developed a friendly policy toward the Indians and tended, in the early days at least, to fulfill with scrupulous honesty the bargains they made.

settlement, which was founded in 1607, lay within the territory of the Powhatan Confederacy, whose chieftain, Waukunsenecaw, left the small white group in peace. When a new wave of settlers appeared, however, his successor, Opechancanough, fought to drive them out. But in 1644 he was decisively beaten.[21] In Massachusetts, peace prevailed between the Indians and the white men for more than ten years, in part because of an illness which heavily depopulated the tribes nearest the shores. Again, however, as the white settlers became more numerous and began to press westward, many tribes grew hostile. While in some cases Indian resistance was temporarily successful, the ultimate outcome was always white victory.

In 1754 the British Crown formulated a policy for dealing with the Indians which took jurisdiction away from the individual colonies or border groups. Under this policy, "the tribes were independent nations, under the protection of the Crown; Indian lands were inalienable except through voluntary surrender to the Crown; and any attempt by an individual or group, subject to the Crown, or by a foreign state, to buy or seize lands from Indians, was illegal."[22] The attempt of the British Government to carry out this policy amidst innumerable local violations increased the antagonism of the colonists, especially those in the border area, toward the Crown. Thus the Indians indirectly contributed to the final issue of the American Revolution.

Period of Control by Treaties: 1778–1871

The policy of the British Crown was in essence taken over by the new American Government. For the first hundred years the relation of the Indian tribes to the federal government was characterized by treaties, nominally negotiated by the government with so-called sovereign Indian nations. Yet whenever the Indians failed to agree with what the government wanted, they were met with military force. Frequently special local groups moved against the Indians quite independently of the national government, as when the Georgia Legislature passed an act confiscating all Cherokee land and declaring Cherokee tribal laws invalid within the state. Persistently when the white people rode roughshod over their own treaties, the Indians fought back, and a number of Indian wars of considerable dimension took place east of the Mississippi. The Seminole War in Florida and the Black Hawk War in the Illinois Territory, in which Lincoln fought, were among the more famous. The final outcome east of the Mississippi was that most of the Indian tribes were forced into the newly established Indian Territory (now the state of Oklahoma). The exceptions were a few small, relatively harmless bands in Maine, New York, Virginia, and Florida, and a consider-

---

[21] From *Indians of the Americas,* by John Collier, copyright, 1947, by John Collier (New York: Mentor Books, The New American Library of World Literature, Inc., 1947), p. 114.
[22] *Ibid.,* pp. 116–117.

able number of Cherokees in North Carolina, who put up so much resistence that they were let alone in the wilds of the Smoky Mountain Region.

West of the Mississippi, much of the story of Indian-white relations centers around, first, the situation in California following the gold rush and, second, the subjugation of the Plains Indians throughout the vast Midwest. In California the white men in search of gold forced the Indians out of any area they wanted. From 1851 on, the federal government negotiated treaties with many local tribes by which the Indians agreed to surrender more than half of California. These treaties, because of frontier political pressure, were never ratified by the Senate, and the government subsequently sold to white people much of the land pledged to the Indians. The subjugation of the Plains Indians beginning about 1870 is described by Collier:

First there was military assault, on slight pretexts or no pretexts at all, and the government exploited tribal rivalries in order that Indians should kill Indians. The limited and disciplinary war customs of the Plains turned into total warfare, aimed at annihilation, with the United States Army as the driving power. The tribes were finally beaten, however, not through overwhelming numbers or superior armament (though these existed) but through starvation after the whites had destroyed the buffalo. . . . That revelry of slaughter, which had no sportsmanship in it, was recognized as a war measure against the Indians and was deliberately encouraged.[23]

Reservation Period: First Phase; Forced Assimilation

In 1871, Congress decreed that no Indian tribe "shall be acknowledged or recognized as an independent nation, tribe or power, with whom the United States may contract by treaty,"[24] thus marking the beginning of a definitely new phase in Indian-white relations. The Indians were now wards of the federal government, a unique status for any minority group in the United States. The policy and practices of the Indian Office from this time on were aimed at weakening the tribal organization of the Indians, destroying their culture, and forcing the assimilation of Indians as individuals into the normative American way of life. After several years of public and congressional debate, a new land policy was adopted with the passage of the famous Dawes Act in 1887. This legislation empowered the President to divide the lands of any tribe by giving allotted individual portions to family heads or other individuals. But the plots so allotted were to be held in trust for twenty-five years, after which they were to become the unrestricted property of each owner. In the meantime they could not be sold. The object of this program was to force each Indian breadwinner to become a self-supporting individual by working his own land. In the meantime the Indians were to be supported directly by the government.

[23] *Ibid.*, p. 133. By permission of the author.
[24] Ray Allen Billington, *Westward Expansion* (New York: The Macmillan Co., 1949), p. 668. Ch. 32, "The Indian Barrier," pp. 651–670, describes the history of Indian-white relations from 1860 to 1887.

The land allotment policy was extremely disastrous to the Indians. For one thing, they did not possess the technical knowledge needed to make their holdings pay. And they lacked the credit to acquire materials needed to operate the land. Further difficulty resulted from division of land through inheritance. Finally, the policy called for selling any "surplus" left after allotments to white people. While some Indians made an attempt to make a living on their allotments, many chose the easier course of leasing their land to whites. White graziers, for example, would rent a large number of contiguous allotments and then operate a range. Over the entire period in which this allotment policy was in effect (1887–1914), the lands held by the Indians were reduced from about 138,000,000 to some 47,000,000 acres.[25]

Another phase of the policy of forced assimilation concerned the educational program. Indian children at school age were taken out of their tribal homes and placed in boarding schools, where the use of Indian languages and the practice of Indian ways, such as dress and hair styles, were forbidden. The curricula of the schools were largely that of the white schools, without any adaptation to the particular needs of the Indians. In Macgregor's opinion, whatever practical training the Indian children obtained either for making a living or making better homes was gained from the labor they performed to help support the school.[26] Thus a mediocre school system tried to prepare Indian children to live like white people, while in fact most of them would return home to live as Indians.

In retrospect this first phase of the Indian reservation policy can be seen as a failure. When it was replaced by the New Deal policy in 1934, it is a fair question whether the over-all Indian problem was any nearer solution than in 1887. From the economic point of view the Indians were a pauperized people. The education which the younger Indians had received had made them marginal individuals not yet ready to take their place in the white American world but also unsettled for Indian life. The health of the Indians was subnormal, though it had improved somewhat toward the later part of this period. This policy failed because it attempted the rapid, forced acculturation of one cultural group to another, a procedure which social science now knows to be impractical. It is least surprising that such a policy should have failed with the Indians, whose cultures were more divergent from white American culture than that of any other minority. Many well-meaning white people could not understand why it should be so difficult to teach Indian men to be hard-working, competitive, economic individualists— to the white American the proper way of economic life. That Indians should desert their jobs when working for white people in order to participate in

[25] Ward Shepard, "Land Problems of an Expanding Indian Population," *The Changing Indian*, p. 76.
[26] Gordon Macgregor, "Indian Education in Relation to the Social and Economic Background of the Reservation," in *The Changing Indian*, pp. 116–127.

their tribal ceremonies was construed by many whites to be an example of the Indian's incorrigible laziness.

The first reservation policy further fell short of its object because of inefficient administration. The Indian Service, particularly in its earlier years, was not conspicuous for the high standards of its personnel. Nor was a particular interest in Indians and their welfare a prerequisite for employment in the Service. Furthermore, the appropriations granted it were inadequate. Even when well-intentioned officials attempted to carry out some sort of policy, they were beset with powerful pressures from special interests to twist the policy to the latter's advantage. Finally, underlying all these factors was the characteristic race consciousness of dominant-status Americans, which saw Indians as "colored" peoples and therefore, like all nonwhites as inferior. The color prejudice militated against the adjustment of even the more acculturated Indians to white society.

During the 1920's constant pressures were brought to bear by certain vested white interests to enact legislation which would have expropriated further the rights of Indians to their resources. These efforts were defeated and as one result of the publicity attending the hearings in this connection, a comprehensive study of the problems of the administration of Indian affairs was undertaken (1927) by a private agency, the Institute for Government Research, at the request of Secretary of the Interior Hubert Work. The findings of this study, usually known as the Merriam Survey, went far to create a more favorable attitude toward the Indians.[27] In the Hoover administration, government policy was oriented toward a more genuine concern for Indian interests. This changing attitude was most specifically expressed in a revamped educational program for Indian children.

Reservation Period: Second Phase; the "New Deal"

The phrase "New Deal," coined to characterize the early years of Franklin D. Roosevelt's administration, was peculiarly apt with reference to Indian affairs. While the time was ripe in 1933 for reorganization of Indian policy, the sweeping character of the changes undertaken at this time was in considerable measure due to a long-standing sympathetic interest in Indians of the new Secretary of the Interior, Harold I. Ickes, and to the appointment of John Collier as Commissioner of the Bureau of Indian Affairs.

Behind the efforts which culminated in the passage of the Indian Reorganization Act, sponsored by Senator Burton Wheeler of Montana, was a new philosophy concerning Indians held by the new Commissioner and strongly supported by the new Federal Administration. In essence, this philosophy aimed at integrating Indians into the national life as Indians, to make Indian groups self-sustaining and yet retain as much of their tribal

[27] Institute for Government Research, *The Problem of Indian Administration* (Baltimore: Johns Hopkins Press, 1928).

culture and group identification as was consistent with life in a modern civilized nation. Collier not only admired the Indians as persons but felt that much of their culture should be preserved, that there was a place for Indians as Indians in a multigroup democratic society. He expressed his philosophy thus:

> The new Indian policy . . . seeks to reinstate the Indians as normally function-ing units, individual and group, into the life of the world. It makes them equal in the management of their own affairs and the direction of their own lives.
> On the purely cultural side, only sheer fanaticism would decide the further destruction of Indian languages, crafts, poetry, music, ritual, philosophy, and religion. These possessions have a significance and a beauty which grew patiently through endless generations of a people immersed in the life of nature, filled with imaginative and ethical insight into the core of being. . . .[28]

The point of view of the new commissioner was reflected in the Indian Reorganization Act passed by Congress in 1934, the chief provisions of which are as follows:

1. With certain qualifications, Indian societies were to be empowered to under-take political, economic, and administrative self-government.
2. Land allotment was to be stopped, and under certain conditions, additional lands could be added to current holdings.
3. A system of agricultural and industrial credit was to be established, and the needed funds were authorized.
4. An Indian Civil Service was to be established and provisions for the training of Indians themselves in administration and the professions were called for.

The Reorganization Act called for the acceptance of its provisions by each tribe individually, determined on the basis of a referendum using secret ballot. Those who voted to accept could organize under it for self-govern-ment and could organize themselves as a federal corporation to conduct economic enterprise.[29]

Progress Under the Indian Reorganization Act

The new deal for the Indians meant considerable strides in economic re-habilitation, increasing tribal self-government, and a slow but steady rise in the welfare of Indians as a whole. By 1948 a total of seventy-three tribes had received charters of incorporation, which meant that with the economic assistance of the government and the technical advice and approval of the Indian Service these groups improved their economic welfare and gained experience in helping themselves. Some tribes through loans have been able to purchase additional lands or to put hitherto unused acreage into effective use. One major problem has been to prevent too great a depletion of Indian land resources because of the desire of many Indians to sell their land to

[28] From Report of House of Representatives Subcommittee on Appropriations for the Interior Department, 1934.
[29] Collier, *Indians of the Americas*, pp. 157–158.

non-Indians or to lease it without adequate safeguards against deterioration. Marked increases in the requests by Indians, some with individual holdings, to sell their lands were reported by the Bureau in 1948 and 1949.[30]

By 1948 a total of ninety-three tribes had adopted written constitutions and had begun to assume larger political self-government. Typically there is a Tribal Council which suggests measures of administration and approves or rejects proposals of the Agency staff. It has considerable control of the tribal finances and appoints a Tribal Court of Indian Judges, which tries all cases of criminal law except those involving the ten most serious offenses, over which the Federal court retains jurisdiction. Nevertheless, the great gap between tribal legal and political practices and those of the white democracy could not be closed at once. For example, it was the practice of both the Navaho and the Papago to decide important matters by face-to-face meetings of all concerned in which the issues were discussed until unanimity was reached, in contrast with the system of majority decision under white democracy. It was clear that the goal of self-government for the Indians had to be approached by degrees.

Although Congress enacted a law in 1924 making all Indians citizens, seven states barred Indians from voting until about 1940, either by discriminatory laws or interpretations of laws. Following 1940, five of these states began to allow Indians to vote by not enforcing these statutes. Court decisions in Arizona and New Mexico in 1948 opened the door to full voting privileges for Indians, and since then Indians there have generally had the right to vote.

Education for Indian children has been continually improving. From 1950 to 1960 the number of Indian children enrolled in schools increased from 26,716 to 133,316; over the same period the percentage of Indian children attending public schools, rather than the federally operated schools for Indian pupils alone, increased from 50 per cent to 63.5 per cent.[31] It is of especial interest to discover that in 1959 some twenty-five tribes themselves provided scholarships in higher education totalling about $500,000.[32]

Despite this improvement the Indians have a long way to go to approximate national norms. The task force assigned by President Kennedy to recommend Indian policy for his administration found that "the bulk of the reservation Indian population is less well educated than other Americans, has a shorter life span, and has a much lower standard of living."[33]

Recent Trends in Official Policy

A considerable reversal in the Indian policy and program occurred in the

[30] Annual Report of Secretary of the Interior, 1948, pp. 369–392.
[31] Annual Report of the Secretary of Interior, 1960, p. 97.
[32] Annual Report, 1959, p. 235.
[33] Report to the Secretary of Interior by the Task Force on Indian Affairs, July 10, 1961, p. 2.

'50's. Efforts to speed up the process of liquidating the government's responsibility to the Indians took the forms which may be designated as "relocation" and "termination."

Relocation   In 1952 the Bureau of Indian Affairs started what was called the Voluntary Relocation Program, under which reservation Indians, either individually or in family groups, who desired to move to industrial centers for permanent employment and settlement were offered financial and other assistance to enable them to relocate. A reason for adopting this program was the fact that most Indian tribal lands were inadequate to permit viable economies with a rapidly growing population. By 1960, some 35,000 reservation Indians had thus been relocated in various industrial areas ranging from the West Coast to the Midwest. These relocated Indians are employed at the lowest occupational range and live in the poorer sections of the cities often inhabited largely by other minorities. Estimates of the extent to which the Indians remained in relocation or returned to the reservation vary. The Bureau of Indian Affairs in 1955 put the number of the relocated Indians who had up to this time returned at about 24 per cent; The Association on American Indian Affairs on the basis of its survey of the relocation program gives a much higher percentage of returnees.[34]

As with any program of this sort, the results vary with the attitudes and efficiency of the officials operating the program at local levels. Many Indian leaders, as well as such friends of the Indians as the Association on American Indian Affairs, favor this program in principle. This latter organization feels that the program could be improved by (1) making it clear that relocation opportunities are available to those Indians who really want it without any undue pressures being exerted; (2) improving liaison with local community agencies in the cities of relocation in order to facilitate the adjustment of the resettled Indians; and (3) not stressing the point of permanence in relocation.

Even if substantial numbers of relocated Indians do return to the reservations, the experience will have been educational and the returned members may contribute to the improvement of tribal conditions through their increased acculturation. The main concern of the friends of the Indians is, however, that the relocation program shall not be viewed as a "solution" of the Indian problem, that its operation shall not deflect effort from the more basic problem of aiding the reservation Indians to develop viable economies, working out their own problems and being free to determine how much of their traditional cultural heritages they wish to retain.[35]

Termination   The termination policy stemmed from a resolution by Congress passed on August 1, 1953, which stated in part:

---

[34] La Verne Madigan, "The American Indian Relocation Program," The Association on American Indian Affairs, 1956. Based on the findings of a relocation survey team.
[35] *Ibid.*

. . . [I]t is the policy of Congress, as rapidly as possible, to make the Indians within the territorial limits of the United States subject to the same laws and entitled to the same privileges and responsibilities as are applicable to other citizens of the United States, to end their status as wards of the United States, and to grant them all the rights and prerogatives pertaining to American citizenship. . . .[36]

Following passage of this resolution, efforts were made to order or to persuade tribes to request termination of their relation to the federal government. This would have meant in many instances dissolution of tribal organizations and the division of tribal assets among the several members. In view of the lack of acculturation of most Indians to the normative American way of life, especially to the norms of economic self-reliance, termination might well have resulted in the demoralization and pauperization of the Indians of many tribes. Alarmed at this prospect, friends of the Indians protested the policy and it was revised. Indian groups were not to be pressured to terminate unless they themselves wanted it and were developed to a point where they could carry on their own affairs. Thus in fact only a few tribes were actually terminated, the most important being the Klamaths of Oregon and the Menomines of Wisconsin, both owners of large tracts of valuable timber.[37]

In the latter part of the Eisenhower Administration, official policy veered back toward the principles embodied in the 1934 Indian Reorganization Act, particularly removing pressure on tribes to terminate. Governmental policy is now directed toward increased financial aid and technical assistance to Indian tribal corporations to improve their capacity to support themselves; increased education, especially vocational training to enable Indians to increase their income by working off the reservation in nearby white communities; and encouragement of the location of new industries near the reservations for Indian employment. The health functions of the Bureau of Indian Affairs were transferred to the United States Bureau of Public Health in 1955. All indications are that the Kennedy Administration will pursue the same policies even more vigorously under the direction of Philleo Nash, long-time student of Indian life, as the new Commissioner of Indian Affairs. It now appears that the Indians will not be pressured into terminating their relation with the federal government.

The Indians and their non-Indian friends face the constant need for combatting the pressures of special business interests ever ready to secure for themselves the valuable land, forest, and mineral resources owned by Indian groups. A recent example is of South Dakota ranchers who, according to Madigan, bring every possible political pressure to enable them to secure nearby Indian lands at the cheapest possible price.[38]

[36] House Concurrent Resolution 108, 83rd Congress, 1st Session.
[37] See Oliver La Farge, "The Enduring Indians," *Scientific American*, February, 1960, 202: 37–46.
[38] La Verne Madigan, "Indian Survival in the Great Plains," *Indian Affairs*, No. 22, September 1957. *Indian Affairs* is a newsletter published by Association on American Indian Affairs, Inc., providing information on developments affecting Indians.

INTERPERSONAL RELATIONS BETWEEN INDIANS AND WHITES

The attitudes of white people toward Indians in the United States have varied widely, perhaps more so than in regard to any other minority. In the past these attitudes ranged from conceiving of the Indian as a "noble savage" to picturing him as a "savage beast." The one extreme is expressed in literature of the Hiawatha type and in many children's books, and in the Indian lore incorporated in such groups as the Boy Scouts. The opposite extreme is expressed in the stereotype of Indians as cruel warriors who enjoyed scalping white people. As the Indians became "tamed" and pauperized, the range of white attitudes tended to swing from benevolent pity and sympathy to disdain and contempt. In the absence of adequate systematic data on the point, we venture the hypothesis that in this century there has been a rough correlation between the attitudes of white people and their proximity to the Indians. By this we suggest that the concept of the Indian as a noble, mistreated person is more frequently found among those white people whose picture of the Indians has been derived from secondary sources, and the notion of the Indian as an inferior, lazy fellow is more widely prevalent among whites living in areas close to reservations.

Race consciousness has played a part in determining white American responses to Indians, though there are some indications that negative white reactions to the Indian's "color" have been less intense than with other racial minorities. The census definition of the Indian given earlier suggests that mixed-bloods with Indian genetic lineage may "pass" as whites much more easily than Negroes. Bogardus' social distance studies support the above statements. In 1926, out of forty different ethnic groups ranked in order of their acceptance by a sample of native-born Americans, Indians ranked twenty-fifth, below most of the European ethnic groups and well above all of the other nonwhite groups.[39] In 1956 the same author found the Indians occupying approximately the same relative position, twentieth among thirty ethnic groups. Of the nonwhite groups only the nisei had forged slightly ahead of the Indians.[40]

From these general observations we turn now to review interpersonal relations between Indians and their white neighbors as revealed in studies of particular Indian tribes. Reservation Indians have come in contact with four categories of dominant-status white people: Indian Service personnel assigned to their reservation; traders; missionaries; and white employers for whom some of the Indians work and white neighbors among whom they sometimes dwell.

[39] Emory S. Bogardus, *Immigration and Race Attitudes* (Boston: D. C. Heath & Company, 1928), p. 25.
[40] Emory S. Bogardus, "Race Reactions by Sexes," *Sociology and Social Research*, Vol. 43, p. 441. In the later studies the foreign-born and native-born Japanese are listed separately.

The Indian Service Personnel

The relations of the Agency staff members to their Indian wards have varied with their own personalities and attitudes toward their task, from warm friendships to purely official and impersonal contact. Spicer found that teachers did not usually become intimately integrated with the Indian life in their school community and that the effectiveness of Agency medical workers to get Indian acceptance of modern health methods depended on their attitude toward Indian beliefs. "Nominally, every staff member . . . is accessible to any Indian who desires to talk with him, but relatively few Indians seek such contacts."[41] Kluckhohn and Leighton found that, while some of the employees of the Indian Service were motivated by a genuine desire to help the Indians, many others took the position because it was the best they could get and not because they had real interest in Indians. "Many are highly conventionally prejudiced, and of limited imagination and flexibility."[42]

The Traders

Because the traders on the reservations are the white people with whom the Indians become best acquainted, they symbolize the white world to the Indians. On the Navaho reservation some traders are very fond of the Indians and perform a wide variety of friendly services; others "have mercilessly and shamefully exploited the Indians' ignorance of markets and of simple arithmetic."[43] While the role of traders is declining as the Indians get to town more often, nevertheless they "are still significant in helping the Navahos market their goods, in encouraging native handicrafts, and in otherwise promoting the economic development of the tribe."[44]

The Missionaries

In their zeal to teach the Indian children English, the mission schools in some instances have forbidden pupils to speak their native tongue anywhere near the school. When Kluckhohn and Leighton found that missionaries had made few practicing converts to Christianity, they attributed the failure in large measure to "their efforts to suppress native custom or to urge strenuously the substitution of white customs, oftentimes in spheres which seem to the Navahos outside the province of the missionaries."[45] The resistance, and sometimes ridicule, which the missionaries encounter in trying to make the

[41] Rosamund Spicer, in Joseph, Spicer, and Chesky, *The Desert People* (Chicago: University of Chicago Press, 1949), p. 103.
[42] Clyde Kluckhohn and Dorothea Leighton, *The Navaho* (Cambridge: Harvard University Press, 1947), p. 107.
[43] *Ibid.*, p. 79.
[44] *Ibid.*, p. 80.
[45] *Ibid.*, pp. 81–82.

Navahos give up their traditional ways is illustrated in the following comment of a young mission school graduate:

> That missionary came here today and tried to make my husband buy a mar-
> riage license, but my husband said he didn't have a dollar. He has been trying to
> get my brother to buy a license for a year. The other missionary tried for two
> years and got tired of it. His wife said, "We're married all right. We don't need
> any paper. You tell him you don't know, you'll have to ask your wife—then he
> won't talk so long to you."[46]

Among the Papago, too, missionaries were found not to have much influence. On the other hand, the Dakotas became almost completely Christian-
ized—in part, as Macgregor suggests, because their own religion was more
akin to that of Christianity than that of many other Indian groups, and in
part because, in its principles at least, Christianity was the one aspect of the
white man's culture which defined Indians as equal to whites.[47]

White Employers and Neighbors

In the Papago area "the general public looks upon these Indians as a
lower-class group with a tendency toward drunkenness, and, though they are
not subjected to as marked social discrimination as are Negroes, they must
endure a certain amount of racial prejudice."[48] In the vicinity of the Pine
Ridge Reservation Macgregor found the neighbors of the Dakotas reacting
to Indians in accord with class position. Middle-class whites looked on
Indians generally as inferior but were more accepting of the few whose education, employment, and social behavior were more like their own; a certain
segment of the lower class tended to accept Indians as equals.[49]

Since World War II, reservation Indians have been increasingly going off
the reservation to work in nearby towns at menial jobs. White employers
have generally found them satisfactory workers, though slow. A frequent
complaint is illustrated in the following: "Navahos are good workers but not
steady. . . . They disappear for days at a time to attend a sing or to help
their families out."[50] Such a comment by white employers indicates the inability of the white people to realize that going out into the white man's
world of work presents a considerable problem of adjustment for Indians.
As Spicer put it, "Working on a definite schedule in the white fashion is not
a normal life for the Papago, but he seems to be able to adjust, perhaps because he likes the wages, which give him a higher cash income than most
people can earn on the reservation."[51] However, the same writer found some

[46] *Ibid.*, p. 82. Reprinted by permission of the publishers.
[47] See Gordon Macgregor, *Warriors Without Weapons* (Chicago: University of Chicago
Press, 1944), pp. 85–104.
[48] Joseph, Spicer, and Chesky, *The Desert People*, p. 110.
[49] Macgregor, *Warriors Without Weapons*, p. 84.
[50] Kluckhohn and Leighton, *The Navaho*, p. 11.
[51] Spicer in *The Desert People*, p. 110.

of the employers adjusting their work to enable the Indians to return home periodically and providing better working and living conditions in order to make the Indians more contented and steadier in their work.

A picture of white-Indian relations in the bi-racial community of "Fruitland," New Mexico, in 1954 is presented by Sasaki:

> There existed evidences of intergroup tension. On the one hand many whites, mostly persons who employed Navahos or worked with them, expressed considerable resentment over the Indians' irresponsible behavior. On the other hand, the Navahos began to feel that they were being discriminated against by employers and by the police. Many not so directly involved also began to stereotype Navaho behavior because of the activities of a few. The record of arrests appearing three or four times a week in the local newspaper revealed the same Navaho names. Although no open brawls occurred between Navahos and whites, the Indians were frequently arrested for fighting among themselves and for intoxication. The town's general growing pains were affecting the Navahos in particular.[52]

However, certain white officials in Fruitland—"men who had spent several decades as traders to the Navahos and thus were able to speak their language—were all active in their own ways of promoting intercultural understanding."[53] They taught the Navahos the value of the vote and helped get their children into public schools.

THE IMPACT OF MINORITY STATUS ON INDIANS

In the case of other minorities, we have noted how the pressures to acculturate to normative American life and the frustrations engendered by discrimination have imposed strain on the personality organization of members of minority groups and the development of the personality of their children. The same phenomenon exists among Indians, although there are some differences in their situation. Reservation Indians have the security of identification with their tribe. They likewise have the advantage of the special guidance and protection of the Indian Service. Nevertheless, the gap between their cultures and that of the world around is so much wider than in the case of most other minorities that even with this special assistance the strain of adjustment is great. In the case of those Indians who go off the reservation into the white world either temporarily or permanently, the problem of adjustment is still greater. Illustrative of ways in which Indians react under these difficult circumstances are the following comments of Kluckhohn and Leighton concerning the Navahos:

> Different sets of Navahos (depending partly upon age, schooling, location of residence with respect to intensity of non-Navaho contacts, and other factors) have shown different major responses to the insecurities, deprivations, and frus-

[52] Tom T. Sasaki, *Fruitland, New Mexico: A Navaho Community in Transition* (Ithaca, New York: Cornell University Press, 1960), pp. 198–199.
[53] *Ibid.*

trations of the immediate past and especially to the "between two worlds" problem. . . . Some focus their energies upon trying to be as like whites as possible.
Some find relief in becoming followers of vocal leaders. Others dissipate much
hostility in factional quarrels or scatter their aggression in family fights, in phan-
tasies about witchcraft or in attacking "witches," in verbal and other indirect
hostilities toward whites, or they turn their aggression inward with resultant fits
of depression. The culturally patterned releases in humor and in "joking relationships" with certain relatives continue to play some part. The central response of
certain individuals is in flight—either in actual physical withdrawal or in the escape
of narcotics, alcohol, and sex. Still others turn to intensified participation in rites
of the native religion and to new cults (e.g., peyote). Partial solutions are achieved
by a few individuals by rigid compartmentalization of their lives and by various
rationalizations.

Those who have set themselves to follow the white man's trail find themselves—
as have representatives of other minority groups—in a (rationally) odd dilemma.
While as youngsters they are rewarded by school teachers and others for behaving
like whites, as adults they are punished for having acquired skills that make them
competitors of their white contemporaries. The more intelligent ones had, by early
maturity, realized that their education would bring them into conflict with or isolation from their own unschooled relatives. But the experience of being turned on
by their white mentors comes as a painful surprise. They find they are seldom
received on terms of social equality, even by those whose standards of living,
dress, and manners they have succeeded in copying almost perfectly. They learn
that they must always (save within the Indian Service) expect to work for a salary
at least one grade lower than that which a white person of comparable training
and experience receives. They overhear remarks by those same groups of whites
who had goaded them to give up "those ignorant Indian ways." "You can never
trust these school boys." "Give me a 'long hair' every time. They may be dumb
but they are honest and they work hard." "Educated Indians are neither fish nor
fowl. They give me the creeps." Rejected by the white world they have made so
many emotional sacrifices to enter, some attempt a bitter retreat to the Navaho
world. Others, in sour disillusionment, abandon all moral codes. Still others achieve
a working (but flat and empty) adjustment.

Navahos are well aware of the difficulty of their situation. Surrounded by
powerful pressures to change, they know that indifference and withdrawal can no
longer serve as effective responses. They are conscious of the need to develop
some compromise with white civilization. But doubt as to the best form of compromise makes them angry and anxious. Thus suspicion and hostility are becoming
a major emotional tone of their relationships with whites.[54]

Indian recognition and resentment of minority status is seen in a small
Fox reservation group near Tama, Iowa.

The Mesquakie are partly insulated from the penalties of lower status by their
life in a separate community, but as more and more adolescents attend the Tama
High School, and as the educated young people try for the first time in Fox history
to get jobs which are more than skilled or unskilled, they are confronted painfully,
even heartbreakingly with the problems of status. . . . [In the words of one
Mesquakie interviewed:] "If you're around here long enough, you'll see how it

[54] Reprinted by permission of the publishers from Clyde Kluckhohn and Dorothea Leighton, *The Navaho*, pp. 113–115.

is. . . . These people here don't give the Indians much chance to do anything. . . .
When a boy gets out of school, well they don't like that naturally. Makes them
mad. . . . In the high school is the worst place of all. . . . There was a girl there
(the only Indian girl in the class) everytime she got up to talk, all of a sudden
everything is quiet, all quiet. Well, that poor girl had to quit."[55]

Tribal Interrelationships

Since each Indian tribe has a separate society with its own particular culture, each has looked on the others with the characteristic "in-group" attitude of ethnic groups toward one another. Navahos consider Pueblos to be
effete town dwellers, and the Pueblos regard the country-dwelling Navahos
as ignorant and barbaric. The Papago look on the Apaches as mean and
cruel, although they admire their prowess as warriors. Thus, because of their
tribal insularity and ethnocentrism, the sense of the solidarity of all Indians
as opposed to whites has been comparatively weak. However, just as changing conditions have brought each Indian tribe more in contact with white
people, so they have increased social contacts between the tribes. Among
the Navahos can be found more or less systematic exchange of goods with
many other tribes. For example, "the Navahos trade rugs and silver to the
Utes for the baskets used in the Navaho ceremonies . . ."[56] Furthermore
there is considerable interest shown by neighboring tribes in each other's
ceremonies. The Papago, for instance, "never tire of watching the Yaqui
pascola dancers perform."[57] In the off-reservation boarding schools, Indian
children of different tribes are brought together, further facilitating inter-
Indian acculturation. Boarding-school romances often lead to intertribal marriages, which the elders, of course, do not favor but to which they are apparently becoming reconciled.

Indians and Other Minorities

Concerning the Papago and the Mexican Americans, Spicer observes:

Mexicans are known to the Papago as "Smarties" (*chuchkam*), and relations
between the two groups vary. At present Mexicans living in the United States and
the American Papago usually meet on friendly terms. Several factors tend to draw
them together: in the towns both groups do the same kind of low-paid work; they
are equally discriminated against by the white Americans, who frequently cannot
tell them apart; and they often have a common religion in Catholicism. A Papago
will trade at a Mexican store in preference to an American. When he is working
in a town, he will live either with his tribesmen in "Papago Town" or with Mexicans (and perhaps lower-class white Americans). Papago in Tucson live in the
"Barrio Libre" along with Mexicans and Yaqui.[58]

[55] *Documentary History of the Fox Project, 1948–1959*, directed by Sol Tax, edited by
Fred Gearing, Robert McC. Netting, and Lisa R. Peattie. (Chicago: University of Chicago Department of Anthropology, 1960), p. 58.
[56] Kluckhohn and Leighton, *The Navaho*, p. 76.
[57] Joseph, Spicer, and Chesky, *The Desert People*, p. 95.
[58] *Ibid.*, p. 95. By permission of the publishers, University of Chicago Press.

The Navaho study reveals in general a similar pattern of relations between these Indians and their Mexican-American neighbors. Mexicans often protect Indians from Anglo law in such minor offenses as drunkenness. While it is rare for Mexicans in towns to invite Indians to their homes, in rural areas intimate, neighborly relations between the two groups are more frequent. On the other hand, gangs of Mexican youth often beat up and rob Indians, and bloody fights occur between small bands of these two groups. It is of considerable interest that Kluckhohn and Leighton note that violence of this sort hardly ever occurs between either of these minorities and the Anglos.[59]

In our discussion of the Negroes we saw the tendency of minorities to deflect their frustration through aggression toward other members of their own group. In the Fox area we find the more socially accepted minority "taking it out" on a lesser minority.

Status becomes a bitter thing, that one must defend what status one has. Thus the young Mesquakie are strongly anti-Negro. This mechanism is shown by a couple of young Fox who spent a great deal of spare time in the Army searching out Negroes who were passing as Indians and beating them up.[60]

TRENDS AND PROSPECTS

While the conditions of welfare which prevail among Indians constitute a serious situation, the critical problem is how to effect the integration of Indians into American society as equal and self-reliant citizens. The major issue revolves around the concepts of cultural pluralism versus total assimilation. Should Indians be encouraged to integrate into American society as Indians, as groups retaining their group identities and as much of the distinctive cultures as can be successfully adapted to a self-reliant group life? Or should they be encouraged to acculturate as rapidly as possible to the typical American way of life leading to complete assimilation, amalgamation, and the disappearance of Indian society and culture? The student of minorities will appreciate that in issues of this sort, adherence to either of these views is often motivated by self-interest rather than concern for the Indians. For example, some Indian Service personnel may favor the non-assimilation viewpoint because it would require the Indian Service as a special agency for a longer period. On the other hand, it is clear that some of the supporters of rapid assimilation have designs on Indian properties and resources. Even among specialists on Indian affairs with long records of sympathetic interest in the welfare of Indians, differences of opinion on the

[59] *The Navaho*, pp. 77–78.
[60] Documentary History of the Fox Project, p. 58. By permission.

issue prevail.[61] Those who favor integration through cultural pluralism believe that there is much in Indian culture which should be preserved or modernized and that the Indian societies should be retained. Since former Commissioner Collier, as we have seen, holds this view, during his administration the policy of the Indian Service was directed to this end. The Indian specialists who incline to the policy of integration of Indians through their complete assimilation argue that Indians will not be in fact autonomous members of our society until they cease their Indian ways.

On the basis of our study of minorities, we bring to bear upon this issue two considerations. The present situation of Jews in the United States, and of certain minor religious sects, suggests that it should be theoretically possible for Indian communities with modernized Indian cultures to become self-reliant in the economic and political sense in due time. In democratic society, if this is what Indians themselves continue to want, democratic principle logically calls for protecting their right to such a solution. On the other hand, whether by this course they could shed completely their minority status is debatable. By remaining culturally differentiated and racially visible, by associating primarily with other Indians, and by comprising a numerically small proportion of the national population, Indians will remain highly vulnerable to dominant discrimination.

The situation of the Indians in the United States at the present time may be summarized as follows:

1. The Indians are minorities in two respects. They are wards of the government in a manner distinctive from all other American groups. They are also minority people in the manner of other minorities. That is, they are categorically discriminated against by white Americans wherever they live in numbers in the proximity of whites.

2. The Indian population is growing at a much faster rate than the national population, and at a rate too great to be adequately supported by the areas now assigned to them.

3. Thus while Indian welfare is improving, greater progress is retarded by the inadequacy of their present material resources for the growing Indian population and by the lag in modernization of their material culture.

4. The Indian groups are becoming increasingly self-governing.

5. The Indian population, in general, still shows a marked tendency to remain Indian in the cultural and social sense. No large-scale tendency to pass over into the non-Indian society and to lose their tribal identification is yet discernible.

6. The strain imposed on Indian groups by the pressure to acculturate, on the one hand, and the desire to remain Indians, on the other, manifests itself

[61] See John F. Embree, "The Indian Bureau and Self-Government," *Human Organization*, Vol. 8, No. 2, Spring, 1949; and John C. Collier, "The Indian Bureau and Self-Government: A Reply," Vol. 8, No. 2, Summer, 1949.

in the behavioral difficulties of many Indian persons. In the case of those Indians either working off the reservations or residing in white communities, discrimination against them as Indians aggravates still further their personality maladjustment.

7. As with other minorities, the progress of Indians toward full equality is retarded by the pressures of vested interests among the dominant group. This factor, however, operates with peculiar force in the case of Indians because of their ownership of valuable lands and mineral resources.

TOPICS FOR PROJECTS AND DISCUSSION

1. Point out as many ways as possible in which the situation of Indians in the United States differs from that of the other minorities with physical visibility.
2. Discuss the significance of the "forced" assimilation policy practiced by the Indian Service from 1878 to 1928 in relation to its contribution to the science of human relations.
3. Discuss (a) color, or race, consciousness, on the part of white people in relation to the Indians, and (b) the direct economic interest of certain white groups as a factor affecting the status and welfare of Indians in this country.
4. Study any pertinent material you can find to verify or disprove the following hypothesis: The prevalence of unfavorable and discriminatory attitudes on the part of whites toward Indians varies directly with the nearness of white communities to Indian reservations. Report your findings.
5. Do you think it possible for Indian groups to become ultimately self-reliant and still retain any of their distinctive ways of life? Develop whichever position you take.

SUGGESTED READING

Aginsky, Burt W. "The Interaction of Ethnic Groups: A Case Study of Indians and Whites. *American Sociological Review*, April, 1949, 14: 288–293.
> *Finds the only workable solution to be "functionally integrated participation" of Pomo Indians into surrounding white society.*

Collier, John. *The Indians of the Americas.* New York: Mentor Books, The New American Library of World Literature, Inc., 1947.
> *The story of Indian-white relations in the Western World, told by the inaugurator of the "new deal for the Indians," as former Commissioner of Indian Affairs.*

Driver, Harold E. *Indians of North America.* Chicago: University of Chicago Press, 1961.
> *A comprehensive comparative description and interpretation of native American cultures from the Arctic to Panama.*

Gearing, Fred, Netting, Robert McC., and Peattie, Lisa R., eds. *Documentary History of the Fox Project, 1948–49.* Chicago: Department of Anthropology, University of Chicago, 1960.
> *A complete report of research on a particular group of Fox Indians near Tama, Iowa.*

Hagan, William T. *American Indians*. Chicago: University of Chicago Press, 1961.
    A brief study of Indian-white relations from colonial times to the present.
Kluckhohn, Clyde, and Leighton, Dorothea, *Children of the People*. Cambridge: Harvard University Press, 1947.
    A systematic study of the personality development of the Navaho child.
Thompson, Laura. *Culture in Crisis*. New York: Harper & Brothers, 1950.
    An exceptionally complete study of the Hopi Indians. A good example of co-ordinated research in social science.
Sasaki, Tom T. *Fruitland, New Mexico: A Navaho Community in Transition*. Ithaca, New York: Cornell University Press, 1960.
    Studies the process of acculturation of Navahos under increasing contact with white people.

16

The Peoples of Hawaii

Hawaii is a part of the United States where intergroup relations are unique. Its extensive ethnic and racial heterogeneity can be seen in Table 15, where the ethnic composition at specified dates is shown. Although the dominant status of the white people of Euro-American background over the peoples of Oriental origin was well established when Hawaii became American territory, intergroup relations have continuously been distinguished by the absence of any legal or public discrimination. Nonofficial discrimination, however, by the white residents against both the native Hawaiians and the successive immigrant groups has been equally evident. The absence of formal discrimination has led many writers and students to picture Hawaii as a paradise of interracial relations; the informal discrimination has led others to view it less favorably.

With so many different peoples to consider, the problem of consistent nomenclature arises. With the exception of the Caucasians, the peoples involved can be identified by the names used in Table 15. By "Hawaiians" we shall mean the descendants of the native group present in the islands when white contact was first established. All others we shall call by their nationality names. Rather than designating the white dominant group by the racial term "Caucasian," we use the name bestowed on them by the native Hawaiians, "haoles," the meaning of which is "stranger." This label has come to be restricted to the first strangers to appear in Hawaii, the Euro-American

TABLE 15

Population of Hawaii by Ethnic Components at Specified Intervals and by Per Cent of Total, 1960[1]

	1853	1884	1900	1920	1950	1960	1960 % of Total
Hawaiian	70,036	40,414	29,799	23,723	12,245	102,100(b)	16.1
Part Hawaiian	983	4,218	9,857	18,027	73,845	—(b)	—
Caucasian	1,687	16,579	26,819	49,140	114,793	202,230(a)	31.9
Portuguese	87	9,967	18,272	27,002			
Other Caucasian	1,600	6,612	8,547	19,708			
Chinese	304	18,254	25,767	23,507	32,376	38,197(a)	6.3
Japanese		116	61,111	109,274	184,598	203,455(a)	32.1
Korean				4,950	7,030		
Filipino	5			21,031	61,062	69,070(a)	10.9
Puerto Rican				5,602	9,551		
Negro			233	348	2,651	4,953(a)	0.8
All Other	62	1,397	648	310	1,618	12,305(c)	1.9
Total	73,137	80,578	154,234	255,912	499,769	632,772(d)	100.0

[1] See Andrew Lind, *Hawaii's People* (Honolulu: University of Hawaii Press, 1955), p. 27 for the data through 1950.
(a) U.S. Census, 1960. PC(A. 2)–13, Table 1, p. 13.
(b) Estimate by the Department of Planning and Research, State of Hawaii as of April 1, 1960.
(c) The Hawaiian components are subtracted from the U.S. Census "All Other" category, leaving the "All Other" largely Korean.
(d) Since the Hawaiian figure in the 1960 column is estimated, the totals do not add up to the exact census count.

whites, and their descendants, and not to others who subsequently immigrated to the islands. It identifies white people of American or northwestern European descent.

Presenting the changing ethnic composition of the population of Hawaii in graphic form offers difficulties. While it is true that official figures by ethnic composition have been recorded since 1853, changes in the basis of classification, reflecting changing social realities, have been made over the years, as is illustrated in Tables 15 and 16. The changes are reasonably clear, however. (1) Between the time of first white contact in 1778 to about 1850, there were only small numbers of haoles residing in the Islands, with an essentially homogeneous native Hawaiian population. (2) From about 1850 to 1930, successive waves of immigrant peoples produced wide ethnic heterogeneity, as reflected in Table 15. The larger immigrant waves were Chinese, Japanese, and Filipino, in that order. At various times other ethnics have found their way to Hawaii in response to the demand for plantation labor. Portuguese, Puerto Ricans, and Koreans came in sufficient numbers to be classified as separate groups in population tables. There have been, in addition, Spaniards, Germans, Islanders from scattered areas of the Pacific, and Russians.[2] (3) During this period the native Hawaiian population declined. Outmarriage of Hawaiians with other ethnics was so extensive that by 1930 the "Part-Hawaiian" began to exceed the pure Hawaiian category. (4) During this period also the Japanese came to a position of numerical predominance among all the ethnics. (5) By 1940 the proportions of the ethnic components were showing a tendency to stabilize. (6) Since World War II the proportion of the Caucasian population has been increasing. Whereas in 1950 the Japanese comprised about 37 per cent and the Caucasian component 25 per cent (including the Puerto Ricans), by 1960 both groups were at about 32 per cent. Table 16 throws light on the sources of change in Hawaii's population during the decade 1950 to 1960. The reader should bear in mind that this table includes the civilian population only, military *dependents* being included but military *personnel* not included. It will be noted that the net increase in the civilian population of Hawaii for the decade was estimated at 103,000. Nearly 40 per cent—or an estimated 40,000 —of this civilian population increase is attributed to the military dependency category. About 85 per cent of this military dependency category is white. It will be noted also that during this period the growth of the Japanese population was retarded by a net migration loss of 17,200, whereas the Caucasian population had a net migration gain of 17,300.

The story of ethnic intergroup relations in Hawaii will be divided into three periods: (1) the period of European invasion and the decline of

---

[2] See Andrew Lind, *An Island Community* (Chicago: University of Chicago Press, 1938), p. 194.

TABLE 16

Components of Change in the Civilian Population, by Ethnic Group and Military Dependency, For Hawaii: 1950 to 1960 [3]

(Provisional estimates. Independently rounded; hence they may not add up exactly to indicated totals.)

ETHNIC GROUP AND MILITARY DEPENDENCY	CIVILIAN POPULATION		COMPONENTS OF CHANGE, 1950 TO 1960			
	APRIL 1, 1950	APRIL 1, 1960	ALL COMPONENTS	LIVE BIRTHS	DEATHS	NET MIGRATION (a)
Total	579,900	476,900	103,000	160,700	30,200	−27,500
By ethnic group:						
Hawaiian (b)	102,100	85,600	16,500	42,500	5,900	−20,100
Caucasian (c)	157,200	104,900	52,300	42,700	7,600	+17,300
Chinese	37,800	32,200	5,600	8,400	2,400	−400
Filipino	67,700	60,500	7,200	17,500	3,500	−6,800
Japanese	202,300	184,100	18,200	45,300	9,800	−17,200
Other groups (d).........	12,800	9,600	3,100	4,300	1,000	−300
By military dependency:						
Military dependents	60,100	20,000	40,000	36,000	1,500	+5,500
Other persons	519,800	456,900	63,000	124,700	28,700	−33,000

(a) Includes net gain or loss from military inductions or separations.

(b) Includes part Hawaiian.

(c) Includes Puerto Rican.

(d) Includes Korean, Negro, Samoan, and other groups.

[3] Estimated by Department of Planning and Research from Hawaii 1950 and 1960 census data and information supplied by the State Department of Health and the United States Air Force, Army, Coast Guard, and Navy. Slightly adapted.

Hawaiian civilization, from 1778 to about 1850, when the immigration of
Asiatic people began; (2) the period of haole dominance over both the
Hawaiians and the other subsequent immigrant peoples from 1850 to the
second World War; (3) the period of the rise in status of the nonhaole
population, which characterizes the years since World War II.

THE DECLINE OF THE HAWAIIANS

At the time of the first white contact with Hawaii in 1778, the archipelago
was inhabited by a people of Polynesian origin and physiognomic features,
who had brown skin, black hair, and were considered handsome by Caucasians. Their society, though preliterate, was highly elaborated. Early estimates of the native population in 1798 placed the number at about 300,000,
but contemporary scholars believe it to have been far less than this. They
suggest that the early explorers saw only the settlements near the coast and
based their estimates of the total population on the assumption that the
interior was just as densely populated. It is now known that the island of
Hawaii, for example, where so much of the interior is covered by bare lava,
was quite sparsely populated. The Hawaiians had developed a distinctive
way of life suitable to themselves and with sufficient resources available to
sustain them. Within a century after the coming of the white man, this
civilization was virtually destroyed. The population declined almost to the
point of extinction, and the relatively small group of white newcomers supplanted the natives as the controlling element in the further development of
Hawaii as an insular community.

Except for the missionaries, the few Euro-Americans who came to Hawaii
before the middle of the nineteenth century were motivated almost entirely
by economic interests. First confining themselves to trading, the whites
gradually became interested in cattle raising and rice growing—introduced
first by the Chinese—and finally in sugar growing, destined to become the
economic foundation of the future Hawaii. Thus they came to seek permanent tenure of more and more valuable lands.

The reactions of the Hawaiians to the Haoles were compounded chiefly of
awe and friendliness, both of which aided the haoles in gaining their immediate ends. The technological superiority of the haole evoked admiration
from the natives and helped establish haole prestige. As Burrows writes,
"They [the natives] seem to have made the generalization that because the
foreigners were superior to them in certain points of technology, they were
superior in everything."[4] Although some native groups did oppose the haoles
as they encroached on their land, in general, infiltration was accomplished
peacefully. In 1845 an act was passed prohibiting aliens from acquiring fee

[4] Edwin G. Burrows, *Hawaiian Americans* (New Haven: Yale University Press, 1947),
p. 17.

simple title to land.⁵ Like the Indians in the United States, however, when this act was repealed in 1850, native Hawaiians sold their land for ready cash.

During the period here under review and beyond it, the native Hawaiian population declined at a staggering rate. From the early explorers' estimate of 300,000 in 1788, the numbers declined so that in 1950 only about 12,000 pure Hawaiians were recorded. The low point for the continued native and part-Hawaiian total was reached in the 1900–1910 decade. Since then the part-Hawaiian group has shown a vigorous growth.

Adams has summarized the causes for this phenomenal population decline: (1) the sanguinary wars which continued for seventeen years after Captain Cook's first visit; (2) the introduction by foreigners of diseases new and highly fatal to the natives; (3) the hardship and exposure incident to new relations with foreigners, such as cutting and carrying candlewood, service on whaling ships, and the contributions of foodstuffs required for trade; (4) the serious disorganization of production through trade and contacts with the foreigners; (5) the disruption of the old moral order; and (6) the inability of a primitive people to meet the requirements of the new situation promptly.⁶ In short, it is clear that this rapid decimation of the Hawaiian population was influenced by haole infiltration, even though haoles as a group or as individuals did not directly contribute to it nor desire it.

In this early period a pattern of interracial relations began to emerge quite contrary to those established by north Euro-Americans in their imperialist expansion elsewhere. The number of white people in Hawaii was quite small. They came from various nations and no one nation had gained ascendancy. Hawaiian political autonomy, although influenced by white intrigue, was maintained. The power situation called for treating Hawaiians with due respect and with at least formal equality. Furthermore, the white population was predominantly male, and thus many of those who remained married Hawaiian women. Intermarriage was further facilitated by the freedom regarding marriage within the loosely organized native Hawaiian system.⁷ Thus many conditions in the Hawaiian situation conspired against the drawing of a color line by the white people. Haole prestige, obvious even in the early days, was based more on social class position than on race consciousness. For the study of dominant-minority relations, this is the most significant development in the early period.

⁵ *Ibid.*, p. 40. At that time, land was owned by the king. In 1848, a division of the land gave some of it to the people.
⁶ Romanzo Adams, *Interracial Marriage in Hawaii* (New York: The Macmillan Co., 1939), p. 7.
⁷ *Ibid.*, pp. 46–48.

THE ESTABLISHMENT OF AMERICAN HAOLE DOMINANCE

In the latter half of the nineteenth century, white people established a firm control over Hawaiian society. Nationalistic rivalries among the whites from imperialist nations were resolved in favor of the Americans. Agitation in the islands for annexation to the United States then arose, ultimately producing a revolution and the formation of a provisional government favorable to annexation. Official transfer of sovereignty from the Republic of Hawaii to the United States occurred on August 12, 1898.

Economic Dominance

Control over the Hawaiian economy by American haoles had been substantially accomplished through the concentration of control over the elaborated plantation system and its auxiliary financial and shipping enterprises. This control was vested substantially in five corporations.

[The Big Five] act in the capacity of factors or agents for all but three of the sugar companies operating in Hawaii, and have substantial stock holdings in these companies. Together, the Big Five control about 96 per cent of island sugar production. Largest of these agencies is American Factors, Ltd., which was formed in 1918 to take over the business of the German firm of H. Hackfeld & Company, and which in 1945 represented nine plantations responsible for 30.8 per cent of the total sugar produced. The others are C. Brewer & Company, Ltd., with 23.5 per cent; Alexander & Baldwin, with 20.8 per cent; Castle & Cook, Ltd., with 14.5 per cent; and Theo. H. Davies & Company, Ltd., with 6.9 per cent. The agency system is less used in the pineapple industry, although some of the Big Five have an interest in that industry. The Big Five have holdings in other important enterprises such as public utilities, docks, shipping companies, banks, hotels, department stores, and affiliated concerns. Power is held not only through direct stock ownership but through financing and supply contracts, through holding companies, through complicated land-leasing systems, through control over transportation agencies, through personal interfamily relationships, through trusteeships, and through a web of interlocking directorates.[8]

This great economic development in Hawaii under American corporate direction would not have been possible without an additional labor supply. But because of the population decline there were not enough Hawaiians. Furthermore, the natives did not make good plantation workers. Burrows writes, "The whole idea of steady work for wages was so foreign to their old culture that it had no value to appeal to them. . . . When an Hawaiian was hired to work on the plantations, he would work, as a rule, only until he had enough money to buy what he wanted at the moment, and to give his friends a good time."[9] The labor problem was solved by the importation, either under contract or by active persuasion, of a succession of immigrants

[8] Ralph S. Kuykendall, and A. Grove Day, *Hawaii: A History* (New York: Prentice-Hall, Inc., 1948), pp. 271–272. By permission.
[9] Burrows, *Hawaiian Americans*, pp. 41–43. By permission of the publishers, Yale University Press.

from various parts of Asia and elsewhere. The order of succession of these ethnic groups is seen in the population composition in Table 15—the Chinese, the Portuguese, the Japanese, and, considerably later, the Puerto Ricans and Filipinos.

This process of immigration to Hawaii developed into a pattern. The need was for cheap and tractable labor. Each new ethnic group would at first serve as plantation workers. As its members became better adjusted to island life, some, growing discontented with their menial lot, would desert the fields for the city or return home. Thus the planters needed constant replacements. As the numbers of any one ethnic group increased, the characteristic antagonism arose, first showing itself among competing workers. The planters' strategy was to try new ethnic sources in order to allay public antagonism against any one group. Another circumstance which suggested this course of action was that the longer any group of workers stayed in Hawaii, the less tractable they became.

While the growth of a strong labor movement in Hawaii is a recent development, there was some organization among workers and some attempted strikes in the early nineteenth century. An ethnically divided working group, however, was not likely to develop strong labor solidarity.

The drawing of racial lines in labor activities has, indeed, been one of the chief causes of lack of labor solidarity. Early in the century, the policy of denying to Orientals membership in the skilled trades unions smashed all hopes for effective organization, for a "one-nationality" union arouses prejudice and may be crippled by competing workers from another national or racial group, who will work for lower wages or even act as strikebreakers. Discrimination has been charged; it was once a common saying in Hawaii that there are three kinds of payment for the same kind of work—what *haoles* pay *haoles*, what *haoles* pay Orientals, and what Orientals pay Orientals. Racial loyalties have conflicted with labor-group loyalties, although racial antagonism in Hawaii has never been acute. Language difficulties and differences in culture and outlook have further divided allegiances to working-class ideals.[10]

Although after annexation, contract labor became illegal, the planters still managed to locate and control the inflow of the additional labor supply needed.

Political Dominance

Wherever the economic control of an area is highly concentrated in relatively few hands, the same economic interests in large measure control the politics and government. While it is true that under American rule all the formal democratic institutions of the American governmental system were established, practically all students of Hawaii conclude that the Big Five controlled the political life of the Islands from annexation to World War II. Illustrative are these remarks of Barber:

[10] Kuykendall and Day, *Hawaii*, p. 275.

Moreover, they [the Big Five] are represented indirectly in the political affairs of the Territory, members of the legislature being linked with the Big Five, either through former association (or as in the case of the Speaker of the lower House, through being legal counsel for the sugar industry), or through the bonds of kinship.[11]

In spite of the fact that the nonhaole groups combined constituted a majority, they did not until about 1930 begin to challenge haole political domination. Although the Japanese were by far the largest of the ethnic groups, "it was not until 1930 that a number of Japanese-American candidates appeared in the primaries."[12] It will be recalled that federal law made foreign-born Orientals ineligible for citizenship.

INTERGROUP RELATIONS

The pattern of intergroup relations established in Hawaii before World War II involved haole social dominance over and discrimination against the nonhaole ethnic groups. The reality of the formal, institutionalized pattern of racial equality in Hawaii is attested by practically all writers on Hawaii. There are no Jim Crow rules in Hawaii; no segregation in schooling; no laws against intermarriage. However, practically all writers indicate that beneath the surface there are indications of prejudice and discrimination in which race consciousness is a predominant factor. Burrows writes:

. . . throughout their school years the Hawaiian born of Oriental stock have become more and more American. The process was favored by an atmosphere kindlier toward their race, and more tolerant of racial and cultural differences, than that of the American mainland. But when they got out of school, and set out to win their way toward prosperity, as good Americans are expected to do, they met with a rude shock. They found that the tolerance and friendliness among races, for which Hawaii has been justly celebrated, prevailed only within limits, and at a price. The price demanded by the dominant haoles—never in so many words, but nevertheless insistent—has been cheerful acceptance by other peoples of a subordinate place.[13]

Referring to haole relations with the Japanese, Bradford Smith cites instances of occupational and social discrimination.

Discrimination appears in social life as well as in business. . . . The principal of a Honolulu school told me that in sixteen years as a teacher . . . he had come to know only three or four haoles well enough to enter their homes, and all of them

[11] From *Hawaii, Restless Rampart*, by Joseph Barber, Jr., copyright 1941, used by special permission of the publishers, The Bobbs-Merrill Company, Inc., p. 46.
[12] Bradford Smith, *Americans From Japan* (Philadelphia: J. B. Lippincott Co., 1948), p. 166.
[13] Burrows, *Hawaiian Americans*, p. 85. By permission of the publishers, Yale University Press.

were from the mainland. Even in the faculty lunch rooms racial lines hold in the table groups.

Social considerations also affect advancement in jobs. A plantation manager wanted to appoint a Nisei chief electrician. If he did, the Nisei and his family would move into a house in the supervisor's area and his wife would have to be invited to social affairs with the other supervisors' wives. The ladies refused to do this. So the man was not appointed.[14]

The dominance of the haoles over the other ethnic groups was in considerable measure a function of their class position. The upper class was composed almost entirely of haoles. Most of the other haoles were in the middle class. The smaller number of lower-class haoles were, or were descended from, sailors or other occasional travelers who decided to stay there, some of whom belonged in the "beachcomber" category. In occupational upgrading and in wage rates within the same job levels, nonhaoles were discriminated against. How much this discrimination was based on "race consciousness" is a difficult question. Judged by comparison with Euro-Americans on the mainland United States, the haoles certainly showed less negative reaction to "color." Intermarriage between whites and Orientals and Hawaiians occurred frequently throughout the period, in part a consequence of the excess of males in the haole group. Before annexation, Hawaii classified its residents on the basis of nationality rather than race. After annexation the territorial government did classify Euro-Americans as Caucasian, and the offspring of a mixed marriage was classified as belonging to the non-Caucasian parent's group. In a plantation community where the differentiation of haoles as the upper class was strongly marked, Norbeck found the distinction between the haoles and the Japanese and the Filipinos to be more often thought of as cultural rather than racial.[15]

Status distinctions developed among the nonhaole groups themselves. The main Hawaiian gradient was haole-Chinese-Japanese-Filipinos. Native Hawaiians were interspersed but generally toward the bottom. Puerto Ricans and Portuguese also had a generally low status. In a study of the race preference of the Japanese in Hawaii, Matsuoka found the first preference to be their own kind, followed by "other Caucasians," Chinese, White-Hawaiians, Korean, Hawaiian, Portuguese, Filipino, Puerto Rican in order. "In general, preference depends not on physiognomy but on socioeconomic status."[16] Within the nonhaole groups, status differences had significance. Among the Hawaiians, the families descended from chiefs were superior to the commoners; among the Chinese, the Punti were superior to the Hakka; and the "regular" Japanese considered themselves above the Okinawans.

---

[14] Bradford Smith, *Americans from Japan*, p. 166.
[15] Edward Norbeck, *Pineapple Town* (Berkeley and Los Angeles: University of California Press, 1959), p. 118.
[16] Jitsuichi Matsuoka, "Race Preference in Hawaii," *American Journal of Sociology*, 1935–36, 41: 635–641.

Nonhaole Reaction to Haole Dominance

How did nonhaoles as individuals and as groups react to haole dominance? Burrows analyzed three types of reaction by the minorities to the stress and frustration engendered by minority status: aggressiveness, withdrawal, and co-operation.[17]

Aggression This had not been characteristic of any of the groups except the Hawaiians at the two periods of their maximum stress: around 1830, when the haoles were rapidly assuming dominance, and in the period of the 1880's, when haoles assumed control of the government. The only form of aggression which had been at all common among the minorities was the mildest one of grumbling.

Withdrawal The extreme forms of withdrawal were more frequent among Hawaiians than among Orientals. Such reactions were manifested in happy-go-lucky apathy, such as drinking extensively and taking life easy—going fishing and strumming the ukulele, for example. Extreme withdrawal was manifested in religious reversion, either in the revival of traditional Hawaiian rites and practices or the embracing of new cults.

According to Burrows, "recreation reversion" gained ground during the last generation in pronounced forms.[18] This mildest form of withdrawal was illustrated by the revival of interest in the traditional culture of the nonhaoles' native lands: among the Hawaiians the revival of ancient pageantry, the hula, and folklore; among the Chinese, the revival of Chinese drama and music; among the Japanese, the revival of Japanese arts, of which dancing was the most popular. While the withdrawal response was more common than aggression, it was still confined to a minority of the persons in the groups involved.

Co-operation Co-operation was the main reaction to haole dominance. For the most part, it involved passive conformity to the demands placed on the nonhaoles by the haoles. In fewer instances it took the form of asceticism, where the individual meticulously avoids all that is forbidden and drives himself to do his full duty. During the war this reaction expressed itself often among Japanese-American soldiers who drove themselves to heroic martyrdom in acts "above and beyond the call of duty."

The Acculturation of the Nonhaole People

Despite these reactions, the pattern of acculturation of the minority ethnic groups went on. The children of immigrant Orientals were being acculturated rapidly to the haole way of life. All the native-born were educated in public schools of a modern American type. "By 1940, approximately 65 per cent of the American citizens of Japanese ancestry over the age of twenty-five had completed eight or more years of American schooling as

[17] Burrows, *Hawaiian Americans*, Part II.
[18] *Ibid.*, pp. 167–198.

compared with only 30 per cent in the entire population of the Territory."[19] The public school system encouraged all its pupils to conceive of themselves as full-fledged members of a free and democratic society. As the native-born came of age, which did not occur before 1920 in any considerable number, except for the Chinese and Hawaiians, they began to participate more actively in political life. Illustrative of the American orientation of the native-born Japanese in comparison with their foreign-born parents, is Bradford Smith's comment on nisei reaction to issei attitudes toward Japan's informal war against China after 1931. "The Nisei resented the partisanship of their parents. They resented anything which set them apart from other young Americans. They resented the contributions to Japanese militarism. Family arguments grew bitter, family relations more strained."[20]

Like the earlier Chinese, the more enterprising Japanese moved from agricultural work into the cities, and there have shown upward occupational mobility. "By 1930 the Japanese were operating 49 per cent of the retail stores in Hawaii and provided 43 per cent of the salesmen. . . . Fifteen per cent of the Japanese gainfully employed in 1940 were in preferred professional, proprietary, and managerial occupations as compared with 13.7 per cent of the total population."[21]

The war gave great impetus to this process of acculturation through the opportunity it offered to participate in the common community war activities and through the improved economic welfare it afforded.

The Rise of the Nonhaoles

World War II marked a turning point in Hawaiian intergroup relations. The circumstances of war introduced new tensions, which were of a temporary nature. However, the war further accelerated certain trends which had begun in the period of haole dominance.

The exigencies of war brought to the islands an influx of mainland civilian workers and military personnel not accustomed to Hawaii's pattern of race relations.

As early as 1940 the mounting tide of defense workers, which was to more than double the size of the civilian population of Caucasian ancestry in Hawaii within six years, had begun to make its impact upon the sensitive balance of race relations within the territory. Despite the fairly frequent instances of "shacking up" with local girls, the defense workers generally were highly critical of the free and easy association of the various racial groups in the Islands. Most of them came with fixed ideas, derived from experience with the Negro in the South or with the Oriental and the Filipino on the West Coast. Although living in Hawaii, the psychological barriers they brought with them, along with the limitations imposed

[19] Andrew Lind, *Hawaii's Japanese* (Princeton, N.J.: Princeton University Press, 1946), p. 18. By permission of the publishers, Princeton University Press.
[20] Bradford Smith, *Americans from Japan*, p. 147.
[21] Lind, *Hawaii's Japanese*, pp. 17–18. By permission of the Publishers, Princeton University Press.

by their occupations and their segregated residence, prevented most of them from really becoming "at home" in Hawaii.[22]

The onset of World War II placed the Japanese in Hawaii in a peculiarly difficult situation. As the largest of the archipelago's ethnic groups, the Japanese had always been something of a threat to many of the haole population. It was almost inevitable that in consequence of the attack on Pearl Harbor, suspicion of their possible disloyalty should arise. Andrew Lind, sociologist at the University of Hawaii, made an intensive study of the situation of the Japanese in Hawaii following Pearl Harbor.[23] He reports that numerous stories of alleged sabotage by Hawaiian Japanese aiding in the success of the Pearl Harbor attack and of other sabotage activities were widely circulated through the islands and on the mainland United States. On the whole, however, he finds that the stories were given more credence on the mainland than in Hawaii itself. As we pointed out in Chapter 9, Hawaiian authorities imposed limited restrictions on those Japanese who were enemy aliens but not on the whole group. As to facts concerning the Japanese, Lind cites from a number of official sources to the effect that there was no evidence of sabotage on the part of Hawaii's Japanese.[24] The generally cooperative behavior of the Japanese, including the service of many Hawaiian Japanese young men and women in the armed forces, demonstrated their loyalty to the United States. "The net effect of the war upon the Japanese," writes Lind, "has been clearly to hasten and assist their participation in the broader life of the Hawaiian community."[25]

Toward Economic Democracy

We have noted the absence of any substantial unionization of nonhaole labor in Hawaii. As late as 1935 the membership of all unions was only 500. Between then and the Pearl Harbor attack, the number grew to 10,000. While the active list dropped to 4,000 during the war, largely because federal government regulation virtually dictated wages and working conditions at high levels, its postwar growth has been very rapid. "In 1947, two years after V-J Day, there were 47 organizations in the territory affiliated with the American Federation of Labor, 18 with the CIO (including five I.L.W.U. locals), 4 independent unions, and 5 government employees' organizations. Total membership claimed by the unions, exclusive of governmental employees, was 55,000 to 60,000."[26]

[22] Andrew W. Lind, "Recent Trends in Hawaiian Race Relations," *Race Relations*, Vol. V, Numbers 3 & 4 (Dec. 1947, Jan. 1948), p. 60. By permission of the publishers, Fisk University.
[23] Lind, *Hawaii's Japanese* (Princeton: Princeton University Press, 1946).
[24] *Ibid.*, pp. 43–46. Among the authorities quoted are Henry L. Stimson, Secretary of War, the Federal Bureau of Investigation, the Army Intelligence in Hawaii, and the Police Chief of Honolulu.
[25] *Ibid.*, p. 53.
[26] Kuykendall and Day, *Hawaii*, p. 283.

The significance of this postwar development of unionism to race relations in Hawaii has been summarized by Lind.

The sudden spread of the labor movement in Hawaii since the close of the war has widened somewhat the breach between the haole elite and the combined non-haole laboring groups. The plantation character of Island economy has long given rise to the myth that the haoles had a monopoly of the preferred positions, while the nonwhite groups performed only the menial tasks and occupied the inferior positions. The rapidly expanding labor unions, particularly those on the plantations, have drawn their membership as well as their lay leadership chiefly from the nonhaole groups, and the subsequent conflicts between the unions and the employers have reenforced the sense of a schism on racial lines. Actually, of course, the professional leadership in the unions is largely Caucasian, and an increasing proportion of the recently acquired wealth in Hawaii is held by non-haoles. As time goes on, it will become progressively more difficult to maintain even the fiction of a racial hierarchy in Hawaii.[27]

TRENDS AND PROSPECTS IN HAWAII

Since World War II, Hawaii's nonhaoles have taken such rapid strides toward assimilation that Lind was able to conclude that "The peoples of Hawaii are becoming Hawaii's people."[28] By 1950 only 15.2 per cent were foreign-born, the Koreans with 25 per cent and the Filipinos with 55 per cent being the only ethnic groups in Hawaii exceeding this.[29] It follows that most of the nonhaoles speak English. The fact that the territorial government stopped collecting data on this after 1930, when 85 per cent were literate and 75 per cent spoke English, indicates the increasing English literacy. The proportion of the total population who were citizens in 1950 was 65.7 per cent. The Filipinos had the lowest percentage of citizens of the large ethnic components, 14.9 per cent. This has been followed by an increasing participation of the nonhaoles in political life. In view of the 40 per cent Japanese population, many Caucasian Americans, both mainland and insular, were disturbed by the prospect of the Japanese controlling Hawaiian politics, but Lind finds no substantial evidence that Japanese participation in politics has had this effect.[30]

Acculturation of the Japanese
Some notion of the acculturation of the Japanese can be gleaned from the study of Pineapple Town, bearing in mind that this plantation community is not as typical as Honolulu.

[27] Lind, "Recent Trends in Hawaiian Race Relations." By permission of the publishers, Fisk University.
[28] Lind, *Hawaii's People*, p. 107.
[29] *Ibid.*, p. 81.
[30] *Ibid.*, pp. 91–92.

Western foods are dominant in nisei diet even though rice is always served. Amusements of the nisei bear little relation to Japanese pursuits, although social dancing is rare. The higher ranking, supervisory nisei belong to the golf club and with their wives bridge playing is a mark of social status. While they have all been taught the Japanese language, nisei are rarely proficient in it because they use it little. While giving their children a Japanese and an English name, nisei parents usually address them by the latter. Japanese cultural survivals are usually found on ceremonial occasions such as weddings and funerals but this is largely in deference to their parents' wishes.

In basic personality traits, the traditional Japanese cultural influence is noted in the prevalence of the following: punctiliousness in meeting obligations; reciprocity for any favors done; social distance, or reserve in social relations; sensitivity to ridicule; and the undisputed mastery of the husband in the home, however more freely the couple may associate in public.[31]

With reference to the religious acculturation of the Japanese, Kolarz writes:

Although many of the young second and third generation Japanese are Christians, Buddhism is by no means dead on the islands. . . . But Buddhism has changed in the Hawaiian atmosphere. It is more and more adopting the English language. Certain hymns have similarity to Christian hymns. Some Buddhist temples have introduced pews, candles and pulpits . . . A Buddhist from Japan would probably be appalled at such a sight.[32]

Further indices of the assimilative process going on in Hawaii can be found in occupational differentiation, in income, in residential distribution, and in intermarriage.

Occupational Differentiation

Each immigrant group started as agricultural laborers (except the Negroes, who are the newest arrivals); successively each group moved urbanward and to other occupations. This occupational shift, which has involved upward mobility as well, had been effected in part by the changing economic structure, especially the decline in the proportion employed in agriculture. Whereas in 1932 there were 51,427 workers employed to produce about a million tons of sugar at a yield of 19.9 tons per acre per employee, in 1952 there were 18,193 workers involved in producing about the same number of tons at a yield of 56.1 tons per employee.[33] By 1961, the number of plantation workers had dropped to about 12,000. With the increasing mechanization of agriculture, both the wage rates and the status of farm workers have risen. A summary of the occupational differentiation is put thus by Lind:

[31] Adapted by permission of the publishers from Edward Norbeck *Pineapple Town*, pp. 96–100.
[32] Walter Kolarz, "The Melting Pot in the Pacific," *Social Process in Hawaii*, 1955, 19: 23–26.
[33] Lind, *Hawaii's People*, p. 66.

Within little more than half a century the Chinese have run the full cycle from an immigrant labor group to one in which unskilled labor is almost nonexistent. The Portuguese and Japanese in that order followed the Chinese in pushing out of the laboring class, and by 1930 the Portuguese had only 30.1 per cent of their employed males left in that class, while the Japanese had a somewhat higher proportion. The slower rate of upward movement among the Filipinos is reflected in the fact that twenty-five years after most of them had arrived in Hawaii more than half of their employed men were still in the laboring class. This is obviously no reflection upon the Filipinos, but rather a reflection of the changed economic conditions of the Islands.[34]

Even with the Filipinos the proportion who worked as laborers declined from 80 to 54 per cent between 1940 and 1950, whereas the proportion engaged at the operator level increased from 8 to nearly 20 per cent. At the highest occupational status level—professional and technical—the continued high ranking position of Caucasians is seen in the 17.0 per cent of this group employed. The Chinese come next with 10.7 per cent; the Hawaiians and the Japanese are nearly even at 5.7 and 5.5 per cent; and the Filipinos are at 1.2 per cent.[35]

Income

As would follow from the occupational mobility indicated above, the income of the nonhaole peoples has been rising. "Census data available only for 1950 indicate that the sharp distinctions which once existed between the average income of the several ethnic groups are much less clearly drawn than formerly."[36] Acquiring the necessary skills for effective competition has been easier for the immigrant groups than for the Hawaiians; and among the immigrants, the Chinese, the Koreans, and the Japanese have enjoyed an advantage over the Portuguese, Puerto Ricans, and Filipinos, which Lind attributes to the variation in cultural traditions of the various groups.

Residential Differentiation

As the successive groups of immigrants moved toward the cities, like immigrants generally, they formed ethnic residential colonies. But in Honolulu at least these colonies tended to fuse more quickly, so that the boundaries between the ethnic colonies have been less sharply marked off than in mainland cities. For example, while Honolulu's "Chinatown" was still visible in 1950, only 10 per cent of the city's Chinese population lived there. The Japanese have been able to maintain their separate communities longer than the other ethnic groups because they have a much larger population. The upward economic mobility of the Oriental groups has caused the scattering of a given group in clusters representing economic levels. For example, in

[34] *Ibid.*, p. 73, 75.
[35] *Ibid.*, p. 78.
[36] *Ibid.*, p. 95.

the mid-twenties a cluster of better-off Chinese established a neighborhood in a higher-class area. Before long this area was invaded by other Orientals, and some of the most prosperous Chinese moved to still higher-class areas. In summary, Lind states: "All of the five largest ethnic groups are represented in all 61 per cent of the census tracts in Honolulu in 1950.[37]

Intermarriage

As we turn to consider the ultimate test of the assimilative process, intermarriage, it is pertinent to recall that marriage across ethnic or racial lines has never been prohibited legally in Hawaii. Any disposition toward racial exclusiveness is better reflected in the actual rates of intermarriage. Fortunately, accurate statistics of intermarriage are available since 1912. According to Lind, "They provide a clear and vivid account of the slow but steady process by which the many races of Hawaii are losing their separate identity. . . ."[38] As Table 17 shows, for 1912 to 1916, the percentage of all marriages that were interracial was 11.5 per cent, whereas from 1957 to 1959, the percentage was 36.4.[39] Over the years the heavy male ratio in each new immigrant group promoted outmarriage, which later tended to decline as the sex ratio of each group became more equitable. But this meant only a temporary reversal of the trend toward intermarriage. By 1950, 18.9 per cent of Hawaii's population was considered of mixed racial ancestry.[40] Except for the part-Hawaiians (already mixed) each ethnic category shows an increasing trend toward intermarriage, including the Japanese, who have shown the strongest tendency toward ingroup marriage.[41]

Throughout the years of haole residence in Hawaii, intermarriage first with native Hawaiians and later the Oriental groups has taken place. Over the time in which accurate figures of intermarriage are available, outmarriage of haole males has been increasing. In 1912–1916 the percentage of outmarriage (as a percentage of all marriages involving Caucasians) was for Caucasian males 17.3 per cent; in 1957–1959, the comparable percentage had more than doubled, to 38.5 per cent. The ethnic outmarriage of Caucasian females has been far less frequent, and showed little change until the postwar period. Since 1949, however the percentage of Caucasian brides marrying non-Caucasian grooms has more than doubled. For 1957–1959, the outmarriage rate for Caucasian brides was 20 per cent. The much lower rate of haole female outmarriage as compared with male outmarriage is con-

[37] *Ibid.*, p. 59.
[38] *Ibid.*, p. 103.
[39] The figures are not strictly comparable here, since for the earlier period there are twelve ethnic categories and for the later period only eight.
[40] Lind, *Hawaii's People*, p. 25.
[41] See C. K. Chan and Douglas Yamamura, "Interracial Marriage and Divorce in Hawaii," *Social Forces*, October, 1957, 36: 77–84, for more detailed discussion of intermarriage.

TABLE 17

Interracial Marriages as Percentage of All Marriages, 1912–1959

		1912–1916*	1920–1930*	1930–1940	PER CENT OUT-MARRIAGES 1940–1949**	1950–1953†	1957–1959††
Hawaiian	Grooms	19.4	33.3	55.2	66.3	76.7	87.6
	Brides	39.9	52.1	62.7	77.2	78.0	86.6
Part-Hawaiian	Grooms	52.1	38.8	41.0	36.9	39.6	42.3
	Brides	66.2	57.7	57.9	64.2	58.0	59.0
Caucasian	Grooms	17.3	24.3	22.4	33.8	35.6	39.5
	Brides	11.7	13.8	10.7	10.2	14.7	19.1
Chinese	Grooms	41.7	24.8	28.0	31.2	41.0	49.0
	Brides	5.7	15.7	28.5	38.0	42.5	50.0
Japanese	Grooms	0.5	2.7	4.3	4.3	7.4	11.2
	Brides	0.2	3.1	6.3	16.9	17.6	21.8
Korean	Grooms	26.4	17.6	23.5	49.0	68.8	74.0
	Brides	0.0	4.9	39.0	66.7	72.3	76.0
Filipino	Grooms	21.8	25.6	37.5	42.0	42.0	48.5
	Brides	2.8	1.0	4.0	21.0	30.0	42.0
Puerto Rican	Grooms	24.4	18.6	29.8	39.5	48.4	47.3
	Brides	26.4	39.7	42.8	50.3	59.9	63.0
Total		11.5	19.2	22.8	28.6	31.0	36.4

* Derived from Romanzo Adams, *Interracial Marriage in Hawaii*, pp. 336–339.
** Bureau of Vital Statistics, July 1, 1940–June 30, 1948, and calendar year 1949.
† Bureau of Health Statistics, calendar years 1950–1953.
†† Bureau of Health Statistics, calendar years 1957–1959. State of Hawaii, Department of Health.

sistent with the principle that women of a higher status group less often out-
marry than do the men. On the other hand, the doubling of the rate of
outmarriage of haole women in a decade is substantial testimony to the
rising status of nonhaole people. A more precise indication of the possible
degree of ethnic prejudices in the matter of marriage requires data on the
class distribution of outmarrying Caucasian men which, unfortunately, is
lacking. Of Pineapple Town it is asserted that a "haole should have a spouse
who is a haole, speech free of any trace of Pidgin English, and he should
avoid intimate social relations with most nonhaoles."[42]

Ethnic Discrimination

Studies since World War II indicate the continuance of subtle discrimination by haoles against the nonhaole peoples. In one study made of a business firm, it was found that the nonhaole employees felt, and in fact were,
discriminated against in getting higher-ranking jobs. The haole top people
say there is no discrimination but then go on to defend not appointing
"colored" to high position as "good business." A tendency to import mainland Caucasians for top jobs was noted also. The educated nonhaole felt
ready for higher position and showed anxiety and tension when it was not
forthcoming.[43]

A study of the reactions of nonhaoles to the Wilder murder case further
revealed the feeling on the part of Orientals toward discrimination. The
case involved the murder of a wealthy white woman by two native Hawaiian prison escapees. Interviews with the nonhaoles brought out their belief
that Hawaiian justice was racially unequal. The comparison was made with
the lesser penalty imposed on two haole youths who in the same year had
murdered two Chinese peddlars. The interviews further revealed a generalized antagonistic attitude toward haoles as "big shots" who took land away
from the Hawaiians and exploited immigrants.[44]

A recent study of ethnicity in relation to housing reports a limited degree
of discrimination by owners of private property in the rental market.[45] It
was found that 40 per cent of the landlords sampled showed no policy of
differential treatment on the basis of ethnic preference—that is, they neither
preferred any ethnic group as tenants nor rejected outright any group.
About 30 per cent showed a preference for a single ethnic group, generally
their own. Caucasian landlords made more use of the category "restricted"

[42] Norbeck, Pineapple Town, p. 118.
[43] Evelyn Yama and Margaret Freeman, "Race Relations within a Business Firm in
Honolulu," Social Process in Hawaii, 1954, 18: 19–25.
[44] Bernard L. Hormann, "The Significance of the Wilder or Majors-Palikiko Case," Social
Process in Hawaii, 1953, 17: 1–12.
[45] Harry V. Ball and Douglas S. Yamamura, "Ethnic Discrimination and the Market
Place: A Study of Landlords Preferences in a Polyethnic Community," American Sociological Review, 1960, 25: 687–694.

than did the Chinese or Japanese landlords. The highest percentage of rejections as tenants was accorded the Negroes, with Puerto Ricans and Filipinos as the next two most rejected groups; the Hawaiians occupied an intermediate rejected position; and the Japanese, Caucasians, and Chinese received the lowest percentage of rejections (in part related to the fact that these groups are also the landlords). This study was designed to determine the extent of purely economic factors, as well as ethnic discrimination, in affecting the landlord preference in choice of tenants. The findings suggest that neither discrimination nor the lack of it is primarily affected by economic reasons. On the one hand, these researchers feel the study suggests that "the more general practice of non-discrimination was in a large measure the result of a positive orientation toward the moral creed of assimilationism."[46] On the other hand, the same market conditions which "permit" individuals to practice discrimination—for example the availability of many Japanese permitting Japanese landlords to prefer Japanese tenants—also bear on the nondiscriminators.

HAWAII AND MAINLAND UNITED STATES

Recent developments have brought Hawaii into closer relationship with mainland United States. Each of these developments has some bearing on ethnic relations throughout the nation.

Trends in Migration

Along with the virtual cessation of large-scale immigration to Hawaii has gone a change in the pattern of migratory interchange between the islands and the mainland. Until 1930, migration from mainland to islands was far greater than the opposite. Since 1930, the intermigration has increased. For the twenty years from 1930 to 1950, Hawaii showed a slight net loss in this process. Nonwhite migration to the mainland has been increasing. In 1870, of Hawaiian-born residents residing in mainland United States, 7.7 per cent were of nonwhite lineage; by 1950 the corresponding percentage was 21.5 per cent.[47] Table 16 shows a substantial net loss in the in-out migration of the Japanese and Filipinos in the 1950–1960 decade.[48] On the other hand, during the same period there was a substantial net gain in haole population in Hawaii through migratory interchange.

Tourists

We have noted the increase in tension in intergroup relations during

[46] *Ibid.*, p. 694.
[47] Robert C. Schmitt, "A Century of Hawaiian Out-Migration," *Social Process in Hawaii,* 1956, 20: 38–46.
[48] This may not be entirely exchange of population within the United States.

World War II with the considerable influx of mainland Americans temporarily stationed in civilian or military assignment. With the increase in the
popularity of Hawaii as a tourist area, the presence of a substantial number
of mainland tourists is a regular feature of the Hawaiian scene. Lind has
speculatively considered the impact of tourists on Hawaii's ethnic relations.

The tourist is a somewhat unpredictable individual, and his effect upon the
local scene is therefore difficult to define and evaluate with precision. In most instances he comes with the racial attitudes and prejudices of the home community,
but as a tourist, he is also seeking to escape from conforming values which his
family and friends inevitably impose. Thus the tourist may arrive in Hawaii with
the same stereotyped attitudes as the military, but being in search of adventure
and stimulation, he may also discard these prejudices with surprising ease.[49]

Negroes in Hawaii

An interesting development to observe is the reaction of Hawaii's people
to the small but increasing number of Negroes now living there. The first
enumeration of Negroes in Hawaii was 233 in 1910; by 1940 there were still
only 255 recorded; but by 1960 there were 4,943. Lee believes that the failure of the census figures to show a greater increase in the number of
Negroes in the Islands between 1910 and 1949 is attributable to the tendency of many of the few Negroes there to "pass" under other ethnic designation—for instance, part-Hawaiian.[50] The substantial Negro growth since
1940 resulted from military and defense assignments. Eventually pressure
was brought to bear on federal officials to curb Negro assignments, a pressure coming particularly from the Hawaiians. Lee further found that, while
Negroes were definitely at the bottom of the socioeconomic hierarchy and
tended to be rejected as a group by all the other peoples, nevertheless, when
an individual Negro could "transcend his mainland-acquired sensitivity to
discrimination" enough to make constructive contributions to the general
community life, as an individual he was accepted without discrimination.[51]
Kalish studied the comparative attitudes toward Negroes of a mainland and
Hawaiian student sample. He found less prejudice among the Hawaiian students toward Negroes than in his mainland sample. The local chapter of the
National Association for the Advancement of Colored People disbanded because "there seemed to be no need for it"; yet he noted also the feeling that
the Negro is "low man on the totem pole" and that Negro-white inter-
marriages are strongly frowned on.[52] It will be recalled that a previously

[49] Lind, "Changing Social Relations in Hawaii," *Social Process in Hawaii*, 1954, 18: 1–9.
[50] Lloyd L. Lee, "A Brief Analysis of the Role and Status of the Negro in the Hawaiian
Community," *American Sociological Review*, 1948, 13: 419–437.
[51] *Ibid.*
[52] Richard A. Kalish, "A Comparison of the Hawaiian and Mainland Attitudes toward
the Negro." *Social Process in Hawaii*, 1956, 20: 16–22.

cited study of ethnic preferences of landlords found more prejudices against Negroes as tenants than for any other ethnic group.[53] Despite this it is significant that only 40 per cent of the landlords sampled indicated definite rejection of Negroes as tenants. The tentative conclusion appears to be that the general lesser prejudice in Hawaii against nonwhite people has mitigated the characateristic mainland prejudice against Negroes but has not eliminated it.

Hawaiian Statehood

Hawaiian statehood came at a time of rapidly increasing democratization of ethnic intergroup relations in the United States. The admission to statehood in 1959 is in itself a reflection of this democratic trend, since the polyethnic composition of the former territory's population had been an important factor delaying the change in political status. Interestingly enough, one of the first two United States senators from Hawaii is of Chinese lineage, and its first congressional representative is of Japanese background. It should be expected that congressional representatives from Hawaii, of whatever ethnic lineage, would join forces with their colleagues in sponsoring legislation aimed at protecting the civil rights of all ethnic groups.

SUMMARY

In summary the relations between ethnic groups in Hawaii may be interpreted by reference to the basic social changes in the Islands' social and economic history. In the relatively short span of less than 200 years, Hawaii has changed from an aboriginal, self-sustaining, isolated, stone-age culture to a modern, urbanized, commercial, industrial community linked closely to international trade. In the early part of this process there was a dichotomized, semi-feudalistic type of society, with an upper-class haole component and the natives (with due deference to the native rulers) and the immigrants as lower class. The dominant haoles possessed a value system in which capitalism, political democracy, and Christianity were basic. These values generated social forces which resulted in a structural revolution, the rise of middle-class nonhaole components which are now merging into a nonethnically differentiated middle class through increasing intermarriage. Among the noneconomic developments which have contributed to this change were (1) the maintenance of political control by native Hawaiians for over a century following discovery; (2) the development of a free and integrated public school system based on the American model; (3) the introduction of American political conceptions with the constitutional guarantees of the equality of all before the law; and (4) the missionary influence.

---

[53] Ball and Yamamura, "Ethnic Discrimination and the Market Place."

This social revolution was undergirded by economic developments: (1) the mechanization of agriculture, forced by acute labor shortages in World War II and later by union pressure; (2) an increase in commercial activities which made for rapid urbanward movement of population to the island of Oahu and the city of Honolulu. As Yamamura puts it:

In this setting there gradually grew the conception, forced by the profit motive, that talents should be utilized irrespective of race to maximize efficiency of operation. The circular reaction of tremendous technological advances and its impact on industrial operation, which promoted the extension of educational opportunities for all and the growing demand for more technically efficient workers, have done much to break the traditional stratification of immigrant groups into the lowest occupational levels. And out of this process has developed a substantial middle class of diverse racial stocks.[54]

Finally, the influx of mainland haoles since 1940 has done much to change the image of the haole in the minds of the immigrant groups. Seeing haoles in the unaccustomed roles of laborers and behaving in ways less typical of "upper-class" Caucasians has caused the other ethnic groups to depreciate the image of the all-powerful dominant haole and, reciprocally, to raise their own group self-conceptions.

SOME IMPLICATIONS FOR THEORY
OF DOMINANT–MINORITY RELATIONS

The Power of the Mores

The power of mores alone as a factor influencing the course of dominant-minority relations is strongly illustrated in the Hawaiian situation. From a particular set of circumstances in the early haole-nonhaole relations, a formal pattern of racial equality developed and as through the years it became explicit and traditional, it has operated persistently against the many forces present in Hawaii pressing in the opposite direction. In contrast, in the mainland South, other circumstances conspired to establish the mores of inequality and segregation. The mores, once established, become powerful factors to check the many influences in the Southern situation operating toward the undermining of caste.

The Cumulative Effect of Democratic Political Institutions

The Hawaiian story well illustrates the persistent effect of political democratic institutions in creating still more democracy. It is doubtful that the haole group in Hawaii at the time of annexation foresaw that the introduction of free education and the democratic franchise in Hawaii would, in

---

[54] Douglas S. Yamamura. Quoted from correspondence with the authors, who are highly appreciative of Dr. Yamamura's many comments which have been adapted in this summary.

time, lead to the challenge of haole dominance by the colored peoples of Hawaii. Yet it now seems clear that the rise of nonhaoles to complete equality in status cannot be prevented without explicit reversals in democratic institutions.

Ambivalent Effects of the Private Enterprise Economy

The drive for private profit in the Hawaiian economy led to the search for labor amenable to low wages and easy to control. The fact that this labor was procurable from sources with a degree of minority status based on racial difference further strengthened employer purposes. On the other hand, technological change, shortage of labor in an expanding economy, and the consumption potential of the labor groups in a competitive situation led to increase in the economic welfare of nonhaole groups as a whole and the increasing allocation of higher functional roles to particular nonhaoles. Thus the dynamics of capitalism produced ambivalent effects on interethnic relations.

TOPICS FOR PROJECTS AND DISCUSSION

1. Compare and contrast the development of dominant-minority relations in Hawaii with those which developed in the Northeastern states as a result of the mass immigration from southern and eastern Europe. Explain any contrasts you find.
2. How do you account for the contrast in the manner in which the dominant groups treated the Japanese in Hawaii and on the Pacific Coast during World War II?
3. Discuss the question, Why was Hawaii not admitted to statehood earlier? What changes in the situation appear to account for its admission in 1959.
4. Analyze the relation of the changes in the economy of Hawaii during the twentieth century to the developments in ethnic intergroup relations.
5. Design a list of questions to be used in interviewing mainland Americans who have spent some time in Hawaii aimed at obtaining their reactions to ethnic relations in the islands. If possible, try out your schedule on several persons, selecting those who were there a considerable time.

SUGGESTED READING

Adams, Romanzo. *Interracial Marriage in Hawaii.* New York: The Macmillan Co., 1937.
> *While primarily concerned with intermarriage, the book contains much material on general intergroup relations in Hawaii.*

Ball, Harry V., and Yamamura, Douglas S. "Ethnic Discrimination and the Market Place," *American Sociological Review,* 1960, 25: 687–694.
> *The findings of research designed to determine the extent of ethnic discrimination in Honolulu as indicated by landlord preferences for or rejection of tenants on the basis of their ethnicity.*

Kuykendall, Ralph S., and Day, A. Grove. *Hawaii: A History.* New York: Prentice-

Hall, Inc., 1948.
    A brief history of the Islands, treating the subject in a way useful to the student of sociology.
Lind, Andrew. *Hawaii's People*. Honolulu: University of Hawaii Press, 1955.
    The most comprehensive treatment of the trends in ethnic relations in Hawaii, including extensive statistical data up to 1953.
Norbeck, Edward. *Pineapple Town*. Berkeley and Los Angeles: University of California Press, 1959.
    An anthropological study of a pineapple plantation community in Hawaii.

17

Catholic-Protestant Relations

Since the American population before 1820 was predominantly Protestant, it is not surprising that among the cultural differences by which the Irish and, in later immigration, many other nationality groups were identifiable was their Catholicism. Most of the Oriental immigrants were not only non-Protestant, but also non-Christian. The one large ethnic group which we have not yet considered, the Jews, is often classified as a religious rather than as an ethnic group. Since the relations between Jews and Gentiles in the United States is so large a topic, it will be dealt with in considerable detail later. In this chapter, let us direct our attention toward evaluating the role of religious difference per se as a determining factor of dominant or minority status. Such an inquiry is logically called for in any systematic analysis of America's minority situations. Special significance, however, arises from the fact that the acculturative process has narrowed the range of general cultural difference among American minorities, while the basic religious difference between Protestant, Catholic, and Jew remains.

PRELIMINARY CONSIDERATIONS

One preliminary consideration involves the definition of persons in religious terms. Who are to be considered Protestants and who Catholics? For our discussion of religious difference as a factor in intergroup relations, the religious designation applies in a broad sense. A person is a Protestant who comes from Protestant lineage, from a Protestant family which is identified

with an ethnic background generally considered Protestant. Whether an
individual person from such a group is a member of a Protestant church or
not or whatever may be the degree of his religiosity is not of much moment
in counting the size of the Protestant group. While there may be some relation between active participation in church life and antagonism toward
other religions, there is no research material to support any hypothesis in
this connection. The definition of Catholics follows the same broad line as
in the case of Protestants. As compared with the number of Protestants who
are church members, far more of all the persons of Catholic background
belong to a parish, although again there is wide variability in participation
in religious life. In connection with dominant-minority relations, it is the
typical religious designation of the ethnic group which is involved. Thus
both Irish and Italians are considered "Catholic" ethnic groups, even though
there have been some conversions to Protestantism.

A second preliminary consideration concerns the distinction between religious difference as a basis of intergroup antagonism and conflict and as a
basis of dominant-minority relations. Here we should not assume that religious difference necessarily leads to conflict. While modern European history
does contain abundant evidence of conflict between religious groups, a number of nations have by now reached a point in which widely varying religious groups live together amicably in the same national community. Neither
should it be assumed that all conflict which divides on a religious basis is of
the nature of dominant-minority conflict. For example, an American Protestant may oppose the viewpoint of Catholics in his community on civic issues
for reasons not reflecting any dominant stereotype of Catholics. He may
only be exhibiting a deeply held concern for the issues involved, for example, the separation of church and state. Strictly speaking, Protestant behavior is "dominant" only when there are indications that it assumes an inferiority or unacceptability of Catholic or other persons as real Americans by
virtue of their religious identification. Even when this occurs, it is colored by
class attitudes, local political power struggles, and the historic position of predominantly Catholic groups. While admittedly it is difficult in practice to
distinguish between Protestant opposition to the Catholic church as an institution and Protestant discrimination against Catholics, we believe it useful to approach the subject with this distinction in mind.

Another preliminary consideration has to do with the relative importance
of religion per se in the total cultural difference which provides cultural
visibility of the minority to the dominant. This we shall later develop by
comparing two large Catholic ethnic groups, the Irish and the Italians.

The Plan of Inquiry

The most precise evaluation of the place of religious difference as a factor
determining status in the United States was made by Warner and Srole in

1945.[1] Drawing upon the available material of others, as well as their "Yankee City" data,[2] these authors set forth a "Scale of Subordination and Assimilation" as follows. After first dividing all ethnic groups into five racial types, they then divide within each racial hierarchial type on the basis of Protestant and non-Protestant. Next they divide on the basis of whether the group is English-speaking or non-English-speaking. The important point for the topic at hand is their conclusion that Protestantism always takes prestige and precedence over non-Protestantism and that being Protestant (the racial types being equal) rates higher than speaking English. For example, among light Caucasoids the English-speaking Protestants rank higher (highest of all) than all Catholics, and Protestants who do not speak English rank higher than Catholics who do speak English. There is considerable doubt that this schema, if applied rigidly, is still valid. For example, in Baltimore and Louisiana, old English and French Catholic families have maintained prestige from colonial times. Nevertheless we find that in adapted form it furnishes a plan for systematic pursuit of our inquiry.

PROTESTANTISM AND DOMINANT STATUS

English Protestants

Identification with an ethnic group which is Protestant is generally considered to be a mark of dominant status in American society. This status prestige of Protestantism derives, as we have noted, from the fact that the earlier settlers were English Protestants and that until 1820 they comprised an overwhelming majority of the population. Protestantism itself has been and still is highly differentiated, and this differentiation from time to time has precipitated oppositions and antagonisms within its own ranks, which manifest some of the characteristics of a dominant-minority situation. Indeed, religious intolerance was a marked feature of colonial history; persecution of sects which branched off from those first established, or of new sects which migrated directly from the Old World, was common.

In 1656 there appeared in Boston two Quaker women, Mary Fisher and Anne Austin. By law Quakers had been adjudged as not "of the people," and so these two were immediately imprisoned. Their books were burned. They were examined for witch marks. For five weeks they were confined in a dark cell, denied a candle and all communication with the outside world was forbidden. Eight other Quakers who arrived later in the year were similarly treated; their imprisonment continued until a ship bore them away.[3]

The principle of the separation of church and state and the right of reli-

[1] W. Lloyd Warner and Leo Srole, *The Social Systems of American Ethnic Groups* (New Haven: Yale University Press, 1945), p. 288.
[2] See Ch. 4 for a description of Yankee City.
[3] Everett R. Clinchy, *All In The Name of God* (New York: The John Day Company, 1934), pp. 30–31. By permission.

gious freedom had been established in the Constitution of the United States. Thus, legally, at least, all English-descended Protestant groups were of equal status. After 1820, however, new sects arose from within this ethnic population whose dissidence from the normative sects was so extreme as to incur persecution—the Mormons, for example. Since it does not appear that such dissident sects now occupy minority status according to our concept of minority, such religious groups do not further engage our attention.

Protestant Non-English-Speaking Peoples

The leading Protestant Caucasoid non-English-speaking ethnic groups in the United States have been the Germans, the Dutch, the Swedes, the Norse, and the Danes. We have already noted their more rapid assimilation as compared with the southern and eastern European peoples, who were largely Catholic. Because their general cultural kinship to the English is so much closer than that of the Catholic nationalities, it is impossible to evaluate precisely the relative importance of the factor of Protestantism among the many others. At the time of their great migration, their Protestant denominationalism was broadly distinguishable from the established English and Scotch denominations. Lutheranism was predominant. But since these peoples appeared on the scene well after the principle of religious tolerance among Protestants was established, their sectarian divergence from the main English denominations seems to have been of little significance. Too, the fact that they came after the beginning of the first great Catholic ethnic migration, that of the Irish, seemed to identify them more closely with other Protestants. It is interesting to note that Warner and Srole say of the Armenians in "Yankee City," a much more strikingly divergent cultural group, that their similarity in background "lies only in a religious affinity between the Armenian Apostolic Church and the Episcopal Church, which led to affiliation between the two and more rapid acculturation of the Armenian group."[4]

Immigrant Sects

In contrast to the "home-grown" minor Protestant sects discussed above, there have been a number of European dissenting sects who migrated to the United States during the nineteenth century and who came here primarily for the purpose of escaping persecution in their homelands. Most of these sects which were not English were of German or Swiss derivation, among them the Dunkers, a dissident Baptist sect establishing their first colony in Germantown in 1719; and the Mennonites, the first group of which also

---

[4] Warner and Srole, *The Social Systems of American Ethnic Groups,* p. 100. In view of the very small number of Armenians in "Yankee City," it would be unwise to assume that their status throughout the United States would be similar to that found in "Yankee City."

settled in Germantown, in 1683. Several Mennonite groups migrated from Russia, to which their ancestors had moved from Germany under the promise of economic assistance and religious toleration by Catherine the Great. Persecuted by later rulers, they came to the United States, settling largely in rural areas. Among the Mennonites in the United States, schismatic tendencies were so pronounced that in the twentieth century there were seventeen distinctive religious organizations which had broken off from the original Mennonite church.[5]

Among the small religious communistic sects, those not of English derivation were, again, primarily of German background. The Ephrata, Pennsylvania, colony was established by a German immigrant; and the Amana Society, established near Buffalo, was inspired by religious movements in Germany. In 1803 a German immigrant from Wurtemburg founded an experimental communistic sectarian community called Harmony, in Butler County, Pennsylvnia. The members later moved to New Harmony, Indiana, in 1814, and in 1824 sold their property to Robert Owen. Moving then to Economy, Pennsylvania, the group survived until 1903.[6]

Our interest in these immigrant sects lies in whether they are or have been minorities as we employ the term, and particularly in whether they have been discriminated against categorically. The studies made of these sects do not provide all the materials we would like for this purpose. Studies of the Amish and of the Molokans, however, are helpful.

The Amish   The Amish are a European-bred religious sect whose dissidence from Protestantism traces back to the Mennonites and ultimately to the Anabaptists. Of their religion Nimkoff writes:

> [They] believed that religion was an individual matter, and that neither an elaborate ecclesiastical machinery of salvation nor a political organization could take the place of a living faith as a means of access to a loving Father. [They] rejected infant baptism and baptized only upon confession of faith. They believed in absolute religious toleration. They held the doctrine of nonresistance, believing that only love and good will could successfully combat such evils as spring from human passion and hatred. They had a strong sense of otherworldliness. They interpreted the Scriptures literally. They stressed the need of living a pure life.[7]

Although the Amish are commonly thought of as Pennsylvania Dutch, they are in fact descended from Swiss, German, and Dutch lineage. Their first settlement was in Germantown, Pennsylvania, and they are still identified with Lancaster County in that state. But they have spread out in colonies intermittently located in the central United States and Canada, and are now estimated to number approximately 25,000.

[5] Elmer T. Clark, *The Small Sects in America*, rev. ed. (New York and Nashville: Abingdon-Cokesbury Press, 1949), p. 187.
[6] *Ibid.*, p. 139.
[7] Meyer F. Nimkoff, *Marriage and the Family* (Boston: Houghton Mifflin Co., 1947), pp. 242–243. By permission.

The central facts about the Amish most pertinent to our interest are that their religion and their whole culture are one and inseparable; and that being a dissident sect with long experience in being persecuted, they in fact desire only a limited acculturation. For this purpose their choice of rural areas to establish their separate community life was felicitous. The studies of the Amish made by outsiders dwell more on their culture than their relations with other groups; hence we lack materials to evaluate the dominant group relations with them. In the areas where they live, the Amish are highly visible by their garb and tonsorial customs. The men wear ankle-length cuffless trousers and white muslin shirts. Single and married men are distinguished by the fact that the latter never shave. It is inevitable that the native population should consider the Amish odd and poke fun at them. Yet it is questionable if they are actually discriminated against. In spite of religious taboos which preclude the use of modern techniques in agriculture, they have been reasonably prosperous, and for this they are respected. Their chief conflict with the larger community has been in connection with education and, in wartime, with military service. The Amish do not consider education beyond the eighth grade essential and they prefer to educate their children themselves. Nimkoff writes, "Recently a group bought an old discarded one-room schoolhouse, and are sending their children there to a private teacher rather than to the new consolidated PWA school with modern equipment."[8] Aside from these particular matters, the presence of the Amish creates no special community problems. They are largely let alone—which is what they desire. There are no indications that any of the Amish-descended people who wish to forsake their parental culture and to become assimilated into general community life would meet with barriers from the dominant status elements.

The Molokans   An immigrant sect more divergent in cultural background than those considered above are the Molokans. Between 1905 and 1907 about 5,000 persons known as Molokans fled from Trans-Caucasia because of religious persecution and settled in the United States. Their largest single colony, in Los Angeles, was made the subject of comprehensive study by Pauline V. Young.[9] The first group of Russian peasants to become Molokans dissented from the Russian Orthodox Church over 250 years ago. Like the other immigrant sects their entire culture is integrated with their religion, and their desire to maintain their distinctive religion developed a strong collective consciousness shutting them off from others. The Molokans, however, differed from the other immigrant sects in having selected an urban milieu, a fact which made it more difficult for them to hold their young people to the faith. In general, their experience in adjustment to American life was

[8] *Ibid.*, p. 251.
[9] Pauline V. Young, *Pilgrims of Russian Town* (Chicago: University of Chicago Press, 1932).

similar to that of other immigrant groups in urban areas, except that their strong desire to retain their religion retarded the process of assimilation.

Pattern of Sects The interrelation of these immigrant sects with the larger society appears to follow a general pattern. The sect typically isolates itself spatially from the rest of the society by choosing a rural locale and attempting to develop a self-contained economy. By limiting its contact with the outside world, the sect reduces to a minimum occasion for conflict. Such conflict as has arisen characteristically has involved the failure of the members of the sect to perform certain civic duties required of all citizens which were contrary to the tenets of the sect. Otherwise there is little evidence that these sects have been discriminated against in the typical manner of the minorities that are our concern in this book. Neither is there any indication that persons from such sects who desire to become part of the larger community find any barriers to their assimilation. In this connection it is to be noted that all the sects mentioned were composed of people of north European background and that despite their dissidence, they were, after all, Protestant Christians.

"Colored" Protestants

The most conspicuous exception to the prestige status of Protestantism is the position of American Negroes, who are preponderantly Protestant yet in most places occupy the lowest status of all the minorities.[10] Perhaps no other fact in the whole minorities picture documents the vastly greater significance of race consciousness as a determiner of minority status than this. When race is involved, all other factors pale into insignificance. Below, in another context, attention is drawn to an increasing conversion of Negroes to Catholicism. Insofar as this is due to a greater willingness of Catholics to admit Negroes to mixed parishes, there arises the interesting possibility that Negroes raise their status by transferring from the dominant prestige religion to the minority prestige faith.

Further light on the relevance of religious difference in affecting minority status when race is involved may be obtained by considering the religious affiliation of Orientals. By 1946, of the native-born Japanese 32 per cent were Christian and of the foreign-born 22 per cent.[11] A recent study reveals that 7.5 per cent of the Chinese in the United States are members of Christian churches.[12] Most Oriental Christians are Protestant, but, since the beginning of this century, the Catholic missionary order of Maryknoll has

[10] Jessie Bernard, *American Community Behavior* (New York: The Dryden Press, Inc., 1949), p. 252.
[11] *The Evacuated People*, United States Department of the Interior, War Relocation Authority (Washington, D.C.: Government Printing Office), p. 79, n. d.
[12] H. R. Cayton and A. O. Lively, *The Chinese in the United States and the Chinese Christian Churches* (National Council of the Churches of Christ in the United States of America, 1955).

also maintained schools for Orientals in the United States. Since Christianization of the Orientals was carried on through separate churches, while it contributed to their acculturation, there are no indications that it changed their status.[13] We have as yet no studies to indicate the extent to which the Orientals who have moved out into the general community are being integrated into the dominant congregations.

CATHOLICISM AND MINORITY STATUS

Catholicism in American society dates to colonial times. At the time of the Revolution it is estimated that there were about 25,000 Catholics in the colonies—16,000 in Maryland, 6,000 in Pennsylvania, and the rest scattered.[14] In most of the colonies, the Catholic Church was proscribed, and even though subsequently the Constitution assured equal status to all religions, some states continued these discriminatory laws and practices into the nineteenth century. Thus the outlook for Catholicism was not promising but, since the number of Catholics was relatively small, Catholic-Protestant relations did not loom as a major social phenomenon in predominantly Protestant America. With the advent of the great Irish immigration, however, the situation was considerably changed.

Anti-Catholicism

Organized anti-Catholicism arose after 1840, having one of its first expressions in the American Party, better known as the "Know-Nothing Party." This was part of the Native American movement which became an organized effort to delay the naturalization of foreigners and thus remove what was conceived of as the threat of Irish Catholic supremacy. As Kane has indicated, priests were forbidden to enter schools or hospitals to administer the last sacrament or to instruct the young in their religion.[15] Public schools used anti-Catholic textbooks, which ridiculed Roman Catholicism, the Pope, and the Irish. Catholic churches and property were destroyed. Kane observes, "In this case a constellation of situational factors—the first stream of Irish immigrants, increased visibility of Catholicism and Catholic power, competition for jobs, the Native American movement and other factors—were stimuli external to the organism—but organized with a special relatedness to Protestant-Catholic relationships. Both sides defined the situation as one threatening their group welfare, and accommodation disappeared in

[13] S. F. Miyomato, *Social Solidarity among the Japanese in Seattle*, University of Washington Publications in the Social Sciences, Vol. 11, No. 2 (Dec. 1939), pp. 99–104.
[14] Will Herberg, *Protestant-Catholic-Jew* (Garden City, N.Y.: Doubleday & Co., Inc., 1956), p. 137.
[15] John J. Kane, "Protestant-Catholic Tensions," *American Sociological Review*, October, 1951, 16: 663–672.

favor of conflict."[16] Later manifestations of organized anti-Catholicism were the American Protective Association, organized in 1887, and the new and revived Ku Klux Klan, developing after World War I. This latter organization, with considerable strength outside the South, was strongly anti-Catholic, as well as against Jews and Negroes.[17]

Ever since the great Irish migration, anti-Catholicism has been expressed in unorganized fashion—in private conversation and humor in Protestant circles, in refusals to admit Catholics into certain clubs and organizations. Well into the twentieth century, notices of jobs have occasionally carried the stipulation that no Catholics need apply.

As we indicated in our preliminary considerations, with the advent of many other immigrant groups from predominantly Catholic countries, all of whom experienced discrimination, it became increasingly difficult to determine how far it was their Catholicism as distinct from their foreignness which was the basis of dominant discrimination. While good test cases would be Germans or Hungarians where there are considerable numbers who were divided religiously, there are no materials to help us to determine whether the Protestant members of these groups rose in status faster than Catholics. However, some further insight into this problem may be gained from comparing two large Catholic immigrant groups, the Irish and the Italians, both of European origin.

The Irish as Catholics

In the general story of native-immigrant relations in Chapter 4, the earlier minority status of the Irish was indicated. Also noted in the community studies cited was the special role they came to play as leaders of ethnic groups, especially those of Catholic persuasion. As the first great Catholic group, the Irish had approximately a generation of adjustment to life in the United States before subsequent Catholic ethnic peoples appeared on the scene. With this experience they became adept at politics, especially on the local level. The common bond of Catholicism with the others enabled the Irish to gain sufficient strength to wrest control of government in many Northeastern cities from the dominant native group and eventually to play a leading role in state and national politics. Finally, within the Church itself the Irish acquired a dominating role among both clergy and laity.

Through the years, Americans of Irish descent have become assimilated. The "Yankee City" Irish by 1933 had distributed themselves through all classes except the topmost level.[18] In formal association and in cliques, the Irish intermingle extensively with Protestant peoples. It appears that persons

---

[16] *Ibid.*, p. 164.
[17] For a more detailed account, see C. F. Marden, "Secret Societies," in Joseph S. Roucek, *Social Control* (New York: D. Van Nostrand Company, Inc., 1949), Ch. 12.
[18] Warner and Srole, *The Social Systems of American Ethnic Groups*, p. 93.

of Irish Catholic lineage intermarry with Protestants, especially in the
middle- and upper-class levels, more than do the other Catholic ethnic
groups. It is also common knowledge that romances across these lines are
often opposed by both sets of parents. From the Irish side, opposition arises
out of intense loyalty to Catholicism. While on the Protestant side the opposition may contain residual elements of antipathy to "aliens," it is also frequently based on the very real problems which Protestant-Catholic marriages precipitate. The assimilation of the Irish is further attested by the
lack of in-group solidarity which their variable class statuses have accelerated. Concerning this the "Yankee City" study finds as follows:

Internally, the Irish group is now differentiated according to position in the city's
class system. The growing identification with class level and the usual manifestations of extreme class distance have served to break up the Irish group's inner
cohesion. The result is seen in the sharp antagonisms which exist between the
Irish of the two lowest classes (lower-lower and upper-lower) and of the two
higher classes (upper-middle and lower-upper). The former refer to the latter as
"lace-curtain Irish," a term with reproachful connotations, and associate them with
the Hill Street "codfish aristocracy." The higher-class Irish, when aroused, will
apply to the Irish of the lower classes the familiar epithet, "shanty Irish." The
lower-middle-class Irish seem to keep to the fence in this conflict between the two
class factions in the group.[19]

Earlier studies of minorities refer to the Irish as the highest ranking
minority. On the basis of the above discussion we advance the hypothesis
that the Irish are no longer a minority at all. The two main elements which
provide some common bond of union among the Irish in America are the
vestiges of anti-British attitude and their identification with Catholicism.
The former was manifested in the spring of 1950 by the "snub" given
by the city administration to the Protestant Premier of North Ireland
when he visited New York City. The prominence of the Irish in Roman
Catholic leadership is in part a function of their relatively higher economic
and political status. But above and beyond this, they continue to display evidences of being the most intensely loyal and devoted to the Church of all
the Catholics in America. Because this is their only remaining basis of "visibility," it follows that to any extent to which the Irish are now, or may be in
the future, a minority, it will be as Catholics and not as Irish. The above
evaluation of the Irish as Catholics may be set in contrast with the status of
Italians as Catholics.

The Italians as Catholics

Of the later immigrant groups the Italians were numerically the largest.
In Chapter 4, their minority status was attested. The Italians are generally
considered an all-Catholic ethnic group, yet in most of the literature con-

[19] *Ibid.* By permission of the publishers, Yale University Press.

cerning dominant reactions to the Italians their Catholicism appears to be a less marked consideration. This may be in part because of their subordination, as with the French-Canadians in New England, to the Irish Catholics, a situation which has caused the Protestants to think of Irishmen rather than of other ethnic groups when the subject of Catholicism arises. In communities where the numbers of Italians warranted the setting up of separate Italian Catholic parishes, the lower prestige rating of these parishes in relation to the Irish has been apparent. Again, the domination of the Irish in the Roman Catholic Church in America when placed against the traditions of Catholicism which the Italians brought with them, precipitated other conflicts. In southern Italy, local Catholicism had many adumbrations in the form of local superstitions which were less tolerated by the Irish priests than by the Italian clergy. In Italy the communicants were not accustomed to large regular contributions to the Church; in the United States such contributions are expected. In Italy the Italian men were not in the habit of attending church as regularly as the Irish, or in other ways actively identifying themselves with religious functions. In view of all these circumstances, it is not surprising to learn that Dr. Tolino, after considerable study of the matter, concluded that, in 1939, of the 6 million Italian-descended people in the United States, only about one-third were "good Catholics"— that is, attended church regularly and went to confession.[20] Another contrast was seen in the difference concerning parochial schooling. "In school too, the two groups hardly met, for the Irish filled the parochial and the Italians the public school. . . . Most Italians, much less faithful in carrying out religious precepts, sent their children to parochial school only when the latter was more conveniently located."[21]

The above considerations suggest that what distinguished Americans of Italian descent in the dominant stereotype was their "foreignness" and their Italianness rather than their Catholicism. Nevertheless, however much less intense and active their manifestations of Catholicism may be, Italian Americans for the most part remain Catholics. More Italian children are now attending parochial schools. There is little indication of their conversion to Protestantism. It may be, therefore, that as the Italians become more assimilated in general to the normative dominant culture, they, like the Irish, will retain visibility largely as Catholics only. This possibility is further strengthened by the circumstances in the process of their assimilation leading to greater residential, occupational, formal associational, and romantic contacts first with other Catholic ethnics.

While the Irish and the Italians have been used as illustrations in this connection, it is probable that considering the other European Catholic

[20] The Rev. John V. Tolino, "The Future of the Italian American Problem," *Ecclesiastical Review*, 1939, 101: 211–232.
[21] Caroline F. Ware, *Greenwich Village* (Boston: Houghton Mifflin Co., 1935), p. 132.

ethnic groups would lead to a similar conclusion. The foregoing analysis suggests that however much the other forms of reciprocal visibility upon which dominant-minority relations rest may appear, the distinction between Protestant and Catholic will remain a fixed difference in the foreseeable future. That this difference has been an aspect of minority situations in the past is clear. We turn now to consider the contemporary trends.

TRENDS IN CATHOLIC–PROTESTANT RELATIONS

An interpretation of the trends in Catholic-Protestant relations since the restriction of immigration requires keeping in mind our preliminary distinction between intergroup tension which results from institutional conflict and discriminatory conduct based on a dominant-minority situation. On the one hand, it appears in general that, ignoring short-time fluctuations, discrimination simply because they are Catholics against Catholic persons who apply for jobs, houses, or admission to social clubs has markedly declined. Illustrative of this decline in discrimination against Catholics are the results, indicated in Table 18, of a survey of restrictions stipulated in job orders placed with a sample of employment agencies. It is seen that restrictions against Catholics are negligible. The survey noted the appearance in the 1957–1958 period of the stipulation that the applicant be "All American," which was a new code name for "white, Gentile," and apparently did not connote rejection of Catholics. On the other hand, there is a less clear answer to the question of whether conflict between these two numerically major religions has increased or decreased. The Roses and Kane believe it has been increasing.[22]

TABLE 18

Restrictions in Job Orders 1956–1957 and 1958–1959[23]

	1956–1957	1958–1959
Total number of job orders	218	303
Total number of firms	202	258
Restrictions against Jews	142	83
Restrictions against Negroes	62	162
Restrictions against Orientals	43	47
Restrictions against Catholics	2	2
Restrictions against Mexican-Americans	18	44
Restrictions against minorities (use of code term "All American," meaning "white Gentile.")	......	30

[22] Arnold Rose and Caroline Rose, *America Divided* (New York: Alfred A. Knopf, Inc., 1948), p. 324, and John J. Kane, "Protestant-Catholic Tensions," *American Sociological Review*, October, 1951, 16: 663–672.

[23] *Rights*, Vol. 2, No. 6, April-May 1961, p. 52. A periodic report published by the Anti-Defamation League.

Areas of Conflict

The more sharply focused opposition between these two great religious groups appears to have been initiated by new activity from the Catholic side evoking more articulate reactions from the Protestant side.

Perhaps the most important field of church competition is between Protestantism and Catholicism. Until recently the United States was a missionary field for the Catholic Church. That is, priests were sent from abroad to take care of Catholic parishes in American communities. . . . The Catholic Church was too busy keeping its members in line and establishing itself in their communities during the transition from Old World to New World to devote itself to converting others. Besides, proselytizing was scarcely possible with foreign-born priests.

Now that it is more secure, however, and has definitely established itself in American community life, the Catholic Church has become aggressively evangelistic. It seeks converts from other churches.[24]

Especially pertinent to the minorities field is the fact that in religious competition for new members, the Catholic Church has made a special effort to win over American Negroes, with noticeable success, as we have mentioned. The Catholic Church enters this competition with certain advantages, notwithstanding the fact that Negroes have been overwhelmingly Protestant, 70 per cent of them Baptist alone. The Roman Church has a long tradition of freedom from racism. Being primarily rooted outside the South, the Church has not been identified with Southern Protestant segregation. In the North, Negroes have been admitted to white Catholic parishes far more widely than into white Protestant congregations. "In St. Louis, for example, while Washington University continued to exclude Negroes, St. Louis University, a Jesuit institution, opened its doors to them."[25] One of Bernard's astute observations is to suggest that the Catholic Church understands better than the Protestants that appeals in the modern world should be directed toward groups. "The Protestant group, with its evangelistic emphasis on the individual and on revivalism, still acts as though individual mentalities were the most important factor. The Catholic Church, with a more urban background, recognizes that a collectivist mentality now prevails."[26] Finally, it may be noted that in its efforts to integrate Negroes into white parishes, the centralized authoritarian organization of the Catholic Church is highly advantageous. A student of one of the authors reported eye-witness observation of the consternation and indignation arising in a predominantly Italian parish when, with no warning at all, at a particular Mass a strongly Negroid-appearing priest presided. Although in the Northeastern city concerned considerable tension existed between colored and white, nevertheless the parish quickly reconciled itself to the new situation.

[24] C. C. Morrison, "Roman Catholicism and Protestantism," *Christian Century*, May 12, 1946, 63: 747. By permission.
[25] Bernard, *American Community Behavior*, p. 253.
[26] *Ibid.*, p. 249.

As would be expected, this somewhat aggressive Catholic behavior generates indignation among Protestants. However, effective counter-aggression is hampered because of the lack of a centralized organization. Among the Protestant clergy are a considerable number who hold the most unequivocal views against discrimination and segregation, but these individual ministers are less able to change the practice of their church against the wishes of the congregation, because for American Protestantism there is no central authoritative body which determines policy.

Catholic-Protestant opposition has arisen also over stands taken by each organization on certain specific issues. From content analysis of a leading Protestant weekly, *Christian Century*, and an influential Catholic journal, *America*, for the first six months of 1939, 1944, and 1949, Kane found an increasing number of articles in each publication critical of the opposing religious organization. He considers this "some evidence" of growing Protestant-Catholic tension.

These tensions find verbal expression in criticism of Catholicism in foreign lands and the implication appears to be that were Catholics a majority in terms of power, American policy toward Protestantism would parallel Spanish policy. . . . Catholics are attacked for using their power and influence in economic, social, and political areas as a means toward achieving control of the country. These criticisms specifically involve federal aid to education, censorship of the media of communication, and appeals to the state legislatures to prevent passage of laws contrary to Catholic dogma.[27]

Another frequent source of conflict between the two religious groups is in the area of family relations—for example, concerning laws about divorce and the dissemination of contraceptive information. Intermarriage also is a source of tension. In general both groups look with disfavor on marriage outside their own faith. The Catholic Church exerts strong pressure to assure that the children of an interfaith marriage will be reared as Catholics and, if possible, the non-Catholic spouse converted to Catholicism. Protestants resent the unwillingness of the Catholic Church to compromise.

RELIGION AND CULTURAL PLURALISM

Herberg's analysis of the religious situation in mid-century United States is highly pertinent to our consideration of religion in relation to dominant-minority relations. (1) He finds that with increasing assimilation of the European immigrants except in religion, religious difference—Catholic, Protestant, Jewish—has replaced ethnic difference as a major differentiation of the American population. (2) In the process of adjustment to American society, both Catholicism and Judaism, originally foreign, became "Amer-

---

[27] Kane, "Protestant-Catholic Tensions," p. 670. By permission of the Editors of *American Sociological Review*.

icanized." "Foreign observers sometimes find the various American religions more like each other than they are like their religious counterparts." For example, "The Catholic church in America has tended to be activist in a way which borders on what Pope Pius XII in 1950 described as the 'heresy of action': the notion that the world can be saved by external activity."[28] The extensive social welfare program of the American Catholic Church illustrates this more worldly focus. Herberg adduces support for the opinion that American Catholicism has accepted the basic principle of separation of church and state, contrary to the traditional position of the Church. (3) The United States is experiencing an "upswing" in religion as measured by such criteria as membership and participation in established churches, the higher status accorded clergymen, and the revival of cultural interest in religion. A 1954 poll is cited showing that 95 per cent of the people sampled identify themselves as having a definite preference for one of the three great religions (68 per cent Protestant, 23 per cent Catholic, 4 per cent Jewish).[29] (4) The secularization of all three religions has proceeded so far that the theological distinctions which serve to distinguish them give way to a common belief which is essentially a belief in the American way of life. "Belief in God" and identification with a congregation of one of the established religions qualifies an American as religious and as a "good" American at the same time. Thus Herberg concludes that all three of the religions are now considered equally American and their adherents all equal Americans.

From the point of view of our inquiry, Herberg's analysis suggests the elimination of ethnic differentiation and its replacement with religious differentiation. Among the larger minorities, the main exceptions are Negroes, who, as we have seen, remain substantially segregated from the main American community, whether Protestant or Catholic; and the two large Catholic Spanish-speaking aggregates, Puerto Ricans in the Northeast, and mexicanos in the Southwest, who are not as yet integrated.

Assuming acceptance of Herberg's thesis of the equality of these three religions does not preclude competition and conflict between them. As we have seen, there is sharp conflict between Protestant and Catholic religious organizations. But this conflict appears more now as that of two forces with fairly evenly balanced power, and in its interpersonal aspects, between persons occupying equal social status (within class). Hence it is more similar to the political conflict between Republicans and Democrats, in which the opponents view each other as formidable adversaries, not as superior or inferior people.

Religious pluralism is consistent with American political democracy on the assumption that the adherents of the different religions are fundamentally Americans first, as are Republicans and Democrats. The conflicts

[28] Herberg, *Protestant-Catholic-Jew*, p. 95.
[29] *Ibid.*, p. 59.

noted above between Catholic and Protestant manifest themselves through the respective religious leaderships and far less often affect the interpersonal relations between the rank and file of the respective laities.

The presidential campaign of 1960 and the election of the first Catholic president, John F. Kennedy, reflected the trend toward religious pluralism. There were, of course, many indications of the traditional Protestant prejudice against Catholicism during the campaign. A University of Michigan post-election survey estimates that Kennedy lost 1,500,000 votes because of his religion. However, there were also many Protestant churchmen according to the Presbyterian *Outlook* and the Protestant Council of New York City who urged the voters to elect whom they felt was the more qualified man irrespective of religion.[30] As a candidate, Kennedy himself met the religious issue directly by stating that he considered federal aid to parochial schools to be unconstitutional and that he did not favor the United States having an ambassador to the Vatican. More generally, he stated to a group of Protestant ministers at Houston, Texas, that he would resign as President if he could not make every decision in the national interest without regard to outside religious pressures.[31]

At the very beginning of President Kennedy's administration, the issue of federal aid to parochial education was raised again when the new administration's bill to provide federal financial aid for public education was introduced in Congress. Opposition to the enactment of this legislation focused on its failure to allow any financial assistance to private and parochial schools. In public debate on this issue the opposition has been voiced largely by Catholic clergymen and laymen, with rejoinders in support of the principle of separation of church and state coming from both Protestant and Jewish religious circles. Thus this long-standing issue in American political life continues to be a source of Catholic-Protestant tension.

TOPICS FOR PROJECTS AND DISCUSSION

1. Select some religious group in your community which is considered a sect as distinguished from a denomination. Study its situation with the purpose of determining whether or not its members are a minority as the term is used in this book.
2. What issues have arisen in your community in the past ten years concerning which different religious groups have tended to oppose one another? Describe the situations and analyze them.
3. Debate the question "Are Catholics in the United States today a minority?" in the light of our use of this concept.
4. As a research project, interview a sample of middle-class Catholics with a questionnaire designed to determine the extent to which they associate with non-

---

[30] The *New York Times*, September 9, 1960, p. 1, and September 15, 1960, p. 28.
[31] The *New York Times*, September 13, 1960, p. 1.

Catholics. The project could be extended by selecting a sample of middle-class Protestants and similarly measuring the extent of their association with Catholics.

5. As a term paper project, study the history of anti-Catholic movements in the United States with the purpose of delineating the social and psychological characteristics of the Protestant groups manifesting intense prejudice against Catholics, and of indicating the social conditions or circumstances under which anti-Catholicism rises or falls.

SUGGESTED READING

Bernard, Jessie. *American Community Behavior*. New York: The Dryden Press, Inc., 1949, Chapter 18, "Culture Conflict: Denominational."
> *An analysis of conflicts within Protestantism and Catholicism and the conflict between the two religious groups.*

Billington, R. A. *The Protestant Crusade, 1800–1860*. New York: The Macmillan Co., 1938.
> *A study of the origins of American nativism and its development to 1960.*

Herberg, Will. *Protestant-Catholic-Jew: An Essay in American Religious Sociology*. Garden City, N.Y.: Doubleday & Co., Inc., 1956.
> *An analysis of the three leading religions in the United States and their relations to each other.*

Kane, John J. "Protestant-Catholic Tensions." *American Sociological Review*. Vol. 10, October 1951, pp. 663–672.

Myers, Gustavus. *History of Bigotry in the United States*. New York: Random House, 1943.
> *An extensive account of organized activities of a nativist, anti-Catholic, and anti-Semitic character in the United States.*

Underwood, Kenneth W. *Protestant and Catholic*. Boston: The Beacon Press, 1957.
> *A field study of Protestant-Catholic relations in a Massachusetts city following a specific incident.*

18

Jewish-Gentile Relations

The persistence of the Judaic tradition as a minority religion in western Europe from the days of the Roman Empire to the present is one of the greatest demonstrations of the survival of a value system in history. It has also occasioned the development of the most complex pattern of dominant-minority relations in modern times. Territorial conquests have subjected or dispersed the Jewish people throughout their history. With the struggle of non-Jews to establish the power of western Christianity, eastern Christianity, and Islam, the religious issue was kept primary. The Jews experienced recurrent persecution, formal restrictions on residence, occupation, and civic status throughout most of Europe until the seventeenth century and in some areas even longer. Persecution occurred in eastern Europe in the nineteenth and early twentieth centuries and, within living memory, in western Europe in the countries under Nazi domination. Such a remembered past alone, even if there were no other factors, of necessity strengthened Jewish bonds of identity.

The situation of the Jews in various times and places has encompassed every aspect of dominant-minority relations. The history of the Jews in the ancient world included the experience of being a colonially conquered people. Early in the Christian era they were driven out of their homeland. In this period, usually referred to as the Diaspora, or "Dispersion," and in the succeeding eighteen centuries, they were dispersed throughout the whole civilized world. The persistence of segregated colonies of Jews created a pattern of cultural minorities.

The particular historical developments of the twentieth century have added other dimensions to the position of Jews as a minority. When the National Socialist Party undid for Germany all the gains made in western European social thought since the Age of Enlightenment and exterminated six million Jews, the bonds of identity of Jews throughout the world, which had loosened under two centuries of improved civic status, were reestablished and intensified. The founding of the state of Israel has given many Jews a Jewish political identity and affected the feelings of Jews in other countries.

One cannot consider Jewish-Gentile relations without this historical perspective. It accounts for the fact that Jews have been identified, and have identified themselves at various times and in various places, as a religious minority, an ethnic minority, and a "racial" minority.

THE JEWS IN AMERICA

No other minority in America has acculturated more rapidly and contributed more to the dominant culture than the Jewish minority. It is not their history in western Europe alone which has influenced the position of Jews in American life. The periods and circumstances of their migration here have contributed to developments within the Jewish minority and to the attitudes of American Gentiles toward Jews.

The growth of the Jewish population in the United States falls into three main periods, the first two of which involved substantial increments through immigration, and the third of which showed smaller migration but an excess of births over deaths. The three periods are (1) from colonial times to the beginning of the great migration after 1880; (2) from the great migration to the passage of the restrictive quota act of 1924; and (3) from 1924 to the present.

Jewish Immigration to 1880

The history of Jewish immigration to North America began with the arrival of twenty-three Sephardic (Spanish-Portuguese) Jews—men, women, and children who settled in New Amsterdam in September, 1654, interestingly enough, according to Goldberg, "as fugitives from South American bigotry."[1]

By the time of the American Revolution, individual Jews or Jewish families were to be found in nearly every colony. "Jews organized religious

[1] Nathan Goldberg, "Population Trends Among American Jews," *Jewish Affairs* (New York: American Jewish Congress, April, 1948), Vol. II, No. 5. See also Bernard D. Weinryb, "Jewish Immigration and Accommodation to America," *The Jews: Social Patterns of an American Group* (Glencoe, Ill.: The Free Press, 1958), p. 4 ff.

communities in Georgia in 1733, in Philadelphia in 1745, in Charleston in 1750, and in Richmond in 1790."[2]

Most of these early Jewish migrants were merchants and fitted very well into the colonial merchant society. According to Weinryb, some had experienced *de facto* political freedom in the Netherlands, England, or the West Indies before coming to America. By the time of the American Revolution and the first decades of the nineteenth century, many were indistinguishable in appearance, manner, and behavior from the rest of the merchant population.[3]

The colonial Jews settled mostly in cities, not only in large cities, but in hinterland towns as well. Rebecca Gratz, daughter of Michael Gratz of Philadelphia and granddaughter of Joseph Simon of Lancaster, Pennsylvania, was a famed beauty and hostess in Philadelphia in the early nineteenth century. She is rumored to have been the model for Rebecca in Scott's *Ivanhoe*. Scott knew of her through their common friend, Washington Irving.[4]

The nineteenth-century Jewish immigration was largely from Germany and Austria. Whereas the colonial Jews had tended to be of the merchant class and of high educational status (either Hebrew or secular), the German migration up to 1840 was primarily of less well-educated, small-town German Jews.[5] After 1840 there was an important German-speaking Jewish group, from Germany and Austria, whose members were liberal intellectuals, including many of the so-called "forty-eighters," who migrated for political reasons. This group, more German in identification than Jewish, served as a link between the German Jewish immigrants and the cultural organizations of other (Gentile) Germans in America.[6] Through their influence, German culture provided the context for the values of the Jewish elite of the period and a model for the small craftsmen and peddlers who comprised the bulk of the German-Jewish migration.

The Immigration from Eastern Europe: 1880–1914

The great eastern European Jewish migration began about 1880 and increased to a flood which was stemmed by World War I and the policy of restriction which followed it. About a half million Jews came to the United States between 1881 and 1898, and about a million and a half between 1898 and 1914. Most of them came from the Russian Empire, which included Poland and the Baltic States.

Under Russian policy these migrants had experienced persecution or the

[2] Goldberg, p. 5.
[3] Weinryb, "Jewish Immigration and Accommodation to America," p. 9.
[4] Gladys Meyer, *Free Trade in Ideas: Aspects of American Liberalism Illustrated in Franklin's Philadelphia Career* (New York: King's Crown Press, 1941), p. 41, n. 77.
[5] Weinryb, "Jewish Immigration and Accommodation to America," p. 12.
[6] *Ibid.*, p. 13.

threat of persecution, attempts at forced conversion, and residential segregation. In eastern Europe the most common pattern of living they had experienced was that of small trading communities, exclusively Jewish, surrounded by Gentile peasantry. Adapted to living an ecologically separate Jewish life in eastern Europe, eastern European Jewish migrants transferred the pattern of a Jewish traditional life to the United States. Nevertheless, despite their traditionalism, the migrants represented the poor and the unlearned or the restless; the rich, learned, and well-established stayed home.

These eastern European Jews, despite differences among them which will be indicated later, came from communities (*shtetle*) in which the total normative structure was governed by Orthodox Judaism. Within these villages high status went to those learned in Talmudic studies (available only to males). Wealth was also highly regarded, but less so than learning. In contrast with this elite, the common people (*prosteh*), who were the craftsmen, unskilled workmen, peddlers, and the like, had markedly lower status. In addition to being religion-centered, the culture was strongly family-centered. The authority was patriarchal, with the activities of the women restricted to domestic responsibility and ceremonial religious participation in the home. The language spoken (Yiddish) was a dialect which combined Hebrew, German, and Russian words with regional incorporations. This folk culture was a rich, warm, earthy, and witty expression of the life of a minority which had stabilized over time its cultural relation to the larger society.[7]

The Jewish immigrants came to stay. "Only 7.1 per cent of Jewish immigrants to the United States between 1908 and 1914 left the country compared with one-third of all other immigrants. Indeed, this proportion of departures fell to 1.7 per cent in the case of Jews between 1915 and 1943, while it rose to an average of 42.3 per cent for other immigrants."[8]

Since Jews more frequently came as families, or the husband and father sent for his wife and relatives as quickly as possible, the sex composition of the Jewish population had a lesser excess of males than that of other immigrant groups of the period.

Recent Jewish Immigration

The more recent Jewish immigration includes those who came to America after the ascendance of the Nazis in Germany, those able to escape in the upheaval and displacement of World War II, and the "remnants of Israel," people from concentration camps and displaced persons centers after the war. The exact volume of this migration cannot be derived from official

---

[7] Mark Zborowski and Elizabeth Herzog, *Life Is With People* (New York: International Universities Press, Inc., 1952). This study of "the Jewish little-town of eastern Europe" was part of the Columbia University Research in Contemporary Cultures, under the late Ruth Benedict.

[8] Goldberg, *Population Trends Among American Jews*, p. 7.

statistics, since religion has been deleted from statistical classification for immigration. It is estimated that about 10,000 Jews have been coming annually since the early nineteen thirties. These immigrants have tended to be very different from those of the earlier migrations. They have come originally from eastern as well as western Europe, some of them making their second or third migration in an attempt to survive displacement in their home territory. They represent a higher educational and status level than the eastern European migration of the pre-World War I period.[9]

Population Characteristics of the Jewish Minority

Accurate data on the size of the Jewish population also is difficult to obtain. A 1959 estimate places the total population of American Jews at 5,367,000.[10] Approximately 75 per cent of the total American Jewish population live in large metropolitan areas: Baltimore, Boston, Chicago, Cincinnati, Cleveland, Detroit, Los Angeles, Miami, New York City, Newark, Philadelphia, Pittsburgh, St. Louis, and San Francisco.[11] One stereotype of Jews has described them as an urban people, which is not entirely correct historically. Contemporary research is beginning to discover a variety of historical ecological *loci* for Jews; they have been land owners, villagers, artisans, and administration personnel in feudal estates, and so on.

While the greater opportunity afforded Jews in the larger cities is one reason for their concentration in urban areas in the United States, another is the preference for living with their co-religionists in a large enough subcommunity either to feel protected or to continue the rich pattern of interaction which has characterized Jewish community life. It is part of Jewish religion that the good Jew is concerned responsibly with community well-being. For some Jews this has been directed toward the life of the Jewish subcommunity. For others, especially for wealthy Jews, it extends to the larger frame of reference of the American secular world.

The almost exclusively urban concentration of American Jews suggests a smaller average family size and a lower birth rate than that of the general population, and consequently a higher proportion of the aged in the Jewish population.[12]

The significant aspects of Jewish demography are these: (1) Jews in the United States comprise less than 5 per cent of the total population; (2) present population trends indicate the Jewish population is growing less rapidly than the general national growth; (3) no radical change has occurred in the urban concentration of Jews within the country.

---

[9] Weinryb, "Jewish Immigration and Accommodation to America," pp. 21–22.
[10] *American Jewish Year Book* (New York and Philadelphia: The Jewish Publication Society of America, 1960), p. 3.
[11] Ben B. Seligman, *et al.*, "Some Aspects of Jewish Demography," in *The Jews: Social Patterns of an American Group*, p. 46.
[12] *Ibid.*, pp. 54–55.

JEWISH TRADITIONS AND INSTITUTIONS

Within the American Jewish population there are differences according to the history of each population group. The greatest of these is among the elite descendants of the Spanish-Portuguese population, the western European Jews, and the eastern Jews. In Europe these differences were reflected in the ways the Jewish people related to their religious tradition and to the outside world. In America they have become predominantly status differences, linked with the period of migration, just as the date of migration has affected status differences for all American settlers.

Jews are divided by their religious affiliation into three groups: Orthodox, Reform, and Conservative. Orthodox Jews keep as closely as possible to the Mosaic Law and its Talmudic elaboration. This means that they observe their Sabbath (Saturday) as a day of absolute abstention from the work of the other six days. For example, they refrain on the Sabbath from using transportation, from cooking, and from secular reading. Orthodox Jews keep the traditional dietary laws, which include prohibitions of particular kinds of foods and ritualistic regulations concerning the preparation of food. Within Orthodoxy there are some sects, the largest of which are the Hassidim, which are distinguished by their dress, hair style, and the character of worship. Orthodoxy is characteristic chiefly of the Spanish-Portuguese elite and the older generations of the eastern European immigrants. In recent decades it has had a revival among Jewish intellectuals.

Reform Judaism is an outgrowth of the philosophy of Enlightenment as it affected Jews primarily in Germany. The Reform movement attempted to adapt Jewish religious life to the dominant Protestant model without losing the essential characteristics of Judaism. This means that it is altered legally and ritualistically, leaving theology unchanged. Some Reform Jews adapt to the dominant culture in observance of Sunday as the Sabbath, and have incorporated in their temple services such modifications as organ music, mixed choirs, and the unsegregated seating of women. The Reform movement in the United States has its main center in Cincinnati and has grown among the German Jewish population. Despite some inroads from Conservative Judaism, it is still the dominant pattern for Mid-western and Southern Jews.

Conservative Judaism represents a compromise and is in part a protest against the extreme modification initiated by the Reform Jewish movement. Less rigid than Orthodox Judaism, it has nevertheless retained much of the liturgical emphasis of Orthodoxy and some of the social practices which preserve the distinctiveness of the Jewish community. Conservative Judaism has often been the comfortable solution for the second and third generation descendants of Orthodox Jews in America.

Jews as a historic minority have been attracted in many instances to movements of social protest. There are many Jews who have embraced a social ideology which rejects religion but who still identify themselves as Jews, either out of love for traditional Jewish culture or from a consciousness of themselves as a designated minority.

The great characteristics of Judaism are both contributive and divisive in the total society. Judaism is responsible for the establishment of the first pure monotheism. As a scripture-based religion, it has maintained literacy and learning as a permanent value, which has been a principal factor in the survival of the Jews as a religious minority. The Jewish religion does not emphasize individual salvation, but rather group salvation. It does not allow a personal image of God, but rather casts the ideals of religion as abstract principles, such as Justice, Mercy, Righteousness, which are the attributes of God. Such a religion, with its group emphasis, logically requires of the Jew that he be a contributor to the community, that within his power he aid its preservation and development, that no individual Jew be left outside the shelter of community concern. The secularization of this ideal is responsible for the fact that Jews have often contributed more of their wealth to the secular community in proportion to their numbers than have Christians.[13]

Another aspect of the fact that Judaism is group oriented is the dogma that the Jews are a "chosen people." This is often misinterpreted to mean that the Jews believe they are better than others. Its religious meaning is rather that the Jews, through their conscious enlightenment about the nature of God and their purification by suffering, have a special role to play in the universal realization of the ideals that are the core of their belief. This dogma, however, often operates as a self-segregating force, and as a divisive factor between Gentiles and Jews.

The Jewish Family

The cohesiveness of the family is one of the strongest characteristics of the Jewish group. This derives in part from the emphasis in Jewish religion on marriage and family life, as well as adaptations of this tradition in such a practice as early (and, in former times, arranged) marriage, and in part from the mutual aid and protection of the extended kinship. Jewish families on the whole live in the nuclear pattern, keeping in closer touch with their relatives, visiting more frequently, and being more willing to aid a promising relative than is characteristic of the dominant pattern.[14] Among the older generation of eastern European Jews, there is the beloved stereotype of the Jewish mother who will sacrifice everything for her family.

Male and female roles are sharply defined, even though American Jews encourage the education of women and their participation in community affairs. Authority in the family is in the hands of the men. For religious Jews, it is important to have sons, since certain rituals can be carried out

[13] Cleveland Amory, *Who Killed Society?* (New York: Harper & Brothers, 1961).
[14] Stanley R. Brav, *Jewish Family Solidarity: Myth or Fact?* (Vicksburg, Miss.: Nogales Press, 1940).

only by males. Even where this religious emphasis is no longer stressed, the high valuation of sons seems to persist. Though Jewish religion takes a strong stand against out-marriage, there has been some out-marriage in modern times.[15] But descendants of the historical priestly class (Cohanim) and Levites specifically may not even marry converts.

The Jewish Occupational Pattern

Accurate estimates of the occupational distribution of Jews are difficult to make, since they must be compiled from studies of different localities, where the job classifications are often not comparable. Some data, however, can give an indication of the character of the Jewish labor force.

According to Seligman, it appears that a smaller proportion of the total Jewish population is part of the labor force than is true of the general population. It is suggested that this may be related to such factors as the longer period of schooling for Jewish children, or to the emphasis on the domestic role of women.[16]

The Jewish male labor force in most of the communities for which we have data appears to be higher in proportion to the general population in the employer and self-employed class. Classifications by industry indicate a concentration in the wholesale and retail trades. Although it is a popular belief that Jews are found most frequently in the professions, community studies which provide occupational information show the manufacturing (proprietary and managerial) group greater than the professional in most cases.[17] If we consider the nationwide pattern of Jewish occupations, the exclusive occupational emphasis of Jews on the professions seems to be less than has been generally believed. "In more recent years proprietorship has been of first rank in virtually all the Jewish population studies included here, with clerical occupations second and professional work in third position."[18]

Jews as a group have a higher average age than the rest of the population. Since the older age groups in this country have a higher proportion of professionals, semiprofessionals, proprietors, managers, and officials, this is a factor which must be taken into account in considering the proportions of the Jewish labor force in these categories. In the female labor force in 1950 the Jewish urban population approaches the proportions found in the general labor force.

The Jews in American Politics

In Europe most of the Jews who were at all politically active, after restric-

---

[15] Fred L. Strodtbeck, "Family Interaction, Values, and Achievement," in *The Jews: Social Patterns of an American Group*, pp. 147 ff.
[16] Seligman, "Some Aspects of Jewish Demography," pp. 70–82.
[17] *Ibid.*, p. 73.
[18] *Ibid.*

tions on political participation were removed, adhered to the moderate democratic movements of the times.[19] But some Jews were attracted by nineteenth-century radicalism, mainly because traditional religious barriers were presumably irrelevant in these movements. In American politics there never was any primary anti-Semitism and consequently throughout the nineteenth century Jews could participate in any political organization to which their interests inclined them. During the Civil War, Jews were among partisans in the South as well as the North, and within both major parties. The number of Jews before 1880 was so small that they were viewed and viewed themselves as individual voters, rather than as group representatives. Generally, though, all American Jews of this period recoiled from participation in any of the extreme movements, such as the radical Abolitionist movement and the Know-Nothing movement.[20]

After 1880, however, the immigrants from eastern Europe were strongly influenced by radical intellectuals, and for a period Jewish workers and their leaders formed the backbone of the Anarchist and Socialist movements in this country. Partly this was due to an over-reaction after the suppression of political liberty they had experienced under the Tsarist government. "When the Jewish intellectual came to the United States, he was suddenly given an opportunity to theorize openly and to his heart's content. He took full advantage of it: for many years, the Lower East Side [in New York City] was one big radical debating society."[21]

In the 1930's the sons and daughters of eastern European immigrants began to graduate from college and enter business and the professions, thus limiting the Jewish working class more and more to the older generations. With educational and occupational improvements, social distinctions between German Jews and east European Jews of the younger generation were modified. Radicals became more moderate and conservatives more liberal. The social fusion of "uptown" and "downtown" resulted in what Cohn calls "American Jewish Liberalism," which soon identified itself with the New Deal, especially as Franklin D. Roosevelt became the symbol of opposition to Hitler. By 1936 even the conservative Orthodox Jewish press supported Roosevelt.[22]

While Jews in the United States have become politically integrated in their communities, most of them tend to comprise a liberal bloc. Cohn believes that this is an expression of the insecure place Jews feel they have in the Gentile world. The establishment of the state of Israel has sharpened their scrutiny of American government policies, and attitudes toward Israel are reflected in political choices.

[19] Werner Cohn, "The Politics of American Jews," in *The Jews: Social Patterns of an American Group*, p. 619.
[20] *Ibid.*, p. 620.
[21] *Ibid.*, p. 621.
[22] *Ibid.*, p. 622.

THE JEWISH SUBCOMMUNITY

Wherever any considerable number of Jewish people reside in an American community there has developed a separate Jewish substructure, usually called the "Jewish community," which has a characteristic relation to the larger Gentile community. Sometimes these are actual ecological communities that have developed through residential discrimination or self-clustering; in other cases residence is dispersed, and the network of social relationships constitutes the Jewish community. There have been many studies of Jewish communities in different parts of the United States. Over 200 communities are affiliated with the Council of Jewish Federations and Welfare Funds, many of which have been studied from one point of view or another.[23]

A large percentage of American Jews have middle-class status and, like the rest of the American urban middle-class, Jews are moving to the suburbs. Let us study briefly the origin and growth of a typical suburban Jewish community.[24]

The Jewish Community of Park Forest

Park Forest is a post-World War II planned community south of Chicago. The men of the community were earning from $4,000 to $10,000 a year in 1949, when the study was made. Among 1,800 families, about 25 per cent of them Catholic, the Jewish community numbered just under 150 families. Of these, about 20 (15 of them mixed marriages) rejected all relationships with the formal Jewish community.[25] The Jewish group was made up of young, highly educated, second-generation Jews of eastern European parentage, most of whom had achieved or were likely to achieve with continued prosperity upper middle-class income status.[26] Park Forest Jews lived like other Park Foresters. They wore the same fashions, ate the same food except on special occasions, and participated with other Park Foresters in the culture of the "young moderns." The Jewish families were scattered, with rarely two Jewish families in adjacent houses.

Soon after these young Jewish families arrived they aligned themselves in a number of cliques, which in a remarkably short time formed a network through which news and gossip could be communicated. Gans points out that "The Jews form a cohesive in-group and tend to behave differently toward a member of the in-group than toward a non-Jew, in many cases reserving the intimacy of friendship for the former."[27] He then describes the

---

[23] See Sklare, *The Jews: Social Patterns of an American Group,* for articles based on the reports of many of these studies.
[24] Herbert J. Gans, "The Origin and Growth of a Jewish Community in the Suburbs: A Study of the Jews of Park Forest," in Sklare, pp. 205 ff.
[25] *Ibid.,* p. 206.
[26] *Ibid.,* p. 209.
[27] *Ibid.,* p. 210.

process by which Jews attempted to recognize other Jews. They were aided in this by a Protestant minister who conducted a religious survey and informed interested Jews who the other Jews in their neighborhood were.[28] Although there was no automatic progression from recognition to acquaintance to friendship, in many cases the desire to associate with other Jews was implied from the first. In general it was a matter of only four to eight weeks before people said they had friends whom they saw regularly.

Sociability patterns did not become exclusively Jewish, but in about half the cases it was pointed out that "best friends" were Jewish. This was defended on the ground that sociability as a primary leisure activity should permit relaxation and self-expression, which was more likely when Jews associated with Jews.

The development of the formal community began with the organization of a B'nai B'rith lodge and a chapter of the National Council of Jewish Women. Attendance and active participation in the Council of Jewish Women was soon greater than in B'nai B'rith, reflecting, according to Gans, the women's greater desire for Jewish companionships.[29] Nearly a year after the new suburb of Park Forest had been occupied, some of the leaders in B'nai B'rith met one evening to discuss setting up a Sunday school, which was to be part of a synagogue, either Reform or Conservative. The women in the Council, however, refused to help form a congregation and insisted that all they needed at the time was a Sunday school. Thus began four months of discussion, argument, and conflict.

In other groups such conflicts can often be explained in terms of power struggles between two socio-economic strata or ideological factions. In the Jewish community, however, they may signify conflicts between groups representing different stages in the ethnic adjustment to American life. . . . In Park Forest, where almost everyone is native born and acculturated to a large and similar extent, the history of the conflict over the Sunday school may be explained as the ascendency of a new type of formal Jewish community, the *child-oriented* one. This contrasts with the traditional Jewish community, which may be described as *adult-oriented.*[30]

The child-oriented group was successful in creating a school with a historical approach to Judaism rather than a liturgical and theological one. The Sunday school thus became an institution through which to transmit norms of ethnic culture and symbols of identification, whereas the home and family were regulated according to secular, middle-class behavior patterns. Some parents, in expressing their reasons for choosing this kind of Sunday school, pointed out that a Jewish child should know how to identify himself in relation to his Catholic and Protestant playmates. A number wanted their children to know the Jewish tradition so that they could later make a choice as

[28] *Ibid.,* p. 212.
[29] *Ibid.,* p. 213. However, it should be pointed out that this greater organizational activity of women is a general suburban pattern.
[30] *Ibid.,* p. 215.

to whether or not they wished to remain Jewish. Others saw Sunday school as providing a defense against later psychological hardships arising out of the minority position of Jews. And some parents were concerned about the fact that, although they selected their intimate friends from among the Jewish group, their children chose playmates without regard to ethnic or religious origin. Although a synagogue was not yet established at the time of Gans' study, there was already considerable discussion of one. The reasons for wanting a synagogue were not entirely religious. For many it was to be a symbol of group respectability or of Jewish solidarity.[31]

This suburban community of young Americans reveals facets of Jewish acculturation which contrast with the Jewish subcommunities of a generation earlier. Perhaps this is best shown in the adaptations made in the Park Forest congregation finally established in 1951. The congregation was designated as "Eastern European Reform." It combined a permissive attitude toward practices in the home which involve the sacrifice of secular pleasures (food restrictions and so forth), Conservative ceremonies, Hebrew reading, and responsive singing. The temple kitchen was not kosher but did not serve pork. The rabbi, who was from eastern European background, had been trained as an Orthodox rabbi but later had changed to Reform. A lecture series on secular Jewish topics attracted good attendance. Otherwise, large attendance occurred mainly on the high holy days.

GENTILE DISCRIMINATION AGAINST JEWS

For purposes of analysis, it is essential in discussing Gentile behavior toward Jews to make a distinction between those more ordinary and less intense sorts of discrimination which are widely manifested by Gentiles among whom Jews live, and the phenomenon of anti-Semitism. Anti-Semitism as a term came into use in Europe during the 1870's to denote social and political agitation, sentiments, and acts directed toward Jews.[32]

Up to that time, hostile attitudes and behavior against Jews were thought of as anti-Judaism, with the implication that it was based on the fact that Jews were not Christians. But beginning with 1870, a shift in the ideological content of antagonism toward Jews began, in which the religious difference played little part. Hostility against Jews on racial, social, economic, and political grounds in varying times and in various places replaced the rationale of religious difference. Organized movements against Jews became an important weapon in European political struggles. In Germany, for example, anti-Semitism became a part of the protest of insecure middle-class elements against the excesses of capitalism, on the one hand, and against the rising

---

[31] *Ibid.*, pp. 224–225.
[32] Benjamin Ginsberg, "Anti-Semitism," *Encyclopedia of Social Sciences*, Vol. 1 (New York: The Macmillan Co., 1930), pp. 119–125.

socialist trend, on the other. In Russia in the late nineteenth century, Jews were discriminated against by law, and the Tsarist government made little effort to curb periodic pogroms. In the Hitler Reich, anti-Semitism as a political weapon reached its climax with a systematic program designed to annihilate the entire Jewish population.

Against this harsh background of European anti-Semitism the treatment accorded Jews in the United States, as we shall presently describe it, appears in a so much more favorable light that the milder discrimination encountered here has been regarded by many Jews themselves, as well as by many Gentiles, of minor significance. Nevertheless, careful study of Jewish-Gentile relations in this country reveals not only persistent and prevalent minor discrimination but, since 1917 at least, the persistence of anti-Semitism in significant segments of the American population, latent at times but periodically becoming active. In this section we shall first describe the major fields of discrimination against Jews and then trace the fluctuating course which opposition to Jews by American Gentiles has followed.

The fields in which Gentile discrimination against Jews operates are those for which statistical evidence is the most difficult to document. No one doubts that many Jews incur social discrimination, occupational discrimination, discrimination in the opportunity for higher education, and in choice of residence. But the data are lacking to provide a definitive measure of these phenomena. Further difficulty in this connection arises because the methods employed in such discrimination are frequently not in the open. Nevertheless, a typical pattern of discrimination against Jews is seen in all the American communities where Jews exist in any considerable number.

Social Discrimination

Most characteristic of all is the prevalence of social discrimination against Jews. While Gentiles are generally civil and friendly to Jews in civic and economic life, in various ways they draw subtle lines against association in informal group life on a plane of equality. Gordon cites the testimony of a Christian businessman in Minneapolis which epitomizes the general pattern. "Most of my business associates are Jews . . . they invite me to play golf with them at their golf club. I have accepted their invitation on many occasions. But it has never occurred to me to invite them to join me in a game of golf at my golf club."[33] In many communities Jews are not admitted to exclusive clubs, where membership denotes the social prestige of its members.[34] And on most college campuses where Jewish students are present in numbers, fraternity and sorority membership is divided on an exclusive Gentile and

[33] Albert I. Gordon, *Jews in Transition* (Minneapolis: University of Minnesota Press, 1949), p. 48.
[34] See Carey McWilliams, *A Mask for Privilege* (Boston: Little Brown & Co., 1948), p. 123, for a documented instance.

Jewish basis.[35] Social discrimination is further seen in the many hotels and vacation places which discourage Jewish clientele.

Whether these kinds of social discrimination, irritating as they are to Jews, impose any serious handicap on their equality of opportunity depends on whether they affect indirectly more serious matters, such as occupation and choice of residence. McWilliams has argued cogently that exclusion from social clubs where the contacts made are important factors in business success is an indirect economic discrimination.[36]

Occupational Discrimination

While 78 per cent of all the complaints over a period with the wartime Federal Fair Employment Practices Commission were filed by Negroes, the next most numerous group involved Jews. The statistics of the New York Commission Against Discrimination were similar in this respect. Another approach to this matter is to look at the actual pattern of employment of Jews at the upper economic levels. At a time when anti-Semitism was high, Fortune magazine in 1936 summarized the position of Jews as follows:

They [Jews] play little or no part in the great commercial houses . . . they have an inconspicuous place in heavy industry. . . . Something of the same situation exists in automobiles. . . . The coal industry is almost entirely non-Jewish. . . . Rubber [and] shipping and transportation are equally non-Jewish. . . . In brief, Jews are so far from controlling the characteristic of present day American activities that they are hardly represented in them at all.

To find Jewish participation in industry it is necessary to turn to the light industries. And even there, it is necessary to turn from the manufacturing to the distributing end . . . the clothing business is the spectacular and outstanding exception to the statement that Jewish industrial interests are generally in the minority. . . . Jews are a definite retailing minority over the country. . . . At the most, half the opinion making and taste influencing paraphernalia (newspapers, radio, movies, theater) is in Jewish hands.[37]

In view of the high level of education among Jews and their desire for economic success, one would expect a reasonably proportionate distribution of Jews in all fields of business life. The fact that they are seldom employed in big corporations appears only to be explained by discrimination. The apparent over-representation of Jews in professional life suggests that Jews incline toward the higher-ranking occupations which are open to them and where they do not have to be hired by someone else. But very often professionally employed Jews occupy a marginal position in these occupations.

[35] Alfred McLung Lee, *Fraternities Without Brotherhood: A Study of Prejudice on the American Campus* (Boston: Beacon Press, Inc., 1955).
[36] For an analysis of patterns of social discrimination throughout a century of American history, see John Higham, "Social Discrimination Against Jews in America, 1830–1930," *Publication of the American Jewish Historical Society*, Vol. XLVII, No. 1 (Sept., 1957).
[37] "Jews in America," Fortune, Vol. 13, No. 2, Feb. 1936. The above material was adapted from pp. 133–136. By permission of the publishers of *Fortune*.

Jewish physicians have difficulty acquiring certified ratings for medical specialties, and few Jewish accountants and lawyers are employed by large firms.[38]

Educational Discrimination

There is no denial of education to Jews in public schools anywhere in the nation. There are, however, strong indications of limited discrimination in college and graduate schools. In a survey of the admissions practices of 700 liberal arts colleges, Dodson found sufficient evidence to conclude that a quota system is in effect in nearly all of them, even though the officials denied it in all but a few instances.[39] Medical schools indicate that the number of Jewish enrollees has been reduced approximately 50 per cent in the last twenty years, which obviously cannot be accounted for on the basis of a decline in qualified Jewish applicants.[40] Patently, discrimination in admission to professional schools places Jews at a disadvantage in the free competitive choice of an occupation.

Discrimination in Other Fields

Evidence of discrimination against Jews in choice of residence is less convincing, although there is no other adequate explanation of their absence from certain middle- and upper-class sections than prejudice. While restrictive covenants have been directed mainly at Negroes and Orientals, they have also been written to exclude Jews. More frequently, pressure is brought on Gentile residents not to sell to Jews.

We have noted the continued existence of a pattern of Gentile discrimination against Jews in the United States. It has seemed that sporadic outbursts of violent anti-Semitism occur in areas where patterns of general discrimination against Jews are a constant feature of Jewish-Gentile relations. Perhaps the failure of many liberal Gentiles and also of many Jews to recognize this point is what made the Nazi holocaust a tragic surprise to so many people of both groups. Jews were nowhere (where they existed in any numbers) more nearly assimilated to a Gentile national life than in Germany. Yet there did exist in Germany the ordinary forms of discrimination out of which, under appropriate economic and political conditions such as accompanied the rise of Hitlerism, anti-Semitism could find fertile ground. This suggests the uncomfortable possibility that a recurrence of anti-Semitism may be implicit in any national society where Jews still possess minority status.

[38] Eli E. Cohen, "Occupational Status and Occupational Structure," *American Jewish Year Book*, 1950, 51: 65.
[39] Dan W. Dodson, "Religious Prejudice in Colleges," *American Mercury*, July, 1946, 63: 5–13.
[40] Frank Kingdon, "Discrimination in Medical Colleges," *American Mercury*, Oct., 1945, 61: 391–399.

ANTI – SEMITISM IN THE UNITED STATES

We shall now consider the beginnings and subsequent course of anti-Semitism in the United States. As we shall see, the visible manifestations of this phenomenon show ebbs and flows in intensity which suggest that, as a state of mind, anti-Semitism has remained latent in particular segments of the Gentile population beginning with the decade of 1870.

The increase of social discrimination cannot be understood without reference to ideological factors. Yet there is no close correlation between the incidence of discrimination and anti-Semitism in its most virulent forms. Both the anti-Semitic ideology and discriminatory practice received impetus from the rise in Jewish immigration. However, the two forms of hostility took separate courses. Discrimination steadily increased from 1870 to World War II, whereas anti-Semitism rose and fell cyclically.[41]

Social Anti-Semitism

Until the 1870's there was little spectacular anti-Semitism in this country. In 1877, Joseph Seligman, the New York banker, was refused accommodations for his family at the Grand Union Hotel in Saratoga Springs. This is one of a number of incidents arising in this decade which provide the first overt manifestations of anti-Semitism. Since Seligman had lived in this country since 1837 and had been offered the post of Secretary of Treasury by President Grant, the refusal to accord him accommodations hitherto granted suggests the development of a new attitude toward Jews, which was to gain momentum.

Economic Anti-Semitism

The great immigration of Jews after 1880 did not provoke any strong anti-Semitic activity. This may be due in part to the fact that so many Jews in New York concentrated in the needle trades, removing themselves from general competition and insulating themselves in their self-developed ghettos. The real upsurge in feeling against Jews as economic competitors appears to have started after 1900, reaching a high peak at the outbreak of the first World War. In Severson's study of discriminatory want ads, one finds that beginning in 1911 "ads requesting 'Christians only' or 'Gentiles only' appeared at the rate of 0.3 per 1,000, rose to 4 per cent in 1921, to 8.8 in 1923, to 13.3 in 1926; averaged 11 per cent from 1927 to 1931; dropped to 4.8 per cent in 1931, and then rose to 9.4 per cent in 1937." Severson's thesis is that it was not immigration per se, or cultural conflict, which developed this latent prejudice but rather "that the particular exigency of the occasion was the coming into the clerical labor market, particularly of girls into typing and stenography, of second-generation east European immigrants."[42]

[41] John Higham, "Social Discrimination Against Jews in America," p. 31.
[42] Quotation taken from A. L. Severson, "Nationality and Religion in Newspaper Ads," *American Journal of Sociology*, January, 1939, 44: 545.

Political Anti-Semitism

Anti-Semitism similar to that known in Europe, political in its implications, more organized, and more vitriolic in its propaganda, began to arise about 1917. In the few years following the close of World War I, large quantities of anti-Semitic literature identifying Jews with the rising European revolutionary ideology appeared; the new Ku Klux Klan arose in the North, with its generally antiforeign orientation including anti-Semitism; the Fellowship Forum distributed widely copies of the forged Protocols of the Elders of Zion; and Henry Ford commenced his anti-Semitic campaign through the publication of the *Dearborn Independent*.[43]

That these new anti-Semitic activities had an effect is indicated by an increase in various incidents of which the following are illustrative.

The board of directors of a Milwaukee golf club asked eight Jewish charter members to resign.

The secretary of the Chamber of Commerce in St. Petersburg, Florida, announced that the time had come to make St. Petersburg "a 100 per cent American gentile City."

Several large real estate concerns in New Jersey, New York, Georgia, and Florida were found to have restricted new subdivisions against Jewish occupancy.

Of more than passing interest in this period was President Lowell's graduation address at Harvard in June 1922, in which he advocated quotas against Jews. While the trustees of Harvard later rejected this suggestion, it was painfully apparent that the quota system was spreading.[44]

Abating somewhat during the late 1920's, anti-Semitism rose again in the early 1930's as the Depression intensified. Strong has indicated that there were 121 organizations actively spreading anti-Semitic propaganda during 1933 and 1940.[45] In the late 1930's anti-Semitism began to be used for the first time openly in political campaigns. The manager of the nativist third party in the 1936 Presidential election is quoted by McWilliams as stating, "the trouble with this country now is due to the money powers and Jewish politicians."[46]

While the sweeping victory of Franklin D. Roosevelt in 1936 temporarily set back the agitation, it resumed with new intensity in the late 1930's and continued until Pearl Harbor. Involved in this activity were the Christian Front, led by Father Charles Coughlin, and the Silver Shirts, directed by William Pelley. In a period of nineteen months before July 31, 1938, Pelley

---

[43] Donald S. Strong, *Organized Anti-Semitism in America* (Washington, D.C.: American Council on Public Affairs, 1941), p. 15.
[44] McWilliams, *A Mask for Privilege*, pp. 38–39. By permission of the publisher Little, Brown & Co.
[45] Strong, *Organized Anti-Semitism in America*, pp. 146–147.
[46] McWilliams, *A Mask for Privilege*, p. 42.

mailed approximately three and a half tons of anti-Semitic propaganda from his headquarters. All of this organization and propaganda obviously cost a good deal of money, and though the program was conducted by relatively unimportant people, it occasionally received support in high places. For example, McWilliams quotes Congressman John Rankin as stating to Congress that "Wall Street and a little group of our international Jewish brethren are still attempting to harass the President and Congress into plunging us into the European War."[47] It is interesting to note that this new crescendo in anti-Semitic propaganda was correlated with the increasing strength of the Nazi movement in Europe.

During World War II overt manifestations of anti-Semitism disappeared. They were considered inimical to the war effort and were discouraged by the government. Furthermore, the ideological inconsistency of supporting anti-Semitism while fighting the arch Jew-hater, Adolph Hitler, had some deterrent effect. In the few months following the end of World War II, however, the Fair Employment Practices Committee noted an increase in discrimination against Jews in employment. However, a *Fortune* Survey, which had found the incidence of anti-Semitism in the adult population to be about 9.3 per cent in 1943, found it to be 8.8 per cent in 1946.[48] Organized anti-Semitic activity failed to resume its prewar intensity, although it was far from dormant. The *American Jewish Year Book* for 1950 noted a tendency for individual agitators to combine operations and to favor the distribution of inflammatory literature to holding meetings and demonstrations.[49] These trends indicate that the agitators were having a more difficult time.

This fluctuating course of anti-Semitic behavior suggests that it is more responsive to changes in socioeconomic conditions in the national community than to changes in the behavior of Jews. Such conditions are manifold and we can rarely single out one factor as being the sole determinant. At times it may appear that economic changes have a direct bearing. For example, in the first of the periods of marked discrimination, 1910–1914, the competition of increasingly Americanized Jews for employment in white-collar positions began to be felt by Gentile workers. At other times conflicts in ideologies loomed as the more significant factor. Thus the rise in anti-Semitism following World War I seems related to the spread of radical philosophy in this country, which raised anxiety in the middle classes. The sharper political orientation of the anti-Semitism of the 1930's occurred at a time when legislation was enacted which made the position of the working class more secure and, in consequence, increased the anxieties of the other economic levels.

[47] *Ibid.*, p. 46.
[48] *Fortune,* "The Fortune Survey," Feb. 1946, 33: 258.
[49] American Jewish Yearbook, 1950, 51: 110.

Although there has been a decline in anti-Semitism since World War II, not all has been quiescent. The most dramatic instances have been symbolic acts against institutional property. Acts of vandalism against Jewish property or molestation of Jewish persons are not new. They occurred during World War I and again during the late 20's and early 30's.[50] This particular kind of anti-minority behavior in the post-World War II period seems to reflect other and in some degree more subtle pressures in the society than war, depression, and international tension. The most recent example of such outbreaks occurred early in 1960. Beginning with an incident in Cologne, Germany, on December 24, 1959, a wave of vandalism and desecration spread through the United States for nine weeks. There were 643 incidents, nearly two-thirds of which involved only the painting of swastikas. About 60 per cent of the incidents occurred in cities with more than 100,000 inhabitants. Not all these acts were directed toward specific Jewish targets. For example, schools and churches were in some instances defaced. The larger the community, the higher the proportion of Jewish targets. The pattern was not consistent throughout the United States; Arizona had an unusually high number of incidents in proportion to its population and its Jewish population, whereas some large cities, such as St. Louis, Newark, New Orleans, Buffalo, and Indianapolis, had hardly any. In the South, states which had made some token effort at desegregation had more incidents than those which had not integrated at all or had made considerable progress in integration.[51]

As for explanations, anxiety in the face of as yet unstructured social change may be inferred as one precipitating factor in the pattern of the Southern outbreaks. The swastika epidemic, however, appealed almost solely to one section of the population—adolescent boys. It was clear from interrogation of the offenders that some of them were expressing direct anti-Semitic feeling. For others, however, this was not the case. It is worth asking what kind of academic, vocational, and personal pressures our society exerts on urban children of this age group that can lead them to engage in this type of destructive activity.

The Stereotype of the Jew

Since the Jews have been a minority people for so many centuries in western society, they are probably more stereotyped than any other minority in American life. The traditional stereotype involves both "racial" and cultural characteristics. In its most derogatory form it is based on an exaggeration and distortion of traits of the segregated medieval Orthodox Jew. This

[50] Charles Wagley and Marvin Harris, *Minorities in the New World* (New York: Columbia University Press, 1958), p. 221.
[51] David Caplovitz and Candace Rogers, *Swastika 1960* (New York: Anti-Defamation League of B'nai B'rith), pp. 28–30, pp. 51–52. It will be useful to the student to compare this type of behavior with the analysis of riots in Chapter 20.

stereotype is so virulent and persistent that it is revived in every major anti-Semitic outbreak. Cultural characteristics are often translated into imputed personality traits in the stereotype. Thus it is said that Jews are exploitative (of non-Jews), emotional and unreserved in speech and gesture, aggressive and competitive, clannish and conspiratorial.

It will be seen that the stereotype differs in important ways from that held by white people concerning other minorities. To illustrate, comparison may be made with the white stereotype of the Negro. Whereas the Negro is considered lazy, the Jew is considered too ambitious; whereas the Negro is considered mentally inferior, the Jew is considered smart. On the other hand, one notes some similarity in the stereotype of the Japanese and the Jews with respect to aggressiveness and the conspiratorial tendency.

Further consideration of the Jewish stereotype reveals that the Gentile concept is not altogether consistent. Jews are considered by some as ruthless capitalists, by others as Marxist radicals. They are criticized on the one hand for being too clannish and on the other for wanting to move into Gentile society.

Another kind of stereotype of the Jews is that of the small trader. It will be noted that wherever there are strangers in marginal economic positions, similar stereotypes arise about them. In Chapter 2 we mentioned that the post-Civil War Yankee trader in the South was assigned characteristics similar to those of Jews. A recent article points out similarities in the stereotype of the Jewish marginal businessman, the Christian Armenian peddler (the rug dealer) in America, the East Indian small merchant in South Africa, and the Chinese local trader in South East Asia.[52] Often marginal enterprises are the only ones to which a newcomer or minority person has access. People in these businesses have role characteristics demanded of them (aggressiveness, and so forth) necessary to success in high risk enterprises, and naturally they will contrast with those of people who are already established.

Are the Jews a Race?

In Chapter 3 we discussed the fact that "race" as used popularly is a social and not a scientific category. We pointed out that present genetic theory accepts only the fact that certain genetic traits are reinforced by isolation and in-marriage. There seems to be little evidence that Jews were ever totally biologically separated from the surrounding peoples. Even initially in Palestine it is probable that the strong prohibitions against out-marriage were a defense against a considerable intermixture. The goal was preserving the religion, not purity of descent, except as this is characteristic of all tribal peoples.

[52] Irwin D. Rinder, "Strangers in the Land: Social Relations in the Status Gap," *Social Problems*, Winter, 1958–1959, 6: 253–260.

As the Jews dispersed, the people with whom intermixture occurred became progressively more differentiated in physiognomic features. The Ashkenazim, especially, who were dispersed through northern Europe and from whom most American Jews are descended, are a blending of Nordic and Alpine with eastern Mediterranean traits.[53] The other main branch of Jews, the Sephardim, lived long in Spain and the Mediterranean region and through in-marriage tended to develop a degree of physical distinctiveness from other Jews. People of this appearance are often referred to as the "classic" Jewish type, but they are often indistinguishable from other eastern Mediterranean peoples. "The wide range of variation between Jewish populations in their physical characteristics and the diversity of the gene frequencies of their blood groups render any unified racial classification for them a contradiction in terms."[54]

Shapiro, who has examined all the research, anthropological and medical, on the biological traits of Jews, makes the following comment:

I suppose that one of the reasons, aside from political and cultural ones, that incline many people to accept readily the notion that the Jews are a distinct race, is the fact that some Jews are recognizably different in appearance from the surrounding population. That some are not to be identified in this way is overlooked and the tendency, naturally enough, is to extend to all the stereotype of a part. This process occurs in so many other situations it is scarcely surprising that it does here too.[55]

Are American Jews an Ethnic Group?

American Jews, as a total population, cannot be considered an ethnic group. As we pointed out in Chapter 2, the term *ethnic* refers usually to shared culture patterns which are the primary focus of group identification. We also considered that variants of the dominant national culture may be called ethnic. In the case of minorities, shared sentiments need not stem from other previous cultural origins, but may spring from adaptation over time to stabilized minority status.

In analyzing the factor of ethnicity among those Jews for which the concept applies, one must consider region of origin before migration, status position in the dominant society, and perhaps to some extent affiliation within the Jewish religious pattern. The outstanding example of ethnicity among Jews is that of the eastern European Jewish migrants. As we have already pointed out, the conditions of settlement in the last two centuries, when western European Jews were moving into larger and larger participation in the several national cultures within which they lived, led eastern

---

[53] Carleton S. Coon, "Have the Jews a Racial Identity?" eds. Isacque Graeber and Steuart Henderson Britt, *Jews in a Gentile World* (New York: The Macmillan Co., 1942), p. 33.
[54] Harry L. Shapiro, *The Jewish People: A Biological History* (Paris: UNESCO, 1960), pp. 74–75.
[55] *Ibid.*

Jews to maintain and elaborate a particular mode of "Jewish" culture. Even within this eastern group there were what could be called "ethnic" differences, as between Lithuanian Jews and Silesian Jews. The roles allowed Jews in these two sections of eastern Europe made for a different emphasis in the preservation of Jewish tradition. Nevertheless, most of the people of both groups were Orthodox village Jews who retained the elaboration of religious behavior in the routines of daily living. Those who were not Orthodox were not religious at all, but many kept the traditional practices outside the synagogue out of habit or affection. By the dominant society they were perceived as one homogeneous culture group. The homogeneous ecological subcommunities in America characteristic of this period of migration strengthened the *ethnic* identification of eastern European Jewish migrants, especially in the urban pattern of work and living where there were also other ethnically identifiable groups.[56]

Western European Jews were as a whole more acculturated to the national cultures within which they had lived. This was especially true of those who had achieved a secure middle-class position before they migrated. In the next generation the less privileged Jewish immigrants from western Europe followed the model of the acculturated from their own home country, but it is hard to determine to what degree, if at all, these migrants were perceived, or perceived themselves, as having a cultural ethos. As we have noted, the valuation of German culture was very high for German Jews. Many of them were part of a cultured elite at a time when American intellectual life ascribed high value to German thought and German education. Western European Jews did not adhere to a Jewish cultural tradition or to an historic pattern of accommodative values, except to the degree that most of them chose to shun alignment with any extreme positions in the social issues of their day. When they came to America, these were the people among whom the Reform religious movement spread.

The Sephardim, although they usually remained Orthodox, lost the quality of ethnicity according to their degree of education and status. There are pockets of Balkan Sephardic Jews in New York City which are tiny ethnic communities. There is also a Sephardic elite which, though Orthodox, has been able to separate the sacred from the secular, and has become in the secular spheres of behavior indistinguishable from the dominant society.

In America the number of Jews living in distinctive "Jewish" cultural patterns is decreasing. Nevertheless, since the persecution by the Nazis and the establishment of the state of Israel, there has been a revival of Jewish culture. The Jewish language is now classical Hebrew; few of the younger generation can speak Yiddish. The revival of Hebrew as a spoken language

---

[56] That some of this persists is evidenced in a study of the needle trades. See Will Herberg, "The Old-Timers and the Newcomers: Ethnic Group Relations in a Needle Trades Union," *The Journal of Social Issues*, 1953, 9: 12.

has led in part to the establishment of Jewish parochial schools in which young people can be bi-lingual, and to a large number of Jewish youth groups which arrange for periods of work or study in Israel. Many Jewish young people today learn Israeli songs and dances, some of which originated with the establishment of Israel but many of which contain the traditional folk elements of east European Jewry. Thus the new Jewish culture, Israel-oriented, is not necessarily religious. But there has also been a revival of Jewish religion in America which is not necessarily related to the cultural revival. Even the Reform synagogues occasionally incorporate more traditional elements in the services. The religious revival, however, is an aspect of the considerable religious revival throughout America. Religious affiliation now establishes for Jews, as it long has for Protestants, identity and respectability in the community.

The Jews as a Minority

It is important to distinguish between an ethnic group and a minority. Difference of religion does not constitute an ethnic group. No cultural designation can subsume all American Jews. And as we have already pointed out, the racial designation is fallacious. The Jews are to be considered a *minority,* and it is because of their position in the dominant culture. Since they have been a minority so long, they have become a traditional object which dominants can use as the projected source of anxieties and discomforts. As a historic minority, many Jews have developed compensatory attitudes for their protection. These run the gamut from strong interdiction on out-marriage and the preservation of close kinship ties to identification with other movements of protest against social injustice.

During the early years of this century some writers saw the Jewish problem as a cultural one, and believed assimilation to be the ultimate goal, in harmony with the general theory of assimilation. (We shall discuss this further in Chapter 19.) It is true than many Jews have assimilated into the dominant culture and intermarried, both with and without conversion to Christianity, but because of their historic situation there is always the risk that the rule of descent will be applied to them more rigorously than to other European groups. The experience of the Jews under the Nazis has strengthened the in-group resistance to assimilation insofar as it implies denial of Jewish descent, or conversion. There are many Jews who claim that any person of Jewish ancestry, no matter how many generations remote, is still a Jew.

Marginality

Because Jews have acculturated to the surrounding dominant culture effectively and rapidly, problems have been created by the combination of the increasing subtlety of discrimination against them and their reactive defenses. One effect of this has been to create a large number of individuals of marginal status. Kurt Lewin examined some problems of marginality among Jews and found that the young persons who had been brought up with the least sense of Jewish identity found themselves in the most disturbing *internal and external* positions with regard to being Jewish. Many experienced "self-hatred," which was an expression of bitterness at an "inherited" handicap.[57] It is the dilemma of the marginal young people that has in part been responsible for the revival of practices intended to strengthen Jewish identity.

Why Does Anti-Semitism Persist?

There are different degrees of intensity of anti-Semitism, different rationalizations for it, and social science is discovering different levels of motivation. Before we indicate these different levels, it is important to point out that the problem of Jewish-Gentile relations can probably never be divorced entirely from the historical tradition. In our opinion, and contemporary evidence seems to bear this out with regard to the Soviet Union, even a revolutionary reorganization of society will not automatically solve the problem. A literate tradition, unlike the oral tradition of a folk society, can never entirely lose historic attitudes and the awareness of historic problems. This affects Gentile and Jewish thinking alike.

We have already discussed some of the forms in which anti-Semitism expresses itself. We are here interested in the psychological dimension which leads people either spontaneously to express anti-Semitic sentiments, or to be receptive to organized anti-Semitic efforts.

Much of what are popularly considered individual psychological reactions really constitute appropriate behavior within given social-structural situations. All groups with a highly developed sense of identity perceive other groups as different from themselves (in-group, out-group relations.) Thus many spontaneous sentiments are construed as anti-Semitic, though they do not necessarily carry with them any inner committment or virulence. They may, however, lay the base for mobilizable sentiments if a stable situation is in the throes of change.

Another type of anti-Semitism is related to the larger minority problem of competition between those whom the dominant culture favors and the able members of any minority. It is obvious that many less able people are retained in occupational positions by the practice of discrimination. Occupational discrimination furthermore has social concomitants, involving choice of mate, club membership, social admission, and so forth. The local community power structure is reinforced by this web of relationships. The end product is an effect on general public policy.

[57] Kurt Lewin, *Resolving Social Conflicts* (New York: Harper & Brothers, 1948).

A popular interpretation of anti-Semitism derives from the so-called "scapegoat" theory, which attributes the need to project blame for personal and social difficulties on somebody else. Here the historic position of the Jews makes them particularly vulnerable to being used as scapegoats, although a comparable attitude was not unknown toward the Japanese through World War II among people on the West Coast. There are different levels of insecurity in which this operates, one of which is insecurity of status, such as the threatened loss of middle-class occupation and style of life, where the individuals feel, correctly or incorrectly, that a competitive threat comes from the minority members. Paul Massing has analyzed this factor with regard to the growth of anti-Semitism before the Nazis took over in Germany and in the subsequent support given the Nazi leadership.[58] A recent study of the Nazi leaders has demonstrated that in one way or another these were all marginal men in their societies.[59] What we see from this is that organized anti-Semitism can be aroused in a threatened stratum of the society, and that leaders emerge from those who are less well integrated in the society than the general population of their age group.

The prejudiced personality has been studied from the viewpoint of both sociology and psychiatry. The study of the authoritarian personality which we present in Chapter 19 suggests that certain types of upbringing create this personality need, and that children in authoritative situations where they feel helpless are more apt to be prejudiced than children given freedom to express themselves, to be inventive and exploratory. A person brought up in this manner, it appears, attempts to repress fear, weakness, sex impulses, and aggressive feelings in order to be approved of by the punishing parents. He then compensates by attributing these "bad" repressed impulses to others whom society holds in less esteem, whether or not there is any basis for it in their behavior. Wherever the social situation provides a target for derogation, the repressed wishes will be assigned to the derogated person.

The reduction of anti-Semitism, in the light of what we have said, needs to be approached in different ways, depending on the sources of the anti-Semitic attitudes. Thus it may involve varying aspects of social integration or it may be a problem at a deep level of personality structure.

THE OUTLOOK FOR JEWISH – GENTILE RELATIONS

There has been a considerable decline in discrimination against Jews, particularly in occupational positions and residence patterns, in the last thirty years. Most of the Jews in the United States are now native born. Differences between the people of the nineteenth and twentieth-century migra-

[58] Paul Massing, *Rehearsal for Destruction* (New York: Harper & Brothers, 1949).
[59] Ithiel da Sola Pool and Daniel K. Lerner, *The Nazi Elite* (Stanford, Calif.: The Stanford University Press, 1956).

tions are diminishing as the generations rapidly acculturate, and the strengthening of Jewish identity has broken down certain traditional status barriers between western and eastern European Jews. We do not know what proportion of Jews disappear through assimilation. We do know, however, that, temporarily if not permanently, within the Jewish group the goal of assimilation in the sense that this would support out-marriage or conversion has diminished.

The solutions confronting the American Jew other than total merging with the dominant society are the establishment of acknowledged and accepted cultural pluralism or religious pluralism. The cultural pluralism for Jews in American society is unlike that of minorities such as the American Indian, which involves a wish for territorial enclaves with minimal adaptation to selected technology of the dominant society. For the Jews, as a significant part of western culture, the bond is a modified and adapted historic value system and behavior which they hope to preserve. The problem is whether any pluralism which embraces many facets of culture will not in the end create a situation such as that envisaged by the "separate but equal" arguments for dominant-minority relations.

One other possibility seems to be emerging. It is that of religious pluralism within the historic American tradition of religious freedom. It may well prove possible that Jews can maintain their own identity as Jews provided this is accepted as nothing but a religious affiliation. Such a development will undoubtedly, however, bring about modifications within the religion, as signs already indicate.

TOPICS FOR PROJECTS AND DISCUSSION

1. Elizabeth Taylor converted to Judaism when she married Eddie Fisher. Is she now a "Jew"?
2. Discuss the effects of the establishment of the State of Israel on the position of Jews in the United States and in the world.
3. Write a biographical sketch of an American Jew who has made a significant contribution to law, humanities, science, business, or the arts. Describe how his interest was aroused and assess his achievement. (Suggested names: Benjamin Cardozo, Albert Einstein, Julius Rosenwald, Leonard Bernstein.)
4. Discuss the role of Jewish Americans in helping other minorities in the United States—for example the activities of the Rosenwald Fund or the Anti-Defamation League of B'nai B'rith.
5. Describe instances of hidden discrimination that you have encountered or read about. How can these be changed?
6. Analyze the types of people attracted to anti-Semitic movements and the social circumstances which give rise to these movements.
7. Discuss generational conflicts of American Jewish young people. Are these similar to the conflict of generations throughout the society, or are they in some way special in the Jewish group?

SUGGESTED READING

Caplowitz, David, and Rogers, Candace. *Swastika 1960: The Epidemic of Anti-Semitic Vandalism in America.* New York: Anti-Defamation League of B'nai B'rith, 1961.
> *An analysis of the outbreak of defacing buildings.*
Lee, Alfred McClung. *Fraternities Without Brotherhood: A Study of Prejudice on the American Campus.* Boston: The Beacon Press, 1955.
> *A report on the effect of the fraternity system at the present time on the attitudes of members.*
Kramer, Judith, and Leventman, Seymour. *Children of the Gilded Ghetto.* New Haven: Yale University Press, 1961.
> *A study of the processes of acculturation as between generations of Jews in a midwestern city.*
Lowenthal, Leo, and Guterman, Norbert. *Prophets of Deceit.* New York: Harper & Brothers, 1949.
> *A study of the techniques of the American agitator as gathered from the speeches and writings of leaders of American anti-minority movements.*
Shapiro, Harry L. *The Jewish People: A Biological History.* Paris, France: UNESCO, 1960.
> *The most up-to-date statement of the physiological traits of the Jewish people.*
Sklare, Marshall. *The Jews: Social Patterns of An American Group.* Glencoe, Ill.: The Free Press, 1958.
> *A book of readings covering many aspects of Jewish life in the United States—cultural, social, religious.*
Zborowski, Mark, and Herzog, Elizabeth. *Life is With People.* New York: International Universities Press, Inc., 1952.
> *Two anthropologists reconstruct with great sensitivity and warmth the eastern European Jewish village as a culture and way of life.*

Part III

Conclusion

In this concluding section, we view the over-all situation of dominant-minority relations in the United States in the light of the development of sociological theory, and of the trends and policies affecting minorities. In Chapter 19 we discuss the current theoretical orientation to questions of dominant-minority relations as contrasted with the theory of a generation ago. In Chapter 20 we synthesize the problems described for the individual minority groups into an over-all interpretation of dominant-minority relations in periods of normal stability and in times of social stress. The concluding chapter discusses the achievements and problems of social policy in behalf of minorities.

19

Sociological Theory and Dominant-Minority Relations

There is no established cohesive body of theory of dominant-minority relations. Since they are one dimension in basic patterns of social interaction, any theory of minorities must develop as a particular focus, in harmony with the general development of social theory. The major concepts with which contemporary social scientists analyze dominant-minority relations have been presented in Chapter 2. In this chapter we wish to consider some questions which are being raised about older assumptions in American sociology regarding dominant-minority relations, and some insights which have been provided by more recent theory and research.

First we present briefly a "classic" approach to "race and culture contacts." We then discuss some of the key concepts of this earlier approach, illustrating from subsequent writings the search for a more accurate definition of terms. To show the process of theory building we then present illustrations of hypotheses based on a limited range of data, which are applicable to dominant-minority relations. Finally, from three contemporary theorists who have developed general systematic sociology from three very different approaches, we present some specific contributions drawn from their larger work which are significant for the analysis of dominant-minority relations.

Not all theory about human behavior that is relevant to dominant-minority situations is the special province of sociology. Anthropologists, with their concern about culture and culture contacts, and psychologists and psychiatrists, with their focus on the dynamics of behavior of individuals and groups, have also contributed to deeper understanding of dominant-minority interaction. Here, however, we are concerned with the special insights contributed by sociologists. Throughout our book, although we have taken cognizance of personality and culture factors, we have emphasized the social structure of American life and its effect on minorities. We are more interested in the dilemmas of institutional behavior than in the psychological roots of behavior. We are more concerned with the institutional barriers to equality of opportunity than with the attitudes of one group to another, except as these attitudes affect the social system.

A CLASSIC APPROACH — THE PARK-WIRTH SCHOOL

Robert E. Park,[1] more than any other sociologist in the first half of this century, attempted to formulate generalizations about race and culture and to relate them to a general theory of society. Park's work in this field, together with that of his colleague, Louis Wirth, made the first major impact on theory of dominant-minority relations. The work of these two men and others associated with them as colleagues or students comprise what has been called the Park-Wirth school of thought about "race relations."

Park's systematic analysis of society revolved around what he felt to be the three basic modes of human interaction: co-operation, competition, and conflict. Race and culture contacts were subsumed under this system. He attempted to explore the diversity in race and culture contacts, from those of accommodative peace to those of open conflict. Park's assumptions were the evolutionary beliefs which were the critical intellectual issues of his period. With this evolutionary orientation, Park saw relations between dominants and minorities as moving through a definite cycle, with one outcome, the assimilation of the minority into the dominant society. The inevitability of this cycle, its sequence, and its ultimate conclusion have been challenged in contemporary writing, as we shall show.

Several of Park's analyses have contributed to the permanent frame of theory of dominant-minority relations and have been validated or expanded by subsequent theory and research. One of the most significant of these is the concept of the marginal man. Park also saw that prejudice is to be separated from discrimination, that it cannot be dispelled by knowledge alone, that it rises in periods of social change as individuals and vested interests resist change in the status of minorities or, otherwise threatened, vent hostility on a vulnerable minority. Park was also interested in the effect of

[1] Robert E. Park, *Race and Culture* (Glencoe, Ill.: The Free Press, 1950).

urbanization on conflicts between races and nationality groups. Extensive study of urbanization is just now being undertaken. Urban patterns of living have changed since Park's day. Whereas Park felt that urbanization increased tension between dominants and minorities, contemporary research may indicate that this is not always so.

Both changing social conditions and new theoretical analyses can lead to the support of or the redefinition of older concepts and theories.[2]

THE REFINEMENT OF CONCEPTS

If we are to analyze dominant-minority relations, sociology must come to some agreement about the meaning of terms describing the major modes in which dominants and minorities relate to each other. Park saw these major modes as patterns of *interaction:* competition, conflict, accommodation, assimilation, proceeding through that sequence. If, however, one is interested in the continuing structured relationships between dominants and minorities, the basic terms which need to be agreed upon are those describing *stabilized forms of adaptation,* and *goals,* of minorities in their minority status: accommodation, acculturation, assimilation.

Accommodation

Since Park emphasized the interaction between dominants and minorities, he saw accommodation as a temporary suspension of conflict. A subsequent emphasis is contained in the definition of accommodation by Kimball Young and Raymond W. Mack: "a condition, a state of equilibrium between individuals or groups in which certain working arrangements have been agreed on or accepted."[3] We would stress *accepted* rather than *agreed on,* thus emphasizing that accommodation is a mode of adaptation about which the minority has no choice. It is the adjustment by the minority to conditions over which it has no control. "The Southerner keeps watching all the time for germs of unrest in the Negro community. He preserves the machinery of caste controls in a state of perpetual preparedness, and applies it occasionally as an exercise or demonstration. In this system, Negroes *have* to accommodate individually and as a group."[4] Myrdal's study brings out in various contexts a point often neglected in the discussion of accommodation: that accommodation has two separate but related components, the external or behavioral element, and the internal or attitudinal change. These

[2] For a re-evaluation of Park by a contemporary sociologist, see Seymour Martin Lipset, "Changing Social Status and Prejudice: The Race Theories of a Pioneering American Sociologist," *Commentary,* May, 1950, pp. 475–479.
[3] Kimball Young and Raymond W. Mack, *Sociology and Social Life,* 2nd ed. (New York: American Book Company, 1962). See *Glossary,* p. 489.
[4] Gunnar Myrdal, *An American Dilemma* (New York: Harper & Brothers, 1944), p. 768. Italics in original.

two levels of adaptation have been much discussed in the literature on acculturation, but it has not been recognized as equally true for minorities who have had to accept an accommodative position. There is ample evidence in the history of slavery and in the subsequent post-Reconstruction history of the Negro that much accommodation was external only.

Another major unexplored area is that of the social effects of accommodation. Whereas social psychiatry has explored a little the effect on minority individuals of living in an accommodative pattern, the study of the effect on the total society, dominants and minorities alike, has not been adequately considered. For example, there is some reason to believe that we could find a correlation between an accommodative pattern of dominant-minority relations and political apathy of both dominants and minorities within that structure.

Acculturation

All contemporary writing on acculturation takes cognizance of the two levels on which cultural characteristics must be acquired when an individual is divesting himself of one culture and accepting another. These have been described by the terms "manifest" versus "intangible," or "behavioral" versus "attitudinal," or "external" and "internal." Whereas these distinctions are commonplace, little attention has been given to the selectivity involved in taking on new cultural traits, whether external or internal. There is very little known about the resistances which may arise at the introduction of a new culture trait or about specific conditions affecting the traits which are accepted or rejected. For example, there will be a difference of behavioral and/or attitudinal acceptance or resistance according to whether culture traits are forced upon a people or are received voluntarily by them. It will make a difference whether or not there is social or political inequality between groups. The analysis of acculturation must be refined to take cognizance of the situations within which acculturation occurs.[5]

Warner and others have claimed that acculturation is apt to occur more quickly when two cultures are similar. Here the differentiation between behavioral and attitudinal needs also to be made, as is pointed out by Broom and Kitsuse.[6] They call attention to the fact that the manifest behavioral culture traits of a minority may be markedly different from those of the host society, but this does not mean that the attitudinal ones are necessarily disparate. They cite the example of the Japanese, and account in this way for the relatively rapid acculturation of Japanese-Americans despite many different external modes of behavior in Japanese culture.

[5] Melville J. Herskovits, *Acculturation: The Study of Culture Contact* (Gloucester, Mass.: Peter Smith, 1958). Appendix, "Outline for the Study of Acculturation," by Robert Redfield, Ralph Linton, and Melville J. Herskovits," p. 133.
[6] Leonard Broom and John Kitsuse, "The Validation of Acculturation," *American Anthropologist*, February, 1955, 57: 44 ff.

Broom and Kitsuse also point out that the person who is taking on a new culture must "validate" his acculturation by having *qualified* and been *accepted* in the major institutional patterns of the dominant society.[7] In order to do this he must also give up any privileged protection or immunities which he has enjoyed by virtue of being a member of a minority. This has been recognized by Frazier and others who have described as "vested interests" the resistances to assimilation of certain status groups within the minority, where incorporation into equal competition with dominants might diminish their advantages. Dominants can equally shut out minorities by patterns of overprotection, by making pets of individual minority members to whom they have some personal tie. In this connection, Margaret Mead, as anthropologist consultant to the Israel Ministry of Health, cautions with regard to the Arab minority:

. . . There seemed to be a tendency to demand for the Arab health services far less local contribution than Jewish communities would make and to treat some Arab nomadic groups with a considerable amount of patronage. I fully realize the delicacy of the problem . . . but I think the only safe course of action is to accord the Arab population the same type of expectation, privilege, and responsibility accorded other Israeli citizens, for over-privilege can be as discriminatory as under-privilege, even though there are fewer immediate ill effects.[8]

Validation is the point at which the move to ultimate assimilation will or will not be made. If minority members reject participation in some but not all the major institutional forms of the dominant culture, they have made a choice for stabilized pluralism, with the ensuing development of particular established patterns of interaction with dominants. There is often a generational battle over the choice of stabilized acculturation versus assimilation.

Assimilation

In a definition of assimilation Park states that "an immigrant is ordinarily considered assimilated as soon as he has acquired the language and the social ritual of the native community and can participate, without encountering prejudice in the common life, economic and political. . . . Assimilation may in some senses and to a certain degree be described as a function of visibility."[9] A problem arises here as to whether or not a minority person is assimilated if he participates only in the secular community institutions of economic and public life, and is debarred in the sphere of social invitation. Another point of view has been that which stresses the interactional aspect of assimilation. Thus Young and Mack define assimilation as "the fusion of

[7] *Ibid.*
[8] Margaret Mead, "Problems of Cultural Accommodation," in *Assignment in Israel,* ed. Bernard Mandelbaum (New York: The Jewish Theological Seminary of America, Harper & Brothers, 1958), p. 113.
[9] Robert E. Park, "Assimilation," *Encyclopedia of the Social Sciences,* Vol. II (New York: The Macmillan Co., 1930), p. 281.

divergent habits, attitudes, and ideas of two or more groups or societies into a common set of habits, attitudes, and ideas."[10] This definition stresses the blending of mutual contributions to the common life. It does not imply that every vestige of the old culture must be abandoned, but it makes no effort to differentiate on what levels old culture sentiments and traits may be retained and a person still be considered assimilated.

Contemporary sociologists stress the fact that, in the end, assimilation depends on dominant acceptance of the minority individual. The question is not only in which spheres of social life a person is accepted; it is also a question of which traits, with what symbolic significance, a host culture will accept, physiognomic or ideological. This last may vary according to the character of the host culture.

Another closely related problem is whether assimilation is the only goal for minority groups. Park believed that minorities and dominants were caught in the same evolutionary process and had no choice. Louis Wirth, in analyzing the problems of the Jewish minority, also saw assimilation as the inevitable outcome, and any alternatives as temporary delays. However, he put the burden of delay on the minority, who are discouraged by rebuffs, or over-aggressive, thereby intensifying both minority solidarity and dominant discrimination.[11]

In a re-evaluation of Wirth's thesis, Etzioni has challenged the *a priori* assumption of assimilation as the only alternative choice.[12] He holds that America is a pluralistic society, and it is illogical not to include cultural pluralism.

This discussion of assimilation suggests that in the writings about dominant-minority relations there is as yet no clear consensus as to which if any sentiments and traits may be retained when a person of minority origin considers himself assimilated and is accepted in all the range of social relationships accorded to a dominant of the same social status.

Pluralism

When we speak of America as a pluralistic society we mean that there are many groups which retain differences derivative from their tradition and some degree of collective identity. In the case of minority groups, this would include some cultural or physiognomic traits. A pattern of pluralism in dominant-minority relations would require that this pattern be acceptable to the larger society and that members of the groups involved be accorded equality in the over-all status scale, regardless of race or ethnicity. Areas in which the validity of pluralism may be tested are religion and education.

[10] *Sociology and Social Life*, 2nd ed., p. 489.
[11] Louis Wirth, *The Ghetto* (Chicago, Ill.: University of Chicago Press, 1928).
[12] Amitai Etzioni, "The Ghetto—A Re-evaluation," *Social Forces*, March, 1959, 37: 255 ff.

Unity under conditions of religious pluralism involves treating religion as a matter of private faith and divorcing it from public policy. In the field of education the issue arises as to whether there can be *any* separate but equal education. Certainly not all Americans will agree that exclusively parochial education of whatever kind can give a successful orientation to the larger society.

An example of how concepts change and are used differently to meet the needs of new social situations is illustrated by the term *integration*. The concept of integration assumes a pluralistic society.

Status

The refinement of theory about minorities has increasingly made use of the concepts of *status* and *role*.

It has been a common assumption in theory of stratification that ethnic identification is one of the factors contributing to position in the over-all status structure of the society. This applies at various class levels. Thus, for example, an Anglo-Saxon chairman of a union local viewed his potential successor as "Polish, but able."[13] In his study of Philadelphia, Baltzell shows that membership in the exclusive clubs of that city, although open more during the last half-century to men who had achieved their position rather than been placed in it by birth, admitted only "token" Catholics and no Jews.[14]

Another aspect of status is involved when two differently evaluated statuses are represented in one person, where one status has low evaluation, and the other high. Everett Hughes cites the example of the Negro physician. In the subsystem he will have high status. In the dominant society as a physician he would also have high status. Does the dominant society treat him as a physician or as a Negro?[15] The answer depends on a number of variables: size of community, region, and so on. In a large Northern metropolitan community Negro physicians are beginning to find a place on hospital staffs where patients are white as well as of other races. It is still rare, however, for a Negro physician in private practice to treat white patients. The more common pattern is, at best, that of treating him as a physician in formal professional associations and as a Negro the rest of the time. Hughes points out that occupational advances of this sort on the part of minority individuals are apt to result in an "elaboration of social segregation."[16]

Warner seems to hold that exclusive membership in the ethnic subsystem

[13] Morroe Berger and John Alexander, "The Grass Roots Labor Leader," in *Studies in Leadership*, ed. Alvin Gouldner (New York: Harper & Brothers, 1950), pp. 174 ff.
[14] E. Digby Baltzell, *The Philadelphia Elite: The Making of a National Upper Class* (Glencoe, Ill.: The Free Press, 1958).
[15] Everett Cherrington Hughes, "Dilemmas and Contradictions of Status," *American Journal of Sociology*, March, 1945, 50: 353 ff.
[16] *Ibid.*

is possible only for those who do not rise above the lower middle class in the larger social system. The rise to higher position implies a break from the ethnic identity and eventual assimilation. His prognosis is that nonracial subgroups, under the motivations provided by the American norm of upward mobility, will eventually disappear. Gordon, in criticism of Warner's evidence that one is frozen at the lower-middle-class ceiling if one remains in the ethnic subsystem, states:

In small towns and cities the number in each ethnic group frequently is so small, in absolute terms, and so few have reached upper-middle class status as a result of general immigration history and the out-migration of many socially mobile members of the second and third generation, that a sub-system composed of upper-middle class ethnics is impossible. Thus those that do reach this status are drawn into Old American social relationships. However, in the larger cities and metropolitan areas, upper middle class and even upper class ethnics are so numerous that they can and do develop their own social systems of primary and associational relationships within the ethnic framework.[17]

In the literature about social mobility there have been a number of ideas brought out which are relevant to dominant-minority relations and which we can indicate only briefly here. Some recent writing has been concerned with the increase in prejudice and discrimination when the members of either the dominant society or of a particular minority are highly mobile. We might expect that the object of prejudice would vary from one status level to another, depending on which minority was competing with a particular stratum in the dominant society. The suggestion is made by Broom and Kitsuse that status competition is the crucial point of dominant-minority tension.[18] This would be the basis for the stereotype which devalues the minority as being "aggressive" or "clever," when, as Merton says, "ingroup virtues become outgroup vices."[19]

Another dimension of the problem of mobility is that of efforts toward group improvement through collective action. Labor organization is an outstanding example of improved status through this means. One of the subtler problems is the relation of dominants to minorities within such collective bodies, of minorities to each other, and of the carryover, or lack of it, of nondiscriminatory patterns from the work situation to the community.[20]

[17] Milton Gordon, *Social Class in America* (Durham, N.C.: Duke University Press, 1959), pp. 111 ff.
[18] Broom and Kitsuse, "The Validation of Acculturation," p. 46. See also, in this connection, Higham's analysis of the Saratoga incident described in Chapter 18. Higham argues that at the time Seligman was refused accommodations, Saratoga was no longer the resort of the upper-class elite but rather of the nouveau riche. "Social Discrimination Against Jews in America, 1830–1930," *Publication of the American Jewish Historical Society*, Vol. XLVII, No. 1 (Sept., 1957).
[19] Robert K. Merton, "The Self-Fulfilling Prophecy," *Social Theory and Social Structure*, rev. ed. (Glencoe, Ill.: The Free Press, 1957), p. 426.
[20] Daniel Bell and Seymour Martin Lipset, "Trade Unions and Minority Problems," *The Journal of Social Issues*, Vol. 9, No. 1 (1953), entire issue.

Marginality

Park was the first sociologist to be concerned with the concept of marginality. He and his students emphasized the role of culture conflict affecting the marginal individual. Thus marginality, in Park's terms, refers to the situation in which an individual finds himself when he still retains values and behavior from the culture group in which he had his early childhood training and subsequently attempts to incorporate other values and ways of behaving derived from experience outside his own group. Stonequist expanded Park's concept of marginality to show alternative individual modes of adaptation to this conflict.[21] The emphasis of these earlier writers was on the conflict engendered in the personality by the attempt to internalize two differing sets of values.

Merton sees marginality as behavior "in which the individual seeks to abandon one membership group for another to which he is socially forbidden access."[22] For Merton the concept of marginality is a special instance of reference group theory.

The term *reference group* was introduced by Herbert Hyman,[23] and has been expanded by Merton and his associates. In his initial article, Hyman pointed out that many individuals tend to identify themselves with a group to which they do not in fact belong but to whom they accord prestige. This group is their point of reference, whose behavior and attitudes they attempt to adopt. Frazier states that in the post-Civil War South there was an invasion of "New England School marms" setting up schools for Negroes, who were able to create a generation of Negroes with the best culture of New England.[24] These teachers were a reference group for their students. But, as Merton comments, such reference group behavior may be dysfunctional to the person's best interests. If his reference group is a closed group to which he can never belong—that is, if he is marginal—his newly adopted behavior may initially lead to confusion.[25] Clyde Kluckhohn found this to be true of some Indians educated at Indian boarding schools, as we cited in Chapter 15. The situation of British and American educated Africans was such until recently.[26] However, if positions in the social structure are open to the person, he will be able to use the new behavior he has learned.

The rigidity or fluidity of the society as a whole will affect how the person is received. If the society has rigid barriers against movement from one

[21] E. V. Stonequist, *The Marginal Man* (New York: Charles Sribners' Sons, 1937).

[22] Robert K. Merton and Alice Rossi, "Contributions to the Theory of Reference Group Behavior," in Robert K. Merton, *Social Theory and Social Structure*, p. 266.

[23] Herbert H. Hyman, "The Psychology of Status," in *Archives of Psychology*, No. 269, 1942.

[24] E. Franklin Frazier, *Race and Culture Contacts in the Modern World* (New York: Alfred A. Knopf, Inc., 1957), p. 309.

[25] Robert K. Merton, *Social Theory and Social Structure*, p. 266 ff.

[26] Frazier, *Race and Culture Contacts*, p. 313.

group to another, the person adapting to modes of a group other than his own will be rejected and ridiculed by the outside group, as Southerners sometimes speak of educated Negroes as "uppity." If the society is less rigid, a Negro who achieves a good job, good manners, and good speech may, in New York for example, be respected by whites and Negroes alike.

Park and Stonequist's approach to marginality supplied sociological dimensions for the explanation of behavior that had previously been viewed as individual deviance and evaluated in moral terms. They wrote at a time when American society was incorporating large groups of migrants of diverse cultural origins. Under Merton the concept of marginality is enlarged, so that it applies not only to individuals of ethnic or racial subgroups but to any individual who seeks entrance to and is denied admission to a group, a stratum, or a community. Merton stresses the role of the excluding group as a new dimension of Park's original formulation.

Roles

There is an increasing interest in sociological theory in role-behavior. A role, as we have seen, is the appropriate behavior associated with a given position in the society. There are socially expected ways of behaving in each society—a father, a student, a priest, a teacher, a chairman, and so on.

The problem of roles in the older theoretical tradition regarding dominant-minority relations was perceived as part of the problem of culture conflict. Handlin has written eloquently on the threatened patriarchal role of the immigrant father, which did not fit the role definition of an "American" father.[27] The first concern with roles, then, was with conflicts in definition of institutional roles between the dominant groups and subcultural groups. Often this may involve the necessity for *role relearning*.

Other writing on minorities has dealt with a second problem of roles: that of *learning new roles*, which are associated with structures and positions that do not exist in the society in which the individual grew up, so that he has had no opportunity to acquire this kind of role behavior in his general social learning. Individuals from folk societies have had to learn the roles appropriate to large-scale technological societies, such as behavior in formal organizations.

Role theory has pointed out that many dilemmas for the individual are contained in the *conflict of roles* he must assume in a complex society. Conflict may occur between the roles of citizen (co-operative in emphasis), entrepreneur (competitive in emphasis), and member of a family (authoritative, or supportive, or subordinate).[28]

Merton has also shown that there may be conflicts within a role-set[29]—

[27] Oscar Handlin, *The Uprooted* (Boston: Little, Brown & Co., 1951).
[28] Robert K. Merton, *Social Theory and Social Structure*, p. 369.
[29] *Ibid.*

that is, the role associated with one position may precipitate conflict because it bears different relations to different reference groups. A school principal has responsibilities to his bureaucratic superiors in the school system, to his teachers, to the children in his school, and to their parents. The interests of these various groups may well contain elements of conflict which affect the principal and can in some circumstances confuse, immobilize, or force difficult decisions upon him.

There are also special roles associated with positions created by the existence of dominant-minority relations. We have spoken in Chapter 18 of the role of German-Jewish intellectual immigrants who served as intermediaries between Germans in Germanic societies in the United States and German Jews.

Role theory is concerned with analyzing roles characteristic of situations found recurrently in comparable situations. Thus, as we mentioned in Chapter 2, Yankee traders invading the Reconstruction South played roles associated with marginal business and were stereotyped with traits similar to the stereotype some Gentiles have of Jews. This passing insight of Lipset's was picked up and expanded by Rinder, who suggested cross-cultural similarities in the role of the stranger-trader, as we described in Chapter 18.[30] Stryker has carried the delineation further in an article which explores the circumstances under which prejudice will develop against these middlemen traders.[31] He compares attitudes toward three groups of these peoples in the nineteenth century: Jews in Germany, Christian Armenians in Turkey, and Parsis in India. Prejudice developed against Jews and Armenians, but not against Parsis. Stryker found that the variable present in the *dominant* society which was absent in the case of Parsis was emergent militant nationalism.

This discussion of the minority trader and the way his role is perceived by the dominant society not only shows the value of a wider conceptual frame in making evaluations of particular social behavior, but the sequence of the discussion from Park, to Lipset, to Rinder, to Stryker is an excellent example of how theory is developed.

MIDDLE – RANGE THEORY

Robert K. Merton has stated that ". . . theory must advance on . . . interconnected planes: through special theories adequate to limited ranges of social data, and the evolution of a more general conceptual scheme adequate to consolidate groups of special theories."[32] We are presenting three ex-

[30] Lipset, "Changing Social Status and Prejudice," p. 477; Irwin D. Rinder, "Strangers in the Land," *Social Problems*, Winter, 1958–1959, 6: 253 ff.
[31] Sheldon Stryker, "Social Structure and Prejudice," *Social Problems*, Spring, 1959, 6: 340 ff.
[32] Merton, *Social Theory and Social Structure*, Introduction, pp. 9–10.

amples of significant middle-range theoretical formulations that contribute
to the analysis of dominant-minority relations.

"The Self-Fulfilling Prophecy"[33]

In this now classic essay Merton explores the phenomenon of the *vicious
cycle*. We have already seen in Chapter 2 that Myrdal dealt with this concept and saw it as a spiraling process. Merton is more concerned with
analyzing how it gets started and what is inherent in its control. Merton's
theory has broader applications than just the vicious cycle, and lends itself
equally well to an analysis of, for example, outbreaks of violence. (See
Chapter 20.)

Starting with the theorem of W. I. Thomas, "If men define situations as
real, they are real in their consequences," Merton points out that the trouble
begins with an incomplete or false definition of the situation. If this false
definition is acted on, it brings about a situation which fits the definition.
His first illustration is of how a bank can be caused to fail when a rumor
starts that it is shaky. The rumor (false definition) brings about a run on the
bank (behavior) that precipitates its failure. His second illustration is of
unions excluding Negroes because Negroes have been strike breakers; then
since they cannot join unions they will obviously have no union loyalty that
would keep them from accepting employment in a shop whose workers are
on strike. Merton's theory illuminates the nature of stereotypes. The dominant group's beliefs (definitions of situations) result in discriminatory actions that so structure the interacting of dominants and minorities that they
force the minority to intensify the derogated behavior and thus give the
stereotype validity. Therefore, stereotypes are never wholly false.

Furthermore, Merton points out that when a minority has been enclaved
in a stereotype—that is to say, a false definition of character and behavior—
the minority individual who behaves in the approved mode of the dominant
group is criticized for so doing. The same behavior is defined differently by
the dominant group, depending on whether it is displayed by one of their
own group or a member of the minority group. What is virtue for the dominant group becomes vice in the eyes of the majority for the stereotyped
minority. If, as Merton cites, a Presbyterian rises from rags to riches, he is
held up as a model. If a Jew does the same he is condemned as being too
acquisitive and too ambitious.

In considering how the circle of self-fulfilling prophecies can be broken,
Merton posits that, logically and ideally, one should begin with a redefinition of the situation. This, however, is not a simple act of will or good will,
for deep-seated beliefs are themselves the products of social forces. He notes
furthermore, the hopelessness of trying to persuade the psychologically disturbed. Similarly, he is less than optimistic about education as the way out.

[33] *Ibid.*, pp. 421–436.

The fact that the educational system is itself part of the normative institutional structure of the dominant society makes it subject to the, at best, "incomplete" definitions that dominants make of minorities.

For this reason, Merton sets his hope for remedy in the deliberate enactment of institutional change. Returning to his initial illustrations of the failure of a bank and action against Negroes, he points out that banking legislation, or the statutory creation of interracial public housing have been effective enacted institutional controls. The original proposition then may be restated in this way: "The self-fulfilling prophecy, whereby fears are translated into reality, operates only in the absence of deliberate institutional controls."[34]

The Authoritarian Personality[35]

For the last several decades there has been a growing literature bringing together psychological and sociological concepts about personality structure. One of the postulates on which such conceptual integration rests is that the individual's early experiences exert a lasting effect on his personality, what he learns as norms (sociology) and how he reacts emotionally to this learning (psychiatry). There is now a wide range of material to document the different modes of child-rearing in different cultures.[36] Looking toward a cross-cultural typology in the field of social structure and personality, one major step has been taken in the formulation of a type: the authoritarian personality. This was first described in the early 1930's by the German philosopher and sociologist Max Horkheimer.[37] The authoritarian personality is one which has been molded by a fear of authority, as for instance in the relationship to a strict patriarchal father whose decisions are binding and often arbitrary, and who punishes for lack of respect. Some cultures, including the Puritan strain in our own, have valued this type of family structure. The child trained in this way responds to all authority as he did to his father, submissively, and as an adult becomes authoritarian in turn. Deeper study of such personalities has shown that obeying arbitrary authority in childhood results in bottled-up fear and resentment. The child who successfully weathers the discipline develops into a man who is frightened by and morally indignant about (and perhaps covertly envious of) people whose behavior is different from the conduct that he has bitterly achieved. His residue of fear and suppressed wish to retaliate can all too easily be mobilized wherever and whenever an appropriate rationalization is supplied.

[34] *Ibid.*, p. 436.
[35] T. W. Adorno, Else Frankel-Brunswik, Daniel J. Levinson, R. Nevitt Sanford, *The Authoritarian Personality* (New York: Harper & Brothers, 1950).
[36] For examples see Margaret Mead, *Childhood in Contemporary Culture* (New York: Columbia University Press, 1958).
[37] Max Horkheimer, "Authority and the Family," in Bernard Stern, *The Family, Past and Present* (New York: D. Appleton-Century Co., 1938), p. 428.

This is one example of an analytic concept in the social sciences which has been tested, in at least one dimension, by a major field study. Under the auspices of the American Jewish Committee, T. W. Adorno, a colleague of Horkheimer, and several associates set out to test the relationship between authoritarian versus non-authoritarian upbringing and degree of anti-Semitic prejudice. They derive from their empirical work a summary profile of the prejudiced and the nonprejudiced personality. The prejudiced personality tries to repress from his consciousness unacceptable tendencies or impulses in himself; the unprejudiced person shows more awareness of his faults and is more willing to face up to them. The prejudiced person particularly attempts to repress fear, weakness, sex impulses, and aggressive feelings toward those in authority—for example, his parents. He shows also a tendency to compensate for this overrepression by manifesting a drive for power and success along conventional lines. The prejudiced seem to gain less pleasure from emotional experience—companionship, art, or music—than the unprejudiced. Outward conformance to conventions is a marked characteristic of the prejudiced; the unprejudiced are more genuinely concerned with discovering a valid ethical value system for themselves. The prejudiced are more interested in achieving power; the less prejudiced seek love and affection as satisfactory ends in themselves. The high scorers on the prejudice scale are extremely rigid in their standards of behavior, intolerant of any deviation from the conventional codes of morals or manners; in contrast, the low scorers are more flexible in their own adjustments to the mores, more appreciative of the complexities of human behavior, and more sympathetic with those who err.

The basis for these two contrasting personality types was found by these research workers to have been established in the contrasting patterns of family life to which the subjects were exposed in childhood. The prejudiced report rigid discipline, with affection made conditional on the child's approved behavior. In the families of the prejudiced there were clearly defined roles of dominance by parents and submission by children, in contrast with families where equalitarian practices prevailed. As the authors put it: "Forced into a surface submission to parental authority, the child develops hostility and aggression which are poorly channelled. The displacement of a repressed antagonism toward authority may be one of the sources, and perhaps the principal source, of his antagonism toward outgroups."[38]

There are social structural implications here which take the analysis of prejudice out of the purely psychological. For even though psychology and psychiatry have given us the insight into the effect of repressed material on behavior, as sociologists we are interested in the kind of family system which is to be normative for our society. The democratic family is not only

[38] Adorno, *et al.*, *The Authoritarian Personality*, p. 482.

logically coherent with the ideal of a democratic society; it is necessary for the functioning of a true democracy.

"Social Structure and Anomie"[39]

In this essay Merton shows how the social structure poses problems of adaptation for individuals in the competitive opportunities offered the members of society. He points out that the person who achieves an honored place in the society is expected to pursue goals which society values, using the means of which the society approves. But other patterns of adjustment occur, depending on opportunity within the society. Some people have incorporated the approved goals into their thinking very early and have been trained appropriately at successive stages in how to pursue them. The boy who goes to a good school, a college of standing, and a recognized school for business or professional training, or becomes associated with a reputable firm may expect, according to his talents, to achieve desirable goals by legitimate means. But the boy who goes to an overcrowded, understaffed school and cannot get into a good college, or any college, will be at a competitive disadvantage in achieving those same goals. He may lower his aspirations but retain the approved means of pursuing such goals as he can attain. He will be good, conscientious, but not so successful. He may on the other hand, retain the goals and abandon the approved means. He may then become a racketeer or a robber baron or a canny politician. He may make a fortune, and perhaps his descendants will endow a college or a church. Or if the barriers are too great or too confusing, he may reject both goals and means. He may retreat into reactive movements, cults, daydreams perhaps stimulated by television or other mass escape mechanisms, or opiates.

The final alternative offered in Merton's paradigm is that of rebellion: the attempt to change both the goals and means. This alternative suggests the association with groups supporting "unofficial values" or counter ideologies. (See Chapter 2.)

Merton has prepared a now well known paradigm[40] which summarizes the choices of adaptation to goals and means.

MODES OF ADAPTATION	CULTURE GOALS	INSTITUTIONAL MEANS
I. Conformity	+	+
II. Innovation	+	−
III. Ritualism	−	+
IV. Retreatism	−	−
V. Rebellion	±	±

Though Merton's theory was not derived from research on minority

[39] Merton, *Social Theory and Social Structure*, pp. 131–160. *Anomie* is a term used to describe a condition characterized by lack of norms.
[40] *Ibid.*, p. 140. By permission.

groups, it does recast in a larger frame some of the substantive materials regarding minority group behavior. It has frequently been observed, for example, that first-generation immigrants have a high rate of mental illness (retreatism) and the second generation a high crime rate (innovation). Our citation of Clyde Kluckhohn's material on the Navahos shows some individuals using several of these alternative adaptations. (See Chapter 15.)

The contribution of this theory is not in labeling the behavior as rebellion or innovation but in providing an explanation of why one might expect to find such behavior more frequently in minority groups than in the dominant group. The explanation, according to Merton, lies in the differential access to the means (education, capital, and so on) for achieving the goals of the dominant culture. According to this theory, as these minorities achieve equality of opportunity, one would expect a decline in such types of deviant behavior.

THREE SYSTEMATIC SOCIOLOGISTS

We have selected three contemporary systematic sociologists for brief mention because each has contributed significant insights that have now become accepted concepts in current writing about dominant-minority relations. Each represents a different approach to systematic sociology. Yet each, in addition to his specific conceptual contribution, in his general analysis, arrives at similar problems in the total social structure which are significant for dominant-minority relations.

Robert M. MacIver

MacIver's main concerns lie in the analysis of society as a mechanism for sustaining an appropriate balance of necessary controls and optimum individual creativity. One of his chief contributions is his definition of the limitations of the role of the state. (We have already discussed this in Chapter 2.) MacIver emphasizes the role of the state as conserver, preserver, and adjudicator of competing *like* interests (economic interests, for example). Like interests are those where the pursuit of its goals by one segment of a society may handicap another segment (with its like interests) in the attainment of these same goals. It is in the regulation of *like* interests that the state finds its function.

MacIver distinguishes like interests from *common* (cultural) interests, where the pursuit of the interest by some members of the society does not detract from the total available to others. Within the sphere of these common interests the state is ill-suited or incapable of functioning effectively.[41] In his differentiation between the nature of competing similar (like) interests of individuals in a society as contrasted with shared (common) interests

[41] Robert M. MacIver and Charles H. Page, *Society* (New York: Rinehart, Inc., 1937), pp. 32–33.

at the cultural level, MacIver opens the way to a redefinition of the problem of cultural pluralism.

George C. Homans[42]

Unlike MacIver's emphasis on society as ordered through the institutional forms of the great associations of men in political life, economic life, and so forth, Homans' point of departure is that of interaction within a group. As Homans points out, at the level of the small group, society has always been able to cohere. Of what then, he asks, does the larger society consist? He distinguishes between an "external system" of relationships related primarily to problems of survival and an "internal system" related to likings and preferences. For Homans, activity, sentiment, interaction, and group norms are the elements which, in various combinations, create both the external and the internal systems. External and internal systems are never totally separate from each other, but difference in order of precedence of the factors distinguishes behavior in the external system from the internal system. Essentially what Homans is accounting for is the type of interaction characteristically related to survival in the larger society as contrasted with the type of interaction which allows the persistence of widely differentiated subgroups within the society. Many of Homans' specific propositions as to types of interaction have laid the theoretical base for efforts in intergroup relations.

Talcott Parsons[43]

Talcott Parsons has attempted the most abstract analysis of social relations to appear in sociological theory. His contribution thus far has been in the more refined specification of relations within the *social* system (as contrasted with systems of ideational or motivational relationships).

Parsons sees a social system as held together by a consensus of central values. The survival of a particular society with its values makes necessary the creation of specific positions which represent the distribution of functions in the society. These might be occupational positions, such as banker, machinist, farmer, private secretary and so forth; or within the kinship patterns, father, aunt, step-mother. These positions are statuses, ranked higher or lower in community evaluation according to how central they are to the preservation of the core values and how limited they are in replaceability. Each status demands the carrying out of a function in a socially defined way. This is role.

Parsons' elaborations of the concepts of status and role have given many new insights into the problems of acculturation. They make possible a more precise description of what must be accepted and what must be left behind,

---

[42] George C. Homans, *The Human Group.*
[43] Talcott Parsons, *The Social System* (Glencoe, Ill.: The Free Press, 1950).

what must be perceived and what must be learned, if one wishes to move from participation in one society to full participation in another. When the increasing volume of small studies using Parsons' contributions is finally brought together and interpreted, we may be in a position to write a more sophisticated theory of dominant-minority relations than has been developed thus far.

Parsons has added a dimension to the discussion of values in distinguishing between "universalistic" and "particularistic" values. For example, a traditional folk society has behavior imperatives dependent on the position of each person in the social system: son toward father, tribesman toward chief, clansman toward clan brother, and so on. These are particularistic in that particular behavior is expected or allowable in relation to each position. Universalistic behavior norms, on the other hand, apply equally to persons regardless of position, as in a court of law, on a team, etc. The social system of some societies may be almost totally particularistic in focus, and this focus highly valued. Large-scale, complex, technological societies have a much stronger value orientation toward universalistic norms. Thus a person moving from one social system to another must internalize not only the *content* of new values, but if necessary a new *way of thinking* as between particularistic and universalistic.

The three theorists we have just presented have taken cognizance, by their respective designations of "like," "external," and "social," of the separation of the secular systems of relationship and the cultural systems of relations. These latter allow, in MacIver's terms, more creative spontaneity; in Homans' terms, more sentiment-engendered interaction; in Parsons' terms, more particularistic values; and in keeping with all three, the possibility of great variety of group life. The cultural sphere is, as it were, terrain for abundant variant flowering, flourishing from a root of common interest, common norms, and established position in the secular order. All three theorists recognize the interdependence of the social and cultural, but all recognize that the spheres are of a different order. Thus the base is laid for the role of culture in our pluralistic society. Even Park, by implication, took this into account in his definition of assimilation as access to and fulfillment of secular community and citizen roles.

Only the experience of America could produce such a theory. Heretofore cultural pluralism has been discussed as if whole cultures, with their sacred and secular systems intact, were to be incorporated in a quasi-federal fashion. The risks of fragmentation, separation, loss of benefit, and eventual instability of the nation-state have been apparent in this older theory, and aroused grave doubts about the support of that kind of pluralistic society. The solution here presented suggests the appropriateness of separating those functions which are uniquely cultural from the totality, allowing their voluntary development in a variety of patterns and strengthening unity in areas of secular public interest. MacIver feels strongly that such a possibility is inherent in the democratic state. It is in the light of these theories that we can then understand Frazier's vision of cosmopolitan urban societies of the future, in which the interaction of people of varying racial and ethnic identification on the basis of equality will lead to a new flow of human creativity.

TOPICS FOR PROJECTS AND DISCUSSION

1. Discuss acculturation as a process related to role relearning and role conflict.
2. From the chapters on the Mexicans and the Puerto Ricans in this book find examples of particularistic values held by these people of Hispanic culture that conflict with universalistic values of the larger society.
3. Write an essay on the self-fulfilling prophecy, using other examples than those used by Merton.
4. From the material on Cornerville in Chapters 4 and 5 of this book, and from the material on American Indians and on the Jewish group, see if you can find appropriate illustrations for each of the positions indicated in Merton's paradigm in "Social Structure and Anomie."
5. What changes have occurred in American society in the last forty years that give occasion for viewing cultural pluralism differently than it formerly was considered.

SUGGESTED READING

Gordon, Milton M. "Social Structure and Goals in Group Relations" in Morroe Berger, Theodore Abel and Charles H. Page, *Freedom and Control in Modern Society.* New York: D. Van Nostrand Co., Inc., 1954.
> *The author analyzes different levels on which cultural pluralism can operate.*

MacIver, Robert M. *The Web of Government.* New York: The Macmillan Co., 1947.
> *The entire argument is an elaboration of MacIver's theory of the state, and the last chapter on the "multi-group" society is especially relevant.*

Merton, Robert K. *Social Theory and Social Structure,* rev. ed. Glencoe, Ill.: The Free Press, 1957.
> *Merton's principal contributions to middle-range theory, including elaborations and further thoughts on the self-fulfilling prophecy, social structure and* anomie, *and reference groups.*

Park, Robert E. *Race and Culture.* Glencoe, Ill.: The Free Press, 1950.
> *This volume of posthumous papers contains Park's central ideas and has an interesting autobiographical essay describing how his ideas developed.*

Parsons, Talcott. *The Social System.* Glencoe, Ill.: The Free Press, 1950.
> *Parsons' elaboration of the structure of the social system. Chapter 3 discusses the various combinations of particularistic and universalistic values found in different cultures.*

20

Interpretation of Dominant-Minority Relations in the United States

In Chapter 19 we related dominant-minority relations to sociological theory in general. In this chapter the task essayed is a narrower one, to interpret dominant-minority relations in the United States, using the specific inter-group relations which have been described.

For this purpose, we shall focus attention on two generalizations for all these manifold situations: (1) In all the specific situations where a different people have come in contact with Americans of unquestioned first-class status, a dominant-minority situation has developed, with the latter as dominant. (2) The structure of the relationship in each case has never been completely stable, and the trend has been toward the elimination of minority status from each people who possessed it. Even though the first of these considerations will engage more attention, the other will be explored as well.

Why is it that all these "strangers" have been accorded minority status, and that so many of their descendants still retain this status. Is this accidental? Is it the natural order of things—the result of some universal principle operating in all situations where people meet? Is it peculiar to Americans, the result of social forces unique in American history, or Western culture? Or is it perhaps a combination of some or all of these factors?

In addition to over-all trends in dominant-minority relations, there are short-term changes related to other internal and external stresses in the society—for example, war or economic depression. These we illustrate and analyze under the category of minorities in times of stress.

We proceed on the assumption that it is not necessary at this point in the development of social science in the United States to give consideration to points of view now generally discarded. Thus we shall assume that the discussion of race in Chapter 3 is sufficient to rule out any conception that dominant or minority behavior is affected by genetic factors. It is taken for granted, too, that there is no "natural" (in the genetic sense) aversion of people of contrasting somatic appearance for one another. Finally, interpretation proceeds on the assumption that no complex pattern of social relationships can be explained by a single "cause." For this reason we should expect, for example, to find a Marxian interpretation of dominant-minority relations exclusively on the basis of class struggle as inadequate to explain dominant-minority relations as it has been to explain the course of social history. We will find it helpful to begin our consideration by examining certain psychological phenomena.

PSYCHOLOGICAL FACTORS

Like all sociological phenomena, dominant-minority relations have their psychological correlates—the attitudes, interests, and motivations which underlie the reciprocal behavior of each group. We are concerned here with the psychology of the members of the dominant group. Dominant behavior may be explained by four general kinds of motivations: (1) the motives generated by the imperatives of the society's culture; (2) the desire to conform to the group; (3) calculated self-interest; and (4) psychological imperatives deeply rooted in the unconscious level of personality.

A basic postulate of social science is that the culture of any society, diffused through group experience, tends to structure the personality of all its members in the mould reflecting its basic values. Thus Zuni culture structures the personality of the individual Zuni to become self-effacing; Chinese culture, to make all Chinese concerned with "saving face"; Dobu culture, to develop suspiciousness in all Dobuans.[1] A comprehensive interpretation of dominant behavior must therefore take into account the basis of the culture of the society in question.

Every normal human being wants to be considered a part of the group and to have a secure place in it; he is constrained to conform to the prevalent practices of his group. In many instances, his conformity lacks any

---

[1] See Ruth Benedict, *Patterns of Culture* (Boston: Houghton Mifflin Co., 1934), for further discussion of the influence of culture on personality. See also *Aspects of Culture and Personality*, ed. Francis L. K. Hsu (New York: Abelard-Schuman, 1954).

specific motivation other than the desire to conform. Indeed, he may conform for this reason even when he possesses strong interest in doing the contrary. Many people discriminate against a minority for no other reason than to stay in the good graces of their fellows or, stated in another way, to avoid group penalties for failure to conform. Ultimately this repetitive conformance becomes habitual and continues more or less unconsciously. This process is best illustrated by children who learn to discriminate against particular groups and simply continue to do so throughout their life.

The intensity of the prejudice against minorities and the degree of discrimination against them varies, however, among the members of a society or a group. Greater discrimination is sometimes due to calculated self-interest, on the whole a rational motive understood at the conscious level of personality. This kind of motivation is illustrated by the role of the slave trader in the colonial slave system, or the housewife who offers a minority applicant for domestic service a lower wage than she would have to offer an applicant of dominant status. The exploitative sexual bargaining of dominant men with minority women is another example.

In other instances, we have seen an intensely hostile attitude toward a minority which does not seem to arise from rational self-interest. This is best illustrated in the personality of the true anti-Semite. Interpretation of the attitudes and behavior of such individuals calls for probing into the dynamics of personality at the unconscious level. Theories of such behavior interpret intense prejudice as one mechanism adopted—unconsciously, of course—by some persons of dominant status possessing a deep-seated or chronic mental conflict or frustration, in order to resolve their neurotic or psychotic feeling. The most general and least complicated of such theories suggests that chronically frustrated people alleviate their frustration by aggression against available minority people. Minorities are convenient objects of this aggression because it is more dangerous to be aggressive against other dominants and because the dominant society is characteristically tolerant of violation of the rights of minorities. It is suggested that the guilt feelings of the dominant may be resolved by projecting the responsibility for evil upon the minority. For example, the businessman neurotically disturbed as a result of attempting to reconcile his aggressive economic behavior with his Christian ethics, resolves the problem by projecting the blame for the general character of capitalist business practice upon Jews. In still another psychoanalytic theory, McLean[2] interprets Southern white behavior toward Negroes as "the loss of a secure dependence on a fixed social system" brought about by the destruction of the slavery system. Assuming the general validity of the modern functional interpretation of neuroses and psychoses, there can be little doubt of its general applicability to the more pathological domi-

[2] Helen V. McLean, "Psychodynamic Factors in Race Relations," *The Annals of the American Academy*, March, 1946, 244: 159–66.

nant behavior toward minorities, however much a particular detailed interpretation may lack verifiability.

SYNTHESIZED INTERPRETATION

A synthesized interpretation of dominant-minority relations appears to us to consider the combined interaction of the following factors and social forces: the universal phenomenon of ethnocentrism and the principle of in-group–out-group interaction, historical circumstances, the dynamics of the private enterprise system, the sustaining influence of tradition, and the dynamics of democracy.

Universal Principles of Group Interaction and Ethnocentrism

The initial stages of interaction between a dominant and a minority group may be expected to follow the well-established universal sociological principles of ethnocentrism and in-group–out-group processes. In order for any society to survive, each member as he grows up must acquire a strong sense of loyalty to and identification with his own people—the in-group. Through this process also each member acquires the conviction that the culture of his own group, its ways of doing things, its values and goals, are the "proper," the right ways and values. It is therefore almost inevitable that when two such in-groups find themselves suddenly faced with the problem of living together in the same area, each should consider the other an out-group and that some antagonism should arise. The immediate harmonious assimilation of two visibly different groups is impossible. Still further, the in-group sentiment requires some degree of sacrifice of individual desires in order to conform to the demands of the society. This involves some degree of repression of individual desires, and the resulting frustrations seek a permissible outlet. An out-group, a different people, afford such an outlet. Thus, for example, the in-group member in wartime, chafing at rationing regulations, may blame the necessity for it on the alleged black market operations of the members of an out-group.

Historical Factors

Since it is sociologically natural for opposition to arise between two peoples living in the same area, the great prevalence of ethnic and racial antagonism in the history of the United States is in no small measure related to the fact that no other nation in modern times has faced so many such situations so often and so continuously. The Parisian French, for example, have a reputation for their indifference to race, but France, as a modern nation, has had no great influx of different peoples to absorb. While, as was pointed out in Chapter 1, southern Europeans have never been as "race-conscious" as northern Europeans, it should be remembered that over the historic period being covered the nations of southern Europe neither faced nor invited the situation of assimilating vast numbers of cultural and racial aliens. In Europe, particularly in the central and eastern regions, hostile attitudes between ethnic and nationality groups create minority problems different from those which have arisen in American history. To an extent then, the prevalence of ethnic and racial antagonism in the United States is due to the unique historical circumstances creating so many potential dominant-minority situations. But, while universal principles explain why intergroup antagonisms arise, and why historical circumstance has presented the United States with unequalled opportunity for their expansion, they do not explain why the outcome has been so unvaryingly of the dominant-minority pattern, and why in each case "white Americans" have been the dominants.

Superior Power

The unvarying dominance of those Americans possessing native status resulted from their possession of superior power. In almost all situations the combination of power factors, superiority in numbers, economic resources, and technological skills is so obvious as to need no elaboration. One exception is the situation of white colonists and Indian peoples in certain areas where the Indians annihilated the whites. In another, the island territory situations where the white Americans were numerically in the minority, their dominant status arose out of their managerial economic position and their ruling political function, a status supported by a homeland power nation. Thus the opportunity to resolve their antagonism with the other peoples by assigning them the status of minorities, if they so desired, lay with the white Americans.

The Dynamics of the Economy

In intergroup relations there is no universal principle that people who are stronger will automatically dominate the weak. If they do so, the motivations for the dominant behavior must be sought in the dynamics of the culture. In American society an important cultural force motivating discrimination is the dynamics of the economic system. Before analyzing how the economy affects discriminatory behavior, some general comment on the system is in order. Historically, the economic system of the West has moved from mercantile capitalism to finance capitalism. In recent years there has been some modification in the direction of welfare capitalism. Its essence, however, is still private enterprise. It is essentially a system in which all individuals strive by competition and bargaining to gain the most for themselves individually. The belief is widely held that the indirect result of this pluralistic striving is to provide the greatest possible economic welfare for the society as a whole. For our purposes, the validity of this belief is irrelevant. What concerns us here is the way the system influences dominant behavior toward minorities.

For this analysis, we will consider human beings strictly in their role as "economic men." (Such a procedure necessarily ignores the total man, who has many other interests than the economic, and the problem of reconciling the other interests with the economic one.) A person acting in his economic role cannot give *primary* consideration to the *common* welfare. The one criterion on which he bases his action is the pecuniary. Decision rests on the answer to the question "What course of action will yield me the greatest economic gain?" Our position is that the dynamics of the economy works both ways under varying conditions and times—sometimes to favor discrimination, sometimes to lessen it. Let us first consider how the system promotes discrimination.

The Entrepreneur
The employing, managerial segment of the American economic order has gained by the presence of minorities in two distinct ways. First, each individual employer wants to get labor at the cheapest possible cost. Minorities are a source of cheaper labor. During the colonial period and after the United States became a nation, vast opportunities existed for highly profitable private enterprise. Full exploitation of these opportunities required far more labor than population growth provided. To start with, African natives were forced to provide that need. During later periods employers have welcomed immigrant newcomers for this purpose. It will be recalled that it was organized labor, not employers, who pressed for restriction of immigration. The differential handicap in wages suffered by minority workers has been partly obscured by the tendency to employ only minority workers in particular occupational functions; for example, Negro cotton workers and house servants, Mexican "beet pickers," immigrants on railroad building gangs. The collective minority status of all the workers helped keep the general wage low. In his pursuit of the cheapest labor, the entrepreneur opposed unionization. If he could not prevent it altogether, he tried to keep union strength at the lowest possible point. Antagonisms between dominant-status labor and minority-status labor, or between minorities themselves, contributed a second advantage to the entrepreneur by weakening the bargaining power of labor. As a closely related point, in a number of instances minority laborers were utilized as "strikebreakers."

While the relations of men in the free enterprise system are primarily competitive and bargaining relations, considerable co-operation with others is a necessary condition to success. Such co-operation takes many forms. The form of most concern to us is that which prompts competitors to maintain common rules of competition. The advantages accruing to entrepreneurs from the presence of minorities are contingent on general co-operation. If one by one, for example, entrepreneurs break the customary "color line," the economic advantage of it would soon be lost. Class-consciousness impels each individual entrepreneur toward conformity with the prevailing patterns of dominant-minority relations, even where the particular employer gets no direct or immediate economic advantage.

Labor

In the prevailing economic system laborers are in competition with each other for jobs and for better jobs. Laborers possessing either dominant status or a higher minority status than other minorities have a differential advantage in this competition. While perhaps in the long run the differential position of all labor would be strengthened by resolving dominant-minority distinctions and opening up union membership to all, the immediate advantage lies in a policy of exclusion. Of further significance is the long experience of labor with depression periods in the business cycle, which gives strong impetus to an individual laborer or his restricted union to maintain job status by any means possible. Discrimination against minorities is one such means. American labor has characteristically discriminated against minorities both economically and socially, although in recent years their position has been changing in this respect.

Indirect Effect of the Private Enterprise Economy

Private enterprise economics also indirectly provides further motivation for dominant behavior. The success of the system lies partly in that it holds out great pecuniary reward for those most successful. From this it follows that wide disparity in wealth and income is an essential part of the system. Consequently, there must be a substantial working class whose pecuniary reward is nominal. For many of the wage earning and low salaried groups the resulting situation inevitably generates a sense of economic deprivation. It is more frustrating to be "poor" in a rich country than to be poor in a poor country. The frustrations thus generated lead people to seek alternative compensations in whatever ways are possible. Dominant status constitutes one such possible compensation. For example, it provides the low income Southern white an ego satisfaction to feel that he is better than any Negro or the low income Anglo-American that he is better than any Pole.

The private enterprise system and the relatively open class system in the United States have provided great opportunity for those born into humble circumstances to achieve higher economic reward and social status, probably to a greater extent than in any other modern nation. For this reason the system has generated strong competitive drives, particularly in the business world. On the other hand, the system offers little security at any level. Therefore there develops among those who acquire this intensely competitive drive a large volume of frustration at not being able to reach the desired level or to be sure of remaining at a level already reached. As we have seen, in Gentile behavior this condition motivates hostility against Jews. The antagonism of some West Coast whites toward Japanese points to a similar interpretation. That this sociopsychological process does not appear in other minority situations may be explained by the fact that, as yet, the other minorities have not reached a point of effective competition in business life.

The connection between the frustrations generated by deprivation and status anxiety and strong antagonism toward minorities is, of course, not automatic. There could be other outlets, such as antagonism toward a foreign nation, or an *-ism*, or in rationally organized efforts to improve one's economic position. But for persons who fear the consequences of opposing those in powerful position, an available minority is a safer outlet for aggression. These indirect effects of the private enterprise system are not, of course, always consciously perceived by the property-holding classes or always consciously exploited for the purpose implied. Nevertheless, the assumption that a vague awareness of the utility of minorities in this regard seems to explain the toleration by the upper-class dominants of the cruder excesses of discrimination displayed by lower-class dominants.

Special Economic Interests

The analysis of economic factors influencing dominant behavior reveals that wide segments of the dominant group gain economic advantages from discrimination against minorities. There are a number of particular interests that profit most highly from the situation. Among these are employers of unskilled labor, of whom large-scale agricultural entrepreneurs would perhaps rank highest. Cotton production in the South, before the introduction of the mechanical cotton picker, utilized Negroes; for large-scale vegetable production, particularly in the Southwest, Mexicans are employed in large numbers; and in general immigrants have supplied the least-skilled labor in the great industrial areas. Other special economic interests are the owners of residential real estate in housing areas more or less restricted to minorities, where the limitation of choice of residence makes it possible to charge exhorbitant rents. Ironically enough, certain minority people themselves have a special economic interest in the maintenance of segregation. For example, Negro ministers, undertakers, and beauticians have a stake in maintaining segregation. While in the long run the removal of all segregation would improve the occupational opportunities of the minority in general, for the present particular persons now earning a living in these ways would stand to lose.

Counterdynamics Favoring Improvement of Minority Status

In spite of the manifold ways in which people, acting in their economic roles under the private enterprise system are motivated to seize the advantages accruing from dominant status, the connection between the two phenomena is not inevitable. Again it is the individualistic and pluralistic character of the system which makes it generate forces in the opposite direction. There are circumstances and conditions where it pays economically not to discriminate. A Southern department store owner may find that it pays to welcome Negro trade and to be civil to Negro customers to keep it. An employer desperately needing labor to fulfill a lucrative contract may be glad to place Negroes in jobs hitherto denied them. An employer may be able to get a better qualified Negro for a job at less money than he would have to pay a white. These entrepreneurs have only to calculate the possible other effects which may offset the advantage, and when the balance appears to favor taking on the minority person, their economic interests lead them to do so. In fact, as has been indicated at many points, in the past decade the total situation has so changed that in an increasing number of instances entrepreneurs have been opening up more opportunities to minorities in employment, even in jobs where they work alongside people of dominant status. While there have been many political and civic pressures which account for this, when the times and the rules change, the practices of the competitive economic man change also.

Finally, it is well to state again that the above analysis has considered the impact of an economic order as though it were the whole societal system, which is, of course, far from so. The total society has also a political order, a religio-moral order, and so on, and they all interact upon one another. Likewise, we have been analyzing the partial responses of the total human being—his economic responses—without reference to the totality of his personality. Man is also a civic being, and as an American holds in varying degrees a belief in the democratic way of life; he believes, however feebly at times, in the brotherhood of man; and he has the capacity to sympathize and to like other human beings irrespective of color and creed. It is this conflict in values within the American man which keeps the structure of dominant-minority relations in flux.

Tradition

In addition to the continued influence of the dynamics of our economic system, the persistence of the dominant-minority pattern is in large measure the product of tradition. It is an elementary principle of social science that, once a pattern of social relationships has been established, it tends to carry on unchanged unless the dynamics of other social forces operate to undermine it. Because this principle is so vital to attacking the problem of minority groups, it is important to apply it to our theme. In addition to the people who in their economic roles have special reasons for maintaining minorities, there are people who hold mythical, stereotyped beliefs about minorities, who manifest prejudiced attitudes, and who in various subtle ways—as mild as repeating a minorities joke—practice discrimination for no other reason than that they have been conditioned that way. Thus a student was heard referring to Gentiles as "white" in contrast to Jews. Traditional attitudes and corresponding behavior patterns, once conditioned, are hard to change in adults. Scientific fact and logic are often unable to dislodge them, especially among the vast numbers who are not trained to think about social phenomena in a scientific manner.

The strength of tradition lies in part in its inclusiveness and its explicitness—it is clearly understood that this is the "right" way of behavior for all good members of the group. In the South, where caste segregation of Negroes is established, the liberal Southerner who desires to have it changed faces the harsh sanctions which tradition can command—ostracism, ridicule, stigmatization as a radical. Nevertheless, tradition is not inflexible. In contrast to dominant behavior enmeshed with economic motives or compelling psychic needs, one finds that dominant behavior of the purely traditional type is more amenable to change, more responsive to intellectual persuasion, more susceptible to scientific evidence, more influenced by broader ethical insights.

Dynamics of Political Democracy

Dominant-minority relations in the United States have always been in a state of flux. The trend of change for any particular group has not always been in one direction. Attention will be given subsequently to certain short-term ebbs and flows, either in status or in the intensity of discrimination practices. One influence in American culture, however, has persistently pressed toward the elimination of minority status and its attendant disabilities—political democracy. Political democracy is a set of beliefs and sentiments which, taken together, constitute what Myrdal has called the American Creed. Among the elements of the creed are the idea that government derives its authority from the consent of the governed and that each citizen is entitled to equal participation in government and to equal protection from it. Furthermore, political democracy is a set of institutions through which the democratic creed is given expression. Among these many institutions, those most pertinent for our consideration are democratic citizenship, democratic government, and public education.

Democratic Citizenship

Democratic citizenship involves both equal opportunity to participate in government and equal protection. Participation includes the right to vote, to join a political party, to run for office, and to be appointed to a government job. Protection includes the right to trial by jury, equal treatment by law-enforcing officers, and equal protection from physical harm or property damage.

European immigrants have been able to acquire all these rights through naturalization, and their descendants born here are automatically citizens.

Mexican immigrants have the same privileges, although local legislation has segregated them in schools and barred them from certain public places. Chinese and Japanese foreign-born have been denied citizenship and the privilege of owning land. Except for a brief post-bellum period, Negroes have been denied many of the privileges of citizenship.

The caste patterning of the administration of government and the intimidation implicit in the caste system often have nullified civic privileges which are not officially denied by local law—for example, voting and jury service.

In spite of these obvious inconsistencies, the basic institutions of political democracy remain to point up the incongruity and, by their continuing existence, press continuously for the abolition of discrimination. During World War II foreign-born Chinese acquired the right to citizenship, and since then the privilege has been accorded all Asian immigrants. Federal Court decisions have step by step narrowed the area of public discrimination which is not specifically considered illegal. The federal government, more recently, has shown increasing vigor in upholding the court decisions and in administering new civil rights legislation, especially in the area of voting. Similarly, more and more states outside the South have enacted legislation and established enforcing agencies making discrimination in the public sphere illegal.

Democratic Government

While effective democratic citizenship itself requires an alert and efficient democratic government to maintain it, emphasis here is on the tendency of democratic government to press further toward its own greater democratization. Politicians, for example, are responsive to all elements of the population in a position to influence elections. Thus in areas of minority-group concentration, the exercise of civic rights permits election of their members to councils and legislatures and their appointment to various government positions. In a study of the rise of Negro voting in Texas, Strong shows how, once Negroes manage to vote in numbers, white politicians begin to bid for their votes. He cites, for example, the veteran Congressman who reacted in 1944 to the court decision outlawing the white primary by stating publicly that Negroes would vote in his district "over my dead body." Yet, "two years later when encountering appreciable opposition in the primary of 1946, he was to be seen putting in an occasional appearance at Negro fish fries and church picnics."[3] Comparison of governmental associations with other associations suggests in the main that the former reveal less discrimination against minorities. In Washington, D. C., the agencies of the federal government are far less discriminatory than the rest of the community. In short,

[3] Donald S. Strong, "The Rise of Negro Voting in Texas," *American Political Science Review,* June, 1948, 42: 510–522.

our thesis is that the very existence of democratic government furnishes a persistent catalyst to further democracy.

Public Education

A strongly established belief of the American Creed is the right of all children in the nation to free public education. The institutional embodiment of this belief is the public school system. Here the children of minorities have been educated at public expense. With three main exceptions, Negroes in the South, Mexicans in some areas of the Southwest, and Indian children on reservations, minority children have not been segregated.

Public education has been profoundly instrumental in undermining minority status. It has been a principal factor in the assimilation of ethnic minorities. In the case of racial minorities, it continues to lead toward their increasing acculturation and improves the group welfare, but as yet has not been sufficiently influential to remove the stigmatism of minority status. But, even in segregated and unequal schools, the education of minority children has one enormously important effect on dominant minority relations: it undermines the dominant stereotype of the minority. Education brings out the varying ranges of talents and abilities which exist in every minority group, and thus makes it increasingly absurd to invoke the stereotype to support the dominant position. Minority valedictorians deflate the myth of categorical minority inferiority.

In its impact on dominant children in unsegregated schools, public education likewise operates to remove the distinctions between dominant and minority. Admittedly the education received for citizenship in the formal curricula is not totally free from prejudiced nuances reflecting the varying attitudes of their teachers. But the process of civic education in a democratic society must outwardly conform to democratic principles. At the minimum, "lip service" must be given against discrimination. Public education works in the same direction also through the association of dominant and minority children on a plane of at least formal equality. Again, we are not unmindful of the formation of cliques manifesting prejudices or the subtle ways in which minority students are frequently kept out of certain school clubs and activities. But by its very nature a public school system in a democratic society cannot officially approve such tendencies. An increasing number of schools outside the South, long before the school desegregation decision, were designing purposive policies to counteract these influences.[4] Finally, the carry-over into adult life of the democratic impact of public education is considerable, though, of course, by no means complete. Many college students liberalized in the cloistered atmosphere of the campus reveal anti-

[4] See Theodore Brameld, *Minority Problems in the Public Schools* (New York: Harper & Brothers, 1946).

Semitic attitudes after several years out in the "hard" world. But it can scarcely be doubted that there is considerable permanent influence.

Summary

The two outstanding generalizations about dominant-minority relations in the United States have been (1) the imposition of minority status on all the "different peoples" coming under the jurisdiction of the nation; and (2) the instability of the dominant-minority patterns thus formed, with the net trend of change in the direction of removing the disabilities of minority status from each minority. An interpretation of the first of these generalizations can be made only by considering a number of circumstances and social forces. Ethnocentrism is a universal phenomenon which engenders some degree of opposition wherever two peoples meet. The historical circumstances which brought so many other peoples in contact with "established" Americans presented the maximum of opportunity for the development of dominant-minority structures. The success of dominant Americans in imposing minority status on all others is due in part to their superior power. The desire to establish and maintain dominance has been powerfully motivated by the dynamics of the free enterprise system, especially in its development up to the first World War. From the viewpoint of entrepreneurs, the exploitation of the possibilities for economic profit in the New World encouraged welcoming new labor willing to perform unskilled tasks. The subsequent minority status of these newcomers contributed to keeping their wages lower, directly by discrimination and indirectly by retarding unionization. Laborers of dominant status in an unstable employment economy were motivated to practice discrimination to protect their tenuous economic status. Indirectly, the individual economic insecurity of many elements in the American economy coupled with the strong urge to rise in socioeconomic status created a large volume of frustration. Discrimination against minorities served to attenuate these frustrations, both by providing the ego satisfaction of having someone else to look down on and by providing an outlet for the aggressive tendencies which frustration generates by projecting them upon minorities. This diversion of frustration also served the economic interest of the entrepreneur. The dynamics of private enterprise do not in all ways and at all times move in the same direction. Changing conditions create situations in which it "pays" for both employer and worker to relax their discriminatory practices. In the final analysis, the relation between the private enterprise system and minority discrimination is not inflexible.

Once established, dominant-minority patterns tend to continue, in part simply because they are traditional, supported by the mores of the dominant community. The tendency to conform is strengthened by conditioning children of dominant status to accept the patterns as "habitual," and by threatening the penalties of nonconformity.

Dominant-minority relations have never been completely frozen. The net trend toward the breakdown of minority status derives primarily from the dynamics of political democracy, from the beliefs in the American Creed and their expression through appropriate institutions. The institutions of democratic citizenship press persistently toward the equal participation of all and the equal protection of all. The process of democratic government also presses continuously for its fuller development, and in so doing affords increasing opportunity for minorities to help themselves. Democratic education tends to break down the dominant stereotype of the minority, an essential rationale for the discriminatory process. Free education for minorities destroys the illusion of their inferiority. Democratic education of the dominant elements further undermines the racist ideology, as does the experience of association with minority students on a relatively equal footing.

DOMINANT – MINORITY RELATIONS IN TIMES OF STRESS

Any general interpretation of the situation of minorities in American life must take into account the vulnerable position of minorities in times of social stress. Throughout American history, we can note the rise and fall of nativist movements among dominants. There have also been small- or large-scale actions against minorities, intended to intimidate or confine a specific minority group. And there have been sudden outbreaks of violence. It is reasonable to assume that any period of great social tension may lead to a recurrence of one or all of these forms of action unless they are sufficiently understood to bring about the development of controls which could avert them.

Nativist Movements

Movements which are organized efforts to revitalize "native" culture and sentiments are now generally recognized to be a special phenomenon of social change. The term "nativist" may apply to a movement within any group, dominant or minority.

A special characteristic of a nativist movement is that it seeks to solve the discomforts which its adherents feel by eliminating what is perceived as alien: persons, artifacts, customs, values.[5] As long as there are visible minorities, they are in a vulnerable position as the target of organized nativist sentiment and action from the dominant group.

Some nativist movements seek to revive and reinstate customs, values, and even beliefs which were thought to be part of the culture complex of earlier generations but are not now present. The Nazis did this with their appeal to *Blut und Boden* (blood—German Aryan; and soil—homeland).

[5] Anthony F. C. Wallace, "Revitalization Movements," *American Anthropologist*, 1956, 59: 264 ff.

The definable stages of the growth of nativist movements have been analyzed by Wallace. At the beginning of the movement the emphasis on excluding alien elements is commonly very low, subordinate to other emphases. Over a number of years the movement grows where individuals or some population group (class, religious, or other definable social group) is experiencing stress. There is a continued lessening of the culture's efficiency in satisfying the needs of this group. The type of leader who reformulates a desirable social system for the group tends to be of the charismatic leadership type, the man with strong personal appeal.

After the movement is conceived and leadership established, it must deal with the establishment of communication and with organization. If it is successful through these initial stages, its success or failure rests on the adequate prediction of the outcome of conflict situations. If it is "unrealistic" about the amount of resistance it will engender, about the consequences of its own and its opponent's moves in a power struggle, it will run the risk of early collapse. Whether its ideology or organization will be viable for long beyond its demise in the power struggle will depend on whether its formulations and structure lead to actions which maintain a low level of stress. This would account for the collapse of defeated political nativistic movements which maximize stress, in contrast with the persistence of religious revivalist or sectarian movements which lower the threshold of stress.

The Riot

A riot is a phenomenon most frequently associated with urban growth and is another symptom of the failure of people to find adequate satisfactions in their social situation. As we have seen, anti-minority riots have occurred from time to time in American history. Two which occurred within a few weeks of each other in 1943 have been analyzed in detail and give us the opportunity to see the common elements in the two situations. These riots occurred in a general climate of anxiety—in this instance, because America was engaged in war. In both instances there was a threatened and actual breakdown of normal civilian control. The outbreaks were each against a minority with clear visibility, and stereotypes were exploited in the mobilization of action. Both riots occurred in cities which had had to absorb a large recent increase in population of the minority which was the target. As Dahlke points out, riots are also more likely to occur when the minority is unwilling to accept its subordinate position.[6] Mass communication media helped mobilize sentiments against the minority.

Let us see what happened in the so-called "Zoot Suit" riots in Los Angeles:[7]

[6] H. Otto Dahlke, "Race and Minority Riots—A Study in the Typology of Violence" Social Forces, Vol. 30, No. 4 (May, 1952), pp. 419–425.
[7] Carey McWilliams, North From Mexico (New York: J. B. Lippincott Co., 1949). Adapted by the authors from Williams' account.

The anti-Mexican riots in Los Angeles raged from June 3, 1943, until June 9. This was wartime; a nearby naval base made Los Angeles the mecca for sailors' leaves. The riots were touched off on June 3 by two incidents. Some servicemen walking through a deteriorated street in a Mexican section of the city were beaten up by a gang of Mexican boys. In a nearby precinct on the same evening some Mexican boys returning from a "club" conference at the police station on how to avoid gang strife were beaten up by a gang of non-Mexican boys. It does not seem as if the two incidents were connected. The police took no immediate action, but then after their regular duty was over, a so-called "vengeance squad" set out to clean up the gang that had attacked the sailors. They found no one to arrest, but great newspaper publicity was given to the incidents and to the policemen who had made the fruitless raid.

The following night about 200 sailors hired a fleet of 20 taxicabs and cruised the Mexican quarter. The Mexican adolescent boys had a fad of wearing long, draped jackets (zoot suits). Four times the taxicab brigade stopped when it sighted a Mexican boy in a zoot suit and beat up the boys, leaving them lying on the pavement. There was no mobilization of police. One police car did intercept the caravan, and nine sailors were taken into custody, but no charges were preferred against them. In the morning papers the war news was pushed off the front page with stories of the night before on a triumphal note of the sailor's move to clean up "zoot-suited roughnecks." The third night, June 5, scores of sailors, soldiers, and marines marched through the Mexican quarter, four abreast, stopping and threatening anyone wearing zoot suits. No sailors were arrested, either by the police, the shore patrol, or the Military Police, although twenty-seven Mexican boys were arrested. In various bars Mexicans were beaten up or their jackets torn off and ripped up. The police announced that any Mexicans involved in rioting would be arrested.

On the night of June 6 six carloads of sailors cruised through the area, beating up teenage Mexicans and wrecking establishments. The police came after them in mopping-up operations and arrested the boys who had been beaten up. In the morning forty-four severely beaten Mexican boys were under arrest.

Whipped up by the press, which warned that the Mexicans were about to riot with broken bottles as weapons and would beat sailors' brains out with hammers, the excitement erupted and two days of really serious rioting occurred, involving soldiers, sailors, and civilians, who invaded motion picture houses, stopped trolley cars, and beat up the Mexicans they found, as well as a few Filipinos and Negroes. At midnight on June 7 the military authorities declared Los Angeles out of bounds for military personnel. The order immediately slowed down the riot. On June 8 the mayor stated that "sooner or later it will blow over," and the chief of police announced the situation "cleared up." However, rioting went on for two more days. Editorials and statements to the press lamented the fact that the servicemen were called off before they were able to complete the job. The district attorney of an outlying county stated that "zoot suits are an open indication of subversive character." And the Los Angeles City Council adopted a resolution making the wearing of zoot suits a misdemeanor.

The tone of the press clearly reflects the war psychology and the support of servicemen. The servicemen themselves were young men away from home, uprooted from the normal community controls in the anonymous and sex-segregated climate of military life. Many of them engaged in actions which would have been unthinkable in their home environment.

The role of the police is to be understood only if one presumes that their refraining from interference was deliberate and related to an entirely different matter. At the time of the riots a police officer was on trial in the courts for charges of brutality. Shortly after the riots, according to Carey McWilliams, a Hollywood police captain told a motion picture director that the police had touched off the riots to give a break to their colleague in demonstrating the necessity for harsh police methods. As a matter of fact, the charges against the officer were dismissed a month later.

The use of the stereotyped image of the zoot suit appeared in all the publicity and what was simply an adolescent fad was linked in the minds of the readers with the characterizations "gang," "roughneck," "subversive," and so forth. The press and the radio leaped on the band wagon and were largely responsible in their unanimity for enflaming the population.

The Detroit Race Riots of 1943[8]

A clash between Negroes and whites on the bridge leading to Belle Isle, a 985 acre recreation area and beach, on a hot Sunday evening, June 20, 1943, touched off nearly a week of rioting in Detroit. There was a history of previous racial clashes in the city. In 1925 a white mob tried to eject a Negro physician from a house he had bought in a white district. In 1941, at the Ford River Rouge plant, Negroes were pitted against white strikers. In 1941, there had been a race riot at the Northwestern High School; in 1942, there had been riots at the Sojurner Truth Housing Project. Over a period of years, Father Charles E. Coughlin, of nearby Royal Oak, had broadcast his campaign of intolerance and "Christian Front." The Reverends Gerald L. K. Smith, and J. Frank Norris, Protestant demagogues of Detroit, had also been proclaiming inflamatory nativist messages. Several weeks before the riot the National Association for the Advancement of Colored People had held its convention in Detroit, and some of the Detroit press took exception to the militancy of some speakers at this meeting.

Once again military personnel were involved in the precipitating incident. Sailors from the nearby naval base were among those fighting on the bridge. According to the senior police inspector, "When the police arrived . . . approximately 200 sailors were fighting with Negroes." This was at 10:30 p.m. Many people, white and Negro, joined the fight, all police precincts were asked to send reserves, and about 5,000 persons were involved. As the crowd was dispersed, small fighting units spread east and west and reports of small-scale rioting from other sections of the city were telephoned to police headquarters. Two rumors immediately spread, one that Negroes had raped and killed a white woman at the bridge, and another, broadcast through the microphone in a Negro night club, which urged the patrons to "take care of the whites who had killed a colored woman and her baby at the bridge."

On Monday, June 21, the congested Negro area of the city called Paradise Valley was the scene of repeated disorder, and injured people were taken to Detroit's municipal receiving hospital at the rate of one a minute. White mobs beat up Negroes leaving a movie theatre and stoned Negro automobiles; Negroes looted stores and attacked white factory workers. A Negro pastor toured Paradise Valley in a sound car pleading for calmness. The Negro representatives early Mon-

[8] Alfred McClung Lee and Norman Daymond Humphrey, *Race Riot* (New York: The Dryden Press, Inc., 1943). Adapted by the authors.

day morning requested the Mayor to call federal troops, but he thought this would not be necessary. The Governor then requested federal troops, but found that he could not get them without declaring martial law, and this he refused to do. The Mayor called an emergency meeting of the Detroit Citizen's Committee (an interracial body). R. J. Thomas, president of the United Automobile Workers, CIO, called an emergency meeting of the union's shop stewards to mobilize the union's opposition to the race riots. The noon edition of a leading paper carried banner headlines that the Negroes had murdered a police sergeant (actually wounded but still alive). White crowds increased, made up chiefly of hoodlums operating under informal but definite leadership, and hunted down stray Negroes. Some high-school students who had been dismissed early, as usual, because of the overcrowding of the school, joined with the band of hoodlums in the anti-Negro crusade. A radio newscaster announced that armed carloads of Negroes were heading for Detroit from Chicago. Ten thousand whites jammed the city hall area pulling Negroes off buses and streetcars. Finally, in the late afternoon, the Governor proclaimed "modified martial law."

On the other side of town, in a racially mixed area, everything was quiet, and a group of high-school students in an integrated high school watched a basketball game. A white Protestant minister and his son took their car and undertook a Negro rescue operation in the area of the riots. By 8:30 in the evening, despite the Governor's proclamation, violence reached a peak. At the Frazer Hotel, a Negro hotel, there was an armed battle between police and Negroes, to the delight of nearly 1,000 spectators. At 9 o'clock the Governor again asked for the assistance of federal troops; informed that his request was not made in the appropriate official form, at 9:30 he repeated the request in the correct form. At 11 he was sent word that federal troops could be made available only on a proclamation from the President of the United States. The Governor telephoned the request to Franklin D. Roosevelt. By 11:30 federal troops had entered Detroit and had the situation generally under control. Fifteen hours had elapsed since the first request for federal troops, and in that fifteen hours irreparable damage had been done.

On Tuesday a weary police dispatcher remarked, "The race rioting has subsided but people's imaginations have not." Six thousand federal troops patrolled the streets and were bivouacked on high-school playing fields and public library lawns. In the Paradise Valley district most Negroes stayed indoors, away from their jobs. On Tuesday night a Negro on his way to the YMCA was shot by a state trooper as he entered the building.

On Wednesday R. J. Thomas of the UAW issued an eight point program of immediate and effective community action to forestall recurrence of race riots in Detroit. The *Detroit Free Press* endorsed the program and pointed out that Thomas was the only Detroiter to come forward with constructive recommendations. On Wednesday evening a mob of 200 hoodlums gathered outside Northeastern High School. In the class of 1943 being graduated that night were twenty-nine Negroes. The principal's parting words warned them not to loiter for congratulations. There had been eight members of the military police at the graduation, and patrolmen outside were holding back the milling white youths. Shouting started a block away, and the policemen abandoned their positions by the school and raced to the spot. In another instant the Negro boys would have been attacked, but four truckloads of soldiers appeared and broke up the mob.

On Thursday, June 24, Congressman Dies, Chairman of the House Committee of Un-American Activities, threatened to descend upon Detroit and conduct a hearing into the cause of the riots. He believed they were caused by Japanese-Americans who had recently been released from internment camps on the West Coast. (American-born Japanese after being duly screened were allowed to leave internment camps and resettle provided they did not enter the prohibited zone of the three West Coast states.) The Detroit newspapers and civic leaders, however, joined in asking Dies to stay away. The Vichy radio in France (Nazi-controlled) hailed the Detroit riots as a revolt that would spread to other cities, and called on the French police to realize the dangers to European civilization inherent in American aims of world domination. In Detroit the first meeting was held to form a permanent interracial citizen's body, which adopted all of Mr. Thomas's proposed program except the final point, that the body should be appointed by the mayor. It was felt that it would be better not to have an official committee, which might be subject to political pressures.

On Friday the Governor's fact-finding committee issued a report indicating that it did not feel the situation warranted a special Grand Jury investigation. The mayor, however, appointed a twelve-member committee of six whites and six Negroes to study the race situation, and the Detroit Council of Churches called on the people of Detroit to observe the following Sunday as a day of penitence.

Detroit was "on probation" over the week end. The next two weeks saw statements by the Mayor and Governor explaining away the delay in declaring martial law and requesting troops. The Lieutenant-Governor pointed out that state troopers could not assist earlier because they were not *properly* requested—in short, each official passed the buck and defended his own branch. The Wayne County prosecutor and the Detroit Police Commissioner made statements on Monday, July 25, accusing the N.A.A.C.P. of being the instigator of the riots, and revived tensions in the city. Labor and Negro and interracial organizations petitioned for Grand Jury investigation, but they met with no response.

The elements of inadequate civilian controls, inflammatory mass communication, and general anxiety are present here, as in Los Angeles. What the Detroit riot shows more clearly, although it was present in Los Angeles too, is the way in which this type of civil violence attracts the hoodlum element.

Many of the factors found in these Los Angeles and Detroit situations of anti-minority outbreaks were seen in our earlier analysis of the removal of the Japanese from the West Coast. All three situations are illustrations of the theory of the self-fulfilling prophecy discussed in Chapter 19. "If men define situations as real, they become, in the absence of institutional controls, real in their consequences."

PROPOSITIONS ABOUT DOMINANT – MINORITY BEHAVIOR

From the extensive research and study of minorities have emerged a number of propositions concerning detailed aspects of the subject on which there is some consensus. In this section, we shall consider some of the more important of such propositions. Robin Williams summarized the field first in 1947 and again in 1957.[9] We draw upon his summaries in part and, for the rest, rely on the previous materials of our own book.

[9] Robin Williams, Jr., *The Reduction of Inter-Group Tensions* (New York: Social Science Research Council, Bulletin 57, 1947). Also Robin Williams, Jr., "Racial and Cultural Relations," in *Review of Sociology*, Joseph B. Gittler, ed. (New York: John Wiley & Sons, Inc., 1957).

Visibility Variables

In general it has long been considered that "racial visibility"—some degree of nonwhiteness in appearance or lineage—has been a stronger barrier to either assimilation or to equality in status than cultural difference. The results of social distance studies show that this continues to be broadly true. However, the more recent ranking of nisei above some less racially visible groups suggest caution against stressing too heavily nonwhiteness as a barrier to assimilation. It is safe to say that Negroid visibility specifically seems still to be the strongest obstacle to full acceptance. Thus our first proposition is this:

1. Negroid visibility is the strongest barrier to the achievement of equal status.

   With reference to cultural visibility it still appears that:

2. The greater the cultural difference of ethnic group from the host group, the slower the rate of assimilation. Among these cultural differences those of language and religion are significantly determinative.

Size and Concentration of the Minority

The following proposition is generally accepted by students of minorities:

3. The larger the size of the minority proportional to the population of the given area, the slower the rate of assimilation.[10]

The rigidity of the Southern caste system appears roughly correlated with varying proportions of the Negro population in the South. North Carolina has a much smaller proportion of Negroes than South Carolina, and the former has a less rigid caste system. Viewed in its entire historical context, the fear in the minds of Southern whites of the sheer number of Negroes in their midst is at least understandable. Most polls have shown that the incidence of anti-Semitism was greatest in the Northeast and the Midwest, the areas of greatest Jewish concentration. Students of the Jewish problem are inclined, however, to be cautious about relating anti-Semitic feeling to any specific phenomena because of the highly symbolic nature of anti-Semitism. The concept of the Jew can be opposed even when Jewish people are not seen.

Closely related to point 3 is the following:

4. Rapid increases in the numbers of any new group increase antagonism toward the group. In consequence, the position of an ethnic group may deteriorate for a time until some new equilibrium is established.

A Negro sociologist once illustrated this point by his own experience. As a graduate student in New York City, he with two other colleagues went to work in the Connecticut tobacco fields to earn money in the summer. These

---

[10] Robin M. Williams, Jr., *The Reduction of Intergroup Tensions*, p. 58. Permission to quote the propositions from this monograph has been granted by the Social Science Research Council.

three Negro young men were well received by their white associates, and played on their ball team. Two years later the young sociologist repeated the experience and found that the whole attitude had changed. Now white people would not associate with him. In the short interval there had occurred a conspicuous "invasion" of the area by Negro people, to which he attributed the change in white attitudes.

Economic Conditions

In a general way the position of minorities improves in economic good times and deteriorates in depression. However, the relationship appears to be more precisely seen in the effect of general changes on particular segments of the population. For the next two propositions, we quote directly from Williams:

5. Conflict is especially likely in periods of rapid change in levels of living. The probability of conflict is increased insofar as the changes have a differential impact on various groups.[11]
6. Among the members of any dominant group the greatest incidence of open conflict behavior toward a given minority will be found among those classes which are most vulnerable to competition from the minority.[12]

Political Conditions

It is a basic postulate of social science that conflict with outside groups intensifies the solidarity of the in-group. When the antagonistic out-group is another nation, the in-group nation shows more unity. Applied to dominant-minority conflict this yields the following proposition:

7. In periods when the nation is preoccupied with the threat of conflict with another nation, the intensity of dominant-minority conflict within the nation declines.

One of the most striking facts revealed in our discussion of the different minorities was the great impetus to advance their position which resulted from World War II. (This despite conditions arising from local stress, as in the Los Angeles and Detroit riots.) The main exception to this proposition is that the position of minorities who may be identified with the enemy may deteriorate, as with the Japanese in World War II. The continuance of another common enemy, "international Communism," has thus tended to furnish an "out-group" upon which to vent hostility in place of domestic minorities. This point is further illustrated by the attempt of reactionary dominants to link several social action groups with Communism, as, for example, some Southern whites attempt to identify the National Association for the Advancement of Colored People as a Communist organization.

[11] *Ibid.*, p. 58.
[12] *Ibid.*, p. 59.

We have placed great emphasis on the dynamics of political democracy as a constant factor persistently operating toward assimilation. The influence of this factor varies, however, in relation to the amount of interest which the particular persons operating the government at any one time have in extending the applications of democracy. To put this in formal statement:

8. The pressures exerted by the dynamics of democracy toward the removal of discrimination vary in intensity with the degree of democratic sentiments held by those in possession of governmental authority.

Minority Behavior

The behavior of a minority is affected by forces generated from within the group itself and by the impact on the group of the manner in which the dominant group treats it. Among the characteristic forms of behavior generated from intragroup life are the following:

9. The minority moves toward acculturation to the norms of the dominant society.
   a. The less culturally different the minority is from the dominant society, the more rapid its acculturation.
   b. The less determined the minority is to retain any parts of its cultural heritage, the more complete its acculturation becomes.

In subproposition 9b above, we have in mind groups like the Amish, and to some extent the Jews, who have shown strong tenacity in preserving their traditional culture. As we have shown repeatedly, it is difficult to evaluate this force because the discrimination from without generates a defensive reaction.

The typical forms of minority behavior which are more clearly interpretable as reaction to dominant treatment embrace the following propositions:

10. Minorities react with sensitivity and withdrawal to dominant discrimination, producing in the personalities of its members in varying degrees of intensity a persecution complex.
11. Dominant discrimination sets in motion a "vicious circle," which tends to increase the prevalence within the minority membership of the very traits considered undesirable by the dominant. This effect varies, however, with the general cultural level of the minority group. The higher the general cultural level of the minority, the more apt it is to struggle against this very effect.

By this we have in mind the behavior of Japanese and Jews who have tempered their competitive behavior with a circumspection growing out of their awareness of the dominant conception of them.

We have noted at various points that as some minorities improve their position they tend to act toward minorities still below them in rank much as dominants have acted toward them. This is in part a function of the process of becoming "Americanized," taking on the normative patterns of behavior of the dominant. But it is also interpretable in the light of the insecure, marginal position which such groups occupy. We have found this kind of behavior often enough to consider it a general characteristic.

12. Minorities in intermediary or insecure status tend to act toward the minorities below them in status in the manner of dominants.

Finally, the variability of "militant" behavior by minorities in their own behalf shows a characteristic mode. Our previous discussion of "protest activity" is one measure of militancy. Our material supports Williams' formulation of this point:

13. Militancy, except for sporadic and short-lived uprisings, is not characteristic of the most deprived and oppressed groups, but rather of those who have gained considerable rights so that they are able realistically to hope for more.
14. A militant reaction from a minority group is most likely when (a) the group's position is rapidly improving, or (b) when it is rapidly deteriorating, especially if this follows a period of improvement.[13]

Dominant-Minority Contact and Prejudice

In his later review of the field, Williams has included propositions on the effect of contact between persons occupying positions of dominant and minority status.[14]

15. The greater the functional proximity of individuals in physical space the greater the likelihood of social interaction . . . even in the presence of quite marked prejudices.[15]

Concerning the previously held hypothesis that contact between members of different groups tends to produce more friendliness when the individuals are of approximately the same class standing, Williams' review finds these propositions, which we have paraphrased.

16. The more competitive the interpersonal relation, the less likely it will produce friendliness.[16]
17. Interactions are more likely to lead to interpersonal liking when the interacting parties have the same or similar values relevant to the type of interaction in which they engage.[17]

THE GENERAL PROSPECT FOR MINORITIES

The trends apparent in our study of America's many minorities point toward the following future developments.

1. A steadily increasing acculturation of all minorities.
2. A continuing decrease in the amount and intensity of discrimination against all minorities in the nation as a whole. Short-term increases in dis-

---

[13] *Ibid.*, p. 61.
[14] "Racial and Cultural Relations." A considerable portion of the new postulates deals with the nature of prejudice and its relation to personality, which is of less sociological relevance than those dealing with contact.
[15] *Ibid.*, p. 438.
[16] *Ibid.*, p. 439.
[17] *Ibid.*, p. 442.

crimination against particular minorities who may move into more homogeneous communities may be anticipated, however.

3. These developments should lead to a reduction in tension in intergroup relations with one conspicuous exception—Negro-white relations in the South. Here interracial tension has markedly risen as Negroes with their heightened aspirational level are vigorously pressing for complete civic equality in a region where the whites are far from ready to grant it. A considerable period of high tension, with sporadic violent incidents, appears probable in the South.

4. Generally, the non-English-speaking European nationalities have moved toward assimilation. In large cities with substantial numbers of any given nationality, there are still some identifiable ethnic subcommunities. For example, there are churches and clubs which are still ethnically labeled, and intimate social relations still show some ethnic delimitation. On the other hand, intermarriage both between the minority European ethnic groups and between these groups and the dominant group has meant that these ethnic subcommunities are becoming vague and attenuated. From the immigrants' grandchildren on, the traditional nationality cultural values and practices seem largely to have disappeared, but common ethnic origin continues to be something of a basis for social relationships. The cultural pluralism remaining from the European immigration is that of Protestantism, Catholicism, and Judaism. We have seen that there are those who believe that already these two previously thought of as "foreign" religions are now viewed as American, so that the adherents of all three great religions are thought of equally as Americans. The ebbs and flows of anti-Semitism historically, both in Europe and in the United States, urge caution in predicting the future of Jewish-Gentile relations.

5. Of the remaining groups now classifiable as minorities, the Puerto Ricans and the mexicanos are still too concentrated geographically and in too low occupational status for prediction as to an assimilationist or culturally pluralistic trend of development. Of the nonwhite groups, the mainland Japanese appear to be the most likely to lose group identity through assimilation, with the Chinese more divided between assimilationist and group identity trends. This leaves the Indians as the ethnic component with the highest possibility of final integration into American society on a pluralistic basis.

The above propositions are based on the assumption that there will be no intervening crisis for the nation generally. We have already observed that the now chronic tension between the free world and International Communism favors the present ameliorative trend in ethnic-intergroup relations. As our analysis of minorities under stress suggests, crisis may precipitate a deterioration in the position of specific minorities.

TOPICS FOR PROJECTS AND DISCUSSION

1. Consult appropriate sources for material on how the English people have reacted to the recent influx of West Indian Negroes to England. Consider parallels and contrasts with Negro-white relations in the United States.
2. Discuss specific conflicts arising between the economic interests and other interests which people of dominant status hold in relation to their behavior toward minorities.
3. What other kinds of "stressfull" situations than those described in this chapter can you think of as likely to precipitate disorderly situations in dominant-minority relations.
4. If you belong to a dominant-status group, indicate how your attitudes toward minorities differs from that of your parents. How do you account for the difference? If you belong to a minority group, indicate how your attitudes toward dominant groups differ from that of your parents. Account for the difference.
5. Which of the propositions about dominant-minority relations stated in the last section of this chapter do you think are least supported by the materials of this book?

SUGGESTED READING

Allport, Gordon. *The Nature of Prejudice.* Cambridge, Mass.: Addison-Wesley Publishing Company, Inc., 1954.
  Part IV of this psychologically oriented treatment discusses the socio-cultural factors influencing prejudice.
Cox, Oliver C. *Caste, Class and Race: a Study in Social Dynamics.* Garden City, N.Y.: Doubleday & Co., Inc., 1948.
  Chapters 21, 22, 23, criticize other theories of race relations from the viewpoint of the author that race relations are one phase of capitalistic exploitation of labor.
Glazer, Nathan. "Ethnic Groups in America: From National Culture to Ideology," in *Freedom and Control in Modern Society,* eds. Morroe Berger, Theodore Abel, and Charles H. Page. New York: D. Van Nostrand Company, Inc., 1954.
  Presents propositions as to the character of nationality groups in the present generation.
Grimshaw, Allen D. "Urban Racial Violence in the United States: Changing Ecological Considerations," *The American Journal of Sociology,* September, 1960, 66: 109–119.
  Shows changing patterns concerning the locales and the participants in race violence since World War II.
Lowenthal, Leo, and Guterman, Norbert. *Prophets of Deceit.* New York: Harper & Brothers, 1949.
  A study of the techniques of the American agitator as gathered from the writings and speeches of American nativists.
Williams, Robin, Jr. *The Reduction of Intergroup Tensions.* New York: Social Science Research Council, Bulletin 57, 1947.
  Summarizes research in the minorities field up to the time of publication.
Williams, Robin, Jr. "Racial and Cultural Relations" in *Review of Sociology, an Analysis of a Decade,* ed. Joseph B. Gittler, New York: John Wiley & Sons, Inc., 1957.
  Summarizes research in the minorities field for the ten years following the same author's previous summary.

21

Minorities and Social Policy

In the preceding chapters we have presented the actual situation of contemporary American minorities and have given an introduction to the concepts with which social science is making an increasingly accurate analysis of dominant-minority relations. In Chapter 20 we showed some differences between conditions of social stability and social stress. Throughout the book we have pointed out the relation of the situation of minorities to historical and contemporary patterns in the total society.

In this chapter we are concerned with changes in dominant-minority relations: how they may be initiated and carried out and what social science can contribute to our understanding and control of factors effecting change in minority status.

Changes affecting minorities occur in two ways. Improvement or decline in the status of one or several minorities, or of minorities in general, may be the by-product of broad changes in the whole society. Or gains or losses for minorities may be the result of conscious efforts.

SOCIAL CHANGE AND SOCIAL PROBLEMS

Social change is continually occurring, regardless of whether or not individuals or groups engage in action to initiate it, to resist it, or to attempt to direct it. Whereas social change probably occurred most often in pretechnological societies through the hazards of nature or of conquest, in contemporary industrialized societies the significant social changes are bound up with advances in technology, the growth of cities, the bureaucratization of economic enterprise in office and factory, and the relations in trade or war with other societies, particularly those of similar technological development. Sometimes, also, social changes have occurred through major changes in attitude and belief, but these are always linked, as cause or result, with new forms of organizing the way of living and working.

Examples of the effect of these general social changes have been cited frequently in earlier chapters. The growth of technology and mass communication has increasingly brought different groups of people into some kind of contact and has diminished for many the sense of strangeness in other ways of living and working. The factory system, an outgrowth of technology, has brought people from many traditions into common work experience, with resulting adaptations of habit and attitude. The growth of cities has made for changing residential patterns and heterogeneity of neighbors in many urban areas. Bureaucratization, with its increasing emphasis on standardized, objective job qualifications, has reduced elements of personal favoritism in employment. The war-time need for manpower and the postwar demand for international personnel has opened opportunities for members of minority groups. The increase in the scientific interpretation of phenomena as a major part of the belief system of modern America, and the hope it proffers for making possible rational attitudes regarding nature and to some extent, human nature, indirectly affects attitudes toward minorities. The configuration of broad social changes at the present moment in the United States is favorable to an improvement in the status of minorities. Reversals in any or all of these trends or the injection of significant new factors will similarly affect minorities and attitudes toward them negatively or positively.

Society is both a process of change and a process of order. Once well established, social structures have a tendency to continue. That social process is inevitably a changeful process has not been as popularly recognized. Furthermore, the era in which we now live is extraordinarily dynamic. It is entirely safe to predict that dominant-minority relations in twenty years will not be just as they are now, whatever social action specifically related to minorities is undertaken.

Another basic sociological principle pertinent to the discussion at hand is that the various separate social institutions in a society are interrelated and that changes in one have reactions on the others. The relationship between these structures is not always harmonious. In fact, in modern societies some of these structures stand in considerable opposition to one another. In general, however, there is a strain toward consistency in a society. This means that each structure can change as a unit only within narrow limits unless adaptive changes are made within other institutions. We have shown, for example, the sensitivity of dominant-minority relations to changes in the economic and political spheres. Social action directed at changing the structure of dominant-minority relations in any single area of life can have only a limited effect unless corresponding changes occur in other areas.

Definition of the Situation

The way change is viewed will vary, depending on how comfortably people can adapt to the changes which impinge on them. This involves how they define the situation. Entering into their various definitions will be such factors as beliefs, values, sentiments, knowledge, interests, personality needs. Whenever enough people who feel discomfort in the adaptations to change assign their discomforts to some specific source, they designate the situation a "problem." Once a problem is named, people in contemporary Western culture expect action to be taken to solve it. With varying degrees of intensity they will organize to protect or to further their interests and their values with relation to "the problem," either by direct action or by the attempt to influence those in power.

Social action, then, is the conscious effort of organized groups to initiate, further, or retard a specific adaptation to situations which they have perceived with discomfort and to have this action further their own values or interests. Undoubtedly, large segments of American society define the situation of minorities as a problem. While not all these people engage in specific direct social action about the minority problem, their attitudes toward it will influence their share in decisions of policy in both public and private life.

The kind of action undertaken will in part depend on the degree to which the definition of the situation is "true" or "false." In Chapter 19 we discussed Merton's concept of the self-fulfilling prophecy, in which false definitions may create conditions whereby they become true. Though there is probably no *true* definition of a complex situation, in the sense of absolute truth, a definition of a situation which attempts to take account of all the factors in their proper proportion is more true than one which neglects factors, oversimplifies, or distorts the relative weight of the various elements. The short-term and long-term success of action, therefore, is related to how true a definition of the situation can be achieved. It is also related to the power to enforce action through influence on legitimate policy-making bodies, or through extra-legal means. Social action always results, in one way or another, in directing social policy.

Ideology, Interest, and Policy

Values in a modern state are most often expressed in political or religious ideology. Of course, there are other values—for instance, familial, economic, or those of social class—which people hold dear. But the value *system* of a society gives greatest emphasis to those values which are most widely shared. The principal values in American life center around political democracy and the Judaic-Christian ethical tradition.

Interests of particular groups, however, often come in conflict with the ideals of democracy and ethics. There is a small group of people in any modern society to whom ideology is always more important than interest. Most people respond in large degree to the appeals of the general value system when it does not touch their special interest, but when they perceive their interests threatened by a social change, they will resist it. Franklin said in *Poor Richard's Almanac*, "Would you persuade, speak of interest, not of reason." Some people nakedly abandon an ideological commitment in favor of protecting their interests, sometimes at all costs. Conflicts of interest and ideology can occur in both those who are threatened by change and those who may benefit from it. There are several modes of behavior, from militant, to moderate, to apathetic, among those whose interests would lead them to resist and also among those whose interests would be promoted by change. Usually, however, rationalizations for action are developed which, for example, define democracy as the rule of the propertied only, or of the white race only, or a religious tradition limited to persons of a particular descent. Thus, in the question of change in dominant-minority relations, people will support policy and engage in action according to how they perceive their interests and how they interpret the central values of the culture, in individual, group, or regional variations.

Four major modes of reacting to the effects of change on minority status are common: (1) There are those who believe that minorities should remain minorities, that the problem is one of keeping them in that status. (2) There are those who hold that the welfare of the depressed minorities should be improved within the framework of segregation, a philosophy followed by some moderate Southerners concerning the Negro. (3) There are those who see a problem only when tension and hostility between groups disturb the peace of the community through disorderly violence. (4) There are those who define the problem in the light of the American Creed and seek adjustment of any conflict of interests and values that may arise.

Social-action groups holding the value system of the American Creed believe that all members of the American national society should have equal opportunity. Since ethnic, racial, or religious discrimination denies equality of opportunity, the central problem, for this group, is discrimination itself; and their objective is therefore to eliminate discrimination. Action groups holding the democratic values stand in clear opposition to those primarily concerned with maintaining discrimination—holders of viewpoint (1). With the other two groups, the democratic social-action group would co-operate at times but frequently differ. While under certain circumstances it might support all-Negro housing projects, the kind of project logically favored by viewpoint (2) above, this group would more properly sponsor an experimental project in mixed housing. Finally, the social-action group seeking to improve minority status might in periods of crisis and tension support viewpoint (3) in establishing order through accommodative procedures, but it would maintain that the long-range cure for such intermittent crises is to eliminate discrimination.

Thus discrimination may be attacked indirectly or directly. By the indirect attack is meant working to improve the general conditions in society known to breed prejudice and discrimination. Among the more important of these conditions, as seen in our general interpretation in Chapter 20, are economic depressions and other economic conditions creating substantial downward social mobility; the ever-present efforts of special economic groups to cultivate discrimination for profit; and the failure of certain governmental officials to uphold vigorously and to implement the democratic institutions they are charged with administering. Persons interested primarily in reducing minority discrimination usually support public policy aimed at creating the general conditions favorable to nondiscrimination.

Direct efforts to reduce discrimination involve attack on the two main sources of discrimination. One source is prejudice against the minorities, prompting discriminatory behavior. The other source is the established patterns of social organization which support discrimination, often in the absence of prejudice. For example, Mr. A from Northtown, with no prejudice against Negroes, buys a store in Southtown. He discovers that it is not customary for Negroes and whites to trade in the same store and that his white clerks will not wait on Negroes. He therefore discriminates against Negro trade even though he has no prejudice and in spite of the fact that, if it were not for the established patterns of the community, Negro trade would be profitable. The variable relations between prejudice and discrimination are indicated by Merton in his formulation of the possible combinations of these two elements in people of dominant status.[1]

Type I. *The Unprejudiced Nondiscriminator, or All-Weather Liberal.* Since this type of person believes unequivocally in the Democratic Creed, he practices what he believes consistently. Obviously such people are logical leaders for social action in the same direction. However, Merton considers the all-weather liberal prone to accept three fallacies. The first, the fallacy of group soliloquy, refers to the tendency for such like-minded people to gather in small groups and reinforce each other's attitudes and convictions rather than joining other groups and influencing them in the desired direc-

[1] Robert K. Merton, "Discrimination and the American Creed," in MacIver, *Discrimination and National Welfare* (New York: Harper & Brothers, 1949), pp. 99–126. The terms "liberal" and "illiberal" used by Merton are based on the degree to which the types illustrated accept or do not accept and practice the American Creed—that is, "the right of equitable access to justice, freedom, and opportunity, irrespective of race or religion, or ethnic origin."

tion. Growing closely out of this is the second fallacy, called the fallacy of unanimity, which is the tendency to exaggerate the extent to which the rest of the community shares their own viewpoint. A third limitation to effective action by all-weather liberals is their addiction to the fallacy of private solutions to social problems. Since he himself has solved the problem, this liberal may not feel compelled to do anything more. Rightly, he feels no guilt for himself.

Type II. *The Unprejudiced Discriminator, or Fair-Weather Liberal.* This is the type of man who has no prejudices against ethnic groups and on the whole believes in the American Creed. But he is primarily a man of expediency, who tends to support discriminatory practices when it is the easier or more profitable course. He does, however, feel guilty about his discrimination. He is therefore capable of cure, because he really wants to be cured.

Type III. *The Prejudiced Nondiscriminator, or Fair-Weather Illiberal.* This type of man does not believe in ethnic equality. Being, however, also a man of expediency, he conforms in situations in which the group sanctions are against discrimination through fear of the penalties which might otherwise ensue. But whenever the pressure against it is removed, he discriminates.

Type IV. *The Prejudiced Discriminator, or the All-Weather Illiberal.* This type is the true bigot. Since he believes firmly that certain minorities ought to be discriminated against, he can be counted on to discriminate as thoroughly as is permitted by the customs and institutions of the community. This type is obviously hardest to change, although the situation varies in relation to the prevailing mores of the area where he lives. When the mores support his position, he is a conformist, and change means making himself open to community criticism. When the mores in general are against him, he is a social deviant, and here change on his part would draw him closer into the general community structure.

THE EFFORT TO REDUCE PREJUDICE

Much has been learned about the various ways prejudice comes about, under what circumstances prejudice can be reduced or eliminated, and the personality structure which uses prejudice to retain a sense of adequacy in the face of internal or external pressure. The simplest distinction is made by MacIver between those who owe their prejudice to the responses learned from their social milieu and those whose prejudice emerges from their own emotional life history.[2] Clearly there is not always an "either-or" dichotomy. Many people lapse into temporary antagonistic expressions toward an outgroup when they are under stress. The test comes in what *action* they take,

[2] Robert M. MacIver, *The More Perfect Union* (New York: The Macmillan Co., 1948), pp. 195–200.

what policy they support, and how amenable they are to revising their opinions. Three approaches to the reduction of prejudice may be mentioned.

The Educational Approach

Education occurs on many levels, the most significant of which is obviously early childhood education, where, under favorable circumstances, the attitudes of parents and school will be incorporated by the young child. If the child has an opportunity to know likeable members of other groups both at home and at school, the base is laid for an attitude which will not easily be subject to categorical devaluation of other groups. Therefore, a great focus of educational effort to reduce prejudice has been to scrutinize the content of school curricula and to ensure school populations made up of all potentially able to do the work, regardless of their descent. One community-wide plan with this purpose is the "Springfield Plan." Inaugurated originally in Springfield, Massachusetts, and subsequently adapted to some other cities, this was an effort supported by citizens and led by the Board of Education which won the support of various other organized groups. The emphasis was on the ideal of "fair play." The program changed the content of both elementary-school and high-school teaching, as well as teacher training in the local college of education.[3]

The attack on traditional subject matter furnishes a good example of one of the areas where sentiments and values resist or conflict with commitment to social justice. For example, an issue which has engaged demonstration and direct action of groups has been the stereotypes of minorities in cherished "classics." In *The Merchant of Venice* the portrait of Shylock clearly represents a sixteenth-century stereotype. There has been controversy over the portrayal of a Negro in *Huckleberry Finn*, which similarly reflects a stereotype of a former time and place. When a teacher interprets the content of a "classic" in relation to the attitudes of the time in which it was written, the stereotypes will not necessarily appear relevant to contemporary life, but how many teachers do so?

The other problem of children's education is the question of school populations. Equal access to the same education for dominants and minorities is, of course, the crux of the question of school integration. Here too one sees the dilemma of many "fair-weather liberals," who believe in the ideology of equal opportunity but for private reasons of one kind or another do not wish to have their children in an integrated school.

Another educational approach is that of general adult education, either through community and professional groups or the broader channels of mass communication. There are a number of organizations primarily concerned with getting facts about minorities before the public. It is very diffi-

[3] *Approaches to National Unity*, eds. Lyman Bryson, Louis Finkelstein, and Robert M. MacIver (New York: Harper & Brothers, 1945), pp. 314 ff.

cult to assess results, but there is general consensus that the presentation of facts has little effect unless those who hear them are already engaged in the issues to which the facts are related. Lectures are apt to be "program fillers" unless there is respect for the special authority of the person who speaks (as with a clergyman and his congregation), and an opportunity to discuss and question. Unless anxieties and perplexities can be brought into the open, those who already agree will go on agreeing and those who disagree will not listen.

We have had few studies of the effect of educational programs on those exposed to them. One, however, was conducted by Dr. Gerhart Saenger on the effectiveness of the UNESCO pamphlet series on race.[4] Students in five colleges in the East and Middle West were given three preliminary tests designed (1) to indicate their attitude toward racial and ethnic groups, (2) to indicate their attitude toward UNESCO, and (3) to measure their democratic-authoritarian character structure. One cross-section then read the pamphlets and discussed them in class; another part of the sample read the pamphlets but did not discuss them in class; and a third (control) group did not read them. All the students were then tested to judge their gain in information and any changes of attitude. The findings showed considerable improvement of knowledge as between those who read the pamphlets and those who did not. Nineteen out of twenty students who had read the assigned material answered more than 60 per cent of the informational questions on the final test correctly, whereas only one in five who had not read the pamphlets could score as well. The greatest change in understanding the nature of prejudice was in the students who had shown the highest prejudice score before reading the pamphlets. Some who had participated in the discussion groups did better than those who had merely read the material, but this varied with the ability of the teacher to direct the discussion.[5] The most prejudiced also showed a significant shift toward lower prejudice on the final projective tests.[6] Finally, a considerable proportion of students indicated further interest in UNESCO, in wishing to have the pamphlets used, in wishing to give money, and to aid research; and a few wished to join action committees or were willing to lead discussion groups.[7]

The Intergroup Contact Approach

A number of organizations seek in various ways to bring together members of different ethnic or racial groups. Sometimes such a group uses as its appeal the common ethical bonds of the major Western religions, as with

---

[4] Gerhart Saenger, "The Effectiveness of the UNESCO Pamphlet Series on Race," in *International Social Science Bulletin,* 1954, 6: No. 3.
[5] *Ibid.,* pp. 11–13.
[6] *Ibid.,* p. 14.
[7] *Ibid.*

the Conference of Christians and Jews, giving adults and often young people of high-school and college age opportunities to meet and discuss their likenesses and differences. Such a program appeals chiefly to middle- and upper-middle-class people, and those who make up the more liberal segment of their social or religious groups.

Other groups are interested in promoting intergroup meetings on a neighborhood basis, usually in connection with a school or neighborhood center. These may take on a more informal character, by which persons of different background have the opportunity to discover each other as individuals through talent nights, international food fairs, or other devices. Either type of intergroup program is undoubtedly good as far as it goes, especially if there is a sustained series of meetings (rather than, as occurs in some places, one occasion a year to celebrate Brotherhood Week). On the whole, however, work in intergroup relations seems to show that the most meaningful associations are more apt to occur when people work together for a concrete goal of benefit to all, as in a Parents' Association, a civic group, a union, or a neighborhood center. The intergroup character is then secondary to the task to be accomplished, and congenial individuals lose sight of differences in their concern for the common goal.[8]

The Therapeutic Approach

The person who experiences the reduction of inner conflict and anxiety as the result of personal psychotherapy usually becomes a more tolerant person. Whereas psychiatry has no sure technique for eliminating prejudice from the insecure prejudiced personality, for many persons the experience of therapy helps locate the source of their anxieties and to minimize displacement of the cause of their discomfort on a handy scapegoat.

There have been a number of attempts to use a group psychotherapeutic approach or at least some of the major principles of psychiatry in activity with groups in order to reduce prejudice. The techniques involved in such efforts are usually safely used only by experienced leaders who have learned to handle hostility and anxiety with enough sureness so that there is neither disruption of the meeting nor contagious panic. This is a technique which seems to have been effective in some situations, but it depends on special leadership, usually professionally trained.

INSTITUTIONAL CONTROLS ON DISCRIMINATION

The emphasis at one time in group efforts by minorities and others to improve the status and opportunities of minorities was primarily directed toward the reduction of prejudice. For some action organizations this is still

[8] Gladys Meyer, *Parent Action in School Integration: A New York Experience* (New York: The United Parents Associations, 1961).

true. Since World War II, there seems to be a shift to emphasis on establishing *institutional controls* which will decrease discrimination. Outstanding recent advances in behalf of minorities have been made with this approach.

Government Controls

The locus of the guarantee of the rights of citizens rests with the government. It must not only protect but, in a democracy, enable full participation. In a federal state like the United States there are several governmental levels which exert some kind of control over what citizens may or may not do. Therefore, controls of discrimination occur at each of these different levels, sometimes, as we have pointed out earlier, with discrepancies between the levels. We shall cite several selected problems to show the role of government at federal, state, and local levels.

On the federal level the most significant recent action affecting minorities has been that of the Supreme Court. The Court is so constituted as to be less subject to popular pressure than the other branches of government. Although the approach to the Court is a lengthy process, once a case is heard by the Court it receives the best guarantee available that it will be heard impartially in the light of the Constitution. The two major Court decisions which have affected minorities since World War II have been the decision on segregated schools in 1954, and the decision outlawing residential covenants in 1948.

The Congress also plays a role in the issue of civil rights. Here, however, regional pressures, economic interests, or political contingencies are often a handicap. The status of federal civil rights legislation as of 1961–62 is an example of this dilemma. Another factor affecting Congress is the degree of minority representation in the composition of the Senate and the House. This is considerably lower than the size of minority populations would warrant.[9]

The office and prestige of the Presidency also affects public policy. Undoubtedly a strong committment to a position of improving minority status in a President of strong leadership has its effect on Congressional action and on popular sentiment.

The administrative structure of the federal government in the hands of the Federal Civil Service has set a precedent for nondiscriminatory employment. Furthermore, and perhaps even more significantly, policy is more influenced than the average citizen realizes by the top bureaucracy in those bureaus which administer affairs affecting minorities, for their personnel usually persists over a longer period of time than in the elected branches of government. Within the Department of the Interior and the Department of

[9] Donald R. Matthews, *The Social Background of Political Decision Makers* (Doubleday Short Studies in Political Science, 1954). Tables on pp. 25 and 26.

Health and Welfare, bureaus such as the Office of Education, the Department of Public Health, and the Indian Bureau work continuously and unspectacularly on the problem of minorities that come within the scope of their responsibility.

In times of emergencies the federal government is allowed extraordinary powers. Since World War I these powers have temporarily benefited minorities in several ways, and there has been some carry-over from emergency action to long-term public policy. The outstanding example of this was the Federal Fair Employment Practices Commission of World War II. This emergency experience led to permanent state commissions in many states. A further carry-over can be seen in the policy of the Kennedy administration prohibiting discrimination in employment in all companies, whatever their geographic location, which receive federal contracts. This affects states where there has thus far been no state legislation against discrimination. An additional feature of the policy with regard to federal contracts is that it includes provisions for no discrimination in upgrading.

One of the ticklish problems of federal action and policy in behalf of minorities is the question of enforcement. We have seen since 1954 the use of the military, the state militia, and federal deputies in the attempt to enforce federal law in the face of local resistance. Undoubtedly the skill and the wisdom with which decisions of enforcement are made and the personnel selected for them affect the increase of pro-minority or anti-minority feeling.

At the state level there have also been actions designed to diminish discrimination. Eighteen states have fair employment practices commissions, though at least one of these has no provisions for enforcement. Most states have copied the New York procedure, which establishes a state commission against discrimination. The commission hears complaints, investigates them, and gives the employer an opportunity to rectify the situation if he has been unwittingly at fault. If he does not comply, a public hearing is held in his community at which the complainants testify. Thereafter, if the employer takes no action, he is brought to court. Very few cases come to court. The State of California reported in August of 1961 that at the end of its first year of operating under such a law, with a similar procedure, all cases but three had been settled by public hearing.[10]

The Metcalfe-Baker Bill, passed in New York State in 1961, shows a state entering the field of discrimination in housing. This law provides that any housing, low-income or middle-income, to which the state has contributed funds may not discriminate.

Local ordinances reflect local differences. It is enough to cite two extremes: (1) New York City has an ordinance against discrimination in hous-

[10] The *New York Times*, August 28, 1961.

ing which affects private as well as public housing. (2) In contrast, local ordinances against trespass have been invoked in attempts to prevent the desegregation of bus terminals in the South.

Integration of Religious Institutions

Within the American pattern of religious institutions the issue of minorities has primarily affected the various forms of Protestantism. As the dominant religion it has tended in the past to reflect, in its various denominations, the customary patterns of the populations it serves. A large segment of the Protestant church belongs to denominations with strong local autonomy; even those branches of Protestantism which have central administration have hesitated to take a position that would offend local parishioners. This has allowed great variation in the pattern of membership in the local church. In the past the major Protestant denominations have tended on the whole to maintain racially segregated congregations, and sometimes denominational nationality branches. The Roman Catholic Church and the Eastern Orthodox Church have also maintained nationality churches, not as a matter of principle but as appropriate to the needs of particular populations. No Christian denomination has denied persons admission to its larger membership because of race or descent, however much individual congregations have sought to remain homogeneous.

Both Protestants and Roman Catholics have long conducted missionary efforts among various minority peoples, notably Asiatics and American Indians. The missionary effort, however, in its nonreligious aspect has been essentially an attempt to improve their welfare without improving their status in the general society, except in individual instances. An exception to this pattern has been the extreme evangelical groups, such as Jehovah's Witnesses, or such non-trinitarian bodies as Quakers and Unitarians. Since Judaism is not a missionary religion, there has been little effort to bring members of non-Jewish descent into the congregations, but Jewish religious leaders, aided by the fraternal organizations of the Jewish community, have been in the forefront of the effort to improve the over-all status of minorities.

Changes are taking place on the religious front. The Presbyterians have elected a national moderator who is Negro. In recent years, Roman Catholic orders in the United States have been admitting members into racially integrated individual religious communities. Although the Church has no mode of enforcement comparable to that of the State, it provides a very strong motivation for breaking down barriers between disparate groups in the society. Its prestige and influence are significant.

Policy Within Economic Institutions

Large businesses and labor unions are the principal economic institutions where it is possible to make policy significant enough to influence the opportunity of minorities. In general it appears that the large businesses have been slow to initiate steps to integrate minorities. When integration of an individual of minority status has taken place spontaneously, it has generally rested on the need for highly skilled personnel, such as chemists and engineers. Some corporations have had a nondiscriminatory policy for the unskilled labor force, though even in such corporations, in the case of Negroes and whites, there sometimes has been segregation within the factory. Since big business represents a conservative force in American life, it might be expected to change more slowly than other segments of the society.

A broader and more direct attack on discrimination has come from organized labor. Not all unions are nondiscriminatory and, even within unions which have a policy opposed to discrimination, problems arise between different populations who make up the membership of the union or who work in a particular shop. We have referred to this in earlier chapters, and it need not be elaborated here. One contrast between business and labor, however, is that, on the whole, labor has supported government measures against discrimination and business has not.

Reducing Discrimination in Prestige and Private Membership Organizations

A focal point of sensitivity for minority members who have achieved high economic position or other recognition is exclusion from membership in organizations which carry status in the community. Such private organizations are often also the seats of informal power. This type of organization, within the concept of American freedom, is not subject to outside institutional controls. Any approach to changing the membership patterns will depend on attitudinal changes. At this point of crucial access to hidden power and prestige, the institutional approach to eliminating discrimination is less valid than the older emphasis on the reduction of prejudice. Clearly, both the strengthening of institutional controls and the reduction of prejudice must be attempted concomitantly if Americans are to think of themselves as a total body of American citizens rather than as dominant and minority.

ACTION ORGANIZATIONS

The National Level

There are nationwide voluntary organizations whose goals are both to promote change and to resist change. Different organizations appeal to different strata in the society, a fact which in part determines their character.

Organizations promoting improvement in the status of minorities may be made up of solely minority membership or may have a broad, inclusive membership. They will have differences in ways of working, as well. An example of an inclusive organization which is moderate and has always worked within the legal framework is the National Association for the Advancement of Colored People. In contrast, the Council on Racial Equality has chosen a more militant approach through demonstration and "passive resistance." There are disadvantages for the solely minority organization, as was illustrated by the dilemma of the nisei organization in World War II, when anti-Japanese dominants continued to classify these loyal nisei with the rest of the Japanese and the Japanese-Americans often regarded them as dubious spokesmen for the entire Japanese group. Mention should also be made of the dilemmas for the individual created by supranational organizations of specific minorities. For the child who is educated in a Zionist home, is Israel the territory of identification, or is America? Does the Negro who is a member of the Pan-African movement pitch his loyalty to territorial Africa and, if so, to which state? There are even the beginnings of a Pan-Indian movement, which seeks to unite the minority Indian peoples of North and South America.

National organizations resisting change may focus on only one or two minorities. On the other hand, we have had organizations whose effort was to minimize the influence of any group other than the white Nordic Protestants. Even respected moderate conservative organizations may, out of their historical tradition, be anti-minority, as for example the Freemasons are still to a degree politically anti-Catholic. One of the major problems of the militant groups that attack one or several minorities is that they rarely abjure extra-legal means to intimidate or drive out the groups they consider undesirable.

The Local Level

At the local level there is a variety of efforts in behalf of minorities. Sometimes there are formal structures, such as citizens' councils, to safeguard minority rights. Other local organizations may be directed toward special purposes which do not primarily involve dominant-minority relations, but which affect minorities, such as housing councils and parent-teacher associations. Perhaps of most significance are local indigenous efforts of citizens to deal effectively with specific local problems.

Citizen Action

An example of citizen action is recorded in its step-by-step development by Julia Abrahamson in *A Neighborhood Finds Itself*.[11] Her account tells of the effort made in the Hyde Park-Kenwood section of Chicago to establish a friendly and co-operative relationship between old residents of the area and Negro families who were buying homes and moving in. The action taken originated with religious groups, Protestant and Jewish. Influences in

---

[11] (New York: Harper & Brothers, 1959).

the area power structure had to be dealt with: businessmen's organizations, the University of Chicago, and the municipal government. One emphasis of the community effort was on the quality of physical standards of the neighborhood that all wished to maintain in order to have a home-owning district, safe for children and congenial for adults. This focus seemed to the residents far more important than the descent of the inhabitants.

The story of Hyde Park-Kenwood is extraordinarily useful in the example it provides of the steps, developments, setbacks, anxieties, and techniques used to meet a change in dominant-minority residential patterns.

Other undocumented instances of similar local efforts are present in other cities. During World War II the mayor of a West Coast city asked for and was assigned a government expert to help develop a plan and a campaign to keep Negroes who were coming to the city for war employment from being forced to form their own restricted quarter. In another city, middle-class white and Negro homeowners formed a homeowners' association to keep old houses from becoming rooming houses and thus changing the "settled" character of the neighborhood. Not all efforts have been without mistakes. One middle-income co-operative housing project set out to build a population that was 50 per cent white and 50 per cent Negro. The white families turned out to be, all but a few, older people without children. The Negro families were younger, with children. The small group of white parents who had children sent them to private schools, and the public school adjoining the development thus became predominantly Negro. This might have been avoided and the goals of an "interracial" housing development more effectively fulfilled if thought had been given to the age composition of the applicants.

Do We Need Experts?

We pointed out in an earlier chapter that special aspects of dominant-minority relations have created positions in the society, usually filled by minority members, to bridge interests and differences. The changes of the past decades have created other intermediary roles, as for example the government representative assigned to the West Coast city during the war. When Negroes began to be integrated into industry, "advisers" or "trouble-shooters" found a function in working with employers and employees. In school integration there has been a place for an adviser from the outside who has no private interest in the adjustments to be made.

There has been a growing number of people who wish to make the field of intergroup relations their profession. Here there are both theory and techniques which are known and can be valuable. We might cite only two examples: (1) Theory of role set, including the potential conflicts within a role set, makes an "adviser" aware of what a manager or an administrator may be contending with, and can show him how he may be able to take responsibility for changes in a way that lessens the pressure on the administrator. (2) Theory of personality, which is part of the training of a good social worker, and the field experience that is part of this training, may make possible the effective handling of the hostility implicit in most situations involving tension.

Little is yet formulated about the role of the expert: how he understands what is expected of him in relation to his motivation and to the structure within which he works. Some seem to know by intuition and long experience. We have not yet determined, however, what ideally should go into the selection and training for this role. We do know, on the other hand, a good deal about the techniques of working with groups, and there is a variety of manuals, pamphlets, and books dealing with techniques. Many schools of education and most schools of social work have courses in community leadership in which the techniques can be learned.

Do We Need Planning?

The experience of crises has led some communities to develop plans to prevent outbreaks of hostility. Lee and Humphrey have outlined programs suitable for this purpose based on a comparative study of riots in Detroit, Los Angeles, and New York.[12] Their proposals may be summarized in three parts.

1. *A Constant Systematic Check on Intergroup Incidents.* Facts gathered after riots often reveal that there was an increased number of small, unnoticed incidents between the two groups before the riot occurred. It is possible to devise an index of incidents which could serve as a sort of barometer of the degree of tension. Periodic checking of the items in the index would serve to warn responsible officials when the tension was rising.

2. *New Accommodative Measures to Reduce Tension.* Having a more specific and regular reading of the intergroup tension barometer affords the opportunity to reduce the degree of tension in its specific and localized manifestations through new accommodative procedures. For this purpose the auspices of a civic biracial committee, independent of the law-enforcing agencies, would appropriately be enlisted. Such a committee would suggest some specific new accommodation and then enlist the support of responsible leaders of both groups in the area for a temporary solution. For example, if fights between adolescent gangs of the two groups were increasing, the biracial committee might propose additional recreational facilities and hiring a recreational supervisor interested in reducing prejudices.

3. *A Plan if Riot Occurs.* If, in spite of all efforts, a riot starts, the city authorities should have a systematic plan to curb it. Lee and Humphrey suggest that the state militia or federal troops be called for. This suggestion

[12] Alfred M. Lee and Norman D. Humphrey, *Race Riot* (New York: The Dryden Press, Inc., 1943). See particularly Part III, "A Program for Preventing Race Riots."

is based on the Detroit experience, where it is clear that in employing force the police manifested distinct anti-Negro bias and did not act impartially.

The effectiveness of planning is also shown in situations such as school integration. Cities like Louisville, which devised a plan and spent a year educating the public and conferring with parents before inaugurating the plan, show that if the full means at hand are used intelligently, changes may be initiated smoothly. Estimating trends and planning in relation to them has become increasingly important in the field of social policy. No large business, of course, would attempt to operate without an assessment of trends. No local community can afford to ignore these either. Large cities concerned with urban renewal are engaged in considerable planning, and the rights of minorities are an important aspect in the construction of such plans.

SOME ISSUES FOR THE LARGER SOCIETY

One of the major issues which must be kept in mind by those who seek to reduce discrimination by government action is the balance of individual liberty and extended state control. The precedent of federal interference in local community action can be disastrous for American society unless the community has enough educated leadership to support the action of the central government. In a period of hysteria or in the hands of irresponsible public officials, extension of federal control is a serious threat to the human rights on which American democracy is built. Therefore, national measures which are enforceable must be accompanied by vigorous programs of public education and, wherever possible, the use of local initiative and local personnel.[13]

Another problem of the larger society is that of the goals in group relations. Is the ideal one in which subcultural differences are to be eradicated in favor of a standardized American? On the other hand, is a goal desirable and praticable in which ethnic groups maintain their own social structures and identity, their values and their behavior patterns? Cultural pluralism, as the history of minorities has shown us, can be of two types. It can involve the total social structure of both primary and secondary contacts—that is to say, intimate and impersonal—as with some American Indians. Or it can be a pluralism which persists only in the family and clique contacts. Each of these presents problems for intergroup relations within the total society.[14]

[13] In this connection see the discussion of the role of the public in issues of national security in Harold D. Lasswell, *National Security and Individual Freedom* (New York: McGraw-Hill Book Co., Inc., 1950), Ch. 7, pp. 154–187.
[14] See the analysis of cultural pluralism in Milton M. Gordon, "Social Structure and Goals in Group Relations," in *Freedom and Control in Modern Society*, Morroe Berger, Theodore Abel, Charles H. Page (New York: D. Van Nostrand Company, Inc., 1954), pp. 153–157.

How the question of cultural pluralism will be resolved in the United States will depend on the developing goals of the several minorities and on the national temper of the total society in the decades to come.

TOPICS FOR PROJECTS AND DISCUSSION

1. Through newspapers and news weeklies explore the history of the Civil Rights Commission of the federal government. What has been its membership, its achievements, and what obstacles has it encountered in developing a program?
2. In your home community what agencies exist for the protection of minority rights or for public education about minority problems?
3. Write a history of the legal efforts which culminated in the 1954 Supreme Court Decision on School Segregation.
4. Discuss the role of religious institutions in improving intergroup relations. Find as many examples as you can of leadership offered by national or local religious bodies in improving the situation of a minority.
5. Collect as many examples as you can of community planning for the improvement or protection of minorities in school desegregation, housing, reduction and control of intergroup tension, and so on.

SUGGESTED READING

Abrahamson, Julia. *A Neighborhood Finds Itself*. New York: Harper & Brothers, 1959.
> *The story of neighborhood integration in a middle-class section of Chicago.*

Frazier, E. Franklin. *Race and Culture Contacts in the Modern World*. New York: Alfred A. Knopf, Inc., 1957.
> *An interpretation of race and culture problems in an international perspective.*

Hill, Herbert, and Greenberg, Jack. *Citizen's Guide to De-Segregation*. Boston: The Beacon Press, 1955.
> *The legal history of the struggle for school desegregation.*

MacIver, Robert M. *The More Perfect Union*. New York: The Macmillan Co., 1948.
> *An eminent sociologist weighs the approaches to improvement of dominant-minority relations*

Meyer, Gladys. *Parent Action in School Integration—A New York City Experience*. New York: The United Parents Associations, 1961.
> *A discussion of the efforts of organized parent bodies to smooth the process of school integration.*

Valien, Bonita H. *The St. Louis Story*. New York: Anti-Defamation League of B'nai B'rith, 1956.
> *A description of the agencies involved in planning for school desegregation in St. Louis.*

Index of Authors

Index of Subjects

Accommodation, 34, 35, 424, 425
Acculturation, 35, 85, 86, 162, 425, 426
Alien and Sedition Acts, 69
Alien Land Holding Laws, 170
Amalgamation, 37
  (*See also* Race crossing.)
"America Fever," 70
American Creed, 16, 38, 470
American Federation of Labor, 305, 322
Amish, as Protestants, 381–382
Anglos (*See* Mexicano-Anglo relations.)
Anderson, Marian, 275
Annexation
  pattern, 6
  of Puerto Rico, 143
Anomie, 436
Anti-Defamation League of B'nai B'rith,
  412
Anti-Semitism
  in the United States, 408–412
  persistence of, 417–418
Apartheid, 7
Argentina, immigration to, 9
Armenians, 80, 380
Assimilation, 36, 91–94, 426–427
Association of American Indian Affairs, 340
Authoritarian Personality, The, 434–436

Black Metropolis, Chicago Negro Community, 257–261

Border Patrol, Mexican, 124–125
Brazil, immigration to, 9
Bridgeton, N.J., Japanese in, 200
Brown v. *Topeka*, 288–289
Burlington, Vt., 77–79

Caste, 43, 231
Caste system of the South
  and class, 235
  effects of, 239–251
  etiquette of, 235
  gains to whites in, 240–241
  methods of enforcing, 236–237
  Negro reactions to, 239–242
Catholic-Protestant relations
  conflict in, 384–385, 389–390
  trends in, 388–390
Catholicism in the United States, 390
  and cultural pluralism, 382
  early period of, 384–385
Catholics in the United States
  Irish as, 385–386
  Italians as, 386–388
  minority status of, 384–388
  and occupational discrimination, 388
Chinatowns, 171–172
  of San Francisco Bay area, 174–175
Chinese Consolidated Benevolent Association, 173–174
Chinese Exclusion Acts, 167, 171

491